GAMES NATIONS PLAY

GAMES NATIONS PLAY

Analyzing International Politics

JOHN SPANIER

SECOND EDITION

PRAEGER PUBLISHERS

New York

Published in the United States of America in 1975
by Praeger Publishers, Inc.
111 Fourth Avenue, New York, N.Y. 10003

This is the second edition of a book originally published by Praeger Publishers in 1972.

Portions of this book originally appeared in a different form in John Spanier's
World Politics in an Age of Revolution.

Library of Congress Cataloging in Publication Data
Spanier, John W
    Games nations play.

    Bibliography: p.
    Includes index.
    1. International relations. I. Title.
JX1391.S7 1975   327   74-11597
ISBN 0-275-33520-8
ISBN 0-275-89060-0 pbk.

Printed in the United States of America

FOR LISA AND DAVID

Love, all alike, no season knows, or clime,
Nor hours, days, months, which are the
    rags of time.

From The Sun Rising by John Donne

Contents

Preface

As its subtitle suggests, the purpose of this book is to teach the reader—primarily the college student—*how to think about international politics.* The average undergraduate takes a course in international politics largely to gain some understanding of the contemporary world and, in particular, of the role played by his own country. Many, of course, are interested in finding out more about particular events and issues, be it the cold war, European integration, Vietnam, the Middle East, the ABM, or SALT. The one thing many students do not expect when they enroll in a course on international politics is abstract analyses of the nature of international politics in order to learn how to *analyze* international politics for themselves. It is precisely because current events so soon become "ancient history" that my aim has been to provide the reader with those tools of analysis that will enable him to analyze tomorrow's events for himself. I hope that, in the end, he will have gained a deeper comprehension of some of the external and internal problems states confront and why frequently they act as they do, whether they are capitalist or Communist, highly industrialized or economically underdeveloped.

Thus, this is a book about the "games nations play." Its objective, moreover, is to convey to the student that there are a number of different ways to think about the subject and not just one way, not simply a "right" way. To this end, the book employs three levels of analysis: the state system, with its balance-of-power emphasis; the national system, with its domestic priorities; and the decision-making system, with its dependence both on the policy-makers' perceptions of reality and on the institutions that formulate and execute policy. This three-dimensional approach, which is a modification of Kenneth N. Waltz's "three images" and J. David Singer's "levels of analysis," enables the student to view a single policy or set of policies from three different—and often conflicting—perspectives. It is hoped that this will afford him a greater understanding of the complexities of the international system, as well as a more sophisticated basis for prediction, criticism, and interpretation. This threefold scheme also reflects my own view that international politics must be analyzed not only in the context of the environment or state system in which they occur but also in terms of how the purposes of nations and their general behavior is shaped by the nature of their societies and the specific policy-makers who conduct foreign policy at a particular time. For the environment has a powerful impact upon states, for example, upon their objectives and the degree of choice they have in choosing among alternative policies; but their internal character and politics too exert a major influence. While somewhat exaggerated, one can paraphrase Clausewitz and say that foreign policy is the conduct of domestic politics by other means.

It should be clear, then, that this book is not a book on American foreign policy or a contemporary diplomatic history. Nevertheless, a sufficient amount of historical material is interwoven for two purposes. One is to give the student a broad picture of the modern era; for, if this is truly a world the present generation did not make, it is nonetheless one with which it must cope. An understanding of the forces and events that have shaped the modern world should help to make this generation more successful in coping with it than past generations have been. Two, and perhaps even more important, analytical frameworks and concepts are useless unless they have some bearing to the "real" world. Some years ago William Newman wrote that "history is useless, or even in a very real sense nonexistent, without some degree of conceptualization of what is to be looked for; at the same time the true meaning and understanding of a concept can only come from a detailed knowledge of those events that are relevant to that concept.[1]

Finally, this paperback "text" is intended to serve as a core volume only. Instead of tying the instructor and students to a large hardback textbook, it frees them to use supplementally a number of the many fine paperbacks on various topics covered in this book—and perhaps others that, owing to oversight, brevity, or lack of time, have been left uncovered.

In writing a book, the author is always indebted to many people. The undergraduates at the University of Florida who over the years have taken my introductory international politics course and been exposed to a number of different ways of organizing the material—and who have often been kind and gentle in suggesting helpful improvements and criticisms—are certainly entitled to a word of thanks. This book has also been immeasurably helped by my editor, Denise Rathbun, whose suggestions on substance, organization, and style were invaluable.

JOHN SPANIER

Gainesville, Florida

---

[1] William J. Newman, *The Balance of Power in the Inter-War Years, 1919–1939* (New York: Random House, 1968), p. ix.

PART ONE

Analytical Approaches to the Study of International Politics

1 Making Sense of International Politics

For Doves and Hawks—as Well as Parrots, Cuckoos, and Vultures

International politics makes no sense to many people. It is the purpose of this book to change that.

It is all too easy to be overwhelmed by the masses of data that bombard us in random fashion throughout our waking hours—newspaper articles, television news, Presidential press conferences, official communiqués—all of which add up to a stockpile of jumbled information. However, these bits and pieces can become intelligible to us when we understand how to organize them. Making sense of international politics, therefore, means—as in other areas of our daily lives—learning how to cope with a fantastic amount of fragmented information. Our perceptions of reality are formed by abstracting from the totality of experience only those parts we consider relevant. Our perception is selective. It is bound to be, because obviously no man sees every aspect of reality; the world is too complicated and perplexing, and each of us is forced to simplify it to avoid being paralyzed by indecision and ambiguity. Most significant, however, is the fact that our perceptions of reality constitute actual models of the real world. Organizing information involves the selection of relevant facts, the arrangement of these facts in some order, and, therefore, their interpretation. A model or conceptual framework thus selects and systematizes the "facts" of international politics, as indeed of all political life, so that "isolated observable phenomena . . . are brought together and related systematically."[1]

We commonly use models to organize our experiences in various ways. On the one hand, a model may serve to help us *explain* why a particular event has occurred by using the model as an *analogy* that has many features in common with the event. On the other hand, a model can help

[1] Eugene J. Meehan, *The Theory and Method of Political Analysis* (Homewood, Ill.: Dorsey Press, 1965), p. 128.

3

us *understand* an event or an object in even more basic terms: a "model" airplane is a representation of a real airplane. Its smaller size allows us to examine the attributes of an airplane in greater detail. Because of the difference in size, however, a "model" airplane is hardly a *true* representation of a real airplane (for one thing, it uses considerably less gas!). But, in its basic features, the model is indeed an airplane and thus can help us get a clearer picture of, for example, how the various parts of the aircraft are related to one another.

More specifically, a model performs certain significant functions in political analysis.[2] The first is the classification of political events and actors into certain groups or categories that correspond to the characteristics of our model. We describe certain political systems, for example, as "democracies," "totalitarian states," "nation-states," or "empires"; or we describe international systems as "bipolar" or "multipolar" state systems. In filing states or state systems into certain categories we must, of course, first describe the characteristics each possesses. This is not always as simple as it sounds. If we wanted to describe democracy, we might list such standard characteristics as competitive parties, regular free elections, majority rule, and minority protection. But, as the performance of American democracy has come to be measured against continued racial discrimination, poverty, urban blight, and environmental pollution, these rather formal features—as well as such informal ones as social pluralism—have of late been widely questioned. In terms of its actual operations, the American political system is frequently described these days as elitist, controlled by big vested interests ("to those who have shall be given"), and committed to the social and economic *status quo*.[3] So how then do we describe democracy? What is the line of demarcation between democratic and nondemocratic states? By democracy, do we mean free elections, majority rule, minority rights, or equality of resources? Suppose that two of these criteria come into conflict—as, for example, when a majority might vote to deprive a minority group of certain rights (as American blacks were long prevented from voting in many parts of the South). And what about such supposedly totalitarian states as the German Democratic Republic (East Germany) and the Democratic Republic of Vietnam (North Vietnam)? Are these democracies? Because people have conflicting ideas of what "democracy" is, these questions may appear to be futile. However, if we develop a model of democracy, we are basically talking about how we use the term "democracy." What does the concept *communicate* to us about the characteristics of a political system? If we find that the concept is too vague to let us differentiate

[2] J. David Singer, "The Level-of-Analysis Problem in International Relations," *World Politics* (October, 1961), pp. 78–80.

[3] Among others, see Theodore J. Lowi, *The End of Liberalism* (New York: W. W. Norton, 1969); Thomas R. Dye and L. Harmon Ziegler, *The Irony of Democracy* (Belmont, Calif.: Wadsworth, 1970); and Duane Lockard, *The Perverted Priorities of American Politics* (New York: Macmillan, 1970).

democratic from nondemocratic systems, then we must either opt for another concept or try to "refine" our notion of what a democracy is.

A second function of a model is to explain political happenings and behavior. We link what would otherwise be seemingly isolated occurrences into meaningful and understandable patterns. It has been argued, for instance, that a democracy acts peacefully unless it is provoked by aggression, but once that happens, its foreign policy tends to turn into a crusade to punish the aggressor so completely that he will never dare attack again.[4] By taking a number of "facts" and relating them—a democracy with peace and a democracy with war—we have offered two explanations of the behavior of a democracy under two quite different conditions. In fact, we have generalized and said that a certain set of conditions will tend to produce a certain type of behavior. Because this generalization may not hold true 100 per cent of the time, we do not refer to it as a "law" of behavior. We call it a hypothesis, and we then test its accuracy by observation and, if possible, experimentation. A model is in this sense a creative act, for its purpose is to construct a framework that the mind can handle in such a manner as to be able to perceive relationships in the form of hypotheses, which can then be tested for their validity. If certain conditions exist, then certain types of behavior are likely to occur. Similarly, one could plan and construct different types of model airplanes and get some idea of what happens when certain fuselage shapes are combined with various types of wings and other design features. For the airplane manufacturer, such models are tested and changed in various ways until they become the basis of the real planes he wants to build.

Finally, a model offers the capacity for qualified predictions of future behavior. This is not as difficult as it might seem. Much depends on the ability to state accurately the conditions under which certain events will occur. We can predict with considerable certainty that if people suddenly notice the building they are in is on fire, they will scramble for the exits; or that if a state is attacked, it will fight back—and, if it is a democratic state and if our above hypothesis was correct, it is likely to fight a total war for the enemy's unconditional surrender. These examples are not intended to suggest that predictions are easy. Indeed, policy-makers who have tried to predict how other states would react to certain acts of their own might at times have good reason to doubt any model's predictive utility. Had President Johnson, for example, been able to predict accurately the costs of the Vietnam war it is doubtful that he would have escalated the intervention so drastically in 1965. Nevertheless, prediction is one of the possible functions of a model, although the model-builder should always be mindful, first, that the possibility of successful prediction depends on the quality of the model (and the information fed into it) and, second, that prediction means not certainties but probabilities.

While it is commonplace to say that most individuals have feelings

[4] George F. Kennan, *American Diplomacy 1900–1950* (Chicago: University of Chicago Press, 1951), pp. 65–66.

and opinions about international events but no organized way of thinking about them, opinions do in fact reflect some pattern of thought: We do not really perceive the international political world as a mere set of random "happenings" that bear no relationship to one another. We "theorize" even while we are unaware of it. For example, at the end of a war we may say the victor should offer the vanquished nation a generous peace treaty. In so saying we may be acting on the implicit theory that a hostile state may change its behavior if the winner holds out a hand of reconciliation. Or we may say that a punitive peace treaty ought to be imposed. This time our statement suggests a belief that the hostile state will repeat its aggressive behavior unless it is severely punished.

The distinction between those who do not conceptualize and those who do may therefore be less valid than the distinction between those who do so implicitly and those who do so explicitly. We must consequently reject the popular distinction between the "doer" and the "theorist"—the former presumably possessing years of experience, knowledge of the facts, and therefore the common sense and intuition needed to solve problems, the latter without experience and therefore allegedly unable to "play it by ear." The truth is that the former's common sense and intuition reflect implicit concepts, which may be reliable or flimsy. The explicit conceptualizations of this text are offered with the hope that they are, on the whole, more reliable than flimsy. In any event, the distinction between the theorist and the doer should be laid to rest by the example of Henry Kissinger, a scholar and teacher who became one of the United States' two or three outstanding Secretaries of State.

This is a book about how to analyze international politics. Thus, although we focus on the world since 1945, it is not the history of this period that is our primary concern. Rather, our aim is to provide a number of conceptual tools needed for the analysis of the relations between nations. We then apply these tools to the post–World War II period because it is the one most familiar to us, the one with which we have grown up, and the one with which we must cope in the future. But presumably the reader will also be able to analyze earlier periods, as well as events that have yet to pass. For unlike many historians who, engaged in detailed examination of the interstate politics of a particular period, tend to regard the occurrences of that period as unique, the product of specific men, social and economic forces, opinions of the time, and other factors, most political scientists tend to look for *recurrent* patterns of behavior. Despite the unique sets of happenings of different historical periods, the political scientist will look for similarities in conditions and behavior.

For instance, we referred to different ways a victor ought to treat a vanquished nation if he wants to avoid a rematch. The fact remains that peace settlements often leave one or more states dissatisfied. If it is the defeated state, the latter may seek to remedy its grievances militarily and also gain revenge for its humiliation if the terms of peace are not changed peacefully. But the "aggressor" may also be one of the former victors, if what it feels to be its interests are not met at the time the peace is made; and its dissatisfaction is likely to be enhanced if its fellow victors seem to make greater gains. These reasons contributed greatly to the outbreak of World War II. Germany, defeated in 1918, and Italy, one of the victors in 1918, joined forces in the late 1930's against the major victors of World War I, Britain and France. On the other hand, the cold war erupted before peace conferences with Germany and Japan could even be arranged. Nor was this accidental: U.S.-Soviet differences over the peace terms helped to precipitate the intense conflict, which was perhaps kept cold only by the desire of both superpowers to avoid a suicidal nuclear conflagration. From these two cases we could suggest two generalizations about state behavior and the occurrence of wars (hot or cold): One, wars tend to result when major powers feel discontented with the peace terms decided upon at the end of the previous war; and two, wars may be spawned by victorious nations quarreling over the terms of peace ending a war just concluded. Thus we move from the examination of a specific war and the specific reasons it broke out to generalizing about certain conditions that, *if* they materialize, *then* are likely to produce war. With such hypotheses in mind, we can now examine a whole series of wars and sort them out according to these and other conditions that tend to lead to war; and in our examinations, we may be able to refine our hypotheses further and suggest more specifically for each condition why sometimes the sequel is war and why on other occasions it is not.

But how can we organize and interpret the "reality" that we call the international political world? We simplify this reality because we cannot possibly describe all aspects of international politics; we must be selective. We isolate and emphasize certain aspects of this reality and throw them into bold relief, thereby enabling us to make a "conceptual blueprint" of the political life among states. In a sense, we act as a painter viewing a panoramic landscape. He cannot draw every detail; rather, he will select and highlight certain parts of the view he sees, relegate others to the background, and omit yet others. The finished picture will be the landscape as seen by the painter's eyes, from his particular physical position and mental perspective. The painting is in this respect, like the model airplane, a partial representation of actuality. If many intricate details are lost in the smaller canvas or model, this is the price we must pay whenever we use a model to help us explain and understand something. A model is always—if we may be excused for mixing metaphors—an "incomplete picture" which emphasizes those features we most want to communicate, the factors we believe are the critical ones in comparing events and objects.

In analyzing international politics we face the same problems of scope and emphasis. What will be our perspective? In this book, we shall employ a three-dimensional view: the state system, the nation-state, and decision-making.[5] The first view considers the behavior of states as it is determined by the environment in which they live and whose rules they must internalize if they are to survive and be secure; the second explains state behavior as the outcome not of conditions external to the state but of its internal nature. Both share a common assumption: behavior is the product of "the system," be that the external state system or the internal one (whether capitalist or socialist, democratic or totalitarian, developed or underdeveloped). The third perspective is that of decision-making: the ways in which the perceptions of specific policy-makers and the organization of the government mold the policies that are decided. The state system does not literally "determine" state behavior; the latter depends on what those policy-makers who are officially responsible for formulating policy see on the stage of world politics. Nor does the character of the internal system inevitably produce just one kind of behavior; different men governing the same domestic system will come up with different sets of policies. The assumption here is that men are not the puppets of impersonal forces that move them in certain directions regardless of individual wishes.

Each of these three perspectives *organizes* the information we have by allowing us to draw boundaries between subjects (as between democracies and totalitarian states), selecting the key factors or variables that allow us to select the relevant data (and leave the rest) in order to put it all together in some meaningful way which aids us in our understanding and explanation of international politics—*at that level of analysis*. Together, these three levels give us a comprehensive picture of the "games nations play"—particularly why they play the game, to a lesser extent how they play it, and some of the efforts they make to regulate and moderate the game, or play it differently or abolish it altogether. Let us now turn to a more detailed look into each of the three levels of analysis, beginning with the model of the state system at the first level. And, hopefully, by the end of this book, the reader will no longer have to rely upon the teacher or news commentator in the paper or on television to analyze world events for him.

[5] The basic organization of this book was suggested by Kenneth N. Waltz's "three images" in *Man, the State and War* (New York: Columbia University Press, 1959). Also see Singer, "Level-of-Analysis Problem." I have made only two changes: One, the order of the three images or levels of analysis has been reversed; and two, Waltz's first image—my third level—consisted of the traditional and behavioral analysis of man, whereas mine emphasizes the official policy-makers and decision-making.

2 The Three Levels of Analysis: A Framework for the Study of International Politics

The Systemic Level

The term "systemic level" refers to the international or state system comprising all existing political units that interact with one another according to some regular and observable pattern of relationship. Some analysts add such phrases as: "[and] all capable of being implicated in a generalized war,"[1] or "[so that] system-centered behavior becomes to a large extent predictable."[2] The reason the term "system" is used is twofold: First, it encompasses all the component units of sovereign states and therefore possesses the virtue of comprehensiveness, the other two levels of analysis being in this regard more limited in scope; second, it focuses on the relationship or interactions among these units and, therefore, on their interdependence. The behavior of each state depends upon the behavior of other states; or, in terms of gamesmanship, every player's move or "strategy"—the set of moves he calculates he must make to win —depends on the moves of every other player. A system, then, is an abstract way of looking at a part of reality for purposes of analysis; hence, we speak of a human being's "circulatory system," in which the parts or "subsystems"—the veins, arteries, organs, and cells—must all work properly if the larger system is to give peak performance or, perhaps, run at all.

In the game of international politics, the key point to remember is that each state in the state system is the guardian of its own security and independence.[3] Each regards other states as potential enemies who might threaten fundamental interests. Consequently, states generally feel insecure and regard one another with a good deal of apprehension

[1] Raymond Aron, *Peace and War* (New York: Praeger Publishers, 1967), p. 94.
[2] Charles O. Lerche, Jr. and Abdul A. Said, *Concepts of International Politics* (Englewood Cliffs, N.J.: Prentice-Hall, 1963), p. 95.
[3] A fuller presentation of the state system model will be found in Chapter 3.

and distrust. The result is that all become very concerned with their strengths or power. In order to prevent an attack, a state feels it must be as powerful as the potential aggressor, for disproportion of power might tempt it to attack. A "balance of power," or equilibrium, however, would make victory in war unlikely. Therefore, equilibrium will in all probability deter attack. "Equilibrium is balanced power, and balanced power is neutralized power."[4] Thus, a balance of power is the prerequisite for each nation's security, if not survival, as well as for the preservation of the system itself. Any attempt by any nation to expand its power and attain dominance or hegemony, which would allow it to impose its will upon the other states, will be resisted. When the balance is disturbed, the tendency will be for responsive action to be taken to return it to a position of equilibrium. In other words, states are actors whose purpose is to play the role the system has "assigned" them in maintaining this equilibrium. If they fail in their assignment by disregarding the operational rule that power must be counterbalanced, they place their own security in jeopardy. *The balance of power is therefore an empirical description of how states do act (or, more cautiously, how most of them, especially the great powers, act most of the time) and also a prescription for states as to how they should act.*

The impact of a shift in the distribution of power is clearly evident in America's involvements in the two world wars of this century and in the cold war. Our historical isolation from European "power politics" during most of the nineteenth century and early twentieth century was the product of a balance of power on the European Continent. The threat to this isolationism stemmed from the possibility that one state or a coalition of states might conquer most of Europe, organize its vast resources in manpower and industrial strength, and use these to menace the United States. England, to protect its own security, had long opposed any state seeking such hegemony and thereby made it possible for the United States to remain what today is called nonaligned. But when, in 1870, Germany was unified and launched a massive program of industrialization, British power declined relative to Germany's growing capability. Indeed, World War I showed clearly that British and French power could not contain Germany. As Czarist Russia collapsed, the transfer of as many as 2 million German soldiers from the East to the Western Front raised the distinct possibility of a German victory. It was at that point that Germany's unrestricted submarine warfare, which included attacks on American shipping, precipitated U.S. intervention, and

---

[4] Nicholas J. Spykman, *America's Strategy in World Politics: The United States and the Balance of Power* (New York: Harcourt, Brace, 1942), p. 21. For a more extensive discussion of the various ways the term "balance of power" is used by analysts, see Ernst B. Haas, "The Balance of Power: Prescription, Concept, or Propaganda," in *World Politics*, July, 1953, pp. 442–77; and Inis L. Claude, Jr., *Power and International Relations* (New York: Random House, 1962), pp. 11–39.

it was this that made it possible to contain the German spring offensive of 1918 and that led to Germany's defeat.[5]

Just over two decades later, America—which, after victory, had retreated into isolationism again—was once more compelled to concern itself with the European balance. The unexpected German defeat of France in 1940 confronted the United States once again with the specter of an invasion and defeat of England despite its large navy. President Franklin D. Roosevelt therefore undertook a number of measures to strengthen Britain to withstand any Nazi assault.[6] He sent fifty old destroyers to help defend the English Channel, and he set up the Lend-Lease program, which made the United States "the arsenal of democracy." But there was no point in "leasing" Britain the war materials it needed unless they got there. Hence, by the time of Pearl Harbor, the United States was already engaged in an undeclared naval war with Germany in the Atlantic. American warships, convoying American supply ships for American troops in Iceland, allowed British merchantmen filled with war supplies to join convoys as far as that island; once there, the British Navy took over escort duty. Later, American merchant ships were permitted to sail to English harbors; the American Navy even reported the positions of German submarines to British warships and shot at the submarines if they allegedly shot first. The balance of power had made this increasing commitment to Britain necessary, even though such actions increased the risk of war with Germany. In fact, war with Germany was merely a matter of time: German submarines would, sooner or later, start sinking American ships in order to compel Britain's surrender. The German invasion of Russia in 1941 briefly postponed the Battle of the Atlantic, and when it did take place the United States was already at war. But had Hitler, in 1940–41, given the order to sink all ships bound for England, President Roosevelt, like President Wilson before him, would have had to ask Congress for a declaration of war.

Nowhere, however, does the *continuity* of a policy and the degree to which the distribution of power *narrows the range of choice* a nation may encounter in its foreign policy show more clearly than in the eruption of the cold war. During World War II, the United States, allied to Russia, believed it had established the basis for a postwar era of harmony and peace.[7] American policy-makers recognized that the Soviet rulers

[5] Edward H. Buehrig, *Woodrow Wilson and the Balance of Power* (Bloomington, Ind.: Indiana University Press, 1955), and Arthur S. Link, *Wilson the Diplomatist* (Baltimore: Johns Hopkins Press, 1957), *passim*, esp. pp. 61–90.

[6] For the period from 1937 to 1941, the most detailed analysis will be found in William L. Langer and S. Everett Gleason, *The Challenge to Isolation*, and *idem*, *The Undeclared War* (New York: Harper & Row, 1952 and 1953, respectively). A briefer study is Robert A. Divine, *The Reluctant Belligerent* (New York: John Wiley, 1965).

[7] William H. McNeill, *America, Britain and Russia—Their Cooperation and Conflict, 1941–1946* (London: Oxford University Press, 1953), written for the Royal

had reasons to be suspicious of the West: Western intervention in the civil war that broke out upon the Communists' seizure of power; the *cordon sanitaire* established by the French in the 1920's in alliance with a number of East European states and aimed at keeping the Russians out of Europe; the West's appeasement of Hitler, especially the Munich agreement, which gave the Nazi dictator Czechoslovakia's Sudetenland—and eventually the rest of the country—and which the Kremlin might well have viewed as a Western attempt to "open the gates to the East." But President Roosevelt believed that four years of wartime cooperation with America and England had dissolved Soviet suspicion of Western intentions and replaced it with sufficient mutual respect and confidence to ensure that possible conflicts between Russia and the Western nations could be resolved amicably.

Thus, before one of the wartime conferences between Prime Minister Churchill and President Roosevelt, an American intelligence forecast of Russia's postwar position in Europe had concluded that the Soviet Union would be the dominant power in postwar Europe:

> With Germany crushed, there is no power in Europe to oppose her tremendous military forces. . . . The conclusions from the foregoing are obvious. Since Russia is the decisive factor in the war, she must be given every assistance, and every effort must be made to obtain her friendship. Likewise, since without question she will dominate Europe on the defeat of the Axis, it is even more essential to develop and maintain the most friendly relations with Russia.[8]

The significance of this forecast is clear: American policy-makers were apparently unable to conceive of the Soviet Union, the acknowledged new dominant power in Europe, replacing Germany as a grave threat to the European and global balance of power. During the war, the U.S. Government therefore did not aim at re-establishing a European balance of power in order to safeguard the United States. It expected this security to stem from a new era of Russo-American good feeling.

At the Yalta Conference with Stalin in February, 1945, amicable relations with Soviet Russia were established. "Uncle Joe" made several concessions on a number of vital postwar issues—such as the United Nations Organization, German occupation policy, and self-government and free elections for the countries of Eastern Europe, as put forth in the "Declaration on Liberated Europe"; and he promised good will for the future. No wonder that at the end of the conference the American delegation felt a mood of "supreme exaltation." President Roosevelt's closest adviser, Harry Hopkins, later recounted:

Institute of International Affairs; Herbert Feis, *Churchill-Roosevelt-Stalin: The War They Waged and the Peace They Sought* (Princeton, N.J.: Princeton University Press, 1957). A shorter study is Gaddis Smith, *American Diplomacy During the Second World War, 1941–1945* (New York: John Wiley, 1965).

[8] Robert E. Sherwood, *Roosevelt and Hopkins: An Intimate History* (New York: Harper & Row, 1948), p. 748.

We really believed in our hearts that this was the dawn of the new day we had all been praying for and talking about for so many years. We were absolutely certain that we had won the first great victory of the peace— and, by "we," I mean *all* of us, the whole civilized human race. The Russians had proved that they could be reasonable and far-seeing, and there wasn't any doubt in the minds of the President or any of us that we could live with them peacefully for as far into the future as any of us could imagine.[9]

The American Secretary of State, Cordell Hull, was even more optimistic: "There will no longer," he said, "be need for spheres of influence, for alliances, balance of power, or any other of the special arrangements through which, in the unhappy past, the nations strove to safeguard their security or promote their interests."[10]

Unlike the United States, with its long isolationist tradition, Russia had been a long-time player of "power politics." The Soviet Union was therefore bound to feel fearful in terms of the state system's norms of behavior. If conflict was inherent in the system, Russia had to assure itself a strong position for the struggle it could expect after Germany's collapse. Russia had, after all, capitulated to Germany during World War I and had come close to defeat during World War II; more than a century earlier, Napoleon had also invaded and almost defeated it. In fact, Russia's experience of and fear of invasion and defeat were quite old, and they left the country, which had never possessed a natural frontier to protect it (as England had with the Channel or America with the Atlantic), with a double legacy: internally, the establishment of an authoritarian government that sought to centralize power in order to provide the country with a better defense and a greater degree of security; and externally, a "defensive expansionism" to obtain "security belts" beyond its frontiers.[11]

Stalin was well aware both of the state system's rules of behavior and of Russia's historical experience. In 1931, even before the German threat had reappeared, he had urged full speed ahead on Soviet industrialization, because

. . . to slacken the pace would mean to lag behind; and those who lag behind are beaten. We do not want to be beaten. No, we don't want to. The history of old . . . Russia [was that] she was ceaselessly beaten for her backwardness. She was beaten by the Mongol Khans, she was beaten by Turkish Beys, she was beaten by Swedish feudal lords, she was beaten by Polish-Lithuanian Pans, she was beaten by Anglo-French capitalists, she was beaten by Japanese barons, she was beaten by all—for her backwardness. For military backwardness, for industrial backwardness, for agricultural backwardness. She was beaten because to beat her was profitable

[9] *Ibid.*, p. 870.

[10] Cordell Hull, *The Memoirs of Cordell Hull* (New York: Macmillan, 1948), 2:1314–15.

[11] Louis J. Halle, *The Cold War as History* (New York: Harper & Row, 1967), pp. 10–19.

and went unpunished. You remember the words of the prerevolutionary poet: "Thou art poor and thou art plentiful, thou are mighty, and thou art helpless, Mother Russia." . . . We are fifty or a hundred years behind the advanced countries. We must make good this lag in ten years. Either we do it or they crush us.[12]

Stalin was right. Hitler almost crushed Soviet Russia, just as World War I had, in fact, helped bring down the Czarist system. And now, as this war was ending, Russia confronted yet another Western power whose population was almost as big as Russia's, whose industrial strength was far greater, and whose enormous military power had, in the closing days of the war, been augmented by the technological discovery of how to split the atom.

Thus, as World War II came to a close and in the months immediately afterward, Russia's actions were largely typical of a great power, irrespective of its ideology: the imposition of Russian control on Poland, Hungary, Bulgaria, and Rumania, turning them into satellites (Yugoslavia was already under Tito's control, and Czechoslovakia was living under the Red Army's shadow); and the attempts to dominate Iran, to effect a breakthrough to the Mediterranean by pressuring Turkey and supporting a guerrilla war in Greece, and demands for the administration of the Italian colony of Libya in North Africa and a share in the control of the Ruhr industry in West Germany while insisting on unilateral control of East Germany. Above all, Soviet power advanced behind the retreating German armies and ended up in the center of Europe.

These were the actions that led to the American containment policy. As weary and destroyed as Russia was by the war, it emerged as the major power on the Eurasian land mass. Its armed forces were reduced—according to Khrushchev's report in 1960—from 12 million to 3 million; Western estimates in the late 1940's were 1 million to 2 million higher, exclusive of approximately half a million security troops.[13] Still, all the other former major powers in Europe had collapsed. Germany was in ruins, France never recovered from its defeat and occupation, and Britain foundered soon after victory. Nowhere in Europe was there any countervailing power. The only such power existed outside Europe. Thus, America may have wanted to turn its back on the international scene and concentrate once more on domestic affairs, and it may have demobilized itself psychologically and militarily (American armed forces were reduced from 11.5 million to just short of 1.5 million men and the military budget cut from the 1945 high of $81 billion to a low of $11 billion in 1948—a full year after the announcement of the containment policy).[14]

[12] Quoted by Isaac Deutscher, *Stalin: A Political Biography* (New York: Oxford University Press, 1949), p. 328.

[13] Thomas W. Wolfe, *Soviet Power and Europe, 1945–1970* (Baltimore: Johns Hopkins Press, 1970), p. 10.

[14] *Ibid.*, p. 11, and Samuel P. Huntington, *The Common Defense* (New York: Columbia University Press, 1961), pp. 33–39.

But this preference was not decisive. The distribution of power in the state system left the nation no choice. It was not what the United States wished to do that was to matter; it was what it *had* to do. A new balance had to be established.

The postwar falling-out among the Allies and their ensuing rivalry was almost a replay of the conflict that occurred after the disintegration of the coalition that had defeated Napoleon. At the end of that lengthy war, Czarist Russia, after an exhausting struggle, ended with soldiers in Paris and a close ally in Prussia. The Czar was particularly adamant about retaining control of Poland (its boundaries were quite different from those of contemporary Poland). All entreaties for him to withdraw his troops behind Russia's frontiers were in vain. (Interestingly, Stalin controlled East Germany, of which Prussia had been a large part before World War II. When an American said to Stalin that it must be gratifying for him to be in Berlin after such a bloody war, Stalin curtly replied "Czar Alexander got to Paris."[15]) It was only after Britain, Austria, and a defeated France signed a triple alliance, reputedly ready to go to war if the Czar remained stubborn, that a new balance satisfactory to all the great powers was worked out (including a part of Poland for the Czar) and ratified at the Congress of Vienna in 1815.

In simple terms, the post-1945 conflict substituted Soviet Russia for Czarist Russia and the United States for Britain.[16] The differences in ideology between the two Russias, or the differences in political complexion and economic systems between the two English-speaking nations, were in the context of the balance-of-power analysis *not* the key factors in breaking up the respective wartime alliances against Napoleon and Hitler and aligning the principal powers on opposite sides. The key issue in each case was the postwar distribution of power. In terms of the state system's logic, even had Russia in 1945 been a capitalist state like the United States (or the latter country a Communist state like Russia), the bipolar division of power after Germany's defeat would have brought on the cold war. They became enemies because, as the only two powerful states left, each had the ability to inflict enormous damage on the other. As Paul Seabury has noted, bipolarity was "a contradiction in which two powers—America and Russia—were by historical circumstances thrown into a posture of confrontation which neither had actually 'willed,' yet one from which extrication was difficult."[17] Or, as Louis Halle has pointed out, the historical circumstances of 1945 "had an ineluctable quality that left the Russians little choice but to move as they

[15] W. Averell Harriman, *America and Russia in a Changing World: A Half Century of Personal Observation* (Garden City, N.Y.: Doubleday, 1971), p. 44.

[16] See, for example, Harold Nicolson, *The Congress of Vienna* (New York: Harcourt, Brace, 1946), and Edward V. Gulick, *Europe's Classical Balance of Power* (New York: W. W. Norton, 1967).

[17] Paul E. Seabury, *The Rise and Decline of the Cold War* (New York: Basic Books, 1967), p. 59.

did. Moving as they did, they compelled the United States and its allies to move in response. And so the Cold War was joined." As Halle suggests, "This is not fundamentally a case of the wicked against the virtuous. Fundamentally . . . we [the observers] may properly feel sorry for both parties, caught, as they are, in a situation of irreducible dilemma."[18]

One point in connection with this level of analysis still needs to be illustrated, namely, that the price of failure to heed the operational rule of balancing the power of a potential opponent is a loss of security and probably war. Churchill once called World War II "the unnecessary war," by which he meant that it could have been prevented if Britain and France had remobilized sufficient forces and acted against Germany's various moves to upset the European balance: the reintroduction of conscription (the German forces had been limited to 100,000 men by the Treaty of Versailles); the occupation of the Rhineland—an area neutralized at Versailles because Germany had twice launched its attacks on France from there; the demand for the return of the Sudetenland— a mountainous area that, despite its sizable German population, was at Versailles given to the new state of Czechoslovakia so that it could better defend itself against its large German neighbor; and finally, the demand for the return of the famous Polish Corridor. Each of these was a move toward changing the distribution of power in Europe in Germany's favor. Conscription would rebuild Germany's military strength. The militarization of the Rhineland would permit Germany to build the Siegfried Line, hold the Western Front against France with minimal strength, and concentrate German power against the countries of Eastern Europe to blackmail them into submission once they could no longer count on their French ally. And the first prize of this policy—the acquisition of the Sudetenland in 1938—dismembered Czechoslovakia, left the rest of that unhappy country prostrate for Germany to swallow a few months later, and strengthened the vise around Poland that was to pressure it into submission.[19]

Not until after Hitler had taken over the whole of Czechoslovakia did England's leaders see the true Hitler and decide that he could not be allowed to go any farther. Hitler, however, believing that England's announced support of Poland was meaningless and that his latest challenge would go unmet as before, attacked Poland. England then declared war on Germany, as did France. World War II thus began under the worst of all circumstances: after Germany's rearmament, the building of the Siegfried Line, the loss of Czechoslovakia, and the demoralization

---

[18] Halle, *Cold War as History*, p. xiii.

[19] William J. Newman, *The Balance of Power in the Interwar Years, 1919–1939* (New York: Random House, 1968); Arnold Wolfers, *Britain and France Between Two Wars* (New York: W. W. Norton, 1966); and Winston S. Churchill, *The Second World War*, vol. I: *The Gathering Storm* (Boston: Houghton Mifflin, 1948), p. 90.

of France's other allies in Eastern Europe—in short, when Germany was no longer the weak power it had been at the time of Hitler's first expansionist moves, in the mid-1930's.

The outbreak of World War II, therefore, stands as a monument to a single lesson: Decent personal motives, such as those of Prime Minister Chamberlain, who wanted nothing more than to spare his countrymen the horror of another war, do not necessarily produce successful political policies. At the very minimum, these require an understanding of the nature of the state system, its demands upon national leaders and the rules of its operation. The American conduct of World War II was to underline the importance of this understanding. American leaders did not expect the Western coalition with Russia to collapse after Germany's defeat. They did not understand that, in terms of the model, once the common purpose had been achieved the partners would have to concern themselves with securing their own protection in a new balance of power; they did not realize that this meant that even during the war each Alliance member, in anticipation of possible future conflict and perhaps even war, needed to take precautionary steps to assure itself of a strong postwar position.

In summing up, three points should be noted briefly at this time about the state system level of analysis. First, to a very significant extent, state behavior can be explained in terms of the ever changing distribution of power in the system. As that distribution changes between any two powers, the behavior and alignment of third powers also change. Thus, according to this analysis, states have a relatively limited range of choice about the kind of foreign policies they adopt. Second, the emphasis on the balance of power as the principal variable explaining a state's conduct suggests that domestic factors, such as a state's political complexion, economic organization, social structure, or role of public opinion, have no noticeable impact on policy. All states are viewed as monolithic units, identical to all other states in interest, motivation, and behavior. Third, perhaps the most appropriate way of summing up our analysis of the state system is to repeat that in many cases the model clearly does seem to explain why states acted as they did. But equally clearly, it does not explain some other very significant instances. By itself, the model as it stands can explain neither British policy in the late 1930's nor American policy during World War II. These examples demonstrate that the systemic model is not as much "scientific" (in the sense that it can account for the behavior of the participating states) as it is *prescriptive*. Our model, in brief, can at times tell us that states did indeed behave as they did behave; but at other times, the best it can tell us is that states did not act as they *should have*.[20] In Inis Claude's words: "From all this there emerges a general principle of action: When any state or bloc becomes powerful, or threatens to become inordinately powerful, other

[20] Charles A. McClelland, *Theory and the International System* (New York: Macmillan, 1966), p. 67.

states *should* recognize this as a threat to their security and respond by taking equivalent measures, individually or jointly, to enhance their power."[21] Because states frequently do not do what they should do, we must look to the other levels of analysis for alternative or supplementary explanations.

The Nation-State Level

As distinct from the state system level of analysis with its emphasis on the *external* determinants of state behavior, the nation-state level attributes this behavior to a state's *internal* characteristics, such as the political system, the nature of the economy, or the social structure. The emphasis here is not on the likeness of states, the similarity of their motives, the insignificant impact of domestic attributes, but on the differences of motivation, attitudes, and internal composition or domestic structure among nations. We therefore categorize states, for example, as capitalist states, democratic states, revolutionary states, new nations, and so forth. Political scientists and diplomatic historians, among others, have frequently attributed certain characteristic patterns of behavior to such typologies.

Let us go back to our example of British policy during the 1930's and the principal point of our earlier analysis: that Britain did not pursue the policy it *should* have. Why? Our second-level analysis suggests one possible answer is that England was a democracy in which mass preferences were expressed regularly through general elections. Successive British governments were, therefore, sensitive to a public opinion and mood that throughout the entire period between the two World Wars were overwhelmingly influenced by the memories of World War I; there was a widespread popular demand that another such bloodletting be avoided if at all possible.

It would be difficult to exaggerate the impact of the cataclysmic experience of the Great War. World War I had been the first total war —with the possible exception of the French Revolution and the Napoleonic Wars—Europe had experienced since the Treaty of Westphalia in 1648 had ended the slaughter of the Thirty Years' War. While Europe had, to be sure, witnessed a number of wars during the nineteenth century, they had been minor and of brief duration. Thus, after the almost 100 years of relative peace since 1815, Europe suffered the shock of another major war and a terrible bloodletting. Once the initial German offensive into France was halted, the war on the Western Front bogged down in the trenches. First one side, then the other tried to break through the opponent's lines; neither was successful. Successive lines of barbed wire protected enemy trenches, murderous machine-gun

---

[21] Claude, *Power and International Relations*, p. 43. Italics added.

and rapid-rifle fire mowed down row after row of advancing infantry. Breakthroughs became impossible.

World War I was not a war of mobility and maneuver; it was a war of attrition—an organized, four-year-long attempt by both sides to gain victory simply by bleeding each other to death. It was an unsophisticated strategy, and the losses were catastrophic. An English attempt to pierce German lines in 1916 resulted in the five-month Battle of the Somme. Although they pounded the German lines for eight days with artillery before the troops were even sent into battle, the British gained only 120 square miles—at the cost of 420,000 men, or 3,500 per square mile. German losses were even greater: 445,000 men. Some estimates place the total Somme casualties at 1.2 million, the highest for any battle in history. At Ypres in 1917, the British bombardment lasted nineteen days; 321 trainloads of shells were fired, the equivalent of a year's production by 55,000 war workers. This time the English forces captured forty-five square miles—at the cost of 370,000 men, or 8,222 per square mile. By comparison, total British Empire casualties during the six years of World War II were almost 1.25 million, including 350,000 dead and 91,000 missing. Approximately 9 million men in uniform were killed during the four years of the Great War, and the number of dead civilians totaled several million more.[22]

But the impact of war cannot be measured by citing statistics of the dead. The real impact can only be understood psychologically. Losses are not just quantitative; they are qualitative as well. A nation can ill afford to lose millions of its men. It can even less afford to lose almost its entire youth. Is it any wonder that the nations of Europe, having lost so many of their men—and especially their young men and the children they would have fathered—also lost their *élan*, their self-confidence, their hope for the future? For the men who would have supplied this vigor and optimism—had they grown up and become the leaders of government, business, labor, and science—lay dead in Flanders Field. And those who returned from the battlefields, where they had left the corpses of their comrades-in-arms, were haunted by the war. In the interwar period, they remained politically passive, withdrawing into their private worlds, avoiding any public involvement. Erich Maria Remarque dedicated his famous novel *All Quiet on the Western Front* to this "generation of men who, even though they may have escaped its shells, were destroyed by the war."[23]

England, its people, and almost all of its political leaders were as a

[22] On the slaughter of World War I, see Theodore Ropp, *War in the Modern World*, rev. ed. (New York: Collier Books, 1962); Hanson W. Baldwin, *World War I: An Outline History* (New York: Harper & Row, 1962); Leon Wolff, *In Flanders Field* (New York: Viking Press, 1958); and particularly the dramatic book by Alistair Horne, *The Price of Glory: Verdun 1916* (New York: St. Martin's Press, 1962).

[23] Erich Maria Remarque, *All Quiet on the Western Front*, translated by A. W. Wheen (Boston: Little, Brown, 1929), pp. 289–90.

result of this slaughter concerned above all with avoiding another war. "No more war, no more war" became their cry. And who could blame them? Prime Ministers Baldwin and Chamberlain were not concerned with their personal survival. They were men of honorable intentions and decent motives, greatly concerned for the welfare of their fellow men and repelled by the senselessness of modern war. It is easy today to sneer at the appeasement of Hitler, but to the survivors of World War I another war could mean only more slaughter and more useless sacrifices, more Verduns and the Sommes. They still heard the "soldiers marching, all to die." And they remembered that the strain of the war had brought collapse to four of Europe's great empires: Austria-Hungary, Ottoman Turkey, Imperial Russia, and Imperial Germany. They also recalled that, despite Germany's grievous losses, its opponents had suffered twice as many—and their populations were smaller than Germany's. If fighting another war would involve another such blood bath, surely they would be signing their nations' death warrants. Their social structures and morale could not absorb such losses for the second time in two generations.

To most men who had lived through the tragic war years, peace thus became a supreme value. The appeasement of Hitler during the 1930's was to them not just the only policy—it was an absolute necessity. Surely it was "saner" to resolve differences with reason than with guns. Would it not be better to understand each other's legitimate grievances and settle differences in a spirit of good will rather than by war? Was it not preferable to make mutual concessions, thereby diminishing distrust and fear and building the mutual confidence that could be the only basis of a firm peace? To ask these questions was to answer them for most of the men who had survived 1914–18. Between the alternatives of appeasement and war, no man of good will and humanity had a choice.

British leaders felt they had no choice anyway. The antiwar mood was far too pervasive: 1933 was the year the students of the Oxford Union passed their resolution refusing "to fight for King and country"; 1935 was the year of the Peace Ballot and a general election in which the Prime Minister, knowing Britain needed to rearm, pledged not to do so because he felt certain that a rearmament stance would have lost the election for the Conservatives; 1938 was the year in which cheering English crowds welcomed back Prime Minister Chamberlain, who, they were assured, had brought them "peace in our time"; and even in 1939, a few months before the outbreak of war and several months after Munich and Hitler's violation of it, the Labour Party—which had been pacifist throughout the 1930's—was still opposing military conscription.[24]

This case study of a single democratic nation's foreign policy remains,

[24] Among others on this period, see Churchill, *Gathering Storm*; Charles L. Mowat, *Britain Between the Wars 1918–1940* (Chicago: University of Chicago Press, 1955); and A. J. P. Taylor, *English History, 1914–1945* (New York: Oxford University Press, 1965).

nevertheless, a single instance and therefore does not provide a sufficient basis for generating broader generalizations about democracies' foreign policy behavior. Klaus Knorr, a political scientist, has however gone beyond one example and has hypothesized that modern industrial societies like Britain—regardless of their earlier war experiences—tend on the whole to be peaceful societies.[25] Before the scientific and industrial revolution, he argues, a state could add to its power and wealth by adding territory and population. But such conquest has become unattractive because the "political and economic leaders of industrial and wealthy countries are now aware that domestic savings and investment and the advancement of education, science, and technology are the most profitable means and the most secure avenues to the attainment of wealth and welfare."[26] Indeed, in modern societies in which leaders are generally responsive to mass preferences, the policy emphasis shifts from "high" policy concerns with security and prestige to "low" policy concentration on wealth and welfare. Economic development, in short, turns the nation's attention and energy primarily toward the further domestic production of "butter" under conditions of peace. Modern societies have evolved into welfare states in which extensive domestic demands on government lower the priority of external aims. These social-service countries are, as a result, primarily inwardly oriented; in the absence of a readily visible threat to their security, they view the spending of large sums on arms as a waste.[27] Popular interest in foreign affairs is at best sporadic, responding to specific crises; only then will money for defensive purposes be allocated. But the aggressive, acquisitive use of force by an affluent state that is geared to public and private expenditures for personal and family comfort will be rare and, if it occurs, disapproved. In addition, such modern societies tend to emphasize values like health, education, and welfare, and these are in conflict with the conduct of foreign policies that emphasize force, killing, or exploitation. Man is not to be treated as an object of aggression or oppression.

If this hypothesis about modernization and foreign policy behavior is

[25] Klaus Knorr, *On the Uses of Military Power in the Nuclear Age* (Princeton, N.J.: Princeton University Press, 1966), pp. 21–23, 29–30, 46–50, and Edward L. Morse, "The Transformation of Foreign Policies: Modernization, Interdependence, and Externalization," *World Politics* (April, 1970), pp. 377–85.

[26] Knorr, *Uses of Military Power*, p. 22.

[27] Walter Lippmann has articulated the role of democratic public opinion more negatively than Knorr. Precisely because of its emphasis on wealth and welfare, Lippmann argues, democracies make it difficult to take the necessary preparations to avoid war.

> The rule to which there are few exceptions . . . is that at the critical junctures, when the stakes are high, the prevailing mass opinion [in a democracy] will impose what amounts to a veto upon changing the course on which the government is at the time proceeding. Prepare for war in time of peace? No. It is bad to raise taxes, to unbalance the budget, to take men way from their schools or their jobs, to provoke the enemy.

Walter Lippmann, *The Public Philosophy* (Boston: Little, Brown, 1955), pp. 19–20.

correct—and given the industrial nature of Nazi Germany, Knorr's hypothesis would probably be more accurate if the term "modern industrialized societies" were preceded by the adjective "democratic"—Britain's policies during the 1930's become even more understandable. For it would by its very nature be an essentially inward-looking nation; and this propensity would have been intensified by the Great Depression. The need to concentrate on domestic problems and do something about the economy—an economy that even before the Depression suffered large-scale unemployment—was bound to make foreign policy a secondary matter. Memories of 1914–18 only augmented this existing scale of priorities, so that not until Hitler made the immense threat to Britain's security clear to both its public and its leaders was this priority of domestic over foreign policy reversed.

The war that broke out in September, 1939, was the second in twenty years to be precipitated by Germany. It was also to become the twentieth century's second total war, a war fought for the total destruction of the enemy and his unconditional surrender. Again, our democratic typology may be used to analyze what happened. George Kennan, a famous American diplomat and scholar, has noted that when democracies turn from their inward, peaceful preoccupation toward the external arena and are compelled to fight, they become ferocious.

> A democracy is peace-loving. It does not like to go to war. It is slow to rise to provocation. When it has once been provoked to the point where it must grasp the sword, it does not easily forgive its adversary for having produced this situation. The fact of the provocation then becomes itself the issue. Democracy fights in anger—it fights for the very reason that it was forced to go to war. It fights to punish the power that was rash enough and hostile enough to provoke it—to teach that power a lesson it will not forget, to prevent the thing from happening again. Such a war must be carried to the bitter end.[28]

Various reasons have been adduced in support of this hypothesis about the warlike nature of democracy once it is engaged in military conflict. If war and violence are considered evil—the very denial of democracy's humanitarian ideals—their use demands a moral stance; when it becomes necessary to resort to force, it must be for defensive and noble reasons. The complete destruction of the aggressor regime, particularly if its way of life is authoritarian (as was Germany's) and therefore by democratic standards inferior, immoral, and warlike, becomes a spiritually uplifting cause. Once destroyed, the vanquished nation can be sent to democratic reform school and transformed into a peaceful state. But beyond this general need for a moral justification lies the reality of war. War disturbs the scale of social priorities of an individualistic and materialistic culture. It separates families; it kills and wounds; it demands

[28] George F. Kennan, *American Diplomacy 1900–1950* (Chicago: University of Chicago Press, 1951), pp. 65–66.

economic sacrifice; and it imposes a degree of regimentation and discipline. If a society that emphasizes individual dignity and the pursuit of individual, family, and social welfare and affluence then must go to war, the sacrifices demanded need to be commensurate with some wholesome, ennobling, and morally transcending goal. Total victory, in this context, becomes the minimum aim.

Whatever the reasons for democracies to fight total wars, the consequences of such wars have, in this century, been dramatic. Kennan has even attributed the Communist seizure of power in Russia to the drive for total victory by the Allies in World War I.[29] After the collapse of the Czarist state during the war, the February Revolution of 1917 established a Provisional Government composed of liberals and moderate conservatives and led by Alexander Kerensky. According to Kennan, if the war had been concluded immediately, the new government might have been able to consolidate its position and Russia would then have been able to evolve in a democratic direction. But Kerensky's government felt honor bound not to break the Czar's pledge to the Western powers that Russia would not sign a separate peace treaty with Germany —which would have left the Allies to confront Germany's overwhelming power alone. And the Western Allies would not release Russia from that pledge. They needed Russia's help to achieve total victory. Yet a conclusion of the war for Russia was a prerequisite for any possible stabilization of the domestic turmoil. The Russian people were weary of fighting. Above all else, they wanted peace. The army had already declared its desire for an end to the massacre by "voting with its feet": Large numbers of soldiers had simply left the front lines and returned home. Even more important, the Provisional Government could not implement a land-reform program while simultaneously trying to conduct a war. Yet this was the key to long-term success. Nine-tenths of all Russians lived on the land, and peasant land hunger had long agitated the Czarist regime and eroded peasant loyalty to the autocracy. In the absence of a serious start on land redistribution, the new government was unable to rally popular support. Lenin exploited these circumstances by promising that when the Communists assumed power they would end hostilities and grant every peasant his own piece of land. In November, 1917, the Communist Party seized power in a second revolution. Russia's continued participation in the war had been fatal for Kerensky's Provisional Government. The incompatibility between Allied war aims and Russia's own domestic needs was thereby resolved in the Communists' favor.

If the Western powers' addiction to total war resulted in the collapse of Russia, leaving it in the hands of a regime that was to become openly hostile to the West, it also made World War II all but inevitable.[30] For, as we now know, a second result of the exhausting wartime experience

[29] George F. Kennan, *Russia and the West Under Lenin and Stalin* (Boston: Little, Brown, 1961), pp. 33–36.
[30] Kennan, *American Diplomacy*, pp. 55–57, 68–69.

of World War I was the grave weakening of Britain and France. A third consequence was the collapse of Austria-Hungary and the birth of a small number of unstable East European states that would not contribute to the continent's equilibrium. Their independence was only a matter of time until Russia and Germany recovered their strength; these two great powers would then share a common interest in destroying the states between them, after which they could engage in a contest for supremacy over the entire area. A final consequence of the complete defeat of Germany was the fall of the Monarchy. Hence, though the Kaiser led his country into war, the new regime created at Weimar led it out, accepting the punitive terms imposed by the Versailles Peace Treaty. As a result, the German people would identify the new democratic Weimar Republic with humiliation and defeat. Amid the great social unrest that followed the runaway inflation of the early 1920's and the Great Depression a few years later, Germany would have no traditional institutions to which to cling as it sought to weather the crisis. These conditions offered fertile ground for Hitler, who sought to gain power by exploiting nationalist frustration, impoverishment, and uncertainty.

If democratic behavior, according to the Kennan interpretation, helped give birth to Soviet Russia, Soviet Russia represented, in a classification coined by Henry Kissinger, a revolutionary state.[31] Whether it is democratic France in the late eighteenth and early nineteenth centuries or Communist Russia in our century, the revolutionary state presents a total challenge to the international order. It repudiates the existing order, because it rejects the domestic structures of the major powers in the system. The revolutionary state's leaders pose two questions: Why do the mass of men live in poverty, ill health, and ignorance? And why is mankind constantly cursed by war? In answer, these leaders point to the *ancien régime*. The majority of men are destitute because they are exploited by a privileged minority. Wars are fought because they pay dividends in the form of enhanced prestige, territorial acquisitions, or economic gains; and while the few profit, it is the masses who are compelled to do most of the fighting and dying. Thus man can be freed from economic exploitation, political subjugation, and international violence only by the destruction of the existing system. Only after the overthrow of the ruling classes in all states can man achieve freedom from want, despotism, and war. The revolutionary state assumes responsibility for the liberation of mankind from its bondage.

Thus, by the very nature of its belief, the revolutionary state is presumably committed to "permanent revolution"—that is, to the total defeat of the prevailing political, economic, and cultural system that has condemned man to eternal slavery. Only a worldwide victory of the "new order" can lead to the establishment of a universal society in

[31] Henry A. Kissinger, *Nuclear Weapons and Foreign Policy* (New York: Harper & Row, 1957), p. 316, and *idem, A World Restored* (New York: Grosset & Dunlap, 1964).

which man will, for the first time in history, be truly free from oppression and need. Characteristic of the revolutionary state as a messianic power engaged in a "just war" to establish eternal domestic social justice and international peace is the proclamation issued by the National Convention of the Republic after the French Revolution:

> The French Nation declares that it will treat as enemies every people who, refusing liberty and equality or renouncing them, may wish to maintain, recall, or treat with the prince and the privileged classes; on the other hand, it engages not to subscribe to any treaty and not to lay down its arms until the sovereignty and independence of the people whose territory the troops of the Republic shall have entered shall be established, and until the people shall have adopted the principles of equality and founded a free and democratic government.[32]

If the typology of the revolutionary state is valid, Stalinist Russia, in the years immediately after World War II, would have viewed the United States not as just another state trapped by the same security problem but as a capitalist state that had to be eliminated. And, in fact, Moscow rejected the notion that national insecurity and international conflict were the result *only*—or even primarily—of the state system. It believed that international antagonism and hostility, as well as domestic poverty, unemployment, ill health, and ignorance, were *also* due—indeed, primarily due—to the internal nature of the system's leading states. Capitalism was the cause of all social evil. Only in a political system in which the Communist Party, representing the exploited majority, the proletariat, possessed control and in which all the forces of production were removed from private ownership so that they could be used for the benefit of all men, instead of for the profit of the privileged few, would mankind finally live free from social injustice, deprivation, and war. As a total critique of capitalist society and a promise to deliver men from evil and bring them domestic justice and external peace, Communism in fact constituted a secular religion of damnation and salvation and conferred upon the Soviet Union the messianic duty of converting all men to the "true faith."

Consequently, according to this interpretation of the foreign policy behavior of a revolutionary state, Soviet Russia was a state engaged in a constant and irreconcilable "holy war" with all non-Communist states, a state seeking hegemony in the state system. Soviet hostility toward the West, it must be emphasized, predated 1945 because it was to a large degree ideological and preconceived.[33] It was a hostility Lenin and Stalin had felt even before they seized power in Russia and before Western governments had adopted any anti-Soviet policies. It was an enmity deduced from first principles and based not on what Western governments

---

[32] Quoted from Carlton J. H. Hayes, *The Historical Evolution of Modern Nationalism* (New York: Macmillan, 1950), p. 40.
[33] Kennan, *Russia and the West*, p. 181.

did but on what they were alleged to be. Western actions were almost irrelevant. Once non-Communist states were declared hostile, and official declarations and policies formulated upon that assumption, it was hardly astounding that Western reactions would be less than friendly and that the Soviet leaders would reap the fruits of the policy they had sown. Communist ideology thus raised the level of mutual fear and suspicion resulting from the state system and caused Stalinist Russia to undertake both "defensive expansionism" (due to its enhanced apprehension of foreign attack) and "offensive expansionism" (due to its determination to shrink the capitalist world). Any *modus vivendi* such as the one finally worked out between Czarist Russia and the monarchies of Britain, France, and Austria-Hungary in 1815 was in the circumstances of 1945 therefore excluded. The war was hardly over when the President of the Soviet Union, Mikhail Kalinin, was saying:

> But even now, after the greatest victory known to history, we cannot for one minute forget the basic fact that our country remains the one socialist state in the world. . . . The victory achieved does not mean that all dangers to our state structure and social order have disappeared. Only the most concrete, most immediate danger, which threatened us from Hitlerite Germany, has disappeared. In order that the danger of war may really disappear for a long time, it is necessary to consolidate our victory.[34]

And in February, 1946, a year before the Truman Doctrine, in what the liberal Supreme Court Justice Douglas called "the declaration of World War III," Stalin warned the Soviet people that further sacrifices were needed in order to increase Russia's industrial strength, for

> it would be a mistake to believe that the second world war broke out accidentally or as a result of mistakes. . . . Actually the war came about as an inevitable result of the development of international economic and political forces on the basis of modern monopoly capitalism. Marxists have repeatedly explained that the capitalist system of world economy contains the elements of a general crisis and armed conflicts, that consequently the development of international capitalism in our time takes place not peacefully and evenly but through crises and war catastrophes.[35]

Thus, according to this second level of analysis, the cold war would have erupted regardless of the emergence of bipolarity, because Russia was now *Soviet* Russia, and its aims and objectives extended far beyond those historically entertained by the Czars.

As with the state-system model, the typologies depicted in this section are intended to be helpful in explaining and predicting the behavior of particular classifications of states. Thus, the hypothesis about the peaceful behavior of a democracy helps in part to explain the reasons for Britain's appeasement of Hitler before World War II and America's

[34] Quoted by Paul E. Zinner, "The Ideological Bases of Soviet Foreign Policy," *World Politics*, July, 1952, p. 497.
[35] *Ibid.*

wartime expectation of a postwar return to normalcy, as well as why both states did not behave as they should presumably have done had they heeded the systemic norms regarding the distribution of power. Presumably, industrialized democracies will look outward only when they perceive themselves gravely provoked by an external challenge that leaves them with little choice but to respond in their own defense against a challenger who has clearly labeled himself an aggressor. Once the challenge has been met, they will again look inward.

Similarly, if it is true that total wars are the kind of wars that democracies fight with a fair degree of domestic unity and moral certitude, as only a high moral purpose can justify a democracy's waging of war,[36] it might have been predictable that the United States would experience internal dissension and moral anguish fighting "limited wars," especially ones that did not begin with a clearly visible and overt aggression and in which its ally was hardly a paragon of democratic rectitude. If a democracy prefers either to abstain from the use of power and concentrate on its business at home or to use its power fully in a righteous cause and get the war over with as quickly as possible in order to return to its domestic affairs, then one might have foreseen that limited wars not soon ended would lead to extreme public opinion bifurcation: on the one hand, those who say the country should never have gotten involved in the first place and should withdraw, and on the other, those who advocate escalation of the conflict to win a quick military victory and then get out. Under these conditions, a President's early popular support for such a war is destined to erode.

The Decision-Making Level

Up to now we have analyzed international politics in terms of such largely abstract units as the state system, which delegates roles to its member units, especially its principal actors, in preserving the balance of power, or of different classes of states. Throughout, we have personified states. But common sense tells us that "the United States" does not make decisions; certain men who occupy the official political positions responsible for making foreign policy decisions do.

It is this level of analysis that is probably most familiar to many people. At election time, we debate the virtues of the leading candidates, their expressed and implied views, their alleged values, groups they may be beholden to; and we watch how they handle themselves on television —whether they have substance, are sincere, remain "cool" under pressure. Apparently, who is President matters. Presumably it affects the priorities between domestic and foreign policies, the kind of foreign

---

[36] This penchant has led Paul Seabury to remark on the ultimate irony: "The pity of this is that in consequence, only huge wars, raising huge ethical issues, are worthy of moral approbation." *Rise and Decline of Cold War*, p. 88.

policies that will be adopted, the extensiveness of foreign commitments, and the weapons to be produced.

We shall emphasize three aspects of decision-making: the policy-maker's perceptions of the world,[37] the different kinds of decisions made, and the various types of decision-making systems. The first of these is very important for the obvious reason that it is the link between the external environment and policy decisions; the real world is the world perceived, whether that perception is correct or not. This distinction between things as they *appear* and things as they *are* raises a key question: Is it the objective environment as such that is important—as we suggested earlier in our analysis of the state system—or is it the policy-makers' subjective perception and definition of that environment that are important? Or, in the terminology of Harold and Margaret Sprout, should we focus analysis on the "psycho-milieu," the perceived world, or on the "operational milieu," the world that exists divorced from decision-makers' values and beliefs?[38] Clearly, the gap between them can range from very large to nonexistent. The operational milieu presumably limits the number of feasible policies that can be implemented to cope with it; nevertheless, alternative policies are likely to remain, and the policy-makers' perceptions will be crucial in selecting a particular course of action.

Thus, Prime Minister Chamberlain not only shared the general British desire in the 1930's to avoid another total war but thought that his policy of appeasing Hitler's demands would achieve that end. The reason: He saw Hitler as one of his own kind, a statesman who like himself was born and bred in a system founded upon nationalism. He could even cite a supporting precedent, for Bismarck, after Germany's unification in 1870, had declared that Germany was satisfied and would thereafter support the new European *status quo*. If Hitler talked in terms of national self-determination, why should he, Chamberlain, not now believe that the new German leader was merely a cruder version of the Prussian aristocrat, and that he, too, would be satiated once he had achieved his apparently nationalistic aims? If Nazi Germany had, in fact, been merely a nationalist state, the differences between it and France and England could probably have been resolved without precipitating a war. But Hitler's Germany harbored aims beyond restoring Germany's 1914 frontiers.

[37] See, for example, Ross Stagner, *Psychological Aspects of International Conflict* (Belmont, Calif.: Brooks-Cole, 1967), and Joseph H. de Rivera, *The Psychological Dimension of Foreign Policy* (Columbus, Ohio: Charles E. Merrill, 1968).

The effects of personality on foreign policy-makers' perceptions may be pursued in Alexander L. and Juliette L. George, *Woodrow Wilson and Colonel House: A Personality Study* (New York: Dover, 1964), and Ole R. Holsti's study of Secretary of State Dulles in Ole R. Holsti *et al.*, eds., *Enemies in Politics* (Chicago: Rand-McNally, 1967), pp. 25–96.

[38] Harold and Margaret Sprout, *The Ecological Perspective on Human Affairs* (Princeton, N.J.: Princeton University Press, 1965), pp. 28–30.

Churchill, on the other hand, was steeped in British history, and he knew that Britain's foreign policy had long been one of opposition to any power seeking to dominate Europe, whether Philip II of Spain, Louis XIV or Napoleon of France, or the German Kaiser. He perceived each of Hitler's limited demands and moves as part of a larger pattern, which would lead to Germany's destruction of the European equilibrium. For this reason he counseled opposition, condemned the Munich agreement, and ridiculed Chamberlain's claim that he had brought back "peace in our time." "We have sustained a total and unmitigated defeat" he said bluntly.[39] Thus, as Churchill himself intimated, had he been the Prime Minister in the late 1930's, World War II might have been avoided. Churchill's perception of Hitler and of Nazi objectives was correct, Chamberlain's mistaken. Possibly Churchill could have explained to the British public the true nature of the Nazi regime, placed the German dictator's repeated demands into their proper perspective, and led Britain to oppose his moves and speed up British rearmament.

The more recent American war in Vietnam illustrates the perception issue even more poignantly. The American intervention in the Vietnam war, which ranks with the Korean War as one of the most unpopular wars in American history, has often been cited as an instance of misperception by both the Kennedy and the Johnson administrations. President Kennedy's Inaugural Address, it is said, was permeated with the sense of the bipolar conflict and confrontation of the 1940's and 1950's.[40] He pledged that the United States was "unwilling to witness or permit the slow undoing of those human rights to which this nation has always been committed, and to which we are committed today at home and around the world. . . . We shall pay any price, bear any burden, meet any hardship, support any friend, oppose any foe, in order to assure the survival and success of liberty." His Administration's conviction that it confronted a united and aggressive Communist bloc was reinforced by its analysis of Khrushchev's famous speech of January, 1961, in which the Soviet leader distinguished among three kinds of warfare: nuclear war, which would end in catastrophe for both superpowers; limited conventional wars, which were dangerous because they could escalate into an American-Soviet nuclear confrontation; and wars of "national liberation," which, he declared, were "just wars" and would have Russia's full support. Not surprisingly, therefore, when such a war was discovered in South Vietnam, the Administration felt that the Russians or Chinese had instigated it and, starting in 1961, it sent in more than 16,000 military "advisers."[41] A few weeks before his death, President Kennedy de-

---

[39] The drama of Munich is captured by John Wheeler-Bennett, *Munich: Prologue to Tragedy* (London: Macmillan, 1948).

[40] Townsend Hoopes, *The Limits of Intervention* (New York: David McKay, 1969), pp. 7–13. A critique in depth of Washington's alleged misconceptions will be found in Ralph K. White, *Nobody Wanted War* (Garden City, N.Y.: Doubleday, 1968).

[41] *Ibid.*, pp. 13–16.

clared that if South Vietnam fell, it would "give the impression that the wave of the future in Southeast Asia was China and the Communists."[42] President Johnson, who relied for his policy advice principally upon his predecessor's counselors, certainly saw it that way and, in 1965, began the massive American intervention.

Critics of the war say that the commitment of half a million troops by Johnson and of the military advisers by Kennedy were both based upon the "old myths" of the cold war instead of the "new realities" that had begun to emerge in the middle 1960's.[43] One of these new realities was that the Communist bloc was badly fragmented along nationalistic lines. An extension of Hanoi's control to South Vietnam did not therefore mean parallel extension of Soviet or Chinese power; indeed, it was contended, a nationalistic Communist Vietnam would be a barrier to an extension of Chinese power. Nor would the loss of Saigon mean the collapse of neighboring nations; whether a successful guerrilla war would occur in these countries depended on their indigenous conditions. Even successful counterguerrilla war in South Vietnam would therefore not necessarily "teach the Communists a lesson" and rule out other such conflicts if internal factors in some of these states were conducive to wars of national liberation. In short, if the perceptions of the policy-makers during the Kennedy-Johnson period had more accurately reflected the changing nature of the international system, the United States could have avoided becoming involved in South Vietnam.

Different policy-makers are, of course, involved in different types of decisions. We will distinguish two kinds of decisions and policies: crisis and program (this distinction, while specifically discussed here in the context of American foreign policies, is broadly applicable to other democracies).[44] Crisis policy refers primarily to great-power confrontations, especially direct American-Russian confrontations, and program policy to annually debated and funded policies such as foreign aid or defense spending. In the American governmental system, crisis policy is usually handled by the executive branch and program policy by both the executive and legislative branches. Of these, crisis decisions are, in the nuclear age, the most crucial, because their mismanagement could well precipitate a nuclear conflict. A crisis by definition refers to some action of another state that the policy-makers of the target nation see as threatening to their vital or security interests; it is also a crisis because the threat is unexpected and because rapid counteraction is seen to be required.

[42] Tom Wicker, *JFK and LBJ: The Influence of Personality upon Politics* (Baltimore: Penguin Books, 1969), p. 192.

[43] Among many others, see J. William Fulbright, *The Arrogance of Power* (New York: Vintage, 1967), Part II; Arthur M. Schlesinger, Jr., *The Bitter Heritage* (New York: Fawcett, 1967); and Theodore Draper, *Abuse of Power* (New York: Viking Press, 1966).

[44] Roger Hilsman, "The Foreign-Policy Consensus: An Interim Research Report," *Journal of Conflict Resolution*, December, 1959, pp. 376–77.

Crisis decision-making, whether in the cold war period or in the pre–World War I era, has received a fair amount of attention and study, and many hypotheses have been offered—some rather obvious, others more suggestive and stimulating. Although it is clear that crisis decisions need considerably more study, some of the existing hypotheses[45] are: that in moments of crises, decisions are made by a few men (the President, selected official advisers, and trusted friends and counselors from outside the government); that, as decision-making "goes to the top," the foreign policy bureaucracies are "short-circuited"; that the decision-makers feel under enormous pressure because crises tend to be short-lasting phenomena, and this further raises the already high level of tension; that inaction is assumed to permit the situation to worsen and the disposition is therefore to act; that consequences of nonviolent responses are depreciated and the effects of violent action overestimated; that policy-makers tend to have relatively little information at their disposal, and the less information they have, the greater their reliance on broad stereotypes or emotional images of the enemy; that they will see themselves as possessing few alternative courses of action and the opponent as holding a number of options; and finally, that the executive policy-makers, feeling the need to act quickly, will tend not to seek legislative approval because it may entail lengthy debate that would rule out speedy action and, therefore, demoralize domestic and allied morale.

Clearly, if American or Soviet policy-makers in a confrontation do not, for example, have sufficient time to obtain information and evaluate the meaning of their opponents' intentions, as well as to plan their tactics to meet the threat of their security while simultaneously avoiding the ultimate catastrophe of a nuclear war, a dangerous miscalculation becomes a definite possibility. During the 1962 Cuban missile crisis, President Kennedy's Administration had one week for deliberation.[46] Had it not received intelligence photos of the Soviet missile construction before the installation was completed, had it instead been confronted by a Moscow announcement of Soviet missile strength in Cuba accompanied by a renewed demand for the West to get out of West Berlin, nuclear war might have erupted. Washington might perhaps have decided to bomb the missile sites, as some of Kennedy's advisers counseled in the early stages of the deliberations, but that would have killed Soviet personnel and the Kremlin might have felt compelled to retaliate to avenge the Soviet dead.

By contrast, program decisions on basic courses of policy involve a far larger number of participants and take longer. In the United States, again, this means first of all the various foreign policy bureaucracies;

---

[45] Ole R. Holsti, "The 1914 Case," *American Political Science Review*, June, 1965, pp. 365–78, and Glen D. Paige, *The Korean Decision* (New York: Free Press, 1968), pp. 273 ff.

[46] For further analysis of the Cuban missile crisis, see Chapter 5.

these have grown to two score agencies, each with personnel abroad, each reporting to different departments, and all competing for money and influence—especially for influence in the White House. This is a noticeable change from 1781, when the Continental Congress established a Department of Foreign Affairs to carry out "all correspondence and business" with other states and authorized it to hire "one or more clerks." Second, and of growing importance as Presidents have increasingly wanted to direct American foreign policy, are those members of the White House staff concerned with national security affairs and led by the President's personally chosen assistant. A third set of decision-makers is Congress, especially the Senate. Power, however, is highly dispersed among committees in both chambers, which are, in addition, frequently jealous of one another. To mobilize the various factions in Congress in support of his policies is, therefore, a time-consuming and often a frustrating affair for a President, tempting him to make his own policies and to sweep Congress along in the name of national unity. Fourth are the many interest groups—economic, veteran, religious, and others—that may be interested in influencing policies of concern to them. Finally, on the outer fringes, is the "public," whose opinions or moods the different policy-makers take into account in varying degrees, depending on the particular foreign policy issue and the scope of public interest. Where there is little interest, the decision-makers are relatively free to pursue the course they believe best; when there is a great deal of interest, when mass opinion is aroused and does not fully support government policy, the freedom of the responsible officials is more restricted.

There is one final distinction among different kinds of governmental structures that needs to be stressed: Governmental organization for decision-making leaves its imprint upon the policy "output" in a number of different ways. Henry Kissinger has, for example, argued that the personal experiences of the Soviet leaders in a totalitarian system affect their attitudes toward foreign policy. The absence of a constitutionally defined way of political succession (to the positions of real, as opposed to formal, power) means a continuous conflict over policy and power at the apex of the Soviet political structure. The rules of the game are usually quite nasty, inasmuch as climbing upward usually means the elimination of one's opponents. Stalin murdered most of his former rivals and associates, Khrushchev purged many of those who helped him into power bureaucratically, and Brezhnev and Kosygin deposed and then denounced their former mentor, Khrushchev. The requisites for upward mobility in the Soviet system of government are therefore an enormous appetite for power, a single-minded dedication to its attainment, a willingness to denounce colleagues and confront the unpleasant, even dangerous, consequences of losing. "Nothing in the personal experience of Soviet leaders would lead them to accept protestations of goodwill at face value. Suspicion is inherent in their domestic position. It is unlikely that their attitude toward the outside world is more benign than toward their own colleagues or that they would expect more consideration from it."[47]

This nonideological analysis based upon the interactions among the Soviet political elite would suggest, for instance, that long, tough, and patient bargaining is needed when negotiating with the Soviet leadership. Making concessions in order to earn good will and elicit later reciprocal concessions is thus a poor bargaining strategy. The Soviets are unlikely to respond. Only a strategy of *quid pro quo* for each item will have a chance of success, and that only after the Soviet rulers are on the one hand convinced of the opponent's firmness and that no more concessions can be extracted and, on the other hand, that their self-interest is incorporated in any resulting agreement. Material interests are not sacrificed on the altar of good will and fellowship.

Interestingly enough, it was precisely upon such avowals of good will that President Roosevelt relied to dissipate Soviet suspicions of the West. Roosevelt, a man of great personal charm and persuasiveness, was addicted to personal diplomacy. He could say "my friend" in eleven languages, and soon after meeting Stalin he was calling him Uncle Joe.[48] The President never doubted his ability to win Stalin's cooperation for the postwar world. He was too shrewd a politician and too good at manipulating men to fail; mutual good feeling and some hard bargaining had won over many an obstreperous Congressman. The difficulty was that Roosevelt's technique, so well suited for success domestically, could not be equally successful in the quite different international arena.

> Disagreements in domestic affairs were over means, not basic objectives. All Americans desired a healthy economy, an end to unemployment, and a broadening of security among the whole population. There were no disagreements that could not be faced and thrashed out by reasonable men of good will. But how different the conduct of international affairs, especially in the emergency conditions of a world war. The nations in uneasy coalition against the Axis disagreed not only on the means of winning the war, but also on fundamental objectives for the future. Differences were too profound to be dissolved by geniality, and disgruntled allies, unlike subordinates, could not be ignored. Roosevelt either forgot these truths, or else believed that his power to make friends was so irresistible that all opposition could be charmed out of existence. He was wrong.[49]

The more common type of effect of governmental organization upon the policies that emerge from them is often popularly discussed in terms of such broad categories as totalitarian (or dictatorial) governments ver-

[47] Henry A. Kissinger, *American Foreign Policy* (New York: W. W. Norton, 1969), pp. 36–37.
[48] Richard Hofstadter, *American Political Tradition* (New York: Vintage Books, 1954), p. 316.
[49] Smith, *American Diplomacy During Second World War*, p. 9.

sus democratic governments. The former, it is sometimes claimed, have certain advantages over the latter because power and decision-making are highly centralized, and they can therefore act quickly and flexibly, adjusting policies as circumstances arise or change and harnessing the resources necessary to support foreign policy objectives. Democratic governments, on the other hand, are said to be deliberate, slow to change their minds once decisions have been made, and sometimes unable to muster the necessary resources because of the electorate's demands for the prior satisfaction of domestic needs. One of the earliest and most astute observers of the United States, Alexis de Tocqueville, suggested that a democratic government would be incapable of persevering on a fixed course of foreign policy; such policy would be constantly at the mercy of domestic politics and the momentary whims of public opinion. Whether democratic governments are thus handicapped in their competition with dictatorial regimes is, of course, a matter of judgment, and of continuing debate among scholars and laymen alike.

The Three Levels

The question that remains is, Which level of analysis should be used in understanding international politics? In this book, the answer is that we shall be using all three. While the state-system level will be fundamental, it cannot by itself sufficiently explain the world politics of the postwar era. To understand why, let us look one final time at three different and previously mentioned historical experiences that have molded our present-day world.

First, as we stressed earlier about British policy toward Germany in the late 1930's, first level analysis will tell us that Britain did not adopt the policies it ought to have adopted; and that was largely due to the pacifist mood of British public opinion and Prime Minister Chamberlain's misperception of Hitler's intentions. In brief, second and third level analyses explain why London pursued the policies it did. And we have also suggested that if Churchill had been the leader of His Majesty's Government, war might have been avoided, for Churchill perceived Hitler's aims correctly. Had the British leader been able to explain the dire threat to the island nation's security to the British public with his customary eloquence and persuasiveness, Britain might have stood up to Hitler.

But is this a likely analysis of what would have happened? This is doubtful. The memories of World War I were too vivid, the desire to avoid its repetition too strong. Chamberlain's policy of appeasement was in fact very representative of the temper of British opinion. How horrible, he had said in a radio address when war with Germany over Czechoslovakia loomed near, that the British should be digging trenches and trying on gas masks because of a quarrel in a faraway country between people of whom they knew nothing.[50] When Hitler's message that he would see Chamberlain at Munich arrived, the Prime Minister was addressing the House of Commons; interrupting his speech with the news, he was cheered by the House. "At once pandemonium broke forth. Everyone was on his feet, cheering, tossing his order papers in the air, some members in tears. It was an unprecedented and most unparliamentary outburst of mass hysteria and relief, in which only a few did not join."[51] Upon his arrival back from Germany, he was met by a jubilant crowd. And Roosevelt sent a message. "Good man," he wired.

Perhaps the most significant and symbolic aspect about Churchill during the late 1930's was precisely that he was not a member of the Government. Like Cassandra, he stood with a small group warning of "the gathering storm" over Europe. But Britain did not want to hear him. Churchill was widely condemned as a warmonger in the 1930's. Even when war erupted, Churchill did not take over the Prime Ministership from the man whose policies had failed so dismally. Chamberlain did not fall until after Germany's unexpected takeover of Denmark and the defeat of British forces in Norway in the spring of 1940. In brief, it took both the outbreak of war and a disaster to make Churchill Prime Minister. Thus, while the state-system level of analysis could prescribe what Britain should have done, the nation-state and decision-making levels can best explain and could have predicted what did happen. The state-system level correctly predicted that failure to play by the rules of the game would mean a loss of security and, in this instance, the necessity to fight a war for its recovery. But the climate of British democracy ruled out doing what should have been done. As this example shows, moreover, one must be careful not to exaggerate the importance of a nation's leader. Foreign policy is not simply a reflection of his preferences and perceptions. He makes policy within the confines of a state system, a national political system, and a specific policy process.

Second, immediate postwar U.S. policy provides a striking example of the mutually reinforcing nature of all three levels of analyses. "Rarely has freedom been more clearly the recognition of necessity," Stanley Hoffmann has said, "and statesmanship the imaginative exploitation of necessity. America rushed to those gates at which Soviet power was knocking."[52] While at the nation-state and decision-making levels the policy-makers ended up doing what they had to do, this was by no means a certainty at the end of World War II. A period of eighteen months passed after the surrender of Japan until the official declaration of the containment policy, although throughout 1946 American policy had been changing slowly toward an anti-Soviet stance. Perhaps the time lag

---

[50] *Times* (London), September 28, 1938, and Wheeler-Bennett, *Munich*, pp. 157–58.

[51] Mowat, *Britain Between Wars*, p. 617.

[52] Stanley Hoffmann, *The State of War* (New York: Praeger Publishers, 1965), p. 163.

involved in the reversal of American policy from its wartime policy of alliance with the Soviet Union is not surprising. Democratic opinion does not normally shift overnight. The American desire for peace, symbolized by the massive postwar demobilization, was too intense. Hostile Soviet acts were needed if the American admiration for the Soviet Union, the result of its heroic wartime resistance, was to be transformed. Not until Britain's support for Greece and Turkey was withdrawn in early 1947 did President Truman confront the fact that only the United States possessed the countervailing power to establish a new balance that would secure both Europe and the United States while preserving the peace. Whenever in this century British power had weakened and German power stood on the verge of attaining European hegemony, the United States had become involved to re-establish the equilibrium; with Britain's complete collapse after two world wars, the United States had no choice but to take over Britain's former responsibility.[53]

President Truman also showed that he had a keen awareness of the strategic significance of the Eastern Mediterranean. When General Eisenhower, at a meeting with the President, showed his concern that Truman might not fully understand the gravity of the course he was embarking on in an area so far removed from the United States, the President responded by pulling an obviously well-worn map of the Middle Eastern area out of a desk drawer and proceeding to give a group of top government officials, including Eisenhower, a reportedly "masterful" lecture on the historical and strategic importance of the area. Finishing, he turned to Eisenhower and good-humoredly asked whether the general was now satisfied; Eisenhower joined in the laughter and said he was.[54] By later going before a joint session of Congress and explaining to the whole country the new situation facing the United States, President Truman was able to mobilize both Congressional and popular support. In this example, therefore, the state-system level is of primary importance in explaining American policy. The nation-state and decision-making levels tell us how accurately the policy-makers perceived "reality" and how they were able in a democratic society to mobilize popular support for the new containment policy.

In the remainder of this book, the three levels of analysis are divided between two sections. Part Two focuses on the first level, the state system; in Part Three we concentrate on the second and third levels. In fact, the division is not quite that neat. While analyzing the state system, we cannot separate it, for example, from the policy-makers' perception of the system or from crisis decision-making. And in analyzing the second and third levels, it is not always possible to keep the specific political system apart from the decision-making institutions and processes. Nevertheless, our broad distinction between the external environment in

[53] For a detailed account of America's assumption of its new role, see Joseph M. Jones, *The Fifteen Weeks* (New York: Viking Press, 1955).

[54] *Ibid.*, pp. 63–64.

which states exist and the internal characteristics of the specific actors remains.

Human Nature and War

It is necessary to deal briefly with one final point in this chapter: human nature. As an explanation of the international system, it was deliberately omitted; yet, because of its recent revival as a popular interpretation and "ultimate" reason for the almost incessant international conflicts and wars of the twentieth century, it deserves a few words. Periodically, human nature—or, rather, man's aggressive instinct—is resurrected as the explanation for wars and violence. Many years ago, Freud asserted

> that men are not gentle, friendly creatures wishing for love, who simply defend themselves if they are attacked, but that a powerful measure of desire for aggression has to be reckoned as a part of their instinctual endowment. . . . *Homo homini lupus*; who has the courage to dispute it in the face of all the evidence in his own life and in history? This aggressive cruelty usually lies in wait for some provocation. . . . In circumstances that favour it [it] manifests itself spontaneously and reveals men as savage beasts to whom the thought of sparing their own kind is alien.

Who can doubt Freud's claim, given man's history from Genghis Khan to Hitler, or man's use of such horrible modern weapons as atomic bombs and napalm against his fellow man? Life, Freud continued, is a struggle between Eros, which seeks to unite man, and Death, whose principal derivative is the instinct for aggression. "And it is this battle of the Titans that our nurses and governesses try to compose with their lullaby-song of Heaven!"[55]

Freud's attribution of conflict and war to man's inherent aggressiveness has in recent times received support from studies of animal life. Their instinct for aggression, seen not merely in Freud's way, as a means of destruction, but also as a means of preserving the various species, is claimed to be universal. It applies to man as well as to animals, and it is said that we would recognize this if we but possessed the humility to recognize that our behavior too obeys the laws of nature and that man is not unique and was neither born in innocence nor possessed of a noble soul. Man is, in the final analysis, a naked ape. Or, as Robert Ardrey has suggested, our ancestry is rooted in the animal world and our legacy was bequeathed to us by the killer apes. "Man is a predator whose natural instinct is to kill with a weapon, [an animal with] an overpowering enthusiasm for things that go boom."[56]

[55] Sigmund Freud, *Civilization and Its Discontents*, translated by Joan Riviere (Garden City, N.Y.: Doubleday, 1951), pp. 60–61, 75.
[56] Robert Ardrey, *African Genesis* (New York: Dell, 1967), pp. 1, 325.

Others have attributed man's strife with his fellow man to a human nature based on a desire for power. Hans Morgenthau, the foremost proponent of "realism" among American political scientists interested in the study of international politics, states that this "lust for power" is as basic a human drive as the drive to live and propagate. The "struggle for power," he writes, "is universal in time and space."[57] But all societies establish rules of conduct and institutional means for controlling these power drives (such as competitive examinations and elections) either to divert the individual drives into channels where they will not endanger the society or to weaken and possibly suppress them. The result, Morgenthau contends, is that most people cannot satisfy their desire for power within the nation; they therefore project their unsatisfied aspirations into the international arena and identify themselves with their country's power drive. Feeling impotent and insignificant domestically, the citizen gains a sense of pride and satisfaction from his nation's power and its successful use. "My country, right or wrong" becomes the normal response to his country's foreign policy; and he calls those who disagree disloyal, if not traitors.[58] "International politics, like all politics, is [therefore] a struggle for power," although the political actor seeks to conceal the true nature of his actions by justifying himself ideologically in terms of moral and legal principles.[59]

Morgenthau's view received the prestigious support of J. William Fulbright, former Senator and Chairman of the Senate Foreign Relations Committee. The causes of war, the Senator suggested, may have more to do with pathology than politics, with irrational pressures of pride rather than rational calculations of advantage. It is not so much the defense of great principles, territories, or markets that has precipitated conflicts and hostilities among states as "certain unfathomable drives of human nature" which he terms the "arrogance of power." Powerful nations, confusing their power with their virtue, tend to believe that they have been selected by God or history to make other states equally wise, happy, and rich. In short, they seem to have a psychological need to prove that they are bigger, better, and stronger than other nations. All nations, capitalist or Communist, democratic or totalitarian, presumably suffer from this arrogance.[60]

The key question, however, is whether international politics can be ascribed so simply and directly to "human nature." A number of points might be made. First, the whole concept of instinctual behavior is questionable. This does not mean that biological factors cannot be important in explaining human behavior, but psychologists and others generally see this behavior as intimately related to social or environmental factors.

[57] Hans J. Morgenthau, *Politics Among Nations: The Struggle for Power and Peace*, 4th ed. (New York: Knopf, 1967), pp. 25–33, 97–105.

[58] *Ibid.*, pp. 97–105.

[59] *Ibid.*, pp. 83–86.

[60] Fulbright, *Arrogance of Power*, pp. 4–9.

Second, even when aggressive behavior—whatever its cause—manifests itself, such aggression can be expressed in various ways. Konrad Lorenz, for example, suggests that man's fighting behavior may be redirected through such other channels as sports; in the case of nations, such instincts may be rechanneled into the competitive peaceful development of space or underdeveloped countries.[61] Third, it is questionable whether one can argue from animal to human behavior and, even more, from individual to collective behavior. If man, individually or collectively, were really motivated by his aggressive instinct or power drive, how can one explain Sweden's policy of neutrality, India's nonalignment, America's historical isolationism, or Britain's appeasement of Hitler? More fundamentally, however, why do events on some occasions result in war while at other times they do not?

Perhaps if man were constantly at war, this state of affairs might well be attributed to his "nature." But man does not always fight; he also enjoys peace, although perhaps less so in this century than in some previous centuries. If man's nature causes war, then his nature must surely also be the cause of the periods of peace that he experiences. To attribute both war and peace, however, to man's nature is hardly helpful in analyzing why nations are sometimes at peace and other times engaged in conflicts. Human nature is, in fact, too broad an explanation.[62] By explaining everything, it explains nothing. The factors that produce conflict and warfare among states must therefore be found in man's social and political behavior, and we can explain this behavior in international politics better by the use of our three levels of analysis.

[61] Konrad Lorenz, *On Aggression* (New York: Bantam Books, 1967), pp. 269–73.
[62] Kenneth N. Waltz, *Man, State, and War* (New York: Columbia University Press, 1959), pp. 27–28.

PART TWO

The State System

3 The State System as an Analytical Model

The Principal Actors

The primary political actor in the state system is the sovereign *nation-state*. The number of these national units has more than doubled since 1945, when there were fifty-one member states in the United Nations —most from Europe and related areas, twenty from Latin America, only twelve from Asia and Africa. Twenty-five years later, the economically underdeveloped states from Asia and Africa alone constituted more than half of the total U.N. membership. If the Latin American states were added, the economically underdeveloped countries constituted a sizable majority. All together, including states that are not members of the United Nations, there are more than 140 states today.

States can be categorized according to, one, their power and, two, the extent of their interests beyond their own frontiers. Power "makes ambitious projects feasible and increases their chances of success; weakness constrains, restrains, and limits choice and independence."[1] It is assumed, according to this description, that a state will define its purposes, and the policies to realize these purposes, on the basis of how much power it has. It follows that the extent of a state's interest beyond its borders is thus a function of its capacity to act in the entire state or global system, or only in one or more of its geographical regions or subsystems. States can consequently be divided very broadly into "great powers" and "small powers"; but considering the large numbers of states and the variations in how much power they possess, this division is oversimplified. The hierarchy or structure of the state system is more complex. But note that the criterion for classifying states is "power."

At the top of this contemporary hierarchy are the two superpowers, the United States and the Soviet Union, which both possess the capabil-

[1] David O. Wilkinson, *Comparative Foreign Relations* (Belmont, Calif.: Dickensen Publishing, 1969), p. 27.

ity to act throughout the whole state system; their interactions at the top of the international "pecking order" will greatly affect, if not determine, the policies of more states than will the interactions of any lower-ranking members.[2] Thus, one of the paradoxes of the post–World War II state system has been that it has simultaneously witnessed a massive expansion of states—approximately 100 new states—and a significant contraction of primary actors, such as the superpowers, in the system.

Underneath these two powers are the second-rank powers, Britain, France, West Germany, China, and Japan, whose capacity to act in one or more of the regions beyond their own is relatively limited. The first three of these, pre–World War II members of the great power club, have recovered from their collapse after 1945, but they can play a world role again only if they succeed some day in proceeding beyond the economic unity of the Common Market, whose leading members they are, to a political and military unity of a United States of Europe. Communist China is still only potentially a superpower, and, while Japan already has the economic-technological potential and population base to become a leading actor once more, political factors still prevent Japan from defining for itself a political and military role consistent with its already existing potential power.

Middle-rank powers, like Italy and Spain in Europe, or potential second-rank and perhaps even superpower states, such as India in Asia or Brazil in Latin America, have even less capacity today to act beyond their own areas. Near the bottom of the hierarchy are the minor powers, Norway, Rumania, Egypt, the Philippines, Malaysia, and Cuba, whose roles are by and large limited to their specific subordinate system, as well as mini-powers like South Vietnam, Tunisia, Syria, the Dominican Republic, or Zaïre and Chad (both in Africa), which have relatively little influence in their own region or, what is more likely for the large number of states in this category, virtually no impact at all.

It has been suggested by some writers that states of different rankings may be differentiated not only by their power and scope of interests but also by differences of behavior.[3] States roughly equal in power—regardless of regime, according to Spiegel—behave similarly; states very unequal in power act differently. Robert Rothstein has specifically warned that a small power is not a great power writ small, that its behavior is different in kind, not just in degree, from its bigger brethren. Thus a first-rank power can occasionally make a mistake without disastrous results, for it can, once it has realized its error, exercise its great capability to correct the earlier blunder. But a small power does not usually have that luxury; a mistake may well be fatal. A great power can, more often than its small colleague, wait a little longer to see if its adversary

[2] Steven L. Spiegel, *Dominance and Diversity* (Boston: Little, Brown, 1972), p. 19.

[3] *Ibid.*, and Robert L. Rothstein, *Alliances and Small Powers* (New York: Columbia University Press, 1968).

will really attack; its margin of safety—and this was perhaps truer in the age before nuclear weapons—was greater, and thus it was less likely to be tempted to strike pre-emptively. "It means, in sum, that the margin of error is small or nonexistent: to choose incorrectly may end the possibility of free choice. A lapse in vigilance can be fatal. Procrastination or 'muddling through' appears to be ruled out."[4] One need only look at Israel's two pre-emptive strikes at Egypt and its allies in 1956 and 1968 as its Arab neighbors appeared to be getting ready to launch war; and one need only contrast this to 1973, when for political reasons Israel decided not to strike first and as a result suffered heavy casualties and loss of prestige in the consequent fighting, which, in turn, affected its negotiating strength in the subsequent attempts to achieve a more lasting peace.

There are also, it needs to be pointed out, other ways that states can be categorized. Classification as we saw during our brief discussion of second-level analysis, can depend on types of government or the stage of development, as developed or rich and underdeveloped or poor countries; or we can classify states according to objectives, such as the protection of *status quo* as opposed to revisionist or expansionist aims; possession goals (those things that states cherish for themselves) as distinct from milieu goals (which aim at shaping the conditions in the state system in which all states must live).[5] However, the above distinctions are not as clear and simple as they might appear. Power, to go back to that, is frequently difficult to calculate, and a nation's ambitions do not necessarily expand or decrease as its power increases or declines. Further, it is often difficult to separate ends and means. Is power merely the means to gain control of, for example, new territory, or is the newly acquired territory the means to enhance the state's power as an end in itself?

In any event, in terms of our power distinction, we can say that the great powers have always been the primary actors in the state system. During the nineteenth century, the Concert of Europe was composed exclusively of the great powers; they were the self-appointed board of directors of the European "corporation," meeting from time to time to deal with significant political problems that affected the peace of Europe. This special great-power status and responsibility were reflected in the League of Nations Covenant, which gave such powers permanent membership on the Council; the Assembly, composed of the smaller nations, was expected to meet only every four to five years. In those days, "the world seemed to be the oyster of the great powers."[6] After Germany's second defeat, their privileged status and obligations were again recognized in the U.N. Charter provision that conferred upon the

[4] Rothstein, *Alliances and Small Powers*, p. 5.
[5] Arnold Wolfers, *Discord and Collaboration* (Baltimore: The Johns Hopkins University Press, 1962), pp. 73–75.
[6] Inis L. Claude, Jr., *Swords into Plowshares* (New York: Random House, 1956), p. 53.

United States, the Soviet Union, Britain, France, and China (which at the time was still controlled by the Nationalists) permanent membership on the Security Council. The General Assembly was again not expected to play a major role in the primary function of preserving the peace. Interestingly enough, these same five states were, by 1971, when Communist China was admitted to the U.N., the only members of the nuclear club. Still, the British, French, and Chinese nuclear forces were minuscule compared to those of the superpowers; and, in fact, the military and political utility of these small forces was widely questioned.

There are in the state system also a number of actors other than nation-states. The United Nations, because it includes most existing states, may be called a *universal actor*. But it remains an institution that, like the international system, is composed of individual states and therefore reflects their conflicts and tensions. It is certainly not a supranational organization or world state, with a will and power of its own transcending those of its members. Nor is it likely to become one in our time. There are also a number of *regional actors*, like the Arab League or the Organization of African Unity. But the attempts of the Arab and African states to work more closely together on a regional basis have produced only limited successes, in part because cooperation has been hampered by traditional national rivalries and jealousies (although this appears to have changed for the Arab states since 1973).[7] Both types of actors fall in the classification of international organization, one dealing with problems in the entire state system, the other with a particular subsystem. In international organizations decisions are made by negotiations between the member states.

Only in Western Europe has there been a serious move away from nationalism and toward forming a *supranational actor* composed of several states who will one day transfer the authority of their own governments to the new federal government which will be established supra or above them. Decisions will from then be made by this government; they will not be products of bargaining among the members' governments. Starting in 1950 with the integration of the coal and steel sectors of their economies, and proceeding to the founding of the Common Market in 1958, West Germany, France, Italy, and the Benelux countries (Belgium, the Netherlands, and Luxembourg), and after 1973 Britain, Denmark, and Ireland, have advanced toward a single economy. The "spillover," which, it was originally assumed, would proceed from the economic to the political sphere[8] and form a larger cohesive European actor, has however lagged behind. For the moment, the states of Europe remain sovereign states acting in accordance with their specific national interests.

Increasingly visible in the international arena since World War II

---

[7] J. S. Nye, *Peace in Parts* (Boston: Little, Brown, 1971).

[8] Ernst Haas, *The Uniting of Europe: Political, Social, and Economic Forces, 1950–1957* (Stanford, Calif.: Stanford University Press, 1958).

has been the *transnational actor* which, while its headquarters may be in a specific country, operates across many frontiers.[9] The most prominent has been the multinational corporation, the huge industrial firm that owns and controls manufacturing plants in foreign countries. Its proponents argue that this type of corporation will make the state irrelevant, because it transcends national boundaries in its operations, tying nations together with the strands of economic benefit while relegating interstate issues of security and prestige to the dustbins of history. Other quite visible transnational actors with an impact on international politics are organizations as venerable as the Catholic Church and as unruly as the Arab terrorists (or Palestine Liberation Organization, as they call themselves). Finally, and in contrast to this class of actors, is the *subnational* one—the business lobby, the ethnic movement, or the officer corps— which seeks to affect policy through influencing the national government. Thus, there are multiple actors in the international system, but for the present and the immediate future the most important actor remains the state.

The Anarchical Nature of the State System

If the first characteristic of the state system is that it is composed of states, the second is the absence of both a central government that makes legitimate policy decisions and a single political culture. Their absence is indeed a primary reason why one so often hears it said that international conflicts are settled with bullets while domestic differences —at least in democratic political systems—are resolved by the ballot. Admittedly, this distinction is oversimplified. Not all quarrels between states result in war; most are settled without even invoking the threat of violence. Nor are all domestic clashes of interest settled without force or violent disturbance, even within contemporary Western democratic political systems. Of the 278 wars fought between 1480 and 1941, 28 per cent were civil wars.[10] In the post–World War II period, political violence and disorder were frequent in the new nations in the formerly colonial areas of the world, suggesting that, where legitimate central governmental institutions and a commonly shared political culture had not yet been achieved, domestic politics tended to resemble international politics! Nevertheless, to the extent that we can fairly draw a clear-cut distinction between politics within nation-states and politics between nation-states, and sum up the principal distinction between politics in these two arenas by the ballot-bullet metaphor, it may be accounted for by several reasons. One is the presence in Western systems of an execu-

[9] Robert O. Keohane and Joseph S. Nye, Jr., eds., *Transnational Relations and World Politics* (Cambridge, Mass.: Harvard University Press, 1972).

[10] Hans J. Morgenthau, *Politics Among Nations: The Struggle for Power and Peace*, 4th ed. (New York: Knopf, 1967), p. 490.

tive branch of government to administer and enforce the law. The significant point about the executive is that it normally holds a preponderance, if not a monopoly, of organized violence with which it can legitimately implement the law, protect society, and discourage potential rebels. The executive controls the armed forces and national police, and it disarms the citizens of the nation by regulating the ownership of arms and forbidding the existence of private or party paramilitary forces. Domestic peace is, therefore, always armed. If the executive loses this superiority of power, either because all or part of the army refuses to support it, as in pre-Hitler Weimar Germany or pre-Franco Spain, or because other political parties arise that possess their own armed forces, as the Nazis or Communist Chinese did, the government may be challenged and the nation plunged into civil war.

Western political systems also institutionalize a legislative process through which conflicts of interests within a society, articulated by political parties and interest groups, can on the whole be channeled and resolved peacefully. The term "legislative process" is used rather than "legislative branch" because the latter does not legislate by itself. In all Western political systems, it is the leader of the majority party who, as President or Prime Minister, draws up the legislative program to be submitted for approval to the Congress or Parliament. In legislation, too, therefore, the executive plays the leading role. The significance of the process of legislation, in any event, is that lawmaking is essentially synonymous with the issue of domestic war and peace. The most controversial, significant, and bitter conflicts in society revolve around the question of what the law should be. The legislative process, to put it in a somewhat different way, revolves around the basic issue of politics, which—as Harold Lasswell once summed it up—is "who gets what, when and how." Other political scientists have used more formal language, such as the "allocation of values." Should there be a redistribution of wealth? Should blacks be granted full equality in American society, and should discrimination in interstate travel, housing, and employment be removed? Should the poor or the unemployed, the aged, the sick, or the hungry receive some kind of help? Should labor be permitted to bargain collectively? These questions pose major social issues and arouse strong passions. Yet they are unavoidable; in a pluralistic society, new demands are continually being advanced, and these must be satisfied to some degree if violence is to be avoided. A political system that does not respond, that does not allow peaceful change, will sooner or later erupt in revolution. It must either meet important aspirations of rising and discontented new strata with sufficient speed or confront violent upheaval. If discontent is widespread enough, the executive's superiority of power cannot prevent the government's fall, because the army and police are largely recruited from the population; in the ultimate breakdown of the society, they are unlikely to suppress their own people.

Finally, a judiciary, together with the other two institutions, helps maintain expectations of individual and social justice. Violence, domestic or international, is normally an instrument of last resort. While hope remains that peaceful change is possible through existing political processes, rebellion will usually be avoided. But just as there is no international executive with a monopoly of organized violence, nor any international legislative process that helps provide for peaceful change, the state system lacks an international judiciary that, like the American judiciary, especially the Supreme Court, has the authority to help preserve this sense of justice and, together with the executive and legislative branches, seeks to ensure peaceful change.

The state system not only lacks effective political institutions that integrate and regulate the behavior of states but also lacks an international political culture comparable to the one existing within most Western states. Individuals within such countries possess a number of common political values and attitudes, particularly toward such fundamental issues as the legitimacy of the government and the way in which major political decisions should be made. National politics is therefore conducted within a system whose members share, whether consciously or not, a high degree of allegiance and a socially sanctioned code of behavior that forbids certain types of actions destructive of "law and order"; they conduct their public business according to widely understood "rules of the game." People obey the law because they agree that the government has the right to govern, not because the government has at its command superior power and the individual is fearful of punishment. "For, if force creates right," Rousseau wrote, "the effect changes with the cause: Every force that is greater than the first succeeds to its right. As soon as it is possible to disobey with impunity, disobedience is legitimate and the strongest being always in the right, the only thing that matters is to act so as to become the strongest." But, Rousseau continued, "the strongest is never strong enough to be always the master, unless he transforms strength into right and obedience into duty."[11] If government is considered legitimate, even people who disagree with the content of a law will obey it because they acknowledge that the government has the authority to decide policies for the entire society.

Instead of broad agreement that buffers and limits areas of conflicts so that they do not shred the whole social fabric, the only common values of what might perhaps be called a minimal "international political culture" of the state system are survival and security, which *maximize* division and conflict between nations. In short, the primary loyalty of the nation-state is to itself. The principal systemic restraint and control is the power of other states; otherwise, states are free to pursue their purposes. The basic condition of the system in these circumstances is therefore

[11] Jean Jacques Rousseau, *The Social Contract* (New York: E. P. Dutton, 1947), p. 6.

one of potential war among its members; at least, there is a higher expectation of violence than in national political systems.[12]

International Politics as a "State of Potential War"

The third characteristic of the state system follows from this decentralized or anarchical nature. Each state in this condition can rely upon itself, and only upon itself, for the protection of its political independence and territorial integrity. In a condition of what might also be called "politics without government"—perhaps the shortest way of summing up the distinction between international and domestic politics—the issue of who gets what, when, and how is decided not by a national government recognized as legitimate but by the interactions of states in a system whose basic rule is "every state for itself." Man's highest secular loyalty being to the nation, policy-makers of all states will be intensely committed to the maintenance of national security, the prerequisite for the enjoyment of the nation's values, its "way of life" or "core values." If it is further correct that the external milieu is anarchical, posing a constant danger to this way of life, policy-makers responsible for protecting the nation will react fearfully against perceived threats to their country.

More specifically, we might say that states living in an environment in which none can acquire absolute security are bound to feel insecure and are therefore driven to reduce their sense of insecurity by enhancing their power. As with man in the Hobbesian state of nature, so with states in the state system: They are haunted by the continual fear and danger of *violent* death.[13] It is the resulting mutual fear and suspicion that states feel for one another that produce "power politics." When a nation sees its neighbor as a potential foe, it will try to deter a potential attack by becoming a little stronger than its neighbor; the latter, in its turn, will also fear an attack and, therefore, feel that it too must be strong to deter one or, if deterrence should fail, win the resulting conflict. The insecurity of all states in the system, in short, compels each to acquire greater security by engaging in a constant scramble for increased power. But, as each state watches its neighbor's power grow, its own sense of insecurity

---

[12] That the domestic system in the United States, for example, assumes people will generally obey the law voluntarily is clearly shown by the contrast between the limited number of police (national, state, and local)—certainly not enough to deal with massive resistance to the law—and the number of men in the armed forces for use outside the United States. For an interesting analysis contrasting the willingness of governments to use force against other governments with their reluctance, if not unwillingness, to use it against their own populations, see E. E. Schattschneider, *Two Hundred Million Americans in Search of a Government* (New York: Holt, Rinehart & Winston, 1969), pp. 17–22.

[13] Thomas Hobbes, *Leviathan* (New York: E. P. Dutton, 1950), p. 104.

will recur; it then tries all the harder to gain even greater strength. The result is that each state is faced with a "security dilemma."[14]

The state system thus condemns each state to a continuing struggle for power because each faces a security dilemma. Nations seek power not because the maximization of power is their goal; they seek it because they wish to guard the security of their "core values," their territorial integrity and political independence. And they act aggressively because the system gives rise to mutual fear and suspicion: each state regards its brother state, so to speak, as a potential Cain.[15] The dilemma inherent in the state system is essentially one of "kill or be killed," of strike first or risk destruction. In this context, it does not take much for one state to arouse and confirm another state's apprehensions and thereby to stimulate the development of reciprocal images of hostility, which each will find it easy to validate by the adversary's behavior. Conversely, these images will be hard to dislodge by even friendly acts; indeed, such acts may well be construed as an indication of weakness and therefore may be exploited.

Perhaps a more apt way of stating this almost compulsive concern with power, which is shared by all states, is to talk of the high potential for violence in the anarchical state system. For in its decentralized circumstances, the use of the threat of violence or actual resort to violence is in the end the only way one state can impose its demands on other states or, conversely, resist demands imposed on it by others. If we follow our earlier argument that in domestic politics government performs an allocative function, we might say that *in international politics coercion and/or force takes the place of government*. It is for this reason that the international system has been characterized as being in a state of potential war; it is war, or the constant possibility of war, that all too frequently determines who gets what and when. In an environment of conflicting demands in which there is no recognized and legitimate means for the nonviolent resolution of these differences, it is the power of the respective adversaries—a power that in the last resort means the power to win war, should one erupt—that will settle the distribution of the matters being disputed and contested.

David Singer has identified ninety-three international wars between

---

[14] John H. Herz, *International Politics in the Atomic Age* (New York: Columbia University Press, 1959), pp. 231–32.

[15] The "very realization that his own brother may play the role of a Cain makes his fellow men appear to him as potential foes. Realization of this fact by others, in turn, makes him appear to them as their potential mortal enemy. Thus there arises a fundamental social constellation, a mutual suspicion and a mutual dilemma: the dilemma of 'kill or perish,' of attacking first or running the risk of being destroyed. There is apparently no escape from this vicious circle. Whether man is 'by nature' peaceful and cooperative, or aggressive and domineering, is not the question." John H. Herz, *Political Realism and Political Idealism* (Chicago: University of Chicago Press, 1951), pp. 2–3.

1816, the end of the Napoleonic War and the beginning of the modern nation-state system, and 1965 (a war in order to be listed had to have 1,000 battle casualties). Fifty of these were interstate wars, and fifty-three were imperial and colonial wars. War occurred in 126 out of these 150 years; 144 nations spent a total of 4,500 "nation-months" (one month spent in battle) fighting, and casualties, excluding civilians, for this period were 29 million killed. There were 6.2 wars in the "average" decade, interstate war beginning every 3.0 years and an imperial or colonial war every 3.5 years. Most of the wars took place in Europe (sixty-eight). Britain and France each fought in nineteen, Russia in fifteen. The United States fought six foreign wars: the Mexican-American, the Spanish-American, the Philippine Insurrection, two World Wars, and Korea. (Vietnam began in 1965, the year in which Singer's study closed.)[16] Thus, the characterization of international politics as a state of potential war does not seem amiss historically. For even had there been far fewer wars, it remains true, as Hobbes suggested, that

> . . . war consists not in battle only, or the act of fighting but in a tract of time . . . as it is in the nature of weather. For as the nature of foul weather lies not in a shower or two or rain, but in an inclination thereto of many days together, so the nature of war consists not in actual fighting, but in the known disposition thereto.[17]

The Balance of Power as a System

The final characteristic of the state system, following from the security and power problems confronted by all states, dictates that if states wish to deter potential attackers and assure their own independence and their ways of life they will pursue "balance of power" policies. The assumption of the balance of power, and the reason why it is sought, is the fear that if one nation were to gain a predominance of power, it might impose its will upon other states, either by the threat of violence or actual use of violence. In Arnold Wolfers's words:

> Under these conditions of anarchy the expectation of violence and even of annihilation is ever-present. To forget this and thus fail in the concern for enhanced power spells the doom of a state. This does not mean constant open warfare; expansion of power at the expense of others will not take place if there is enough counterpower to deter or to stop states from undertaking it. Although no state is interested in a mere balance of power, the efforts of all states to maximize power may lead to equilibrium. If and when that happens, there is "peace" or, more exactly, a condition of stale-

16 J. David Singer and Melvin Small, *The Wages of War* (New York: John Wiley, 1973).
17 Quoted in William Ebenstein, *Great Political Thinkers*, 3d ed. (New York: Holt, Rinehart & Winston, 1960), p. 368.

mate or truce. Under the conditions described here, this balancing of power process is the only available "peace" strategy.[18]

The term "balance of power" is often used in loose and contradictory ways. It may, for example, be used to refer to any actually existing distribution of power between two states, whether this is a balance or equilibrium or not; an approximate balance; a situation of imbalance, meaning either a superiority or inferiority of power as in the sentences "the balance has shifted toward Egypt" and "the balance has shifted away from or against Israel."[19] However, as we will use the term here, it refers to a "balance of power system" in which any shift away from equilibrium in the state system leads to countershifts through the mobilization of countervailing power. While this suggests a mechanism like the "invisible hand" (as in the classical free market), which would preserve the equilibrium, this element and the systemic nature of the balance of power are further explained by Wolfers in a passage that, although long, is worth quoting in full:

> While it makes little sense to use the term "automatic" literally, as if human choices and errors were irrelevant to the establishment, preservation, or destruction of a state of equilibrium, there nevertheless is a significant element of truth in the theory of "automatism" which is valid even today. If one may assume that any government in its senses will be deeply concerned with the relative power position of hostile countries, then one may conclude that efforts to keep in step in the competition for power with such opponents, or even to outdo them, will almost certainly be forthcoming. If most nations react in this way, a tendency towards equilibrium will follow it; will come into play whether both sides aim at equilibrium or whether the more aggressive side strives for superiority. In the latter case, the opposite side is likely to be provoked into matching these aggressive moves. Forces appear therefore to be working "behind the backs" of the human actors, pushing them in the direction of balanced power irrespective of their preferences.[20]

In short, states cannot be trusted with power, for they will be tempted to abuse it. *Unrestrained power in the system constitutes a menace to all other member states. Power is therefore the best antidote to power.* The fundamental assumption, of course, is that power will not be abolished, that it is inherent in a system denoted by competition and rivalry,

18 Arnold Wolfers, *Discord and Collaboration*, p. 83. For contrary interpretations correlating peace with a superiority of power and war with a balance, see A. F. K. Organski, *World Politics* (New York: Knopf, 1956), pp. 325–33, and Geoffrey Blainey, *The Causes of War* (New York: Free Press, 1973), pp. 112–14.

19 A discussion of the different meanings of the balance of power will be found in Morgenthau, *Struggle for Power*, pp. 161–3; Ernst B. Haas, "The Balance of Power: Prescription, Concept, or Propaganda?" *World Politics*, July, 1953, pp. 442–77; and Inis L. Claude, *Power in International Relations* (New York: Random House, 1962), Part I.

20 Wolfers, *Discord and Collaboration*, p. 123.

and therefore that the principal "task of keeping war-making potential under control [is] the problem of the management of power."[21]

Power thus begets countervailing power, but note its twofold aim. The first is the protection of the security of each state, not the preservation of peace. To be sure, most states normally feel secure when they are at peace, but peace is the product of a balance acceptable to the leading powers because it assures their individual security. This the reason why, historically, their preferences for peace have not been unqualified and why, when they believed their security endangered, they have sacrificed peace. No major nation has wanted "peace at any price," at least not until the atom bomb. Inasmuch as war was not tantamount to committing suicide before 1945, war was one principal instrument of preserving the balance. If a nation forgets to distinguish between peace and security and gives a higher priority to peace, as did Britain in the 1930's, the end is likely to be disaster.

The second aim is to protect the state system as a whole. The rationale underlying the balance of power is the protection of each participating state. One way of ensuring this is to prevent the emergence of a preponderant state. Another way is to preserve the state system as a whole upon the assumption that to protect the individual state is to preserve the system of which it is a member. States are therefore rarely eliminated by the great powers. The most prominent exception, which almost confirms the rule, is, of course, Poland. Having the misfortune to lie surrounded by Russia, Austria-Hungary, and Prussia—and, later, between Soviet Russia and Nazi Germany—Poland has been divided several times to maintain a balance between its neighbors. More common is the action of the victors at the end of the Napoleonic War. Despite twenty-five years of warfare, the costliest Europe experienced since the Thirty Years' War, which ended in 1648, France was neither eliminated nor punitively treated. A lenient peace treaty was signed so that France would once more take its place in the family of European states and contribute to its preservation. A vengeful France, on the other hand, might have started another war instead of contributing to the European system's peace and stability.

By contrast, the Versailles Peace Treaty ending World War I was a harsh one. At least, Germany considered it punitive, and many regard it as a central reason why that nation remained a threat to the stability and peace of post-1918 Europe. Had Britain and France signed a treaty of reconciliation or modified the Versailles pact in the 1920's, when Germany was still weak, the German Republic might have weathered the Depression and become a pillar of support for the European settlement. Instead, Hitler was able to exploit German nationalism to help him achieve power, mobilize support for his regime, and proceed to destroy the Europe of Versailles. Ironically, it was only when Germany threat-

[21] Claude, *Power in International Relations*, p. 6.

ened to use force that the Western powers sought to appease Hitler; but by then German ambitions and power had outgrown any possibility of being satisfied.

The United States learned from this interwar experience. It signed a generous peace treaty with Japan after World War II and treated West Germany in a spirit of reconciliation. And in the subsequent postwar containment policy, in which its former enemies figure prominently, the United States accepted the premise that Russia was a *permanent fixture* on the international chessboard. The aim of containment was not to eliminate Russia. There was no reason to believe that this would end America's international involvements any more than had the prior elimination of Hitler's Germany. The aim of containment was merely to prevent further Soviet expansion. The expectation was that with time the Soviet Union would "mellow" and become easier to coexist with. In the long run, there was even the possibility of another realignment as the power distribution in the system would change again.

War and Peace as a Continuum

We usually think of war and peace as two quite distinctly different conditions, separated by a formal declaration of war. Our analysis should by now have shown this to be incorrect. We characterized the state system, with Stanley Hoffmann's phrase, as a "state of war" and then slightly amended it to read a "state of potential war."[22] Thus it is more accurate to think of war and peace as existing on a continuum along which states have a series of conflicting interests of increasing scope and intensity. Some of these will be resolvable by peaceful negotiations, but somewhere along the line a point will be reached where one side will feel that the demands made upon it are excessive, that it can no longer offer any concessions without endangering its own security; but the adversary will not be satisfied with a rejection of its demands. At this point along the line one side feels—or possibly, both sides agree—that peaceful bargaining will not resolve their dispute and decides to continue bargaining over the terms of their coexistence—who gets what—by war, "the continuation of politics by other means."[23]

Peace, in short, is not an absolute, but conditional. If a state can preserve its security in peace, it will do so; but if it cannot do so, it will invoke force as the instrument of last resort, as Britain finally did when Hitler attacked Poland. Once fighting erupts, and this is not as frequently preceded by an official declaration of war as may be thought,[24] it will continue until at least one side attains satisfactory terms he can live with peacefully (as in the two World Wars, in which the van-

22 Stanley Hoffmann, *The State of War* (New York: Praeger Publishers, 1965).
23 Blainey, *Causes of War*, pp. 115–19.
24 *Ibid.*, pp. 170–73.

quished parties had to surrender unconditionally) or, more frequently since 1945 and the era of limited wars, both sides reach a new set of mutually acceptable terms and conclude the war, an event often symbolized by an official peace conference in which the new postwar balance of power is registered (at the end of World War II, the conflict over this balance began so quickly after the cessation of hostilities that no formal conference was ever held). But the key point is again that peace is conditional. The peace negotiations from 1968 to 1973 between North Vietnam and the United States, for example, could have led to peace at any time during those years; but neither side was willing to accept the other side's *terms* of peace. Thus the fighting, or the bargaining, continued, since it held out the promise to each side of better or more acceptable terms later. *The price of peace was of greater concern to them than peace itself.* This is what normally results in war between states in the first place and, therefore, the war will not end nor peace be restored until its cost is, at the very minimum, tolerable, if not satisfactory.

War and peace, in any event, are hardly mutually exclusive conditions. Political conflict continues from one to the other; so does bargaining. The axiom "when diplomacy stops, war starts" is, therefore, simply untrue. Bargaining, which in peace time is called diplomacy, continues once the shooting starts. War is not normally an alternative to negotiations; it is bargaining carried on more violently. Power, especially military power, is always present. Although we talk of peaceful negotiations, power stands in the background—"on guard"—and when needed is brought to the fore to be invoked as a threat; and if that is insufficient, it will be openly used as force. Power is omnipresent. Peace and war, therefore, have much in common. "Diplomacy without armaments is like music without instruments."[25]

Peace, in this context, thus becomes difficult, perhaps impossible, to define, because it has many different meanings. In our terms, it may simply denote an absence of hot war (at least, large-scale war as distinct from more limited kinds of war), but not the absence of major political conflict and rivalry, including the rather intense form of competition that in our age has been called "cold war." In the state system, the struggle for security is fundamental, and, by and large, an increase in security and power for one state is viewed by its rival as a decrease of security and power for itself (we shall later qualify this statement and see that in practice this is not always true). It also needs to be stressed that the reverse side of the coin of conflict among states is cooperation among states. In their competitive pursuits, for instance, opposing states seek allies with whom to collaborate; even between the rivals themselves there is a degree of cooperation, as, for example, American-Russian arms control agreements and trade pacts. International politics is thus a *mix of conflict and cooperation*, although it must be noted that this latter

[25] Frederick the Great, quoted by Blainey, *ibid.*, p. 108.

characteristic occurs *within the context of an adversary relationship.* A state wants to add the strength of allies to enhance its power position in order to compete better; an arms control agreement may reduce the level of armaments, reduce international tensions, and make the world a slightly safer place to live in, but these agreements are signed, after all, by states whose weapons are aimed at each other because they are political rivals. But peace, to many, signifies the absence of precisely these types of competitive relationships. Words such as *détente* or *rapprochement* suggest not only the absence of much conflict and war but a high degree of genuine cooperation, if not indeed harmony, among states. Still, both of these attempts to define peace remain negative; note our repeated use of the word "absence."

There are positive ways of specifying the conditions of peace. Later we shall analyze a number of different attempts to regulate who gets what, when, and how within the structure of the state system and transform that system itself in order to reduce the conflict inherent in the contemporary decentralized anarchical system. We shall look at the role of the United Nations, which embodies the hope that man will turn his swords into plowshares; it also provides an institutional parliamentary-type setting where nations meet and *should* resolve their differences in a spirit of concern for mankind as a whole rather than in a selfish regard for their own national portions of mankind. But even the expectation of peaceful and orderly change is not quite satisfactory for some observers; peace, they insist, should include the expectation of social justice for all men. (For some revolutionary groups, who do not expect this to come about peacefully, the concern with social justice as they define it is so intense that they are quite willing to sacrifice peace and human life to obtain it.) In the final analysis, however, some maintain, a true peace will occur only at a yet higher level, that of a world government. Such a government would more fully institutionalize the processes of change than a U.N. ever could, plus a global community in which national differences and jealousies disappear and all humanity shares the blessings of peace, prosperity, and freedom. Reasons for differences among men will appear to evaporate and a lasting peace exist for the first time in history.

This futuristic definition of peace, however, presumes the transformation of the existing state system. Until that happens, it is probably wiser to rely upon our model of the current system for an understanding of international politics and a prescription for policy. Existing at the opposite end of the world government spectrum, the state system model remains a model of a primitive political system whose primary feature is an anarchy moderated by a modicum of order imposed by the balance of power.[26] Its fundamental assumptions are that nation-states place a

[26] Robert D. Masters, "World Politics as a Primitive Political System," *World Politics*, July, 1964, pp. 595–619.

high value on national security in order to protect their "core values"; that states will react fearfully against threats to their security and therefore seek to enhance their power; that states are responsible only to themselves, and self-help is the fundamental rule of the game; and that their relationship is determined by the interaction of their respective strengths.

The Four Characteristics of First-Level Analysis

Analyzing the games nations play from the state-system level will give us certain very specific perspectives on the behavior of states. The first is *the focus on the interactions of states revolving around the axle of the balance of power.* Systemic change affects the behavior of all member states. Whenever the system becomes unbalanced, trouble follows. When Britain weakens and can no longer contain a continental power seeking European hegemony, a previously isolationist power, the United States, must step in and play Britain's role. When Germany in the center of Europe is destroyed, a conflict erupts between two previous allies, both superpowers on the periphery of Europe. Eliminating a troublesome member does *not*, therefore, guarantee the end of trouble and conflict. Nor can it. *To alter the structure of the system is to change everyone's behavior;* the new distribution of power merely leads to new alignments. But the competition among the states continues.

A second characteristic of analyzing international politics at the systemic level is that it minimizes domestic factors in explaining states' behavior. *The system imposes a high degree of uniformity of behavior upon states, regardless of their domestic complexion.* The same basic interests and motivations are ascribed to all members. The "necessity of state" overrides such different national attributes as political culture, economic organization, or class structure—or, at least, it is supposed to. Thus the systems analyst will examine internal variables only if they seem to have interfered with how a state *ought* to have behaved.

In this connection, the systemic model also tends to minimize the importance of ideologies, which are generally considered as justifying whatever states do. States are motivated largely by their security interests and are therefore concerned with preserving or enhancing their power. Ideology is seen as a function of this interest.[27] For example, despite its antifascist and anticapitalist ideology, Communism did not prevent Russia from aligning itself with France in 1935, then with Nazi Germany in 1939, and, in 1941, with the United States and Britain against its previous ally. And after the war, Soviet Russia acted very much like Czarist Russia in its postwar expansion into Eastern Europe and in its attempts to extend its power into the Eastern Mediterranean area. Ideology, in

[27] Morgenthau, *Politics Among Nations*, pp. 83–86.

short, did not prevent Moscow from behaving in typical balance-of-power terms based upon *Russian* security interests. Indeed, the wide range of policies seemingly compatible with a specific ideology is cited as evidence that ideology is essentially a rationalization of policy rather than a motivation for it.

This de-emphasis of ideology, then, suggests that the analyst of world politics need pay little attention to what policy-makers *say* about their policies. Clearly, they will say whatever will make their actions look good. They will talk in terms of freedom, national self-determination, liberating peoples from Communist or capitalist slavery, and bringing about a world of peace, law, order, and justice. But such verbalization should not be confused with the concrete interests that are the real, underlying reason for the state's behavior. Indeed, the analyst assuming that state behavior is the product of an ever changing distribution of power can, according to Hans Morgenthau,

> retrace and anticipate, as it were, the steps a statesman—past, present, or future—has taken or will take on the political scene. We can look over his shoulder when he writes his dispatches; we listen in on his conversation with other statesmen; we read and anticipate his very thoughts. . . . We think as he does, and as disinterested observers we understand his thoughts and actions *perhaps better than he*, the actor in the political scene, does himself.[28]

Whether Morgenthau is correct or not, the de-emphasis of ideologies and statements of intentions does tend to reduce the probability that international politics will be viewed as a morality tale, a conflict between good and evil, and it refocuses attention on the security dilemma shared by all states living in an anarchical environment in which they see other states as potential enemies and are, therefore, bound to be concerned with their power vis-à-vis one another.

A third characteristic is the emphasis on *the limits the system places on the policy choices states possess.* Some observers refer to this as "system determined" behavior. While this phrase may understate the degree of a state's "free will" or the range of choice a state may in fact possess, it is a healthy reminder that for states, as often as for individuals, the available options depend on the external reality—in this case, the distribution of power. "The choice with which governments are in fact confronted is not that between opting for the present structure of the world, and opting for some other structure, but between attempting to maintain a balance of power and failing to do so."[29]

Finally, and closely related, is that the systemic perspective allows us to see *why the continuity of policy* is a characteristic of the foreign policies of so many nations. The political complexion of a great power—such

---

[28] *Ibid.*, p. 5. Emphasis added.
[29] Hedley Bull, *The Control of the Arms Race* (New York: Praeger Publishers, 1961), p. 39.

as Russia—may change, as may its perception of its role in the world and its definition of objectives. But it still lives in a system where neighbors to the east and west remain the same; so, therefore, does Russia's need for securing Eastern Europe, because Russia, Czarist or Communist, has no natural protective barrier, as Britain with the English Channel, or Italy and Spain with mountain ranges. The system, in other words, places constraints upon its members and presents them with only a limited number of options and, in some situations, no options at all. As we shall see, the degree of constraint and the foreign policy alternatives available to a state in responding to the external environment depend on the particular distribution of power.

4 Systemic Structure and Stability: From Bipolarity to Bipolycentrism

Distributions of Power and Stability

Analysis at the state-system level, we have suggested, focuses upon the distribution of power as the key to explaining and understanding the behavior of states. More specifically, we can now add, this first-level analysis suggests that there is a relationship between the number of great powers or "poles," the degree of choice states have among alternative policies, and the *stability* of the entire system. Stability may be defined in terms of the absence of any nation's predominance, the survival of most member states, and the absence of a major war. This last point needs special stress since the concept of the balance of power assumes that war is an instrument—admittedly, an instrument of last resort—to preserve the equilibrium in the system or restore it if it has been upset. Perhaps, therefore, a stable system may be said to be one that retains the principal characteristics of the system and in which the differences among states are usually settled peacefully. An unstable system, by contrast, is prone to violence.

One of the distributions of power witnessed in recent times is bipolar. This structure, in which the major states are grouped around those two among them whose strength is so far superior that they are recognized as "superpowers," leaves the principal adversaries feeling such a high degree of insecurity that they are virtually "compelled" to react against one another's external threats. The reason is that in such a distribution of power the balance is constantly at stake. Each superpower, fearing that its adversary will achieve hegemony, and that such a hegemony may be irreversible, will be extremely sensitive to the slightest shifts of power. Neither, in the perception of the other, can make an "innocent move"; each will see any move by the other—even if defensively motivated—as a deliberate and hostile attempt to enhance its position, and thus counteraction is inevitable. In this condition, which might almost be called "institutionalized paranoia," a gain of power and security for one will be

61

seen as a loss of power and security by the other. Even moves in areas which are not normally considered to be of vital interest to the other superpower will be opposed for symbolic and psychological reasons. Each fears a "domino effect"—if one of his allies, friends, protégés, or satellites falls, others will follow—thereby upsetting the equilibrium. Each state's attention is therefore riveted upon its rival. When one pushes, the other feels compelled to push back. Both are "trapped." Neither can advance or retreat—at least in areas where it has some control over the situation. Positions must be held. In a bipolar system, in short, states feel they have few policy options and little choice. Drawing lines or "frontiers" between their respective spheres of influence, and then preserving this territorial *status quo*, becomes the heart of the bipolar struggle. Consequently, bipolar politics is the politics of confrontation and recurrent crises.[1]

Is a bipolar system, then, stable or unstable? The answer would seem to be evident from the basic rule of behavior in a bipolar structure: Oppose any unilateral attempt by the adversary to upset the balance of power. If he pushes, push him back. The attendant arms races, spurred by the constant fear that the opponent might achieve an irreversible power advantage—in which case the "game" is over for the other side— the almost frantic search for allies, the cohesiveness of the principal alliances, the attempts to undermine the opposing "camp" while preventing defections from one's own through interventions, all mean frequent crises, occasional limited wars, and the persistent threat of a general war. For these reasons, bipolarity has usually been adjudged an unstable system.

A multipolar, in contrast to a bipolar, system comprises at least three essential actors; some theorists have said that approximately five equally great powers are needed.[2] Such a system, it is asserted, is characterized by more restrained behavior. With a larger number of great-power actors, states possess greater mobility to align and realign themselves. Thus compared to bipolarity's *simple* and *rigid* division, multipolarity is *complex* and *flexible*. Alliances last only for short periods and are created for specific purposes; as the equilibrium changes, alignments change too. In comparison to bipolarity's confrontations and crises in which the antagonisms of the two powers are constantly reinforcing one another, multipolarity's greater opportunity for possible combinations and shifting around reduces the risks of mutually reinforcing hostilities between various "players." One's allies today may become tomorrow's adversaries and

---

[1] There is considerable disagreement about the dangers and virtues of bipolarity. For the former, see Morgenthau, *Politics Among Nations*, pp. 346–47, and for the latter, see Kenneth N. Waltz, "The Stability of a Bipolar World," *Daedalus*, Summer, 1964, pp. 881–909.

For a suggestive comparative study of bipolar struggle between Athens and Sparta, see Peter J. Fliess, *Thucydides and the Politics of Bipolarity* (Baton Rouge: Louisiana State University Press, 1966).

[2] Morton Kaplan, *System and Process in International Politics* (New York: John Wiley, 1957).

allies once more the day after tomorrow; since you may thus need your present opponent as an ally in the future, hostilities cannot be allowed to become too intense. To put it another way: Because individual states will have changing relationships with so many other states, they will have cross-cutting loyalties.[3] A member of one alliance will share common as well as conflicting interests with his partners, but he is also likely to have an overlap of interests with some members of the opposing coalition. This will lower any animosity felt toward any specific state or cause.

Closely related to this reasoning is the argument that the more numerous the actors, the less attention any one state can give to another. Whereas in a bipolar system the contestants watch each other unfailingly, "the average share of available attention for any one conflict drops sharply as soon as there are more than three power centers in the system, and more gently after there are more than five such centers." More specifically, it was argued, if a conflict requires at least 10 per cent of a government's critical attention for it to engage in behavior that might involve armed conflict, then the "minimal attention ratio for an escalating conflict would have to be 1 : 9, since it does not seem likely that any country could be provoked very far into an escalating conflict with less than 10 per cent of the foreign policy attention of its government devoted to the matter."[4] A system with eleven approximately equal great powers would thus be able to avoid major conflicts. To sum up: Whereas bipolar systems are prone to crises and the eruption of war, multipolar systems because of their flexibility and maneuverability are more likely to maintain peace.

Extensive Bipolarity, 1947–62

THE INITIAL CONFRONTATION

Bipolarity was the kind of balance that, as we saw earlier, emerged from the ashes of World War II, and the first feature of this balance was its *extensive* or global nature. Anticipating a postwar conflict, Russia consolidated its positions in the areas of Eastern and Central Europe from which the German forces had retreated and, around the periphery of its new position, probed for weak spots to enhance its power for the expected forthcoming struggle. Russian domination of Poland and the Balkans meant that Russian power lapped the shores of the Aegean, the Straits of Constantinople, and—through its still close relationship with Yugoslavia—the Adriatic. In the period from the end of the war to early 1947, the Russians also attempted to effect a major breakthrough into the Middle East, which Napoleon had called the key to the world.

[3] Karl W. Deutsch and J. David Singer, "Multipolar Power Systems and International Stability," *World Politics*, April, 1964, pp. 392–96.
[4] *Ibid.*, pp. 396–400.

And well he might, for the area links Europe, Africa, and Asia. The power that dominates the Middle East is in an excellent position to expand into North Africa and South Asia—and thereby into the rest of Eurasia and Africa—as well as to outflank Western Europe, dependent as it is on Middle Eastern oil. Russian attempts to control the area, however, predated the discovery of oil. It was an interest shared by Czar and commissar.

This time, the Russians focused first on Iran, trying to convert it into another satellite.[5] Moscow then demanded the cession of Turkish territory, a naval base in the Dardanelles, and the severance of Turkey's ties with Britain; finally, the Communist revolt in Greece, squashed by British troops in 1944 as Greece was being liberated from German occupation, started anew. The loss of Greece would have left Turkey and Iran outflanked and exposed. If Greece collapsed—and by early 1947 the reports from that nation indicated that it was likely to do so in a matter of weeks—Washington expected it would be only a question of time until its neighbors to the east crumbled. But the fall of Greece would not only affect these neighbors; it might also lead to an increase of Communist pressure on Italy. With the largest Communist Party in Western Europe, Italy would then be faced with these Communist states to its east—Yugoslavia, Albania, and Greece. To the northwest lay France, with the second largest Communist Party in the West, four Communists in the government, and the biggest Communist trade union in Western Europe.

While the security of all of Western Europe might thus be endangered, the immediate danger lay in the eastern Mediterranean. The Soviet aim to control this area was highlighted by its demands that the city of Trieste, situated at the head of the Adriatic, be yielded to Yugoslavia and that Italy's former Northern African colony of Libya be placed under Soviet trusteeship. Given these moves, the stakes in Greece became immense. Whether the United States would meet the Soviet challenge, however, did not become a pressing question until, on the afternoon of February 21, 1947, the First Secretary of the British Embassy in Washington visited the State Department and handed American officials two notes from His Majesty's Government. One concerned Greece, the other Turkey. In effect, they both stated the same thing: Britain could no longer meet its traditional responsibilities in those two countries. As both were on the verge of collapse, the import of the British notes was clear: A Russian breakthrough could be prevented only by a major American commitment.

February 21 was thus a turning point in international politics. On

---

[5] Truman was especially outraged by this, for Iran was Russia's ally during World War II, its chief utility being to serve as the pipeline through which needed American war supplies were shipped to Russia. Without these supplies, Truman felt, Russia would have been defeated. Harry S. Truman, *Memoirs* 1: *Year of Decision* (New York: Signet Books, 1965): 605–6.

that day, Great Britain, the only remaining power in Europe, acknowledged its exhaustion, and the cold fact of a bipolar world suddenly confronted the United States. On March 12, in a historic address to a joint session of Congress, President Truman publicly committed the United States to the protection of Greece and Turkey.[6]

It had taken eighteen months since the surrender of Japan and the end of the war for the United States to reassess its policy toward the Soviet Union. Although President Truman would, in 1946, exasperatedly say that he was "tired of babying the Soviets" and that the only language the Russians understood was "how many divisions have you?"—and although he had been present on the platform in Fulton, Missouri, in March of that year when Winston Churchill became the first Western public figure to talk openly of the "iron curtain" descending across the European Continent—American policy had not yet shifted fundamentally toward the kind of Anglo-American alliance against Russia for which Churchill was calling.[7] Demobilization continued in this interim period, and the draft came to an end. American opinion was, significantly enough, shocked by the English wartime leader's speech, but as the year progressed this opinion began to shift with rapidity. Still, the Soviet threat described by Churchill was not widely recognized. American positions on specific issues became firmer, the assumption being that, if the United States took a tougher bargaining stance, the Soviet leaders would see the futility of their obduracy and agree to fair compromise solutions. But the idea that a struggle for a new balance of power had erupted was not yet widespread at the top levels of the American Government. Not until early 1947 did the moment of truth arrive, with the United States announcing a new, broad-scale policy of containment.

BIPOLARITY IN EUROPE

This policy of containment focused not only on Greece and Turkey but also on Western Europe, as Soviet control of Eastern and Central Europe was perceived as constituting a direct threat to the security of the West. Just as Russian leaders were bound to see the establishment of a rival power's influence in Eastern Europe as a menace to their country's security, so American policy-makers were bound to view the extension of Russian power into the heart of Europe as a threat to their security. As Averell Harriman, the American Ambassador to Moscow at the time of Yalta, told Washington, in a cable sent before that meeting, his concern was not so much Eastern Europe itself, for it could be

[6] Joseph M. Jones, *The Fifteen Weeks* (New York: Viking, 1955), and Truman, *Memoirs* 2: *Years of Trial and Hope* (Garden City, N.Y.: Doubleday & Co., 1956): 104–9.

[7] Truman, *Years of Trial and Hope*, p. 606. For this transitional period, also see Seyom Brown, *The Faces of Power* (New York: Columbia University Press, 1968), pp. 31–45, and John Spanier, *American Foreign Policy Since World War II*, 6th ed. (New York: Praeger Publishers, 1973), pp. 32–36, 38–44.

argued that this area was not vital to American interests; rather, what bothered him was that when a country began, by strong-arm methods, to extend its influence beyond its borders in the name of security, it was unsure where the final line would be drawn. Once it was accepted that the Soviet Union had the right to move on its immediate neighbors to enhance its security, what was to prevent "defensive expansionism" into the countries that then formed its new neighbors?[8]

This did not mean that American leaders feared a Soviet military invasion of Western Europe. Such a contingency could not be entirely ruled out, but it was the possibility that Western Europe's weakness, demoralization, and economic collapse would be exploited by Moscow that disturbed Washington. Two world wars had drained Europe of all its energies. What remained in 1945 was a badly battered and destroyed Europe,

> . . . a curiosity unique in all time. Here was a community of 300,000,000 men who had developed a civilization so unbalanced that they could not possibly survive as a civilization on their own resources. The vital margin of their food supply, almost all the fibers they used to clothe themselves, the tea at breakfast, the evening coffee, rubber sheathing and copper wires, liquid fuels—all of these products that Europeans not only enjoyed but could not live without came from overseas on the cycling tides of trade. . . . For a century the community had unthinkingly relied on invisible strands of trade which brought these necessities to the home ports in return for what Europe could ship out; these strands had seemed once as rugged and strong as bonds of iron. Now they were cut. With the strands cut, Europe threatened to sink, or rather to plummet, directly out of modern civilization.[9]

The central difficulty was that the Europeans were basically in a position of being unable to earn sufficient funds, particularly in dollars, to buy the commodities they needed for their recovery and reconstruction. There was little chance of competing extensively against mass-produced American goods. Yet the United States possessed most of the items Europe needed for its reconstruction—such as wheat, cotton, sulphur, sugar, machinery, trucks, and coal. At the same time, the United States was so well supplied with everything that it had little need to buy much from abroad. Europe was therefore confronted with an ominous "dollar gap" —and its fate seemed to be hunger and cold and loss of hope. The American response was the Marshall Plan, which granted Europe a massive program of economic aid. As the doctor to an economically sick Europe, the United States prescribed as the main part of the cure a $17 billion injection (the patient recovered with $12 billion). Only in this manner was Europe to restore, and even surpass, its prewar agricultural

[8] W. Averell Harriman, *America and Russia in a Changing World: A Half Century of Personal Observation* (Garden City, N.Y.: Doubleday, 1971), p. 34.

[9] Theodore White, *Fire in the Ashes: Europe in Mid-Century* (New York: William Sloane Associates, 1953), pp. 46–47.

and industrial production, earn its way in the world, and regain its political vitality and military strength.

If Europe was dependent on America for its recovery, America needed Europe for its security, as two world wars had already demonstrated. In 1949, therefore, the United States established the North Atlantic Treaty Organization (NATO) and extended its protection to Belgium, Canada, Denmark, France, Great Britain, Iceland, Italy, Luxembourg, the Netherlands, Norway, and Portugal. Greece, Turkey, and West Germany became members at a later date. But even before the formation of NATO, the United States and the Soviet Union began their struggle over Germany.[10]

As a result of Allied agreements, the eastern section of Germany fell into Russian hands at the conclusion of the war; the western sector, with its larger population and greater industrial capacity, was occupied by the Western powers. As Europe's economic collapse became clearer and the cold war intensified, it became necessary to lift Germany out of its economic stagnation and make its industry contribute to the general economic recovery of Europe. The necessity of West German support in the cold war persuaded America and Britain to let the Germans take a more active part in running their own country, thus foreshadowing the eventual establishment of a West German Government and West German rearmament. But first Germany needed a sound currency, for without that its economy could not recover. The subsequent currency reform carried out by the United States Military Government became the basis of West Germany's amazing economic recovery.

To forestall Germany's revival, the Russians blockaded West Berlin in a test of strength with the West. If the Allies could be forced out of Berlin, German confidence—and, of course, French and British confidence—in the American commitment and ability to protect Europe would be undermined. The Berlin crisis, were it not met, might undermine the entire American position in Europe and nullify America's postwar efforts to rebuild Europe as a partner in the conflict with the Soviet Union. An intensive airlift by American and British forces was mounted, the blockade was lifted, and the test was met.

The United States had transformed a situation of weakness into one of strength. It had drawn a frontier between the American and Russian spheres of influence and had demonstrated that it was in Europe to stay. In the meantime, the Greek civil war had ended when Yugoslavia, which had been aiding the guerrillas, was ejected from the Soviet bloc in 1948; the Yugoslavs had thereupon terminated aid and refuge for the guerrillas. By 1949, Europe no longer provided opportunities for guerrilla warfare, coups d'état, or attempts at subversion. To cross the demarcation line drawn by the United States was to risk total war, and this risk was hardly one the Soviet Union was willing to assume.

[10] Wolfram Hanrieder, *The Stable Crisis* (New York: Harper & Row, 1970).

BIPOLARITY IN ASIA

Asia was a more profitable area for political and military exploitation. Most countries there had only recently emerged from Western colonialism, and their nationalistic and anti-Western feelings were strong. In late 1949, Nationalist China collapsed and a Communist government was established on the mainland. It had been beyond the capacity of the United States to prevent this, largely because Chiang Kai-shek's regime had been corrupt, reactionary, and inefficient. A government whose principal support came from the landowner could not meet peasant aspirations for land, and the peasants constituted four-fifths of China's population. Aid to Europe had stood a good chance of achieving its objective of restoring Britain and the Continent's health and strength; the Truman Administration, however, felt that no reasonable amounts of aid could restore a government that had lost the confidence of most of its own people.[11] Chiang's demise, however, weakened the Western position in Asia, shifted the balance, and created a vacuum that attracted Russian attention.

In June, 1950, the North Korean Communists marched across the 38th Parallel to attack South Korea. At the end of World War II, the Russians had occupied the northern half of Korea in order to disarm the Japanese; they had stayed long enough to place a Communist regime in power. The attack, which could not have been launched without Soviet knowledge, encouragement, and support, was seen by Washington as a threat to the entire containment or balance-of-power policy. If the aim of this policy was indeed to prevent further expansion of Soviet power, American policy-makers calculated that a refusal to help their protégé regime in the South could only whet Stalin's appetite and tempt him to devour other areas. Failure to meet the Soviet challenge was also seen as affecting not only Soviet behavior but that of our allies as well. For, if the United States did not measure up to the test, the Kremlin would have succeeded in demonstrating Soviet strength and resolution, and, conversely, America's timidity and unreliability. Consequently, if the United States abandoned Korea under the threat of force, America's European allies might conclude that they, too, would be abandoned in a similar crisis. The recently signed NATO alliance would undoubtedly collapse. The Europeans might dismiss as valueless Washington's treaty pledge to protect them and turn instead to neutralism. As neutrals, they would be subjected to increasing Soviet pressure and eventual domination. Virtually the entire length and breadth of Eurasia would then be under Sino-Soviet control. Japan, too, would have no choice but to turn to neutralism if the United States did not go to the defense of South Korea. Mainland China having just fallen to the Communists, the

[11] Tang Tsou, *America's Failure in China, 1941–50* (Chicago: University of Chicago Press, 1963).

United States wished to rearm Japan to create a new situation of strength in the Pacific, but the precondition for transforming Japan into an American ally was the protection of its security. Hence, all "frontiers" were thought to be interrelated.[12]

Korea was America's first "limited war," a painful and frustrating three-year experience, in defense of part of that "frontier" around the periphery of the then still cohesive Sino-Soviet bloc. The 38th Parallel, like the frontier lines drawn in the Eastern Mediterranean and Central Europe, registered the respective Western and Communist spheres existing at the end of World War II; together, they reflected the position of Allied and Soviet armies in 1945. The next frontier drawn, in Indochina, did not. After Japan's surrender, the French tried to reimpose colonial control on Indochina only to find that, in an age of decolonization, such attempts were futile. Worse, in the attempt, all nationalists were driven into the arms of the Communist-led Vietminh movement. A long and bitter guerrilla war erupted from 1946–54. While the United States was initially unsympathetic to France because of its refusal to give Indochina independence, the attack on South Korea led it to send large-scale military and economic aid to the French.

In Korea, the issue had been the suspected Soviet support for the North Korean Army and the belief that the conquest of South Korea would increase Soviet power. But in Indochina the issue was nationalism. The goal of Ho Chi Minh, the Vietminh leader, was to free Indochina from French colonial rule. To be sure, he was a Communist, but he was no more a puppet of Moscow than Mao Tse-tung. However, the Korean War and Communist China's intervention in that war led American policy-makers to view all Communist states as part of a single cohesive bloc led by Moscow, pursuing expansionist goals. The French effort to reimpose colonial control on Indochina, initially viewed by Washington with disfavor, now became transformed into an anti-Communist war in which France was fighting on behalf of the "Free World." In the context of American-Soviet conflict, then, even former peripheral American interests became symbolically important. Thus, when the French suffered defeat in Vietnam, the United States considered intervention, although President Eisenhower finally decided against it. A negotiated peace at Geneva in 1954 resulted in the division of Vietnam at the 17th Parallel. Another line, like the 38th Parallel in Korea or the one drawn through the middle of Germany along the Elbe River, now divided yet another country.[13] Admittedly, one provision—significantly enough, left unsigned—of the Geneva agreements provided for nationwide elections to unify the country, but the new non-Communist government of South Vietnam, led by Ngo Dinh Diem and supported by the United States, did

[12] John W. Spanier, *The Truman-MacArthur Controversy and the Korean War*, rev. ed. (New York: W. W. Norton, 1965), pp. 23–30.

[13] Melvin Gurtov, *The First Vietnam Crisis* (New York: Columbia University Press, 1967).

not consider itself bound by a provision in the negotiation of which it had not participated. And meanwhile, the 17th Parallel had, it was hoped, become part of the extensive frontier dividing the Communist from the non-Communist world.

The challenges and responses between 1946 and 1954 over Iran, Greece, Turkey, Berlin, Korea, and Indochina, along with the continuous confrontations and crises after that period over the islands of Quemoy and Matsu off the Chinese coast and over Berlin almost constantly from 1958 through 1962, hung "hands off" or "cross at your own risk" signs all around the Eurasian continent to deter transgressions of such lines in order to avoid any possible miscalculations that might ignite the highly combustible postwar system.

Intensive Bipolarity, 1947–62

THE ARMS RACE

The bipolar balance was not, however, merely extensive in geographic scope. It was also *intensive*, as demonstrated by the arms race, the scramble for allies, the cohesiveness of the principal respective alliances, and the sensitivity each superpower showed to possible defections from its camp. The precariousness of that balance was bound to render the two superpowers sensitive to any changes in military strength. Indeed, the change in nuclear technology made them hypersensitive, because it fundamentally changed the manner in which military strength could be employed. Historically, force has been used either to deter wars or, once wars have erupted, to win them. In prenuclear times, when no weapons were so destructive that their employment threatened their user with extinction, the critical test of military policy had been less the prevention of hostilities than the ability to attain victory once they had broken out. The gains to be won seemed to outweigh the cost of fighting. War was therefore considered a rational instrument of national policy. Nuclear arms, however, threatened the very substance of life military force was supposed to protect. Total war thus became suicidal and irrational.[14] The result was paradox. On the one hand, the chief threat to the state system has always been the possibility of dominance by one power or one bloc; to prevent this, war has been a principal and ultimate means. On the other hand, war—total war—now threatened the very existence of the state system; the "instrument of last resort" to assure the security of all the members now threatened them, if used, with extinction. Hence the only remaining utility of all-out war as an instrument of policy lay in the threat of its use precisely in order to assure its *nonuse*—in short, deterrence. This, in turn, required that the enemy must at all times be con-

[14] Bernard Brodie, *Strategy in the Missile Age* (Princeton, N.J.: Princeton University Press, 1959), remains the finest introductory analysis of the changing nature of warfare in the twentieth century.

vinced that the costs of an attack would be wholly disproportionate to any conceivable gains; hence the utility of the threat of virtual total destruction. Only in this way could deterrence be made permanent and the one mistake—which would be one too many—be avoided. This means that military strength is required so that it will *not* be used and the best of strategy becomes not victory in war but the prevention of war. The outbreak of all-out hostilities would signal the failure of strategy.

Each of the two superpowers must therefore constantly concern itself with maintaining its offensive superiority, for its adversary must never doubt that he could be destroyed. The "balance of terror," in short, is *not* automatic. Strategic bombing might well be decisive in the nuclear age, and the American-Soviet capacity to inflict mutually mortal wounds might give each side a vested interest in not *wanting* to fight a total war. But this desire to avoid war does not suffice of itself. The crucial prerequisite for the *pax atomica* is not "the bomb" but the delivery system. If deterrence is to function effectively, the opponent must never have any doubt that the bombs can be delivered on target. He must always fear that any attack he launches will result in his own atomization. Nuclear stockpiles thus demand the development of effective delivery systems. The offense must remain superior to the defense. Because defensive measures are constantly being improved, the maintenance of this offensive edge requires continuing and unrelaxing effort.

In these circumstances, each power tends to be consumed by the constant fear that a technological breakthrough might grant its opponent a temporary advantage that could be exploited to end the conflict on his terms. Both are highly industrialized nations with sophisticated technological knowledge, so this possibility of a breakthrough is seen as a very real threat by each protagonist. And rightly so. For the marriage of such knowledge to intense mutual fear leads to a fantastically large investment of resources and skills in the development of ever newer arms, in order that the offense be kept ahead of the defense and, on the other hand, that the defense catch up with the offense. Thus the proverbial arms race becomes a *series* of arms races as technology constantly devises new weapons.

As the United States and the Soviet Union throw one weapons system after another into the effort to maintain at least a balance of terror, neither dares fall behind in either the discovery of new physical relationships or in the application of scientific knowledge to military hardware and political-military strategy. Thus, by the end of the first decade of the Cold War, about 50 per cent of the engineers in the United States and 25 per cent of the scientists were employed by the federal government, either directly or on contract, and about 65 per cent of the scientific research in universities and 57 per cent of that in private industry were government-financed.[15]

15 Warner R. Schilling, "Scientists, Foreign Policy, and Politics," *The American Political Science Review*, June, 1962, p. 288.

The result has been an intensive effort to design delivery systems with high performance characteristics. Because of the rapidity of technological change in delivery systems, this has required constant attention. Thus the bomber, which came into its own during World War II, was already on the way out less than two decades after the end of the war. No sooner had one bomber been designed, produced, placed in service, and the crews trained, than it became obsolescent. Compare this with prenuclear delivery systems. The Flying Fortress, the workhorse of the U.S. Army Air Corps, was in use before the nation entered World War II, and it was still being flown at the end of the war in Europe. Only in the last stage of the air war against Japan did the Superfortress come into service. In the nuclear age, it was soon outmoded as the need for an intercontinental bomber developed. The B-36, with its six piston motors, four jet engines, and a range of 10,000 miles, answered this need. But its slow top speed of just over 400 mph soon made it vulnerable to fighter attack, and it had to be replaced by the B-47, a pure jet bomber with a speed of over 600 mph. Because the B-47 was a medium-range bomber, it could operate from the United States only if refueled in the air, so it flew mostly from overseas bases in Europe, North Africa, the Middle East, and the Far East. Overseas bases were within range of the Soviet Union's sizable force of medium-range bombers; continental American bases were still beyond the range of Soviet bombers in the early and middle 1950's. Consequently, yet another intercontinental bomber was necessary. The United States therefore developed the B-52, whose eight jet engines gave the bomber a speed of over 650 mph and a range exceeding 6,000 miles. This bomber subsequently became the backbone of the Strategic Air Command. The B-47 was retired after about a decade; the B-52 survived in ever dwindling numbers into the 1970's.

By the late 1960's, the backbone of deterrence was the intercontinental missile flying at 18,000 mph. These, too, went through several technological changes: from liquid fuel to solid fuel; from a small single warhead with a "small" payload—less than one megaton—to a larger payload, to multiple warheads. Each new weapon, of course, cost more than its predecessor, with the result that these arms races became ever increasing financial burdens for both superpowers. Yet, in the extensive and intensive bipolar system, the superpowers felt that they had little, if any, choice about what they had to do to preserve the balance of power.

ALLIANCES, EAST AND WEST

The search for alliances was also the result of superpower fear of the slightest change in the balance of power. Alliances, in this context, served three functions: to draw frontiers, to give the superpower a legal reason for intervention to preserve the territorial *status quo*, and to add power to that of the protector. The United States, particularly, showed great zeal in finding allies. Indeed, it has sometimes been accused of suffering from "pactomania," of indiscriminately collecting allies whether they were strategically placed or not, strong or weak, developed or underdeveloped. All in all, the U.S. collected over forty allies in all corners of the world except sub-Sahara Africa.

NATO was, of course, the principal American alliance, and its potential collective power was very great. Because the need for an American commitment to Western Europe to protect U.S. security had already been demonstrated by two wars, the heart of the Treaty stated that the parties agreed that an armed attack against one or more of them in Europe or North America would be considered an attack against all of them. Europe had become the "first line of defense." The knowledge that the United States would fight to preserve Europe's freedom was intended to deter a Soviet attack. Instead of again standing by and allowing the balance of power to be upset—and thereby once more becoming drawn into war—the United States now committed itself to the preservation of the European balance in peacetime. The American perception of a Soviet threat was, moreover, shared by all alliance members, and after the outbreak of the Korean War apprehension about a possible military attack increased, making rearmament seem necessary. In response, President Truman appointed General Eisenhower to serve as Supreme Allied Commander in Europe, and all member nations began to rearm themselves.

The very success of NATO tempted the United States to organize multilateral military alliances in other areas of the world—but with little success. Thus, after the French debacle in Indochina in 1954, the United States founded the Southeast Asia Treaty Organization (SEATO) to defend the South Pacific area—excluding the British colony of Hong Kong, which presumably would be defended by Britain, and the Nationalist Chinese base of Formosa, which was considered America's responsibility, a responsibility formalized by treaty the same year. (A protocol to the SEATO treaty later extended the organization's protection to Vietnam, Laos, and Cambodia.) The signatories were the United States, Britain, France, Australia, New Zealand, the Philippines, Pakistan, and Thailand. There were thus only three Asian members. Britain was a reluctant member, because India, a leading Commonwealth member and spokesman for the nonalignment of the new nations, opposed the treaty; France's influence in the area was diminishing rapidly; Australia and New Zealand, also Commonwealth members, were already protected by the United States under the ANZUS Treaty of 1951 and, in any event, were hardly Asian countries. Of the Asian states to join, the Philippines had traditional ties to the United States, Pakistan wanted arms and allied help against its archrival India, and only Thailand was genuinely concerned with the Communist threat, because the French defeat in Indochina had brought that threat nearer to its frontiers. Thus, unlike NATO, SEATO contained neither the most important nations in the area nor a true mutuality of interest.

India, Burma, Ceylon, and Indonesia did not join. Having just emerged from Western colonialism, they were unwilling to be tied once more to the West through a military alliance. For this reason alone, the inclusion of the Western colonial powers was a mistake. Besides, these Asian countries' colonial experience did not include Russian imperialism. Nor had the new China yet infringed on the territories of the former colonies. Hence, a threat from Russia or China was not for them an immediate fear. Their greatest concern was to remain nonaligned in the cold war, to concentrate on their nations' modernization.

Because for most Asian nations the Communist threat was not a reality, American policy did not inspire much confidence in Asia. U.S. support for Chiang's discredited regime and its refusal to recognize and deal with Communist China—then still considered peaceful and progressive by most of its neighbors—seemed to them unrealistic. American backing of the French in their fight against the Vietminh—who, like the Communist Chinese, were regarded as more nationalist than Communist—suggested that the United States opposed progress and the spirit of the times. To the Asians, as Louis Halle has noted, U.S. policy in regard to China and Indochina put it in the untenable position (particularly for a Western power) of defending China against the Chinese, Vietnam against Vietnamese, and Asia against Asians.[16]

In short, unlike NATO, SEATO was an alliance lacking the principal nations of the area and organized against a threat they did not themselves recognize. In effect, if SEATO was anything it was a unilateral attempt by the United States to deter further Communist expansion. As a non-Asian alliance for the defense of an Asian area, its chief purpose was to warn the Communists of America's stake in that portion of the world. And if the United States felt its security in the area threatened by direct or indirect Communist extension of power, SEATO provided America with the opportunity for unilateral intervention to hold the frontier in this area of the world. While the Treaty formally committed the United States *only* to consultation with other treaty members in case of aggression, Secretary of State Dulles was to insist that under SEATO the United States was committed not only to resist overt attack, but also to prevent and counter covert subversion from within.[17]

Another multilateral treaty organized by the United States was the Middle East Treaty Organization (METO), also known as the Baghdad Pact. Actually, it was an alliance among Britain, Turkey, Iran, Iraq, and Pakistan. Not wishing to become involved in the Arab-Israeli conflict, the United States did not join, but cooperation was so close that it was a member in all but name. As Dulles saw it: "Many of the Arab League

16 Louis J. Halle, *The Cold War as History* (New York: Harper & Row, 1967), p. 304.

17 Quoted in Walter LaFeber, *America, Russia, and the Cold War, 1945–66* (New York: Wiley, 1967), p. 167.

countries are so engrossed with their quarrels with Israel or with Great Britain or Greece that they pay little heed to the menace of Soviet Communism. However, there is more concern where the Soviet Union is near. In general, the northern tier shows awareness of the danger."[18] Dulles notwithstanding, METO was plagued by some of the same problems as SEATO. Turkey was already a member of NATO, and Pakistan, whose concern remained India and not Communism, was a SEATO partner. Iraq was a traditional rival of Egypt for Arab leadership, and Britain, thrown out of Egypt, joined the alliance to protect its strategic and economic interests in the area. Thus, contrary to Dulles, a common perception of a Soviet menace was lacking.

Instead, the pact aroused rivalry. Egypt's Nasser in particular saw METO as an attempt both to preserve Western power in the area and to support a competitor. He therefore set out to destroy it. Arab hostility to the influence of an old colonial power, coupled with intra-Arab rivalries and major political schisms within the nations of the area, helped undermine METO. In Iraq, the pro-Western leaders had little popular support, and in 1958 the government was overthrown. Baghdad left the Pact. Above all, the bipolarization of Arab politics that resulted from the founding of METO gave Russia a wedge into the region. Such intra-Arab rivalry between the more revolutionary and the more conservative regimes would probably have occurred anyway, but by its alliance with some of the latter the West hastened the split while at the same time setting itself up as an easy and visible target for the militant Arab governments. This situation was ready-made for the Soviet Union, which linked itself politically—by means of military aid and economic assistance—to the anti-Western Arab countries.

These were not, of course, the only American alliances. There were other multilateral alliances, such as the Rio Pact, providing for collective self-defense of Latin America, as well as a good many bilateral alliances, such as those of the United States with Nationalist China, South Korea, and Japan. Russia too was concerned with allies, although not nearly to the same degree as the United States, perhaps because Moscow's relationships with other Communist countries have been primarily at the Party, rather than state, level, and thus it did not necessarily need formal alliances. The Warsaw Pact, which was organized as a formal alliance only after West Germany's entry into NATO in 1955, existed as a "nonalliance" for several years prior to that inclusion. There was never a question of Eastern Europe's close relationship with Russia. Similarly, even had the Sino-Soviet Treaty of 1950 never been drawn, there would have existed close relations between the two great Communist powers —at least until their schism opened. Almost all the states who were members of the UN in 1955, before the admission of many of the new states, had been signed up by either the U.S. and England or Russia.

[18] Quoted in Brown, *Faces of Power*, p. 78.

ALLIANCE COHESION

The principal alliances were also highly cohesive, so much so that they were commonly referred to as "blocs." Bipolarity left the NATO countries little choice, for the countries of Europe were militarily and economically completely dependent upon the United States. West Germany, of course, had only one option besides possible neutralization and reunification under Soviet auspices—which was really no option. Facing the Red Army to the East and occupied by the Western Allies, it aligned itself with the latter to gain the political support and help so necessary for its reunification, security, and economic recovery, as well as for its "moral" rehabilitation in the eyes of its neighbors. In the immediate postwar period, France thought it did have options. Bordering on a larger and more powerful country, France wished to see Germany broken into a number of smaller states. Unable to elicit Allied support for such a policy, it advocated control over German industry instead. As Moscow was also concerned with the rebirth of German power, France hoped to gain Soviet support for this course of action. Indeed, during the years immediately following the war, Paris thought it could act as a mediator between Moscow and Washington. But Russia was uninterested in French overtures; like the United States, the Russians were using the issue of German unification to bid for German support, for, in the bipolar confrontation, Germany's potential strength was sought by both superpowers even as the defeated country still lay in ruins. France was, therefore, unable to play the role of mediator; threatened by Russian power, it had to move under America's protective wing.

Britain's case provides an even better illustration of the "tightness" or intensity of bipolarity. The Labour Party, which had been elected right after the war, came into power with ideological preconceptions antithetical to traditional foreign policy. As a convinced democratic socialist party, it opposed capitalist foreign policy and was committed to international working-class solidarity and the repudiation of an allegedly immoral "power politics" with its ultimate reliance upon armaments. Thus the rank and file of Labour Party members were shocked by their leaders' foreign policy. For, as seen earlier, the United States did not wholly confront the demands of the bipolar world until February, 1947. Until then, it had been Britain that had condemned Soviet actions in Eastern Europe and helped Greece and Turkey to oppose the Soviet Union. Thus, the Labour Party leadership adopted the historic British policy of opposing any nation seeking European hegemony. Furthermore, aware of Britain's weakness, the leadership tried from the beginning to enlist American support. In brief, Labour acted as any pro-capitalist Conservative Government would have done by aligning socialist Britain with a capitalist nation that, by definition, should have been the enemy, against a socialist power that, by definition, should have been a peaceful and nonexpansionist state. The realities of the state system had rendered such slogans as "Left understands Left" and "no enemies to the left" obsolete and underlined the continuity of foreign policy despite the ideological differences among policy-makers. Labour leaders recognized the environmental restraints existing for postwar Britain and made the necessary adjustments to them. Above all, to the consternation of many of its followers Labour fell back on the traditional technique of power politics. Because the Labour Party's foreign policy was not dictated by socialist ideology, the party was to be deeply divided on foreign policy issues, especially after it began Britain's rearmament in the wake of Korea. But this internal cleavage also testifies to the "socialization" of a nation's leadership, which may not perceive the external reality correctly but soon finds it must adjust to environmental demands and pressures.[19]

In fact, once the bipolar state system had aligned countries such as Germany, France, and Britain, bipolarity transformed them on occasions into what one analyst has called a "penetrated political system . . . in which non-members of a national society participate directly and authoritatively, through actions taken jointly with the society's members, in either the allocation of its values or the mobilization of support in behalf of its goals."[20] All three European countries received massive economic assistance for their recovery and all were pressured by the United States to rearm. Washington therefore participated authoritatively in these societies' distribution of resources among their many different foreign and domestic policies.

The cohesiveness of the Soviet bloc is perhaps less surprising. Later, as the extensive and intensive bipolarity began to erode, some of the satellites became more independent of Soviet controls, especially in the domestic arena. Until then, however, the controls at the Party and governmental levels were relatively easy to apply. All the East European states were penetrated systems.[21] First of all, the satellite leaders were appointed by Stalin, which meant that the men had proved their loyalty and devotion to Stalin. A strong incentive for them to remain loyal was the knowledge that the Soviet dictator could—and frequently did—effect purges against them. Stalin usually held only bilateral "consultations" with his viceroys, so that each set of Party leaders faced him alone. Assured that the other satellites had already given their support to whatever policy Stalin was discussing, they inevitably endorsed the policy too. A second lever of control was the Soviet ambassador in each satellite, who maintained a close watch on the Party leadership and kept Moscow

[19] Michael R. Gordon, *Conflict and Consensus in Labour's Foreign Policy* (Stanford, Calif.: Stanford University Press, 1969), pp. 1–44, 102. Also Leon D. Epstein, *Britain—Uneasy Alliance* (Chicago: University of Chicago Press, 1954).

[20] James N. Rosenau, "Pre-Theories and Theories of Foreign Policy," in R. Barry Farrell, ed., *Approaches to Comparative and International Politics* (Evanston, Ill.: Northwestern University Press, 1966), pp. 63–66.

[21] Zbigniew K. Brzezinski, *The Soviet Bloc: Unity and Conflict*, rev. ed. (New York: Praeger Publishers, 1961), pp. 104–37.

informed. Knowing that the ambassador's reports on their performance reached Moscow regularly, the satellite leaders generally checked their views and evaluations with the ambassador to ensure favorable reports. A more obvious instance of close supervision by the Soviet Government was found in the command of the armies. The Polish Army, for example, was for many years headed by Russian General Rokossovsky; less open, and more typical, was the appointment of Russian officers to high command positions in the Czechoslovak Army. The Red Army itself remained in the background, but its presence was a constant reminder that it was there to be used—if necessary.

There was also close cooperation between Soviet and satellite secret police. In addition, the Soviet secret police apparatus maintained its own independent structure in Eastern Europe. Whenever it considered Soviet security to be at stake, it could arrest any nationals of the satellite countries. Finally, Soviet political and military domination was reinforced by economic control. Stalin established joint companies in which the shares and profits were to be divided on a fifty-fifty basis between the Soviet Union and each satellite nation. In reality, however, these joint companies were merely vehicles for Soviet exploitation of the economy. Another economic institution, the Council for Mutual Economic Aid (COMECON), was to be the economic equivalent of the Cominform (the postwar successor to the Comintern). The principal concern of COMECON was to coordinate trade among the states of the socialist camp. The treaties governing these trade relations specified what goods the satellites had to deliver to the Soviet Union and at what prices. COMECON, in brief, served as another instrument of Soviet exploitation. All phases of the satellites' lives, then, were subject to close Soviet supervision, including their foreign affairs. Relations with the West, in particular, were "guided" by Moscow. Foreign policies were dictated, and discussion, let alone disagreement, was futile and perhaps dangerous.

Naturally, such complete subordination and exploitation led to strong popular resentment and anti-Russian feelings,[22] although during the early years these remained hidden underneath the surface harmony and comradeship of "proletarian internationalism." Only one state opposed the Stalinist pattern of imperial control: Yugoslavia. In order to discourage other potential challenges to Soviet primacy, Stalin expelled Tito from the Cominform in 1949. At the same time, actual and potential leaders throughout Eastern Europe were dismissed from office, publicly tried, and in many cases executed. But the issue dramatized by the Tito-Stalin conflict—how to organize the new socialist camp—remained.

With the Soviet Union determined to expel any Communist state that rejected its "vanguard" position, there was bound to be a conflict

[22] Ghita Ionescu, *The Break-Up of the Soviet Empire in Eastern Europe* (Baltimore: Penguin Books, 1965), pp. 39–86.

with the new China in the long run.[23] Historically, the relationship between Czarist Russia and Imperial China had hardly been that of equals. During the nineteenth century, the Russians, who had by then already extended their domain to Siberia and the Pacific Coast, expanded farther eastward and southward.[24] In 1860, they founded the city of Vladivostok ("Ruler of the East") on former Chinese territory, and, in the last decade of the century, they began to construct the Trans-Siberian Railroad. Taking advantage of the weakness of Imperial China, the Czarist government gained the right to lay the track through Manchuria and to control the management and finance of the railway. The Chinese Eastern Railroad thereby became a principal instrument for the expansion of Russian influence in northern Manchuria. The Russians also penetrated China in Sinkiang and Outer Mongolia and occupied the island of Sakhalin. In fact, Czarist Russia's territorial gains and concessions in China exceeded those won by Britain and France.

But the new China considered itself the Soviet Union's equal and potentially one of the world's great powers. Furthermore, like Yugoslavia, it possessed a Party and army independent of Russia. China could hardly be transformed into a satellite. Indeed, one of China's prime objectives was to restore its own unity, status, and strength. For much of the 2,000 years preceding the Communist takeover, China as an imperial power had exercised hegemony over large areas of the Far East, Central Asia, and Southeast Asia. China was the "Middle Kingdom," receiving tribute from the surrounding states. The Chinese have always been convinced of their primacy in Asia as well as of their cultural superiority; non-Chinese were regarded as "barbarians." Such an attitude naturally bred a sense of superiority and condescension toward other nations, similar to that generally harbored by the West toward the non-Western (formerly colonial) peoples. But China's goal in its determination to be a great power was not limited to playing a pre-eminent role in Asia; the new China's second aim was to play a major role in determining the Communist bloc's over-all policies.

The question this posed for the Russians, bearing on the future of the Sino-Soviet alliance, was whether they should permit China to *share* the leadership of the bloc. Stalin's successors after 1953 were particularly anxious to relieve developing tensions by granting China and Mao greater status within the Communist movement. Symbolically, Chou En-lai, as the representative of the Chinese Communist Party at Stalin's funeral, walked side by side with Malenkov and Khrushchev behind the carriage bearing the Soviet dictator's body; and he stood among the

[23] David Floyd, *Mao Against Khrushchev* (New York: Praeger Publishers, 1963), and Donald S. Zagoria, *The Sino-Soviet Conflict 1956–1961* (Princeton, N.J.: Princeton University Press, 1962).

[24] For a brief commentary on the depth of Russian fear and hatred of China, stemming from the Mongol invasion, see Harrison E. Salisbury, *War Between Russia and China* (New York: W. W. Norton, 1969), pp. 29–38.

Soviet leaders on the balcony of Lenin's tomb, from which the eulogies were delivered, rather than with the other foreign Communist leaders.

In turn, the Chinese closely supported the Soviet Union on foreign policy. When the Russians ran into trouble with their satellites in 1956, the Chinese interceded to reconcile Moscow and Warsaw while also approving of the military suppression of the Hungarian revolt. The Chinese purpose was very clear: to preserve a united Communist bloc and strengthen it under the Soviet Union's leadership against American "imperialism." As the strongest Communist power, the Soviet Union was the bloc's obvious "center," although China was claiming co-leadership. In effect, during this period the Chinese were seeking the establishment of a Sino-Soviet high command that would wage an effective *coalition* campaign against the capitalist enemy.[25] This was the crucial Chinese assumption—that the Soviets would wage a militant anti-Western foreign policy. It was only as the Soviet Union became generally more cautious in behavior and began to move closer to the United States on arms control and other issues that Peking began to move away from Moscow, eventually attacking it for having sold out the Revolution. Not surprisingly, however, during these bipolar days Russia and China saw the imperialist countries as a united entity and feared being "encircled by world capitalism"; similarly, Washington during this period saw the Communist world as a monolithic "world conspiracy" and opposed any Communist extension of power anywhere in the world, including in Korea and Vietnam. For, during the days of extensive and intensive bipolarity existing during the first decade of the cold war, an extension of power by a bloc member was viewed as, in reality, an extension of American or Soviet power. Since each viewed the other as a bloc, such an extension had to be opposed.

DEFECTIONS AND INTERVENTIONS

Another index of each superpower's sensitivity to changes in the bipolar balance was its sensitivity to any actual or attempted defections from its respective bloc. Each bloc was to be guarded from within like a fortress; bloc loyalty had to be assured. Simultaneously, each superpower suspected the other adversary of intending to undermine its own sphere. Thus, for example, the United States helped (through the CIA) to overthrow what it deemed to be a Guatemalan pro-Communist government, which had received weapons from the East; sought unsuccessfully to topple Castro's regime in Cuba after the Cuban leader had tied his island politically and economically to the Soviet Union; sent troops to prevent the victory of alleged pro-Castro, pro-Communist elements in the Dominician Republic; helped finance opposition to the Marxist government of Allende in Chile and thereby helped to topple it; often

[25] G. F. Hudson, Richard Lowenthal, and Roderick MacFarquhar, eds., *The Sino-Soviet Dispute* (New York: Praeger Publishers, 1961), p. 4.

"interfered" in European and other elections to the extent of making it clear which party (obviously the pro-American one) it favored; and supported South Vietnam's refusal to participate in the 1956 countrywide election stipulated by the 1954 Geneva agreements because it feared that the election would go to Ho Chi Minh's North Vietnamese regime rather than to the American-supported Diem regime. On the other side, the Soviets seized power in Czechoslovakia in 1948 to "fill out" their Eastern zone; suppressed the East German revolt in 1953; threatened to crush the Polish uprising; and did crush the Hungarian revolution in 1956 and the Czechoslovak experiment in 1968. Similarly, they have refused to allow the East Germans to express their views on the issue of a reunification with West Germany through free elections and have ignored the Yalta obligation to permit free elections, with all parties represented (except those that collaborated with Nazi Germany). Finally, when American forces crossed the 38th Parallel and advanced into North Korea during the Korean War, China intervened—both to guard its security and to preserve a Communist regime—and similarly the North Vietnamese support for the Vietcong in the South increased American counteractions as South Vietnam disintegrated and a Communist victory appeared increasingly likely.

Bipolycentrism and the Cold War After 1962

Limited Adversary Relationship

The exact moment when the extensive and intensive bipolarity began to change is difficult to pinpoint. Perhaps it could be dated from 1957, when the Soviet Union tested the first ICBM and greatly enhanced its capacity to hit the United States. The transformation was certainly clear after the 1962 Cuban missile crisis, when both powers realized how close they had come to stepping over the brink and, symbolic of their changing attitudes, signed a limited test ban treaty in 1963.

The nature of this transformation was to result in: one, increasing superpower cooperation on military and political issues; two, the loosening of the formerly rival blocs into less cohesive alliances; and, three, the rise of actors not aligned with either of the superpowers' principal alliances. But while bipolarity has passed, the new distribution of power has not become truly multipolar, or polycentric, either. Perhaps the post-bipolar system might more accurately be described as *bipolycentric*. The power of the two nuclear giants, even without their nuclear arms, remains immensely superior to that of their respective allies; there is no rough equality of power as in the multipolar model or in past historical systems. Indeed, it was the United States and the Soviet Union that were the principal "producers" of security in this system; their allies were the "consumers" of this security. (So too were the nonaligned new nations;

in the absence of the American-Russian balance, these would have been unable to remain unentangled and would have lost their collective identity as the "third world.") Because these producers, as the principal rivals in the system, were deadlocked in a balance of terror—a deadlock which in itself required increasing cooperation and a lowering of international tension to maintain—their allies regained a measure of freedom for diplomatic independence and maneuver. As with weaker states throughout history, they took advantage of this stalemate between their stronger colleagues and became once again centers of independent foreign policy decisions. As Henry Kissinger has said, "Polycentrism is on the rise not because the world has ceased to be bipolar, but because with respect to nuclear weapons it essentially remains so."[26]

This bipolycentrism differs from traditional multipolarity in one significant respect: States do not shift from one alliance to a counteralliance and back again. In bi-polycentrism, the new centers of foreign policy decisions have remained formally in alliance with their respective superpower, upon which they remain, in the final analysis, dependent for their security (China is, however, a significant exception); but these allies have also to varying degrees rebelled against the superpower's intra-alliance hegemony, and they have asserted their own interests more vigorously.[27] This psychological revolt means that relationships among states have become far more numerous and complex than during the bipolar days when the interactions between the two cohesive alliances were conducted largely by the United States and the Soviet Union. Thus each superpower can—and does—establish links to its rival's secondary allies, taking advantage of intra-alliance differences in order to weaken its adversary. By the same token, the secondary states seek to use these links and others with the secondary powers in the opposing alliance in the expectation of enhancing their bargaining capacity within their own alliances. They might be far weaker militarily than their protector, but by moving diplomatically out of the latter's embrace and toward its competitor, or by being difficult and obstructing their own alliance, they seek to gain sufficient influence to achieve at least some of their objectives. Thus even in the absence of mobility from one coalition to the other, the increasing political cooperation of the two superpowers, the degree of movement possible *within* the "free world" or the "socialist world" for the secondary powers plus their increased crossing of cold war lines has apparently produced the same kind of moderate behavior as in a multipolar system.

It was above all the increasing awareness of the dangers of bipolar confrontations and nuclear warfare that most moderated the cold war and changed the behavior of the United States and the Soviet Union. Both

[26] Henry A. Kissinger, *The Troubled Partnership* (Garden City, N.Y.: Anchor Books, 1966), p. 16.

[27] Herbert S. Dinerstein, "The Transformation of Alliance Systems," *American Political Science Review*, September, 1965, pp. 596–97.

superpowers drew the same conclusion from their common fate of being, in Robert Oppenheimer's words, "two scorpions in a bottle." In short, both had every reason to avoid stinging one another. Churchill called this the "balance of terror" and said survival would be the twin brother of annihilation; a German author referred to the common fate of the superpowers as "the interdependence of doom."[28] By the mid-1950's, the policy-makers drew the logical conclusions. In 1955, President Eisenhower proclaimed that there was "no alternative to peace." Shortly afterward, Khrushchev, the then Soviet Party leader, declared that Lenin's prophecy of an inevitable war between Communism and capitalism had become outmoded through modern technology. The leaders of both nations, in brief, recognized the starkness of their alternatives: coexistence or nonexistence. Thus Russia and America became increasingly cautious in their external behavior as they realized that the crucial issue was their ability not to mobilize their power but to *exercise it with restraint*.

Admittedly, this increasing cautiousness in foreign policy did not come about all at once. Feeling that the balance of power was changing in Russia's favor—after the 1957 Soviet space achievements and the testing of the first ICBM before the United States—Khrushchev tried to pressure the Western powers to get out of West Berlin. He failed to achieve this objective, although he won a number of tactical successes. It was only after Cuba in 1962 that the two nuclear giants transformed their new-found common consciousness of the catastrophe of nuclear warfare into the realization that they had a common stake in the preservation of peace and needed to cooperate with one another for the purpose of "arms control." Containment had all along been the American goal; and, with their increasing awareness of the fatal nature of nuclear weapons, the Russians, too, increasingly talked of "peaceful coexistence" as more than a temporary tactical device to put their adversaries off guard.

More specifically, after the Cuban crisis the two powers established a "hot line" between the White House and the Kremlin for instant communications during crises and agreed to a limited ban on the testing of nuclear weapons, to a prohibition against nuclear weapons in space and on the sea beds, and to a ban on proliferating them to other nations here on earth. In the realm of strategy, they sought to stabilize their mutual deterrence. This was by no means easy. Because of their continued existence in the state system and the dependence of the global balance upon their strengths, their need to protect themselves continued to inspire mutual suspicion. Thus they remained gripped in an "action-reaction" arms cycle. If one saw its opponent as offensively superior and sought increased protection and enhanced deterrence with antiballistic missiles (ABM's), for example, the other interpreted the first's increased defensive capacity as an offensive threat to itself because of the

[28] W. W. Schütz, quoted in John H. Herz, *International Politics in the Atomic Age* (Chicago: University of Chicago Press, 1951), pp. 111–12.

possibility that it might weaken its own deterrent capability. Each therefore sought ABM's to ensure that enough of a retaliatory force would survive an initial enemy strike, irrespective of the size of the attacking force. At the same time, the ABM build-up had a "feedback" result: a further accumulation of missiles with multiple warheads, because each side now felt it needed more missiles to penetrate the enemy defenses to deliver its retaliatory blow.

On the other hand, however, both superpowers had to confront harsh realities. First, both recognized the danger that a large-scale deployment of new offensive and defensive arms might produce an atmosphere of uncertainty in the calculation of the balance of power. A resultant miscalculation might then make one power think that the balance was turning against it, thus inducing it to strike first before it became too late. Second, both were burdened with the fantastic yet ever mounting costs of new weapons and the need for resources for nonmilitary purposes. The agreement of the United States and the Soviet Union to negotiate to find out if they could reach an accord on limiting their respective offensive and defensive arms would have been inconceivable in the days of intensive bipolarity; the mutual distrust would have been too high. By the late 1960's, however, American and Soviet leaders were far more conscious of the degree to which their *common interests cut across their continuing conflicts*, and thus, while they began to deploy the new weapons, they at least professed a desire to halt the ever spiraling arms build-up. The most dramatic result of this awareness was their subsequent agreement to limit the number of antiballistic missiles each could deploy, and to freeze their respective land and sea-based offensive intercontinental missiles while they continued to negotiate an equitable strategic arms balance, and finally in 1974 to place a ceiling on the numbers of missiles and bombers each side could have for the next decade.

Simultaneously, this new relationship meant that each superpower needed to discipline its allies and abstain from actions that might jeopardize the peace. Thus the United States has restrained Nationalist Chinese forces on Formosa from attacking the mainland; it did not intervene in Hungary in 1956, or in Czechoslovakia in 1968, to help the anti-Soviet revolts; it compelled its two closest allies, Britain and France, to halt their attack upon Egypt in 1956; it negotiated with Moscow bilaterally over such issues as Berlin and mutual and balanced force reductions in Europe, even when its major allies were opposed; and it signed the limited test ban treaty and negotiated the antiproliferation treaty despite the open opposition of France and, in the latter case, the reluctance of West Germany. Similarly, the Soviets refused to extend their nuclear umbrella to Chinese Communist efforts to capture Formosa; to China's rage, they vehemently opposed Peking's attacks upon India in 1959 and supported India diplomatically when the conflict erupted again in 1962; they did not allow the Arab-Israeli War of 1967 to turn into a direct Soviet clash with the United States, although the Arabs attempted to make it so in order to avoid defeat; and, until just before the 1973 Middle East war, they had refused to send Egypt and Syria the offensive arms they had requested; despite Vietnam, Moscow's accusations against Washington as a warmonger were mild (considering it was bombing and mining the harbors of a "fraternal" state), and Russia persisted in improving its bilateral relations with the United States—in fact, dramatically so during the Nixon period; and, in Latin America, it opposed Castro's strategy of attempting to overthrow governments through guerrilla warfare.

Stabilizing the military environment, and therefore lowering international tensions so that sparks in this highly flammable world would not ignite it, has thus become part of the new pattern of Soviet-American relations. Admittedly, it is not the total pattern. The two superpowers continue to have major conflicts that could eventually diminish their limited cooperation; arms negotiations could fail, and new cycles of yet more technologically advanced and sophisticated weapons could occur; quarrels such as the one between Israel and Egypt and other Arab states, in which the Soviet Union seeks to exploit existing Arab nationalism and anti-American animus in order to dislodge Western influence throughout the Middle East and substitute its own—as in the Yom Kippur War of 1973—are bound on occasion to test severely the new cooperation and bring on possible confrontations. There will undoubtedly be failures and setbacks. Yet it is this trend to cooperation, so different from the pattern of intense hostility of the first decade of the cold war, that is significant. The relationship has changed from one of total hostility toward one another to a *"limited adversary" relationship of conflict and cooperation.*

ALLIANCE DISINTEGRATION

This changed American-Russian relationship, resulting from their mutual antisuicide pact, began to erode the cohesive bonds of each superpower's principal alliances.[29] For one thing, in the case of America's European allies, this new situation of nuclear stalemate coincided with the rebirth of European self-confidence and political assertiveness. When the Marshall Plan was launched and the NATO alliance formed, the European states were weak and exhausted. The transatlantic "harmony" and NATO "unity" of the first few years were therefore based on an unequal power relationship. Confronted on the one side by a powerful United States and on the other side by the immense power of the Soviet Union, the Continental allies became dependent upon their protecting superpower. It was the superpower that possessed the real power and responsibility and, in the final analysis therefore, defined *their* interests as well as its own. If it decided, for example, to rearm West Germany—as

[29] The degree of "integration" is studied by Francis A. Beer, *Integration and Disintegration in NATO* (Columbus: Ohio State University Press, 1969).

the United States did after the Korean War erupted—that became allied policy. If France or any other country objected—and virtually every one of the European allies did—there was little more that they could do about it than object. Though the nations of Europe were America's friends, they also felt themselves in these circumstances to be its client states.

Britain, with its linguistic and cultural ties to the United States, as well as the recent close wartime cooperation, felt this dependency somewhat less keenly. The special relationship between the two English-speaking peoples served Britain as a psychological buffer against the realization that its days as a great and independent power were past. Its appearance as a major world power was further bolstered by its leadership of the Commonwealth. Not until the failure of the Suez invasion during the Arab-Israeli war of 1956—a failure in which British conventional military impotence and inefficiency were compounded by the strong American and Commonwealth opposition—were these illusions exposed and did Britons become both conscious of their real weakness as an independent "power" and their very high degree of dependence upon American support and good will.

For the French, by contrast, their lack of importance within NATO was emphasized by the resurgence of West Germany. The latter's recovery reinforced France's subordinate status within the Western alliance. Washington paid more attention to Bonn than to Paris, because West Germany was the stronger and more central of the two powers. Thus France found itself well behind Britain and West Germany and just a step ahead of Italy and the Low Countries. For France, feeling itself to be an American satellite, a united Europe based upon Franco-German reconciliation and unity was, not surprisingly in these circumstances, seen as an alternative to remaining subservient to the United States. It was the means by which France could gain sufficient strength to acquire an equal voice with the "Anglo-Saxons" in NATO and by which the nations of Europe could someday re-exert their prestige and influence in the postwar age of the superpowers.

In short, opposition to American hegemony constituted one strong motivation that from the very beginning was inherent in the movement to create a United States of Europe. This movement, having started with the French-proposed European Coal and Steel Community in 1950, had by 1958 picked up momentum and resulted in the Common Market. Until that moment, Europe's dependence on America and, generally, European acquiescence in American policy had seemed quite normal to American policy-makers. Washington never questioned that American strategists should have sole responsibility for Europe's defense and that Washington diplomats should decide Europe's political future. But in reality it had always been only a matter of time until Europe, which was eventually to include Britain, would rebel. It was in the nature of an alliance of very unequal power relationships that the weaker members would again seek to play a major role as they regained some of their pre-war status. French President de Gaulle's assertive posture toward the United States after 1958 was symbolic of Europe's revolt against its subordinate status in NATO and an expression of hope that Europe would at some future date once more be master of its own destiny. In that sense de Gaulle had become "a self-appointed spokesman for the new nationalism that has come in the wake of European union."[30]

The other factor eroding the formerly cohesive strands of the NATO alliance stemmed specifically from the nuclear balance between the two superpowers. Among other things, now that the United States is itself vulnerable to a nuclear strike, the American commitment to the defense of Western Europe is viewed by its allies as increasingly less credible than when the United States possessed an atomic monopoly or, later, a far greater capability to strike the Soviet Union than the Russians had to strike the United States. But since Sputnik in 1957 the Europeans have seen the United States become more and more cautious as by 1970 it moved toward *détente* with a Russia that had by then gained strategic parity. What they, as nonnuclear powers, have feared even more than being left undefended against a major possible Soviet incursion or diplomatic threat—and they recognize that the latter is far more likely than the former—is that Washington, as the principal nuclear power upon whose strength and determination the defense of Western Europe has continued to rest, would make a tacit or actual deal at their expense in order to continue and strengthen its bilateral relations with the Soviet Union. The fact that Britain and France have built their own small deterrents and that West Germany seeks a voice regarding the use of the American deterrent testifies to the doubts of the principal U.S. allies about the protection their interests will receive in the future. Paradoxically, the nuclear balance also has the opposing effect of eroding the fear of war, which had previously cemented the alliance, thereby tempting each country to go its own way in the belief that its security was assured and that it did not therefore have to do its protector's bidding.

The changing American-Soviet relationship has also had a profound impact upon the Sino-Soviet alliance. China's friendly relations with Russia during the early years of their association to a large extent had depended upon the Kremlin's pursuing a militant anti-Western, especially anti-American, policy. When this policy changed (as Russia increasingly turned toward minimizing the risks of war), so did China's relationship with Russia. For the Chinese—at least, until 1971, when Sino-American relations began to thaw—continued to press for a more activist and militant policy which would keep up the pressure on the West. The Chinese were apprehensive lest the Soviet Union's fear of war be so great that it would shrink from challenging the West and, in

[30] Ronald Steel, *The End of Alliance* (New York: Viking, 1964), p. 79.

the process, lose its revolutionary fervor. For if the use of violence, in the form of threats and wars of national liberation, were foresworn because of anxiety that any spark might ignite a global conflagration, attempts to change the *status quo* by pressure tactics would also be reduced. And this would, Peking asserted, be a betrayal of the Communist cause; indeed, Peking charged, a "no-win" policy was tantamount to American-Russian cooperation to isolate and contain China, which proclaimed its continued commitment to its revolutionary vows.

China also carried over into its dispute with the Soviet Union something of the spirit of the Middle Kingdom, between heaven and earth —not quite up in heaven, but well above the other states in the world. Sensitive to pre-Communist China's humiliation and shame at the hands of the colonial powers, the new China was a proud country, determined to be a great power and redress outstanding grievances inflicted by foreigners. Considering itself Soviet Russia's equal as a large, potentially powerful member state in the socialist world, insisting that Moscow consult Peking in formulating a united and comprehensive anticapitalist political strategy, it felt hurt and angered by the Russian leaders' determination to decide policy unilaterally not only for Russia but the Sino-Soviet bloc, as it was then known. One way China attempted to show that, if Moscow would not seek Peking's help and approval in foreign policy decision-making, it could not make policy against Peking's wishes was by attacking one of Russia's most important friends, India, claiming that some of India's frontier territory belonged rightfully to China. The Soviets refused to take a position.[31] The Chinese charged the Russians with betrayal for not condemning "reactionary" India and for refusing to support an ally. China resumed its attack in 1962, when it roundly defeated the Indian forces. Again, the Russians refused to support China. The Chinese retaliated by repeatedly raising the question of the territories that they claimed were Chinese but had been seized by, among others, the Czars. The implied threat was obvious.

Both Russia and China have since then strengthened themselves militarily along the lengthy Sino-Soviet frontier and clashed briefly on a number of occasions. But Moscow has not limited itself to reinforcing its Far Eastern Central Asian and Outer-Mongolian borders; it has also signed a treaty of friendship with India, supported it in the Indian-Pakistan War of 1971, and openly and repeatedly announced its desire for an Asian alliance. Even Moscow's extensive support of Hanoi during the Vietnam War has been not only to assist a fraternal state in trouble but also to decrease China's influence and reinforce Vietnam's ancient resistance to Chinese domination. Polemically, the Sino-Soviet schism has descended to the verbal intensity and undiplomatic insults of the early cold war. Moscow now accuses Peking of Hitlerite ambitions and behavior—and Peking returns the compliment in kind in what an

---

[31] Tass statement, September 9, 1959, quoted in Floyd, *Mao Against Khrushchev*, pp. 261–62.

English observer, Edward Crankshaw, has called the "new cold war."[32]

Not only has the Soviet Union been faced with a Sino-Soviet schism, but it has also confronted increasing demands for national autonomy in Eastern Europe. Stalin had left a legacy of popular resentment and hatred for Russia in the "people's democracies," and this confronted his successors with a serious dilemma. If they preserved the Stalinist conception of empire, they would only intensify the existing dissatisfaction and opposition to Soviet exploitation and Soviet-imposed rapid industrialization, with its neglect of the people's standard of living and peasant agriculture and its attendant police terror. On the other hand, what if the Soviet leaders relaxed their grip on the satellites too much? Might this not stimulate further demands for concessions until Soviet authority had been whittled away? Could they safely eliminate the worst abuses and the most oppressive features of the Stalinist systems without disintegrating the bloc? While suppression produced resentment, concessions might create popular defiance and self-confidence. This is exactly what happened. By relaxing its grip, Moscow stimulated the demand for even greater independence. The Soviet-controlled thaw soon became an uncontrolled flood. Poland revolted, as did Hungary. The Red Army almost intervened in Warsaw; in Budapest it did so, because the new Hungarian regime wanted to defect from the Soviet bloc, and the Soviets feared that if this were allowed, the "domino effect" would destroy their security belt in Eastern Europe.

Nevertheless, after 1956 the Soviets increasingly accepted greater degrees of domestic autonomy and even some independence in foreign policy for its satellites—as long as they remained loyal to the Soviet bloc and supported Russia in its struggle with China. It was Rumania that most strongly asserted itself against Moscow and Peking and demonstrated the degree of national freedom made possible largely by the Sino-Soviet rift. It boldly declared that all bloc members should control their own economic lives and suggested that the presence of Soviet troops on the soil of Warsaw Pact members was no longer justified. The Rumanians reduced Russian cultural influence, increased trade with the West, maintained amicable ties with Peking, granted official recognition to West Germany (the first Communist country to do so), supported Czechoslovakia when it tried in 1968 to assert greater control over its domestic and foreign policies, and condemned Moscow for crushing Prague militarily when the Russians felt the Czechs had gone too far. Symbolic of his relative independence, the Rumanian Premier received President Nixon on a state visit in 1969 and then followed this up by visiting the White House. Short of further Budapests and Pragues— which hardly would help the Kremlin's reputation—the Soviet Union had more and more to deal with Eastern Europe on a basis of a limited give and take, hoping to retain ultimate control but acquiescing in a re-

[32] Edward Crankshaw, *The New Cold War: Moscow v. Peking* (Baltimore: Penguin Books, 1963).

duction of its authority throughout the area. Albania was the only exception. It had aligned itself with Peking, partly out of fear that a Soviet-Yugoslav rapprochement might be arranged at Albania's expense, since Belgrade had cast its eye eagerly in Albania's direction.

It was the erosion of the once solid bonds of these alliances that tempted both superpowers to try divide-and-rule tactics upon one another's coalitions. When Stalin threw Yugoslavia's Tito out of his bloc, the United States immediately supplied Tito with economic and military aid. Yugoslavia was an example to the other countries of Eastern Europe of an independent, rather than Russian-controlled, Communist nation. It was hoped that they would be stirred to loosen the Russian chains. When Poland did so in 1956, American economic help was again provided. Since then, "bridge-building" to the more independent of the former satellites—but not intervention—has been a continuing policy. And, in 1971, the Nixon Administration signaled a major change in American–Communist Chinese relations as the President announced he would visit the People's Republic on the mainland. Similarly, the Soviet Union has tried hard since de Gaulle's Presidency to exploit France's general opposition to American policies in Europe and elsewhere in order to weaken NATO further, to isolate West Germany, and to decrease U.S. influence in Europe. And in the Western Hemisphere, Russia supported Castro—before the Cuban leader declared himself to be a Communist—to weaken "hemispheric solidarity." Each power has tried to give the nations in the other's spheres of influence a vested interest in maintaining a relationship with itself so as to reduce alliance cohesion; for the secondary powers in the rival system, such a relationship creates the possibility of greater leverage with their leader and, in the Eastern bloc, economic rewards from the West.

Similarly, the secondary powers have also established links with one another. Rumania and France, Pakistan and Communist China, West Germany and several of the East European states are all again typical examples of the attempts by secondary states to use such links to try to enhance their bargaining ability with their protectors. Cross-cutting loyalties and pressures have thus been created. Of course, they can also act more directly. France under de Gaulle and Greece during the Cyprus crisis of 1974, for instance, withdrew their forces from NATO; Peking attacked India during the Khrushchev era to undermine Moscow's policy toward nonaligned India and Hanoi launched its 1972 spring offensive to rupture the Kremlin's *détente* with America. These are some of the ways in which the secondary states seek to enhance their influence within alliances characterized by gross disparities of power and domination by superpower policy interests; it is because the superpowers do not always take into account the interests of their allies—indeed, on occasions seem to go contrary to them—that the latter "oppose and try to undermine their protectors' policies. Such opposition is a symptom of weakness, not strength.

THE ROLE OF NEW NATIONS

This polycentrism was even further accentuated by the increasing role of the new non-Western nations. These nations could not escape the cold war once the earlier extensive and intensive bipolarity shifted the area of the American-Soviet conflict from Europe to the underdeveloped countries. The superpowers, reluctant to engage in direct conflict, channeled their conflict into the "safer" competition for the loyalty and support of these new nations. The third world thus acted as a kind of safety valve. Not only was the superpowers' confrontation diverted from areas where their respective vital interests were greatest and the possibility of hostilities were thus equally great, but among the principal instruments of this competition were economic aid and technical assistance. Undoubtedly, in a bipolar world, nonalignment was a position that was likely to augment benefits for the new states, and the chief benefit they sought was funds for their programs of modernization. In short, the Soviet Union and the United States acted as suitors in pursuit of the hand of the beautiful, but still unattached, maiden. By occasionally seeming to promise itself without ever actually making a commitment, the new nation in turn made the most of its bargaining strength. For each suitor was thereby compelled to show his ardor and "prove his love"—with his pocketbook—and this tended to enhance the volume of economic aid the new nation received. But for this American-Soviet competition, they would in all likelihood have received far less. Such aid also diminished the new nation's economic and political dependence on the West. The farther a nation moved away from the West, the more eagerly did the Soviet Union offer it aid. Conversely, the more resistance it showed to Communist seduction, the wider did the United States open its coffers. Tactically, then, nonalignment allowed the newly born weak state to enhance its influence in the state system beyond the power it actually possessed. In that sense, their exploitation of American-Soviet rivalry turned out to be "nothing more than the traditional scavenger policy of small powers in new clothes."[33] In short, they were acting on the age-old policy of small states that seek to extract maximum benefits from powerful friends.

Yet this third world, lying between the two rival blocs, was also an occasional source of great tension and, therefore, of confrontation when the superpowers were tempted to interfere in conflicts that erupted in these regions. Conflicts arose from various sources: from a new nation's strife with a former colonial master (as Egypt and Britain); from two or more regional states (as Egypt and Israel, Pakistan and India); and from domestic instability (as in the Congo). These conflicts presented problems to the United States and the Soviet Union, because each was

[33] Robert L. Rothstein, *Alliances and Small Powers* (New York: Columbia University Press, 1968), p. 254.

likely to be friendly with some of these states or because they supported opposing states in the various areas or domestic factions within some of the countries. Because neither felt that it could afford to permit the other to gain a major advantage that might perhaps result in regional dominance, intervention by one meant intervention by both. Indeed, if one superpower thought the other might intervene, it would feel compelled to intervene preventively—even if the other had initially had no such intention.

For the underdeveloped countries, the greatest danger stemming from the bipolar competition was their involvement in this great-power conflict and the risk they ran of becoming satellites of one or the other. They therefore sought shelter in the United Nations, using it to protect themselves through "preventive diplomacy"—that is, keeping local belligerents in the third world apart or defusing threatening situations that might otherwise attract American or Soviet intervention. By this means, they hoped to keep the two superpowers from extending the cold war to their soil. Because such an extension could spark a larger conflagration, the United Nations, supported tacitly or explicitly by one or both of the superpowers whose survival would be at stake if such a conflagration were started, performed the vital function of "system maintenance" in the "Balkans" of the second half of the twentieth century.

THE IMPACT OF CHANGE

The upshot of all these changes was that relationships between enemies as well as allies became more complex, and international tensions were generally reduced. The degree of perceived security threat was no longer as intense, and thus the policies that needed to be adopted were correspondingly less self-evident. In short, alternative policies were available. In the extensive and intensive bipolar system, for example, U.S. intervention and increasing military commitment in Vietnam would not, as far as one can speculate on the matter, have become more of a major political issue than the Korean intervention. In a system in which each alliance was still a cohesive bloc and each superpower highly sensitive to the slightest alteration of the balance, the United States would have equated a Vietcong victory with an extension of Soviet power. Whether the war in South Vietnam had started as a genuine civil war or as North Vietnamese aggression in the guise of a civil war would have been irrelevant. The basic issue would have been that a Communist success would have been equated with a significant loss of American security. The defeat of a client state at least in part created by the United States, to which the United States had pledged itself, however vaguely, would have been perceived as undermining the credibility of other American commitments, driving allies into neutralism, and possibly enticing the Soviets and Chinese into expansionist probes elsewhere.

It is because America's chief policy-makers apparently still thought in these terms in the early and middle 1960's that they have been so widely criticized. That President Kennedy could, in his Inaugural Address, talk as if the world were still bipolar, that he could attribute a "war of national liberation" to Soviet or Chinese instigation, or that he and his successor could still think in terms of the domino effect in Southeast Asia are, according to the critics, evidence that they were making policy on the basis of the "old [cold war] myths" rather than the "new realities." In a period of American-Soviet relaxation of tensions and disintegrating alliances, policy-makers confront a more complicated world. Was the war, in fact, a civil war or disguised Northern aggression? Would a win for the Vietcong really be a gain for Russia or China, or neither? Would a united Communist Vietnam, with its great sense of national pride, contain Peking's influence in Southeast Asia or act in concert with Peking, or possibly alone, to extend Communist influence farther southward and eastward? Can guerrilla wars or "wars of national liberation" be "exported" to other lands or not? Would American security be diminished by a loss of South Vietnam, and possibly of other Southeast Asian nations? If diminished, would the loss of security be relatively minor or sufficiently great to warrant American intervention? If intervention were called for, with about how many troops and at what cost in lives and money? And were conditions in South Vietnam such that these forces could be successfully employed? One's answers to these and other questions depend upon one's perception of this more complex world; the origins of this war; the relationship of the Vietcong to Hanoi, Moscow, and Peking; the impact on American security; the costs to be paid for specific external gains; and the importance of domestic versus international problems. No wonder the massive American intervention became a topic of such fierce and widespread domestic debate among policy-makers and general public alike, for there was no longer an obvious single set of answers.

Extensive bipolarity, or "globalism" as it came to be called, had made sense as long as any Communist expansion had meant an addition to Soviet strength. It was one thing to "fight Communism" as long as there was only one Communism to fight. But once Communism was a many-splintered thing, was the extensive role as "world policeman" still necessary? Now that there are many "Communisms," the United States has to decide whether all Communist states are still its enemies or, at least, whether all are equally hostile to America and equally threatening to its interests. Which Communist state does it "fight" now? More specifically, what changes in the state system's power distribution could it now safely allow and where, if anywhere, does it still have to draw "frontiers"? This is the crucial question. A bipolycentric system presents American policy-makers with some difficult questions to which there are alternative responses. Vietnam has certainly clarified this much for the post-Vietnam period.

5 Values, Priorities, and Policy Choices

The Values States Seek

A principal difference between bipolarity and bipolycentrism is the degree of choice a state perceives itself to have in devoting attention and resources to the pursuit of values other than security. Arnold Wolfers offers a suggestive analogy:

> Imagine a number of individuals, varying widely in their predispositions, who find themselves inside a house on fire. It would be perfectly realistic to expect that these individuals, with rare exceptions, would feel compelled to run toward exits. General fears of losing the cherished possession of life, coupled with the stark external threat of life, would produce the same reaction, whatever the psychological peculiarities of the actors. Surely, therefore, for an explanation of the rush for the exits, there is no need to analyze the individual decisions that produced it. The situation would be different if one or several members of the group had not joined the stampede, but had remained unmoved after the fire was discovered or had even failed to perceive it. Such "deviationist" behavior, running counter to expectation, would justify and require intensive psychological inquiry.
>
> A different situation would arise if, instead of being on fire, the house in question merely were overheated. In such a case, the second prerequisite of compulsion—serious external danger—would be absent. The reactions of different inhabitants might range all the way from hurried window-opening and loud complaints to complete indifference. To formulate expectations concerning behavior in an overheated house, one would need intimate knowledge of the varying individual predispositions and of the symptoms by which they could be recognized.[1]

A bipolar system tends to resemble a house on fire. The principal actors feel a high degree of insecurity; indeed, they may perceive their survival

[1] Arnold Wolfers, *Discord and Collaboration: Essays on International Politics* (Baltimore: Johns Hopkins Press, 1965), pp. 13–14.

as being at stake. Thus their individual behavior tends to be similar, regardless of their individual characteristics. *In bipolar circumstances, security becomes a key value*, because the policy-makers' perception of the nature of the state system closely reflects its objective condition. Moreover, the impact this has on domestic affairs was aptly stated by President Johnson: "The agony and the cruelty of the American Presidency in the last half of the twentieth century is that, whatever the purposes of its incumbent at home, the world will not permit the occupant of the office—nor the American people themselves—to attend the needs of this society without diversion."[2] This was in a sense already true even before the post-1945 bipolar days. President Wilson's progressive New Freedom program was ended by World War I. President Franklin Roosevelt had to turn from New Deal reforms to the problems of World War II. After 1945, President Truman sought a Fair Deal but soon became occupied with the historic reorientation of American foreign policy. And President Johnson wished to create a Great Society but was overwhelmed by Vietnam.

One analysis has rather bluntly stated that, since World War II, "foreign policy concerns tended to drive out domestic policy."[3] Perhaps it would be more accurate to say that domestic affairs were relegated to a secondary status during much of this period. Indeed, in a bipolar system, the nation confronts so many foreign policy problems that a much overworked President does not even have the time for all these issues. One of President Kennedy's advisers has called the American intervention in Vietnam an example of the triumph of the politics of inadvertence. President Kennedy, he has remarked, was so busy with more pressing problems during 1961–63—mainly foreign problems such as Cuba, Berlin, Latin America, the preservation of the European alliance, nuclear testing, and the threatening Communist expansion in Laos—that the increasingly grave situation in Vietnam was never thoroughly examined and debated. Instead, American military "advisers" were committed to Vietnam on a piecemeal basis to help the South Vietnamese against the Vietcong and to prevent the situation from collapsing. As the political and military situation continued to deteriorate, however, more advisers were sent, until American power and prestige became so deeply involved in South Vietnam that, by 1965, President Johnson, whose foreign policy advisers were all Kennedy-appointed men, felt he could not permit a Vietcong victory, and so he began an even larger direct intervention with American forces.[4] If a Vietnam must first become critical in order to compete against other pressing foreign situations for Presidential attention, it is hardly surprising that many domestic problems suffered.

[2] Lyndon B. Johnson, "In Quest of Peace," *Reader's Digest*, February, 1969, p. 222.

[3] Aaron Wildavsky, "The Two Presidencies," *Trans-action*, December, 1966, p. 8.

[4] Tom Wicker, *JFK and LBJ: The Influence of Personality upon Politics* (Baltimore: Penguin Books, 1969), pp. 195–208, and *The Pentagon Papers* (New York: Bantam Books, 1971).

Hence, in 1963 the Secretary of the Interior tried to talk to President Kennedy about issues of conservation but, after seeing him, remarked, "He's imprisoned by Berlin." Conservation was secondary to conserving the nation. "That son of a bitch [Khrushchev] won't pay any attention to words," Kennedy remarked bitterly about Berlin. "He has to see you move."[5] It was deciding which moves to make that "imprisoned" the President. Apart from election talk, domestic affairs usually received attention only when they also became critical, and so indeed they tended to become after long neglect and insufficient application of intellectual and economic resources. During the 1960's, internal problems drew increasing attention, often because their urgency was dramatized by violent activities. Occasionally, indeed, it seemed as if only ghetto riots and burning, student demonstrations, and peace marches would draw public attention and elicit some response and results.

The primacy of foreign policy was especially evident in the national budget. From 1946 to 1967, according to Senator Fulbright, the government spent $904 billion, or just over 57 per cent of its budget, "for military power" and $96 billion, or 6 per cent, for "social functions," such as health, education, welfare, labor, and housing.[6] The missile build-up of the first half of the 1960's, the Vietnam war of the second half, the funds in excess of $30 billion spent to land a man on the moon and demonstrate that it was the United States, and not the Soviet Union, that was first in space—all ensured the continued investment of vast funds in foreign policy and defense issues.

But in a bipolycentric system, states feel that they have greater choice in arranging their priorities. Objectively, states face different degrees of insecurity:

> In international politics, the house is not always, nor everywhere, on fire although the temperature may not be comfortable, even under the best circumstances! This means that danger as well as opportunity for gain, and fear as well as appetite, are not constants but important variables. . . . Where less than national survival is at stake, there is far less compulsion and therefore a less uniform reaction.[7]

While in a bipolar system the objectively existing degree of security threat is likely to be close to the subjectively perceived threat, in multipolar and bipolycentric systems the degree of insecurity a major actor thinks it confronts is likely to be lower. And in such a condition, security, while remaining an important value, will no longer almost automatically be granted the same priority. *Instead, security will find itself increasingly competing against important other values that states also pursue.* For, as Arnold Wolfers has remarked, security is essentially a negative value tantamount to the absence of insecurity. Efforts to ob-

[5] Arthur M. Schlesinger, Jr., *A Thousand Days: John F. Kennedy in the White House* (New York: A Fawcett Crest Book, 1967), p. 363.

[6] *New York Times,* August 20, 1967.

[7] Wolfers, *Discord and Collaboration,* p. 15.

tain security are therefore experienced as a burden, and nations will be inclined to keep this burden at the lowest level consistent with their sense of "adequate protection." Thus, in a *non*bipolar system, it would not be true that over a long period of time foreign policy will tend consistently "to drive out domestic policy."

What are the most common values or objectives that states generally seek? The first and most basic, as we have stressed throughout, is security. At the very minimum, this term refers to the territorial integrity and political independence of a state. Because some frontiers do change over time, states may redefine the meaning of "territorial integrity" from time to time. Poland, for example, has different frontiers to the East and West from those it had before World War II and no longer thinks of its integrity in terms of the prewar boundaries. Communist China, on the other hand, frequently refers publicly to the Chinese territories seized by the Russian Czars during the last century and wants to renegotiate the "unequal treaties" that compelled earlier Chinese rulers to accept those losses. Russia, however, claims that the present frontier between the two countries is final. Security also includes a country's political independence which, negatively, means its freedom from foreign control and, positively, refers to the preservation of whatever domestic political and economic system or "way of life" prevails. Security means not merely the maintenance of a state's physical security but also the perpetuation of the values, patterns of social relations, life-styles, and varied other elements that give each state its unique identity.

This simple point is worth a little elaboration. Earlier we briefly analyzed how the United States became involved in the two world wars and the cold war. Notice that we emphasized that the threat which precipitated U.S. involvement on all three occasions was the possibility that one power—Germany twice, Russia once—would establish its domination over Europe. We should note two additional points: This threat had little to do with ideology, certainly not Communism since Germany once represented monarchical conservatism and once fascism; nor was it related to physical danger, for neither Germany on either occasion or Russia after 1945 had weapons that could reach and destroy the United States. American intervention came because on each occasion American leaders saw the domination of Europe by a nondemocratic—indeed, *anti*democratic—great power as a threat to America's security as a particular kind of nation and as a threat to the kind of world environment in which the United States could most comfortably live.[8] As President Franklin Roosevelt summed it up in explaining his decision to aid England in 1940–41, the United States should not become a lone democratic island surrounded by totalitarian seas to its East and West (Roosevelt included Japan's threat in East Asia in his descriptive phrase). What he meant was that to defend itself in such circumstances, the United States would have to turn itself into a "garrison state"; democracy would have to be

[8] Raymond Aron, "Is Isolationism Possible?" *Commentary*, April, 1974, p. 42.

dumped overboard. He also meant that as a *democratic* state the nation wished to preserve an international order in which democracy could flourish; committed to this milieu goal, the United States could not stand by and watch one democracy after another snuffed out by hostile antidemocratic regimes. The result would be a hostile external environment, incompatible with American conceptions of the just and unjust.

One additional point about security as a value is worth repeating: As is true when we speak of the other values to be discussed below, we are talking of a *degree* of security that allows a state to feel *relatively* safe; conversely, we accept as a fact of life that all states have to live with a degree of insecurity. (There is no such thing as absolute security in the state system, at least not short of universal conquest and the destruction of all other independent states, an unlikely possibility.) Since all states have to "live dangerously," the question is how much security do they feel is essential to protect their "non-negotiable" vital interests?

Let us turn to some other basic values states pursue when their security needs seem satisfied. One of these is welfare, the prosperity or the economic well-being of the nation and its citizens. Welfare, like security, is a relative value. The frequently used phrase "the revolution of rising expectations" refers to the unrest in many ex-colonial countries that are economically underdeveloped; the absolute gains in their standard of living since independence have only served to make them more aware of the yet higher standard of living possessed by the Western nations that were once their colonial masters. The desire for the "good life" is not limited to these new states. The drive for even higher economic growth rates and increased gross national product (the total value of a nation's total production and services) is shared by the highly industrialized and urbanized states. Every few years the Russian leaders promise their long-suffering compatriots that at the end of this or that five-year plan or decade their standard of living will be comparable to that of the United States, the nation whose economic and social system they denounce as exploitive and inhumane. One of the benefits of Europe's economic integration efforts was to expand greatly the "economic pie" so that all classes in society, particularly those near the bottom of the social structure, could share in a new general prosperity.

In the West, indeed, it might well be said, until the recent concern with environmental problems, mostly the by-products of industrialization, economic growth was the chief, if not sole, criterion for social policy. Raising everyone's living standards, by attempting to distribute more of an ever rising GNP to those previously neglected or denied was at the heart of all modern Western welfare states' social policies, including those of the United States. Attempts to redistribute existing or only a slowly growing wealth among different classes or segments of society would have precipitated intense social conflict; rapidly expanding the "economic pie" so that everyone could have a larger share of it avoided such conflict while satisfying the vast majority of groups and people.

The foreign policy implications of a nation's higher standards of living are several: It tends to confer upon it a certain pre-eminence and makes other nations want to copy it; it allows such a country to use its capital, technology, trade, and skills to advance its interests; Marxist scholars claim that the attainment of wealth is, in fact, the prime purpose of a capitalist state's foreign policy.

A third value important to many states is prestige. Precisely because prestige is, as we shall see later, closely related to power, prestige may be defined as a nation's *reputation* for power among its fellow states. Thus prestige is of special concern to would-be great powers; they expend major resources and efforts in quest of it and often even more to avoid its loss. When the Russians first put a Sputnik into orbit and particularly after they sent the first man into space in 1961, their achievements were widely interpreted throughout the world as a loss of prestige for the United States, for American power—especially in weaponry—was based to a very large extent on its technological ability and innovation, an area in which until then the United States was deemed to be far superior to Russia. President Kennedy reacted to the Soviets' man in space by setting America's goal as placing a man on the moon before the end of the 1960's in order to recoup American prestige. The effort cost over $30 billion.

The American intervention in Vietnam is a less successful and even more costly effort to prevent the loss of prestige that Washington saw as attending the defeat of South Vietnam, a loss it was unwilling to entertain lest it erode the credibility of American power and commitments in other, perhaps more significant, areas than Vietnam. As one Pentagon memorandum written by an Assistant Secretary of Defense put it:

70 per cent—To avoid a humiliating U.S. defeat
20 per cent—To keep South Vietnamese territory from Chinese hands
10 per cent—To permit the people of South Vietnam to enjoy better,
    freer way of life.[9]

Smaller states, however, are hardly unconcerned with their own prestige. New states are indeed very sensitive to this consideration. Are they being treated with the same respect and dignity accorded older and more venerable states, or are they still being treated with the contempt or condescension of preindependence days? Yet it is also probably true that prestige or such synonyms as pride and greatness are often considered desirable goals in themselves by both national leaders and people. One of India's motivations in becoming the world's sixth nation to explode a nuclear device was certainly prestige.

A fourth value or objective, which some states pursue more than others, is the protection and/or promotion of ideology. An ideology is a set of beliefs that claims to explain reality and prescribe a desirable future state of existence for society and the world in general. Revolutionary

[9] *Pentagon Papers*, p. 432.

ideologies, particularly, are concerned with long-range goals that should be actively promoted domestically and internationally.

Thus in the nineteenth century protected by the balance of power in Europe, the United States, regarding itself as a New World with a morally superior political system to the regimes of the Old World, chose to isolate itself from possible contamination from the European nations. In the twentieth century, by contrast, as it has increasingly been sucked into the Old World's quarrels as Britain's power weakened, the United States has engaged Germany and Russia in order to repulse the threats of despotisms and preserve an amicable external environment in which democratic values, including the ones that had blossomed in Europe, could survive and flourish. On the other hand, revolutionary regimes, such as France after her democratic revolution and Russia after the Bolshevik revolution, energetically sought to expand their influence and power in the international system in order to convert it to their respective new faith. Whereas America, particularly in the last century, believed that its task was primarily to create a beacon of freedom at home which would serve as a shining example for the rest of mankind to follow, the French and later Russian leaders wished to make sure that history would march their way by helping it along wherever and whenever possible, if necessary by imposing upon a reluctant mankind the faith that would make it free and assure its secular salvation. One crucial problem, however, that arises for states that harbor universal goals and, therefore, expect to transform both themselves and the existing state system is that these aims frequently conflict with short-term and daily aims like security, with the result that unlimited revolutionary interests tend to become subordinate to limited national interests and demands. Marx, to use but one example, presumably becomes less important than Machiavelli for the men in the Kremlin.

The Competition of Values

If these are some—although by no means all—of the principal values states seek as "possession goals," the resulting conflict among these values within each state suggests that *all too often the acquisition of more of one value comes at the cost of another*; values are frequently incompatible with one another. One such conflict is between security and welfare or, in more colloquial language, guns and butter. Realistically, the more a state spends on maintaining military forces, the less it can spend on foreign aid, on construction of schools, hospitals, and roads, on education, vocational training, and a "war on poverty." The more taxes it needs to buy bombs, the less the taxpayer has left to buy a new house or car, purchase family insurance, go to Europe on vacation, or send his children to college. Nations have limited resources, even if these are great, and they must make choices; and the choice is not usually *either* guns *or* butter but *how many* guns and *how much* butter. The question then becomes: How many more guns will yield how much of an increase in relative security—taking into account the fact that the opponent is also likely to increase the number of his guns? Or conversely, how much *less* butter is a possibly small additional increase in security worth, assuming it is an increase? If such a reduction in butter, for instance, depresses the quality of life in the society and perhaps its cohesion as a functioning entity, will the extra arms have enhanced its security, even if the opponent does not or cannot match it in arms? These have been the kinds of questions widely and frequently asked in the United States since the late 1960's.

Another set of competing values for a country like the United States is security versus democracy. This has both domestic and external implications. If a democratic nation really sought to maximize its security, it could start at home by establishing a "garrison state": The young would be drafted into military service and the older people into work in factories producing war materials; all would be subjected to a strict discipline and orthodoxy that would squash diversity of opinion, and those who differed with the official viewpoint would be sent to prison camps as security and loyalty risks; all resources, except those used in producing the necessities of life, would be channeled into military production; and the power of the government would be centralized in the hands of a few leaders. Democratic values, competing political parties and opinions, the entire way of life would fall victim to the organization of the nation for maximum military security. As a matter of fact, those who feel that the "military-industrial complex" dominates the American political process suggest that, while things have not yet gone that far, the purposes of American democracy have already been distorted. Wrongly perceiving security threats almost everywhere, the United States has become a weapons culture dedicated to the invention, production, and deployment of ever newer arms, the enrichment of the large corporations, and the subsidizing of its entire economy; in the process, it has neglected its poor, barely made an effort to resolve the nation's terrible racial problem, continued to ignore its environment, and alienated a sizable minority of its educated youth.

The external implications of the clash of security and democracy are starkly evident when a democracy allies itself with undemocratic states. If it really believes in its values, can it associate itself with dictatorial states without impugning its own cause? On the other hand, should it confine itself only to allies blessed with the same political values, even if this should jeopardize its security by failing to take advantage of the strategic position, economic benefits and added military strength that could have been offered by certain undemocratic states? During World War II Churchill welcomed Russia as an ally after Hitler became their common enemy. Russia might not be a democracy, the Prime Minister said, but to beat Hitler he would sup with the devil—although he did admit that he would use a long spoon.

Still, this alliance was brought about by Germany's attack on Russia. After 1954, however, and the outbreak of the cold war, the United States made alliances with many undemocratic regimes—Turkey, Greece, Spain, Nationalist China, Brazil, Portugal, to name some of the more prominent—in the pursuit of the containment of Russian and Chinese Communist power. Indeed, containment began with the Truman Doctrine, which somewhat ironically pictured the threat to Turkey and Greece from the Soviet Union as a conflict of democracy versus totalitarianism. The Turkish and Greek regimes were hardly models of democratic purity. Were President Truman's declaration and American policy hypocritical because they were inconsistent with the values of American democracy, or was the United States acting as the bipolar distribution of power after World War II obliged it to act? President Truman's action demonstrated clearly that he believed a democracy could align itself with undemocratic governments in strategically located areas at a moment of perceived danger to American security. It can, of course, be defended in terms of keeping open these countries' option for a possible future evolution to democracy, an option perceived by American policy-makers as foreclosed if they were controlled by Soviet Communism. But this was largely a rationalization.

Thus, while the Truman Doctrine committed the United States to the support of "free peoples," America's security after 1947 was often adjudged incompatible with sustaining freedom in other countries. Only in Western Europe were security and self-determination seen as compatible; and in Eastern Europe, it was safe to push the principle of self-determination since its application would mean the retraction of Soviet power. In the meantime, it allowed the United States to point out that the Russian-controlled People's Democracies were a farce. But outside of Europe, safety and equilibrium came first. In two limited wars the United States defended governing regimes that were far from stamped with the seal of good democratic housekeeping; the issue, as American policy-makers saw it at the time of intervention, was American security vis-à-vis the Soviet Union or Communist China, not the worthiness of the Seoul or Saigon government.

The central question all these examples of conflicting values raise, of course, is: What price security? The means of securing a nation's territorial integrity may be incompatible with the values by which it lives. Should a nation root out all possible "security" risks at home, even if under the broad criteria established for a security program innocent people may be hurt, and even if the resultant fear of expressing any criticism of governmental actions leads to a stifling of free speech, which could be followed by such other measures as the censorship of books and the banning of debates on "controversial" topics? Is a democratic nation, in allying itself abroad with patently undemocratic countries, augmenting its security, or is it weakening itself? Can a democratic state, for instance, launch a preventive war, firing the first shot, or survive the creation of a "military-industrial complex" with its alleged vested interest in continued high international tension as the reason for its existence and the condition for its survival? In short, in a nonbipolar distribution of power, policy-makers and public alike will be deeply divided over the character of the state system, the values—or, rather, the exact *mix of values*—the nation ought to preserve, the means to achieve these interests, the level of external commitments, and the priorities between foreign and domestic policies.

One conflict of values is continuous, however, regardless of the distribution of power—namely, peace versus security. We said earlier that one of the purposes of the balance of power is to preserve each state's security, not to obtain peace *per se.*While states generally prefer security *and* peace, they would sacrifice the latter if it were necessary to their security. But because this is a sacrifice of a dearly held value, policy-makers in fact have on important occasions placed the cart of peace in front of the horse of security. Thus Britain and France in the 1930's were concerned for their security. But they also feared a repetition of the Great War, which could bring about their collapse. Security in those circumstances seemed to depend not upon going to war but upon preserving the peace at almost any price. But security and peace were in this instance clearly incompatible goals. Britain and France, by identifying the one with the other and making peace an exclusive priority, therefore ended up appeasing Hitler and helped him upset the balance against themselves.

In the nuclear age, this dilemma of peace versus security has in one sense been resolved by making the two values synonymous. But in another sense the dilemma has sharpened. To the extent that the balance of power still depends largely, if not primarily, upon the superpowers' military strength, the balance is now maintained by the threat of using total force rather than its actual use. The danger of an eruption of a total war does, however, remain. It may not come, as we shall see below, from a coldly calculated premeditated attack; it may come instead from miscalculation as a result of the rapid technological changes of weapons, inept "crisis management," or the escalation of a limited war. But such a total war can hardly be fought for the enhancement of a nation's security; it will only doom the contestants to extinction. Britain and France during the interwar period had already sensed this and were therefore willing to go far—too far, it turned out—to avoid an all-out war. Since World War II, both the United States and the Soviet Union have, as their past behavior has shown, ruled out total nuclear warfare as an instrument of policy. For both know that peace and security have become inseparable. The crucial question, however, is how national power can be employed so that it can simultaneously preserve security *and* peace.

The Price of Détente

The need in the nuclear age to remain secure and yet maintain the peace sharply poses the question of what price is to be paid for what the Soviets call "peaceful coexistence." This issue came very much to the fore as the Nixon Administration moved, in the popular phrase, "from confrontation to negotiations." When the Republicans came into office in 1968, their purpose was, as Henry Kissinger explained it, the establishment of what "the President has called a structure of peace . . . an international system less geared to the management of crises, less conscious of constant eruptions of conflict, in which the principal participants operate with a consciousness of stability and permanence." Kissinger emphasized that this "puts a particular obligation on the two great nuclear powers that have the capacity to destroy mankind and whose conflicts have produced so many of the crises of the postwar period."[10] The new relationship sought by the Administration, soon to become known as *détente*, stressed the reduction of the danger from a continuing arms race, which could be achieved only in the context of a more restrained competitive behavior. *Détente* thus meant a lower level of international tensions, even an attempt to codify the terms of competition; it meant not only a continued rivalry but also superpower cooperation in the field of arms control, as well as in other political, economic, technical, and scientific areas.

Yet the improvement of American-Soviet relations has keenly raised the issue of the competing values the United States seeks: Has *détente* been purchased at the cost of justice and the democratic values America has long professed to stand on, take pride in and defend in the world? In the days before *détente*, liberals used to advocate a thawing of cold war tensions because they expected it to relax the vigilance of Soviet totalitarianism and create at least a degree of freedom for Soviet citizens. What has happened instead is that *détente* has produced a partial return to Stalinism. Ideological orthodoxy, censorship, and the squashing of dissent has increased as party ideologues, military conservatives, and, especially, the secret police have been concerned that American liberals could be right that *détente* might create pressure for change and possible demands for fewer restrictions and less supervision, which, these groups in Russia fear, will threaten the foundations of the Soviet state.

In the United States, this price for *détente* came to be symbolized in the early 1970's by the Soviet author Alexander Solzhenitsyn and the issue of Jewish emigration to Israel. Solzhenitsyn, a severe critic of the

[10] *New York Times*, June 23, 1973.

Soviet system (and also of Western democracy, for his solution for Russia is a return to a traditional paternalistic Russian autocracy), also became a critic of *détente* by warning against the dangers of appeasement à la Chamberlain.[11] Nevertheless, his courage in speaking out despite the obvious personal danger, as well as the eloquence of his words of criticism of the Soviet regime, evoked worldwide sympathy. The Kremlin, instead of imprisoning him and creating a martyr, finally exiled him to the West. The Jewish emigration issue arose because many Jews, discriminated against in Russia, wanted to go to Israel, but the authorities made emigration extremely difficult by imposing a very high, often unpayable, tax on the emigré, as well as through other measures. Although on an informal basis the Russians suspended their restrictions and allowed many Jews to leave as part of an attempt to seek better relations with America, where Jewish groups were very aroused about this issue, some members of Congress sought to tie an improvement of American-Soviet commercial relations to a Soviet agreement permitting "the right to emigrate." The Nixon Administration opposed this linkage.

So the central issue of *détente* for many, including liberal intellectuals and hard-nosed Senators, was the role of morality in foreign policy. No issue could have struck more at the core of the meaning of U.S. policy. The critics of the President and Kissinger argued that their position was, at best, amoral. The United States, they said, being the kind of country it is, cannot close its eyes to injustice, whether it exists in the Soviet Union or Brazil. American foreign policy, they said further, must have a moral basis if it is to have any real meaning; America cannot pursue a foreign policy divorced from its ideals. As the playwright Arthur Miller has said, *détente* has been "sterilized of any human meaning," a "*détente* that suppresses human liberty is a travesty. It not only sells out American ideals but encourages the Kremlin to repress its critics and deny its people freedom and dignity."[12] The trouble, in short, was precisely that U.S. policy did not—and had not for a number of years—concern itself with issues of right and wrong, freedom and slavery.

It was not that the critics of *détente* did not appreciate the Administration's attempt to create a safer and stabler world, but the central question was whether that end would justify any means in attaining it. Was the basic aim of U.S. foreign policy survival at any cost? If, by comparison, Britain's pre–World War II policy of appeasement had worked and a British-German *détente* had followed, could the British with good conscience have accepted a peace bought at the price of millions of Czechs, German Jews, and other persecuted groups? Can a democracy make peace with states whose principles and domestic organization are abhorrent to Western man? Could the United States, toward the end of World War II and right afterward, really have shown no concern over Eastern Europe as a Soviet sphere of domination de-

11 *Ibid.*, September 12, 1973.
12 *Ibid.*, July 5, 1974.

spite all the atrocity stories about Russian behavior and the brutality with which the Soviets exerted their influence? Would the United States not have denied its very essence if it had shown indifference to these events because good Soviet-American relations depended on remaining silent? (Revisionist writers contend that U.S. interference in Eastern Europe brought on the cold war, but they have never been willing to face the implications of noninterference despite the fact that they profess to be democrats and humanitarians.)

Does "moral" in this context mean that states with antithetical values cannot coexist in peace except at a cost of "selling their souls"? The principal danger to the world is the disaster of a nuclear holocaust; only one failure would be one too many. Therefore reducing tensions between the superpowers and attempting to a degree to regularize their continuing rivalry is imperative. *Détente*, Kissinger has argued, "is a process of managing relations with potentially hostile countries in order to preserve peace while maintaining our vital interests. In a nuclear age, this is in itself an objective not without moral validity."[13] *Détente* does not, however, mean the end of U.S.-Soviet political competition, a sharing of common values, or approval of one another. At most, the United States can expect Russia to keep agreements and behave responsibly (as Washington tried to clarify to Moscow by placing U.S. forces on alert during the Middle East War of 1973 when it looked to the President and Kissinger as if the Russians might send troops in to prevent an Israeli rout of the Egyptian forces). But, the proponents of *détente* argue, this state of relations cannot be made dependent upon a transformation of the Soviet domestic structure. Indeed, to put such public pressure on the Soviet rulers for domestic reforms is to encourage their rejection, resistance, and bitterness (comparable to that which would be engendered in the United States if the Soviets announced that the price of *détente* for us would be the immediate and full realization of equal opportunities for all blacks in education, housing, and employment); it might also endanger those leaders favoring *détente*, as well as the *détente* itself, which remains in the long run the best hope for the emergence of forces for change in the Soviet Union. The United States does not have to condone what the Soviet Union does internally. But American policy does have to face the basic question, which, as Kissinger phrased it, is "whether and to what extent we can risk other objectives—and especially the building of a structure of peace—for these domestic changes."[14] President Nixon summed up the argument as follows:

There are limits to what we can do, and we must ask ourselves some very hard questions. . . .

What is our capability to change the domestic structure of other nations? Would a slowdown or reversal of *détente* help or hurt the posi-

---

[13] *Ibid.*, March 8, 1974.
[14] *Ibid.*

tive evolution of other social systems? What price in terms of renewed conflict are we willing to pay to bring pressure to bear for humane causes?

Not by our choice but by our capability, our primary concern in foreign policy must be to help influence the international conduct of nations in the world arena. We would not welcome the intervention of other countries in our domestic affairs and we cannot expect them to be cooperative when we seek to intervene directly in theirs. We cannot gear our foreign policy to transformation of other societies. In the nuclear age our first responsibility must be the prevention of a war that could destroy all society.

Peace between nations with totally different systems is also a high moral objective.[15]

In early 1975, Moscow renounced its trade agreement with the United States because Congress had tied the pact to the principle of emigration. The dilemma of coexistence—the choices among competing values, all of which it would be desirable for the United States to enhance—thus remains. The Soviet Union, too, confronts this dilemma as, on the one hand, it recognizes the need for coexistence while, on the other hand, its ideologically defined long-range aim remains the elimination of the capitalist states, a mission whose seeming abandonment some—including the Chinese Communists—have condemned as a betrayal of Communist values.

[15] *Ibid.*, June 6, 1974.

6 Power, Deterrence, and Diplomacy

The Nature of Power

"Power," "great power," "superpower," "balance of power"—we have all used these terms repeatedly. Yet at no point have we stopped to inquire into the nature of power. In one sense, there hardly seems a reason to do so, for power is a term with which we are all familiar; it seems so "obvious" what power is. When the United States lands soldiers in the Dominican Republic to stop a political faction judged by Washington to be infiltrated by "pro-Castro Communists" from capturing control of the government; when the Red Army invades Czechoslovakia to throw out the Prague government whose Communist sympathies are suspect in Moscow; when the United States demands the withdrawal of Soviet missiles in Cuba; when Russia demands that West Berlin be turned into a "free city" (free of the Western allies, that is)—we all know that power is being exercised.

It is a fact of life that some nations are more powerful than others and that international politics has generally been the story of the games played by these stronger members of the state system.[1] Everyone is also aware that the adjectives "more powerful" and "stronger" refer essentially to military capacity. No one thinks of Belgium or Burma as "powers"; their military strength, by either conventional or nuclear standards, is puny. The label "power" has historically been awarded by states to a colleague that has made a successful military debut. Until such a moment, who could have known of that state's "power"? In the absence of its exercise—and successful exercise at that—the state's power is in abey-

[1] Only recently has this assumption about the great states as primary actors been questioned by some analysts. See Stanley Hoffmann, *Gulliver's Troubles or the Setting of American Foreign Policy* (New York: McGraw-Hill, 1968), pp. 26–43. For a response to Hoffmann, see Kenneth N. Waltz, "International Structure, National Force, and the Balance of World Power," *Journal of International Affairs* 21, No. 2 (1967): 220–28.

ance. But military victory confers a *reputation for power*. In the nineteenth century, Prussia's two rapid victories, the first over the ancient and redoubtable Austro-Hungarian Empire in 1866, and the second over Europe's strongest continental power, France, in 1870, left no doubt that the newly unified Germany was now not only *a* power to be reckoned with but, in Europe, *the* power. America's defeat of Spain in Cuba in 1898 and Japan's defeat of Russia in 1904–5 similarly conferred greatpower status on these newcomers on the international stage. World War I confirmed these rankings.

Conversely, a military defeat such as the one suffered in 1940 by France, which had already been bled white during the 1914–18 war, puts a nation's reputation for power in jeopardy. It may not even have to be a defeat; just the fact that a great power is unable to win a conflict with a lesser power will hurt its prestige. Perhaps it should not have indulged in such a conflict in the first place, but once it has done so its ability to exercise power effectively is one of the issues at stake. Britain's inept use of force against Egypt during the Suez War in 1956, for example, made it plain to Conservative Party leaders that it was no longer a first-rank power and that as a nation-state its status and influence could become great once more only if it joined Europe. Thus, a few years after Suez, Britain, a country that had long regarded Europe's division as requisite for its own security, made its first application to join the Common Market. Just as Britain might have been better off had it not intervened in Egypt, so might America also better have avoided entanglement in Vietnam. Once ensnared, Presidents Johnson and Nixon found it difficult to untangle themselves from the war in large part because of the high priority they gave to the "credibility of American *power*."

There are, of course, variations on this theme of victory and defeat. Thus, during the 1960's, when all-out war was no longer a true test of a nation's power, the "space race" became a substitute for the physical test of battle. In 1960, Presidential candidate Kennedy pounded home the message that America's second-rate performance in space during the Eisenhower years meant that the nation was not yet aware of the global political and psychological impact of what, in the bipolar context, was a competition in space. The first manned Soviet satellite to orbit the earth in April of Kennedy's first year in office convinced him that a secondrate, second-place effort was not consistent with his country's role as a world leader and a great power whose reputation was based to a very large extent on its industrial-technological abilities. The technology in this new sphere had become symbolic of the reputation for power, as well as the way of life, of the United States and the Soviet Union. Kennedy immediately ordered a review of various space projects in which America could surpass Russia.[2] The most likely seemed to be landing a man on the moon, and, in May, the President announced that this ob-

---

[2] Theodore C. Sorensen, *Kennedy* (New York: Bantam Books, 1966), pp. 589–92.

jective would be achieved before the end of the decade. In July, 1969, the first men stood on the moon. And while they talked of having come on behalf of all mankind, their shoulder patches read U.S.A.

An international power image may also change as a result of policy decisions taken primarily for internal reasons. Hence, Stalin's massive purge of the Soviet general staff in the late 1930's was thought by Western observers to have left the military weak to the point of ineffectiveness, with the result that Russian influence on the world scene plummeted. The French then estimated Poland to be stronger than Russia, and later, when France and Britain were already at war with Germany, they almost took on Russia as well when they decided to help Finland in its courageous defense after the Red Army attacked that country.

Two points are very important about these examples. The first is the popular identification, generally shared by policy-makers, of power with military capacity—regardless of whether the estimate is based on power overtly applied, peacefully demonstrated (as in parades, maneuvers, or space shots), or held in the background while adversaries bargain. Thus, when books are written on power, they bear such titles as *The War Potential of Nations.*[3] Because war has historically been the *ultima ratio* of power in interstate politics, this emphasis on military strength is hardly surprising. The Prussian general Clausewitz, in his classic definition, called war the continuation of political relations by other means; turning this phrase around, peace might be called the continuation of the last war by other means. Earlier, we suggested that the state system, unlike most modern Western domestic political systems, is characterized by a condition of potential warfare. Each state's concern with its military power has thus historically been an acceptable standard of behavior. And it is military power that today, because of its enormous contemporary destructive ability, most needs to be controlled and managed. To be sure, there are—as we shall see—other ways of exercising power, especially by economic means. But coercion and the use of violence by states to achieve their ends in a system of politics without government has long been of primary significance as a substitute for the governmental allocation of values.

The second point about these examples is that *power is what people think it is.* In the instances of military successes or failures, it is how policy-makers in other states perceive the country that has just won a victory or suffered a defeat. And, as the Kennedy space effort demonstrated, it may not only be how foreign statesmen evaluate another nation's power, but how a particular nation's decision-makers think *other* states will think about its power status that is important. A *reputation for power will confer power*, whether that subjective evaluation is correct or mistaken. Thus one can overestimate or underestimate an adversary's

[3] Klaus Knorr, *The War Potential of Nations* (Princeton, N.J.: Princeton University Press, 1955), and *idem, Military Power and Potential* (Lexington, Mass.: D.C. Heath, 1970).

power. But in either case, one is likely to act in terms of *perceived power*; the result may be trouble.

If one overestimates an opponent's power, one may not act when one should. Britain and France consistently overestimated German power in the 1930's. Their policy-makers remembered German military prowess in World War I, and Hitler tended, by his bold behavior and aggressive speeches, to reinforce this impression of German power. He knew how strong Germany really was, but he bluffed well. More recently—as we shall see later—between 1957 and 1960, Washington tended to overestimate Soviet power in the struggle over West Berlin; Khrushchev also bluffed well.

On the other hand, one can underestimate an opponent's power, only to be rebuffed or to become involved in a protracted conflict the cost of which is not "worth" the gains initially expected. The Vietnam war will long remain a painful reminder of this lesson. As a Presidential candidate, Nixon called North Vietnam a fourth-rate power. But it is precisely this war with a fourth-rate power (which we shall analyze at some length in the next chapter) that testifies to the care with which policy-makers and interested laymen must calculate power. Who, before 1965 and the large-scale American military intervention in South Vietnam, would have doubted that it was but a matter of weeks, at most months, before the world's greatest military power would clobber North Vietnam, one of the world's smallest powers, a "half-country" with less than 10 per cent of the U.S. population and virtually no industry—in short, "a bunch of peasants"? Yet these peasants fought one of the finest and best-equipped American armies of all time to a stalemate.

Hence power—before a conflict erupts into war—lies in the mind. And it is the battlefield that usually testifies to the correctness or incorrectness of the perception of power. A parallel to Vietnam is the United States during the interwar period, when others, especially Hitler, underestimated American power. Having retired once more into isolationism after World War I, the United States was not an active participant in the state system, and its power—the ability to affect the behavior of other nations in accordance with its own objectives—was by and large discounted, particularly by Nazi Germany, which was preparing for war with France and Britain. America pursued few world political objectives; it wished merely to be left alone. Consequently, it was ranked low in the great-power hierarchy, behind Britain, France, Germany, Russia, and Japan. Yet, objectively, it was undoubtedly the world's number one power, far stronger than Germany or its Western opponents.

Thus a distinction must be drawn between subjective or perceived power and objective or actual power. In the latter calculations, quantitatively measurable components such as population, industrial production, guns, and the like are totaled. We are, of course, oversimplifying the matter. Even these individual components are not always easy to give a specific weight to; and because power is composed of the total of these components—for example, large population and major industrial capacity are added up because neither without the other amounts to very much—such calculations can become difficult. This is even truer if one includes less tangible factors such as national character or morale, the quality of a country's government or its diplomacy.[4] Yet policy-makers obviously cannot afford to forgo adding up these and other components in their concern with the power balance, however difficult this calculation may be. But the question concerning the relationship between objective and subjective power remains.

Policy-makers within one country may, of course, vary in their evaluations of another country's power. To select one more example from the 1930's, let us look at the German calculations of French power. The German military was particularly impressed by France's strength. It knew the size of the French forces and the total number of divisions that could be mobilized within a number of weeks after the outbreak of hostilities. It also recalled the toughness, skill, and bravery of the French Army during World War I. The German soldiers—and usually the German diplomats as well—therefore tended to caution Hitler in the middle and late 1930's, lest he overreach himself and precipitate another war, which the generals felt Germany would lose. Hitler did not appreciate these attempts to restrain his bold policy, and he finally eliminated the army's leadership, promoting younger officers favorably disposed to his regime and placing the army and the other services under his direct command and control.[5] The Nazi leader was confident that he could afford to be bold. He thought of France as a weak country because it was domestically torn apart by class conflicts and its mentality was defeatist. Hitler turned out to be right with regard to France. Whereas his generals' conception of power was essentially *quantitative* and *military*, his own analysis was basically *qualitative* and *political-psychological*. For Hitler, the normal components of power, such as physical strength, were important only when related to fundamental attitudes and social forces.

Although we know power may be largely based on military capacity and may exist "within the mind," we still have not said what power is. What are the characteristics of power? Obviously, power is a relationship between two or more parties. Specifically, *power is the capacity to influence the behavior of others in accordance with one's own objectives.* Further, power relationships are reciprocal. A influences B and B influences A, but the amount of influence each possesses is not necessarily the same; A's ability to influence B may be much greater than the other way around. Power relationships, while reciprocal, are not therefore nec-

[4] See Hans J. Morgenthau, *Politics Among Nations: The Struggle for Power and Peace,* 4th ed. (New York: Knopf, 1967), pp. 106–44 and 196–201, for an example of the difficulties in evaluating a state's power.

[5] John Wheeler-Bennett, *The Nemesis of Power: The German Army in Politics 1918–1945* (New York: St. Martin's Press, 1954), pp. 333–455.

essarily symmetrical. Moscow invades Prague to change the behavior of Czechoslovakia, or Washington tells the Kremlin to remove its missiles from Cuba; in the former instance, the Soviet Union was clearly the more powerful state, in the latter instance, the United States was the more powerful state, although over all the two superpowers were well matched. Both of these examples suggest that one state has influence over another state when an imbalance of power exists. Peter Bachrach and Morton Baratz have analyzed power relationships in more detail and have said that such relationships exist when three factors are present.[6] First, there must be a conflict of interests or values. If A and B agree on objectives, B will consent freely to A's demands or course of action. Should this occur, we say that A has authority—that B recognizes A's right to set the course of action; but we do not say A is exercising power in relation to B.[7] Second, B must accede, however unwillingly, to A's demands. This is necessary because, though the two may be involved in a conflict of interest, B might simply stand its ground and not comply. In such a case, A must either give up its demands or resort to force. Third, a power relationship assumes that one of the parties invokes sanctions that the other regards as capable of inflicting "severe deprivations" upon itself. The cost of noncompliance for B must be greater than the cost he pays if he complies. It is presumed in a power relationship, as one might expect, that A and B are clearly communicating or signaling to each other and, most important, that the threatened state B believes the adversary A's threat of sanctions is credible and not a bluff.

Coercion occurs when a threat to punish by peaceful sanctions becomes a threat to punish with violent means. If the attempt to carry out a coercive threat is made, we speak of *force*. If B complies when A exercises coercion, the use of force is unnecessary; A must resort to force only if B does *not* comply with A's demands. When A resorts to force, he admits his failure to attain his objectives by only threats of punishment. For example, a country will resort to force to prevent an upset of the balance of power or restore it if an imbalance has occurred. The U.S. involvements in two limited wars in Asia came after U.S. help to protégé governments did not suffice to deter a direct, overt attack in Korea and the organization of a revolutionary war in South Vietnam; American interventions were intended to prevent perceived disequilibriums. Britain's

[6] Peter Bachrach and Morton S. Baratz, *Power and Poverty* (New York: Oxford University Press, 1970), pp. 17–38. Also see Charles A. McClelland, *Theory and the International System* (New York: Macmillan, 1966), pp. 68–88, and K. J. Holsti, *International Politics: A Framework for Analysis* (Englewood Cliffs, N.J.: Prentice-Hall, 1967), pp. 191–209.

[7] Earlier, in chapter 2, I suggested that people in modernized Western states obey government not simply because it is superior in power but because they feel it possesses *authority*. Government has the right to govern because most people share certain common political values and attitudes, especially about the way political decisions should be made and the legitimacy of the government; therefore, even those who may not like certain laws and policies usually comply with the laws.

declaration of war in 1939, on the other hand, was intended to restore an equilibrium already upset by Hitler's succession of military moves. But one important point needs to be re-emphasized: *The use of force can at times result in a loss of the reputation of power.*[8] If the sanctions, once applied, do not inflict as severe a deprivation as A's threat has implied, future compliance by B with A's demands is less likely.

We can now speak of three characteristics of power: *power as primarily military capacity, power as essentially perceived power, and power as coercion and force.* These three characteristics will provide the focus for our analyses of deterrence, arms control, crisis management, and limited war. And we shall see that *the nuclear balance of power emphasizes these three characteristics far more than did the calculations of power in prenuclear times.* Indeed, I shall later refer to the balance of power as the balance of resolve *and* capability.

The Multiplication of Power

The military component of national power has always been important, for, as E. H. Carr wrote, "war lurks in the background of international politics just as a revolution lurks in the background of domestic politics."[9] Ironically, it was democracy, which was expected to abolish war, that multiplied this component of power many times over. One of democracy's assumptions was that only irresponsible rulers were belligerent, that wars were for them merely an enjoyable—and quite profitable— "blood sport." It was the people who paid the price for wars with their lives and taxes. Thus, if the peace-loving people could hold their rulers accountable, wars would be eliminated and peace secured. Democracy would bring an era of good will—of individual freedom and social justice at home, of peace and harmony abroad. The world would be safe for democracy—because it would be democratic. Government by the people, of the people, and for the people would ensure perpetual peace.[10]

Instead, democracy was tied to nationalism and the two gave birth to the "nation in arms." Once men were freed from feudal bondage and granted the right to some form of self-government, they were thrust into a close identification with their nation. And if men now equated their well-being with that of their nation, it was only reasonable that the nation should be able to call on them—its citizens—for its defense. Not

[8] See below, Chapter 7, under heading "American Power and the 'Rules of the Game' in Vietnam."

[9] Edward Hallett Carr, *The Twenty Years Crisis* (London: Macmillan, 1951), p. 109.

[10] See, for example, Immanuel Kant, *Perpetual Peace*, translated by Carl J. Friedrich and added as an appendix to his book *Inevitable Peace* (Cambridge, Mass.: Harvard University Press, 1948), pp. 251–52.

surprisingly, the French Revolution, which broke the intermediary bonds of the traditional society and brought men into immediate contact with the nation-state, and which revered the norms (if not the forms) of democracy, produced the first system of universal military service. If men's supreme loyalty was to the nation, the "nation in arms" followed logically. Democracy and nationalism thus enabled France to mobilize fully for total war—and to fight a war to destroy its opponents completely.

This was one reason the Congress of Vienna reacted with such horror to the Revolution, for it had unleashed mass passions and all-out war. Previous wars had been restrained because men had identified not with the nation but with smaller units—the town or the manor—or with universal ties—the Church. The mass army, fired by nationalism, was unknown until the Revolution. The armies of the *ancien régime* were composed largely of mercenaries and such lowly elements of society as debtors, vagrants, and criminals—men who were animated neither by love of country nor by hatred of enemy, but who fought because they were paid or compelled to do so. States lacked sufficient economic resources to maintain sizable armies. Indeed, their tactics were determined by the need to limit expenses; thus, the emphasis was on maneuver rather than pitched battle, to keep casualties low. But the Revolution enlisted popular support, and soldiers began to fight in defense of their country. "A new era in military history now opened, the era of cannon fodder."[11]

It only remained for the Industrial Revolution to produce the instruments enabling men to kill each other in greater numbers. Modern military technology brought total war to its fullest realization.[12] Mass armies could be equipped with ever more destructive arms, and nations could therefore inflict progressively greater damage on each other in shorter and shorter periods. It took thirty years for the states of Europe to slaughter half the population of Central Europe in the seventeenth century. It took only four years in the second decade of the twentieth century for the European nations to bleed each other into a state of exhaustion and, for some, collapse. "Mankind," Churchill wrote after 1918, "has got into its hands for the first time the tools by which it can unfailingly accomplish its own extermination. . . . Death stands at attention, obedient, expectant, ready, if called on, to pulverise, without

[11] Bertrand de Jouvenel, *On Power*, translated by J. F. Huntington (Boston: Beacon Press, 1962), p. 148.

[12] The interrelationship between war and industrial power is well treated in John U. Nef, *War and Human Progress* (Cambridge, Mass.: Harvard University Press, 1950), and Richard A. Preston and Sidney F. Wise, *Men in Arms: A History of Warfare and Its Interrelationships with Western Society*, rev. ed. (New York: Praeger Publishers, 1970), pp. 176 ff. For the impact of democratization and industrialization on American military performance, see Walter Millis, *Arms and Men* (New York: New American Library, 1956).

hope of repair, what is left of civilization. He awaits only the word of command. He awaits it from a frail, bewildered being, long his victim, now—for one occasion only—his Master."[13]

It was not until the ascendancy of strategic air power—and ultimately the development of atomic weapons—that man found it possible to accomplish his own extermination. World War I provided the stimulus for the development of air power. The British and French reaction to the war, as we know, was to avoid another war. But if this were to prove impossible, they would fight a defensive war only; the French symbolized this mood by building the Maginot Line. The Germans, on the other hand, rethought their approach to war. The answer was the *Blitzkrieg*— that is, a war conducted with lightning speed. Mobile land forces— meaning largely *Panzer* or tank divisions—in combination with tactical air power would smash the enemy's lines and break through into the open and undefended areas in his rear. The infantry would advance in the wake of this one-two punch and mop up the enemy's broken and confused forces. Thus the German military leaders, unlike their French and British (and, indeed, American) counterparts, were able to comprehend the impact on military tactics of the airplanes and tanks that had appeared late in the previous war. They realized their possibilities and thought of a unique manner in which a combination of the two could restore to warfare the mobility that had been lost during the Great War at such an enormous cost of life.

Both these reactions to World War I, different as they were, nevertheless shared one fundamental assumption: that the decisive engagements of a future war would be fought on land. A third view of the conduct of warfare rejected this assumption, maintaining that the key battles would be fought in the air. If, as World War I had shown, the defensive force had gained a seemingly lasting superiority over the offensive forces, then the only quick and effective way of breaking the stalemate on land and of achieving victory was to attack the enemy's home front from the air. The target would be his cities. If these were heavily bombed, two objectives would be achieved: First, the industrial strength that sustained his armies in the field would be smashed; and second, the morale of the civilian—presumably less hardened to the rigors of war than the front-line soldier—would be broken. The role of the army and navy was to be strictly secondary: to perform a holding operation on the ground while the air force pulverized the enemy's urban and industrial centers and compelled him to surrender. The development of big bombers and bombs was inherent in this line of thinking. The greater the explosive power of the bombs, the more destructive would be the impact of each strike.

It was in World War II that strategic bombing was first tried. The key to victory, however, turned out to be, as the Germans had predicted,

[13] Winston S. Churchill, *The Second World War*, vol I: *The Gathering Storm* (Boston: Houghton Mifflin, 1948), p. 40.

the combination of mobile ground power with tactical air support: armored divisions—essentially tanks, with some mobile infantry and artillery—cooperating closely with fighter aircraft. This tank-fighter combination restored the mobility and offensive momentum to warfare that the trench warfare of World War I had lost; and because the thrust and speed of the attack led to quicker victories on the battlefield, casualty rates were reduced. The Germans succeeded brilliantly with this *Blitzkrieg* tactic in Poland in 1939 and on the Western Front in 1940.[14] A year later, they almost defeated the Soviet Union with the same tactic, but the Red Army, helped by the bitter Russian winter, held the Germans at the gates of Moscow and Leningrad and finally turned the tide against Germany at Stalingrad in 1942. The British and American forces, after their invasion of France in 1944, also used this combination of mobile land forces and tactical air power with great success. It was not accidental that most of the best-known generals of World War II were "tank generals." Such figures as Rommel, Guderian, and Patton gained their fame not because they were first-rate strategists but because of their brilliant tactical handling of the tank and the spectacular results they achieved.

By contrast, strategic air power proved largely ineffective until the final phase of the war, when the outcome had already been decided. There were several reasons for this. Germany—like Russia—was a land power whose senior service was the army. It was thus natural that the Germans should think of war as land warfare and that air power should be assigned to support ground operations. Air power therefore was not thought of as a service operating independently of the army and navy.[15] Consequently, while the Germans did build up a bomber force, it was not sufficiently large at the beginning of the war, or by the fall of Dunkirk in May, 1940, to knock England out of the war. And because the Luftwaffe failed to establish command of the air over the Channel and the southern counties, there was no invasion of England.[16]

The second reason for the failure of strategic air power was technological. Strategic air war theorists had believed that a bomber equipped with guns to ward off attacking fighters would always get through; they had not foreseen that fighters, guided by radar, would be extremely effective in finding their quarry and shooting it down. By the time of the Battle of Britain (1940–41), the Royal Air Force possessed the famous Spitfires and Hurricanes that proved the vulnerability of bombers. Later, this was to be equally true for British and American bombers in their attacks upon Germany. The U.S. Army Air Force, whose officers were particularly enthusiastic devotees of bombing, learned this lesson soon after American bombers started operations against Germany from English bases, in late 1942. The British by then had already begun bomber

[14] Telford Taylor, *The March of Conquest* (New York: Simon & Schuster, 1958).
[15] *Ibid.*, pp. 24–25, 366.
[16] Peter Fleming, *Operation Sea Lion* (New York: Simon & Schuster, 1957).

operations against Germany. Because British four-engine bombers were heavier and therefore did not carry as many guns for their protection as American bombers, they operated largely at night. The Army Air Force was confident, however, that it could "do the job" by day. U.S. Flying Fortresses and Liberators were heavily armed and could fly high. After its air power in England had been built up and it had gained some bombing experience, the Air Force decided to prove the bombing theory by attacking a single target, the city of Schweinfurt, where the Germans had concentrated their ball-bearing production. If the factories producing ball bearings could be destroyed, the German military machine would be disastrously—and probably fatally—wounded.

The attacks on Schweinfurt proved instead to be disastrous for the attackers. The number of planes brought down by German air defenses was very high. The lesson was clear: Repeated attacks against such well-guarded targets could end in heroic suicide for the bombers and their crews. Schweinfurt was a grim reminder that fighter defenses could be effective and that even armed bombers needed fighter protection. The Flying Fortress—the name itself a symptom of the overweening confidence of American officers that the bomber would always get through—was not, in fact, self-sufficient.[17] After Schweinfurt, the Air Force ordered the production of long-range Thunderbolt fighters. Until they were ready to escort the bombers (in early 1944), sustained, long-range, daylight precision bombing against military targets in Germany was halted. Only the British continued heavy night raids, which turned out to be largely indiscriminate city bombings—attacks on civilian populations and industry.

In the four years that elapsed from the German victory in France to the Allied invasion of France, independent strategic bombing did not produce spectacular results, let alone win the war. While the bombing of urban centers destroyed large sections of big cities, it did not seriously affect essential war production because most such bombing was directed at the centers of cities, while the industries—at least in Germany—were on the outskirts. Even when factories were hit, more damage was done to the buildings than to the machinery inside—as, for instance, at Schweinfurt—and the Germans were quick to restore needed factory buildings to maximum working capacity. Indeed, the postwar United States Strategic Bombing Survey found that German war production—for instance, of fighters—increased up until late 1944. And at least one reason for this was that Allied bombing, by destroying nonvital factories and services, allowed the Germans to channel labor and resources to the war industries. Nor did German morale suffer critically. The civilians—"the soldiers on the home front"—proved to be tough and resilient; indeed, the aerial attacks tended to unify the population, as the Allies should have known after the German attacks on Coventry and London.

[17] Millis, *Arms and Men*, pp. 259–60, and Bernard Brodie, *Strategy in the Missile Age* (Princeton, N.J.: Princeton University Press, 1959), p. 115.

Inevitably, over time and after repeated bombing raids, some decline in civilian morale did occur, but this had no vital impact on the behavior of the working population, who still went to work as usual. (No doubt the threat of reprisals by the Nazis against those workers who failed to show up exerted a strong influence.)[18]

Thus, the results of city-bombing were not rewarding. The predicted collapse of war production and civilian morale did not occur. The evidence of the period prior to the 1944 invasion would therefore seem to be negative. During the last phase of the war in Europe, however, strategic air power came into its own, and its impact was devastating. Interestingly enough, though, its primary use was no longer city-bombing. The selected targets bombed by the Allied air forces, now very large and escorted by fighters, were transportation complexes and the centers of the chemical–synthetic oil industry, both of which proved extremely vulnerable. Road, railroad, and canal transportation were brought to a virtual standstill. For a highly developed economy, this turned out to be fatal. How could the coal that stoked the furnaces be brought to the factories? And how could more weapons and ammunition be brought to the front? Moreover, the attacks on the oil industry reduced oil production drastically, and production of aviation and motor gasoline was even more seriously affected. Thus, while fighter-aircraft production rose, there was less and less gasoline available for flight training or combat flying. Similarly, on the ground, German tanks lacked sufficient fuel, and their effectiveness in battle was thereby severely hampered.[19]

Strategic air power did not achieve devastating results until it was realized that the highly specialized and interdependent entity that is a modern economy is an extremely sensitive structure. The denial of one essential element can cripple it, *if* there is no substitute for that one element—a necessary qualification since, in a highly industrialized economy, advanced technology can usually produce a substitute. It has been said that a nation's industry is not like a building, to be destroyed, but like a tree, which can grow new branches when old ones die. An economy is less a structure than a process or set of activities and purposes that can be undertaken in a variety of ways; the loss of one element in this process is seldom irreparable. But what substitute is there for destroyed railroad lines—when barges and road transportation are also under continuous heavy attack? Or for a synthetic oil industry—itself already a substitute? Where is the substitute for the substitute? And how quickly can it be found?

Whatever the shortcomings of strategic bombing during World War II, however, the atomic and hydrogen bombs have since left no doubt that air power would play the decisive role in any future total war. Cities —indeed, whole nations—could be laid waste in a matter of hours, if not

[18] See Brodie, *Strategy in Missile Age*, pp. 120–24, 131–38.
[19] See *ibid.*, pp. 109–20, and Georges Blond, *The Death of Hitler's Germany* (New York: Macmillan, 1954), pp. 105–6.

minutes. The effectiveness of that kind of strategic air power against a highly urbanized and industrialized society is no longer a matter of dispute. Nuclear bombs have the capacity to impose a degree of destruction that would make World War II bombing attacks appear trivial by comparison. The atomic bombs dropped on Hiroshima and Nagasaki (20 kilotons, or 20 thousand tons of TNT) were within a few years surpassed in destructive power by new weapons produced by both the United States and the Soviet Union. Kilotons were replaced by megatons (1 million tons of TNT). A single U.S. Strategic Air Command B-52 bomber carries an average of 25 megatons of explosive power—which represents 12.5 times the entire explosive power of all bombs dropped during World War II, including the two atomic bombs![20] And the B-52 could carry a 50-megaton bomb, if the United States possessed one, as Russia does.[21]

The total estimated American nuclear stockpile by the time of the Cuban missile crisis in 1962 was approximately 35 kilomegatons (35 billion tons of TNT)—"enough bang to provide 10 tons of explosive power for everyone in the world. In the form of TNT this much explosive power would fill a string of freight cars stretching from the earth to the moon and back 15 times (approximately 240,000 miles each way)."[22] The estimated Soviet stockpile in 1962 was 20 kilomegatons. The Soviets have tested the world's largest bomb—58 megatons—and claim that their stockpile includes 100-megaton bombs. Actually, a bomb can be made as large or as small as desired—up to 1,000 megatons, or a "giga-ton." Moreover, it is cheap to increase the yield of a bomb. It costs $750,000 for a 100-kiloton atom bomb, $1 million for a 1-megaton hydrogen bomb, $1.1 million for a 10-megaton bomb, and $1.2 million for a 100-megaton bomb; above 10 megatons, each additional ton of explosive costs about a penny. In short, bombs come in true economy sizes.[23] However, it is not necessarily true that the larger the bomb, the more effective it is; while a larger bomb may cause greater damage, the amount of damage does not increase proportionally with the size of the bomb. A 10-megaton bomb is sufficient to incinerate any large city, and two 25-megaton bombs dropped several miles apart will cause more extensive damage than one 50-megaton bomb.

A nuclear explosion has three effects: blast, thermal, and radiation. The blast, or shock wave—the almost solid wall of air pressure produced by an explosion—resulting from a bomb exploding in a city will collapse all wooden buildings within 6 miles of ground zero for a low-altitude

[20] Arthur T. Hadley, The Nation's Safety and Arms Control (New York: Viking Press, 1961), p. 4.

[21] New York Times, August 14, 1963.

[22] Hadley, Nation's Safety and Arms Control, pp. 3–4. The American stockpile was so large that in January, 1964, President Johnson ordered a 25 per cent cutback in the production of enriched uranium and closed four of the fourteen American reactors producing plutonium. This was followed by a further cutback of 15 per cent in April, 1964.

[23] Ralph E. Lapp, Kill and Overkill (New York: Basic Books, 1962), p. 37.

1-megaton bomb, 14 miles for a 10-megaton bomb, and 30 miles for a 100-megaton bomb. For brick buildings, the comparative figures for the same bombs are 4, 9, and 18 miles; and for sturdier buildings, the distance ranges from 3 to 12 miles.

The thermal impact is even more devastating. The heat generated by a 1-megaton bomb is tremendous, producing second-degree burns of the skin up to 9 miles from ground zero; a 10-megaton bomb has the same effect up to 24 miles, a 100-megaton bomb up to 70 miles.[24] Moreover, the heat would in most cases ignite wooden houses—as, for instance, those in many suburbs—and other combustible objectives over about the same range. World War II demonstrated that the real danger from fire, even when started with ordinary incendiary bombs, is the resulting "fire storm."[25] In a fire storm, the intense heat from the fire rises, heating the air in turn. The pressure differential between the hot and colder air sucks in fresh oxygen to feed the hungry flames, and the process builds in intensity. Air rushes in at ever greater speeds until wind velocity surpasses gale force. The flames, whipped by the wind and fed further by the gas, oil, and other incendiary materials of the homes and streets of the burning city, leap upward, stabbing high into the air, enveloping the stricken area. Everything burns in this tomb of heat and flame. There is no escape. Those who have not yet been crushed in their shelters will be asphyxiated by a lack of oxygen or by carbon monoxide poisoning; if they seek to escape into the burning streets, they will sear their lungs, and their bodies, exposed to the intense heat, will suddenly burst into flame. During the attack on Hamburg, the fire storm caused a ground temperature of 1,400°F. Indeed, near the center of the fire storm the temperature exceeded 2,200°F. A 100-megaton bomb could cause fire storms up to 75 miles from the point of explosion; woods, trash, and dry leaves all provide kindling.

The third effect of a nuclear explosion, the radiation impact, can be maximized by a ground burst or low-altitude explosion. The resulting fireball—the large, rapidly expanding sphere of hot gases that produces high and intense heat—scoops up the debris and converts it into radioactive material. The fireball of a 10-megaton bomb has a 6-mile diameter. The heavier particles of debris fall back to earth within the first few

[24] *Ibid.*, pp. 51–52, and Scientists' Committee for Radiation Information, "Effects of Nuclear Explosives," in Seymour Melman, ed., *No Place to Hide* (New York: Grove Press, 1962), pp. 98–107.

[25] A vivid account of a fire storm is given in Martin Caidin, *The Night Hamburg Died* (New York: Ballantine Books, 1960), pp. 80–105, 129–41. The German estimate of those killed in Hamburg was 60,000. The American B-29 attack on Tokyo on March 9–10, 1945, burned up 16 square miles and killed 84,000 people, most of whom were burned to death or died from wounds caused by fire. By contrast, the Hiroshima atom bomb killed 72,000 people. The most destructive attack ever, however, was the two-day Anglo-American bombing of Dresden in February, 1945, in which 135,000 people were killed. On this, see David Irving, *The Destruction of Dresden* (New York: Holt, Rinehart & Winston, 1964).

hours. The lighter particles "fall out" during the following days over an area whose size depends on the size of the explosion, the surface over which the explosion occurs, and the meteorological conditions. The American 15-megaton thermonuclear explosion of 1954 in the Pacific caused substantial contamination over an area of 7,000 square miles (equivalent to the size of New Jersey). Under more "favorable" conditions, the fallout could have covered an area of 100,000 square miles (equivalent to New Jersey plus New York plus Pennsylvania). Such fallout, moreover, can emit radiation for days, months, or even years. The ability of this radiation to kill depends on the number of roentgens a human being absorbs.[26] A dosage of 100–200 roentgens causes radiation sickness—a combination of weakness, nausea, and vomiting; this is not fatal, although it can result in disability. At 200 roentgens, the radiation becomes very dangerous: Disability is certain, and death can come within a month. At about 300 roentgens, the possibility of death increases until, at 500 roentgens, death is certain for 50 per cent of those exposed to the radiation. Above 600 roentgens, the number of deaths goes up and they occur more rapidly.[27] Radiation also has two other effects: It can cause cancer, and it can cause genetic transmutations that may affect following generations.

It would therefore appear that, in the case of nuclear weapons, the World War II problem of failing to hit a target industry or of damaging only the buildings but not the machinery they house no longer exists. An entire city can now be eliminated with a single bomb. Thus, a coordinated nuclear attack on a nation's major urban and industrial centers would be catastrophic, reducing everything to rubble and leaving the population dead or injured, with little hope of help. Most hospitals, doctors, nurses, drugs, and blood plasma would be destroyed; so would the machinery for the processing and refrigeration of food and the purification of water. There would be no transportation left to take survivors out of the smoldering ruins and into the countryside; most, if not all, of the fuel would also have burned. Estimates of those killed in such a coordinated strike on a modern industrial nation range from 30 to 90 per cent of the population, depending upon the yield, the heights of the explosions, weather conditions, civilian protection, and preparations made to cope with the aftermath of such an attack. It has been estimated, for instance, that a Soviet attack employing 260 H-bombs with a yield of 1,500 megatons against 224 American strategic targets would, in the first day, result in a minimum of 50 million dead and 20 million more injured. The estimate of those killed in a Soviet 20,000-megaton attack is 95 per cent of the country's population.[28] President Kennedy's Secretary of Defense stated that "even under the most favorable circumstances"

[26] Lapp, Kill and Overkill, pp. 53–54.

[27] Ibid., p. 77.

[28] Harrison Scott Brown and James Real, Community of Fear (Santa Barbara, Calif.: Center for the Study of Democratic Institutions, 1960), pp. 20–23.

fatalities would run "into tens of millions." Estimates have run from 129 million to 149 million casualties.[29]

The psychological impact upon the survivors would be as devastating as the physical destruction. The elimination of a nation's larger cities, the deaths of tens of millions, the wrecking of its industries, communications, and transportation system—all would be bound to undermine any remaining sense of self-confidence of those who were still alive. A nation in ruins is not likely to retain its *élan vital* or entertain any optimistic expectations for the future. It has taken Europe, and especially France, more than forty years to recover from the psychological wounds of World War I and the loss of its younger generation on the battlefields. Recovery after World War II was made possible by extensive infusions of American economic aid, yet European wounds and losses were minor compared with those a nation would suffer during a nuclear attack. For the result would be not only the destruction of cities but the disorganization of all social life.

> Any society operates through confidence in an orderly succession of events, either natural or social. A catastrophe is an interruption in what has come to be considered natural. The panic it often produces is the reflection of an inability to react to an unexpected situation and attempt to flee as rapidly as possible into a familiar and, therefore, predictable environment. If a familiar environment remains, some confidence can be restored. Most natural catastrophes can be dealt with, because they affect only a very small geographic area or a very small proportion of the population. The remainder of the society can utilize its machinery or cooperative effort to come to the assistance of the stricken area. Indeed, such action tends to reinforce the cohesiveness of a society, because it becomes a symbol of its value and efficiency. The essence of the catastrophe produced by an all-out thermonuclear war, however, is the depth of the dislocation it produces and the consequent impossibility of escaping into familiar relationships. When all relationships, or even most relationships, have to be reconstituted, society as we know it today will have been fundamentally transformed.[30]

Indeed, it may be even worse than Henry Kissinger has suggested. For in 1974, it became known that nuclear war could possibly destroy the ozone layer in the stratosphere. This layer protects all living things from the sun's ultra-violent radiation; thus, in addition to death, destruction and radiation, nuclear war and extensive ozone depletion could destroy the food chain of plants and animals upon which man depends for his survival as the ultraviolet rays disintegrate protein molecules.

One must logically conclude that modern nuclear warfare is irrational. Nuclear technology has so vastly augmented the scope of violence and destruction that total war can destroy the very nation that wages it. The

[29] See Robert S. McNamara's statement in *New York Times*, January 28, 1964.
[30] Henry A. Kissinger, *Nuclear Weapons and Foreign Policy* (New York: Harper & Row, 1957), p. 79.

impact of this new power on the conduct of international politics has been revolutionary.

The Assumptions Underlying Deterrence

The balance of power has historically had two purposes: the deterrence of war (at least when states were secure, for otherwise they have tended to reject "peace at any price"); and, if hostilities could not be prevented, defending oneself and winning the war. Nuclear technology has fundamentally changed the manner in which military strength can be used to attain an approximate equilibrium to prevent an expansionist power from dominating the international system.[31] Nuclear weapons now ensure that any total war will risk the very substance of national life. Rather than helping to preserve civilization, the new instruments of violence threaten to destroy it. What possible goal would be "worth" the cost of self-immolation? How could a nation defend its political independence and territorial integrity if, in the very act of defense, it might well sacrifice the life of its nation? Nuclear war can know no victors; all the contestants must be losers. *Thus, total wars may be in accord with weapons of limited destructive capacity, but they are incompatible with "absolute weapons."* The first conclusion to be drawn from this general principle is that the principal function of strategic military strength in the nuclear age becomes the *deterrence* of an all-out attack. In other words, its chief purpose now is to prevent any attack from occurring, rather than to defend the nation after it has become engaged in hostilities. The opponent is threatened with such massive retaliation that he dare not attack. The assumption is that, faced with the risk of virtual suicide if he attacks, he will desist, since the price he would have to pay for any possible gains would be far too high. This extraordinary situation is paradoxical: Military capacity must be strong, but it must be strong so that it will not have to be used. Its most important role is in its peacetime impact; if war erupts, it will have failed. The decisive test of arms is no longer vanquishing the enemy in battle; it is not to have to fight him at all.

In the nuclear age, moreover, this deterrence must be perpetual. Obviously, there can be no margin for error. In previous periods of history, if a deterrent did not perform its assigned function, war resulted. Because no weapon was so destructive that failure spelled extinction, such mistakes were not irreparable. The crucial problem for the military was, therefore, the reverse of today: It was not so much whether it could prevent the outbreak of hostilities, but whether it could win the war once the country was mobilized. This is no longer true, since the superpowers, on the one hand, possess overwhelming and devastating power

---

[31] Glenn H. Snyder, "Balance of Power in the Missile Age," *Journal of International Affairs,* 14, No. 1 (1960): 21–34.

and, on the other, are completely vulnerable to attack and destruction. Nuclear technology and national rivalry, not religion and good will among men, may thus bring mankind peace on earth: a *pax atomica*—perpetual deterrence for perpetual peace.

If deterrence is a feasible strategy in the nuclear age, it also fitted the post–World War II bipolar age of drawing lines and preserving them as "frontiers" separating the superpowers' spheres of influence. Indeed, the fundamental assumption of deterrence is the acceptance of the territorial *status quo*. This acceptance is based either upon the justice of the general international settlement or, if not its justice, upon a belief that it at least provides for stability. The contrast between the interwar and postwar years again clarifies this difference, *for deterrence could not have worked in the 1930's.*[32] Not only was there in Britain and France a strong antiwar feeling, but there was also a sizable guilt complex about the Versailles peace settlement. In other words, the victors who had drawn up the settlement began to feel that they had wronged Germany and therefore that Hitler was a spokesman for legitimate German grievances. For instance, at Versailles the Allies had said that Germany's military limitation was only the first step toward a more general reduction of armaments. But after two wars with Germany—that of 1870 and the 1914–18 conflict—France was actually more concerned with maintaining its military strength than with disarmament. Hitler could therefore pose as the spokesman of an aggrieved Germany that had, in good faith, "accepted" a large measure of disarmament while its former enemies, despite their avowals, had not. A great power and the equal of France and England, Germany was being treated as a second-class state; all it asked was to be treated fairly. Hitler's other claims were advanced in the context of the democratic principle of national self-determination, the very basis of the Treaty of Versailles. This principle had not been implemented fully; like other principles, when applied it ran into competing principles. National self-determination had been violated in the Rhineland, the Sudetenland, and the Polish Corridor, primarily for security reasons. Hitler could thus invoke a fundamental Western principle against the West in order to undermine the post–World War I settlement.

On what basis could France and England deny him any of these claims? Were equality and national self-determination all right for themselves but not for anyone else? Hitler's claims were recognized as just. Who could really say that he was insincere and that he was using the Versailles principles cynically? Had not the West—as Hitler repeatedly pointed out—violated its own principles? Was not the German leader therefore justified in demanding that the two Western powers

[32] Evan Luard, "Conciliation and Deterrence: A Comparison of Political Strategies in the Interwar and Postwar Periods," *World Politics*, January, 1967, pp. 167–89; see also Arnold Wolfers, *Britain and France Between Two Wars* (New York: Norton, 1966), and Wheeler-Bennett, *Munich*.

correct the inequalities they had written into the peace treaty? No wonder the Western powers, because of these tactics, felt guilty about Versailles. They had preached one thing and practiced another; and they had thereby placed the moral validity of the Versailles settlement in jeopardy. Thus France and especially Britain felt that if war were to erupt it would be *their* fault for clinging too stubbornly to the territorial settlement defined by Versailles. Hitler's frantic speeches could be explained away in terms of the vigorous German resentment at the unjust treatment dealt it by France and England.

In other words, Hitler shrewdly disguised his aim and paralyzed the will of his opponents to act against him. Each challenge confronted them with the question of whether they wanted to fight to preserve a morally dubious *status quo*. After the horrors of World War I, the answer was obvious. Why should a war be fought to defend unjust positions, especially if it could be avoided? If Hitler was a nationalist who only wanted the return of German territory, would not the satisfaction of his demands for national self-determination end his claims and gain his support for the preservation of the European balance and peace?

A post–World War II generation that thinks of Hitler as a warmonger has forgotten that, to their predecessors of the 1930's, this was not so apparent. Hitler could announce Germany's rearmament while pledging Germany's willingness to renounce all offensive weapons or disband its entire military establishment—if only other nations would pledge to do the same. He could denounce a treaty with a neighbor while simultaneously issuing assurances that it was his own fondest hope to sign a non-aggression pact with that same neighbor. He "solemnly" guaranteed other countries' frontiers, promising not to interfere in their internal affairs, and he never tired of declaring that his present claim was the last one he would ever make. Ironically, Hitler became a most effective spokesman for "peace." To his contemporaries, Hitler often appeared to be sincerely and honestly dedicated to resolving all problems that might stand in the way of peace in Europe. His constant refrain was that Germany would never break the peace.

The post–World War II period was different. No peace treaty with Germany was ever signed. (In 1970, Russia and West Germany signed a treaty in which the latter recognized the territorial *status quo* that had existed since 1945.) Furthermore, as every age learns from the immediate past—for it is this past that constitutes "experience"—American leaders after 1945 blamed the "unnecessary war" on the policy of appeasement. The failure of this policy was attributed to the insatiable appetites of dictators; feeding them a few choice morsels merely whetted their appetite for more. For anyone confronted by Stalin, it was all too easy to think of him as the Russian Hitler. In more impersonal terms, both men were thought of as leaders of totalitarian regimes whose very dynamic was "permanent revolution." The first comparative scholarly analysis of totalitarianism by Sigmund Neumann in 1942 concluded that totalitarian dictatorships were "governments for war. The analysis of their inner structure . . . has proved conclusively that the permanent evolution of perpetual motion is the driving force of totalitarianism. Expansion is of its essence. The rise, development, and survival of modern dictatorships are inextricably tied up with continuous dynamics."[33] Russia's postwar behavior seemed only to confirm this conclusion.

The first requirement of policy under these circumstances was to hold fast. Changing frontiers was considered appeasement that could only undermine the peace. In the earlier period, changing frontiers and appeasement were expected to build a more solid foundation for peace; conversely, preserving the territorial *status quo* was considered the sure way to war. After 1945, the division of Germany, for instance, was not "just," but both superpowers could live with it. At least it provided a degree of stability in Central Europe. The cold war was essentially a means of drawing frontiers and then preserving them. Thus, when a challenge to the *status quo* occurred, the response was to demonstrate firmness rather than make concessions. To give in was only to make the situation worse.

Thus "all the most important issues in dispute—Berlin, Germany, Formosa, the offshore islands—have remained in dispute even twenty [or thirty] years after the end of the war. There have been no 'betrayals.' But there have been no settlements either."[34] The problem of the postwar world has been to learn how to live with problems, not how to solve them. Once asked whether he hoped to be remembered for having achieved a settlement of the Berlin problem by the end of his time as Secretary of State, Dean Rusk answered that he was not that vain. His ambition was to be remembered in history for succeeding in passing the Berlin problems he found upon entering office down to his successor intact.[35] But even without the vivid memories of the 1930's, the bipolarity of the postwar period would have led the United States to fear the loss of dominoes and to support the frontiers between the respective spheres of influence. The Soviet fear of a row of collapsing dominoes was equally great. Moscow was constantly concerned about Eastern Europe and prepared to use force to preserve its hegemony there. Both superpowers carefully guarded against defections. Violence has mainly been used to preserve or restore the *status quo*, not to transform it. Thus history and the nature of the post-1945 world combined to produce a policy of preserving lines and demonstrating firmness. This capacity to prevent changes in the *status quo* ought perhaps to be called *negative power*. Its purpose was to prevent expansion and to deny territorial changes where this negative power could be brought to bear. (Later, we shall

---

[33] Sigmund Neumann, *Permanent Revolution*, 2d ed. (New York: Praeger Publishers, 1965), p. 257.

[34] Luard, "Conciliation and Deterrence," pp. 174–75.

[35] Roger Hilsman, *To Move A Nation* (Garden City, N.Y.: Doubleday, 1967), p. 41.

analyze positive power—or "compellence"—to affect changes in the *status quo*.)

A second assumption underlying deterrence, an assumption independent of the political conditions in which deterrence may or may not work, was that the policy-makers on both sides were rational—that is, that they could calculate the costs and gains of any moves they contemplated and could keep a situation from getting out of control. In the nuclear era especially this implies that they can calculate that the gains to be had from destroying the adversary are completely disproportionate to the costs their side would have to pay. "It is sometimes stated," writes Herman Kahn,

> that even an adequate . . . deterrent would not deter an irrational enemy. This might be true if irrationality were an all-or-nothing proposition. Actually, irrationality is a matter of degree, and if the irrationality is sufficiently bizarre, the irrational decision-maker's subordinates are likely to step in. As a result, we should want a safety factor in . . . deterrence systems so large as to impress even the irrational and irresponsible with the degree of their irrationality and therefore the need for caution.[36]

But in the 1930's, the British were not so sure. On the one hand, they thought of Hitler as rational, believing that he would settle down once he had been appeased; on the other hand, they thought of him as really irrational—that is, reckless enough to engulf Europe in flames. If the Nazi leader was really such a raving maniac, it was the better part of valor to satisfy his demand for national self-determination and give him his "last territorial demand in Europe." Schelling has compared political leaders who either are or feign to be irrational with some of the inmates of mental institutions. Referring to the inmates, he noted that these people "are either very crazy or very wise, or both, [because they] make clear to the attendants that they may slit their own veins or light their clothes on fire if they don't have their way"—and so may get their way.[37] When this suicidal technique is used politically, the threat is intended to suggest that the "fire" will also burn those who are threatened. This is not unlike an airplane hijacking, when Arab terrorists, for example, threaten to blow up the plane unless the pilot does what he is told. This is surely irrational in the sense that blowing up the plane will kill them too. But as fanatics they manage to convey this impression of irrationality, and their threat therefore becomes credible.

No American policy-makers in the postwar period thought of Stalin or

[36] Herman Kahn, *Thinking About the Unthinkable* (New York: Horizon Press, 1962), pp. 111–12, and Thomas C. Schelling, *Arms and Influence* (New Haven, Conn.: Yale University Press, 1966), pp. 229–30. It might be added that by "irrationality" Kahn means to suggest more than "crazy" and presumably, therefore, it includes recklessness; it also includes panic or nervousness or fear on the part of policy-makers at a moment of crisis, in contrast to cool-headed calculation.

[37] Schelling, *Arms and Influence*, pp. 37–38, and *idem, Strategy of Conflict* (Cambridge, Mass.: Harvard University Press, 1960), p. 17.

his various successors as irrational. Quite the contrary. In the rationale for the containment policy, George Kennan, analyzing the sources of Soviet conduct, talked of the impact on Russian behavior of both Communist ideological perception and Russian history:

> The Kremlin is under no ideological compulsion to accomplish its purposes in a hurry. Like the Church, it is dealing in ideological concepts which are of long-term validity, and it can afford to be patient. It has no right to risk the existing achievements of the revolution for the sake of vain baubles of the future. The very teachings of Lenin himself require great caution and flexibility in the pursuit of Communist purposes. Again, these precepts are fortified by the lessons of Russian history: of centuries of obscure battles between nomadic forces over the stretches of a vast unfortified plain. Here caution, circumspection, flexibility and deception are the valuable qualities; and their value finds natural appreciation in the Russian or the oriental mind. Thus the Kremlin has no compunction about retreating in the face of superior force. And being under the compulsion of no timetable, it does not get panicky under the necessity for such retreat. Its main concern is to make sure that it has filled every nook and cranny available to it in the basin of world power. But if it finds unassailable barriers in its path, it accepts these philosophically and accommodates itself to them. The main thing is that there should always be pressure, increasing constant pressure, toward the desired goal. There is no trace of any feeling in Soviet psychology that that goal must be reached at any given time.[38]

Studies of the "operational code of the Politburo" have confirmed this appraisal.[39] The Kremlin did not believe in "adventurism" or "romanticism." It counseled against being "provoked" by the enemy into an untimely or unwise move to advance. It suggested that, with every plan for advance, there must be a provision for retreat. And Chinese Communist foreign policy behavior has been equally cautious—as distinct from Peking's verbal militancy.

Conversely the Russians, first by their actions and later by their words, demonstrated that they believed American policy-makers to be rational as well. The early years of the cold war, when the United States held an atomic monopoly, were also the years of pressure on Iran and Turkey and of the Greek civil war, the *coup d'état* in Czechoslovakia, the use of Communist parties and Communist-controlled unions to try to undermine the Marshall Plan, and, of course, the North Korean aggresssion. This last particularly showed that the Russians were not fearful of a retaliatory attack on Moscow. Even in 1957–62, when massive retaliation had become a two-way street but the Soviet leaders *knew* that American strategic power remained vastly more destructive than Russia's, the So-

[38] George F. Kennan, *American Diplomacy 1900–1950* (Chicago: University of Chicago Press, 1951), p. 118.

[39] Nathan Leites, *The Operational Code of the Politburo* (New York: McGraw-Hill, 1951), and *idem, A Study of Bolshevism* (Glencoe, Ill.: Free Press, 1953), pp. 27–63.

viet leadership felt confident that it could raise tensions *without* provoking the United States. As long as this tension was not raised too high, it felt able to control the risk of war. To ensure that tensions would not get out of control, the Soviets either left themselves a diplomatic escape hatch or were willing to make timely withdrawals in case they had underestimated the American reaction. The Cuban missile crisis testifies to the Soviets' confidence that, short of a major provocation—from which they carefully abstained—they could challenge the United States without fear of nuclear response. Khrushchev later distinguished between American "madmen" and "realists" in Washington, the former allegedly believing that Communism must be eliminated and that this must be done by military force, the latter committed to coexistence and arms control. It was the latter group that was in power in Washington.

The Diplomacy of Coercion

Deterrence is not just a military technique. In fact—following our earlier distinction between deterrence and defense—deterrence is a *diplomatic concept*, while defense is the military one. Because the soldier's primary test has been on the battlefield, his primary professional concern has been with weapons or capability and the application of violence. Deterrence obviously needs a capability to support it, but its test lies not in its use but in the *threat* of its use. The actual application of force to beat the enemy is replaced by the *exploitation of potential force* to dissuade the potential aggressor from striking. Deterrence is, in other words, a psychological concept because it employs coercion to *affect an opponent's intentions*.[40] It is his state of mind that must be influenced. The skills required to do this are not those the military has acquired in its training; rather, they belong to the responsible civilian policy-makers.[41] For what we are talking about when we stress this civilian-directed manipulation of the threat of violence is diplomacy.[42] The capacity to hurt

---

[40] Schelling, *Strategy of Conflict*, pp. 3–10.

[41] Symptomatic of this fundamental change from the conduct of war to the implementation of deterrence through the exploitation of coercion is that virtually all the seminal thinking on the resort to military force short of actual employment has been by civilian intellectuals. The student interested in what is usually referred to as national security affairs does not go to the works written by the generals and admirals but to the civilian experts, mostly academicians, who as political scientists, historians, mathematicians, and physicists have concerned themselves with issues of strategy. Since the word strategy, historically defined as the use of battles to achieve the objectives of war, is now more concerned with what one of these experts, Thomas Schelling, has called "the manipulation of risk," it is to their writings that we turn. By taking the mystery out of a subject that civilians have usually felt was understood only by professional soldiers, men such as Bernard Brodie and Henry Kissinger have transformed the interested layman into an expert and permitted him to question the soldier's judgment on matters of strategy, force levels, and weapons.

[42] Schelling, *Arms and Influence*, pp. 1–34.

or destroy with nuclear arms—as well as to reward "good behavior" by withholding this capacity to hurt—provides a state with a *capacity to bargain*.

Bargaining by means of violence—rather than coercion—sometimes occurred during wartime before the nuclear era. An example from World War I was Germany's strategy of attrition on the Western Front. Unable to break through Allied lines, Germany would deliberately select a city important to the French and fight not so much to capture it as to destroy the manpower France would pour in to hold it. Thus, in a ten-month battle, Verdun cost France 535,000 casualties while Germany, a nation with almost twice France's population, lost 427,000 men.[43] If France wanted to avoid further such staggering losses, Germany was in fact saying, it had only to accept Germany's terms. A more recent example from World War II would be the bombing of Japan. By the time heavy air attacks began in the spring of 1945, Japan had already lost the war. Its navy and merchant marine no longer existed, and its troops on continental Asia were cut off. Even if every Japanese war firm had still been producing, the troops could not have been properly supplied; as it was, the raw materials Japanese factories needed could not even be imported any longer. What was needed was to bring home to Japan's leaders the simple fact that the war was lost and there was no point in further resistance. The bombing of Japanese cities, climaxed by the atomic attacks on Hiroshima and Nagasaki, was intended to help make this clear. By suggesting that if it continued the war Japan would be completely devastated, the Allies informed the enemy what behavior of his would bring more punishment and what behavior would end the violence.[44]

But these examples are exceptional. During both world wars, the Allied aim against Germany was the destruction of its forces and the government's unconditional surrender. Total military victory was the objective. Only after this had been achieved were terms imposed on the defeated enemy, at least when the victorious nations (as after World War I) could agree on terms. Bargaining occurred only after the war (if one can call negotiating with a completely defeated opponent bargaining). *The exercise of military power was thus largely seen as an alternative to bargaining, not as a process of bargaining.*[45]

Nuclear arms, however, make it no longer necessary to defeat the enemy in battle first. He knows that he can be immensely hurt; he does not have to engage in war to make this discovery. Indeed, he shares a *common interest* with the party seeking to deter him in avoiding war. Therefore, the ability to inflict great pain can be exploited diplomatically

[43] See Alistair Horne, *The Price of Glory: Verdun 1916* (New York: St. Martin's, 1962).

[44] Brodie, *Strategy in Missile Age*, pp. 127–31, 138–43; see also Herbert Feis, *Japan Subdued* (Princeton, N.J.: Princeton University Press, 1961), p. 185.

[45] Schelling, *Arms and Influence*, pp. 15–16.

before the eruption of war.[46] Modern technology has thus enhanced the importance of "threats of war as techniques of influence, not of destruction; of coercion and deterrence, not of conquest and defense; of bargaining and intimidation."[47]

A few general comments about diplomacy are necessary before analyzing it in more depth. Diplomacy is frequently represented as mutually exclusive with force. "When diplomacy ends, war starts" and "While states talk, they are at least not fighting" are two commonly expressed notions. Yet, as stressed earlier, in reality diplomacy and force are linked. War is, as Clausewitz defined it, the continuation of diplomacy by other means; peace, on the other hand, may be defined as the continuation of the last war by other means. Diplomacy as a means of resolving differences among states does not necessarily have to have military support. Conflicts on occasion can be settled merely by offering rewards or "carrots." But, in the final analysis, "it is an illusion of posterity that past international settlements were brought about entirely by reasonableness and negotiating skills." The author of those words, Henry Kissinger, goes on to say:

> In a society of "sovereign" states, a power can in the last resort vindicate its interpretation of justice or defend its "vital interests" only by the willingness to employ force. The motive force behind international settlements has always been a combination of the belief in the advantages of harmony and the fear of the consequences of proving obdurate. A renunciation of force, by eliminating the penalty for intransigence, will therefore place the international order at the mercy of its most ruthless or its most irresponsible member.[48]

Thus military power, as a coercive instrument and sometimes as a violent instrument, is more often than not an inherent part of diplomacy in an essentially anarchical system in which the expectation of the threat or actual use of violence is a permanent feature of international life.

Nor is diplomacy synonymous with compromise. Resolving differences among states somewhere between the initial proposals advanced by each side—but not necessarily halfway between them—is not its only purpose. Diplomacy can be used for many different purposes.[49] Propaganda is a frequent aim in the age of mass participation in politics and the ability of the mass media to reach vast numbers of people. Summit meetings, for example, with all the buildups and expectations surrounding them, are a particularly fruitful source of propaganda; so are such "motherhood" issues as disarmament conferences (who, after all, is against disarmament?). Other diplomatic aims may range from maintaining some contact with an adversary (the United States and Com-

[46] *Ibid.*, p. 22.
[47] *Ibid.*, p. 33.
[48] Henry A. Kissinger, *Nuclear Weapons and Foreign Policy*, pp. 4–5.
[49] Fred Iklé, *How Nations Negotiate* (New York: Harper & Row, 1964), pp. 26–58.

munist China in the 1950's and 1960's) to gaining intelligence and deception (U.S.S.R. negotiating with Czech leaders just before intervening in Czechoslovakia in 1968). More specifically, in a bipolar context diplomacy has been much concerned with confirming the *status quo* or lines drawn between the Soviet and American spheres through deterrence, crisis management, and establishing restraints in limited war, as this and the next chapter will elaborate. In a system with more poles, diplomacy as a means of negotiating differences, clarifying areas of common interest, or maneuvering is more likely to be stressed.

Finally, diplomacy is not always conducted by individuals officially designated as diplomats who sit around a table attempting to settle their nations' contrasting points of views. In our age it is often conducted by civilian policy-makers, some politically elected, most politically appointed to key foreign policy-making positions, whose prime responsibility is the formulation of the policies the diplomats and military officers help carry out. In addition, diplomacy is not always, as immediately comes to mind when we think of diplomacy, a process in which each side submits explicit proposals which provide the basis for the subsequent formal negotiations; in our age much diplomacy is conducted tacitly, that is, each side signals its intentions and expectations to the adversary by its actions but never sits down with him and *formally* negotiates with him. Yet they manage to arrive at "tacit agreements."

The achievement of deterrence through the manipulation of coercion is part of this new form of bargaining. It is one thing, however, to try and influence an opponent not to resort to violence, and quite another to make him believe that you will actually go to war to defend the objective he wants, considering the price such a war will exact. To put it more bluntly: How can the opponent be made to believe that your threat is *credible*? One principal answer: Make a credible commitment.[50] A number of different techniques—such as staking one's reputation and making automatic commitments—may be used to communicate this to an opponent. The former technique consists of making a commitment that involves a nation's honor and prestige, its bargaining reputation, and the confidence of its own public and allies. Once having made a threat involving these values, it will be hard not to carry it out; and having done it publicly, in full view of the world, this will be particularly so. Staking a reputation is particularly important when a nation is involved in both continuous and intersecting negotiations. Continuous negotiation means that any issue will probably be one of a number of issues that will be negotiated simultaneously or in the future with the same country; intersecting negotiation refers to yet other issues that are or will be negotiated with other countries. In both cases, staking a reputation is intended to persuade the adversary with the argument: "If I make a concession, this will lower my bargaining reputation with you (or other countries), and

---

[50] Schelling, *Arms and Influence*, pp. 43–55, and *idem*, *Strategy of Conflict*, pp. 21–28.

you (or they) will expect me to concede in future negotiations. Therefore, even if I would like to satisfy you, I cannot retreat." In the repeated Berlin crises, as we shall see, the United States has always felt its reputation to be at stake; if it withdrew from West Berlin the Russians would, Washington felt, demand further concessions, and the NATO allies would be discouraged and demoralized.

Staking one's reputation, then, is a commitment from which there can be no retreat because it is too costly not to honor in terms of one's reputation for power. The automatic commitment, on the other hand, is one from which it is physically impossible to retreat. This kind of commitment has been likened to "burning one's bridges." An opponent may not find your commitment credible if you can withdraw; but if there is no bridge across which to retreat and if you have no choice but to fight, he may find the threat in support of your commitment credible. The story is told that prior to World War I, during staff talks between the British and the French military, a French officer was asked by a British colleague how many of his own country's soldiers he would need; he replied that he needed only one. This soldier would then be so placed that on the first day of a war with Germany he would be killed, thus ensuring Britain's entry into the war. One of the purposes of an American army stationed in post–World War II Europe has been to serve this "tripwire" function; the American lives lost should the Red Army attack would leave this country no choice but to fight. The enemy, knowing this, will be deterred. The ultimate but imaginary automatic commitment is Herman Kahn's fantasy doomsday machine, which would blow up the whole world if the enemy fired his nuclear weapons—even if the defender were caught by surprise. By way of contrast, one need but note that the Korean War erupted after the United States had withdrawn its forces and left no specific commitment to defense. Indeed, the officially announced U.S. defense perimeter excluded the Korean Peninsula.[51] But the main point remains: The "power to bind oneself" is the crucial factor in any bargaining situation.

Two important points need to be underlined with respect to bargaining by means of credible commitments. These and other tactics are in support of commitments that presumably leave the defender no choice as to his course of action should the opponent move despite the warnings and threats communicated to him. The deterrer "relinquishes the initiative"; he has made it known that he will stand firm regardless of cost, and the responsibility for the next move and the responsibility, therefore, for precipitating a conflict is now up to the other side. The deterrer's "initiative that forces the opponent to initiate" thus becomes the crucial coercive instrument. But in real political life irrevocable commitments are rare, for states seldom deliberately take inflexible stands from which they cannot retreat if the adversary stands firm and hostil-

[51] Spanier, *The Truman-MacArthur Controversy and the Korean War* (Cambridge, Mass.: Harvard University Press, 1959), pp. 16–21.

ities appear to be both imminent and undesirable. Threats are usually more ambiguous and commitments somewhat more porous. Irrevocable commitments may indeed place the choice of war or peace on the adversary; but they also surrender the initiator's control over events. A mixture of firmness and flexibility is therefore a more normal pattern of interaction.[52]

The other point is that the term "balance of power" underlying this kind of bargaining situation would be more useful analytically if it were divided into a *balance of resolve* and a *balance of capability*.[53] For bargaining the deterrer's requirements are threefold: the possession of capability, the willingness to use it, and the evaluation of both of these by the potential attacker. Power, however massive, is ineffective without the disposition to employ it; and even when these factors are present, they will still fail to deter unless the adversary perceives their presence. Why, it was asked earlier, did World War II erupt? We saw that the answer was Britain's policy of appeasement. The German–French/British military balance was not as lopsided throughout the late 1930's as the swift German victory in the spring of 1940 would lead one to believe.[54] What was more significant was the balance of resolve. Even after Britain had publicly pledged assistance to Poland if Germany attacked it, Hitler continued to perceive a lack of British determination. After years of appeasement, this was not surprising. Perhaps it is more surprising that British leaders felt that the Nazi leader would see their commitment as credible. Since World War II, the paradox is surely that both superpowers know that a nuclear war would devastate them, and yet each one's ability to impress the other with his willingness to run the risk of different levels of violence and, if necessary, to ascend the "escalation ladder"[55] to the rung of a strategic nuclear strike has become *the* critical factor in the balance of terror.

A *stable* balance thus depends upon one intangible and one tangible variable. The intangible element of this balance is particularly hard to evaluate. Each power's perception of the other's resolve is likely to fluctuate with time and specific occurrences. Khrushchev's image of American determination was apparently sufficiently lowered by Kennedy's early efforts—the acceptance of a neutralist coalition, including Communists, in Laos; the failure to support with American forces the abortive Bay of Pigs landing by anti-Castro Cuban refugees; the inaction at the time of the building of the Berlin Wall—so that he was tempted in 1962

[52] See particularly the two chapters entitled "Resolve and Prudence" and "Freedom of Choice" in Oran R. Young, *The Politics of Force: Bargaining During International Crises* (Princeton, N.J.: Princeton University Press, 1968), pp. 177–265.

[53] Glenn H. Snyder "Crisis Bargaining," in Charles F. Hermann, ed., *International Crises* (New York: The Free Press, 1972), p. 232.

[54] This is well analyzed by Newman, *Balance of Power in Interwar Years*, pp. 112–22, 131–46.

[55] The metaphor is from Herman Kahn, *On Escalation* (New York: Praeger Publishers, 1965), pp. 38–41.

to establish a missile base close to American shores, despite the Monroe Doctrine and in the face of Kennedy's warning about the establishment by another power of a base in the Western Hemisphere.[56] After 1962, American resolve was once again established.

Thus, the danger is that if one side (A) acts—or does not act—consistently with the other's (B's) image of how, if A were determined, A should act, B's resolve may increase and B may push again, expecting A to retreat. The latter may do so, knowing that this is expected; A's resolve, as a result, may further decline. But if at some point A vows to stand firm instead of retreating once again and, like Chamberlain, fails to make that commitment credible to B, war will erupt because of miscalculation. The balance of resolve may therefore be unstable in two respects: one, an inclination by one side toward retreating; and two, a propensity to produce hostilities when this side decides to demonstrate its will but fails to communicate the credibility of its resolve to the opponent.

It is not surprising, therefore, that both of the nuclear giants have been continuously concerned about the credibility of their commitments and have tended to see the commitments each of them has made as interdependent.[57] For it follows that if a specific commitment to preserve a particular line or "frontier" is no longer credible, regardless of how distant or unimportant it may seem, B may then come to believe that other commitments made by A are no longer believable; and this may entice B to seek further expansion of his power, since he expects that he can cross a particular line with impunity. It is, of course, true—as the critics of the disastrous commitment in Vietnam have repeatedly stressed—that a nation's interests and commitments are not all equally important and that they are scaled hierarchically on the basis of some criteria of security. Therefore, a country's defaulting on some commitments that are of lower priority does *not* signal the adversary that there will be a lack of resolve to honor more important commitments (had South Vietnam not been defended, this line of argument maintains, it would not have meant that West Berlin would not be defended). In the abstract this qualification of the "interdependence of commitments" is correct. But two key questions remain: One, how can B always be sure of A's ranking of his priorities; and two, even if B can make some pretty good guesses, will A's yielding of a lower priority commitment not tempt B to test A's resolve in an area of greater importance? After all, he cannot without testing really know whether A's determination will indeed be stronger. The

[56] Elie Abel, *The Missile Crisis* (New York: Bantam Books, 1966), pp. 24–26, 28, and Young, *Politics of Force*, pp. 79–80, 87. Khrushchev's explanation in his "memoirs" emphasizes only his desire to defend Cuba from an alleged American invasion. For an evaluation of this motivation, see Arnold Horelick, "The Cuban Missile Crisis: An Analysis of Soviet Calculations and Behavior," *World Politics*, April, 1964, pp. 365–69.

[57] Schelling, *Arms and Influence*, p. 56.

failure of A to honor a commitment in one area, in short, may be seen by the potential attacker as an indication that other commitments also may not be honored because states generally feel that their over-all reputation is more important than, and relatively *independent* of, the specific interest and commitment being challenged.[58] "Weakness is weakness."

One final point needs to be added in connection with the intangible nature of power. The test of deterrence, as was emphasized, is in terms of things that do *not* occur. Precisely because it is impossible ever to say with absolute certainty why an event did not occur—or even that it might have and did not—and because one therefore cannot prove that "nonevents" are due either to a specific weapons system or to resolve shown in support of specific commitments, both issues have, in an open society, increasingly given rise to differing evaluations; and, as the price—in money and in lives—for preserving deterrence has become increasingly taxing and agonizing, these questions have generated intense debate.

Arms Control and the Stability of Mutual Deterrence

Tangibly, there is a need for *forces-in-being* that can implement the "massive retaliation" with which the deterrer threatens his opponent should he be tempted to strike. Before World War II, states normally had some existing military forces with which they hoped to prevent an enemy attack; but these were never near to the strength of the forces they could mobilize after war broke out. Inasmuch as war was not fatal, there was no reason to keep large and expensive forces continuously ready. Plowshares were converted into swords after the attack. This was particularly true for the United States. Protected by two oceans, and not therefore subject to invasion or even air attack, it had the time to mobilize its vast power after it had become involved in war. But nuclear deterrence required peacetime readiness of *all* the forces that would be required for retaliation if an enemy attack occurred. For the enemy must never doubt for even a moment—if deterrence is to be permanent—that he would be committing suicide should he strike first.

The need for an offensive superiority is therefore constant and in turn requires unfailing concern with effective delivery systems. The difficulty is in the rapid technological changes that have occurred about every five years since 1945. These, like the factor of resolve, have become a critical factor affecting the stability of the nuclear balance of power. Even the early nuclear delivery systems tended to destabilize the postwar equilibrium because of the ability of fast bombers to launch a surprise attack. It is true, of course, that even before the development of high-speed bombers surprise attack had been possible. The Germans had achieved it against the Russians in 1941, despite the large-scale movement of

[58] Snyder, "Crisis Bargaining," pp. 232–33.

troops to Poland it necessitated; and the Japanese were highly successful at Pearl Harbor a few months later. The speed of postwar bombers, however, made such an attack even more feasible, particularly as it would no longer have to be preceded by massive troop or ship movements. Because forces-in-being were absolutely essential for deterrence, and bombers constantly flew training missions, the potential victim's first knowledge of an impending attack was not likely to come before planes approached very near to, or crossed into, his territory. Thus, while the United States, for instance, sought to deter a Soviet attack by threatening to drop enough bombs virtually to wipe the Soviet Union off the map, its threat might be meaningless if most American bombers were to be destroyed in a surprise attack. The surviving bombers might not be able to retaliate with sufficient destructiveness. Not all of them would have enough fuel to reach their targets. Soviet fighters and ground-to-air missiles, alerted for the arrival of the bombers that did reach Soviet territory, would be able to shoot down many, if not most. The few that managed to penetrate Soviet defenses might no longer be able to impose catastrophic damage. The resulting damage might, indeed, be acceptable to the Soviet leaders if it would mean, once and for all, the elimination of their deadliest enemy and its ability to destroy the Soviet Union.

The vulnerability of bombers to a nuclear Pearl Harbor, in short, rendered the balance of power or mutual deterrence very unstable because of the high dividend their destruction would pay to the side striking the initial blow. Possessing the bombs was not enough by itself to ensure that the balance would not result in war. The possibility of eliminating the opponent's retaliatory bombers—bombers above ground being "soft" targets—constituted a powerful incentive to attack. The consequent balance of terror was therefore "delicate." What conditions might instigate an opponent's first strike against one's retaliatory force? And what could be done to prevent this and "stabilize" mutual deterrence?[59] These were the questions to which students of "arms control" addressed themselves in the late 1950's. Arms control rejected the feasibility of general disarmament and assumed that neither conflicts among states nor nuclear weapons would be abolished;[60] instead, man's best hope for earthly salvation lay in the "control" of armaments. In a competitive state system, deterrence was recognized as the only feasible policy. It had to be improved, however, to be made "safe."

Arms control thus supplemented the more traditional defense policies, as its aim was identical: to protect the national security by deterring war. Whereas disarmament stressed the reduction of a nation's military *capability*, either completely or partially, arms control emphasized the

[59] The continuing concern with this issue in terms of different strategies and changing weapons systems is elaborated by William W. Kaufmann, *The McNamara Strategy* (New York: Harper & Row, 1964).

[60] See below, Chapter 8.

elimination of American and Soviet *incentives* to strike first. Two presuppositions underlay arms control; one, that despite the continuation of their political conflict both nuclear powers shared a *common* interest in avoiding nuclear war; and two, that, although the basic tensions were due to political antagonism, the nature of the delivery systems increased tensions even more because they provided a strong and *independent* incentive for a first strike.[61] This incentive was simply the paramount importance of hitting first, for to come in second was to lose; to be caught off guard could be fatal. Policy-makers thus seemed to have no choice but to initiate a strike.

If the only defense was indeed the offense, then a *pre-emptive strike* was a particular danger during crisis periods. Such a contingency differs from a *preventive strike*, in which the aggressor coolly calculates beforehand to strike at his opponent in the belief that he possesses the capacity to obliterate him; the attacker picks a specific date and then sends his force on its way, irrespective of any possible provocation. But in a pre-emptive blow, the attack is launched in order to forestall the enemy's initial blow. The aggressor in this instance believes that his opponent is about to hit him; he therefore launches his strike in order to destroy the enemy's forces before they take off. The attack occurs as a result of moves on the *other side* that are interpreted as menacing.[62]

The role miscalculation might play in precipitating a pre-emptive strike becomes clear. The sign that an opponent is about to launch an attack is likely to be ambiguous. He might be taking measures not to attack but to render his strategic force less vulnerable and thereby to enhance his deterrent stance. For instance, he might send many of his bombers into the air in order to avoid having them caught on the ground; by rendering them less prone to sudden destruction, he was trying to caution the other side against launching an attack. But his action could easily be misinterpreted as a possible prelude to attack. In a situation of mutual vulnerability in which the "nice guy" finishes last, delay could prove fatal. Offensive action was therefore the only wise course: " 'Self-defense' becomes peculiarly compounded if we have to worry about his

---

[61] Fine introductions to the field of arms control can be found in Hedley Bull, *The Control of the Arms Race*, 2d ed. (New York: Praeger Publishers, 1965), and Thomas C. Schelling and Morton H. Halperin, *Strategy and Arms Control* (New York: Twentieth Century Fund, 1961).

[62] In Schelling's words:

The "equalizer" of the Old West [the pistol] made it possible for *either* man to kill the other; it did not assure that *both* would be killed. . . . The advantage of shooting first aggravates any incentive to shoot. As the survivor might put it, "He was about to kill me in self-defense, so I had to kill him in self-defense." Or, "He, thinking I was about to kill him in self-defense, was about to kill me in self-defense, so I had to kill him in self-defense." But if both were assured of living long enough to shoot back with unimpaired aim, there would be no advantage in jumping the gun and little reason to fear that the other would try it.

Schelling, *Strategy of Conflict*, pp. 232–33. Emphasis in original.

striking us to keep us from striking him to keep him from striking us."[63]
What is important, therefore, is not what A *intends* to do, but B's *perception* of A's intentions. And in this type of hair-trigger situation, the interpretation would not be conservative. Because the survival of the nation would be at stake, the worst has to be assumed. The strategic bombers of both sides were, of course, ready at all times to take off on their missions. When one side placed a sizable number of them in the air, the possibility of a sudden attack increased. Even defensive actions intended merely to enhance one's deterrent power might thus serve to intensify international tensions and perhaps touch off a nuclear conflagration. Paradoxically, then, the very weapons intended to deter nuclear war might well precipitate this catastrophe.

The crucial problem arms control had to answer in these circumstances was how a preventive war and pre-emptive strike could be forestalled. The remedy, as already suggested, was to render each side's retaliatory or second-strike forces invulnerable. (The vulnerable bomber deterrent was a first-strike force. If it were surprised on its bases, most of it could be wiped out; the fact that it had to be used first created the dangerous situation of mutual trigger-happiness. A second-strike force is one that can absorb an initial blow and *still* effectively perform its retaliatory task. The deterrent force that matters is, in brief, that part of the force left after an enemy attack, not the size of the force that existed before the attack.) The best method of attaining this, it was thought during the bomber era, was to develop a well-protected retaliatory force composed primarily of solid-fuel missiles that could be fired instantly. They could be dispersed more easily than bombers, which are generally concentrated on a relatively small number of bases whose location is easily discernible. Missiles could also be hardened—that is, buried in concrete silos that could withstand great pressure. Finally, and most important, missiles could be moved around constantly so that the enemy would never know their exact location. Mobile missiles, such as the Polaris, which are carried under water on nuclear-powered submarines, are virtually impossible to hit. To the extent that an enemy in a first strike would seek to destroy such mobile missiles, an oceanic system would have the additional advantage of moving an initial strike—or at least a good part of that strike—away from the land or the "zone of the interior."

The importance of the dispersal, hardening, and mobility of missiles lay in the fact that these deprived a surprise attack of its rationale. The entire justification for a first strike had been to surprise the opponent's "soft" bombers on the ground and destroy them. But when the opponent's retaliatory power consists entirely or primarily of mobile, solid-fuel, long-range missiles, it is impossible to know where to hit in order to destroy this retaliatory capacity. Obliterating the enemy's cities would benefit the aggressor very little if he still retained this capacity. Surprise,

---

[63] *Ibid.*, p. 231.

therefore, no longer confers any significant advantage to the side that hits first. Conversely, to the extent missiles become largely invulnerable —particularly under water—there is no longer any incentive for a pre-emptive blow. The enemy's first strike cannot destroy the ability to strike back. The fact that a second-strike force remains is the best guarantee against war. *Invulnerable deterrents thus stabilize mutual deterrence.*[64] Once the advantage of the initial attack was greatly reduced, if not eliminated, the incentive to strike at all, and therefore the possibility of war, also disappeared.

Four significant points are inherent in this analysis of the achievement of a stable mutual deterrence. First, *the balance of capability does not necessarily require an equality in numbers.* A balance is achieved when both sides have second-strike forces able to destroy the opponent's homeland after absorbing an initial blow. The size that either Moscow or Washington thinks such a second-strike force ought to be may vary quite a bit. Whether one side has 600 missiles and the other 1,000 was never the crux of the nuclear capability equation. The crux was whether you could absorb a first blow and then in retaliation still deliver the *coup de grâce.* Thus if one side had invulnerable weapons, arms control theory would suggest that 600 missiles would probably suffice; on the other hand, if its weapons were vulnerable, arms control would suggest that perhaps 1,000, and perhaps more, missiles would be needed. Arms control, to repeat, does not necessarily counsel a reduction in arms as the disarmament approach. Arms control's primary interest is in eliminating the incentives for attack; whether this requires more or fewer weapons is secondary. But anything above recommended force levels would be "overkill," because once the enemy had been destroyed the capacity to do so a second and third time is pointless.

Second, therefore, *what is particularly significant is that the weapons are the right kinds of weapons.* Historically, the arms one country possessed were a plus factor whereas the opponent's were a minus factor. In the context of arms control thinking, however, weapons that contribute to the stability of the nuclear balance are a plus, *irrespective of which side possesses them;* weapons that detract from this stability are a major factor, again no matter which side owns them. Thus, arms control would suggest that if only one side could invent a new, let us say, invulnerable weapon while the other still had only soft weapons, the former should build some of its new arms and give them to the latter! The logic is that, if this is not done, the side with the vulnerable arms will feel that before things get too bad for it, it had better launch a preventive war; or, in a crisis where it cannot afford to wait and see whether it will be struck, it may do so pre-emptively because this is its only option. Such a transfer of weapons from one power to its opponent is, of course, unheard of and in our nationalistic age would be considered traitorous. Luckily, such a

---

[64] *Ibid.*, p. 232.

transfer in practice is not necessary. Throughout the twentieth century, the great powers have produced new weapons at approximately the same time.[65] After all, their cultural levels are about the same, and their scientific knowledge is at roughly the same stage of development; men ask themselves similar questions and come up with similar answers. The period after World War II, when the United States held an atomic monopoly until the Soviets exploded their bomb in 1949, stands out as a major exception. But both tested their first hydrogen devices within a few months of each other. And the American development of the ICBM has not lagged far behind that of the Soviets.

The third significant point is that, instead of building weapons for the adversary, *the parties to the conflict*—and this has been much more true of the United States than of Russia—*inform each other of their defense posture by a succession of "signals."* Historically these matters were considered state secrets; the less a potential adversary knew about one's military strength and its disposition, the better. But traditional logic has once more been superseded. To reassure an adversary so that he will not be tempted to launch either a preventive or pre-emptive blow becomes the prime consideration. In the United States, of course, there is a great deal of available information through, for example, the mass media, Congressional hearings, and books published on defense and arms control by the civilian defense community. These are supplemented in two ways: by the speeches of high-ranking government officials, from the President and Secretary of Defense to the lower levels of Under and Assistant Secretaries in the major departments concerned exclusively with foreign and military policies; and, even more important, by the actual deployment of specific weapons. Thus, during the 1960's there were continuous speeches telling the Russians why the bomber was being phased out; the accompanying build-up of land- and sea-based missiles was the evidence of a changing strategy and of American concern with stabilizing the military part of the balance. What is said is clearly important, but what is *done* is paramount. Together, the two are intended to influence Soviet perception of American military strategy and —above all—to elicit the appropriate response in order to assure a stable balance of capabilities. As with deterrence and the tactics of commitment, negotiations with the opponent are largely conducted by actions, for it is these that largely convey intentions. But this kind of communication must be two-way; for if one of the two parties refuses to tell the adversary the nature of certain weapons or strategy—in order to exploit the opponent's uncertainty for his own benefit—the uninformed state, in fear of its security and expecting the worst, will very likely undertake acts that may destabilize the deterrent equation. If, of course, the powers

[65] See Samuel P. Huntington, "Arms Races: Prerequisites and Results," in Carl J. Friedrich and Seymour E. Harris, eds., *Public Policy* (Cambridge, Mass.: Graduate School of Public Administration, Harvard University, 1958), pp. 72–73.

still wish to talk directly and explicitly to each other in order to explain their deterrent postures and achieve a formal arms control agreement, they can do so.

The final point brings us back to the issue of the numbers of weapons. While a strategic "balance" does not require equal numbers of weapons and while the right kinds of weapons are crucial for the stability of mutual deterrence, *numbers are not completely unimportant*. Stability is the result of each side conveying to the other as much as possible its defensive intentions. If one thinks the other is building first strike weapons, the stability is endangered. Similarly, beyond a certain hard-to-define limit, a superior number of weapons for one side may be perceived—rightly or wrongly—by the opponent as no longer signifying defensive purposes. Again, he is likely to fear that this many weapons, in comparison to his own, will constitute a first strike threat which is likely to be exploited diplomatically. A large numbers gap could, therefore, affect the balance of resolve. Thus, although a gap in the numbers of strategic arms each side possesses may be tolerable for the balance of capability, it is not an elastic gap; it can only be "stretched" so far.

The above also suggests that there are two different types of arms control "agreements," one informal, the other formal. The U.S. shift from bombers to missiles was justified as making America more secure (a "possession goal"), because it minimized or eliminated the risk of a Soviet first strike; but this shift was also explained by Washington to Moscow as helping to stabilize the nuclear balance and, therefore, of benefit to both (a "milieu goal"). In brief, the public explanations of the deterrent posture and deployment of missiles were intended to induce the Russians to follow the American example. If both sides moved away from vulnerable to invulnerable deterrent systems, the resulting arms control "agreement" stabilizing the nuclear balance was an informal one, arrived at and kept because it was in the interest of both sides to do so. Diplomats had never met, no explicit and specific proposals were ever advanced, and no formal bargaining occurred; rather, the agreement had been arrived at tacitly by mutual example.

On the other hand, other arms control agreements were arrived at by traditional diplomatic bargaining between the United States and the U.S.S.R.: the 1963 limited nuclear test ban, the 1967 outer space treaty, and the 1971 sea-bed treaty, which forbade emplacement of nuclear arms in these areas; the 1970 nuclear nonproliferation treaty; and, most important of all, the 1972 strategic arms limitation treaty (although one part of it was embodied in an executive agreement rather than a formal treaty that would have had to be submitted to the U.S. Senate). For a better understanding of the complexity of arms control, the difficulties of negotiating agreements explicitly, and some of the problems involved, we shall now look in more detail at the strategic arms limitation talks (SALT I and II).

How to Negotiate: SALT

Until the 1972 SALT arms control agreement, the formal agreements achieved were either largely symbolic or a recognition by both Russia and America that they each had a special stake as well as a common interest in the preservation of peace. Agreements were confined to keeping such zones as outer space and the sea beds demilitarized or slowing down the rate of nuclear acquisition by other states. The SALT talks were the first set of serious negotiations to focus on American and Soviet strategic forces and to attempt a formal limitation of the numbers of offensive and defensive missiles each side possessed.

For two such powerful states as the United States and the Soviet Union even to sit down together and negotiate on a matter of common concern—and not negotiate primarily for such side effects as propaganda, deception, or gaining information—they must both *first want an agreement*. However desirable or morally worthy the cause, or however true it may be as a general proposition that states ought to negotiate and settle this or that problem, be it the American-Russian arms race or Israeli-Arab peace, this is unlikely to occur until both parties find the circumstances propitious. One side usually takes the lead in attempting to initiate such negotiations by seeking to persuade the other that it would be more advantageous to negotiate an agreement than to let things go on as they are. The question is whether the side to whom the proposal to settle is addressed agrees that nonagreement will have greater unfavorable consequences than agreement. Remember what might almost be called the first law of preservation in the state system: Be suspicious. One side's gain—and any proposal from a potential adversary is assumed to incorporate advantages for himself—is usually considered the other side's loss. And this fear of a loss is particularly acute in the military sphere, where, as in the U.S.-Soviet bipolar strategic realm, each is hypersensitive to the possibility of being left militarily inferior. Few arms agreements exist in history precisely because states, driven by their sense of insecurity, prefer to *add* arms to their already existing arsenals to assure themselves that they will not find themselves in such a quandary.

It was the Johnson Administration in the late 1960's that first approached the Russians about the possibility of SALT as both sides stood on the eve of a new set of arms races in defensive and offensive weapons —the antiballistic missile (ABM) and the multiple, independently targeted re-entry vehicle (MIRV), an ICBM with multiple warheads, each of which could be fired at separate targets as the carrying missile keeps on changing its trajectory. In 1964 the Russians had also begun constructing 60-odd ABM launchers around Moscow; and while the Galosh system, as it was named, was not considered technologically advanced, it was assumed that they were working on a second generation of ABMs and that, if successful, an extension of the ABM defenses could probably be expected.[66] Historically, the Russians have always placed heavy emphasis on defense. The Soviet Premier had declared that weapons that might save lives were good weapons and would not, therefore, spur a new offensive arms race, as the Americans contended. By the time the Nixon Administration came into office in 1969, each superpower faced a rapidly changing situation. In 1966 the American arsenal had stood at approximately its 1969 size: 1,000 Minuteman and 54 Titan II land-based ICBM's, 41 Polaris submarines with a total of 656 missiles, and 450 B-52 and 86 B-58 bombers. The Russians at that time had about 250 ICBM's and about 150 bombers capable of hitting the United States. But since 1966 they had increased their missile force fivefold to approximately 1,350 land-based missiles, about 300 more than the United States, and they were continuing this build-up; in addition, they were constructing a fleet of Polaris-type submarines.[67]

These developments clearly affected the issue of the stability of the deterrent balance. It was not so much the numbers of Soviet land-based missiles that proved to be the concern as the impact of these new weapons themselves. Both the Soviet Union and the United States stood on the threshold of acquiring large numbers of MIRVs and ABMs. Their development was, furthermore, related. It was the Soviet deployment of the ABM that led the United States to interest itself in MIRVs. For if ABMs could be engineered to have a high rate of success, the U.S. retaliatory capacity would be seriously diminished—perhaps to the point where the Soviets would dare a first strike because they no longer needed to fear the possibility of virtual suicide. The American answer was to inundate the defenses with so many warheads coming from so many different trajectories that the offense could keep its edge over the defense and therefore continue to make deterrence credible. Hence the MIRV. The Soviets, however, were also developing MIRV, and Washington therefore felt a need for a limited ABM deployment to protect enough of its Minutemen so that, even if the opponent were tempted to hit first and destroyed many of these, enough missiles would survive to assure that the deterrent threat would remain effective.[68]

Of these two new weapons systems, the MIRV was probably the most dangerous for the future stability of deterrence. The MIRV obviously had the advantage over single-headed missiles in providing its side with a far larger number of warheads for the same number of silos and boost-

---

[66] For the Secretary of Defense's report on a renewal of Soviet ABM site construction, see *New York Times*, April 28, 1971.

[67] Institute for Strategic Studies, *The Military Balance 1970–71* (London, 1970).

[68] Jerome B. Wiesner, Abram Chayes, *et al.*, *ABM: An Evaluation of the Decision to Employ an Antiballistic Missile System* (New York: Signet, 1969), and Johan J. Holst and William Schneider, Jr., eds., *Why ABM? Policy Issues in the Missile Defense Controversy* (New York: Pergamon Press, 1969).

ers, even though the individual yield would be far smaller. But this was, as already seen, not necessarily a disadvantage, because two warheads of one-half megaton were likely to cause greater damage than a single one-megaton warhead. Thus, to take the American example, the U.S. plan was to place three independently targeted warheads of about 100 kilotons (five times more powerful than the Hiroshima bomb) upon half of its Minutemen and replace the Polaris missiles on thirty-one submarines with the Poseidon, carrying ten apiece, each of 30 to 40 kilotons. The total number of American warheads would then be increased by 1,500 Minutemen plus 4,960 Poseidons for a total of 6,460. The Soviet Union would likewise increase the number of its warheads.

But this advantage of the MIRV might not outweigh its principal disadvantage, the possibility that MIRVs might become first-strike weapons.[69] Initially developed to help penetrate any ABM system, the MIRV can be engineered so that it can knock out the adversary's silos. Indeed, the Nixon Administration's main worry—and the reason it wanted some missile protection by ABMs—was the Soviet SS-9,[70] of which by late 1969 the Soviet Union reportedly had 280 either deployed or under construction; and the estimated production rate was fifty per year.[71] While the SS-9 could carry a single warhead of between 20 and 25 megatons, it was thought more likely that it would carry three 5-megaton warheads. In addition, the Defense Department believed the missile to have sufficient accuracy, and therefore argued that its purpose was, to launch a first strike, not to retaliate. A large yield and high accuracy presumably would enable the SS-9 to destroy a Minuteman; it was calculated that 425 SS-9s, which Russia could have by 1975, might threaten the entire Minuteman force. By contrast, the first generation of Minuteman 3s and Poseidons were said to be only retaliatory weapons; their yields were claimed to be too small to destroy Soviet missiles protected by silos. Even though that is probably true, a second generation nevertheless could obviously be designed to have larger warheads and also be first-strike counterforce weapons.

The key to nuclear stability, however, remains mutual invulnerability of deterrent forces. Each nation must have sufficient weapons to ride out an attack and be able to retaliate afterward. It is the stability of the balance, then, which is endangered by the MIRVs—if the MIRVs could really knock out so substantial a number of the opponent's retaliatory force. The uncertainty resulting during the period of MIRV deployment would again bring up the chief danger of the bomber period—that

[69] Leo Sartori, "The Myth of MIRV," *Saturday Review*, August 30, 1969. For a critique of this possibility and the lack of any political payoff from any position of strategic superiority the U.S.S.R. might achieve, if that was its aim, see Benjamin S. Lambeth "Deterrence in the MIRV Era," *World Politics* (January, 1972), p. 221 ff.

[70] John W. Finney, "SS-9 Helps Administration Score Points in Missile Debate," *New York Times*, March 24, 1969.

[71] William Beecher, "The Nuclear Arsenals: A Balance of Terror," *New York Times*, November 18, 1969.

of a pre-emptive strike by one or the other side, particularly during crises when each side is jittery enough without having the additional worry of the security of its strategic deterrent.

Here is an instance where, contrary to our rule about arms control communication between the two powers, the Russians clearly did not—and would not—communicate the nature of a major new weapons system to the United States, which in turn led American policy-makers, rightly or wrongly, to draw the worst possible conclusions. The Nixon Administration, therefore, decided that the United States too must deploy ABMs. Interestingly enough, President Nixon, in his speech to the country announcing the establishment of two ABM bases, stressed the arms control factor.[72] Before leaving office, his predecessor had recommended a "thin" ABM system around a number of key cities, ostensibly as protection against the kind of small-scale attack it was thought the Chinese Communists would be capable of by the mid-1970's.[73] Nixon switched the ABM to safeguard not cities but some of the deterrent missile force. Cities, he said, were to be left open as hostages. If the United States defended its cities—and it was known that the Joint Chiefs were eager for a "thick" defense protecting the nation's fifty major urban and industrial areas—the Soviet Union might think it was getting ready for an American first strike. It could, went the argument, risk exposing U.S. cities to Soviet retaliation if those cities were really well protected. The Russians might be enticed to attack before sufficient protection had been provided. Furthermore, Nixon added, by safeguarding a sufficient portion of U.S. strike forces to ensure that the American deterrent capacity would never be in doubt, the Safeguard ABM need not spur a Soviet reaction leading to a new arms race. The Soviet retaliatory capacity against the U.S. population, in other words, would remain unaffected. The United States would therefore remain deterred. Only the Soviet ability to launch a successful surprise attack against the American deterrent force would be reduced.

Thus, a new set of offensive and defensive arms races seemed likely. Each side feared military inferiority, the United States because it saw the Soviets overtaking the United States in numbers of land-based missiles, rapidly catching up—presumably to surpass—the Americans in quantity of sea-based missiles, and above all endangering the Minuteman with the SS-9; the Soviets because the United States was already multiplying the warheads on both its land- and sea-based missiles while they were still only testing MIRVs, thus giving the United States a vastly superior number of warheads with which to attack, plus the American development of a new, even larger and technologically far better strategic submarine, the Trident, with more longer-range multiple-headed missiles, while Soviet submarines were qualitatively still inferior to the American Polaris and Poseidon submarines. But this common fear of

---

[72] *New York Times*, March 15, 1969.
[73] See below, Chapter 14, for a fuller explanation.

being left militarily inferior had to be balanced against certain other interests, some of which the superpowers shared, which provided counterbalancing incentives for some sort of arms control agreement. In short, the early 1970's was one of those passing moments when common interests and hopes seemed stronger than conflicting interests and fears, thus providing a basis for negotiations to occur.

More specifically, both sides were concerned with the possible destabilization of the nuclear balance. Washington was driven into negotiations by the Soviet SS-9 buildup; Moscow desired negotiations because it reportedly feared a large-scale American ABM deployment. It thereby acknowledged that defensive and offensive weapons cannot be neatly separated as it had maintained before, but stimulate one another. Second, both countries realized the very expensive nature of new arms production and deployments. Spending huge sums of money on weapons confronted both countries with the contentious issue of guns versus butter, although this issue was obviously more public and controversial in the United States where war weariness stemming from Vietnam plus a new awareness of major domestic problems produced a sharp debate on spending priorities between domestic and foreign—especially defense —policies. The American mood of disillusionment with foreign policy supported rather than opposed moves toward a *détente* with Russia. For Russia too, its conflict with China played a role: a desire to relax tensions with the United States in order to concentrate on China and an apprehension that renewed arms races plus rising political tensions with the United States might speed up the U.S. *rapprochement* with China, a possibility President Nixon shrewdly exploited during the arms talks. A lagging Russian economy falling behind the West in the Second Industrial (Computer) Revolution also provided Moscow with an incentive for a relaxation of international tension; it needed Western, particularly American, capital and technology. Common, as well as different but conflicting interests, thus led the two powers to begin negotiations.

But it is one thing for both parties to reach a point where they want agreement, and quite another to turn that wish, which may be qualified with a degree of suspicion, into a *specific settlement*.[74] This takes hard and long negotiations with the constant possibility that specific issues cannot be reconciled and that the talks can break down despite the desire to agree. Let us briefly examine just two such issues. The first was the definition of a strategic offensive missile. From the beginning, the differences on this issue almost stalled the negotiations. The Russians insisted that all nuclear weapons that could reach their homeland were strategic. Thus, they argued, American forward based systems (FBS), such as certain tactical nuclear weapons and fighter-bombers in Europe, as well as in the Mediterranean, were strategic weapons which had to be included in an over-all offensive weapons limitation. The United States

[74] The story of the SALT I negotiations are detailed in John Newhouse, *Cold Dawn* (New York: Holt, Rinehart & Winston, 1973).

rejected the inclusion of FBS in the negotiations, arguing that they were tactical weapons to be used in support of local theater operations and that Washington could not unilaterally decide such a matter anyway in total disregard of its principal alliance partners. Were the Russians genuinely fearful of a strike force that constituted only about 2 per cent of America's total striking capacity, or were they using FBS as a diplomatic tactic to divide NATO? Interestingly enough, the Soviets rejected an American counterclaim to include within the Russian strategic forces the large numbers of medium-range (MRBM) and intermediate-range (IRBM) missiles that the Soviet Union had long aimed at Western Europe.

Even if calling FBS strategic was not a canny negotiating ploy to strengthen the Soviet bargaining position, the subsequent Soviet offer to separate the negotiations on offensive and defensive forces because the former were stalled, and to concentrate only on ABMs, was a very shrewd diplomatic tactic. The fear of many influential Americans that if the United States did not accept this Soviet proposition it would jeopardize even an ABM agreement led to intense pressure from segments of academia, the prestige press, and Congress upon the Nixon Administration to accept an ABM agreement only as at least a partial halt to the arms race. The President refused to budge, however, asserting that to limit the numbers of ABMs without at the same time limiting offensive arms would be to enhance the Soviet Union's offensive capability, which was continuing to increase at a rapid rate. A defensive arms limitation was acceptable to the United States, the President insisted, only if it were tied to an offensive arms limitation. A compromise was reached after Washington refused to move. Negotiations on defensive weapons would be taken up first, but a final agreement would include an offensive weapons limitation.

SALT I therefore incorporated two sets of agreements. The first of these was a formal treaty limiting each side to 200 ABMs, half of which were to protect the capital city of each power (the Soviets insisted on this, presumably not just out of fear of an American attack but apparently even more out of fear of a Chinese attack on Moscow). The other half was to protect missiles. (A protocol added at the 1974 Nixon-Brezhnev meeting cut this number in half and limited each side's ABMs to one site.) This ABM limitation was significant in that it not only forestalled an ABM race but also, by limiting each to relatively few ABM's, ensured the all-important superiority of the offense upon which deterrence rests. (For example, had the Soviets been able to build a large-scale ABM network in the absence of an agreement, the deterrent capability of U.S. submarine-launched missiles, which are not particularly accurate and therefore are best targeted against cities rather than missile silos, might have been gravely weakened.)

On the other hand, the offensive arms limitation was attained (1) by *not* including FBS, Soviet MRBMs and IRBMs, or the intercontinental bombers of each side, an exclusion of clear advantage to the United States, with its far larger strategic bomber force, and (2) by simply freezing the over-all American and Russian offensive missile forces. By and large, this avoided a whole set of complex issues for the moment, postponing them until SALT II, making the SALT I agreement possible. The offensive five-year interim agreement, which was signed by the United States as an executive agreement rather than as a treaty, froze the United States to 1,054 ICBMs plus 656 on nuclear submarines and the Soviet Union to 1,618 ICBMs plus 740 on nuclear submarines. (Actually, provisions for replacing some older land- and sea-based weapons with more missiles to be launched from submarines could change this distribution somewhat.) All in all, given the better than 3 to 1 American strategic bomber superiority plus the U.S. lead in MIRVing, the offensive accord meant that the greater size of the Russian arsenal was matched off against the technological superiority of the American arsenal. Each side, as already mentioned, had the right to make *qualitative* changes to improve its weapons but had to remain within an over-all quantitative agreement, thus preserving "parity" between the two powers. While no on-site inspection to check against violations was decided upon, both sides pledged themselves not to interfere with each other's reconnaissance or spy satellites, which will be the principal means to check compliance with both accords.

In addition, further negotiations were to be held to work out a final over-all offensive missile treaty; clearly, the nuclear warhead ratios, estimated to be 5,700 for the United States to 2,500 for the Soviet Union by the beginning of 1973, would change as the Soviets replaced their current missiles, including the SS-9, with larger missiles capable of carrying up to twenty warheads. Thus the United States was concerned that a SALT II agreement reflect a greater numerical equality in missiles numbers but, in 1972, American negotiators confronted the fact that the Russians, in the absence of a limitation agreement, would continue to build up their offensive capability while the U.S. Congress was in no mood to fund a corresponding American numerical build-up in order to pressure the Soviets to accept a numerically more balanced accord. Thus, to give but one example, the United States was willing to allow the Soviets sixty-two nuclear submarines, twenty-one more than America itself possessed. But, as the U.S. Navy estimated, the Soviets could by the end of the 1970's construct between eighty and ninety submarines; limiting them to sixty-two submarines while the United States still had better submarines and missiles and could base the subs in Europe nearer to Russia, thereby keeping more on station at all times, thus appeared as a good deal. (The Americans' own estimate independently agreed that the Russians had to have sixty-two submarines to keep an equivalent number on station.) The final equation was finally decided in 1974–75.

At that point, the two superpowers agreed on the general principle that parity would mean exactly that: Equal numbers of strategic weapons for each side. Both countries would cap their total number of missiles *and* bombers at 2,400 each (the United States had about 450 bombers, Russia 160), and each would be able to MIRV 1,320 missiles; FBS was not included, a Russian concession. They also agreed that a permanent offensive arms limitation was impossible and that, therefore, their accord would last until 1985, thereby extending the 1972 five-year freeze. The Russian-set ceiling on strategic arms, while higher than the United States had wanted —indeed it would allow the United States to build up to the ceiling—did require somewhat of a cutback of the Russian strategic force. At best, like the offensive freeze in 1972, which allowed the Soviet Union a larger strategic force, SALT II seems to have averted an even larger Soviet build-up. It left until later possible reductions of these sizable American and Soviet forces. More immediately, there were other questions to be settled. For example, the agreement placed no limits on the size and lifting-power or "throw-weight" of missiles, or the number of warheads they could carry. Given the far larger throw-weight of Russian missiles and their ability therefore to carry more warheads than American missiles, would a Soviet land-based force—if most of its MIRVs were placed on this force—constitute a first-strike threat against the U.S. Minutemen, although the Russians were to abide by the 1972 ceiling of 300 on their huge land-based missiles? In turn, would this require the costly replacement of Minutemen with a force of larger U.S. missiles capable of carrying more and larger warheads? Or would it lead to an increasing shift of U.S. strategic forces to the sea and a reduction of Minutemen? The question of preserving strategic stability thus remained a critical issue. Nevertheless, while SALT II was only a ten-year agreement and placed a cap on offensive arms higher than the total existing U.S. forces, SALT I and II together remain an important achievement, a symptom of the need for the two superpowers to work together to avoid war and, at the same time, their continuing distrust of one another and rivalry in the world.[75]

One final point about diplomatic tactics: The Nixon and Ford administrations attempted in many of their diplomatic dealings to link various issues. That is, instead of negotiations limited to one specific area of concern and attempting to achieve some compromise only on that issue, it attempted to link different issues in its negotiations. The belief was that this would create many webs of interdependence between these two strong competitors and that this, in turn would mute their conflict as the different bureaucracies gained a vested interest in American-Russian cooperation. In Henry Kissinger's words,

> we have sought to channel our relations with the U.S.S.R. into a more stable framework—a structure of interrelated and interdependent agreements. Forward movement in our relations must be on a broad front so

[75] For an evaluation of SALT I, see Morton Kaplan, ed., *SALT* (Morristown, N.J.: General Learning Press, 1974), and William R. Kintner and Robert L. Pfaltzgraff, Jr., *SALT* (Pittsburgh: University of Pittsburgh Press, 1973).

that groups and individuals in both countries will have a vested interest in the maintainance of peace and the growth of a stable international order.[76]

The SALT agreement came in part, as suggested before, because Soviet economic needs permitted the United States to link the political-military strategic issue to the economic one, however subtle that linkage might at times have been officially expressed. Other areas of cooperation—in space, health services, environmental problems, and so forth—were all linked to the broader political and strategic issues. Each superpower, then, gets something it wants; progress in one area is conditioned to progress in another.

To sum up, diplomacy, if it is to achieve agreement, whether that agreement is arrived at tacitly or explicitly, whether that agreement is informally understood or formally negotiated and ratified, depends upon a number of conditions: the mobilization of power, the application of the right kind of power to the specific situation, common interests among the adversaries, the ability to exploit these interests into initiating negotiations at the right time, the careful mixing of credible sanctions and desired rewards, and the possession of enough patience, tolerance, stubbornness, diligence, careful preparation, and, probably, a sense of humor, to turn common interests into a detailed, concrete formal accord or informally understood deployment and behavior. What we have seen to be true for the exercise of the threat of violence in support of deterrence, as well as formal bilateral negotiations as in SALT, is even truer for crisis management and limited wars, where the key issues for the policy-makers are, on the one hand, to defend perceived national security interests and, on the other hand, to avoid triggering a nuclear clash by either avoiding violence altogether or keeping it under careful control.

[76] *New York Times*, March 8, 1974.

7 Coercion and Violence as Bargaining Techniques

Crisis Management

The postwar world has been characterized not only by deterrence but also by frequent American-Soviet confrontations and crises. This is not really surprising, for, in drawing "frontiers" and defining their respective spheres of influence, the two superpowers had only each other to watch. While this might at times become tedious, neither could see the other make a push without itself pushing back. Crises are probably unavoidable in an international system whose basic characteristic is anarchy. In a bipolar system, given the sense of insecurity, fear, and suspicion that the two great powers feel lest a move by the other upset the balance and thereby grant it hegemony, the avoidance of crises is particularly difficult. Thus, on the one hand, it may be correct to conclude, as Kenneth Waltz has suggested, that in a bipolar distribution of power "a large crisis now [is better] than a small war later."[1] For a crisis is evidence that the balance is being kept. On the other hand, given its characteristics— a perception of a grave threat to the security of at least one participant, the suddenness and unexpected nature of this threat, the feeling of "players" that they must act quickly, and their heightened expectation of violence—a crisis is obviously dangerous. The alternative to some sort of settlement, however, is so catastrophic in our nuclear age that restraint becomes imperative. The diplomacy of "crisis management," or what has also been termed "coercive diplomacy," in these circumstances becomes a matter of survival.

The very eruption of a crisis suggests that the existing pattern of power has been "significantly disturbed" and that the relationship between the adversaries has become "politically fluid."[2] For example, in

[1] Kenneth N. Waltz, "The Stability of a Bipolar World," *Daedalus*, Summer, 1964, p. 884.
[2] Oran Young, *The Politics of Force* (Princeton, N.J.: Princeton University Press, 1968), pp. 63–95.

1958—the year after Sputnik and the first Soviet ICBM test—the Soviet leaders, feeling that the balance was changing, attempted to exploit diplomatically what they considered to be a military advantage. At the very least, they felt they possessed the strategic nuclear strength to deter any American attack; at best, they might be able to intimidate the United States.[3] The Soviet Sputniks had greatly impressed Americans with their new vulnerability to nuclear attack. SAC was said to be particularly vulnerable to a surprise missile strike, and its credibility was in some doubt both in the United States and among the NATO allies.[4] The Soviets therefore suddenly demanded that West Berlin be "demilitarized" and turned into a "free city" by the withdrawal of Western troops.[5] If the Western powers did not comply by the end of a six-month period, the Soviet Union would turn the approaches to West Berlin over to the East German Government, with which the Western Allies would then have to negotiate the terms of access. If they refused —quite likely, as they did not even recognize the German Democratic Republic—and if they attempted by force to break through a subsequent East German blockade, they were warned that Soviet troops would come to the aid of East Germany. On the other hand, if the Allies did negotiate new terms of access, they would at the same time be jeopardizing their future in Berlin. Their presence in the city by right of occupation stemming from the defeat of Nazi Germany—a right that depended on no other nation's consent—would be transformed into a presence by the consent of East Germany. It was likely that East Germany would then, bit by bit, whittle away Allied "rights."

The balance of resolve was thus at stake, as both Soviet and American policy-makers perceived a changing balance of capability. This is why the test over Berlin was crucial, and why the relationship of the superpowers would remain fluid until the outcome was clear. The threat of war historically, of course, has been one of the most potent means employed by states to gain their political ends. As Salvador de Madariaga said long ago, "The normal wielders of armaments are not the soldiers but the diplomats." This is even more true today. Total war may no longer be considered a rational instrument of national policy. But it is precisely because nuclear war is so devastating that the very prospect of

[3] Arnold L. Horelick and Myron Rush, *Strategic Power and Soviet Policy* (Chicago: University of Chicago Press, 1966), pp. 35–102.

[4] For the analysis by the special Presidential commission established to study the impact of the Soviet development and how the United States ought to deal with it, see Morton H. Halperin, "The Gaither Committee and the Policy Process," *World Politics*, April, 1961, pp. 360–84.

[5] The most detailed analyses in the context of bargaining techniques are James L. Richardson, *Germany and the Atlantic Alliance: the Interaction of Strategy and Politics* (Cambridge, Mass.: Harvard University Press, 1966), Part IV; and Hans Speier, *Divided Berlin: The Anatomy of Soviet Political Blackmail* (New York: Praeger Publishers, 1961). Also, more briefly, John Mander, *Berlin: Hostage for the West* (Baltimore: Penguin Books, 1962).

it can be used diplomatically. It is not the actual dropping of bombs but the threat of dropping them that provides each superpower with a powerful bargaining device. That nation makes limited demands. Knowing that it can deter an attack upon itself, it states that if its demands are not satisfied, it will unilaterally change the *status quo*, and that if its opponent resists this change, it will create—in that vague yet ominous phrase—a "grave situation." (This kind of phrase illustrates our earlier point that it is often best to keep threats ambiguous. It may, as hoped, frighten the adversary and compel him to retreat or offer concessions. But if it does not, the threatener can with reasonable grace climb off the limb he finds himself perched on—unless, of course, he prefers to fight.)

The defender of the *status quo*, however, faces the choice of suicide or surrender. The "incentive" held out to him is the avoidance of all-out war—but at the price of the demanded concessions. This form of coercive diplomacy, also sometimes called nuclear blackmail, is the test of will *par excellence*. A failure of will can result only in the loss of the disputed territory or right; more important, it is likely to have a grave impact upon the defender's allies and even upon the nonaligned states. Again, it is the intangible, or psychological, impact that is considered vital: "For expectations about the circumstances and consequences of war in the minds of nations and statesmen—Americans, adversaries, allies, and the nonaligned—may affect the fortunes of the cold war no less decisively than war itself."[6] Once again power is what people think it is. As President Kennedy stated the issue in 1961:

> The fulfillment of our pledge to that city is essential to the morale and the security of Western Germany, to the unity of Western Europe, and to the faith of the whole free world. Soviet strategy has long been aimed, not merely at Berlin, but at dividing and neutralizing all of Europe, forcing us back to our own shores. We must meet our oft-stated pledge to the free peoples of West Berlin—and maintain our rights and their safety, even in the face of force—in order to maintain the confidence of other free people in our word and our resolve. The strength of the alliance on which our security depends is dependent in turn on our willingness to meet their commitments.

West Berlin was therefore "the great testing place of Western courage and will, a focal point where our solemn commitments and Soviet ambitions now meet in basic confrontation."[7]

The difficulty, though, was in containing those ambitions without precipitating nuclear war. The Soviets could, of course, simply march into West Berlin. But this would constitute clear-cut military action that would unite the West and leave it no alternative but to react with force. The responsibility for the initiation of the use of force, and its possible

[6] Robert E. Osgood, *NATO: The Entangling Alliance* (Chicago: University of Chicago Press, 1962), p. 16.

[7] Quoted in *New York Times*, July 26, 1961.

escalation once Soviet and American troops clashed, would clearly rest with the Russians. The Soviets therefore posed the issue in terms of a series of limited challenges to Western rights. If, on the one hand, those rights were not defended, the West's position in Berlin would be slowly eroded. On the other hand, by exerting pressure on the West to accede to their demands, the Soviets shrewdly placed the burden of initiating the use of force on the West. The Soviets merely made the demands. It was the Western powers that had to decide whether they would stand firm or not, and the decision to stand firm at all times entailed the possibility that force might be needed to back up Western rights; in turn, this included the possibility of nuclear escalation.

The essence of coercive diplomacy, then, is that the defending power, rather than the power demanding change, bears the responsibility for firing the first shot. This very clever maneuver put the West on the spot precisely because of its fear of war. If the Soviets could demonstrate both the impotence of NATO and American hesitancy and fear, they could deal a death blow to West Berlin without firing a shot. If the future of the city looked uncertain, West German businessmen, whose economic support was vital, would not risk investing capital there. The effect would be to bring the economic life of the city to a standstill. If the city appeared to be doomed, West Berliners—particularly the younger people—would leave for West Germany. The exit of Western troops was thus not the only means of "demilitarizing" West Berlin. Undermining the confidence in the United States of the city's citizens and, in general, of all West Germans would suffice. If this were achieved, the Western segment of the city would subsequently wither away, despite the continued presence of Western troops.

The manner in which the United States handled this situation, as well as the substance of the positions it took, was extremely significant. In both instances, the United States more often than not failed to impress the Kremlin that its commitments were credible. There were, to be sure, constant proclamations by the West affirming its stance in the defense of West Berlin. But, since actions often speak louder than words in this type of situation, the real question was at what point the United States would resist Soviet intimidation. For instance, when the Soviet Union followed up its demand for the "demilitarization" of West Berlin with a proposal for a summit conference on a German peace treaty, the United States accepted on two conditions: that the six-month ultimatum be withdrawn and that a preliminary foreign ministers' conference yield fruitful results that would then merely be ratified at the later summit meeting. At that foreign ministers' conference, the Soviets deliberately turned down all Western plans in order to keep up their pressure on the West, and President Eisenhower then invited Khrushchev to meet him in the United States. The six-month deadline had, to be sure, been postponed, although the Soviets denied that it had been an ultimatum; still, the basic threat to West Berlin remained. The

President then reversed his previous position that he would not negotiate under pressure, and this move suggested to Khrushchev that he had been right in not showing a conciliatory attitude toward the West. Indeed, the more bellicose Khrushchev sounded and the more firmly he stood by his demands, the more flexible the Western position became. Obtaining the invitation to visit the United States was a major tactical victory. It brought other rewards as well. It demonstrated his equality with the President and accorded the Soviet Union recognition as one of the two great superpowers. It also deepened the fissures among the Western Allies. The West Germans and the French, fearful that the United States might not stand firm, were worried that Khrushchev and Eisenhower would arrange a deal that would get the United States "off the hook" at Europe's expense—precisely the impression Khrushchev wished to convey.

The substance of the negotiations was handled in a similar manner. During the foreign ministers' conference, the West first offered the Soviet Union a "package plan" linking a West Berlin solution with German reunification. The Soviets immediately rejected this, as their concern was to expel the West from Berlin. The West then retreated to a five-year interim solution providing for free and unrestricted access to West Berlin for civilian and military traffic. In return, the West would not station nuclear weapons in Berlin (hardly a concession, as there was no plan to do so anyway), would accept East Germans as Soviet "agents" for the control of traffic, and would curb propaganda and intelligence activities that "might either disturb public order or seriously affect the rights and interests, or amount to interference in the internal affairs, of others." The West, in short, was seeking to extricate itself from the risk of war by converting its permanent status to a temporary status based on Soviet consent. If, at the end of the five-year period, the Soviet Union refused to renew the agreement or would do so only on conditions unacceptable to the West, the city and the West's position would be in even greater jeopardy, because the right of the West to be in Berlin at all would have been abrogated. While the Western powers did state that, in the event of such disagreement, their old rights would be reinstated, it remains true, as has been observed, that the West, after a five-year interval, would hardly have been likely to defend rights it had not been prepared to defend when it had first been challenged and which had been specifically altered by the interim agreement.[8]

It is also likely that the West's position would, in any case, have further eroded during this five-year period. For example, the West's offer to curb propaganda and intelligence activities in West Berlin was altered by the Soviet Union during the discussion to read that West Berlin was not to be used for "hostile propaganda" and "subversive activities against the Soviet Union, the German Democratic Republic, and other socialist

[8] Henry A. Kissinger, *The Necessity for Choice* (New York: Harper & Row, 1961), pp. 142–43.

states." Because the Soviet Union was likely to define points of view different from its own as hostile and all criticism of itself as subversive, virtually any political news or article, editorial, or radio or television broadcast in West Berlin would fall under these all-encompassing terms as defined by the Soviets. If the Soviets then, in displeasure, threatened to break the interim agreement, would the West impose censorship on all media of communication in West Berlin? If it did not, it would confront the very risk of war it had sought to avoid in the first place; and if it did—for would an editorial be "worth" fighting a nuclear war over?— the West would then have proved its lack of nerve and will to resist piecemeal Soviet encroachment. West Berliners would have been demoralized, and the West's position badly undermined. This would especially have been the case if the West had also acceded to the Soviet demand for a reduction of the West's approximately 11,000-man garrison to a "symbolic" 3,000–4,000 men. This would have constituted a major withdrawal of the Western powers and would have provided more evidence that, at the end of five years, the West would not oppose further Soviet demands, let alone reassert its former rights. If the Soviets did not accept the West's interim proposal, it was only in order to compel the West to continue negotiating under stress and to seek "deWesternization" of Berlin.

Three aspects of the Soviet diplomacy are particularly interesting. First, the Soviets tended to pose each specific challenge in terms of minor points that seemed of little importance, particularly when measured against the risk of nuclear war. Indeed, the issue of Western access and presence in West Berlin was already three years old by 1958. The Soviets had, in fact, after the failure of their earlier Berlin Blockade, resurrected this issue in 1955, when control of civilian German traffic and goods transportation was handed over to the East Germans. During the same year, East Berlin was declared to be the capital of the German Democratic Republic. Shortly thereafter, Berlin was declared to lie "in the territory of the G.D.R." This was, in fact, a challenge to Western authority in Berlin. But at no time was there any response, for each of the acts was so minor. The declarations could easily be shrugged off, as the Western powers remained in Berlin and the city thus could not become East Germany's capital. Was it worth risking a war over whether Russians rather than East Germans handled traffic? And what matter that the East Germans unilaterally announced that Greater Berlin lay in their territory?

Second, it should be noted that each Soviet challenge, no matter how minor it seemed, was in fact important. What appeared to the West to be relatively unimportant issues not worth the risk of war—supposedly this risk was to be accepted only on "major" issues—were vital from the Soviet point of view. To them, Western inaction and willingness not to resist minor demands and changes in the *status quo* meant that the West could perhaps be pressured into larger concessions. Thus, the Soviet reaction to Western inaction was not the desired relaxation of international tensions but a heightening of these tensions. A minor challenge unmet would be followed by a greater challenge on the presumption that, if the West's will to resist was wanting on a small issue, its nerve might also fail on a more important issue as the pressures increased.[9] An excellent example of the Soviet means of augmenting the scale of a challenge can be seen in the events that followed the tragic death of a young German boy, Peter Fechter, shot while seeking to escape from East Berlin over the Wall.[10] For an hour, the East German border guards had left him to bleed to death—in front of American guards, who stood by passively. In reaction, outraged West Berliners stoned the Russian bus that each day carried Russian guards to the Soviet War Memorial in what had been the British sector. Purportedly to safeguard their men from broken glass and stones, the Soviets then notified the Western allies that they would send their guards in three armored personnel carriers. Although the local American command apparently foresaw the harmful effect of Russian armor traveling through West Berlin, it also had received orders from Washington to do nothing that might further raise the already high tension level. The Soviet armored cars were permitted to enter West Berlin. On the third day of such convoys, the Russian soldiers threw open the turrets of their vehicles and stood at attention holding their submachine guns. On the fourth day, an American convoy leaving West Berlin was detained for almost seven hours while the two Russian colonels supervising the detention frequently phoned their headquarters. Ostensibly, the issue was whether the soldiers would dismount to be counted, which they finally did. The real point was, apparently, that the Russians were serving notice: Thenceforth, they would equate their own armored access to West Berlin with that of the Western powers. On the seventh day, when there was no longer any danger of demonstrations, it was suggested to the Soviets that they return to the use of buses to transport their men. They replied that the buses were no longer available. Instead, the Soviets began to build up their "military presence" in West Berlin: On the tenth day, they added two jeep escorts to their three armored personnel carriers, and the next day they switched from the four-wheeled carriers they had been using to six-wheelers. At this point, Washington realized the danger of what was happening and took a firm stand. But some of the psychological damage had already been done.

Finally, each Soviet challenge was an act of definition of *Western* rights, and herein lay the importance of the initial "minor" demand and the subsequently enlarged demand. Each challenge not met established both a more advanced position for the Soviets and the basis for subse-

---

[9] See Speier, *Divided Berlin*, pp. 115–17, for another "minor" example: the annual meeting of the Bundestag in West Berlin.

[10] Daniel Schorr, "The Trojan Troika in Berlin," *Reporter*, September 27, 1962, pp. 25–27.

quent demands. The Soviets' demonstration of their armored access to West Berlin was typical. Another precedent was established in early 1962 when a Soviet officer at a checkpoint on the highway connecting West Germany and Berlin protested his inability to count the American soldiers in a convoy. He suggested that the soldiers dismount to facilitate his count, and they obliged. Again, the issue seemed minor, but the point scored by the Soviets was not, for they sought to establish that they, not the Allies, set the conditions for travel along the access routes to West Berlin. Afterward, the Allies reasserted Western rights by allowing the soldiers to dismount for a count only when the convoy carried a certain number of soldiers. Dismounting was not called off, however; it had become "established procedure." Each challenge thus not only eroded the Western position but also defined Western rights on a descending scale. The most dramatic Soviet act of definition was, of course, the building of the Wall, which divides East and West Berlin. Overnight, the Four-Power Statute, under which the entire city had been ruled by wartime agreement—and which the Soviets had been undermining for years—was eliminated. The Allies, fearful of precipitating an armed conflict, quickly announced that they were now responsible only for their respective sectors—this despite the fact that the Wall was the type of "major" issue on which the Allies had previously suggested that they would "react sharply."

By 1962, the Soviets had apparently become convinced that the United States would not use force to defend its vital interests, and Khrushchev talked openly of America's failure of nerve. The West's passive acceptance of the Berlin Wall was characteristic. So was its verbal reaction: "Negotiations are now more necessary than ever." Another indication was the debacle of the Cuban invasion sponsored by the Central Intelligence Agency.[11] The lesson Khrushchev apparently drew was that the United States talked loudly but carried a small stick, hence it did not seem that the installation of Soviet missiles in Cuba would involve great risk. The Soviet Union merely had to confront the United States with a *fait accompli*, and it would then retreat rather than face a test of will. Past American inaction or ineffective reaction seems to have encouraged the Soviets to continue their probes—and in the instance of the missile installations, the probe was to be 90 miles from the American shore.

On this occasion, however, the United States did react. Why in this instance was the United States successful, particularly when in contrast to Berlin, where it sought only to compel Moscow to *desist* from upsetting the *status quo* and preserve a frontier line, its aim in Cuba was to compel the Soviets to *retreat*? One reason, probably fundamental, was

---

[11] Theodore C. Sorensen, *Kennedy* (New York: Harper & Row, 1965), pp. 326–46; Arthur M. Schlesinger, Jr., *A Thousand Days* (Boston: Houghton Mifflin, 1965), pp. 219–50; and Tad Szulc and Karl E. Meyer, *The Cuban Invasion: The Chronicle of a Disaster* (New York: Ballantine Books, 1962).

that the American motivation to succeed in Cuba was far stronger than that of Russia; the "asymmetry of motivation" favored the United States. For passivity in the face of such a clear menace—underlined by both the stealth and the speed of the Soviet missile buildup—was perceived by Washington as humiliating to the United States, lending credence to repeated Soviet claims that Communism was the wave of the future and that the Soviet Union had become the world's foremost power. It would also have demonstrated American impotence to a watching world, for a United States unable or unwilling to prevent the installation of Soviet missiles in its traditional sphere of influence—as Ronald Steel has observed, the Monroe Doctrine was really a Caribbean Doctrine[12]—would obviously also be thought too weak or fearful to defend vital interests farther away. In terms of U.S. security, Soviet medium-range ballistic missiles (MRBMs) in Cuba would to some degree have enhanced the Soviet capacity for a first strike, as U.S. early warning lines were all positioned in the north to detect a strike across the North Pole. And confronted by American inaction the Soviets might well have shipped many more such missiles to Cuba.

Nonetheless, as President Kennedy recognized, it was less the balance of capability that would be affected than the balance of resolve. Not the strategic balance but the *appearance* of that balance would be substantially altered.[13] In these circumstances, the Soviets would undoubtedly have renewed their pressure on Berlin; they had already announced that they wished to resume "negotiations" on this subject after the American midterm election in November. They would also have furnished "proof" that America's allies in Europe, the Middle East, and Asia could not rely upon the United States in any major crisis. The future existence of these alliances would thus have been seriously jeopardized. And in the Western Hemisphere, this evidence of American impotence would have encouraged Castro and other leaders of anti-American movements, sharply reducing the authority of the "colossus of the North" in Latin America.

All in all, Kennedy felt that the Russians had broken a fundamental "rule of the game" in Cuba. The United States had established no bases in Eastern Europe; it had not aided anti-Russian revolts. In return, the Russians were not to encroach militarily in its sphere of influence. Castro's takeover of power, which resulted from internal Cuban conditions and despite the opposition of the Cuban Communist party, had not represented such an encroachment. Soviet missiles did. If the Soviet

12 Ronald Steel, *Pax Americana* (New York: Viking, 1967), p. 195.
13 The best accounts of the missile crisis can be found in Sorensen, *Kennedy*, pp. 752–809; Schlesinger, *Thousand Days*, pp. 726–49, and Elie Abel, *The Missile Crisis* (Philadelphia: Lippincott, 1966). The most detailed analysis of U.S. policy may be found in Graham T. Allison, *Essence of Decision* (Boston: Little, Brown, 1971). For an analysis of Soviet motivations, see Arnold Horelick "The Cuban Missile Crisis: An Analysis of Soviet Calculations," *World Politics* (April, 1964), pp. 363–70.

action were to pass with impunity, it would have redefined the terms of the whole bipolar competition. There were, of course, major risks involved in demanding the withdrawal of the Soviet missiles, but the consequences of *inaction* were perceived to be disastrous. The Russians had much to gain; but American losses were seen to be even greater, and thus Washington felt that it had no choice but to react in Cuba and demand the withdrawal of Soviet missiles. Hence the asymmetry of motivation, which favored the United States.

A second reason for the American success was the balance of capabilities. In Berlin, for several years after 1957, Washington remained apprehensive that the Soviet pronouncements of the changing balance were true. Khrushchev and his Defense Minister repeatedly proclaimed that the Soviet Union was producing ICBMs "on the assembly line" and threatened the United States with annihilating defeat. "We now have stockpiled so many rockets [ICBMs], so many atomic and hydrogen warheads," Khrushchev said, "that, if we were attacked, we could wipe from the face of the earth all of our probable opponents."[14] Moscow shrewdly exploited the resulting American uncertainty about actual Soviet strategic strength.[15] By 1960, thirty Soviet ICBM tests had been reported in the U.S. press, the Soviets had launched six successful space shots, and Americans knowledgeable about the nation's defense efforts forecast a sizable "missile gap" until the year 1964.

By 1962, however, fears of such a gap had been stilled. Spurred by Khrushchev's statements about large-scale production of missiles and his threats, the Kennedy Administration, upon coming into office in 1961, launched the massive build-up of Minuteman and Polaris missiles, which by 1966 were to total 1,000 and 656, respectively. It also soon discovered that Russian rocket production claims were greatly exaggerated. Moreover, Khrushchev was aware that the Americans knew this. The Russian medium- and intermediate-range missile installation in Cuba could therefore be partly interpreted as a technological shortcut to enhance Soviet strength. Given the imbalance of capabilities, in brief, President Kennedy could be reasonably confident and resolute. The American demand, even though it called upon the Soviet leaders to undo something they had already done rather than only to stop what they were doing, was nonetheless credible.[16] American power and resolve, successfully conveyed by Washington to Moscow during the crisis, reinforced the

[14] Horelick and Rush, *Strategic Power and Soviet Policy*, pp. 50, 58.

[15] The forecast of Soviet and American ICBMs was: 1960, 100 to 30; 1961, 500 to 70; 1962, 1,000 to 130; 1963, 1,500 to 130; 1964, 2,000 to 130. This forecast was based on interviews with persons presumably knowledgeable about the defense effort. The gap would be closed after 1964. Quoted from *New York Times* in *ibid.*, p. 51.

[16] Schelling, *Arms and Influence*, pp. 69 ff. The relationship of the balance of power to attempts at coercion—indeed, the whole strategy of coercion or compellence —is explored in greater detail in the excellent analysis of the Cuban missile crisis in Alexander L. George, David K. Hall, and William E. Simons, *The Limits of Coercive Diplomacy: Laos, Cuba, Vietnam* (Boston: Little, Brown, 1971), pp. 86–136.

asymmetry of motivation to strengthen the American bargaining capacity. Although Kennedy did not foolishly resort to an ultimatum quickly and remained cautious until just before the Russian missiles were to become operational, once he did deliver the ultimatum Khrushchev assumed a conciliatory tone and promised to dismantle the missiles in Cuba and ship them back to Russia. He did not, as some expected, take any retaliatory action in Berlin, where conventional Soviet power dominated. Quite the reverse: Khrushchev followed his Cuban surrender by sounding reasonable about Berlin, too. The balance of resolve and capability, which had been placed in some doubt by Berlin, had once more become settled. American-Soviet relations were no longer "politically fluid."

A third reason why the American threat of coercion was successful was the careful handling of the details of the crisis. To start with, Washington seized and held a tactical advantage by fully exploiting the "initiative that forces the opponent to initiate." Just as in Berlin, where Moscow placed the awesome responsibility of possibly sparking a nuclear conflagration upon its opponent, so Washington reversed this initiative in Cuba.[17] The blockade of any offensive arms cargo left it to Khrushchev to decide whether to break this quarantine and, if so, how. Kennedy, however, managed the details of the blockade shrewdly. Khrushchev had to make the key decisions, but he was not to be affronted in such a way that he would have no alternative but to respond militarily. He was also to be given time to think over what he would do; he was not to be forced into hasty and ill-considered actions. Thus while the Navy wished to intercept out to 800 miles into the Atlantic so that its ships would be out of range of the MIG fighters in Cuba, the President reduced the figure to 500 miles.[18] Furthermore, the first ship to be boarded and searched was not to be one owned and manned by the Soviets. A Russian tanker, which had identified itself and its cargo to U.S. naval ships, was allowed to pass because it was unlikely to be carrying missiles. An East German passenger ship was also cleared. The ship that was finally halted and searched was an American-built Liberty ship, Panamanian-owned, registered in Lebanon, captained by a Greek and bound for Cuba under Soviet charter![19] It was important in a crisis—one of whose chief characteristics is the perceived need for quick decision, which, in turn, could easily result in miscalculation and accident—to slow down the momentum of interactions and introduce "pauses" for careful reflection and calculation.

The blockade also enabled the contestants to preserve some freedom to maneuver—a matter of critical importance in superpower confrontations. On the one hand, superpowers must make commitments that ap-

---

[17] Young, *Politics of Force*, pp. 348–61.

[18] Robert F. Kennedy, *Thirteen Days: A Memoir of the Cuban Missile Crisis* (New York: Signet, 1969), p. 67.

[19] *Ibid.*, p. 82.

pear to surrender their initiative, and they do so to impress the opponent with the credibility of these commitments; on the other hand, should one of them refuse to retreat, the other cannot afford to be caught out on a limb. It therefore must preserve a degree of freedom about its course of action. It can state its basic aim, sound menacing, keep up the pressure—but in order to maintain flexibility it will at first probably take only small steps. If these call forth no resistance, and if its demands remain unmet, it can then take greater steps and escalate. This is how the Soviets sought to erode the Western position in Berlin starting in 1955 and culminating in the demand for a "free city" of West Berlin in 1958. And this is why President Kennedy began with the blockade.

He did have other options to deal with the Russian missiles: a private warning to Khrushchev, a protest at the United Nations, an air strike on the missile sites, or a full-fledged invasion. But the blockade was selected, even though Kennedy realized that, while the blockade might prevent more Russian missiles from entering Cuba, it might not be able to get rid of the ones already on the island. The blockade was intended as a signal of American determination (which a private warning or protest might not have been able to achieve); if Khrushchev then failed to remove his rockets, the pressure could be stepped up. In the meantime, Khrushchev would have to decide his response, while Kennedy could delay the even more agonizing decision on what he would do if the missile construction continued. No great power presents an ultimatum to another lightly. However, Kennedy did escalate the pressure toward the end of the first week of the crisis and informed the Russians that if the missiles were not removed the United States would remove them.[20] He did so, as said before, only as the Soviet missiles reached the point of becoming operational. Even then, he did not present his ultimatum publicly but privately through his brother to the Russian Ambassador in Washington; simultaneously, he gave his personal assurance that the few American missiles in Turkey, which were supposed to have been removed before the Cuban crisis erupted and whose removal the Russians had late in the crisis publically suggested as a *quid pro quo* for the removal of their missiles in Cuba, would soon be dismantled.

One of the more interesting features of the diplomatic communication between the two adversaries was *how*—as distinct from *what*—they signaled to each other. In part, it was public and verbal. In Berlin, from 1958 to 1960, the Russians continuously sounded menacing in order to pressure the West. In the Cuban crisis, Kennedy used his speech to the nation to make the American commitment credible. Indeed, by making his demand publicly, he committed himself and the country's reputation for power. In these circumstances, retreat was difficult without a serious loss of prestige. There were, in addition, important private communications. Messages were passed between President Kennedy and Khrushchev, as well as between Robert Kennedy and the Soviet Ambassador in Washington. Perhaps most important were the go-between meetings

[20] Kennedy, *Thirteen Days*, pp. 107–9, and George *et al.*, *Limits of Coercive Diplomacy*, pp. 115–34.

of a Soviet Embassy official and an ABC television reporter in which the Russian unofficially proposed the bargain that ended the crisis—the removal of the missiles for an American pledge of noninvasion.

But public statements rarely suffice by themselves. In a crisis, communication between the adversaries consists increasingly of the moves they make and the impressions these make on the opponent.[21] The blockade was the President's first move. Troops moving down to Florida, presumably for an invasion of Cuba, SAC's alert—all were intended to signal intentions, expectations, and attitudes.

Things that were *not* done were also intended to communicate messages. Soviet missiles were the issue; Castro and Communism in Cuba were not made an issue. The Russians were not asked to pull out totally and stab Castro in the back as they left. To do so would be to humiliate them and perhaps trigger a reaction. This is also why Kennedy was unwilling either to select a Russian ship as the first to be stopped or to launch a surprise attack on the missile sites; why, having won, he did not revel in his victory but praised Khrushchev's "statesmanlike decision to stop building bases in Cuba [and dismantle] offensive weapons. . . . This is an important and constructive contribution to peace";[22] and why he gave the Russian leader a pledge not to invade Cuba, which he had no intention of doing anyway. As a result, Khrushchev was able to claim that he had sent the missiles to Cuba to defend Castro from an American invasion and, having received a pledge of noninvasion, could bring them home.

There is one final point to be made about superpower confrontations: If a crisis erupts when the existing pattern of interstate relations has been significantly disturbed, the post-crisis period can produce a new stability.[23] While the clash over Berlin, climaxing in the building of the Wall in August, 1961, left the balance of resolve uncertain, the missile crisis of October, 1962, resulted in a Caribbean "understanding,"[24] a new superpower stability, and some significant shifts in alignments in the state system. Both the United States and the Soviet Union had marched to the brink of war, and both had been frightened by the possibility of going over the edge. Within a year, they would agree to the establishment of the "hot line" between Washington and Moscow (for instant communication between the leaders so that, in a crisis, misunderstandings and miscalculations could be prevented—if both sides wished to prevent such miscalculations and refrained from using the hot line for deceptive purposes), to the limited test ban, and to a ban on orbiting nuclear weapons in space. The missile crisis thus stimulated the two

[21] Young, *Politics of Force*, pp. 116–45.
[22] Quoted in Abel, *Missile Crisis*, p. 183.
[23] Young, *Politics of Force*, pp. 89–92.
[24] Whether the understanding about the stationing of Soviet strategic missiles in the Caribbean was in fact well understood by Moscow seems to remain a question (unless Moscow understands but wishes to change it). In 1970, the issue was raised about a possible Soviet base in Cuba for missile-carrying submarines; indeed, the issue went beyond this to the possible stationing of such submarines in the Caribbean area. *New York Times*, November, 1970.

powers to move closer toward each other in order to keep the peace. This greater restraint has, in subsequent years, often been referred to as a *détente*. Symbolic of the changing relationship were the opening of direct Moscow–New York air flights, a new consular treaty, and the Glassboro summit meeting between Johnson and Kosygin, at which the President argued for arms limitation talks. It was this *détente* that widened the Sino-Soviet schism, and, while reducing European fears of Russian power, also stirred their fears of an American-Soviet deal at their cost. The consequences of a crisis may be even more long-range. The Cuban debacle was presumably a major factor in Khrushchev's fall from power in 1964 and one significant reason why his successors, Kosygin and Brezhnev, began a major build-up of the Soviet missile force and navy. In the future, Russia was to possess the capacity to support distant overseas commitments and have the strength to stand up to American demands for retreat. Thus, a crisis may have significant short- and long-run —as well as ambiguous and contradictory—effects on political attitudes, intentions, and the ratio of military forces, even while preserving the *status quo*.

To sum up, coercive diplomacy, used defensively to prevent a change in the *status quo*, falls between deterrence, or the use of coercion to dissuade the adversary from doing something he has not yet started to do, and limited war, or the use of limited force to prevent a forcible change in the *status quo* by restoring it. Coercive diplomacy seeks to persuade the adversary either to stop what he is already doing (as in Berlin) or, more ambitiously, to reverse what he has already done (as in Cuba.) In the latter situation, the demand upon the adversary is greater, and therefore he is likely to be more *disinclined* to comply; consequently, stronger threats, which must be sufficiently credible, are needed to compel compliance. This means that this is a far more dangerous situation than the already dangerous enough situation in which coercive displomacy seeks merely to halt the opponent and lets him keep what he has achieved.

GRADATIONS IN DETERRENCE AND COERCIVE DIPLOMACY[25]

(increasing difficulty from standpoint of the "defender," in terms of pressure on "aggressor" necessary to achieve the desired effect)

[25] From Alexander L. George, David K. Hall, and William R. Simons, *The Limits of Coercive Diplomacy: Laos-Cuba-Vietnam*, p. 24. Copyright © 1971, by Little, Brown and Company (Inc.). Reprinted by permission.

Limited War

If a crisis and coercive diplomacy is one way of attempting to upset the balance of mutual deterrence, the limited use of violence is another. If one of the adversaries or one of its allies can confront the opponent with a less than total challenge to which he can reply *only* with a total response, the nuclear stalemate can be shifted in a piecemeal fashion.[26] All or nothing, war or peace, deterrence or self-destruction are not feasible alternatives. For if either power cannot counter a limited challenge with an equally limited response, it faces the simple but agonizing dilemma: Either it can answer the challenge with total force and risk suicide, or it can decide not to react at all, which would be tantamount to surrender or appeasement. In short, while the all-out use of violence is really irrational, it does not follow that the use of *any* violence is irrational. Indeed, in a condition of nuclear plenty for both principal contestants, the use of limited force—actual or, as a threat, potential—is rational, and, as with crises, the key challenge becomes the limited challenge. A series of such limited challenges could undermine the adversary's position.

Even before the atomic age, no "rational" nation fought an all-out war to defend limited stakes. In 1936, for instance, the French were unable to respond to Hitler's march into the Rhineland—which had been "neutralized," or "demilitarized," at Versailles—because they had prepared war plans only for an all-out war with Germany. Moreover, the implementation of these plans was contingent upon a German attack on France. Unprepared to meet Germany's limited challenge and unwilling to risk a total war, the French did not react, even though the Rhineland was crucial: Once Hitler had fortified the Rhineland by building the Siegfried Line, Germany was in a position to stop any possible French attack and could concentrate its army and air force on its eastern frontier, picking off one after another of the smaller nations in that area and thereby gaining dominance of the Continent. Thus the inability of the French to fight less than a total war—and, admittedly, they were reluctant to fight any kind of war—had a disastrous impact.[27] Instead of avoiding war, France ensured its inevitability as well as that it would occur at a time of Germany's choosing, when it had regained its strength.

Following World War II, the United States enjoyed virtual immunity

[26] The two best introductory books on limited war are Henry A. Kissinger, *Nuclear Weapons and Foreign Policy* (New York: Harper & Row, 1957), and Robert E. Osgood, *Limited War: The Challenge to American Strategy* (Chicago: University of Chicago Press, 1957).

[27] B. A. C. Parker, "The First Capitulation: France and the Rhineland Crisis of 1936," *World Politics*, April, 1956, pp. 355–73.

from attack until the mid-1950's, for the Soviets did not explode their first atomic bomb until late 1949, and the Soviet long-range air force did not begin its major development until 1954. Conversely, the Soviet Union was vulnerable to SAC bombers, whose American bases were supplemented by a global string of bases around the periphery of the Sino-Soviet bloc. Yet, even under such favorable conditions, it was not rational for the United States to fight a total war in response to limited provocation. There was no doubt about the American commitment to resist "aggression," but such resistance was thought of in terms of an all-out war in response to a Soviet first strike. The lack of SAC's credibility in deterring limited Soviet probes was in no way more clearly demonstrated than by the North Korean attack on South Korea in June, 1950. The Soviets were apparently quite willing to resort to force by proxy, despite America's overwhelming strategic superiority. Obviously, they did not expect the United States to retaliate against Russia.

Neither did the Chinese Communists in Indochina in 1954. The French had reoccupied their former colony after World War II and, refusing to grant the nationalist demands for full self-government, soon found themselves engaged in a long guerrilla war with the Communist-controlled Vietminh. With the end of the Korean War, the Chinese Communists augmented their assistance to the Vietminh. The French, attempting to fight a conventional war but unable to find their elusive opponents, occupied Dienbienphu in the hope of luring the Vietminh into the open in order to defeat them in a conventional battle. They were successful in enticing the Vietminh forward, but it was the French who were defeated, and this defeat confronted the United States with a major dilemma.[28]

On the one hand, it thought of Indochina as the "gateway" to Southeast Asia. President Eisenhower described Indochina as "of the most transcendent importance" to American security and compared the effect of the possible loss of the area upon the rest of Southeast Asia to the fall of the first in a row of dominoes; the implication was that, to prevent the dominoes from falling over, the first domino would have to be held up. On the other hand, the Eisenhower Administration was firmly committed to a policy of "massive retaliation." Secretary Dulles believed that the Korean War would never have occurred if the Soviets had known beforehand that the invasion of South Korea would be met with a retaliatory strike against the Soviet Union itself. Future Koreas could therefore be deterred by warning the enemy that the United States would retaliate with an attack on his homeland. SAC was the deterrent of both total *and* limited challenges. Dienbienphu was the test of this policy. The Eisenhower Administration had warned the Chinese Communists not to intervene; its warning had not been restricted to the contingency of open and direct intervention but applied even to indirect

[28] Melvin Gurtov, *The First Vietnam Crisis* (New York: Columbia University Press, 1967).

Chinese aid to the Vietminh in the form of military advisers, equipment, and training for its forces. The crucial issue was the strategic significance of Indochina.

In terms of its declared policy, the United States should have attacked the China mainland after its repeated warnings had been ignored. But Eisenhower was no more willing to do that than had Truman been to bomb across the Yalu River after the Chinese intervened in Korea in late 1950. Clearly, the reason in each instance was the realization that an attack on China could precipitate Russian intervention, thereby triggering a world war. Neither Korean nor Indochinese real estate seemed worth that high a price. Eisenhower's attempt to contain what he perceived as Communist expansion thus failed, and American power and prestige were badly bruised. The French were left to work out the best deal they could get. Surprisingly—and probably because the new post-Stalin government was trying to impress the world with its peacefulness and reasonableness—they managed to "save" Vietnam south of the 17th Parallel.

This experience revealed once more the lack of credibility of the total-war threat. Reliance upon an all-or-nothing strategy paralyzed American foreign policy: The ability to drop atomic bombs on Moscow or Peking was less than useless in deterring or defeating limited incursions. In short, for a threat to be credible, a commitment—if it exists—is not enough. There must also be some sort of *reasonble relationship between the magnitude of the issue at stake and the stated punishment* if the party threatened is to be persuaded to desist. A total war response to an attack on one's homeland is reasonable and credible; the same response in defense of an important ally is a little bit less credible; but would one risk committing suicide for a limited challenge in a country to whom no formal defense commitment exists? The lesson of Indochina—and what should have been the lesson of Korea, according to the critics—was the need for a flexible strategy. Deterrence had to operate effectively against both total and limited challenges. The basic necessity of an invulnerable retaliatory force had to be supplemented by the requirements of limited war—conventional army forces supported by tactical air elements and an airlift capacity to rush troops when needed to any area of the world, plus forces trained in the technique of unconventional or guerrilla war. Only then would attacks at all levels of violence be unprofitable for an adversary; only then could an adversary be deterred or, if not deterred, denied any victories. It was the Kennedy Administration that was to build up the required limited war capability with which to implement the containment policy.

"Limited war" may be defined as a war fought for limited political purposes by the superpower participant.[29] In contrast to the aim of total war, which is generally the complete destruction of the enemy's military forces and the elimination of his government, the objectives of limited

[29] Kissinger, *Nuclear Weapons and Foreign Policy*, p. 140.

war fall far short of total victory and the opponent's unconditional surrender. Perhaps the most obvious goal is the capture of strategically located and/or economically important territory. Thus, in the Korean War, if the North Korean army had captured South Korea, it would have established Communist control over the entire Korean peninsula, and thereby, in the deadly metaphor used by the Japanese, would have "pointed the Korean dagger straight at Japan's heart." It is significant to recall in this respect that the precipitating cause of the Russo-Japanese War of 1904–5 was Russia's penetration of Korea from the Russian sphere of influence in Manchuria. Japan at that time offered to divide Korea at the 38th Parallel, but the Czarist government refused. As a result of this refusal Japan attacked Russia in Siberia. Japanese security demanded that the southern half of Korea remain free of Russian control. In June, 1950, when Japan served as a base for American forces, the United States' reaction was similar.

But territory, as has been stressed before, is not necessarily the principal aim of a limited challenge. More often, a limited challenge is made to test the will and determination of the power defending the *status quo*. President Truman and his advisers certainly saw the North Korean attack in that context, for they compared the North Korean attack with Nazi and fascist aggression during the 1930's. In the absence of sufficient information on what was behind the Communist attack, this characterization of Communist states as totalitarian and of totalitarian states as aggressive proved a powerful analogy.[30] Thus a failure to meet the Communist challenge in Korea was seen as affecting both Soviet behavior and that of our allies. If the United States did not measure up to the test, the leaders in the Kremlin would succeed in demonstrating their own strength and resolution, and, conversely, America's weakness, fear, and unreliability.[31] It was expected that America's European allies and Japan—a much sought-after ally once Nationalist China disintegrated—would in these circumstances seek safety in a neutral position.

Hence, even had Korea been geographically unimportant, the challenge posed by the North Korean attack would have required that a stand be taken. "Firmness now would be the only way to deter new actions in other portions of the world," said President Truman. "Not only in Asia, but in Europe, the Middle East, and elsewhere the confidence of peoples in countries adjacent to the Soviet Union would be very adversely affected, in our judgment, if we failed to take action to protect a country established under our auspices and confirmed in its freedom by action of the United Nations."[32] Commitments in the bipolar world were seen by American policy-makers as extensive and interrelated. And the consequences of inaction were viewed as more intangible than tan-

[30] Jay Waltz in *New York Times*, June 26, 1950.
[31] See Harry S. Truman, *Memoirs* I, *Years of Trial and Hope* (Garden City, N.Y.: Doubleday, 1958): 332–33.
[32] *Ibid.*, pp. 339–40. For Vietnam, the view was similar. See *Pentagon Papers*.

gible, related more to political-psychological than to strictly territorial factors.

While limited war was thus seen as one means of maintaining the containment of America's major cold war adversaries, it was also viewed as a way of avoiding the terrible devastation that an all-out nuclear war would inflict. It is, indeed, in this sense that the limited conflicts of the post-1945 era differ from those of past ages. Europe's wars between 1648 and 1914, with the exception of the French Revolution, were also fought for limited political ends. But they were restrained by the absence of large-scale industrial strength, and they were fought on the basis of a technology that lacked the destructiveness of our contemporary age. "To-day, on the contrary, we speak of limited war in a sense that connotes a deliberate hobbling of a tremendous power that is already mobilized and that must in any case be maintained at a very high pitch of effectiveness for the sake only of inducing the enemy to hobble himself to like degree."[33] Limitations on political objectives, in other words, are dictated by nuclear technology.

It has, to be sure, sometimes been argued that a limited war may escalate into a total war. The great powers, whether they are directly or indirectly involved, do not apply all their power. It is therefore true that any restraints operating during a limited war are arbitrary, and it is possible that, rather than suffer a defeat, the side in danger of losing may ignore these restraints and expand the scope of the war. Nonetheless, while each possesses the ability to expand hostilities, the existence of this ability strengthens the common interest of both in avoiding a nuclear holocaust. Certainly, the losing side has no incentive to expand the war all the way. Nations do not seek to escape a limited defeat by initiating a total war they might not survive at all.

But if the losing side is to be willing *not* to escalate limited conflicts to avoid specific losses, the winning side must also forgo any thoughts of gaining a complete victory. The winner on the battlefield is equally responsible for preserving the restraints on the war. The existence of the opponent's state cannot become the issue. Halting his violation of one's own side's interests is the issue. The Korean War provides a good example of this. The United States first sought merely to restore the *status quo*. But once the North Korean forces had been beaten and driven back to the 38th Parallel, the United States, seeing an opportunity to unify all of Korea and destroy a Communist satellite government, enlarged its objective. By turning around the "dagger" once aimed at Japan and by endangering the political survival of the North Korean regime, the United States provoked Chinese intervention.[34] China's entry into

[33] Bernard Brodie, *Strategy in the Missile Age* (Princeton, N.J.: Princeton University Press, 1959), p. 311.

[34] See John W. Spanier, *The Truman-MacArthur Controversy and the Korean War* (Cambridge, Mass.: Harvard University Press, 1959), pp. 84–134, and Allen S. Whiting, *China Crosses the Yalu: The Decision to Enter the Korean War* (New York: Macmillan, 1960).

the conflict escalated the fighting and risked an even greater escalation of the war. But Washington, fearful that to strike back against China *in* China would bog the United States down in a full-scale war on the Asian mainland—if, indeed, it did not precipitate World War III—reverted to its original aim.

This is exactly the opposite of what happened in Vietnam. The First Indochina War, a war of succession in which the Vietminh felt it should succeed the French, had concluded at Geneva in 1954 with the partition of Vietnam at the 17th Parallel. All the principl parties seemed to gain in Geneva—except for the Vietminh. The Russians, helping the French get out of a bad situation, were rewarded by France's scuttling of the European Defense Community, an organization within which Germany was to rearm; the Chinese, included in a major international conference, enhanced their claim to great-power status; and both Communist powers avoided having to decide what to do if, in case Geneva failed, the United States intervened.[35] And the United States, without having to fight another limited war, managed to see to it that half the country was salvaged.

Only the Vietminh lost. Ho Chi Minh was persuaded to settle for half of Vietnam, with reunification to be the subject of elections in two years' time. But this was unrealistic: The election stipulation in the Geneva agreements went unsigned. In Saigon, Diem's new government, which had not been a party to the agreement, denounced it immediately—it was unlikely that it would voluntarily acquiesce in its own extinction. And, in the context of the extensive and intensive bipolarity of the period, there was no reason to expect Washington to preside over Diem's political elimination. The 17th Parallel thereby became part of the international frontier. Nor could Ho Chi Minh really have believed that elections would be held; he was not that naïve. More probably, he expected South Vietnam to collapse, enabling him to pick up the pieces.[36] The Saigon "government" was hardly in control over the lower half of the country. There was not much of a bureaucracy or army. Diem did not even control Saigon, let alone the countryside. South Vietnam was in chaos, while North Vietnam was powerful, confident, a winner, and monolithically organized.

When South Vietnam, to virtually everyone's surprise, did not disintegrate by 1956, the Second Indochina War began in 1957.[37] The Communist leaders in Hanoi still considered themselves the rightful successors to the French over the whole of Indochina and, feeling cheated by the 1954 Geneva agreements, now sought to achieve the goal that their big-power allies had denied them by ending the war when they were winning. Their goal, as North Korea's had been, was total—the

---

[35] Gurtov, *First Vietnam Crisis*, pp. 152–53.

[36] Bernard B. Fall, *Viet-Nam Witness: 1953–66* (New York: Praeger Publishers, 1966), pp. 75–76.

[37] *Ibid.*, pp. 78, 185.

complete elimination of the rival government in the southern half of the country. The apparatus for rekindling the war in the South was already present. The elite of the Vietminh's political and military operators, estimated at about 5,000 men, had gone underground after Geneva; it now became the hard core of the Vietcong. And Vietcong cadres, drawn from the approximately 80,000 South Vietnamese Communist recruits and dependents who had gone north after Geneva, were infiltrated.[38] Washington interpreted the new war as an attempt to overthrow the government in Saigon and "liberate" the South. The result was direct American intervention.

Whereas Washington had by then accepted the principle of division, as with the division of Korea, Hanoi had not and, through support of the Vietcong, was seeking total victory. This meant that the conflict became more difficult to restrain, for in such circumstances escalation appears necessary. Only by imposing more severe sanctions and exacting a greater price for "victory"—and also posing the greater possibility of a rapid escalation into a far larger and more expensive war—can the "escalator" hope that the opponent will back down and limit his objectives. The result is a paradox. On the one hand, limited goals are established to avoid escalation; on the other, if one belligerent goes beyond these goals, escalation is expected to compel him to exercise self-restraint: The escalation, by taking the hostilities one step nearer to all-out war, is supposed to underline the fact that the price of a complete victory is far too high. The paradox becomes painful, however, when, despite the escalation, the adversary persists in seeking a total victory (which, as we shall see, happened in Vietnam).

Whatever the case, the basic restraint that must be maintained during a limited war is obvious—the nonuse of strategic nuclear weapons. Almost equally important is the noninvolvement of American, Russian, and Chinese troops. Again, this is not to say that if these forces clashed total war would be inevitable. But their involvement increases the difficulty of preserving the limitations on the conflict. The great powers seem to be well aware of this second restraint, and the United States and the Soviet Union have been careful to avoid any embroilment in which they might confront each other directly. One of the aims in stationing American troops in Europe was to let the Soviets know that any attack there would inevitably involve the United States in war. In the ground and air corridors to West Berlin, as well as within the city itself, incidents involving a direct clash between American and Russian forces have been scrupulously avoided.

Significantly, the Soviets risked a conflict only in a situation where American forces had been withdrawn—that is, in South Korea. The technique of deterrence—of making credible commitments—was still an art to be mastered in the early days of the cold war. South Korea had not

[38] *Ibid.*, p. 236, and Roger Hilsman, *To Move a Nation* (Garden City, N.Y.: Doubleday, 1967), p. 428.

received such a commitment; it seemed, indeed, as if the United States had abandoned it. Force was thus to become necessary if this failure to use power properly were to be redeemed. Initially, fighting was between troops of the Soviet Union's North Korean satellite and those of the United Nations. Even the Communist Chinese troops that later intervened were not sent officially by the Chinese Government. Peking never declared war and never accepted responsibility for the Chinese troops in Korea, which were declared to be "volunteers." Nor did the United States declare war on North Korea or on Communist China. American troops were regarded as part of the U.N. force fighting a U.N. "police action." The nondeclaration of war and the use of volunteers may well seem to be both minor and obvious disguises. Nevertheless, they play a significant role in keeping wars limited. Again, despite the fact that the Soviet Union was the instigator of the Korean War and supplied both the North Koreans and Communist Chinese with military equipment and diplomatic support, it was no more officially involved in terms of troops than was the United States when it supplied weapons in 1958 to the Nationalist Chinese defending the two islands, Quemoy and Matsu, lying right off the mainland's coastline. And in that instance, the Chinese did not fire on American ships, and American naval guns and planes did not attack Communist shore batteries and nearby airfields.

A further restraint required in limited war is geographical—that is, limited wars have generally been confined to one nation. The Yalu River served as the frontier between North Korea and China in the Korean War, and even after Peking's intervention the war was not extended beyond it. Bombers were not sent to hit the factories, railroads, or military supply depots in Manchuria. In fact, even the bombing of the bridges crossing the Yalu into China was restricted to the North Korean side. Thus, the Korean War was confined to Korea. Similarly, the Quemoy-Matsu crisis was confined to the two islands and surrounding waters, and the Second Indochina War to the Indochina area.

In the case of Indochina, the war was, for the most part, limited to North and South Vietnam, even though the North used Laos and Cambodia as routes for sending troops and supplies southward, and these Communist trails were bombed regularly. In Laos, American aid was essentially limited to providing the neutralist government with air support against its Communist Pathet Lao and North Vietnamese forces on its soil. In early 1971, U.S. intervention in the form of air support for South Vietnamese ground forces attempting to cut the Ho Chi Minh trail was increased. The United States was also bombing heavily in Cambodia where in 1970, five years after American intervention had begun, the Nixon Administration sent ground forces for an eight-week period to clean out North Vietnamese sanctuaries. These, it was alleged, were undergoing a rapid buildup prior to an attack on South Vietnam, which would come at a time when American troops were increasingly being disengaged and Saigon's forces were not yet ready to carry on the fight alone. Presumably, an additional purpose was to support the shaky new Cambodian military government, which—having asked Hanoi to reduce its presence in the country—was also threatened by the North Vietnamese forces. Although the incursions into Laos and Cambodia extended the geographic range of U.S. operations, hostilities were nevertheless confined to the Indochina area, over whose status the fighting had initially begun. This does not mean that, had there been an extension beyond these frontiers, total war would have resulted. It is doubtful that air attacks on Manchuria during the Korean War would have incurred Soviet intervention, because the Soviet Union at the time was strategically inferior to the United States. The American air attacks on North Vietnam that began in 1965 certainly did not precipitate all-out war. Nevertheless, boundaries do serve as clear lines of demarcation and, therefore, as restraints upon escalation. Such lines of demarcation may be set in a number of ways, not the least of which is an "accident of history."

The 38th Parallel is such a case. It had been intended to serve only as a temporary divider between the Soviet and American zones of occupation of Korea until Japanese troops had been disarmed, yet it grew into an unofficially recognized frontier between the Soviet and American spheres of influence. Or they may come about as a result of a series of "tests of resolve." During the Quemoy-Matsu crises of 1958, Peking proclaimed that its territorial waters extended 12 miles out to sea, but the United States rejected this claim, recognizing only the traditional 3-mile limit. American supply ships stopped just short of this limit and then transferred their supplies to smaller Nationalist ships. In turn, the Chinese Communist guns on the mainland fired only at the Nationalists when they crossed within the 3-mile limit.

Whatever the cause, in a limited war each side usually acknowledges that it must allow the other to possess some clearly demarcated "privileged sanctuaries"—inviolable areas in which are held reserve troops, supplies, and air and naval bases. To attack these areas is to risk removing one of the important restraints limiting the scope of the conflict. Manchuria was such a sanctuary for the Communists during the Korean War. While its use as a sanctuary was generally recognized in the United States, especially by those who demanded that Manchuria be bombed, there was little realization that the United States, too, possessed privileged sanctuaries—in Japan and Okinawa. Few took note of the fact, moreover, that the Communists made no attacks on sea transports that supplied American, South Korean, and other allied forces. There were even sanctuaries within the actual area of the fighting: The Communists launched no air attacks on either Pusan or Inchon, the two largest ports through which most of the supplies for the U.N. forces were channeled. If either port had been subjected to frequent bombing, U.N. operations might have been seriously hampered. Similarly, Chinese Communist jet fighters did not attack U.N. troops in the field, United States air bases in South Korea, or aircraft carriers lying off the coast; instead, they limited themselves to the Yalu River area, defending the bridges that crossed it.

In Vietnam, the United States tolerated sanctuaries in Cambodia and in Laos until President Nixon decided that nonintervention jeopardized his strategy of withdrawing American troops while simultaneously seeking to prevent South Vietnam's fall. President Johnson earlier had attacked North Vietnam by air because Hanoi, he felt, should not go unpunished for its direction of and aid to the Vietcong in the South; it might, if hurt enough, be persuaded to desist from its effort. Hilsman has argued that this air war violated a tacit agreement: the United States would refrain from bombing north of the 17th Parallel, while North Vietnam would not infiltrate any, or at least large numbers, of its troops.[39]

A final restraint in limited wars—and this would apply primarily to conventional hostilities—is the nonuse of tactical nuclear weapons.[40] Use of these weapons, which did not become available until the mid-1950's, does not necessarily favor the defending side. A conventional defense is generally calculated to hold an offense three times its size, but tactical nuclear weapons would eliminate this advantage. Given the use of such weapons, if both sides are equally matched in numbers, there is no innate reason why the defender should hold his ground, let alone advance. In these circumstances, tactical nuclear weapons are likely to favor the larger army. It is not that their superior firepower makes them a substitute for manpower. In fact, precisely because they can impose a much higher casualty rate, an army probably must be larger in order to replace its high rate of killed and wounded. Moreover, if the use of tactical nuclear arms were a foregone conclusion, and an adversary therefore resorted to them from the beginning, they might completely overwhelm their victims and attain their political objectives before the defender could mobilize his forces and move them to the attacked area. If the North Koreans, for example, had possessed tactical nuclear weapons, it would have been impossible for the first American troops to fight an effective rear-guard action, reorganize the defeated South Korean Army, and defend themselves for weeks in a narrow beachhead perimeter while waiting to go on the offensive. In such an instance, the enemy's use of tactical nuclear arms and the extremely high casualty rates the United States would suffer if it responded to such an attack could actually prove a *deterrent* to an American response.

More important, though, tactical nuclear weapons are a political liability. Few nations want to be "saved from Communism" by tactical nu-

---

[39] Hilsman, *To Move a Nation*, p. 531.

[40] Arguments to the contrary are presented by Kissinger, *Nuclear Weapons and Foreign Policy*, pp. 174–202 (although he changed his mind in *The Necessity for Choice*, pp. 75–86); Oskar Morgenstern, *The Question of National Defense* (New York: Random House, 1959), pp. 145–54; and Osgood, *Limited War*, pp. 251–59.

clear weapons, which could devastate the "beneficiary." The average tactical nuclear weapon in the NATO stockpile, for example, has a yield five times greater than that of the bomb dropped on Hiroshima. Its tremendous destructive power is its chief political disadvantage. But most important of all, the principal advantage of the *non*use of tactical nuclear weapons is the distinction between them and conventional arms—a distinction as clear-cut as a boundary line and just as vital in preserving the limitations on war. For once this distinction has been erased, where can a new boundary line be drawn? Will the momentum of battle not lead to the employment of ever larger nuclear weapons until the escalation finally results in the use of strategic arms? By contrast, nonuse of tactical nuclear arms is simple and unambiguous and may be easily understood and observed.[41]

In a sense, then, limited wars are another form of arms control, which seeks not only to stabilize mutual deterrence and thereby prevent a nuclear war but also to preserve the restraints on less-than-total military conflicts in order to forestall escalation into total war. But, quite significantly, limited wars are based on a *tacit* diplomatic bargain between the participants to observe certain restrictions and not to exceed them. However ridiculous these restrictions may appear to be from the military point of view, their principal aim is to convey to the opponent the desire to abide by existing limitations and to provide the opponent with some incentive to show a similar restraint. The limitations must be clearly drawn: Precisely because they are *not* formally negotiated but are tacitly agreed upon, it is necessary that the terms be qualitatively distinguishable from possible alternatives.

These, then, are the principal restraints that, if observed, keep limited wars limited. In addition, these restraints tend to reinforce one another; conversely, the more they are violated, the more tenuous the limitation. No single escalation will erupt immediately and automatically into total war. There are different gradations or levels of violence between a landing of U.S. Marines in Lebanon, a Quemoy-Matsu, a Korea or Indochina, and an all-out nuclear conflict between the United States and the Soviet Union. Indeed, the nuclear strategist Herman Kahn has constructed an "escalation ladder" that ascends from the lower rungs of an "ostensible crisis" to what he terms a "spasm or insensate war."[42] The very fact that each restraint violated weakens the over-all capacity to limit the conflict means that when one side does escalate, the step must be taken carefully and slowly. The first U.S. air attack on North Vietnam was reportedly in response to a PT-boat attack on American destroyers in the Gulf of Tonkin; the target was the harbor from which the PT boats had sailed. Later, several air attacks were launched to retaliate

[41] Schelling, *Strategy of Conflict*, p. 75, and *idem, Arms and Influence*, pp. 137–41.

[42] Herman Kahn, *On Escalation* (New York: Praeger Publishers, 1965), pp. 38–41.

for Vietcong attacks on American servicemen and planes in South Vietnam. The next step was to hit North Vietnamese military targets, regardless of attacks on American personnel or equipment in the South. These strikes, it was stressed, were aimed at halting what the government considered Communist aggression against South Vietnam. Thus, the scope of the attacks, initially narrowly confined, was only gradually broadened.

But gradual escalation is a question not only of the nature and scope of the targets but also—as in crises—of timing. After each step upward on the ladder, the careful escalator pauses to see if his opponent will desist as a result of the escalation and the fear that this has presumably induced a greatly expanded, if not total, war. If he does, there will be no need for a further escalation; if not, it may be necessary.[43] Thus the first U.S. air strikes against North Vietnam were north of the 17th Parallel but south of the 19th. When this produced no results, the strikes hit targets north of the 19th Parallel. The important point is that at each rung of the ladder there be time for either tacit or explicit bargaining to occur. The side against which the escalation is directed must have time to evaluate its next move; and it can do this only after it has decided what the escalation signifies about the opponent's intentions.

Revolutionary Warfare

While the above limitations are applicable in both conventional limited wars and unconventional revolutionary or guerrilla conflicts, the latter category constitutes a quite different species of warfare. The Soviets and, particularly, the Chinese Communists, who used it to come into power, call them "wars of national liberation," and they favor them in the underdeveloped or non-Western areas of the world, where they see the need for the people to free themselves from the colonial rulers through armed struggle.[44] It was Khrushchev's 1961 statement about such wars that aroused the Kennedy Administration and inclined it to believe that the war in South Vietnam was instigated by Moscow and/ or Peking and was not simply a nationalist war of unification.

One advantage of national liberation is that such wars do not raise the issue of aggression as clearly as do conventional limited attacks, so the initiators remain free of the stigma of "aggressor." There is no single moment when a major attack across a well-defined frontier or line alerts the United States and its allies, let alone the nonaligned nations.

[43] For a critical view of American escalation, suggesting that the escalations from late 1963 to 1966 occurred to prevent negotiations, presumably to prevent an unfavorable political settlement while the military situation was unfavorable, see Franz Schurmann et al., The Politics of the Escalation in Vietnam (New York: Fawcett, 1966).

[44] Washington Center of Foreign Policy Research, Two Communist Manifestoes (Washington, D.C., 1961), pp. 51–52.

In the conventional war, the aggressor who has prepared for it within the confines of his national territory, channeling his resources into the preparation, has much to gain by attacking suddenly with all his forces. The transition from peace to war is as abrupt as the state of the art allows; the first shock may be decisive. This is hardly possible in the revolutionary war because the aggressor—the insurgent—lacks sufficient strength at the outset. Indeed, years may sometimes pass before he has built up significant political, let alone military, power. So there is usually little or no first shock, little or no surprise, no possibility of an early decisive battle. In fact, the insurgent has no interest in producing a shock until he feels fully able to withstand the enemy's expected reaction.[45]

Furthermore, because the guerrilla forces generally are preponderantly native, not foreign, a guerrilla war has the appearance of being a "domestic" conflict. Finally, guerrilla wars tend to be lengthy. If the guerrillas were as strong as or stronger than their opponent, they would seek to defeat him quickly in a conventional battle. But their very weakness compels them to whittle away at their enemy's strength bit by bit. This process of attrition can go almost unnoticed by the outside world until the last stage of the war, when the guerrillas are poised to achieve the defeat of their by now weakened and demoralized opponent. By then, it is usually too late for effective countermeasures. Waging guerrilla warfare is thus considerably safer than fighting a regular war in the nuclear age.

The ultimate aim of the guerrillas is, of course, the capture of state power *in order to transform completely the social-political structure and economic organization of the nation,* and this is what distinguishes it from civil war, *coups d'état,* and other types of rebellion. That is why guerrilla war is often referred to as a war of "internal conquest," subversive warfare, or, more appropriately, *revolutionary warfare.* In the initial phase of revolutionary war, the guerrillas, as the weaker side, are strategically on the defensive; tactically, though, they are always on the offensive. In order to wear down the enemy, they adopt hit-and-run tactics. Mobility, surprise, and rapid military decisions are characteristic of their operations. They fight only when there is a good chance of victory; otherwise, they do not attack and, if engaged, quickly disengage. Their attacks are swift, sudden, and relentless. There is no front line in such a war. The front is everywhere, and the guerrillas strike anywhere and everywhere. In the words of the man sometimes called the father of revolutionary warfare, Chinese Communist leader Mao Tse-tung, the guerrillas "must move with the fluidity of water and the ease of the blowing wind. Their tactics must deceive, tempt, and confuse the enemy. They must lead the enemy to believe that they will attack him from the east and north, and they must then strike him from the west and the south. They must strike, then rapidly disperse. They must move at night."[46]

[45] David Galula, *Counterinsurgency Warfare* (New York: Praeger Publishers, 1964), pp. 9–10.

[46] *Mao Tse-tung on Guerrilla Warfare,* translated and with an introduction by Samuel B. Griffith (New York: Praeger Publishers, 1961), pp. 103–4.

Guerrilla tactical doctrine is perhaps most aptly summed up in Mao's well-known formula: "Enemy advances, we retreat; enemy halts, we harass; enemy tires, we attack; enemy retreats, we pursue."[47]

Rather than inflict any major or severe defeats on the enemy, these tactics harass, confuse, and frustrate him. The guerrillas do not, in fact, engage in conventional battle until the last stage of the war; they are too weak throughout most of the hostilities. The violence at the physical level is important but, again, it is the *psychological* impact of the war that is decisive. If the enemy cannot be beaten physically, his *will to fight* can still be eroded. And this can be achieved in two ways. Basically, his army can be demoralized. Suffering one minor defeat after another, rarely finding the enemy to engage and defeat in battle, forced increasingly to the defensive by the guerrilla's tactics, the army loses its offensive spirit as it finds that Western conventional tactics are useless. The army's determination to stay and fight declines; its stamina is sapped.

Even more important in undermining the enemy's will to fight is to isolate him either by capturing the support of most of the population or by neutralizing it. Control of the population is essential if the guerrillas are to realize their objective of "internal conquest." The populace provides them with recruits, food, shelter, and, above all else, intelligence; for, if the guerrillas are to surprise the enemy, they must know where to strike and when. They must know all the opponent's moves in order to be able to fight at moments of their own choosing, against smaller groups, and to escape if government reinforcements suddenly arrive.

Victories are naturally one way of impressing the people, who at the beginning of a revolutionary war are likely to be divided into three groups: a fervent minority favoring the guerrillas, a militant minority favoring the government, and a majority of the population—estimated between 50 to 70 per cent—who are neutral. This latter element will remain passive until it becomes clear which side will win. Its neutrality, of course, favors the guerrillas, because it hampers government forces; the people will not provide the latter with the information that is necessary to locate the guerrillas. As the government's troops become demoralized and defensively oriented, as they increasingly appear unable to provide the population with elementary security in their daily lives, the government loses whatever allegiance it had. It is the village peasants, generally removed from any contact with their government, who are most concerned to ensure their own future. If they think the guerrillas will win the war, they are unlikely to antagonize them but instead will cooperate increasingly.

Terror also plays a role in eliciting cooperation. This terror is usually selective, and its aim is to reaffirm the weakness of the government; thus in the main it is applied to local government officials. Obviously, wholesale and indiscriminate terror would only alienate the very people whose

[47] For the Vietminh's seven rules for the conduct of guerrilla warfare, see Otto Hellbrunn, *Partisan Warfare* (New York: Praeger Publishers, 1962), pp. 78–79.

support the guerrillas seek to win, although on occasions wholesale executions or the burning of a village is used to influence the minds and behavior of other villages and towns. The guerrillas will have made their point vividly when they can show the peasants that the government is not able even to protect its own officials.[48] Moreover, by eliminating these officials, the guerrillas break the link between the government and the majority of the people, thus restricting the government's authority mainly to the cities.

Even in the cities, this authority may not be left uncontested. The Vietcong Tet offensive of 1968 infiltrated major South Vietnamese cities and district capitals. The city population was shocked into realizing that it was not safe either. Just as Vietcong control of a village and executions of some villagers who cooperated with, or were on the side of, the government conveyed the message to the peasants that they had better support the guerrillas—or, at the very minimum, remain "neutral"—so the attacks on Saigon and Hué were intended to suggest to their inhabitants as well that they had better be careful about which side they supported. These attacks further undermined confidence in the Saigon government, as well as in the United States; if, after three years of intensive warfare, apparently neither could so much as guarantee the safety of the cities they were supposed to control, why should the population expect any better in the future?

The guerrillas, then, gain popular control in part because they appear to be the eventual winners, in part because of selective terror as well as the more subtle kind of terror that operates when large masses of the population are fearful because they really do not know what will happen to them if the guerrillas win—although many obviously fear the worst. But there is another reason: an effective social strategy and propaganda that manage to identify the guerrillas with a popular cause or grievances.[49] Communist guerrillas do not present themselves as Communists; nor do the people support them because they are Communists or desire the establishment of a Communist state. The guerrillas present themselves simply as spokesmen for existing social grievances and aspirations. If the people are resentful of continued colonial rule or of a despotic native government, the guerrillas take up their cries. If certain classes seek social and economic justice, the guerrillas demand it on their behalf. The guerrillas, in brief, identify themselves as "liberators" and "reformers," promising that they can satisfy the revolution of rising expectations. Thus, in South Vietnam, the Vietcong appealed to the peasants by pointing out that they were working in the landowners' rice fields for the landowners' rather than their own benefit. When the landlords fled to

---

[48] In South Vietnam, for instance, more than 15,000 village officials were murdered between 1957 and 1965. Fall, Viet-Nam Witness, p. 293.

[49] Jeffrey Race, War Comes to Long An (Berkeley: University of California Press, 1972), pp. 141 ff.; Heilbrunn, Partisan War, pp. 145–46; and George K. Tanham, Communist Revolutionary Warfare (New York: Praeger Publishers, 1961), p. 143.

the cities, the Vietcong told the peasants they no longer needed to pay their exorbitant and exploitative rents (or taxes); the peasants owned the land, and the Vietcong would protect them if anyone sought to take it away. The result was a deep schism between the government in Saigon and the peasantry. Not until 1970 was a large-scale land reform program enacted to give the peasants a greater stake in a non-Communist South Vietnam. Such programs, although narrower in scope, had in the past been relatively ineffective. This social strategy, as Jeffrey Race has termed it, is basic to the guerrillas' revolutionary warfare; important as the military component of this warfare is, it is neither the most significant nor the distinguishing characteristic of this particular kind of war, especially as it is waged by Communist parties whose entire social outlook is based on a class analysis and class struggle. Indeed, this struggle begins *before* the military phase of the war begins, as in each village and hamlet the revolutionary party establishes its cells, seeks local control and support, and thereby diminishes the base of popular support for the government. Thus the fact that a large element of the population tends to be neutral in the war, waiting to see who is likely to win, is not just a matter of the clash of arms but also the result of this *pre-emptive* social strategy. While the revolutionaries' maximum goal is to mobilize the population to fight with them against the government, their minimal aim is to prevent the population from fighting on the government's side against the revolution.

When the war has gone on long enough to win widespread popular support and the government has become increasingly socially isolated and militarily weakened, only a final *coup de grâce* is needed to topple the government. This means resort to conventional battle—*unless* the guerrillas, as in Cuba and South Vietnam (until the U.S. intervention) have already disintegrated the entire governmental structure and authority, even in the capital city. The guerrillas must, of course, be extremely careful in their timing. If they engage in conventional fighting too early, before the enemy army has lost most of its will to fight and before they themselves are properly trained and equipped, they may be badly defeated. On the other hand, if they have the patience and are able to calculate correctly the moment of transition, the war will end in their victory. The defeat of the French forces at Dienbienphu broke France's determination to hold onto its old colony. Yet the French garrison there consisted of only one-fifteenth of the total number of French troops in Indochina, and, though the French suffered 12,000 casualties, including prisoners, the estimated Vietminh casualties were 15,000. Since their total force was not as large as that of the French, the Vietminh clearly had been badly hurt. Nonetheless, this single battle of Dienbienphu sapped France's will to resist.[50] Since 1950, the French position at home in regard to Indochina had become ambivalent, and its military position

[50] Tanham, *Communist Revolutionary Warfare*, pp. 32, 97.

inside Indochina had been eroding; thus Dienbienphu was to prove politically and psychologically decisive. The French determined to end the long and—for them—futile fighting.

It is in this final phase, according to some experts, that the guerrilla forces' need for a continuous external source of support and supply becomes crucial:

A siege-like battle on the scale of Dien Bien Phu, with its heavy requirement for artillery and manpower, would have been unthinkable without the constant supply line from Communist China and without the ease of access of personnel from one country to the other. Not for many years, if ever, could the Vietminh alone have manufactured the artillery necessary for the decisive battle against the French, and it needed the experience and expertise of the Chinese to train the Vietminh soldiery and military leadership, both in China and in Vietnam. In both respects, the advantage of contiguity was vital: Without a common border, the logistic problem of moving men and weapons would have been formidable so long as the French controlled both sea and air. There can be no doubt whatever that China's interest in supporting the revolutionaries, coupled with the common border, was a strong contributing—if not the decisive—factor in the success of the Vietminh.[51]

Perhaps the word "decisive" is a bit strong. The pattern is more complex. The guerrilla war in Greece after World War II did not end in the guerrillas' defeat until after the Tito-Stalin break had deprived them of their sanctuary. No doubt, also, the Chinese Communist sanctuary did play a vital role in the French defeat at Dienbienphu. But the French had already lost the war to the Vietminh by late 1950, when almost the entire northern half of Vietnam had become a Vietminh stronghold. Moreover, the Vietminh received most of its weapons from the defeated French forces. Similarly, by the end of 1967, North Vietnam had infiltrated an estimated 60,000 troops—of an approximate total force of 300,000 insurgents—into South Vietnam.[52] Thus, while Hanoi's role in the direction of the war in the South was by then clear, the war remained basically an insurrection boosted by infiltration. The 20 per cent of the troops supplied by Hanoi did *not* constitute an invasion aided by an insurgency.

Castro, on the other hand, had possessed no sanctuary. He won because the Batista regime had alienated the masses, particularly the urban

---

[51] *Ibid.*, p. 144. Bernard Fall also held the external sanctuary to be decisive: "The success or failure of *all* rebellions since World War II depended on whether the active sanctuary was willing and able to perform its expected role." Yet Fall himself admitted that "the French were definitely the 'aliens' and the Communist-led Viet-Minh forces could count on the instinctive support of the native population." The French were therefore unable to create antiguerrilla forces, and their intelligence was often faulty because they were isolated from the population. See Fall, *Street Without Joy*, rev. ed. (Harrisburg, Pa.: Stackpole, 1966), p. 16.

[52] Sir Robert Thompson, *No Exit from Vietnam* (New York: David McKay, 1969), p. 45.

middle class, and the army just disintegrated. Likewise, the Chinese Communists won because Chiang Kai-shek's regime had lost mass support after the defeat of Japan. To be sure, the Communists benefited greatly from the arms they took (without the Nationalists' permission) from the surrendering Japanese Army, from those supplied by Soviet troops in Manchuria, and from great quantities of American arms captured from the Nationalist forces they had defeated. But fundamentally they were successful because they were able to exploit peasant dissatisfaction. In short, while the external sanctuary may play an important role in guerrilla warfare, as it does in conventional limited war, the "decisive" role continues to be played by the populace.[53]

Guerrilla warfare may at times seem militarily primitive, for the weapons used by the guerrillas by and large do not begin to compare with the highly intricate weapons in Western arsenals. Guerrillas may, of course, receive some similar weapons, but the insurgents' success does not depend on doing so. Politically, however, guerrilla warfare is "more sophisticated than nuclear war or atomic war or war as it was waged by conventional armies, navies, and air forces."[54] More than any other kind of war, it requires a high degree of political intelligence—as does counterguerrilla or counterinsurgency warfare.

> A successful response to the problem posed by the guerrilla is neither simple to plan nor easy, cheap, and quick to carry out. . . . Basically, the problem is a political one; to attempt to understand it in purely military terms is the most dangerous kind of oversimplification. Guerrillas are a symptom rather than a cause. Lasting success requires a viable political settlement, and even operational success over a period of time demands the proper political framework for effective action.[55]

Counterguerrilla—or counterrevolutionary—warfare, thus must also rely upon the political and psychological effects of military actions. The first requirement is, of course, to impose military defeats on the guerrilla forces. The guerrillas need victories to maintain their morale, discipline, and momentum, and continual defeats are bound to have a serious impact. Moreover, the civilian population, witnessing these defeats and no longer sure that the guerrillas may win, will tend to become less cooperative. Such defeats can best be inflicted by the government if the counterguerrilla forces divide the country into a number of areas and flush the guerrillas out area by area. In order to do this, it is necessary to counter the basic mobility and surprise principles of guerrilla warfare—that is,

---

[53] On the decisiveness of civilian loyalties, rather than the external base, terror, or military tactics, see Chalmers A. Johnson, "Civilian Loyalties and Guerrilla Conflict," *World Politics*, July, 1962, pp. 646–61. Also see his interesting *Autopsy on People's War* (Berkeley: University of California Press, 1973).

[54] Griffith, in Introduction to *Mao on Guerrilla Warfare*, p. 7.

[55] Peter Paret and John W. Shy, *Guerrillas in the 1960's*, rev. ed. (New York: Praeger Publishers, 1962), pp. 71–72; see also Charles W. Thayer, *Guerrilla* (New York: Harper & Row, 1963), pp. 42–60.

government forces must find the guerrillas, pin them down, and force them to stand and fight. Once an area has been cleared and, above all, once the cell structure that controls each village has been rooted out, garrison forces composed of regular troops and perhaps militia can be left to guard it. The striking forces must be highly professional, extremely tough, thoroughly trained in unconventional warfare, and mobile enough at all times to seek out the enemy. The British in Malaya, for instance, used squads and platoons that lived in the jungles for months, gathering their own intelligence, ambushing enemy patrols, and cutting supply lines. At the same time, the British held out amnesties to guerrillas who surrendered, and a number of guerrillas, feeling beaten, did accept the amnesties.

Counterguerrilla forces can avail themselves of modern methods of communications, such as radios or walkie-talkies, which allow troops in contact with the enemy to call in reinforcements in an attempt to cut off the guerrillas' retreat. The helicopter can also be valuable, if used properly, as a means of searching out guerrillas; the guerrilla, for a change, feels hunted and is placed on the defensive. The helicopter can also be used to bring reinforcements quickly to the battlefields, thus forcing the guerrilla either to fight or to flee. But the helicopter is subject to certain limitations as well. It is virtually useless at night, and during the daytime its success in finding guerrillas depends on how bushy or jungle-covered the terrain is. Moreover, guerrillas have managed to devise antihelicopter tactics by which they try to knock them out. The helicopter probably does make it more difficult for guerrillas to defeat piecemeal a well-equipped and mobile enemy force, such as that of the United States, or impose a conventional defeat upon it in the final phase of the war.

But no counterrevolutionary war can be won by conventional military means alone: *A purely military solution is an illusion.* It is interesting to note in this connection that the successful guerrilla and counterguerrilla leaders of the past two decades have largely been nonmilitary men.[56] In China, Mao Tse-tung, a student and librarian, and subsequently a professionally trained revolutionary, defeated Chiang Kai-shek, a professionally trained soldier. In Indochina, Ho Chi Minh, a socialist agitator, and General Giap, a French-trained history teacher, defeated four of France's senior generals, including a marshal. Castro was a lawyer, and Magsaysay, who led the counterguerrilla war in the Philippines, was an automotive mechanic who became a politician. In short, the orthodox military officer by and large has been unable to cope with the unorthodox nature of guerrilla warfare.

A second requirement in antiguerrilla warfare is to separate the guerrillas from the population. One technique by which this can be accomplished is to resettle the latter in so-called strategic hamlets. Because

[56] Thayer, *Guerrilla*, p. 69.

people do not enjoy being uprooted from their homes and villages, they rarely go freely. In Malaya, the Communists were being supplied by about a half-million Chinese "squatters" who lived near the edge of the jungle and worked in nearby mines and plantations. All of them were moved, and the Communist guerrillas, left without their source of food, then had to clear sections of the jungle and plant their own. (British RAF planes subsequently searched for these spots and poisoned the crops.) Such a relocation of the population not only isolates the guerrillas but also gives the government an opportunity to prove its ability to remedy the people's grievances and satisfy at least some of their aspirations. The resettled population must learn that they can live in safety and enjoy improved social conditions: some land of their own, electric light, health facilities, education for their children, and a voice in their own government. Otherwise, the people will remain hostile to the government and will probably continue to help the guerrillas as much as possible. If the people are made more secure and given greater opportunities, however, they are more likely to defend themselves against the guerrillas. Once this happens, the war is half won.

The problem here is that the remedy is easy to prescribe but difficult to implement. In Malaya, the resettlement program was relatively simple, despite its large scale. The Chinese, an ethnic minority in Malaya, were easily identifiable. Nor were all Chinese involved in supporting the guerrillas—only the poor squatters, not the urban middle class. The squatters thus were visibly different from the rest of the population and, moreover, lived in a particular area. To find and remove them to areas away from the guerrilla war was therefore simple compared with the task in South Vietnam. There, no such distinct group exists. The strategic hamlet program would have required moving almost 10 million people—obviously a colossal operation. All this effort would, in any case, be useless if the camps did not provide their inhabitants with better living conditions and security. To be effective, the strategic hamlets must instill in the people a reason for supporting the government. Malaya's "new villages" provided such social services; moreover, the 8,000 Communist terrorists were too weak to attack the villages. South Vietnam's hamlets, both before the overthrow of Ngo Dinh Diem in late 1963 and since, failed in both respects. The regime was not particularly concerned with its people's grievances or aspirations. And the guerrillas were strong: The Communists frequently attacked the hamlets and destroyed them, thereby proving to the people that the government could not protect them, no matter what it did.

In the final analysis, the government can win its war against the revolutionaries only if it alleviates the conditions that led the peasantry to support the revolutionary party in the first place. For example, in Malaya the British promised independence; because they had already granted independence to India, Pakistan, and Burma, their word was credible, and the Malayans saw a stake in the struggle. The Communists, by the same token, were stripped of their pose as liberators from colonialism. Many Malays fought alongside British troops. The contrast to Vietnam is striking. In the First Indochina War, the people supported the Vietminh as national liberators because the French refused to grant them full independence. Ho Chi Minh thus became a symbol of Vietnamese nationalism. Anti-Communist Vietnamese who had fought with the French against the Vietminh (as anti-Communist Malays had fought with the British) were never able to compete with Ho for this nationalist identity. After 1954, they appeared to many—including many in the West— as mere puppets of France. This image was reinforced by their lack of social conscience and concern. Indeed, the government's suppression of political opponents, critics of the war, and advocates of a settlement with the Vietcong only fortified this image.

Popular confidence, then, is the *indispensable* condition for successful antirevolutionary warfare. Military countermeasures alone can never be adequate; troops trained in the tactics of unconventional warfare must be supported by political, social, and economic reform. It was this kind of combination that defeated the Communist-led Huks in the Philippines during the 1950's. The government won the allegiance of the peasantry by instituting reforms to improve their lives; the Communist appeal was weakened and the Huks lost their support.[57] A British colonel summed up the essence of counterguerrilla warfare when he said, "There has never been a successful guerrilla war conducted in an area where the populace is hostile to the guerrillas. . . . *The art of defeating the guerrillas is therefore the art of turning the populace against them.*"[58]

The major task of antirevolutionary warfare is fundamentally a *political* one. Guerrillas are a barometer of discontent. This discontent must be ameliorated, for it is the decisive element that determines victory or failure. Guerrillas are not invincible, as the British proved in Malaya and Kenya; on the other hand, they did lose in Palestine and Cyprus. In all four of these counterguerrilla efforts, the British had support among the populations; they also possessed great superiority in numbers of troops and utilized all the usual counterguerrilla techniques, including population resettlement. Yet only in Malaya and Kenya did they win, and, in a sense, the British did not really win in Malaya; rather the Communist terrorists lost as a result of the British grant of independence. The Communist insurrections in Burma and Indonesia in the late 1940's failed because of a similar lack of popular support.

Perhaps the French experience in Algeria offers the clearest illustra-

[57] See Frances L. Starner, *Magsaysay and the Philippine Peasantry: The Agrarian Impact on Philippine Politics, 1953–1956* (Berkeley and Los Angeles: University of California Press, 1961). For views of the contrasting situation in South Vietnam, see Bernard B. Fall, *The Two Viet-Nams: A Political and Military Analysis*, rev. ed. (New York: Praeger Publishers, 1964), and Denis Warner, *The Last Confucian* (New York: Macmillan, 1963).

[58] Quoted in Heilbrunn, *Partisan War*, p. 34. Emphasis added.

tion of this basic point, for the French actually won the military war against the Algerian guerrillas. By 1960, the Algerian National Liberation Army no longer possessed even a battalion-size unit. By the end of the war in 1962, the Algerian guerrillas had, according to French Army sources, fewer than 4,000 troops left (10,000 according to other, more sympathetic, French sources) out of a total of almost 60,000 three years earlier.[59] French military tactics were, in short, as effective in Algeria as they had been ineffective in Indochina. Nevertheless, the French lost the war because it was *politically* "unwinnable." The Algerian population was hostile; so were France's NATO allies and the nonaligned states. The suppression of a nationalist movement was politically unpalatable and unfeasible in an age when the legitimacy of all former colonial nations to rule themselves was almost universally recognized and asserted. It is understanding that in certain circumstances war is revolution that allows us to understand why conventionally used military force tends to be self-defeating.

American Power and the "Rules of the Game" in Vietnam[60]

One might have suspected from this prescription for counterguerrilla warfare that it would be difficult for the United States to wage this kind of warfare if it had to intervene in Vietnam. U.S. military leaders were, first of all, trained orthodoxly. They saw this war, like other wars, as essentially a military undertaking, not a political one.[61] All that needed to

[59] Fall, *Two Viet-Nams*, pp. 346–47. The Algerian example also clearly demonstrates that the use of counterterror is not successful in ending guerrilla warfare.

[60] This section is not concerned with judgments on whether the United States should have intervened in Vietnam. It focuses only on the manner in which force was used. Judgment is, of course, implicit in such an analysis. Ultimately, it reflects back on the issue of the original intervention, for if the conclusion is that force was exercised ineffectively—indeed, counterproductively—one conclusion that might be deduced is that the intervention should have been avoided in the first place. This, to be sure, is a pragmatic, not a moral, judgment. For moral and legal judgments on the war see, among others, Telford Taylor, *Nuremberg and Vietnam: An American Tragedy* (New York: Bantam Books, 1971), and Richard A. Falk, Gabriel Kolko, and Robert J. Lifton, eds., *Crimes of War* (New York: Vintage Books, 1971).

This writer's final pragmatic judgment on Vietnam is much the same as Donald Zagoria's in *Vietnam Triangle: Moscow, Peking, Hanoi* (New York: Pegasus, 1967): namely, that American strategy and tactics raise "serious doubts in my mind whether we as a nation have the wisdom, the skills and the manpower to cope with civil wars" (p. xiii).

[61] General Lewis W. Walt, the assistant commandant of the Marine Corps, confessed in 1970 that, when he visited Vietnam in 1965, he did not understand that the war was primarily a guerrilla war. Rather, he thought of it in terms of the more conventional wars, such as World War II and the Korean War. *New York Times*, November 18, 1970. General Wheeler, the Chairman of the Joint Chiefs of Staff, held the same opinion, as reported by Hilsman, *To Move a Nation*, p. 426.

be done, they felt, was to apply American technology and "know-how" to the problem. Admittedly, it was hard to conceive of the world's mightiest nation, with its sizable army led by well-trained officers, supported by the might and knowledge of American industry, and administered by Robert S. McNamara, perhaps the most keen-minded Secretary of Defense the country ever had, as unable to defeat a few thousand black-clad Asian guerrillas. It was easy to indulge in the "illusion of omnipotence." The country had, after all, beaten far greater powers. France's earlier failure was seen in terms of the alienation of Vietnamese nationalism and an army that was not as well equipped or led and had poor air support. None of these factors, presumably, would hamper the United States.

Hubris, the Greek word for overweening pride, however, proved to be a great impediment. In effect, the United States felt so powerful and so sure of success that it believed it could defeat a guerrilla war, fought according to specific "rules of the game," by simply *changing the rules* and fighting according to its *own*, or the American, concept of war.[62] And this concept emphasized the achievement of victory through the attrition of the enemy's forces. The soldier's concern was "strictly military"; politics was not his business. This division of labor suggested that the crucial political war would by and large be ignored until after the achievement of a military triumph. Then, and then only, would the Saigon government carry out the necessary political and social reforms. (Of course, if the guerrillas could be destroyed by such purely military means, reforms would be unnecessary later. Why should Saigon bother?) The additional advantage that the military saw in its conduct of the war was that America would be fighting the war, thereby avoiding the difficulties and frustrations of cooperating with Saigon's ineffective army, which was expected only to stay out of the way. Such a policy and ordering of priorities were to be a recipe for failure. For surely the war could not be won *primarily* by foreign troops but only by an indigenous army with a will to fight and support from a sizable portion of its people.

In any event, the American strategy adopted in South Vietnam from 1965 to 1968 was one of search-and-destroy to defeat the North Vietnamese forces, the assumption being that once they had been destroyed the Vietcong guerrillas could be mopped up as they fought on alone. Translated into daily operations, this strategy allocated 80 per cent of American forces to the Central Highlands and frontier areas in which only 4 per cent of the population resided. More than 90 per cent of the people lived in the Mekong Delta and coastal plain, and it was in those areas that the guerrilla war was being fought.[63] As America sent in more troops to decimate the North Vietnamese forces, Hanoi matched the

---

[62] Thompson, *No Exit from Vietnam*, pp. 13–17.

[63] Henry A. Kissinger, *American Foreign Policy* (New York: W. W. Norton, 1969), p. 102.

buildup. The U.S. aim was *physical* attrition; Hanoi's was *psychological* exhaustion.[64] The battles American forces won and the heavy casualties they inflicted could not, as a result, be transformed into lasting political success. And Washington could not avoid a seemingly interminable war that would sooner or later erode the patience of the American public. Indeed, the search-and-destroy strategy, by scattering troops all over the place and leaving the cities undefended, just begged the Vietcong to attack them. The dramatic Tet offensive of 1968 not only pointed out the folly of American strategy but also forced Americans to ask whether the war could be brought to a successful political and military conclusion at all.[65] Psychologically, Tet was the beginning of the end for the United States in Vietnam, as American opinion, already beset by doubts about the wisdom and costs of the war, became increasingly disillusioned. It was America's Dien Bien Phu, sapping Washington's will and determination. It was not a military defeat; quite the contrary, as the Vietcong lost its elite forces.

The heart of revolutionary warfare—control of the population—was rejected by the American command as requiring too defensive a strategy. Not only did it necessitate gradual clearance of guerrillas from one zone after another, it also required providing security on a continuing basis in each cleared zone, and this meant keeping the troops there. The population could then be separated from the guerrillas, the guerrilla political cell structure flushed out, and necessary reforms carried out to win the people's allegiance. Such a strategy is, of course, slow and fundamentally static. It is not dramatic in yielding big body counts and weapons losses; it is at odds with the military's offensive image of itself, and it subordinates military considerations to political and psychological ones. Yet a 30 per cent clearance of South Vietnam with the attendant provisions of security plus reform for the local population brought to it by a government that showed it cared would have contributed more to ending the war than the continuous search-and-destroy operations that cleared areas by defeating the enemy, only to move on to search for him elsewhere, while the guerrillas returned and continued to control the population. Had American forces, in fact, been able to start destroying the Vietcong infrastructure controlling South Vietnam's villages, the Vietcong and Hanoi would have seen their control begin to wither, and this would have provided them with a greater incentive to accept a political settlement of the war before their village cells were destroyed. The casualties they suffered were no comparable incentive.[66] Manpower was the price the guerrillas expected to pay for success; as harsh as it sounds, the dead were replaceable. The cells, built up over a twenty-five-year period, were not so easily replaceable.

Such an American enclave strategy might also have turned the mo-

[64] *Ibid.*, p. 104.
[65] Thompson, *No Exit from Vietnam*, pp. 70–74.
[66] *Ibid.*, pp. 51, 57–58.

mentum of the war against the guerrillas as the peasantry saw and benefited by its results; word of government and American successes might
then have spread ahead of the areas freed from Vietcong control. It is
perhaps not too much to say that, but for the helicopter, such a strategy
might at least have been considered; perhaps it might also have been
adopted—out of necessity—had not the U.S. forces possessed the mobility afforded by the helicopter. But the American love of gadgetry, the
desire to own the latest in technology in order to be as "modern" and
"efficient" as possible, was shared by the army; and it enabled the army
to adopt an irrelevant strategy. American officers apparently had not
heard the axiom that a conventional army in a guerrilla war loses if it
does not win, while guerrillas win if they do not lose. But winning in the
context of this kind of warfare demanded a strategy that gave priority to
political and psychological factors. Instead, America had a strategy guaranteed to lose. *Technology could not change the rules of revolutionary
warfare.*

Characteristically, the military told itself that it was not winning the
war because of the men and weapons coming from North Vietnam. In
this way, the military could avoid diagnosing its faulty strategy in the
South, the only place where the war could be won. In the United States,
political leaders focused on the North Vietnamese sanctuaries, believing
these had to be attacked to gain a successful conclusion to the war. They
knew that counterguerrilla wars could be lengthy affairs. In Malaya,
where the Communist terrorists had almost no outside help and little
or no support from the Malays or wealthier Chinese, it took 80,000 British and Commonwealth troops, plus 180,000 Malay special police, con-
stables, and village militia members, twelve years (from 1948 to 1960)
to defeat only 8,000 guerrillas.[67] In the Philippines, it took five years
(1947 to 1952) to defeat the Huks. And after President Magsaysay died,
the corrupt Garcia Administration faced a revival of Huk activities, so
that when President Macapagal took office in 1962, he had to order
mop-up operations. But Americans like to win their wars quickly. President Johnson could recall the more direct challenge in Korea. Within
one year, Americans were fed up with "Truman's war" and the continuation of the apparently futile loss of American lives. This mood, moreover, contributed to the defeat of the Democrats in the 1952 Presidential
election. A long-drawn-out, indecisive engagement does not fit the traditional American all-or-nothing approach, and guerrillas can exploit this
impatience. Not permitting the enemy to take shelter within his main
sanctuary thus seemed one possible way of ending the hostilities reasonably quickly and, therefore, a justifiable reason for breaking one of the
principal restraints of limited warfare.

The concept of graduated escalation in limited wars was thought of as
a means of influencing the adversary's will by a process of bargaining on

[67] Fall, *Two Viet-Nams*, p. 341.

ascending levels of violence in order to give him an incentive to agree to acceptable terms and conclude hostilities.[68] In brief, Hanoi was to be punished for its role in the war and made to pay an ever increasing price until it would desist when it had suffered enough. The air force was to be the instrument for administering this punishment. But the task was beyond the ability of the air force; indeed, the political consequences of the air war against North Vietnam have to be judged as disastrous. The reasons are several.

First, air power's ability to affect successfully an enemy's capacity to fight lies in its ability to attack the sources of his supplies and his supply lines to the battlefield; it requires that the army then engage the enemy on the battlefield in continuous combat.[69] The sources of supplies in Vietnam, however, were Russia and China; and it was the enemy who generally chose the time and length of engagement in this unconventional warfare. This left only the trails running to South Vietnam and, of course, roads, rivers, and a few factories in North Vietnam. But the trails, covered by jungle, were hard to find and ran largely through Laos and Cambodia; long periods of bad weather and the lack of an all-weather fighter-bomber (except for the F-111, which came into service late and then was plagued with constant problems) only added to the difficulties of interdiction. As for bombing the North, it could

> succeed in wiping out all North Viet-Nam's conventional industrial and military targets, but it would probably have little immediate effect on its armed forces. After all, they [the guerrillas] successfully fought the French for eight years from hidden guerrilla bases and without making use of electric-power plants and railroads. . . . Lest it be forgotten, the United States Air Force was unable successfully to interdict Communist supply operations in Korea despite the fact that all conventional targets had been effectively destroyed.[70]

In Vietnam, as in Korea, supplies kept on coming. Indeed, the flow of men and ammunition increased, and the trails were not even used to full capacity.

The real difficulty with the bombing campaign of 1965–68 would seem to have been the concept of graduated escalation. It is perhaps doubtful that it can be made to work against an underdeveloped country; an industrial state simply has more to lose. No doubt, there must be some level of punishment that would affect even an underdeveloped nation's will. But in Hanoi's case, the motivation to succeed the French in all of Indochina was so tenacious, had been held so long, had been fought and

[68] The attempts to force Hanoi to cease and desist in South Vietnam before the large commitment of ground forces in July, 1965, are catalogued in the Pentagon study of the intervention. See *Pentagon Papers*.

[69] Townsend Hoopes, *The Limits of Intervention* (New York: McKay, 1969), pp. 75–79.

[70] Fall, *Two Viet-Nams*, p. 402.

sacrificed for so many years, and had been so near to fulfillment on more than one occasion—only to be repeatedly betrayed—that the will to fight on was intense. General Giap, victor of Dienbienphu and strategist of the war in the South, had a shrewd political estimate of the Western democracies' determination to continue fighting an inconclusive war for very long: "The enemy will pass slowly from the offensive to the defensive. The blitzkrieg will transform itself into a war of long duration. Thus, the enemy will be caught in a dilemma: He has to drag out the war in order to win it and does not possess, on the other hand, the psychological and political means to fight a long-drawn-out war."[71] Whereas in Cuba the Soviets calculated that the cost of noncompliance with the American demand to pull out the missiles was greater than the cost of complying, in Vietnam Hanoi calculated that the cost of noncompliance with the Johnson Administration's demands—to desist in its military activities in the South and pull its troops back to the North—was less than the cost of complying. The North Vietnamese were willing to pay the price of bomb damage, civilian casualties and heavy losses in military manpower (600,000 men from 1965 to 1968 out of a manpower pool of 5 million, according to Hanoi, 863,577 according to the Pentagon)[72] for not having to give up their fundamental belief that they were the rightful heirs of French power throughout all of Vietnam, if not all of Indochina.

It can perhaps be argued that more bombing and quicker escalation would have raised the price for noncompliance higher than that for compliance. Perhaps. What we do know is that, in the three years of air war against North and South Vietnam, the air force dropped three times the total tonnage dropped in Europe and the Pacific during World War II (at a cost of 50 cents per pound of bomb, or a total cost of $3 billion!).[73] We also know that the bombing (particularly the use of antipersonnel devices) more than any other issue deeply divided the country at home and aroused widespread antagonism in even friendly Western nations. To have bombed Hanoi "back to the Stone Age," as one Air Force general summed up his recipe for victory, would have aroused even greater political hostility.

The bombing of North Vietnam, then, had little effect on Hanoi's determination to continue the fighting or on its ability to infiltrate. Quite the contrary. Hanoi benefited by being bombed! It undoubtedly

[71] Quoted in *Ibid.*, p. 113.

[72] Department of Defense, Office of the Assistant Secretary of Defense for Public Affairs, *Southeast Asia Casualties Statistical Summary* (Washington: Government Printing Office, 1972).

[73] Raphael Littauer and Norman Uphoff, eds., *The Air War in Indochina* (Boston: Beacon Press, 1972). See also Col. James A. Donovan, *Militarism, U.S.A.* (New York: Charles Scribner's Sons, 1970). For a more general analysis of graduated escalation, see George *et al.*, *Limits of Coercive Diplomacy*, pp. 21–30, and, for analysis of the beginning of the bombing of North Vietnam, pp. 144–200. See also *Pentagon Papers* for the development of this strategy.

received greater domestic support for its efforts in the South because, as the Battle of Britain had epically demonstrated, people who are bombarded daily have their backbone strengthened; without the bombing, Ho might not have been able quite so easily to rally his people behind a long war with a high casualty rate.[74] Worse, the bombing made the United States look like a bully and North Vietnam like the underdog. It provided Hanoi with international sympathy and support, and it stirred many an American conscience. It made Hanoi and Vietcong propaganda that their cause was just, and that Saigon's rule was morally and politically unjustified, seem more credible to millions throughout the world. The bombing turned many people out for anti-American demonstrations in various countries, and these demonstrations were just as much a part of the war as the actual battles—and seemingly more decisive. Townsend Hoopes, a Deputy Assistant Secretary of Defense, Under Secretary of the Air Force, and critic of the bombing campaign over North Vietnam, has said that the bombing raised the emotional temperature of the war and made it more difficult to handle the war "politically at home and diplomatically abroad."[75] It shifted the moral onus of the war from Hanoi to Washington. Had there been no bombing of the North and had the war been confined to the South, Hoopes maintains, the dissent against the war might not have become so widespread, bitter, and unmanageable. The bombing, in blunt words, was politically counterproductive.

It was not really until after Tet and the Nixon Administration's assumption of power that the conduct of the war changed in some significant respects and that the *political context* within which the war was fought changed dramatically. For Tet was a turning point not only psychologically within the United States but militarily in South Vietnam. The North Vietnamese surprise blow, while disillusioning much of American public opinion with the nation's involvement in the war, nevertheless resulted in extremely heavy casualties for the Vietcong, killing many of their best-trained and most experienced military cadres, so that by 1970 most of the combat was carried on by the North Vietnamese army instead of the indigenous forces. The replacement of both the U.S. field commander and the President resulted in more of an adaptation to the classical and successful counterinsurgency type of operations in South Vietnam. Vietcong capabilities were gradually reduced, although not eliminated. Politically, the President sought to preserve—as his predecessors had too—an anti-Communist government in Saigon; but he needed to win time at home. Nixon proceeded to withdraw U.S. troops gradually in order to cut casualties, reduce the draft, and thereby lessen domestic opposition; South Vietnamese forces, closely supported by U.S. air power, were to foreclose Vietcong chances of taking over the government in Saigon—the objective of revolutionary war.

[74] Thompson, *No Exit from Vietnam*, pp. 139–40.
[75] Hoopes, *Limits of Intervention*, p. 82.

The result was that in the spring of 1972 the North Vietnamese launched a large-scale attack across the so-called demilitarized zone separating North and South Vietnam, presumably to administer the *coup de grâce* at a time when few U.S. combat troops were left and just before the President's visit to Moscow. This attack was heavily supported by all the implements of modern warfare, such as tanks, which came primarily from Russia. The attack proved successful at first against some of South Vietnam's worst troops (an offensive had been expected, but elsewhere), although when reinforced they rallied later on. Very heavy American air support probably won the day; the North Vietnamese, exposing themselves to conventional warfare with modern weapons with all the logistical needs they involve (bringing up gasoline, artillery shells, and so forth) provided U.S. air power for the first time in seven years of warfare with destructible targets moving in open country. In addition, President Nixon in retaliation for what he defined as a full-scale invasion and clear-cut case of aggression, decided to restart the bombing of North Vietnam—including the use of B-52s against urban and industrial targets which had been off limits during the Johnson years—and mine the harbor of Haiphong to stop all incoming supplies. This latter step is one that President Johnson had constantly rejected, partly because, being a guerrilla force, the Vietcong was less dependent on modern weapons and, more important, because he feared that such a blockade of North Vietnam's principal harbor might precipitate Chinese military intervention. But Nixon's new bombing campaign took place in politically quite different circumstances.

Whereas Johnson had tried unsuccessfully to use Moscow to put pressure on Hanoi, which generally received Peking's support, to help him find a settlement, Nixon used both Russia's and China's needs for a *détente* with the United States to isolate North Vietnam. Nixon, in brief, offered both Communist countries carrots. Although his retaliation risked the very real possibility that the Moscow summit meeting would be called off, the President took the gamble, hoping that Moscow needed the SALT agreement and modern technology to help its sagging economy enough not to jeopardize the summit conference. He also extended to Peking an opportunity to concentrate on what it perceived to be the greater and more immediate Russian threat without simultaneously confronting the United States. Even North Vietnam, while suddenly subjected to a heavy beating with a stick, was offered some carrots; unlike earlier in 1965–68, when North Vietnam had been offered no carrots, only a cease-fire and peace if it pulled out of South Vietnam, it was now offered a complete withdrawal of U.S. forces, including U.S. air power, an opportunity to retain control of those areas it militarily dominated, plus a possible place in a coalition government to be arranged through negotiations among the various parties in South Vietnam after a cease-fire and return of U.S. prisoners of war. Deserted, Hanoi was willing to accept a settlement that eliminated direct U.S. participation in the war and left its future opportunities to capture partial or full control in the South open for a continued political-military struggle with Saigon.

Some Lessons About Power and Diplomatic Bargaining

Vietnam has rather painfully taught a number of key lessons about the power that underlies diplomacy. First, while each state's power is relative to that of whichever state it is in contention with, and *normally* a great power can achieve its objectives when in conflict with a lesser power, one must nevertheless be careful when talking of one state as more powerful than another. In terms of all the normal indices of power —population, natural resources, industry, men under arms, and military weapons—one could have expected the United States to clobber the Vietcong and Hanoi in short order. But the far more powerful nation, with a sizable army and the modern conventional paraphernalia of war, did not "win."

Second, the war stands as a reminder that power is relative not only to the power of other states but also to the specific conditions to which it is applied. Power, in order to be effective, must not only be mobilized but it must be the right kind of power, applicable to the specific conditions at issue. Thus most of America's mobilized power—both its nuclear power and most of its conventional military power—proved useless in Vietnam, because it was inapplicable against a nonindustrialized state in a war with no front lines. And the power that was applied was not as useful as it might have been, because it was applied without much regard for the political context of revolutionary warfare. In terms of the earlier distinction, the United States in Vietnam thought of power in quantitative and military terms rather than in qualitative and political-psychological ones. The guerrillas, on the other hand, related their inferior military strength from the outset of the struggle to such fundamental attitudes and social forces as the appeal of nationalism and the desires for political, social, and economic changes within Vietnam. These forces, which would have existed even in the absence of the guerrillas, were shrewdly exploited by them as "multipliers" of their own power. So were foreign attitudes created by the war itself; these attitudes included those within the United States itself.

Vietnam, in short, will long stand as a reminder of the grave limitations, if not the uselessness, of resorting to force in unfavorable political circumstances. Regardless of one's evaluation of South Vietnam's relationship to American security, or of President Diem and his rule, the very fact that, toward the end of his own days, President Kennedy acquiesced in the South Vietnamese military's overthrow of Diem testified, in Theodore Draper's words, to the political bankruptcy and catastrophic failure of American policy. "Kennedy's decision in 1963 not to block Diem's overthrow was the most deadly criticism of Kennedy's decision in 1961 to back Diem to the hilt."[76] Thus, long before Johnson's massive escalation in 1965, the situation in South Vietnam had clearly become unpromising. General Walter Bedell Smith, head of the American delegation at the 1954 Geneva Conference, once reportedly said that any second-rate general should be able to win in Indochina if there were a correct political atmosphere. Without such an atmosphere, not even a first-rate general could win. Draper was obviously correct when he concluded from this remark that "sound politics in Vietnam was the precondition of military victory, not that military victory was the precondition of sound politics."[77] Resort to force in unfavorable political circumstances, he said, constitutes an "abuse of force" and can only result in political failure. The use of force in such circumstances will result in a loss of a state's reputation for power.

Third, coercive diplomacy as pure coercion makes the task of coercion much more difficult, for it offers the adversary no incentive to settle. But a coercive diplomacy that mixes coercion with rewards reduces the opponent's reasons for continued resistance and may isolate him from his allies. Johnson offered Hanoi nothing while limiting the amount of pressure on North Vietnam through the air war due to the considerable domestic opposition this part of the war had aroused. Given the asymmetry of motivation favoring North Vietnam during the war, which meant an intense commitment to capturing power throughout all of Vietnam, the losses Hanoi suffered during the war were tolerable; by contrast, U.S. motivation to resist this aim eroded fairly quickly as the war dragged on. Hanoi expected a long war; this was inherent in the strategy of revolutionary warfare plus its expectation that democracies could not fight long wars. Nixon, on the other hand, like Kennedy in the Cuban crisis, offered Hanoi rewards while simultaneously greatly increasing the pressure of the air war despite intense public criticisms; most of all, he isolated Hanoi by playing Russia and China off against one another.

Fourth, Vietnam underlines the distinction between negative and positive power. Negative power, the capacity to prevent unfavorable changes in a nation's perceived security interests, seems to be the power that the superpowers wield the most effectively. Both have managed to deter total war and forestall any major changes in the territorial divisions drawn by World War II. The international *status quo* has, on the whole, been frozen since 1945. Most major territorial changes historically have resulted from the threat or use of force. But as the costs of warfare have risen out of all proportion to the objectives that might be achieved, most conflicts have been perpetuated instead of resolved. Preventing changes has become the principal role of the threat or employment of force. By contrast, positive power, the capacity to compel

[76] Theodore Draper, *Abuse of Power* (New York: Viking, 1967), p. 59; *Pentagon Papers*.

[77] Draper, *Abuse of Power*, pp. 29, 30.

favorable alterations in the *status quo*, seems less successful in the post-war period. While the United States succeeded in compelling Moscow to pull its missiles out of Cuba, it clearly failed to force the Vietcong and Hanoi to desist in South Vietnam. The contrast between the American ability to preserve the *status quo* vis-à-vis the powerful Soviet Union and the inability to compel relatively small and puny Hanoi to comply with its demands is startling.

This failure of a superpower to coerce such a minor country as North Vietnam (by contrast, Russia did not try to use force against Yugoslavia when Tito broke with Stalin) is no fluke and, therefore, needs some elaboration. A major reason for the smaller powers' successful wielding of negative power is their capacity to resist pacification. The growth of nationalism since the French Revolution has made it increasingly difficult to conquer *and* pacify foreign territories and populations. The conquered peoples of Europe resisted the Nazi oppressors. If Britain in 1956 had toppled Nasser of Egypt or if the United States had successfully overthrown Castro in 1961, each would have found itself confronting a lengthy and, for democracies, morally and politically repugnant task of pacification. In brief, weak countries with a strong sense of national identity—and foreign attack can be a powerful stimulant of nationalism—can make the use of force against themselves look most unattractive because of their resistant capacity. To be sure, the strong might still prevail over the weak in the long run, but the price of victory might be so high that the objective sought becomes, on balance, not worth it. Pacification can be made costly and difficult by a continued resistance fixed by nationalistic emotions directed against the foreign intruder and occupier.

In addition, the opinions of other countries, as well as segments of domestic opinion in the democratic society engaged in the conflict, tend to inhibit the use of force or, if that fails, make winning a victory difficult, if not impossible. (A Russia can crush a Hungary or Czechoslovakia because, however outraged external opinion may be, domestic opposition has no way of expressing itself politically.) The cost in terms of a loss of external respect and prestige, as well as domestic unity, is too high. For an older, Western, white nation with a colonial legacy to attempt to coerce or use force against one of the new, non-Western, non-white, ex-colonial nations in an age that recognizes the legitimacy of national self-determination arouses a sense of democratic guilt and moral repugnance. One need but note the opposition within Britain and the Commonwealth countries in 1956 to the Suez War, the internal American aversion and resistance to the Vietnam war (as well as criticisms in allied countries), and President Kennedy's apprehension in 1961 that the use of American forces in Cuba would alienate the very progressive elements in Latin America needed for the success of the Alliance for Progress.

In these circumstances, the differences in power between David and

Goliath, if not neutralized, are certainly reduced, because *domestic conditions*—not just external ones—may make it impossible either to mobilize power or use it as the policy-makers might wish; in extreme circumstances, large segments of public opinion may be alienated. Nothing stimulated domestic protest more, as we already know, than the air war against North Vietnam. The Johnson Administration felt itself so besieged on this issue that, for example, it called bombing halts while it ostensibly pursued peace negotiations which, when they failed, could be blamed on Hanoi, thus justifying continued bombing; it also limited its attacks to certain kinds of targets such as bridges and railroad lines, which would avoid extensive civilian damage and loss of life. Nixon, by contrast, was unable to use ground forces any more because of the uproar about U.S. casualties. (The total casualties were about 50,000 dead, spread over a period of several years; ironically, the 50,000 killed on U.S. roads each year elicit no protest.) The blockade plus massive bombing with heavy bombers in 1972 brought an uproar from influential segments of Congressional, journalistic, and public opinion; this was especially true of the Christmas bombing, which Nixon claimed he used to compel Hanoi to accept a cease-fire (which occurred shortly after the bombing, whether due to the bombing or not). Nevertheless, Nixon, in this as in much of his Vietnam policy, tended to do what he felt was right regardless of criticisms; one result was a good deal of Congressional hostility, including an act to limit presidential war powers.

An apt way of summing up this significant point is to re-emphasize an earlier point: that a power relationship exists when one side complies with the demands of the other when it invokes sanctions. In David-Goliath relationships, the asymmetry of motivation favoring the highly nationalistic Davids over the Goliaths beset by inner doubts about the rightness of their cause and the havoc and destruction they create in the name of that cause means that the former calculate that the cost for complying with the Goliaths' demands is far higher than that of not complying; conversely, the latter finally give up because they calculate the cost of continuing their attempts to coerce the Davids is no longer acceptable. The cost is disproportionate to the end to be achieved.

Fifth, the term "negative power" ought not to suggest to us that this is "useless" power. Absolute power, it has been said, equals absolute impotence. Strategic power is useful only as a means of denial, not gain, in the prevailing situation of mutual deterrence. The conclusion sometimes drawn is that military power, no longer equated with a coercive power that can achieve gains, ought to be largely discounted as an important instrument of national policy. Yet the nonuse of strategic power, our analysis shows, should not be confused with a lack of usefulness. As Kenneth Waltz has suggested somewhat ironically, this is like saying "that the police force that seldom if ever employs violence is weak or that a police force is strong only when policemen are swinging their clubs. To vary the image, it is comparable to saying that a man with large assets is not rich if he spends little money or that a man is rich only if he spends a lot of it."[78]

Even if the two superpowers did not possess any nuclear weapons, they would still be superpowers pursuing deterrent strategies; they would certainly go to war no more lightly than they do today. The penalty of a failure of deterrence might not be fatal, but it would nevertheless be enormous. Indeed, they might destroy each other just or almost as much; it would only take longer with conventional arms. The history of twentieth-century war had been marked by the quick growth of the scale of destruction even before Hiroshima. The significance of the use of military power for the negative purpose of deterrence, given the immense consequences of resorting to an all-out conventional or nuclear war, is thus hardly to be denied or denigrated. More important, while deterrent power will—it is hoped—neutralize deterrent power, this does not mean that the value of strategic power in international negotiations has been so reduced that the superpowers are really no longer superior to, or are only equal with, the second-rank powers that possess only puny nuclear forces or none at all. The superpowers remain superpowers because they have immense resources that allow them to maintain not only large strategic forces, but sizable conventional forces, as well as various nonmilitary kinds of power, such as economic power.

Perhaps the distinction between negative and positive power, while analytically very useful, is a little too neat and needs some qualification. The mere existence of strategic weapons has, as we have seen over and over again, a profound impact on the political relations among countries. Power being what people think it is, weapons deployments, numbers of weapons, and innovations in weaponry can have major effects on the willingness of one party to risk challenging the other, the determination of the challenged party to resist, and, as we shall see in the next chapter, the cohesiveness or lack of cohesion of alliances. Robert Osgood has accurately and perceptively noted that

> . . . the most important consequence of a stable or unstable, credible or incredible, posture of deterrence may be, not the prevention or outbreak of overt aggression, but rather the maintenance or loss of prestige and morale, the strength or weakness of political positions and diplomatic maneuvers, or the consolidation or disintegration of the alliance itself. For expectations about the circumstances and consequences of war in the minds of nations and statesmen—Americans, adversaries, allies and the non-aligned—may affect the fortunes of the cold war no less decisively than war itself.[79]

To the extent that the conflict between the two superpowers continues to be waged against a background of *beliefs* about their relative power

---

[78] Kenneth Waltz, "International Structure, National Force, and the Balance of World Power," *Journal of International Affairs*, 2 (1967): 224.

[79] Osgood, *NATO*, p. 16.

by themselves and all other watching states—about whether and how they will use their power, and what are likely to be the consequences— the continuing importance of strategic military power is clear. The Berlin crises after 1958 and the Cuban missile crisis of 1962 occurred precisely in these circumstances, in which the perceptions of power by the adversaries, their allies, and the nonaligned countries were changing. Negative power has a way, then, of becoming positive power, because strategic weapons under some conditions do possess *diplomatic leverage*. They are not, as is so often said, good for nothing but deterrence. This deep political impact of nuclear weapons is very visible in both superpowers' alliance relationships.

8 The Changing Character of Alliances and Nonalignment

The Reasons for Alliances

The shift from bipolarity to bipolycentrism led to changes in the behavior of the superpowers from a total to a limited adversary partnership complemented by increasing cooperation in arms control and other areas. Bipolycentrism also produced changes in the cohesiveness of the principal alliances of each; the same causes that have weakened the bonds of NATO have deeply affected the relations between Russia and China. We shall, therefore, direct our analysis to these two alliances—with some side glances at the Warsaw Pact—and emphasize the similar effects of such environmental factors; later, we shall examine the impact of ideology as a major difference between America's and Russia's alliances.[1]

Alliances have traditionally been a major technique in the balance-of-power politics engaged in by states perceiving common threats. The obvious reason is that allies constitute an addition of the power of other nations to one's own. Since, in the final analysis, this extra strength is desirable if the ultimate test of war should occur, an alliance might be called—in Robert Osgood's phrase—a "latent war community."[2] Western Europe in 1945 was, of course, an area of weakness; Germany in particular, after its total collapse, constituted a "power vacuum" into which Russian and American power flowed. Europe, historically the cockpit of world power, was potentially still powerful. Germany, for example, might

---

[1] See Chapter 11.

[2] Robert E. Osgood, *Alliances and American Foreign Policy* (Baltimore: Johns Hopkins Press, 1968). For other recent analyses of alliances, see George Liska, *Nations in Alliance* (Baltimore: Johns Hopkins Press, 1962); Francis A. Beer, ed., *Alliances: Latent War Communities in the Contemporary World* (New York: Holt, Rinehart & Winston, 1970); and Julian R. Friedman *et al.*, eds., *Alliance in International Politics* (Boston: Allyn & Bacon, 1970).

lie in ruins, but the skills and energy of its workers, the technological knowledge and inventiveness of its engineers and scientists, and the managerial abilities of its industrial executives were still in existence. What Europe needed was resources, rebuilt factories, and new machinery for the recovery of its economic health, political self-confidence, and military strength. To achieve these objectives, American policy gave Europe economic aid under the Marshall Plan, provided it with protection under NATO, and persistently pressured the European states—individually in the postwar era second-rank powers even should they recover—to merge into a United States of Europe.

For Russia, the demise of Nationalist China and the birth of Communist China also seemed to spell an accretion of power for what immediately came to be called the Sino-Soviet bloc. The addition of a sizable fellow Communist state whose potential power was enormous were it ever to industrialize appeared at the time as a major advantage to Moscow. Thus, while Europe, already "modern," was to transform itself into a larger nation to multiply its power, China, already a huge country, needed to modernize itself to realize its potential power.

A second purpose of alliances has been to "draw lines," to leave no doubt in an adversary's mind about which areas are considered vital to oneself and are to be left alone; another way of stating this is to talk of the credibility of commitments. With NATO, the United States for the first time committed itself to a peacetime alliance in order to inform the Soviet Union explicitly which area of the world was judged of vital importance to American security and what actions on Russia's part would precipitate a military conflict. In justifying the Senate's approval of the alliance, Republican Senator Vandenberg, leader of bipartisan support for Democratic President Truman's foreign policy, said:

> In my opinion, when Mr. Hitler was contemplating World War Two, I believe he would have never launched it if he had had any serious reasons to believe that it might bring him into armed collision with the United States. I think he was sure it would not do so because of our then existing neutrality laws. If an appropriate North Atlantic Pact is written, I think it will exactly reverse this psychology so far as Mr. Stalin is concerned if, as and when he contemplates World War Three.[3]

American troops stationed in Europe were to serve as a tripwire to leave no doubt of the U.S. commitment. Indeed, the Marshall Plan had already declared America's interest in Europe, and, even before the signing of the NATO treaty, the occupation troops in Germany had made both powers cautious in their Berlin confrontation during 1948–49. The management of that conflict reflected the unwillingness of both the United States and the Soviet Union to risk a total war. Thus, almost at the start the Western powers ruled out an attempt to reopen the corridor to Ber-

[3] Arthur H. Vandenberg, Jr., *The Private Papers of Senator Vandenberg* (Boston: Houghton Mifflin, 1952), pp. 479–80.

lin by sending troops and tanks to challenge the Red Army. Instead, they limited themselves to an airlift to supply the city with all its needs. The Russians did not challenge this effort, for they knew that if they did so successfully, they might leave the United States and Britain with no alternative but to fight. When the airlift proved that the Allies could amply supply the needs of West Berlin's citizens, the Russians simply called off their blockade. In later American alliances, where no troops have been stationed along a demarcation line—for example, the Southeast Asia Treaty Organization—the signing of the alliance has been intended to convey the possibility of collective intervention or, in the absence of allied support, of unilateral intervention if an Administration were to perceive this as necessary.

For their part, Russia and China signed the Treaty of Friendship, Alliance, and Mutual Assistance, the central provision of which provided Soviet protection for China in the event of an American attack. During the subsequent Korean War, this treaty was a major factor discouraging American air attacks on China as well as U.S. attempts to land Nationalist troops on the mainland once Communist China became involved. Both courses of action were insistently recommended by General MacArthur, and both were rejected as too risky. Washington feared that bombing China and inflicting a defeat upon Russia's principal ally would probably precipitate World War III. China was the Soviet Union's largest and most important ally, and Russian self-interest in the Far East and the necessity of maintaining Russian prestige in the Communist sphere would make it difficult for the Soviet Union to ignore a direct attack upon the China mainland. As Secretary of State Acheson explained, in such instances there were a number of courses the Russians might follow:

> They could turn over to the Chinese large numbers of planes and "volunteer" crews for retaliatory action in Korea and outside. They might participate with the Soviet Air Force and the submarine fleet. [Or the] Kremlin could elect to parallel the action taken by Peiping and intervene with half a million or more ground-force "volunteers"; or it could go the whole way and launch an all-out war. Singly, or in combination, these reactions contain explosive possibilities, not only for the Far East, but for the rest of the world as well.[4]

Soviet deterrence thus worked as well. In Europe, the Warsaw Pact between Russia and the East European countries formalized Soviet control and erased any doubts—if any existed after Russia's longtime interest in a security belt on its western borders had been embodied in the stationing of Red Army troops throughout the area—that it would allow any of its allies to defect or that it would sit meekly by if the United States tried to help any defection attempts.

---

[4] Quoted in John W. Spanier, *The Truman-MacArthur Controversy and the Korean War* (Cambridge, Mass.: Harvard University Press, 1959), p. 248.

For deterrent purposes, an alliance such as NATO, which has already continued past its original twenty-five-year term and is committed solely to preserving Europe's territorial *status quo*, stands in glaring contrast to the alliances of the interwar period. Quite apart from other reasons why deterrence was not a feasible policy against Nazi Germany, a yet unmentioned one lies in the shifts of some states from one alliance to another and the bilateral nature of many of the alliances.[5] France, after all, did try after World War I to establish alliances that would help it contain German power in the future. But Britain would only commit itself to the defense of France's frontier with Germany; it refused to support the French alliances with Poland, Czechoslovakia, Yugoslavia, and Rumania, which were intended to strengthen these countries vis-à-vis Germany's revisionist ambitions in Eastern Europe. Because France, after its blood-letting in World War I, would not take a firm stand that entailed a risk of having to fight another war without Britain, deterrence in Eastern Europe could not be implemented. In recognition of this, Poland signed a nonaggression treaty with Hitler. And Russia, which had an alliance with France, watched as, in 1938, France let Czechoslovakia down, and then switched sides within a year. So a powerful potential ally was lost to France and Britain, weakening deterrence even further. Finally, the British opposition to Italy's Ethiopian adventure alienated Mussolini and drove him into partnership with Hitler. By contrast, the presence of two multilateral, long-term alliances committed to the preservation of the *status quo* in postwar Western and Eastern Europe provided reasonable stability and the protection of each superpower's sphere of influence.

The Impact of Nuclear Weapons: Decreasing Credibility of Commitments and Perception of Threat

When NATO was formed the United States still held a monopoly of atomic bombs; Russia had only just tested an atomic device. Thus America's vows of protection for its allies were highly credible. But this situation began to change in the 1950's and was symbolically demonstrated by the first Soviet ICBM test in 1957, followed shortly thereafter by the first Sputnik, and redemonstrated after 1972 by the SALT agreements on offensive and defensive strategic arms. As the Soviet Union gradually acquired an increasing capability to hit the United States, achieving strategic "parity" in the early 1970's, the credibility of the American commitment to Europe's defense was reduced.

The Europeans know that in these changed circumstances of the mutual capacity to strike at one another, any American President con-

[5] Arnold Wolfers, *Britain and France Between Two Wars* (New York: W. W. Norton, 1966), and Keith Eubank, *The Origins of World War II* (New York: Crowell, 1969).

fronted by Soviet challenges in Europe must face the agonizing choices of suicide or surrender. They know that before the atom bomb one nation could pledge itself to come to another's rescue in the event of an attack and expect, at worst, to lose the war, pay reparations, and possibly lose some territory. They also know that nuclear weapons have changed this situation radically. No nation can be expected to risk its existence for an ally; therefore, the credibility of American pledges is at best uncertain, at worst, meaningless. The fact that the Soviets could strike the United States and impose catastrophic damage means that, in the event of a specific challenge, areas formerly considered of "vital interest" to American security might be reduced to only "secondary interest," not worth defending at the cost of the nation and its comfortable way of life. At the moment of crisis, it might seem better to accept a limited loss by making some suitable denial of the value of the area surrendered. American responses—or, rather, lack of effective response—to Soviet challenges in Berlin in the late 1950's aroused fear in Europe precisely because they were seen as a preview of things to come. A newly vulnerable America would hesitate to defend a West Berlin if the cost of such defense was the destruction of New York, Chicago, Washington, Los Angeles, and San Francisco. Was anything short of an attack on the United States itself "worth" the destruction of these cities?[6]

European concern about the credibility of the NATO commitment rose as the United States from the Kennedy Administration onward searched for an alternative to a suicide-or-surrender massive response to possible limited Communist probes in Europe. The Europeans feared what was at the time called American "nuclear disengagement" from the continent. For the United States emphasized not only that ground forces had to be mobilized to fight limited wars in Europe, as well as outside of Europe, but also that these forces had to be conventionally armed. Such an army, equipped with tactical nuclear weapons, was not thought to be a credible deterrent. In the first place, a limited war fought with tactical nuclear arms would be as devastating for Europe as an all-out strategic nuclear war would be for the United States. Therefore, just as the threat of all-out war by the United States was not considered a sufficient deterrent to a limited Soviet probe, the threat of fighting a tactical nuclear war might not deter the Soviets. Indeed, in as much as they were well aware that the Europeans had no desire to see their lands laid waste for a third time in a century, the Soviets might be tempted to probe on the gamble that America's European partners would prefer to surrender rather than risk virtual suicide. A second reason for using only conventional arms was that once tactical nuclear weapons were employed, the clear-cut distinction between nonnuclear and

[6] Pierre M. Gallois, "U.S. Strategy and the Defense of Europe," *Orbis*, Summer, 1963, pp. 226–49; for a conflicting view from another French military thinker, see André Beaufre, *Deterrence and Strategy* (New York: Praeger Publishers, 1966).

nuclear tactical arms would have been erased, and the possibility of an escalation to strategic nuclear war would increase; the pressure from field commanders to use weapons of larger and larger yields would be great once the original distinctions between nuclear and conventional arms had been eliminated.

From the American point of view—where the concern was to meet limited Soviet challenges *without* precipitating total war—this emphasis on conventionally equipped limited-war forces was, then, an arms-control measure. It permitted the NATO alliance to defend Europe in the event of a limited attack. But the Europeans on whose soil such a conflict would be fought—and here geography led to conflicting perceptions and needs—have viewed this emphasis on conventional warfare as tantamount to a tacit "deal" between the United States and the Soviet Union in which both agree that Europe could be the battleground in any conflict while the homelands of the two superpowers remained out of bounds, protected by their strategic nuclear forces. The Continental countries, understandably enough, from their point of view are also concerned almost exclusively with deterrence rather than defense.

There is an inevitable difference of perspective between ourselves and some of our allies. If the NATO area is looked on as a unit, a strategy that exposes a limited territory to the fluctuations of conventional combat may seem eminently sensible. To the allies on whose territory such a war would be fought, however, a Soviet penetration of even a hundred miles might well spell the end of their national existence. They have compelling incentive to strive for a strategy that poses the threat of maximum devastation for the Soviets. Europeans are almost inevitably more concerned with deterrence than with defense. They will prefer a strategy that seems to magnify the risks of the aggressor rather than reduce the losses of the defender.[7]

Accordingly, the Europeans have generally argued that ground forces should be equipped with tactical nuclear weapons—not in order to fight *after* an attack has been launched, but in order to *deter* the attack entirely. If the danger of employing tactical nuclear weapons is indeed the possibility of escalation, then this very danger constitutes a deterrent, for the Soviets will be as fearful of escalation into a strategic exchange as the Western powers. If the fear of total war is a deterrent because all-out nuclear war has become "unthinkable," then the fear that a tactical nuclear war might ignite a thermonuclear war would also render a war in Europe unthinkable. In brief, what deterrence on the strategic level was for the United States, deterrence on the tactical level became for the Europeans.[8]

[7] Henry A. Kissinger, "NATO's Nuclear Dilemma," *Reporter*, March 28, 1963, pp. 26–27. Kissinger expanded his thoughts on NATO's strategic problems in *The Troubled Partnership* (New York: McGraw-Hill, 1965).

[8] Bernard Brodie, "What Price Conventional Capabilities in Europe?" *Reporter*, May 23, 1963, p. 33.

Thus security was a potent factor in the development of first the British, and then the French, national deterrent forces to protect their respective nation's vital interests in those instances when the United States might deem a particular interest not worth the risk of war. To the degree that, in the nuclear age, the superpower might not risk its existence for the defense of a protectorate's interest, a national deterrent came to be seen by the secondary power as a substitute for an alliance. The question, of course, was whether such a *force de frappe*, whose strike capacity would be only about 5 per cent of that of the United States, could constitute an effective *force de dissuasion?* Were not small independent national deterrents composed primarily of some bombers or a few missiles useless even as first-strike forces (the only way they could be employed, as they would not be strong enough to survive a Soviet first strike to serve as second-strike forces)? Given that the Soviet Union was virtually invulnerable because neither British nor French strategic forces could knock out more than a fraction of the Soviet bombers and missile force, how could they deter a Soviet challenge? Were these allied deterrents therefore any more likely to be used than the far larger and more powerful American deterrent? Indeed, were these forces not a wasteful and useless duplication? President de Gaulle answered these questions in the negative:

"The atomic force with which France intends to equip itself is and will remain," they [France's critics] say, "insignificant in relation to those of the U.S. and Russia. To build it up is thus to waste a lot of effort and money for nothing. And then, within the alliance, the U.S. has an overwhelming superiority, therefore no one should run counter to its strategy through any divergent action."

It is quite true that the number of nuclear weapons with which we can equip ourselves will not equal, far from it, the mass of those of the two giants of today. But since when has it been proved that a people should remain deprived of the most effective weapons for the reason that its chief possible adversary and its chief friend have means far superior to its own? . . .

Moreover, the atomic force has a feature of its own, in that it has an efficacy that is certain and to an extent that is frightening even if it does not approach the conceivable maximum. . . . I only want to say that the French atomic force, from the very beginning of its establishment, will have the sombre and terrible capacity of destroying in a few seconds millions of men. This fact cannot fail to have at least some bearing on the intents of any possible aggressor.[9]

[9] Press conference on January 14, 1963, in *Major Addresses, Statements and Press Conferences of General Charles de Gaulle May 19, 1958–January 31, 1964* (New York: French Embassy, Press and Information Service), pp. 216–17. A critique may be found in Helmut Schmidt, *Defense or Retaliation: A German View* (New York: Praeger Publishers, 1962), and Raymond Aron, *The Great Debate* (Garden City, N.Y.: Doubleday, 1965). The role of nuclear arms in de Gaulle's political strategy is analyzed in Wilfrid L. Kohl, *French Nuclear Diplomacy* (Princeton, N.J.: Princeton University Press, 1971).

Whatever the pros and cons of these arguments over the effectiveness of small deterrent forces, there can be no doubt that they posed a crisis for the NATO alliance. No nation is willing to permit another to risk its own survival on an issue it may not deem vital. The possibility that one member of the alliance might pull all its partners into war, even though none considered the particular issue at stake worth the risk, could weaken, if not dissolve, the bonds of cohesion. Thus, the birth of independent deterrents radically altered the previously existing situation in which the United States had possessed the exclusive authority to decide when to fight and over what issue. Now Britain and France had their fingers on the trigger as well; now Britain and France had the potential to decide for what causes Americans would perish. For America, the risk was new, extraordinary—and unacceptable. Europeans had had no choice but to accept it. They had, of course, protested on those occasions when they felt that the United States might be about to act recklessly and involve them in all-out war. But the final decision had rested in American hands. By acting unilaterally, as in Cuba in 1962, when its vital interests were involved—and thereby risking a war that could have incinerated tens of millions of Europeans—the United States was doing exactly what it did not want the Europeans to do.

The very fact that the United States did not want to be triggered into war against its will reinforced the Europeans in their belief that they must have independent deterrents. Hence, though the United States generally insisted—and continues to so insist—that national deterrents were not needed because the alliance shared common interests, all of which would be defended by the American deterrent, its opposition to these deterrents has been based squarely on its refusal to be drawn into a war against its will. To avoid being triggered into a war against its will, the United States saw the necessity of retaining its virtual nuclear monopoly and predominant position within NATO. For, as de Gaulle perceptively remarked, "countries which do not have an atomic arsenal believe that they have to accept a strategic and consequently a political dependency in relation to that one of the two giants which is not threatening them."[10] For the giant this is, of course, the most desirable relationship, because, as de Gaulle added, "In politics and in strategy, as in the economy, monopoly naturally appears to the person who holds it to be the best possible system."[11]

Nuclear arms also proved a divisive factor in Sino-Soviet relations, but the basic point of their disagreement about the impact of nuclear arms on international politics was the issue of "peaceful coexistence." In the Soviet view, nuclear arms had made coexistence the sole alternative to nonexistence. Implicitly, the Soviets were admitting that nuclear war could upset what Marxism-Leninism called the laws of history—that it

[10] *President de Gaulle Holds Tenth Press Conference*, French Embassy release, p. 8.

[11] *Major Addresses of de Gaulle*, p. 217.

could forestall the final emergence of a Communist world. The Chinese disagreed publicly:

> Whether or not the imperialists will unleash a war is not determined by us; we are, after all, not chiefs-of-staff to the imperialists. [But] if the U.S. or other imperialists . . . should dare to fly in the face of the will of all humanity by launching a war using atomic and nuclear weapons, the result will be the very speedy destruction of these monsters encircled by the peoples of the world, and the result will certainly not be the annihilation of mankind. . . . On the debris of a dead imperialism, the victorious people would create very swiftly a civilisation thousands of times higher than the capitalist system and a truly beautiful future for themselves. . . . Rocketry and so on has changed, as alleged by the modern revisionists [what the Chinese called Khrushchev], the basic characteristics of the epoch of imperialism and proletarian revolution pointed out by Lenin. . . . We believe in the absolute correctness of Lenin's thinking: War is an inevitable outcome of systems of exploitation and the source of modern wars is the imperialist system. Until the imperialist system and the exploiting classes come to an end, wars of one kind or another will always occur.[12]

Khrushchev responded with a blunt comment on the Chinese position:

> Foreign scientists and military experts estimate that the United States now has roughly 40,000 hydrogen bombs and warheads. Everyone knows that the Soviet Union, too, has more than enough of this stuff.
>
> What would happen if all these nuclear weapons were brought down on people? Scientists estimate that the first blow alone would take a toll of 700 to 800 million human lives. All the big cities would be wiped out or destroyed—not only in the two leading nuclear countries, the United States and the U.S.S.R., but in France, Britain, Germany, Italy, China, Japan and many other countries of the world. The effects of a nuclear war would continue to tell through the lifetime of many generations, causing disease and death and the worst deformities in the development of people. I am not saying these things to frighten anyone. I am simply citing data at the disposal of science. These data cannot but be reckoned with.
>
> There can be no doubt that a world nuclear war, if started by the imperialist maniacs, would inevitably result in the downfall of the capitalist system, a system breeding wars. But would the socialist countries and the cause of socialism all over the world benefit from a world nuclear disaster? Only people who deliberately shut their eyes to the facts can think so. As for Marxist-Leninists, they cannot propose to establish a Communist civilisation on the ruins of centres of world culture, on land laid waste and contaminated by nuclear fall-out. We need hardly add that in the case of many peoples, the question of socialism would be eliminated altogether, because they would have disappeared bodily from our planet.[13]

[12] *Red Flag*, April 16, 1960; quoted in David Floyd, *Mao Against Khrushchev* (New York: Praeger Publishers, 1964), pp. 267–68.

[13] Khrushchev's address to the Sixth Congress of the East German Communist Party, January 16, 1963; quoted in Floyd, *Mao Against Khrushchev*, pp. 353–54.

This verbal exchange could hardly be interpreted to mean that the Chinese were for war or the Soviets for peace. To be sure, this was how Khrushchev presented the issue in order to consolidate the Soviet position in the Communist movement and thereby isolate the Chinese. But the issue of war or peace was not that simple. Only a few years earlier, in his power struggle with Malenkov, Khrushchev had himself taken the "hard" line now identified with Peking. Malenkov, successor to Stalin as Prime Minister, had stated that a nuclear war would destroy "world civilization"—that is, both the capitalist and the Communist countries. Denying this, Khrushchev had said that while the Communist states would suffer heavy damage, they would not be destroyed; only the capitalist countries would be eliminated. The thesis that nuclear war would cause the destruction of world civilization was denounced as a capitalist trick to lull the masses into a false sense of security and to allow the capitalists to pose as saviors of peace while they really pursued an aggressive course.[14] Not until after Khrushchev—who had succeeded to Stalin's other and more powerful position as First Secretary of the Party—had toppled Malenkov in 1955 did he reverse himself; at the Twentieth Party Congress, in 1956, he adopted Malenkov's earlier position. Suddenly, he was contending that nuclear war threatened the destruction of the Soviet Union. Perhaps the greatest irony of this dispute is that it had been the Chinese, now accused by Khrushchev of being warmongers, who had first enunciated the principles of "peaceful coexistence" throughout Asia. In 1954 they had spoken out for mutual respect for each other's territorial integrity and sovereignty, nonaggression, noninterference in each other's internal affairs, equality, and mutual benefit.[15]

When one examines actual behavior, it becomes even more difficult to analyze the Sino-Soviet debate in terms of the simple war-peace dichotomy. For despite all the talk of peaceful coexistence, it was Khrushchev who could not refrain from brandishing his sputniks and ICBMs and making them "pay off" politically and psychologically. It was Khrushchev who violated the moratorium on nuclear testing in 1961; it was his nuclear blackmail tactics that on several occasions brought the world to the brink of war; and it was he who repeatedly warned America's allies that he would turn their countries into "cemeteries." Finally, it was Khrushchev who in the name of peaceful coexistence had brought on the dangerous Cuban missile confrontation. This attempt suggested that Khrushchev's concept of peaceful coexistence was less a matter of choice than a necessity for the strategically inferior Soviet Union. Had he been

[14] The Malenkov-Khrushchev dispute over nuclear weapons is analyzed in Herbert S. Dinerstein, *War and the Soviet Union*, rev. ed. (New York: Praeger Publishers, 1962), pp. 65–77.

[15] See A. Doak Barnett, *Communist China and Asia* (New York: Harper & Row, 1960), pp. 100–101.

able to place his missiles in Cuba, he might in fact have been able to treat the American "imperialists" as the "paper tigers" the Chinese alleged they were.[16]

By contrast, Chinese actions hardly matched their militant words. It may be true that the Chinese believe a "truly beautiful future" awaits the world after a nuclear war; and Mao is reported to have stated that even if China lost 300 million people in a nuclear war, it would—unlike the Soviet Union and the United States—still have 300 million people left and would therefore emerge as the world's strongest power. But the Chinese have shown little desire to become involved in a major war with the United States. They probably are quite aware that the nuclear destruction of China's food supplies and cities, however few and however primitively industrialized, would wreck the control system by which the totalitarian government in Peking maintains itself in power. In any case, the Chinese record when it has confronted American power is not one of recklessness but of caution. In the Korean conflict, the Chinese warned that an advance into North Korea would compel them to enter the war, just as the Communist invasion of South Korea had forced the United States to fight. Both sides intervened for the same defensive reason—to prevent the "Korean dagger" from being aimed, and thrust, into their hearts. The first Chinese intervention, in late October, 1950, was a limited one and was broken off in early November. For three weeks there was no contact; then, in response to MacArthur's November offensive, the Chinese counterattacked. Once they were fully committed, the Chinese sought to ensure the "limitation" of the war by refraining from such measures as air attacks on the forces in the field or on the supply ports.

Several years later, the Chinese made two attempts to capture the offshore islands of Quemoy and Matsu in the Formosa Straits; they broke off the action when they realized the American determination to support the Nationalist troops on the islands. The Chinese were actually so cautious that Khrushchev, whom the Chinese were at the time accusing of having become "timid as a mouse," taunted Mao: Pointing to the colony of Macao, which lies off the coast of China and has been controlled by the Portuguese for centuries, and to the British colony of Hong Kong, situated just below Canton, Khrushchev wondered why, if the Chinese pursued the militant policy they were preaching and trying to foist on the Russians, they did not simply take over both islands. Surely they were not fearful of a war with Portugal or Britain.[17]

Indeed Mao's fame, on the basis of both his writings and his actions, has been built upon his concept of protracted warfare. His formula has always been "strategically despise the enemy, tactically take them seri-

---

[16] Floyd, *Mao Against Khrushchev*, p. 67.

[17] *Ibid.*, pp. 328–29. Clearly, to make his point, Khrushchev intentionally overlooked the value to the Chinese—in terms of foreign exchange as well as information—of both foreign enclaves.

ously." Translated into common sense terms, this means that the opponent may be weak, a "paper tiger" or a "giant with feet of clay," but in specific conflicts one must carefully reckon the balance of forces and proceed cautiously. As Mao has himself explained: "Strategically we take the eating of a meal lightly: we know we can finish it. But when actually eating, we do it a mouthful at a time. It would be impossible to swallow the entire feast in a single mouthful. This is called a piecemeal solution. And in military literature, it is called smashing the enemy bit by bit."[18]

In the final analysis, then, these arguments over peaceful coexistence were, and continue to be, somewhat misleading. The Russians and the Chinese have always been "militarily conservative." Military power has never been their principal tool of policy. The Communist concept of the international class struggle is couched in social and economic terms. Admittedly, both subscribe to Mao's dictum that "power grows out of a barrel of a gun." But this does not mean the gun has to be fired. Both have usually employed force politically and psychologically—to threaten, harry, weaken, and isolate enemies—in a variety of situations ranging from nuclear blackmail to guerrilla warfare.

The issue of whether to take a "hard" or "soft" stand[19] has on most occasions also divided the NATO allies, as well as policy-makers within the governments of each of the NATO countries. It seems probable that in every major international crisis since the end of World War II, policy-makers on both sides of the Iron Curtain have divided in this way. And this issue, while it can be simply stated, is in reality a complex one. Whether the policy decided upon is "hard" or "soft," it will in most cases have both advantages and liabilities. There is usually no clear-cut policy offering opportunities without simultaneously creating risks. The challenging or challenged party must always ask at what point the opponent is likely to resist with force and on what scale. These questions obviously require considerable and most careful calculation. And it is on these calculations regarding the level of risks that should be run that Moscow and Peking have differed. For the answer determines both the opportunities that can be exploited and the consequences that may be suffered. If little pressure is applied because the risks seem high, then the gains will be none or small; that is why the Chinese charge the Russians with betraying the Communist cause through a cowardice that leads them to "kowtow" to the United States. If a great deal of pressure is exerted, the "profit" may be higher, but so are the risks; this is why the Russians accuse the Chinese of a recklessness that could provoke the United States into dropping bombs that do not, in the end, distinguish

[18] Quoted in Allen S. Whiting, "The Logic of Communist China's Policy: The First Decade," in Devere E. Pentony, ed., *China, the Emerging Red Giant* (San Francisco: Chandler, 1962), p. 71.

[19] The value judgments implicit in these terms can easily be reversed by calling them "inflexible" and "flexible" stands; the former then implies an obduracy that risks war, while the latter suggests a relaxation of tensions and preservation of peace.

between imperialists and workers. Wisdom in such circumstances counsels caution.

Thus, the increasing caution of the two superpowers made their respective allies apprehensive: They feared that their vital interests, as they defined them, would not be defended or attained and might even be sacrificed to avoid the risk of war. The Chinese were concerned lest Soviet fear of nuclear war become so great that Moscow would no longer use coercion or limited force for offensive purposes. The Europeans were worried that the United States might not even be counted on to prove reliable in protecting the *status quo*. Similar situations thus came into play in both blocs. China on the one side, Britain, France and West Germany on the other, all believing that their interests had become increasingly subordinated to the strategic caution of their respective superpowers. Thus, the two superpowers have attempted to slow down French and Chinese development of national nuclear forces they could not control. France and China, of course, objected to the limited test ban and nuclear nonproliferation treaties, but Moscow and Washington negotiated and signed them despite these protests. And if the secondary powers resort to force, they encounter opposition from the superpowers. Thus America opposed the British, French, and Israeli attack on Egypt in 1956, and Russia opposed the limited Chinese attacks on India in 1959 and 1962 and would not use its nuclear force to help China recover Formosa. Both nuclear powers *and* their secondary allies must pursue their objectives with far less reliance on the use of force. It is not surprising, then, that Paris and Peking "defect." *The two nuclear giants define their own interests and preserve their own policies toward each other despite the demands of their allies* when these upset their own relationship and raise the risk of a military clash. De Gaulle's tactics of defying the United States were typical of the weak; defiance was all he could do while he hoped that, to "win him back," Washington would grant concessions favorable to France. Mao's denunciation of Khrushchev, and later of Kosygin and Brezhnev, was a similar tactic. *But American and Soviet policy is not made for France—or, more broadly, for Europe—and China, which in turn explains their "deviant" behavior as each moved away from the policies of its respective superpower.*[20] And as the superpowers moved closer together to cooperate with one another in various spheres of common interest, and more and more talked to one another while ignoring their allies, the more apprehensive and fearful did the latter become. Europeans constantly articulated the fear that the Big Two, to maintain and improve their bilateral *détente* relationship of lower tensions, would agree to arrangements detrimental to the interests of Europe. China voiced similar objections, going so far as to accuse Moscow of a tacit alliance with Washington to contain and isolate China (it was to divide this alleged alliance that China turned in the

---

[20] Dinerstein, *War and Soviet Union*, p. 595.

early 1970's to the United States), denouncing Russia for having sold out the revolution and proclaiming itself as the true inheritor of Marxism-Leninism while cutting its own bonds with its heretical former ally.

Yet this situation of increasing strategic parity and stable mutual deterrence not only gave voice to fears of being left unprotected but—paradoxically enough—also provided a degree of security to the partners of each superpower. If a stable balance existed, the same feeling that bred the suspicion of the lack of American and Russian credibility also bred the hope that war was impossible and their security assured. In short, nuclear arms had an ambiguous impact: On the one hand, *they increased the sense of insecurity* aroused by the fear of being left unprotected; on the other hand, *they decreased the perception of threat* as the balance was believed to guard against attack or threat of attack. For example, neither China nor France would have challenged its superpower and permitted relations to deteriorate quite as much—particularly in China's case, because the Russians withdrew their economic and military assistance—had they really expected a war. Knowing that a balance exists and that war is unlikely, these powers can simply ignore superpower demands. France, for example, knows that U.S. security interests demand that America safeguard France. Hence, the French do not have to make concessions to gain U.S. protection; they can assume it. (The Chinese, while they lost their fear of an American attack, did become apprehensive of a Russian attack, a fear that ironically drove them toward the United States to enhance their security.) To the obvious displeasure of American policy-makers who "produce" this security, the French can "consume" it while at the same time following policies not in accord with American preferences. They can, in short, exploit the greater maneuverability weaker nations tend to possess in a condition of balance between their stronger colleagues; they will do so by establishing relations with the other superpower—who responds out of a possibility it can divide and rule—as well as with that superpower's allies, whose own maneuverability and influence will thereby be augmented. The most dramatic example of one superpower's former ally approaching the other has, of course, been China; because of its potential power, this case is particularly significant in the long run.

Thus deviant behavior becomes at least a partial substitute for the flexibility of the old multipolar balance in this new bipolycentric balance:

> France wants American acceptance of its claim to primacy in Europe; Soviet or Chinese assent is meaningless. Poland and Rumania require Soviet acceptance of their desire for greater freedom in foreign policy. West Germany or France cannot satisfy that wish, they can only serve as instruments for its accomplishment. Therefore, these approaches to members of the rival alliances are really methods of improving negotiating power against the hegemonic power. The basic impulse is from within the alliance, not from without it.[21]

[21] *Ibid.*, p. 597.

Alliance Inequality and the Intra-alliance Balance

Whatever the merits of this controversy over the role of nuclear weapons in each superpower's principal alliances, one point was clear: Washington and Moscow respectively decided alliance strategy and, therefore, to the extent that the conduct of foreign policy is based on strategy, the foreign policies of their allies as well. The Europeans and the Chinese felt that very largely they were pawns of foreign policies and strategies that were not always in their interests, but their protests were dismissed. Thus in both alliances, the protest against unilateral superpower decision-making grew; however valid the American or Russian strategies were, they were poor alliance politics. Indeed, the weakness of each superpower's partners proved troublesome from the alliances' formation on, although problems did not erupt clearly and publicly until bipolarity was waning. But the reactions of the allies were all but inevitable.

From the beginning of NATO, to analyze that alliance first, the relative weakness of the European states led Britain and then France to develop their own national nuclear deterrents. The aim, in this intra-alliance context, was prestige, not security in the inter-nation environment.[22] Nuclear weapons are, however, regarded in both settings as status symbols. Just as a great power once demonstrated its primary status by acquiring colonies and a strong navy, so, after World War II, it acquired nuclear weapons. For nations that were once great powers and continued to harbor the "great-power syndrome" or saw themselves once more becoming great powers, nuclear weapons were symbols they had to acquire. In their view, not to possess such weapons would be to retreat from greatness, an abandonment of power, and a loss of international respect—and, therefore, self-respect. For, in the nuclear age, was a nation not impotent if it did not own such arms? Could a nation still claim its authority to make decisions on the vital issues of life and death if it were dependent on another power's nuclear protection? National pride, in short, has been a powerful incentive to the development of national nuclear deterrents.[23]

A second reason for developing national deterrents in the context of intra-alliance relations was the belief that nuclear arms would gain the allies a voice in Washington so that they could then influence U.S. policy decisions. At the very minimum, they wished to prevent actions they might deem detrimental to their own immediate interests. In every alliance, common interests bring states together; the individual countries

[22] Britain's development of nuclear arms is described by Richard N. Rosecrance, *Defense of the Realm: British Strategy in the Nuclear Epoch* (New York: Columbia University Press, 1968).

[23] Leonard Beaton, *Must the Bomb Spread?* (Baltimore: Penguin Books, 1966), pp. 49–61.

continue, however, to have their own special interests. Still, one might ask why British policy-makers, for example, believed nuclear weapons would afford them greater influence in determining alliance policy. The answer lies in the nature of an alliance. Because an alliance is presumably an international division of labor, each state supplies certain capabilities to the coalition and, as a result, members become at least partially interdependent. Influence for weaker states in an alliance thus tends to be a function of their *contribution* to alliance strategy.[24] Since American strategy for most of the period dating from the end of World War II relied primarily upon massive—that is, nuclear—retaliation to deter a Soviet attack, the British believed their influence within the alliance would be proportional to their contribution to this nuclear strategy. Britain's early development of a nuclear force was thus not merely a means of satisfying national pride; it was also a means of continuing and strengthening the special relationship with the United States that had emerged from World War II. As former Prime Minister Macmillan explained it: "The independent contribution gives us a better position in the world with respect to the United States. It puts us where we ought to be, in the position of a great power. The fact that we have it makes the United States pay a greater regard to our point of view."[25] Not surprisingly, the French began to realize the value of the development of a French bomb as a means of regaining their great-power status and influence in Washington. Contrary to popular belief, this program was launched *before* de Gaulle became President of France in 1958. France, like Great Britain before it, intended to be one of those select NATO equals who were "more equal" than the others.

If the striving for national nuclear forces was one indication of the former great powers' search for enhanced prestige and influence (West Germany, forbidden to produce nuclear arms, sought greater influence within NATO by contributing sizable ground forces), the drive for a unified Europe by the Continental states was another. Only Britain joined neither the European Coal and Steel Community in 1950 nor the Common Market or Inner Six (West Germany, France, Italy, and the Benelux countries—Belgium, the Netherlands, and Luxembourg) eight years later, largely because, while Great Britain was determined to keep the "Great" in Britain and therefore felt its status required the acquisition of nuclear arms, it never shared with the Continental states their sense of impotence. Britain had not been defeated or occupied during World War II. Emerging from the war as one of the Big Three Powers, it retained a degree of self-confidence, in strong contrast to the Continental states, all of which had experienced invasion, conquest, foreign occupation, and postwar collapse. Thus, at no time between 1950 and 1961 did Britain see any need to join its Continental allies in their efforts

24 Robert E. Osgood, NATO: *The Entangling Alliance* (Chicago: University of Chicago Press, 1962), pp. 349–50.
25 *Times* (London), February 24, 1958.

to integrate in a more powerful union. Their sense of helplessness was reinforced by both the Soviet threat and the predominance of American power. And an atom bomb as a symbol of prestige and an instrument of influence was for them not an immediate prospect. For Britain, whose scientists had been involved in its development, it seemed the obvious weapon to acquire. But, "as British power ebbed, the symbols of power came to be prized above the reality. Like an aging actress, Britain's statesmen and people sought refuge from the harsh facts in an illusion of grandeur [particularly stressing] the Churchillian doctrine of the 'interlocking circles'—the theory that Britain was uniquely placed at the heart of three great blocs: the Atlantic alliance with America, the Commonwealth, and Western Europe. This doctrine carried the flattering implication that Britain really was 'at the still center of the turning world,' buttressed and shielded by innumerable friends."[26]

Britain's "partnership" with the United States and its leadership of the Commonwealth—the one far more powerful than the island nation, the other a shrinking and militarily weak entity—thus allowed it to continue to hide from itself the realities of power and to try to play a role apart from its Continental allies, who did indeed recognize these realities.[27] Not until years after the 1956 Suez debacle and the success of the Common Market did Britain face the prospect that as a single power it would be increasingly ignored. As its strength declined, so would its influence in Washington and Moscow, as well as in New Delhi and Peking. In a world in which continental-sized powers with populations of approximately 200 million or more would be the principal actors, greater and greater attention would be paid to the New Europe. Thus the advantages of joining the Common Market became increasingly clear: A Britain in the Common Market would be a member of a potential superpower comprising a population larger than that of the United States or the Soviet Union, producing more coal and steel than either of the two present superpowers, and absorbing almost half of the world's exports. In the early 1960's, it finally, but still gingerly, tried to join the by then flourishing Inner Six.

For the Six, the effort to create a United Europe was from the outset at cross-purposes with the American sponsorship of an integrated Europe.[28] For Washington, integration was a way of enhancing the West's power. For the European states it was also a way of once more proudly standing on their own feet, defining—and eventually defending—their own interests. By changing the intra-NATO balance between Europe

[26] Michael Shanks and John Lambert, *The Common Market Today—and Tomorrow* (New York: Praeger Publishers, 1963), p. 26.

[27] On Britain's illusions about Anglo-American relations and the Commonwealth, see U. W. Kitzinger, *The Politics and Economics of European Integration* (New York: Praeger Publishers, 1963), pp. 164–77.

[28] This point is well analyzed in Ronald Steel, *The End of the Alliance* (New York: Viking Press, 1962), pp. 10–14, 30, 80–82.

and America, they would enhance their prestige and influence. For France in particular, a United Europe and a more equitable distribution of power within the alliance meant a Continental leadership role and a voice equal to that of the "Anglo-Saxons" in NATO. West Germany, though a stronger power, could hardly provide this leadership, in view of its past history. "It is not necessary to go so far as to assert that 'the European idea has an anti-American flavor,' " George Lichtheim has written, "though it clearly does have such connotations for some influential people in Europe; it is quite enough to realize that its unspoken premises include the belief that Europe has been unduly overshadowed in the [alliance] system built up after 1945 under Anglo–U.S. auspices."[29]

Assertion against the United States was thus inevitable. Just as the young America after the War of Independence had once sought its new identity by asserting itself against the Old World, so the states of Europe, engaged in a "nation-building" experiment that seeks to transcend the frontiers of the old nation-states, acquire a measure of their new sense of their identity by setting themselves off against their closest friend and ally, the United States. In brief, in addition to the impact of nuclear weapons and the perception of a declining external threat, the conflicting purposes of the Europeans (especially those of France) and the United States within NATO were a third cause of the erosion of the Western alliance's bonds.

From 1958 to 1969, French President de Gaulle and—after his resignation from office and death, his successor—Georges Pompidou, until his death in 1974, tended to be the eloquent and often arrogant spokesmen in what was frequently referred to as the conflict between the American idea of Atlanticism—a united Europe closely tied to the United States in a large "Atlantic community"—and the French concept of Europeanness in which the members of the Common Market, or European Economic Community (EEC), first talk to one another and only *then* to the United States as an equal. This concept, widely supported by other Europeans, asserted that there could be no "Europe" if each EEC member first talked bilaterally to Washington.

A keen demonstration of a second-rank power's assertion of itself and the clear-cut confrontation of Atlanticism versus Europeanness may be seen in the French veto in 1963 of Britain's attempt to join the Common Market. While this entry into Europe was hampered by complex economic problems, it was, in the final analysis, political and military factors that proved to be the insuperable barriers. De Gaulle particularly feared that Britain's entry would cause the EEC to lose its European identity, because Britain would be America's spokesman in the Community. Equally, de Gaulle believed that Europe should, as far as possible, be master of its own destiny, and he questioned whether Britain, as the price of entry, would surrender its special relationship with

[29] George Lichtheim, *The New Europe: Today—and Tomorrow*, 2d ed. (New York: Praeger Publishers, 1967), p. 36.

the United States to prove its conversion to "Europeanness." Could it demonstrate this time that it really was sympathetic to the political unification of the New Europe, or, as Britain needed greater access to the Common Market to bolster a slumping economy, were its interests in Europe purely economic? But the crucial and overriding question was whether it would continue to give primary emphasis to its relationship with Washington. It is clear that Washington wanted its "partner" inside Europe. As one writer suggested at the time, America believed Britain would then be in a position to

> act as America's most reliable ally in Europe. . . . Once inside Europe, the British will "manage" it—in the joint interest of Anglo-Saxon powers. This is wishful thinking; the Europeans are in no mood to have their affairs run by people whom they regard as outsiders. If the British count on playing a leading role in the new Europe, they will have to demonstrate to their skeptical partners that in any serious conflict of interest between the two halves of the Atlantic world they can be counted on to come down on the European side.[30]

If a "European" Europe were ever to emerge, and if such a Europe were to control its own fate, it presumably would also have to control its own defense. It was in this field that, in late 1962, the critical test of Britain's Europeanness came, with the U.S. cancellation of the Skybolt program.[31] Up to that moment, Britain's 170-odd bombers at least permitted the appearance of great-power status, if not perhaps the substance. But the British had found it increasingly expensive to keep up with evolving nuclear technology in the key item, the delivery system. In 1957 they had begun to develop their own missile, but it proved too burdensome financially and was therefore scrapped. Instead, the British decided to buy the Skybolt air-to-ground missile from the United States when it became available. The development of the Skybolt was seen as a way of prolonging the life of Britain's bombers, because the missiles could be attached under their wings; if the bombers were unable to penetrate Soviet defenses, the Skybolts could still be hurled at the targets. British prestige, and the Conservative Government's political future, were thus linked to America's delivery of the Skybolt: Failure to deliver would eliminate Britain's national deterrent, thereby humiliating America's closest ally and undermining the Conservatives' self-proclaimed position as the best guardian of British security and the voice that was always listened to in the White House. Yet this is exactly what happened in late 1962.

London's choice was clear: "There was the possibility of going to America and asking for a substitute for Skybolt. There was the possibility of dropping the British deterrent completely. But there was—in

[30] *Ibid.*, pp. 36–37.

[31] The ability to miscalculate so badly the relations among even close allies is dissected by Richard E. Neustadt, *Alliance Politics* (New York: Columbia University Press, 1970).

de Gaulle's mind, at least—a third possibility. That was to go to the French and say: 'Let's produce ballistic missiles together.' "[32] Apparently, de Gaulle assumed that Britain would pay this price as the cost of admission to the European "club": an *entente nucléaire* between France and Britain. In June, 1962, in talks with Prime Minister Macmillan, de Gaulle reportedly intimated that the two countries should join in establishing an Anglo-French atomic force as the basis of a European deterrent that could redress the balance within NATO.[33]

Yet, at the decisive moment, despite its public humiliation by the United States, Britain signed the Nassau Pact. Under its terms, as a replacement for the Skybolt, it was to receive American Polaris missiles, and it would itself provide the submarines and warheads. Britain thereby chose to remain dependent on the United States for maintenance of its "independence."[34] Nassau demonstrated clearly once again that Britain's first loyalty was to the United States, not to the Europeans with whom it was at that very time negotiating for economic and political integration. For fifteen months prior to this, the British had stalled, haggling over the subsidies for bacon and eggs and avoiding a choice between the Commonwealth and Europe. But compelled to choose between the United States and Europe at Nassau, the British Government made the decision in forty-eight hours to hand over to the United States the one contribution it could have made to Europe. The French President reportedly considered that Britain, by allowing one of the vital attributes of national sovereignty—the deterrent force—to become dependent on the United States, had disqualified itself as a European

[32] Raymond Aron, "Size-Up of De Gaulle," *U.S. News & World Report*, April 22, 1963. Also see *idem, Great Debate*.

[33] "After entry into the Common Market, Macmillan said, Britain looked forward to political union with the Six. That would mean close cooperation with France and the Six, not only in foreign policy but also in defense. He spoke for the first time of a European, rather than simply a NATO, defense policy. There was a mention of future Anglo-French cooperation in defense production and research. While no details were discussed or engagements made, de Gaulle emerged with the impression that the door would be open to Anglo-French cooperation in the nuclear defense field after Britain entered the Common Market. There was no indication in the British minutes that cooperation in nuclear arms production, as such, had been discussed. But Macmillan, according to the French minutes, suggested that the two countries coordinate the plans of their nuclear forces for circumstances, should they arise, where the United States might be unwilling to employ its deterrent.

"De Gaulle's conviction, after Champs, was that the British 'had made their choice —for Europe.' " Robert Kleiman, *Atlantic Crisis: American Diplomacy Confronts a Resurgent Europe* (New York: W. W. Norton, 1964), pp. 69–70.

[34] See *ibid.*, pp. 56–59: "Macmillan, back in London, stressed his right to withdraw Britain's Polaris submarines from NATO for national use and insisted that he had retained an independent deterrent. *Administration spokesmen, in Washington, emphasized the multilateral aspects of the agreement and described Britain's withdrawal rights as virtually useless.* . . . At Nassau, when Britain in return for Polaris agreed to commit its deterrent to NATO, it became possible for the first time to offer France equal treatment *without* accepting the concept of a completely independent French nuclear force." Emphasis added.

power. Clearly, Britain still preferred its "special relationship" to Washington. As a result, de Gaulle suspected that Britain, so organically linked to the other English-speaking power across the Atlantic, would play the role of a Trojan horse were it to be admitted to the Common Market.[35] The entrance of Britain, possibly along with some of its partners from the European Free Trade Area (formed as a rival organization to the EEC, but, as it turned out, certainly no competitor), would create a "colossal Atlantic Community under American . . . leadership which would soon completely swallow up the European Community."[36] With this in mind, de Gaulle vetoed Britain's entry. France's Continental colleagues might not have acted or spoken as bluntly, but they nevertheless shared its concern about American hegemony over NATO. Fundamentally, the issue for them was Europe's emancipation from its postwar protectorate status.

The irony was that, with or without Britain (which, together with Denmark and Ireland, joined the Inner Six to form a Europe of Nine in 1973), the absence of an integrated Europe meant that the European states remained dependent upon America. The Six had advanced far along the path toward the goal of greater economic unity and the EEC's success in integrating the members' economies was obvious. Yet, in terms of common defense, the French deterrent was no substitute for the American; here Britain was essential, for only a pooling of the French and British deterrents could create the kind of European nuclear power that could someday develop into a genuine deterrent force. But this in turn assumes the existence of a central government able to determine a European foreign policy and a European military strategy to support it. Such a United States of Europe would be a superpower in its own right, with the capacity to articulate and sustain its own interests. But, while the Europeans are keen to assert their equality with—and independence from—the United States, they have still not decided whether they are willing to pay the price for superpower status: the surrender of national sovereignty and expenditure of sizable funds to buy military power. A de Gaulle may then have been necessary if Europe was to assert its identity and once more play a role in the world, but the confederation he preferred could not balance American power in NATO. Thus the Europeans remain psychologically in revolt against American domination of the alliance,[37] but the prospects for a politically united Europe of Nine are at best ambiguous, at worst dismal (as we shall see later

[35] Edmund Taylor, "After Brussels," *The Reporter*, February 14, 1963.
[36] *Major Addresses of de Gaulle*, p. 124.
[37] Robert L. Pfaltzgraff, Jr., *The Atlantic Community: A Complex Imbalance* (Princeton, N.J.: Van Nostrand Reinhold, 1969), and David Calleo, *The Atlantic Fantasy* (Baltimore: Johns Hopkins Press, 1970), are good and relatively short analyses of transatlantic strains. The most comprehensive treatment of the alliance problems, introduced by almost 400 pages of analysis on American style and politics, is Stanley Hoffman, *Gulliver's Troubles, or the Setting of American Foreign Policy* (New York: McGraw-Hill, 1968).

when we analyze the process of functional supranational integration).

If the Western alliance was predicated on U.S. predominance, Soviet hegemony was also unavoidable in Moscow's relationship with Peking. After the Bolshevik Revolution of 1917, the Soviet leaders considered their party to be the leading party, and, as it was then the only Communist Party to have captured state power, it was natural that non-Soviet Communists tended to defer to it. The role of Moscow as leader of the international Communist movement was reinforced by the failure of the post–World War I revolutions in Germany and Hungary. Moscow refused to believe that these failures had anything to do with the different conditions in the two countries, attributing them instead to poor tactics on the part of local leaders over whom the Kremlin had had little control. The implication was that, had Lenin been in control, these revolutions would have succeeded. All Communist Parties were subsequently subordinated to the Kremlin's leadership and were expected to obey its orders unquestioningly. When, toward the end of World War II, "socialism in one country" became "socialism in one zone"—comprising the Soviet Union, Albania, Bulgaria, Czechoslovakia, East Germany, Hungary, Poland, Rumania, and Yugoslavia (which Stalin later threw out), the twenty-year pattern of Soviet domination and subordination of all other Communist Parties was solidified. Instead of directing only foreign Communist Parties, Moscow now directed entire nations.

The Tito-Stalin conflict was the first portent of the later Sino-Soviet schism.[38] In a sense, the break between Belgrade and Moscow was ironic, for Tito was a Stalinist who denounced the West in the harshest terms; following the war, he had shot down American planes and encouraged the Greek Civil war. In Yugoslavia, he had collectivized agriculture and industry at a rapid race. There were, however, a number of reasons for his conflict with the Russian dictator. First, Tito had gained international fame during the war as a resistance leader; his Yugoslav partisans had resisted the German occupation forces and liberated their country with little or no help from the Red Army. Second, and more important, Tito had built up his own party and army and he was therefore able to resist Soviet attempts to penetrate these; he remained in full control of all the instruments he needed to govern Yugoslavia. Tito's control was a portent of things to come; the Soviet Union could expect trouble in policy disputes with any Communist state whose leaders had won power by themselves, had gained great prestige, and held the instruments of control. China was such a state and Mao was such a leader.

Russia's China policy during World War II had certainly not foreseen the emergence of Mao as a rival to Stalin. Rather, the Soviets reacted to China in terms of Russian national interests that predated the Communist regime. As the price for Russian participation in the war against Japan, Stalin had exacted from the Nationalist regime a guarantee of

[38] Vladimir Dedijer, *The Battle Stalin Lost* (New York: Viking Press, 1971).

the *status quo* in Outer Mongolia and the restoration of the "former rights of Russia violated by the treacherous attack of Japan in 1904." This meant primarily the restoration of Russian influence in Manchuria.[39]

The establishment of the Chinese People's Republic thus posed a serious problem for the Soviet Union. Stalin was determined to preserve Soviet leadership of the new Sino-Soviet bloc and would not accord equality to Communist China. And he had no intention of abandoning the Soviet positions in Manchuria, Sinkiang, or the newly named Mongolian People's Republic. Yet, as leader of the Chinese Communist Party, Mao Tse-tung intended to unify China and, like Tito, controlled his own party and army. Even more than Tito, he had used both to achieve victory in his own country over Chiang Kai-shek and the Kuomintang (Nationalists). What, then, was to be the place of the new China in the Communist state system? How was Stalin to preserve the Soviet Union's territorial rights in China without antagonizing China's leaders and thereby risking a repetition of his experience with Tito?

The Sino-Soviet treaty was Stalin's answer. In it, Russia pledged itself to the defense of the new China, and the two powers pledged themselves to consult each other on important international problems affecting their common interests. But Stalin's customary interpretation of the word "consult," as demonstrated by his "consultations" with the East European People's Democracies, was unilateral decision and declaration followed by automatic and full-fledged support from the other members of the Soviet bloc. The more specific clauses concerning the areas of traditional Chinese-Russian conflict showed that Stalin intended to preserve the Soviet position in China, although he did make some significant concessions. The Russians indicated a willingness to abandon Manchuria as a sphere of influence and they recognized Chinese sovereignty over Sinkiang but gained China's agreement for the establishment of joint companies under the direction of Soviet experts for the exploitation of Sinkiang's oil and metal resources. Such joint companies had served as tools of Soviet control and exploitation in Eastern Europe. In Outer Mongolia, the Chinese had no alternative but to accept the "independent" status of the Mongolian People's Republic. Finally, the Soviet Union lent the Chinese $300 million ($60 million per year over a five-year period) at 1 per cent annual interest;[40] reportedly, Mao had requested a loan of almost $3 billion.[41] The size of the loan must have been a severe disappointment for Mao, who had his own plans for rapid

[39] Treaty provisions may be found in Floyd, *Mao Against Khrushchev*, pp. 213–15. For a detailed analysis, see Herbert Feis, *The China Tangle: The American Effort in China from Pearl Harbor to the Marshall Mission* (Princeton, N.J.: Princeton University Press, 1953), pp. 226–54.

[40] Floyd, *Mao Against Khrushchev*, p. 214.

[41] David J. Dallin, *Soviet Foreign Policy After Stalin* (Philadelphia: Lippincott, 1961), p. 83.

industrialization. Certainly, it would slow China's industrial development.

But, on the whole, as one political analyst has concluded, the Sino-Soviet treaty did not "signify an about-face in Sino-Soviet relations. Some leeway had to be granted to Mao's policies, and Stalin had to accede to a number of Chinese demands. But Moscow succeeded in temporizing and delaying and conditioning the rise of China. Stalin had no reason to revise his basic views about his allies, about the structure of the Soviet bloc, or about his own role as the leader of that bloc."[42] China was assigned to the second rank in the Soviet bloc. But Sinkiang and Mongolia remained potentially divisive issues. Thus Stalin's legacy to his successors was strain and tension with China, as well as with Eastern Europe. As nationalism grew in these countries, such tensions would increase; someday they would threaten the unity of the bloc.

These tensions arose first in Eastern Europe. Stalin had left a legacy of popular resentment and hatred for Russia in the People's Democracies, and this legacy was to confront his successors with a serious dilemma. If they preserved the Stalinist conception of empire, they would only intensify the existing dissatisfaction; opposition to Soviet exploitation and Soviet-imposed rapid industrialization, with its neglect of the people's standard of living and of peasant agriculture and with its attendant police terror, would increase. Indications of the trouble ahead came soon after Stalin's death: In June, 1953, a general strike and uprising occurred in East Germany and East Berlin. The revolt was spearheaded, moreover, by the proletariat, to whose liberation from capitalist chains the Communists were ostensibly dedicated. The chief victims of the rapid industrialization, these workers rebelled against low wages, harsh discipline, and austerity, and they were supported by the mass of the population.[43] The use of Russian tanks and troops to quell the revolt, especially in Berlin, was hardly the best way to impress on the world that Communism was the wave of the future because of its superior way of life. But what if the Soviet leaders went too far in relaxing their grip on the satellites? Might this not stimulate further demands for concessions until Soviet authority was virtually whittled away? Could the Russians safely eliminate the worst abuses and the most oppressive features of the Stalinist system without bringing about the disintegration of the bloc? While suppression produced resentment, concessions might create popular defiance and overconfidence.

The East German uprising allowed the new Soviet leaders little time to consider these questions. A relaxation of the Soviet reins—a "thaw," as it came to be called—was absolutely necessary. Exploitation of the satellites was abandoned. As a result, the thaw became a flood, and Soviet troops almost had to intervene to suppress the Poles and did in fact intervene in 1956 to suppress the Hungarian revolt. Unlike Poland,

[42] *Ibid.*
[43] *Ibid.*, p. 170.

Hungary had tried to defect; and again unlike Poland, Hungary's Communist Party had lost its monopoly of power.[44] The Kremlin was not willing to tolerate either condition. Had it done so, the Soviet empire in Eastern Europe would have "withered away." The Red Army therefore moved in and squashed the rebellion. But the Hungarian revolt had offered dramatic proof that, in the final analysis, the Soviet empire rested on naked force.

The conclusion seemed clear: "National Communism" was unacceptable to the Soviet Union. Completely independent Communist states, such as Yugoslavia, would destroy the unity of the Communist bloc and undermine Soviet leadership. The Soviets were prepared to accept national "adaptations" of the basic laws of socialist construction, but only so long as the resulting diversity presented no challenge to their dominant role in the international Communist movement. Communist states could experiment internally, but only within certain limitations: recognition of the Soviet Union as the leader of the socialist camp; retention of the dictatorship of the proletariat—that is, the Communist one-party state; acceptance of the basic irreconcilability of the capitalist and socialist worlds; and, finally, rejection of an independent, or "neutral," foreign policy.[45] Violation of any of the conditions by a satellite might precipitate Soviet military intervention. To dramatize the point, Imre Nagy and several other leaders of the Hungarian revolt were executed.

It was on this set of restrictions that, twelve years later, the short-lived Czechoslovak experiment foundered. Believing in freedom of speech and the press and even in parliamentary elections and domestic opposition, and seeking to establish formal political and commercial ties to the West in foreign policy, the Dubcek regime aroused Soviet fears that the Czechoslovak Communist Party monopoly control was in jeopardy—and this in a nation neighboring West Germany.[46] (Rumania, which was also developing ties to the West at the time, did not share a border with the Federal Republic, and, in any event, the Bucharest regime was domestically orthodox. Hence, the Soviets left it alone.) Doubtless, Moscow was equally fearful of the impact of a successful Czechoslovak example on the other nations of Eastern Europe, and perhaps even on Russia itself. Thus the Red Army intervened once again and, in the resulting Brezhnev Doctrine (hardly Brezhnev's invention, incidentally), Moscow declared it would not tolerate any regime that by its actions endangered

[44] Zbigniew K. Brzezinski, *The Soviet Bloc* (Cambridge, Mass.: Harvard University Press, 1967), pp. 207–65. An excellent briefer analysis is Ghita Ionescu, *The Break-Up of the Soviet Empire in Eastern Europe* (Baltimore: Penguin, 1965).

[45] See statement issued by the 1957 Moscow Conference of Communist Parties, quoted in G. F. Hudson *et al.*, eds., *The Sino-Soviet Dispute* (New York: Praeger Publishers, 1961), p. 51.

[46] Philip Windsor and Adam Roberts, *Czechoslovakia: Reform, Repression and Resistance* (New York: Columbia University Press, 1969).

"socialism" in Eastern Europe—a matter on which it, of course, would be the judge.

Despite the Brezhnev Doctrine, it is obvious that for most of the states of Eastern Europe "satellite" is no longer the proper descriptive term. Increasing their trade with the West, most of these states have made clear their desire to improve relations with the non-Communist nations. The major exception has been East Germany, and even it seems at last to be moving in this direction. The countries remain Communist, of course. This is a matter of faith and political survival for most of the ruling Communist Parties in Eastern Europe. They do not represent majority will in their respective countries, and, in the final analysis, it is still the Red Army that guarantees their power. Their link to Moscow is thus essential. But these regimes gain a measure of popularity by adapting Communism to particular national conditions and by relaxing pressure in varying degrees. When, as in Budapest in 1956 and in Prague in 1968, this seemed to go too far, Moscow intervened. It too, however, finds itself in a quandary. Short of reimposing Stalinist controls, with all the dangers this would imply, and short of outright military intervention, Moscow really has no means of counteracting the growing trend toward greater independence. For the states of Eastern Europe, the outer bounds to freedom are set by the necessity of remaining loyal to Moscow. The Soviet leadership may not react if these countries open links to the West, but—as Czechoslovakia demonstrated—it is unlikely to permit them to substitute these links for their ties with the Soviet Union; certainly, outright anti-Soviet policies will not be tolerated. The Kremlin thus appears willing to accept a measure of decline in its status and authority and to deal with its former satellites on the basis of a limited give-and-take.[47]

Still, it is one thing for Moscow to deal with the relatively weak states of Russia's security belt, another for it to deal with a potentially powerful Communist China. Even before Moscow had demonstrated its Czarist-like ambitions toward China during the war, its prewar direction of Communist affairs in China had suggested to Mao that to follow Russia's advice was not necessarily wise.[48] In the 1920's, Stalin had ordered the Chinese Communists to join a coalition with the Kuomintang, which, as a nationalist party, sought to unify China by destroying the local warlords and ejecting the colonial powers. In the Soviet Union's view, a united China would best serve Soviet interests because it would divert Japanese pressure from Siberia. In addition, Moscow saw in the coalition a means to infiltrate the Kuomintang and organize the workers

[47] Adam Bromke, ed., *The Communist States at the Crossroads* (New York: Praeger Publishers, 1965); J. F. Brown, *The New Eastern Europe: The Khrushchev Era and After* (New York: Praeger Publishers, 1966); and Andrew Gyorgi, ed., *Issues of World Communism* (New York: Van Nostrand, 1966).

[48] Klaus Mehnert, *Peking and Moscow* (New York: Putnam's, 1963).

in the cities: Hence, the coalition would serve as the spearhead of the revolution. Communist participation in the Kuomintang would enable the proletariat to achieve hegemony in a national bourgeois revolution, bringing about the socialist revolution more quickly. The alliance with the Communists was also useful to the Nationalists. Among other things, the Russian emissaries taught the Chinese Nationalist leaders how to organize their party along Communist lines. But the alliance proved to be only temporary. In 1927, Chiang Kai-shek turned on the Communists in Shanghai and shattered the coalition and Stalin's policy. The idea of basing the Communist Party upon the proletariat died at the same time.

In early 1928, Mao Tse-tung began to reorganize the Party using the peasants, rather than the proletariat, as the revolutionary vanguard—hardly an orthodox approach. Mao has consequently been called a heretic, but in fact he was merely adapting the Leninist strategy for the conquest of power to China's conditions. Lenin himself, after all, had not been averse to exploiting peasant unrest and dissatisfaction to undermine the Czarist regime and its moderate successor. Mao simply went a step farther, organizing the peasants into a guerrilla force to fight against the Nationalists. The principal attraction to the peasants was the Communist policy of land reform: to confiscate the land of the landowners and redistribute it to the poor peasants. Thus the Communists posed as "agrarian reformers": "The Chinese communist movement was a movement of peasants, but not a peasant movement. . . . The communists had to get peasant good-will, as Lenin in 1917 and 1918 had had to get peasant good-will. The only way, for Mao as for Lenin, was to give the peasants what they wanted—the use, on more favourable terms, of the land. But in the 'liberated territories' the political and military hierarchy was firmly controlled by communists."[49]

The Chinese civil war between the Communists and the Kuomintang was temporarily interrupted by the Japanese seizure of Manchuria in 1931 and, again, by the large-scale Japanese attacks on China in 1937. Stalin, interested in seeing that China continued to fight—lest a powerful Japan that had conquered much or all of China establish itself on Russia's Asian borders—ordered the Chinese Communist Party to form a united front with Chiang. But this united front soon collapsed, and the civil war was resumed and fought throughout the rest of the Sino-Japanese war. After Japan's defeat by the Allies in 1945, Stalin again intervened. This time, he reportedly told Mao that the Communists were still too weak to defeat Chiang and should therefore join a coalition government and "bore from within.' Mao is supposed to have nodded his assent, but he then went on to disregard Stalin's advice. He resumed his war against Chiang—and ultimately won.

Mao's victory in spite of Soviet advice was not the only occurrence

[49] Hugh Seton-Watson, *From Lenin to Khrushchev*, rev. ed. (New York: Praeger Publishers, 1960), p. 153.

that led him to question Moscow's political judgment. Quite apart from his determination that China, as a great power, deserved equality with Russia, he felt that Moscow's global Communist strategy needed leavening with Chinese political wisdom. But soon after Stalin's death it became apparent that the Kremlin had no intention of sharing its dominant position. Ironically, it was Khrushchev's attack on Stalin in 1956 that precipitated the Sino-Soviet conflict. The Chinese considered the attack a blunder. Not that they bore any love for Stalin's memory, but they apparently saw the implications of this drastic step more clearly than Khrushchev himself. Partly, no doubt, they were embarrassed by the implications of Khrushchev's denunciation of Stalin, having themselves publicly praised Stalin for years. The disclosure of Stalin's real personality and methods of ruling Russia made the Chinese look foolish. More important, the attack on the cult of the individual might be considered applicable as well to the organized adulation for Mao Tse-tung. Even worse, Khrushchev's denunciation had raised the fundamental question as to whether Stalinism was the product of the late dictator's personality or of the nature of Communist society. Khrushchev had clearly blamed the former and sought to exonerate the latter. But could it not be properly contended that a repetition of Stalin's crimes could be avoided only if some checks were placed on the exercise of totalitarian power? And could such checks be accepted without an undermining of the Party's monopoly of authority? Had Khrushchev, indeed, not placed the legitimacy of the Communist system in jeopardy by his denunciation of the man who, for three decades, had been depicted by Communist propaganda as the wise and humane successor to Lenin and the leader of world Communism? Had he not gravely weakened the international movement by dethroning Stalin, for which Communist state or Party would again trust Moscow's leadership? Had Khrushchev's revelations not thereby stimulated the emergence of "polycentrism"—that is, the existence of several independent centers of decision-making in the Communist world—thus weakening the political unity of the Sino-Soviet bloc?

The Chinese questioned not only the wisdom of Khrushchev's action but also the manner in which he acted. The paradox, as the Chinese saw it, was that, while Khrushchev was denouncing Stalin for the way in which he had exercised his absolute power, the Soviet leader nonetheless expected all Communist Parties to accept Moscow's unilateral decision to downgrade the dead dictator. Khrushchev was thus behaving in a characteristically Stalinist manner. Because the destruction of the Stalin myth discredited not only Russian Communism but the entire international movement, the Chinese felt that they should have been consulted before Khrushchev made his decision. It was, however, not until the events in Poland and Hungary impelled Soviet intervention that the Chinese openly asserted their claim to share in the Soviet Union's monopoly of decision-making authority for the entire socialist camp. In both Poland and Hungary, Khrushchev's decisions had clearly been poor, and the consequences for the unity of the socialist bloc had been disastrous. But the Soviets were determined not to share, making the Sino-Soviet quarrel—and later schism—inevitable, replacing the American-Soviet cold war with a Sino-Soviet cold war.

Transatlantic Economic Conflict

Three reasons, as we have seen, account for the erosion of the NATO alliance: the impact of nuclear weapons, the declining perception of the external danger that brought the alliance into being in the first place, and the reaction to the inequitable power distribution within the alliance. These factors affected the Sino-Soviet alliance as well, but a fourth was as unique to NATO as ideological quarrels were to the Sino-Soviet relations. The additional source of dissent was economic. Whereas in the 1950's and 1960's the alliance's problems were primarily military, in the 1970's economic problems were coming to the surface. While their security was at stake, the members of the alliance drew closer together; but as fear of Russia declined issues of trade and finance within the alliance became more prominent, and they proved highly divisive, although they did not, as did the ideological disputes between Russia and China, cut off virtually all governmental and party relations, which affected all personal and commercial relations as well.

Some NATO problems arose from the formation of the Common Market. The European integration movement was sponsored by the United States in order to add the weight of a United States of Europe in the Western scales of power against the Soviet Union and, later, the Sino-Soviet alliance. The political and military benefits were judged to be greater than the probable effects of economic competition among European nations. But, with the lag in political integration and the increasing European-American political-military differences that arose as dread of the Soviet Union decreased, the economic issues accentuated these differences and made all issues harder to settle.

In one sense, the economic side of the alliance tended to reinforce American dominance. The chief means of laying an economic base for a politically united Europe were, one, to eliminate tariff barriers among the members and offer them the economic advantages of a much enlarged common market and, two, to protect this market by establishing a common tariff wall around all of them to keep out cheaper foreign—largely American—goods while European industries grew in size, technological sophistication, and marketing techniques to become more competitive. Since this tariff wall would make exporting to Europe more difficult, American corporations began to jump the wall instead of seeking a reduction or elimination of tariffs, which would, in turn, demand re-

ciprocal U.S. action. The massive flow of corporate dollars for investment purposes followed as American companies saw huge profits in a
new market larger than that of the United States. Moreover, these companies had an immense advantage over their European counterparts:
They were used to operating in a system composed of different states
with different business regulations and sales patterns, whereas European
companies were used to operating in smaller, less diverse markets. Thus
the most "European" of Europe's companies—that is, the largest companies—turned out to be American corporations. Ironically enough, because of their recognized greater capabilities, these American corporations could obtain more financing from European banks than European
companies; but, of course the U.S. companies had huge financial resources of their own.

When to these advantages was added the American lead in certain
areas of advanced technology, largely the result of the considerable publicly funded research and development stimulated by the cold war, the
competitive edge of American companies was clear—not that their own
investments in newer and better products and their management, advertising, and marketing techniques were not important in themselves.
While American-owned industries in Europe today account for no more
than 6 per cent of the total business activity in any one country, they are
concentrated in a few highly technological sectors that shape the contemporary economy—such as chemicals and oil—and in those sectors
that tend to reshape the environment of the future; American companies
manufacture 75 per cent of all computers used in Europe, thus clearly
demonstrating the American lead in the Second Industrial Revolution
of advanced electronics and the dependence of Europe on U.S. technology. In other areas, American companies produce 33 per cent of all cars
and 35 per cent of Britain's tires; in France alone, they manufacture 40
per cent of the farm machinery, 70 per cent of the sewing machines, 75
per cent of the electrical and statistical machines, and 90 per cent of the
synthetic rubber. Several factors account for Europe's technological lag:
National markets and industries have in the past been too small; both
government and private-enterprise spending on research and development has been insufficient; and managerial training and skills, along
with the general and higher educational system, have been inadequate.
Beyond this technological gap, there is also a psychological, political,
economic, and social gap.[50] In any event, what all this meant was that
economically there was an immense dollar flow to Europe and, politically and psychologically, European concern over what a British Labour
Prime Minister once referred to as "industrial helotry," or slavery, under
American dominance.

Trade relations, like investments, tended to aggravate transatlantic re-

[50] J. J. Servan-Schreiber, *The American Challenge* (New York: Avon Books,
1969), and Pfaltzgraff, *Atlantic Community*, pp. 70–94.

lations.[51] The Common Market was, in a sense, a marriage of French agrarian interests and West German industrial interests, both seeking larger outlets. Thus American farm exports were bound to be affected negatively as more costly European, especially French, agriculture replaced lower-cost American farm produce. Admittedly, American industrial exports rose rapidly during the early years of the Common Market, spurring American economic growth and prosperity, as well as helping keep up high employment rates. But the rapid inflation caused by the Johnson Administration's financing of the Vietnam War and the very high wages earned by American labor helped, one, to drive American firms abroad to look for lower production costs; two, to make American home-produced items so expensive that they began to price themselves out of the international market; and three, to lead American consumers to buy more and more imports (including Japanese goods). The American exports surplus in 1971 vanished for the first time in seventy-one years as the value of imports exceeded that of exports. The dollar flow out of the United States increased as the dollar's domestic purchasing power decreased, while its fixed relationship to foreign currencies meant that European (or Japanese) holders of that money could purchase fewer and fewer products from the American economy. In short, the dollar was overvalued and in 1971 was officially devalued while some other currencies, such as those of Germany and Japan, whose exports to the United States were very sizable, were upvalued; the hoped-for effect was to make American goods and services internationally competitive once more by lowering U.S. prices and drastically raising the prices of products imported to the United States.

In reality, the American trade deficit and therefore the nation's deficit in the balance of payments (the difference between the cost of exports and the import costs, which, if it results in a surplus of money from greater export earnings, is considered good for the economy) continued to get worse. As the dollar outflow grew even more rapidly, banks and corporations—especially those manufacturing and doing business in Europe—speculated heavily, unloading their dollars to buy such stronger currencies as the German mark in the expectation of further devaluations. This greatly exacerbated the financial problems among the principal industrial countries, because it led to further pressure for devaluations and upvaluations, depending on the currencies involved in this speculation. This finally led the Nixon Administration to negotiate further with the other industrial nations in order to establish a monetary system in which all their currencies would be allowed to "float" according to the monetary market pressures. The dollar was no longer to hold a fixed value in relationship to other currencies. The trade surplus was restored once more. Still, given the highly inflationary pressures domesti-

[51] For a critical analysis of America's economic role in the Atlantic Community, see David P. Calleo and Benjamin M. Rowland *America and the World Political Economy* (Bloomington: Indiana University Press, 1973).

cally, doubts about the stability of the American dollar remained; and questions about the fate of President Nixon, the Watergate scandal, and political uncertainty in the United States did not help the dollar. The fantastic rise in oil prices after 1973 settled many doubts; for the United States, as for other industrial countries, the balance of payments became a crisis as money flowed in increasing amounts from the West to the Arab states, threatening the future of all industrial economies.

Dollars flowed out of the United States, however, not only because of the investment opportunities in Europe, cheaper European and Japanese goods, high oil prices, and such other large items as American tourism in Europe; it also flowed out because of U.S. troops stationed in Europe. Even in the 1960's, when exports still exceeded imports, the United States was already running a deficit in the balance of payments. This was due to American political and military NATO commitments, and this deficit, despite a favorable balance of trade, might therefore be termed the price of containment in the area most vital to American security. It was a price that, after the disillusionment of Vietnam, the increasing awareness of many domestic problems that would require substantial funding, the improvement of American-Soviet relations, and the international difficulties of the dollar, many Americans began to think was too high.

Pressure therefore grew in Congress, especially in the Senate, for sizable reductions in the 300,000-man American force in Europe with more than 200,000 dependents. After all, it seemed that the Soviets were more concerned with China than Europe, and that their forces in East Germany and Eastern Europe were large because they had a policing function against internal revolt and loss of control over the area. And was it not also true that a continent whose population and industrial strength exceeded Russia's could devote more of its wealth and mobilize more of its own manpower if it were genuinely concerned with its own defense rather than depend on the United States as much as it does? Did it not seem strange that a Europe of more than 250 million people was still dependent for its protection on a country of just over 200 million people after twenty-five years, against another country whose approximate population is 225 million people, and which is simultaneously in conflict with a country whose size is over 800 million people?[52]

The Nixon Administration opposed what it termed a unilateral withdrawal. A cut in American ground forces of up to 50 per cent meant not only that a limited conventional response to a limited challenge would be impossible, thereby lowering the nuclear threshold, but also that such

[52] John Newhouse, ed., *U.S. Troops in Europe* (Washington, D.C.: The Brookings Institution, 1971) and William T. R. Fox and Warner R. Schilling, eds., *European Security and the Atlantic System* (New York: Columbia University Press, 1973); plus Christopher Bertram, Jr., *Mutual Force Reductions in Europe: The Political Aspects*, Adelphi Paper 84 (London: International Institute for Strategic Studies, 1972).

a pullback from Western Europe would be read by the Russians, as well as the Western Europeans, as an even further lowering of the credibility of America's remaining verbal and legal commitment to Europe's defense. Thus Russia, whose strategic and conventional strength had risen so enormously in recent years, and which had modernized and enlarged its forces in Eastern Europe, would be left in the center of Europe, its might throwing a shadow over the entire Continent, confronting a militarily far weaker Western Europe supported by an increasingly uncredible commitment from the United States, which in an era of parity would not lightly sacrifice its population for Bonn, Paris, and London. A U.S. troop withdrawal in a context of a nuclear standoff would, therefore, leave the European NATO members vulnerable to Soviet political pressure. And since the European countries, like the United States, were democracies whose populations too were tired of high taxes and military recruitment of men in an era of *détente*, it was unlikely that their parliaments would vote for larger military forces and budgets; thus the threat of Western European states' "Finlandization" was a real possibility. (That means that they, as the weaker states, would, like Finland, preserve their independence, but only by avoiding offending the U.S.S.R. with policies Moscow considered hostile. Neutralization of Western Europe would be the minimum Soviet condition.) Were the risks of such an occurrence with its obvious consequences for U.S. security worth chancing, particularly considering that not much money would be saved by the withdrawal of American troops to whose presence in Europe the German government contributed sizable funds and whose return to Europe by an airlift in emergency situations would cost more—unless they were to be disbanded, which the Administration suspected was the real goal of most of those who pressured for their withdrawal? President Nixon insisted that an American troop withdrawal would occur only if the Soviets matched such a pullback in a mutual and balanced force reduction (MBFR), and complex MBFR talks were started between NATO and the Warsaw Pact. Thus economic and financial conditions heavily influenced foreign policy considerations, and vice versa.

It was in these circumstances that Secretary of State Kissinger in 1973 called for a "new Atlantic Charter" to guide relations among the United States, Japan, and Western Europe. No longer weak and exhausted and threatened by a militant Russia, Western Europe was economically prosperous and potentially powerful in an era of *détente*. Fearful that the many differences on defense, economic, and financial issues would be prolonged and create even greater frictions if their resolution were left to the technical experts, Kissinger said that these various problems

> must engage the top political leaders for they require above all a commitment of political will. If they are left to the experts, the inevitable competitiveness of economic interests will dominate the debate. The influence of pressure groups and special interests will become pervasive.

There will be no overriding sense of direction. There will be no framework for the generous solutions or mutual concessions essential to preserve a vital Atlantic partnership.

It is the responsibility of national leaders to insure that economic relations serve larger political purposes. They must recognize that economic rivalry, if carried on without restraint, will in the end damage other relationships.[53]

Perhaps. Not surprisingly, the transatlantic quarrels did not abate despite Kissinger's call. The Europeans in their response—and especially the French—refused to include either the word "partnership" or "interdependence" in a proposed joint declaration on principles governing relations between the United States and the EEC, or in the declaration issued by the latter after its meeting during the energy crisis following the Arab-Israeli War of 1973. (In order to obtain Arab oil, upon which Europe and Japan are far more dependent than the United States, they wanted to put even more distance between themselves and Washington, much to the latter's anger.) Fearing that the call to tackle all the military, economic, and financial issues together as part of a larger whole meant that the United States expected monetary and trade concessions in return for maintaining its troops in Europe—that is, the Europeans would be required to buy them as mercenaries, so to speak—the Europeans responded by suggesting two sets of talks, one on military issues to be conducted within NATO channels, the other on economic-financial issues to be conducted between the United States and a representative of the EEC, although these issues were in fact interrelated. The crisis of the Western alliance thus remained unresolved and will perhaps be unresolvable, at least until the issue of Atlanticism versus Europeanness is settled.

The emergence of a larger economic and perhaps political unit in Europe raises at least two questions: Whether the United States has helped spawn a serious economic rival and whether the underlying assumption of American sponsorship of the European community—namely, that Europe's political interests would be, if not identical, at least compatible with American political interests—was realistic. During the 1973 Mideast crisis, the Europeans did arrive at a large measure of agreement on their common interests. But their consensus did not support the U.S. pro-Israel policy; rather, they sought to avoid alienating the Arabs. Thus Europe's common position, presumably the kind of thing Washington had always desired from a united Europe, was at odds with America's; and this suggested that perhaps the coincidence of interests between the two was not guaranteed and would require far closer consultation and cooperation than had occurred in the past, when the United States had not really confronted the issue that the united Europe it wanted might

[53] *New York Times*, April 24, 1973.

have independent interests.[54] (When this problem had occurred sporadically, as for example with the issue of a possible European nuclear force whose core would be the British and French nuclear forces, Washington had usually balked at this logical conclusion of its policy toward a united Europe.) Even more basically, however, the Secretary of State had raised the single most crucial issue, which touched on the very *raison d'être* of NATO or, indeed, any alliance: Can an alliance forged by a common perception of danger survive when that perception has diminished by substituting "positive shared aspirations"? Or, to phrase it slightly differently, does not a cohesive alliance depend on strong adversary relations with an external opponent; and if that adversary relationship diminishes and the chief power in the alliance is increasingly arranging its own relationship with the chief power in the opposite camp, is an erosion of the alliance not inevitable?

The Nonaligned

In the bipolar world that existed until the late 1950's and early 1960's, before the erosion of NATO and the Sino-Soviet alliance, both blocs sought, as their maximum objective, to enhance their respective strengths by adding the territory, population, and resources of the newly emerged nations—or, at least, the potentially stronger and politically more important new states; their minimal aim was to prevent these states from joining the adversary's bloc. In their competition for the allegiance and adherence of the former colonial states, the Western and Communist states shifted—although not entirely or forever—their conflict from the European frontyard, where they confronted one another face-to-face with their military forces, to the non-Western backyard, where they did not confront one another directly and tended to compete politically, economically, and in unconventional military terms. Nuclear weapons could play no role in this competition, and for neither superpower were interests of paramount importance—such as existed in Europe—involved.

For the new states, all of which were militarily weak and economically and politically underdeveloped, nonalignment with either bloc made tactical sense in the context of this postwar distribution.[55] An "in-between" or third world posture presumably allowed them to maximize their bargaining influence. This was significant in at least two respects. First, the new nations desperately needed economic aid and technical assistance. Second, for nations that had long been Western-controlled,

---

[54] "Z," "The Year of Europe," *Foreign Affairs*, January, 1974, p. 237, and Karl Kaiser, "Europe and America," *Foreign Affairs*, July, 1974, pp. 725 ff. See also Adelphi Papers 70 and 71, entitled *Europe and America in the 1970s* (London: International Institute for Strategic Studies, 1970).

[55] The nature of nonalignment is analyzed in greater detail in Chapter 15.

such aid could reduce their political and economic dependence on the West. When a nation moved away from the West, of course, the Communist states would offer it aid. Conversely, when it became too dependent on the Communists or when it resisted them, an American loan tended to be forthcoming. The middle position in the cold war was therefore politically and economically very useful:

> The possibility of "blackmail" is built into the very structure of Cold War competition. But from the point of view of the excessively dependent, relatively impotent new state, this is not blackmail. It is the equally ancient but more honorable art of maintaining political equilibrium through the diversification of dependence, the balancing of weakness—in short, the creation of an "alternative" lest the influence of one side or the other become too imposing. The attraction of Communist aid is enhanced for radical governments whose wariness of the intentions of the former metropole extends to the "capitalist-imperialist West" in general. Yet [even] conservative governments—Morocco and Ethiopia, for example—are receptive to Communist aid. They want it partly to placate their radical oppositions and to hasten development, but also, one suspects, to pursue the first requirement of operational independence—the creation of a rough equilibrium among foreign influences in the life of the country. Conversely, radical governments that have developed extensive relations with the Communist bloc may seek the re-establishment of compensatory links with the West, as in the case of Guinea and the U.A.R.[56]

For the new states, however, nonalignment is more than a tactical operational rule. It is also a *psychological need.* For these states, because they are new states, are highly nationalistic. During the 1950's, Americans were wont to equate their nonalignment with a moral neutrality in the cold war, but this inference of moral indifference was false. The leaders of the new countries simply viewed the East-West conflict from a different perspective. Their attitudes were bound to be influenced by their colonial experience. During the 1950's, American statements that the global struggle was between freedom and despotism—and therefore a struggle in which all nations must "stand up and be counted"—might well be regarded with some skepticism by those once ruled autocratically by the West.[57] But even had the leaders of these new states seen the cold war in such terms, most of them would have been unlikely to take sides in an alliance. The reason was simply that the cold war was secondary to the new nations' preoccupation with their own development and

[56] Robert C. Good, "State-Building as a Determinant of Foreign Policy in the New States," in Laurence W. Martin, ed., *Neutralism and Nonalignment* (New York: Praeger Publishers, 1962), p. 11.

[57] "We find," Kenya's Tom Mboya has said, "that both Westerners and Russians look at Africans through the same pair of glasses: the one lens is marked pro-Western; the other pro-Communist. It is not surprising that, looking at Africans in this way, most foreigners fail to understand the one great reality about our continent—that Africans are neither pro-West nor pro-Russian; they are pro-African." Quoted in Colin Legum, *Pan-Africanism,* rev. ed. (New York: Praeger Publishers, 1965), p. 13.

modernization. In these circumstances, their foreign policies become essentially a reflection of their quest for national identity and cohesion. Reacting to past colonial domination, they could not join the West in a coalition against the Communist bloc. Only by asserting themselves could they acquire a sense of their own nationhood. Only by rejecting their British or French or Dutch "father" could they gain their feeling of identity. In much the same way, the New Europe has tended to reject its American father—just as the world's "first new nation" once rejected its Old World parentage.

The relationship of nonalignment to the acquisition of national identity is, indeed, interestingly illustrated by American behavior after the United States became independent. It called nonalignment nonentanglement, which even then meant the refusal of the new state to align itself with the former colonial ruler and, in fact, to abstain from a continuing involvement in the quarrels of the great powers. All new states, by refusing to identify themselves with any side, maintain their freedom of action. Indeed, they gain self-recognition by asserting themselves—at the very minimum on a verbal plane—against the great powers. Having gained independence, they seek to preserve their separate identity. That is why the speeches of a Nehru or a Nasser seem to echo John Adams and George Washington. Turning to Washington's Farewell Address, for instance, one reads:

> The great rule of conduct for us in regard to foreign nations is, in extending our commercial relations, to have with them as little *political* connection as possible. . . .
>
> Europe has a set of primary interests which to us have none or a very remote relation. Hence she must be engaged in frequent controversies, the causes of which are essentially foreign to our concerns. Hence, therefore, it must be unwise in us to implicate ourselves by artificial ties in the ordinary vicissitudes of her politics or the ordinary combinations and collisions of her friendships or enmities. . . .
>
> Why forgo the advantages of so peculiar a situation? Why quit our own to stand upon foreign ground? Why, by interweaving our destiny with that of any part of Europe, entangle our peace and prosperity in the toils of European Ambition, Rivalship, Interest, Humor, or Caprice?[58]

Jefferson summed it up succinctly when he said simply: "Peace, commerce and honest friendship with all nations—entangling alliances with none."

Perhaps the best example of "nation-building" through the rejection of the European "father" was the Monroe Doctrine, promulgated in 1823. The doctrine formalized the rejection and demonstrated explicitly that American nationalism—or anticolonialism—was directed not merely at Britain, the former ruler, but at all of Europe. The New World would

[58] See Felix Gilbert, *To the Farewell Address: Ideas of Early American Foreign Policy* (Princeton, N.J.: Princeton University Press, 1961), Appendix, p. 145. Emphasis added.

stand apart from the Old. This formal step of separation was taken at a time when American security was threatened by a possible attempt of the Holy Alliance to help Spain restore control over its former colonies in South America. Despite this menace to its safety, the United States refused to ally itself formally with Britain, the only power capable of protecting it from the Holy Alliance. Because Britain, too, opposed the Alliance, it proposed to the United States that the two countries form a common front against the monarchical reaction it represented—against what was a threat, therefore, not only to American security but also to constitutional government anywhere. The British approached the United States not because the American Navy was strong but because they sought the kind of political support that American diplomats now seek, for instance, from India. Yet, despite the coincidence of American interests with those of Britain, the country refused: American policy remained one of nonalignment. As Secretary of State John Quincy Adams put it, the United States refused to become "a cockboat in the wake of the British man of war."[59]

Instead, it unilaterally proclaimed the Monroe Doctrine—knowing full well that British sea power would support it. Significantly, instead of informing the Continental powers privately that the Western Hemisphere was no longer to be regarded as a preserve for European colonialism, Monroe resorted to "open diplomacy." Clearly, such a public pronouncement was more gratifying to national pride and more insulting to Europe. Of course, it is unlikely that Europe would have respected the doctrine had it not been aware that, rejected or no, England's Navy stood behind it.

Nonalignment in search of identity also tends to be very sensitive—hypersensitive, in fact—to the slightest insult. A new nation may be independent, but its anticolonial mentality fades only gradually. The War of 1812 illustrates this dramatically. British impressment of American sailors was considered an insult to the nation, as it carried the implication that the American flag could not protect those who served it and that Britain continued to view the nation as though it were still a colony. Not surprisingly, the War of 1812 came to be known as the "second war of independence."

Nonalignment, both as a tactic and as a psychological need, depends in the final analysis upon the equitable distribution of power between the great powers. After the War of 1812, and the issuance of the Monroe Doctrine in 1823, there was little competition for America's allegiance. But the contemporary new nations of the postwar era were born into a world of continuing competition for their favors. Nonalignment would not have been feasible if other conditions had prevailed: if the superpowers had ended their conflict and lived in a *détente* or, better yet, an *entente cordiale*; if one superpower had attained hegemony in

[59] Quoted in Dexter Perkins, *A History of the Monroe Doctrine*, rev. ed. (Boston: Little, Brown, 1955), p. 43.

the state system; or if there were more than two great powers and if these had concentrated their efforts on the relationships with their peers rather than the allegiance of powerless nonaligned states. Nonalignment works well in a bipolar distribution of power—at least, until the non-aligned state is attacked or threatened by a great power. Then its security depends upon the support of a rival great power. The need for such support is indeed implicit in the conception of nonalignment.

If bipolarity was conducive to a policy of nonalignment and enhanced the bargaining capacity of the new states, the passing of bipolarity decreased their influence in the international system. First, as the cohesive alliances, East and West, broke up and the superpowers increasingly recognized the need for cooperation in order to preserve the peace, they also became aware that they could satisfy some of their most important interests through this cooperation; thus their competition for the allegiance of the Third World countries declined. Indeed, their nonalignment began in most cases to seem preferable to their alignment. Second, both the United States and the Soviet Union had become disenchanted with economic aid to the nonaligned nations. Economic development seemed so terribly slow and, with the exception of the Arab states, which were wooed with much additional military aid by the Soviets, both the superpowers found the new nations very nationalistic and, therefore, resistant to attempts to convert foreign aid into foreign influence. Third, growing numbers of the new nations' more militant leaders, whose interests were primarily in foreign policy rather than domestic problems and the difficult task of modernization, were deposed by less militant leaders whose basic concern was their nations' development. To the degree that the superpowers also wished to avoid a confrontation, they had found the nationalist leadership more a liability than a tool for establishing their influence. After all, a Nasser might provide the Soviets with *entrée* into the Middle East because he needed Russia for diplomatic support and military aid and training for his army against Israel, but he could also get the Soviet Union into trouble by precipitating a fight that might bring about an American-Russian confrontation in the area. And, despite all the Soviet Union's help for Egypt, Nasser did arrest local Communists. And Sadat, when he succeeded Nasser after the latter's death, turned against Moscow when he did not get all he wanted and moved toward the United States instead—at least for the time being, while Washington could help Egypt realize its political and economic aims. Fourth, rapid multiplication of the new states meant that it became harder to describe the Third World as if it were a monolith whose members all responded identically to the external stimuli of great-power conflict. This had not even been true when there had been fewer nonaligned countries and there was still an East and a West. It was even less true with the proliferation of so many new states and after the passing of bipolarity. Among the new states, a multitude of differences arose, including conflicting views on their policies toward America, Russia, and China. Finally, and somewhat more tentatively, the superpowers appeared to be moving toward resolving conflicts among these smaller powers and trying to work out a settlement for them or with them. Although such negotiations were held under U.N. auspices, it was the United States and the U.S.S.R. that did the negotiating. For, to the degree that they gave priority to their new bilateral cooperation and wished to avoid confrontations brought about by their client states, they had a common stake in bilaterally arranging solutions that would protect their friends' as well as their own interests, yet meet the needs of the other superpower and its friends. While it would be going too far to say that the Big Two can impose a settlement on their client states, it is not going too far to suggest that they can provide the incentives for the latter to want—even if somewhat reluctantly—a settlement. It was in the Middle East, after the Arab-Israeli War of 1973, that this trend first became visible in the American-Russian arranged cease-fire and their post-war sponsorship of the Geneva peace conference to explore if, after four regional wars, a more tranquil peace could be arranged. This trend may become stronger as the two superpowers increasingly hope to avoid confrontations arising from critical situations occurring throughout the Third World. This would be a significant departure from their earlier pattern, should it occur, and in turn it would profoundly affect the future role of the United Nations as a peace-keeping institution.[60]

[60] See chapter 14 for additional comments on the influence of the new states because of their possession of resources needed by the industrial nations.

9 Preserving Peace in the State System: The United Nations and Disarmament

Beyond the Balance of Power?

If the state system is likely to survive for a long time and if inter-state conflict remains a principal characteristic of what remains an essentially anarchical system, does the future of international peace then continue to depend largely on the preservation of a balance of power forged by the superpowers and their allies? No previous balance in history has in the long-run prevented war; no deterrent strategy has been fail-proof. Two world wars and a cold war in just over thirty years (1914, 1939, 1947) are evidence enough; and although the penalty for a failure of deterrence is suicide, will that be sufficient to guarantee perpetual peace? If not, can states, so to speak, go "beyond deterrence" to ensure world peace?

Two frequently suggested solutions to problems of conflict in a strife prone system are the United Nations and disarmament. For many advocates of international organization, a United Nations symbolizes the expectation of an abolition of war for, hopefully, it represents the embodiment of a new spirit of internationalism which will erode national egotism and replace it with a spirit of international cooperation and harmony. In Senator Fulbright's words, the United Nations is an institution to protect "humanity from the destructiveness of unrestrained nationalism" and therefore to be strengthened by subordinating the short-run needs of each country to the longer-run needs of all humanity.[1]

By contrast, disarmament does not address itself so much to the problem of conflict resolution as the extermination of the weapons with which conflicts may be waged. Whereas the U.N. approach stresses a new spirit of accommodation and the peaceful settlements of disputes, disarmament assumes that differences of interests will continue; but if

[1] J. William Fulbright, "In Thrall to Fear," *The New Yorker* (January 8, 1972), p. 59.

nations no longer possess arms, wars will not occur. How realistic are these approaches to making the state system safe for mankind?

The Three United Nations

The United Nations is, unfortunately, not the Great Peacemaker and solver of all problems. The international organization is not a superstate, usurping its members' sovereignty and imposing its will on them. Nor is the United Nations independent of states' national interests and political considerations. Its decisions are not made according to some impartial, nonpolitical, and therefore purportedly morally superior standard of justice. The United Nations is not above politics because it does not exist and act independently of the politics of its members. Rather, the United Nations reflects the political interests, attitudes, and problems of its member states. It does not possess independent authority but is merely the channel through which the power and purposes of its members flows. In short, the United Nations is not a substitute for power politics; it only registers the power politics of the state system. It is a mirror, not a panacea; it has no magic wand by which it can resolve all of man's international problems. It cannot transcend the cold war or the anticolonial struggles. It must function in the world as it exists, and it cannot solve any problems that its members, because of conflicting interests, are not prepared to solve. Its failures indicate only its members' inability to reach agreement.

Because the United Nations is not a superstate imposing its will upon its members but a body registering their political interests, attitudes, and problems, the international organization's functions can be understood best in terms of the changing conditions of the state system. When it was formed, the United Nations reflected the wartime hopes that, once victory over Germany had been won, great-power cooperation would continue and peace would be maintained. Primary authority for the preservation of peace and security in the first United Nations was vested in the Security Council, composed of eleven members, six of them on a rotating basis. The real authority, however, was to be exercised by the United States, the Soviet Union, Britain, France, and China. If they voted unanimously to take enforcement action against aggression, their decision had to be followed by all U.N. members. Thus, through an oligarchical structure that reflected the global distribution of power, the great powers were the masters of the United Nations. Indeed, the United States and the Soviet Union, actually the only two great powers remaining in 1945, were the real masters. Britain was exhausted, France was still recovering from its defeat and German occupation, and China was a weak country embroiled in civil war. As long as the two superpowers could maintain harmony, peace would be preserved.

The security system was thus directed only against the smaller nations; if they disturbed the peace, and if the great powers agreed to take punitive action, they could be squashed. The United Nations was, in the words of one delegate at its first conference, "engaged in establishing a world in which the mice could be stamped out but in which the lions would not be restrained."[2] The veto was to prevent one of the great powers from mobilizing the United Nations against another great power. The United Nations was never intended to be a collective-security organization, inasmuch as going to war to punish a great power's aggression would precipitate another global war. Hence,

> insertion of the veto provision in the decision-making circuit of the Security Council reflected the clear conviction that in cases of sharp conflict among the great powers the Council ought, for safety's sake, to be incapacitated—to be rendered incapable of being used to precipitate a showdown, or to mobilize collective action against the recalcitrant power. The philosophy of the veto is that it is better to have the Security Council stalemated than to have that body used by a majority to take action so strongly opposed by a dissident great power that a world war is likely to ensue.[3]

Great-power conflicts were to be handled *outside* the United Nations under collective self-defense arrangements, which did not require prior Security Council authorization to take individual or joint military action against an attack.

As the two superpowers assumed opposing sides at the beginning of the cold war, the United States sought to mobilize the support of the United Nations for the containment of Russia and thereby to associate its own policies with the organization's humanitarian, peaceful, and democratic values. This transformation from the first to the second United Nations was most dramatically illustrated in Korea. The United States had no choice but to oppose the Soviet Union, but it acted under U.N. auspices. The Soviet absence from the Security Council on the day it voted to intervene enabled it to act. But such an absence was not likely to occur a second time. The United States therefore introduced the "Uniting for Peace" resolution in November, 1950, the purpose of which was to transfer primary responsibility for the preservation of peace and security to the General Assembly should the Security Council become paralyzed by the veto. Constitutionally, this transfer of authority should not have been possible. The General Assembly was granted authority only to debate, investigate, and recommend on issues concerning international peace and security. Even then, it could offer no recommendations affecting matters on the Security Council's agenda; by placing an issue on the agenda, then, the Council could reduce the Assembly to a mere debating society.

[2] Quoted in Inis L. Claude, Jr., *Power and International Relations* (New York: Random House, 1964), p. 59.
[3] *Ibid.*, p. 160, and *idem, Swords into Plowshares*, rev. ed. (New York: Random House, 1964), pp. 80–86.

The Americans argued, however, that the U.N. responsibility for the preservation of international peace and security could not be abandoned just because the Security Council was stymied. If the Council could not fulfill its "primary responsibility" for this function, the Assembly would have to assume this task. It need hardly be added that in the Assembly as it was then constituted the United States could easily muster the two-thirds majorities needed for important resolutions by drawing on the votes of the NATO countries, the older British dominions, the Latin American republics, and one or two Asian states. The Soviet Union, with no veto in the Assembly, was of course constantly outvoted. Yet it was still able to use the Assembly to give vent to its own point of view.

The attempt to use the Assembly to support American anti-Communist policies did not last long. Just as the configuration of power underlying the original Security Council—the wartime alliance—was to be changed shortly after the establishment of the United Nations, so the political alignment at the outbreak of the Korean War was a fleeting one not destined to survive even the war, despite the "Uniting for Peace" resolution. The United States had received U.N. support at the beginning of the war for two reasons. First, an overwhelming number of its members, including the nonaligned states,[4] saw in the North Korean aggression a test of the United Nations itself. If the organization failed to respond, it would follow the League of Nations into the dustbin of history. Second, the smaller powers saw in the transfer of authority on security matters to the Assembly an opportunity to play the enlarged role in U.N. affairs that they had originally been denied by the "lions," much to their resentment. But Communist China's intervention in late 1950 changed this American-sponsored use of the United Nations as an instrument of collective enforcement against the Communist bloc. The involvement of a major Communist power, and the possibility that the U.S. Government might accede to strong domestic pressures to extend the war to China by air bombardment, naval blockade, and the landing of Nationalist forces on the mainland, dramatized the wisdom of the U.N. architects' original intent to prevent the organization's involvement in the military conflicts of the great powers. The danger of world war was simply too great.

In addition, the then twelve Arab-Asian members of the General Assembly were determined to remain nonaligned in the cold war. Their earlier support for American intervention in Korea had been motivated by their concern for the United Nations as an institution. It was essential that North Korea's aggression be met, and because the United States had the strength to take the appropriate measures, the Arab-Asian members had approved of the original American reaction. But they had no desire to participate in taking collective measures against one side or the other, which would in effect have forced them to become allied to one

---

[4] Egypt, because of its feeling that the United Nations had not supported it in the war against Israel in 1947–48, was an exception.

of the cold war blocs through the mechanism of the U.N. voting procedure. The problem was to prevent a military clash between the great
powers and, simultaneously, to avoid becoming aligned in the cold war
themselves. The answer was to shift the function of the United Nations
from enforcement to conciliation.[5] The United Nations was to serve as
an instrument of mediation in conflict situations between the great powers. The original assumption that peace could be preserved by having the
five lions, headed by the two biggest lions, act as the world's guardians
now was replaced with the recognition of the imperative need to keep
the lions from mauling each other to death—and trampling the mice
while they were at it.

A third United Nations was thus born. The first had been dedicated
to preserving the wartime Grand Alliance; the second, which succeeded
it, had been, so to speak, a wing of the State Department. This United
Nations began to die during the Korean War. By exerting great pressure,
the United States could still, in the spring of 1951, obtain the two-thirds
majority needed in the General Assembly for the condemnation of Communist China. Already, though, it had to make concessions to collect
these votes—the price being that it would not follow the condemnation
with additional military or economic measures. Instead, the United
States was to give primary emphasis to the conciliatory efforts of the
Arab-Asian bloc—supported by most of its NATO allies, which were
also concerned about a possible escalation of the conflict—to end the
war. By 1955, the third United Nations—born in 1950, when the six
Arab and six Asian members of the United Nations began to consult
each other regularly about the positions they adopted during the Korean
War—had reached adolescence; and as the number of newly independent members, especially African ones, grew rapidly after 1955, it matured
quickly. In 1955 six new Asian and North African states were admitted
to the United Nations; one year later, four more were added. In 1960,
the number of new states admitted was seventeen, mainly from sub-
Saharan Africa. By 1974, Asian, African, and Latin American states com-
prised three-quarters of the United Nations' 138 members. If both the
American and the Soviet blocs had previously used the United Nations
for their own cold wars purposes, the neutral bloc now employed the
organization to erase the vestiges of Western colonialism as soon as possible. The General Assembly was a particularly good forum in which to
voice anticolonial sentiments and to keep the pressure on the West by
passing, or trying to pass—with the help of the Communist bloc—resolutions in favor of national self-determination.

The new United Nations could not, however, help but become involved in the cold war. The United States and the Soviet Union, to be
sure, did not allow the organization to interfere in *their* clashes. The So-

[5] Ernst Haas, "Types of Collective Security: An Examination of Operational Concepts," *American Political Science Review*, March, 1955, pp. 40–62, examines this
transition from "permissive enforcement" to "balancing."

viets had no intention of permitting the United Nations to intervene in Hungary or Czechoslovakia. Nor would the United States permit the United Nations to become involved in negotiation over the post-1958 Berlin crises, any Cuban problems,[6] or even Vietnam. East-West issues were debated only; no action was taken. The superpowers handled their own direct confrontations. But on the periphery of the cold war, the United States and the Soviet Union were constantly tempted to interfere in the conflicts stemming from the end of colonialism. Such interference, by threatening the peace and involving the neutrals in the cold war, was bound to lead the nonaligned nations to take protective action. The United Nations to them was more than a political platform. It was also a shelter in which they sought refuge from great-power pressure. They thought of this third United Nations as *theirs*, and they were determined to use it to remain nonaligned. The chief function of the United Nations thus became one of "preventive diplomacy"[7]—that is, the stabilization of local conflicts *before* either of the superpowers could become involved and thereby provoke its antagonist's intervention as well. Or, to state it negatively, preventive diplomacy was intended to keep American-Soviet clashes from extending beyond the cold war zone. At the same time, by containing the cold war, it would safeguard the new nations' independence and permit them control over their own future. Thus the mice were to keep the lions apart before they began to grapple with each other and trample the mice to death while they fought. The chief means of stabilization was the establishment of a "United Nations presence" in these peripheral quarrels. The United Nations, in short, became a fire brigade. In a highly combustible world, it rushed to potential fire-hazard areas to contain and douse the initial flames. It did so not by dousing the fire—which the United Nations could not do—but by using its presence to signal to the world that a fire was imminent or had already broken out and needed to be put out quickly.

PREVENTIVE DIPLOMACY

In a real sense, the United Nations has thus performed a crucial arms control function in a highly combustible world. But for the United Na-

---

[6] In the case of Cuba, only after the Cuban missile crisis had already been resolved was the organization to be used—and then it was to check that all Soviet missiles were removed from Cuba. But because Castro refused to submit to international inspection and the United States had no doubts that all the missiles had been shipped back to Russia, the United Nations remained uninvolved.

[7] Andrew Boyd, *United Nations: Piety, Myth and Truth* (Baltimore: Penguin Books, 1962), pp. 85 ff; Inis L. Claude, Jr., *The Changing United Nations* (New York: Random House, 1967), pp. 23 ff; Arthur L. Burns and Nina Heathcote, *Peace-Keeping by U.N. Forces: From Suez to Congo* (New York: Praeger Publishers, 1963); and Linda B. Miller, *World Order and Local Disorder* (Princeton, N.J.: Princeton University Press, 1967).

tions to perform this role, it has needed not only superpower support, or at least acquiescence, but the active support and participation of the Third World countries. The latter's contribution to systemic stability comes in response to two conditions. The first is that the problems of the non-Western states tend to spill over into the international arena. This may result, for example, from the disintegration of a state, as happened in the Congo after it attained independence in 1960; in the resultant attempts to reunify it, the competing factions turned to outside help. Or it may be due to a clash of regional states—although former colonial powers may be involved—that have friends in the different superpower camps. This happened during the Israeli-Egyptian War in 1956, when France and Britain intervened militarily on Israel's side and the Soviet Union supported Egypt diplomatically—and even talked of sending its missiles winging toward Paris and London. The second condition is that these types of problem tend to attract the Soviet Union and the United States, thus leading to a possible confrontation, with all its attendant dangers of a military clash. The two superpowers are attracted, of course, because the outcome of these problems may be to bring to power a group one country likes and the other dislikes, or a regional expansion that may benefit one and hurt the other. If one of the two nations is unwilling to tolerate what it may consider, in terms of the global balance of power, a local or regional setback, it will intervene; or, if it fears that if it does not intervene its opponent might, the result may be a preventive intervention. In both cases, it risks counterintervention. Thus the conflicts that arose on the peripheries of the American-Soviet rivalry have tended to be drawn into the extensive confrontations of the two superpowers.

The Suez crisis of 1956 provides a good illustration of this tendency of conflicts emanating essentially from the end of colonialism to spill over into the cold war zone. Egypt had been a British protectorate from 1881 to 1936, when it was granted independence. Britain retained control of the Suez Canal, though, and in effect maintained its dominant position. But mounting Egyptian nationalism and a corresponding rise in anti-British feelings afterward eventually led Britain to relinquish its Suez military base in 1954, although not its control of the Canal. The moment British troops had withdrawn, President Nasser launched an energetic anti-Western campaign to eliminate all "colonial" governments in the Middle East and North Africa. Success would, of course, make him the leader of all Arabs and give him control of most of the Arabian oil. Once Egypt became the strongest Arab state, it would have tremendous bargaining power, since Europe, especially Britain, was dependent on Middle Eastern oil. The United States and Britain were alarmed by these attempts to eliminate Western power and influence in the economically and strategically vital Middle East, particularly since Nasser leaned increasingly toward the Soviet Union, for whom the Middle East provided a means of outflanking NATO without a shot being fired. Therefore, shortly after Nasser extended diplomatic recognition to Communist China, the United States withdrew its offer to finance the Aswan Dam, which was to irrigate much of Egypt's weather-beaten soil and thus help its economic development. Nasser's reaction was to nationalize the Suez Canal, claiming that he would use its income to build the dam.

Britain now felt compelled to act. If Nasser were allowed to seize Suez with impunity, it felt, other Arab governments would appropriate Western property—particularly oil property; nor would any pro-Western Arab government be safe from overthrow by pro-Nasser elements within their countries. Britain—joined by France, which wished to stop Egyptian shipments of arms to the Algerian nationalists to be used against France —gained the opportunity when Israel attacked Egypt. This moment occurred after Nasser's famous arms deal with Russia, made with the stated purpose of driving Israel into the sea. The consequent hostilities threatened to develop into a major war as the Soviet Union, which shared Egypt's interest in expelling the West from the Middle East, threatened to send volunteers to Egypt and even to rain atomic rockets on London and Paris.

The possibility of Soviet intervention naturally brought forth an American response. The United States disapproved of its allies' attack on Egypt, feeling that it smacked of nineteenth-century colonialism and would alienate the new nations. U.S. support for the British and French action would have allowed the Soviet Union to pose as the friend and defender of the new nations. The United States therefore voted with the Soviet Union in the Security Council to condemn Britain and France's aggression and to call upon them to desist. At the same time, it could not stand by and let the Soviet Union send military "volunteers" into the Middle East, let alone attack Britain and France, so a warning note was sent to Moscow. Yet could the Soviet Union, posing as Egypt's protector, really remain inactive in the event of American intervention without endangering its good relations with the other nonaligned states? At the very least, then, the situation was dangerous.

In 1973 there was almost a replay of this situation. In October Egypt and Syria attacked Israel during the highest Jewish holiday, Yom Kippur, the Day of Atonement. Egypt was now ruled by Anwar Sadat, an Egyptian nationalist but a more moderate figure than Nasser, who had been an Arab nationalist or Pan-Arabist before his death. The country had become increasingly frustrated by Israel's continued occupation of Egyptian territory up to the East Bank of the Suez Canal. This territory, captured by Israel in the Six Day War in 1967 after Nasser had precipitated a showdown with a series of political and military moves, looked as if it may remain in Israeli hands for a long time. Israel had no incentives to surrender it. After the war in which it had established its independence, Israel had had to fight for survival in 1956 and 1967. The Arab states continued to be hostile to its existence, and Nasser, the only Arab leader of stature who could have mobilized popular support throughout the Arab world for a compromise settlement recognizing Israel's exist-

ence as a fact that could not be undone, refused to play the role of peacemaker. Instead, allying himself with Jordan and Syria, he had in 1967
proclaimed Egypt ready for the "final struggle." But, even after having
lost yet another war, he refused to sit down with Israel and negotiate a
settlement; the defeat did not therefore bring peace, only another cease-
fire.

But Israel thought it was a peace of sorts. It felt itself to be militarily
superior and therefore not likely to be attacked. The American-Soviet
détente also benefited Israel since the United States did not exercise any
pressure on it to give up the captured Egyptian and Syrian territories.
The Soviet Union, needing American technology, investments, and trade
for its own sagging economy and wanting a SALT agreement, was also
in no position to call down pressure upon Israel or to give active political
and military support to the Arab states. Moscow, by limiting its support
for North Vietnam despite the American blockade and bombing in the
spring of 1972, had achieved better relations with Washington and was
not about to permit Cairo to jeopardize these relations any more than it
had allowed Hanoi to do so when the latter had launched its spring offensive. Indeed, having supplied North Vietnam with the arms that had
helped it launch that offensive and jeopardize better Soviet-American
relations, Moscow made sure that the offensive arms Cairo wanted for an
attack on Israel were not delivered; only Egypt's defenses were bolstered.
The territorial *status quo* thus became frozen.

But Sadat was unwilling to live with this *status quo*. For one thing, he
was subject to increasing domestic pressures, especially from the army
and university students, to seek revenge against Israel; external pressures
from the more militant Arab states, like Libya, and nonstate actors, such
as the various Palestinian guerrilla movements, were also severe. Thus
Sadat, an unglamorous figure succeeding the beloved and charismatic
Nasser, was in danger of being overthrown; pro-Soviet Egyptian leaders
were particularly anxious to replace him as Sadat began to reduce and
then eliminate their influence and undertook measures to attract foreign, including American, private capital to rescue Egypt's stagnate
economy from Nasser's "Arab socialism." Above all, Sadat realized that
if Israel was to be compelled to abandon the Arab territory captured in
1967 he had to look elsewhere than Moscow. Only the United States,
Israel's friend, could help him achieve this goal; and this emphasis on
the return of the 1967 territory suggested a reciprocal willingness to recognize Israel's existence. But Israel, skeptical after its previous bitter experiences, subject to constant guerrilla attacks, continuously denounced
by Arab militants, did nothing; to Israel, Sadat was merely talking, wanting the return of territory that, once returned, would only strengthen
him for yet another war. The United States, too, did nothing after Sadat
in 1972 threw the Soviet advisers to his military out, thereby trying to entice Washington to take the initiative in seeking a peace agreement.

Sadat, frustrated, his power endangered, therefore launched the Yom

Kippur War, which took Israel by surprise and achieved initial success in crossing the Suez Canal and driving into the Sinai Desert. But, once Israel recovered from its shock and had driven the Syrians back from the Golan Heights, its forces concentrated on Egypt, crossed the Suez Canal to the West bank, and moved to cut off supplies to the Egyptian forces on the East bank and encircle them. At this point, the United States and Russia agreed upon a cease-fire resolution in the U.N. Security Council, the United States because it felt that no peace could be arranged if Egypt were again humiliated in war—indeed the psychological boost derived from its initial successes had to be preserved if it were expected to make any concessions in a peace settlement—and Russia to avoid an Egyptian defeat that might compel Moscow to enter the war to rescue its client state.

Indeed, this almost happened as the shooting continued and the Israelis drove to encircle and destroy the Egyptian army on the Eastern side of the Suez Canal. Sadat now requested the United States and the Soviet Union to use their own forces to impose their cease-fire resolution. When the United States declined to intervene with its forces and Russia threatened to do so unilaterally, the two superpowers confronted one another as American military forces were placed on a worldwide alert. Another highly flammable situation existed.

One more illustration, this time stemming from the disintegration of a new state once it emerged from colonial rule, is provided by the Congo crisis. The Republic of Congo (now Zaïre) became an independent state in 1960. But the Belgians, unlike the British and the French in most of their colonies, had not trained native leaders to take over for them. Complete disorder soon broke out when the native army rioted. The Belgian settlers fled, and to protect them Belgium flew in troops. The Congolese Prime Minister, Patrice Lumumba, interpreted the Belgian action as an attempt to restore its colonial rule. He appealed to the United Nations to compel the Belgians to withdraw. The Soviets immediately supported his appeal and condemned Belgium, accusing it of acting as the front for "NATO imperialism." An even more serious situation developed when the province of Katanga seceded. Katanga's rich copper mines were the Congo's main source of revenue, and the secession thus threatened the survival of the entire nation. But the Katanga mines were owned by the powerful Union Minière du Haute-Katange, which supported the secession. This company, representing Belgian and British capital, helped the provincial President Moïse Tshombe build up a large army led by Belgian and other European officers. Lumumba demanded that the United Nations crush Tshombe's mercenary army and help him restore Congolese unity.

When his demand went unheeded, Lumumba appealed to the Soviet Union to help him against the "colonialists." He received both Russian diplomatic support and Russian military supplies, and it looked as if Moscow would establish a base from which it could further expand its influence in Africa. This possibility was not much reduced when Lumumba was dismissed from office by the Congo's President, whom the United States supported in its efforts to prevent the establishment of a Soviet foothold in Central Africa. The Soviets, however, refused to recognize his successor, contending that only Parliament had the right to dismiss Lumumba and that since it had not he was still the Congo's legitimate Prime Minister and must be restored to his office. Lumumba's subsequent murder exacerbated the situation.

The national coalition government formed in early 1961 thus faced a major crisis from its beginning, a crisis that could only benefit the Soviet Union unless a solution was found. The government, committed to a policy of nonalignment in foreign policy, had as its first objective national reunification. Failure to achieve this goal would undermine its authority and lead to its collapse through political failure and financial weakness. The transfer of power to a more radical pro-Communist government would then be a real possibility. Or the central government, to head off its own collapse, might itself turn toward Russia, just as Lumumba had done earlier. In either case, there would be a Soviet-American confrontation in the Congo.

It is in such situations outside the cold war zone, then, where the two superpowers are drawn in and threaten the peace of the world, that the third U.N. plays its most important role. And just as the Security Council had been intended to be the focus of authority in the first United Nations, and the General Assembly the focus in the second, the Secretary-General was to be the principal actor in this third United Nations. No longer merely the prime U.N. administrative officer, the Secretary-General, in partnership with the nonaligned nations, became its leading political officer. It was Dag Hammarskjöld who, by establishing the precedent of the U.N. presence in troubled areas, first assumed the role that has been described as "custodian of brushfire peace." The most dramatic form this presence has taken has been the "nonfighting international force" whose purpose is basically not military but political. The size of the force, drawn primarily from states not involved in the dispute, and its firepower are not as significant as its political presence, which forestalls the influx of Soviet or American forces. Thus, in the Suez crisis, the U.N. Emergency Force (UNEF) supervised the withdrawal of British, French, and Israeli troops from Egypt in 1956. It did not seek to compel their withdrawal through combat. The cease-fire agreement was the prerequisite for its use. Yet the fact that the force was available made it easier to obtain British, French, and Israeli agreement to withdraw. Once the withdrawal had been completed, fewer than 5,000 U.N. soldiers were left to guard the Israeli-Egyptian frontier and maintain the peace in that area. Symbolically enough, it was Nasser's demand that these forces be withdrawn in 1967, leaving Egypt and Israel to confront each other once more directly, that led to the Six Day War. Similarly, the interposition of U.N. forces between Israeli and Egyptian troops ended the crisis emanating from the American-Soviet confrontation during the 1973 war; and it was these U.N. forces that remained between the hostile forces on both the Egyptian and Syrian fronts as the U.S. Secretary of State patiently negotiated disengagements of the combatants as a prelude to a formal Geneva peace conference under joint American-Russian sponsorship.

At least two conditions are imposed on such an international force. First, the nation upon whose territory the force is placed to show its "presence" must grant permission for its entry. The host nation thus has some control over the composition of the international force and can exclude troops from nations it considers unfriendly or undesirable. It can also demand the withdrawal of these troops, as Egypt did in 1967. Indeed, Nasser's army just shunted them aside. Even had the Secretary-General not agreed to their withdrawal, he would have had no option; UNEF was a small force and not fit for fighting. The second condition is that the U.N. force may not intervene in any purely internal conflict. Thus, in Egypt in 1956 and 1973, the force was not employed to impose a specific settlement on Nasser or Sadat in order to calm the international situation. It merely disentangled the combatants. The U.N. presence was not intended to deal with the causes that precipitated the two wars; it dealt only with their effects. This was also true in the Congo—although with a special twist, for it was precisely the U.N. refusal to interfere in the domestic politics of the Congo that created most of the difficulties. After the Congo had disintegrated, the head of the "national" government insisted that the UNEF be employed to squash the secession of the province of Katanga. In the end, the international organization could not isolate itself from the Congolese civil war. The effect of the U.N. nonintervention was to freeze the Congolese schism and, because Katanga's rich copper mines were the nation's major source of revenue, ensure the collapse of the Congo. The U.N. forces therefore eventually did fight and squash the secessionist province. The second condition of domestic nonintervention is thus a qualified one.

The nations of the Third World, it must be noted, can perform this preventive diplomacy function *only* if the superpowers permit them to do so. The fundamental assumption underlying the pacifying role of the nonaligned states is that both the United States and the Soviet Union wish to avoid adding new areas of conflict to the cold war because of the high degree of risk. Their desire to avoid nuclear war gives them a vested interest in keeping peripheral conflicts limited and under control. Thus, they will at least acquiesce in the establishment of a U.N. presence: "It cannot be done *against* the major parties; it cannot be done *by* them; it can only be done *for* them and by their leave."[8]

Four alternative courses of action in conflicts that do not involve di-

---

[8] Inis L. Claude, Jr., "Containment and Resolution of Disputes," in Francis O. Wilcox and H. Field Haviland, Jr., eds., *The U.S. and the U.N.* (Baltimore: Johns Hopkins Press, 1961), pp. 101–28. Emphasis in original.

rect American-Soviet confrontations are possible in implementing preventive diplomacy. The United Nations may take a pro-Western action, an impartial neutralizing action, no action at all, or a pro-Soviet action. Obviously, the American preference is in that order, with the Soviets preferring the exact reverse. Neither extreme is really feasible, but the difficulty is that the United States stresses the impartial, neutralizing action of the remaining alternatives, while the Soviet Union prefers inactivity. The reasons are obvious. The United States fears that inactivity will either produce a Soviet advantage or lead to a collapse requiring American intervention and Soviet counterintervention. It also hopes that impartial neutralizing action will result in pro-American results. Conversely, the Soviets hope that inaction will produce pro-Soviet results while avoiding American intervention, and they fear that the course preferred by the United States might indeed produce results detrimental to Soviet interests.

In terms of these calculations, preventive diplomacy, by limiting the scope of conflicts in marginal situations and by seeking to stabilize such situations, has on the whole served American purposes better than Soviet ones. In Egypt in 1956 and 1973, the U.N. forces helped pre-empt a possible Soviet intervention; and in the Congo U.N. intervention eliminated the bridgehead the Soviets had established. The Soviet Union, therefore, was frustrated and bitter. From its perspective, the moving force in both crises, especially the Congo, was the Secretary-General, and the results of his actions only served to demonstrate the need for a Soviet veto over his actions. In the aftermath of the Congo, the Soviets thus proposed a "troika" plan, which was intended to achieve just this goal by means of the appointment of three secretaries-general, each of whom would represent one of the major blocs in the world. By this plan, the Soviets sought to supplement their actual veto in the Security Council and their virtual veto in the General Assembly (where the Soviets can now usually find enough votes among the nonaligned states to prevent a two-thirds majority vote against them) with a hidden veto at the top of the Secretariat. This would ensure that the United Nations could not be employed in any way detrimental to Soviet interests.

Thus, the Kremlin's reaction to the U.N. intervention in the Congo was a growing disenchantment with the international organization in its peace-keeping operations, and, in fact, it refused to contribute any funds for these operations. The nonaligned states, to be sure, have shown no such disenchantment. They unanimously opposed the "troika" plan to hamstring the Secretary-General, for they value the organization as the protector of their independence and "neutralist" position in the cold war. Because of Russia's refusal to pay for U.N. peace-keeping operations and American insistence that Moscow pay if it did not wish to lose its voting rights in the General Assembly, the U.N. became deadlocked. It remained so until Washington saw that it would receive little support for stripping Russia of its voting rights in the Assembly and was willing to recognize instead the principle that no great power must pay for operations it regards as detrimental to its interests. It is inconceivable that the United States would be any more likely than Moscow to support financially operations that are injurious to its national interests. Indeed, at the time the United States abandoned its position that Russia must pay, Washington declared that it too reserved the right not to pay for future peace-keeping operations of which it disapproved. While this may at the time have been a face-saving way out of an awkward situation, the United States went beyond the Russians and reduced its contribution to the United Nations as a whole, not just for its peace-keeping forces, when in 1971 Communist China was seated in the international organization. At a time when President Nixon was seeking a *rapprochement* with Peking, the U.S. House of Representatives reacted to this event by deciding unilaterally, and in clear violation of U.N. Charter, to cut the American share of the U.N. budget from 31 to 25 per cent. The Senate restored the cut, but the U.S. Government did notify the General Assembly, which assesses its 130-odd members states, that America wished to negotiate a reduction of its contribution to no more than 25 per cent.

Another interesting result deriving from the Big Two clash over the Congo was the revival of the Security Council as the focal United Nations organ. If Russia could not be assured of majority support in the General Assembly—and the 1971 vote on seating Peking also demonstrated that the United States could not be certain of majority support either—and if Russia could not control the Secretary-General, then it would be better to keep peace-keeping operations in the Security Council, where, with judicious restraint in the use of the veto, Moscow could keep some degree of control and influence over whatever the Council decided to do. If it did not act with restraint there, as the history of the U.N. had shown, this Council function merely shifted to another U.N. organ where Russia had less influence and no veto. Symptomatic of this reverse shift to the Security Council was the U.N. force in Cyprus, whose function was to keep the Greek and Turkish communities from transforming their mutual ethnic fears and hatreds into a full-scale war. Again, like Russia, the United States after 1966 could no longer be certain of controlling the Security Council, as it had been able to do in the first United Nations, because in that year a number of nonpermanent members were added to the Council. Events in 1974 suggested a similar loss of American influence in the General Assembly and the use of that body for purposes detrimental to American interests. Thus it is perhaps not surprising that during the Yom Kippur War of 1973 the two superpowers cooperated through the Council in passing a cease-fire resolution; that they agreed to sponsor jointly under United Nations auspices the Geneva peace conference of the Arabs and Israelis; or that they followed a similar procedure when Greece and Turkey almost came to war in 1974 over Cyprus.

What the United Nations Is

In conclusion, a number of points are worth restating about the United Nations. One, the U.N. is *not* a means of eliminating power politics and rising above such a crude and vulgar means of conducting world affairs. To idealize the U.N., to expect it to be "above that sort of thing," to be superior in its morals and general demeanor to the nation-states that are its members, is not only unwarranted but likely to breed the kind of disillusionment and cynicism that follow from the disappointment of unrealistically high expectations and can only result in a decline in the support the U.N. needs to carry out its highly important arms control function in an instantly inflammable world. Conversely, it is untrue that the U.N. is useless, a mere debating society. After all, the U.S. Congress is a debating society too; it spends a lot more time talking than it does passing legislation. But the debates there, as in the U.N. organs, serve the purpose of articulating clashing views, making the public aware of the key issues that are likely to be troublesome, and educating it on these specific problems (and, as in the Congress, the U.N. also allows the representatives from the various national constituencies to get together informally, see if their conflicting interests are amenable to resolution, and arrange compromises out of the public limelight).

Two, if the U.N. reflects the real world, and not the fanciful and ideal world many of its onlookers and proponents want to see in it, it should not be too surprising that all nations follow their national interests in the policies they advocate, regardless of how moralistic and altruistic the rhetoric. Thus, characteristically, when Russia was in a minority during the first United Nations, it could repel, so to speak, majority resolutions in the Security Council only through using the veto power that it as one of the five permanent members (Russia, America, China, England, and France) possesses. It indeed cast a lot vetoes, in good part because the United States, using diplomacy as a tool of propaganda, would repeatedly introduce issues in the Council to which it knew Russia would object. Thus, precisely because the U.N. is associated in the popular mind with idealism, the United States placed Moscow in a position of seemingly obstructing the peaceful works of the organization and America itself with the majority in the pursuit of all that is good and true. Conversely, the United States did not have to cast a veto; it had majority support. In using a majority vote to reject Soviet proposals, it used what has been called a "hidden veto"—a negative vote hidden underneath majority rule and a democratic cloak. Not until after 1966, when the nonpermanent members had been added to the Security Council, thereby jeopardizing U.S. majority control in that body, did Washington begin to cast a few vetoes itself. Both superpowers, although it is still easier for the United States, now negotiate with the other Council members to mobilize majority support. Thus a state's national interests dictate its voting behavior, as was already suggested earlier in the example of the payment or nonpayment for the U.N. peace-keeping operations. U.S. voting behavior in the Council then, despite the paucity of vetoes up till now, is not much different from Russian behavior with its plethora of vetoes. And faced with the possibility that the majority of underdeveloped countries might form a hostile anti-Western coalition, the United States in late 1974 informed the General Assembly of the erosion of popular and congressional support for the United Nations in the United States.

Three, if the U.N. does represent its constituent members with all their problems, and if these nations pursue their national interests in the organization, it also follows that the U.N. will on occasion reflect a double standard of judgment. Israel can strike back at one of its Arab neighbors in retaliation for brutal guerrilla attacks and outright murder, and it is as likely as not to find itself condemned by a majority of U.N. members since the Arab states, as both underdeveloped and Muslim nations, have lots of friends. But the guerrillas and the Arab state harboring them will not be similarly chastised. The United States' second veto was cast when, in retaliation against the murder by Palestinian terrorists of several members of the Israeli Olympic team in Munich in 1972, Israel exacted reprisals and was about to be condemned for its retaliatory raid. Similarly, when Israel shortly thereafter forced down an Arab airliner suspected of carrying one of the leaders of these terrorists it was condemned; when a few years earlier Algeria had forced down an airliner carrying Katanga's formerly troublesome Moïse Tshombe, by now the Congolese Premier, not a word of chastisement was heard from the U.N. building on New York's East River. And while South Africa is a constant subject of condemnation, the underdeveloped states have yet to condemn Uganda for 90,000 estimated murders or the persecution and expulsion of 60,000 Asians or Burundi for over 100,000 reported Hutus killed within its borders.

Four, as the last two points have suggested, the U.N. does not represent a "world public opinion" which allegedly restrains state behavior. Most states in the world can hardly be considered democratic, although many of them do use the word in their names. Most states are authoritarian, whether civilians or military men are in charge; public opinion has no means to express itself on national issues in such countries. Nor do such countries allow competing parties or a free press and other mass media; thus the masses hear only what the government wishes them to hear. In addition, a government's public views may not reflect its private views. For example, during the Vietnam War. India's leaders were officially condemning the United States for the war, but they told Vice-President Humphrey in private during a 1966 visit that "it was absolutely essential that we were there. Because without us being there, China would be a menace that no one could control. That's all they could see, was China." (Interestingly enough, that was the Kennedy-

Johnson view as well, and if India perceived the meaning of the civil war in Vietnam in the context of Communist China's expansion, it is perhaps less surprising that the U.S. Government from 1961 on did so as well.)

In any event, this absence of a world public opinion reflects the presence of many nations with numerous historical traditions, philosophies, ideologies, and political and moral standards. Thus there is little consensus among countries as to what is moral or immoral, what are acceptable standards of behavior, certainly nothing equivalent to those that exist in modern Western political systems. What does exist is a set of *governmental* views and opinions, and these are often mistaken for "world public opinion." When a government in the U.N. solemnly declares that "our people wish to express their outrage" or whatever else they may be expressing, it is the government's opinion wrapped up as the *vox populi*, which, in democracies, is often mistaken for the *vox dei*. A state is, admittedly, sensitive much of the time to what other states will think of its actions, and it may take such prospective reactions into account in planning what its aims are, how they are to be achieved, and how publicly it will explain its policies. Concern for other states' opinions is an everyday affair of which the extensive public relations propaganda efforts by each country are the symptom. And no state relishes a critical U.N. vote against itself, given the popular image of the U.N. as a "good" organization symbolic of man's desire for peace. Nevertheless, when governments feel genuinely strongly about an issue they will go ahead, regardless of what set of *national* opinions are expressed in the General Assembly and Security Council of the U.N., as the Soviet invasions of Hungary and Czechoslovakia or India's defiance of a cease-fire resolution in its 1971 war with Pakistan clearly demonstrated.

Five, and perhaps most significant, the U.N. has been very adaptable in a world of flux. Like the American Constitution, it has up to now proved very flexible and pragmatic in changing with the times. It was established originally upon the assumption of great-power cooperation, but with the added safeguard that, if they could not cooperate, it was better to cast a veto rather than attempt to ride roughshod over a great power with a majority vote and then try to enforce it. It was preferable to paralyze the Council and prevent action since that would reflect the real stalemate that in fact existed outside the U.N.; to have abolished the veto might have removed the Council's inability to act, but it would also probably have meant war. When one great power opposes another, it is the better part of wisdom to attempt to negotiate differences rather than to outvote it and then enforce the majority decision. In any event, the U.N. did not in its area of primary responsibility, peace-keeping, stay permanently paralyzed. The function was first shifted to the General Assembly, then to the Secretary-General, and then back again—or so it would seem—to the Security Council. As a result of this flexibility, the U.N. has demonstrated a vitality that its predecessor, the League of Nations, during the period between the two world wars, never exhibited. It has survived and performed some vital functions during three decades of changing American-Soviet relations, the large-scale births and entry into the international organization of many new states, and the subsequent division between the rich and poor countries or, to use another of those shorthand phrases, the North and the South (as distinct from the Russo-American or East-West conflict). Presumably it will continue to survive in the at least equally rapidly changing world of the future. With China now a member of the Security Council, will the veto again paralyze the Council? Will the great powers in the emerging tripolycentric system of the immediate future be more tempted to by-pass the organization and perhaps impose settlements directly on those problems in which they are not immediately involved, or will they continue to use the U.N. to find settlements? Will they, in addition, also perhaps bring in *their* problems for a full airing and possible resolution?

The answers to these questions remain unknown, but the U.N. may well survive and thrive within the parameters allowed it by the superpowers. As a peace-keeping organization, as distinct from a peace-making institution, it has performed yeoman service in preserving the state system. It was the former function that the Charter emphasized, while the latter function increasingly fell upon the superpowers, as the Arab-Israeli situation after the 1973 war and the Cyprus situation in 1974 clearly demonstrated. (In the latter, the European members of NATO worked closely with the United States to pressure both Greece and Turkey not to go to war and to calm their volatile ethnic quarrel on the island.) Indeed, the parameters will not be completely set by the superpowers and secondary powers; for the lesser states, the U.N. will serve as an arena where they can publicly announce great-power pressures and mobilize counter pressures; and for the underdeveloped countries not blessed with oil or similarly scarce and demanded resources, the international organization remains the forum in which they can publicize the multitude of grave problems they confront and try to coax larger funds and other kinds of assistance for their modernization from the industrial states.

The danger for the vitality and viability of the United Nations, at least as suggested by a number of actions by the General Assembly in late 1974, stems from the failure of that body to observe its own Charter and decisions, and in the process possibly transform the international organization into an anti-Western fourth U.N. It was the dangerous Middle Eastern situation that first suggested this likelihood. The Assembly invited the head of the Palestinian Liberation Organization, a non-state actor whose acts of terrorism and hijacking the Assembly had debated only a few years earlier, to address it. Indicative of the Assembly's mood, it treated the PLO leader Arafat as a head of government and greeted him with sustained applause while limiting the time for Israel's reply, which was delivered to a virtually empty body. Simultaneously, the same Arab-African majority, supported by the Communist states, barred Israeli participation in the previously nonpolitical United Nations Educational, Scientific, and Cultural Organization. In addition to these actions, the Assembly ousted South Africa from its session for its racial practices after the Security Council, which exercises the ultimate suspension power, had refused to do so. And finally, the Assembly debated who was to represent Cambodia, the *de facto* government in Phnom Penh or the exile government of Prince Sihanouk in Peking. One of the principal sponsors of this pro-Sihanouk resolution was the General Assembly's Algerian President, whose decision it had been to treat the PLO chieftain as a head of government and curb Israel's right to speak on the Palestinian issue, a ruling upheld by a large Assembly majority. Previous Assembly Presidents had acted with greater restraint and balance, regardless of their personal preferences or their nations' official positions.

The implications of this behavior, *if* it represents a trend, were several. The United Nations was founded to incorporate existing governments; other guerrilla leaders, including those of Algeria, were not invited to the organization or given observer status even where it appeared likely that they might someday establish a government. More important, governments were U.N. members because they in fact governed certain territory and population; they were not chosen to become members because they represented certain kinds of governments or practiced certain enlightened or virtuous policies. Fair Deal America, Democratic Socialist England, Stalin's Russia, and Chiang Kai-shek's China were among the U.N.'s founding members; membership was clearly not a question of the purity or nobility of their governments. Today, Burundi and Uganda are members, as well as democratic Israel; the two former states are not excluded for their brutal internal practices. To start excluding governments or limiting their right of debate because a current majority of U.N. members objects would signify a radical transformation from the original and long-standing U.N. aim of including all governments so that their views may be represented and aired and formal and informal exchanges of different opinions occur. It would not only impede the Assembly's work. It would embitter states and either paralyze the Assembly's capacity to decide or render its resolutions, which are of an advisory nature only, useless; and, in the final analysis, it would alienate Western and especially American support. As the U.S. Ambassador to the U.N. explained:

> These resolutions are sometimes adopted by Assembly majorities which represent only a small fraction of the people of the world, its wealth, or its territory. Sometimes they brutally disregard the sensitivity of the minority. . . . Each time that this Assembly makes a decision which a significant minority of members regard as unfair or one-sided, it further erodes vital support for the United Nations among that minority. But the minority which is so often offended may in fact be a practical majority, in terms of its capacity to support this organization and implement its decisions.[9]

[9] *New York Times*, December 7, 1974.

The Assembly's actions in the Middle East may also enhance the possibilities of war in that area and, because of their relations with the Arab countries and Israel, precipitate a superpower clash. This would be tantamount to a reversal of the third U.N.'s aims of helping to prevent a military clash or, if it occurs, to try and end it before the United States and the Soviet Union might intervene directly. It was the Assembly that in 1947 had recommended that Palestine be partitioned to avoid the increasing Arab-Jewish bloodshed. The founders of Israel had accepted this compromise suggestion; the Arabs had not, and it was this rejection of the U.N. plan and the consequent Arab refusal to recognize Israel's right to exist that remained the cause of the three wars that erupted after Israel's establishment. This unwillingness to recognize Israel's right to exist appeared to change in the wake of the 1973 war, especially on the part of Egypt. The Arab-sponsored resolution reaffirming the Palestinians' right to independence and representation at peace talks may, however, make Israel more distrustful of negotiating, constrain Egypt's diplomatic flexibility, fortify the Arab hardliners, and make a renewed war more likely. This is not because the Palestinians have no rights—rights that have admittedly often been denied or overlooked by Israel as well as the Arab states—but because of the General Assembly's failure to "insist on the concurrent rights of the State of Israel, and in the Assembly's blind acceptance of a definition of Palestinian rights laid down by a self-annointed leadership . . . which continues to reject the U.N.'s own partition principle, i.e., Israel's right to exist"[10]—a right reaffirmed in the 1967 Security Council resolution which was supposed to be the basis of the Arab-Israeli peace talks.

If the above actions should represent a future trend, the relevance of future General Assembly resolutions will be placed in doubt. The authority of a majority composed of many small nondemocratic states, whose financial contributions to the U.N.'s upkeep is minimal, will be widely questioned—in the West, at least. For such a possible fourth United Nations is likely to be essentially anti-Western, especially anti-American; by perhaps casting the United States in the lonely minority role that Russia occupied in the first United Nations, it will help alienate American opinion and financial support, which has already been cut. Indeed, it will make it more necessary for Washington to consult Moscow and, ironically, may drive the United States—like Russia—back into the Security Council; or the United States may increasingly bypass the United Nations to elicit Russian cooperation, e.g., pressuring the PLO into a more accommodating stance. Yet the real danger stems not from superpower cooperation and their imposition of the terms of settlement upon client states but of failing to avoid in such an inflammable area as the Middle East a confrontation and the catastrophe of a nuclear war, which up to now they have managed to avoid both bilaterally and through the United Nations.

[10] Editorial, *New York Times*, November 23, 1974.

Disarmament to Declaw States

From the moment the first atomic bomb exploded, the central question of our time has turned on whether this "absolute" weapon can be compatible with the continued existence of man organized in nation-states. If nations are unwilling to relinquish their sovereign rights, or at least adopt a new spirit of accommodation, within the United Nations, might not some future quarrel spark a global conflagration that would leave the world in ruins, its smoldering ashes a monument to man's scientific genius and to his malevolence toward other men? The Spanish philosopher Ortega y Gasset once wrote that man was "lord of all things, but he is not lord of himself." The devil in George Bernard Shaw's *Man and Superman* put it even more poignantly, long before Hiroshima:

> And is man any the less destroying himself for all this boasted brain of his? Have you walked up and down upon the earth lately? I have; and I have examined Man's wonderful inventions. And I tell you that in the arts of life man invents nothing but in the arts of death he outdoes Nature herself, and produces by chemistry and machinery all the slaughter of plague, pestilence, and famine . . . when he goes out to slay, he carries a marvel of mechanism that lets loose at the touch of his finger all the hidden molecular energies, and leaves the javelin, the arrow, the blowpipe of his fathers far behind. In the arts of peace Man is a bungler. . . . I know his clumsy typewriters and bungling locomotives and tedious bicycles: they are toys compared to the Maxim gun, the submarine, torpedo boat. There is nothing in Man's industrial machinery but his greed and sloth: his heart is in his weapons. This marvelous force of life of which you boast is a force of Death: Man measures his strength by his destructiveness.[11]

If Shaw is correct, our first level of analysis could lead us only to a rather gloomy prediction for the future. For, given the conflict inherent in the state system, nuclear war is only a matter of time. But one can logically draw several other prescriptions from our model that would deal with the power and security dilemma inherent in the state system and avoid the ultimate catastrophe. One of these recommended solutions is general and complete disarmament. Even before Hiroshima, it was apparent that in a competitive system political conflict was accompanied by arms build-ups; these "arms races" had a tendency to erupt in warfare. In an increasingly destructive century, the question has been whether it would not be safer for all nations to disarm. If nations main-

[11] George Bernard Shaw, *Man and Superman* (Baltimore: Penguin Books, 1952), p. 145.

tain their arms, is war not inevitable sooner or later? Had not all previous arms races sparked wars? The answer seemed as obvious as disarmament seemed a solution, particularly in the nuclear age. Armaments were no longer a means of protecting nations; and only disarmament could guarantee national security. Failure to disarm would mean that sooner or later the nuclear powers will clash and fight. The goal, therefore, must be total or quantitative disarmament; even a partial or qualitative disarmament of a specific type of weapons, such as nuclear arms, would not suffice.

However *theoretically* feasible disarmament might seem to the problem of conflict in the state system, it is unlikely to be the answer to the dilemma of nuclear weapons in a world of political conflict. In the first place, there can be no such thing as *total* disarmament. This is more than a mere semantic problem. In assessing a nation's strength and capacity to wage war, as we know, one must take into account—along with the number of men under arms and the weapons they possess—geographic position, population, natural resources, productive capacity, and scientific ability, all of which are equally important. Military power is only one aspect of a nation's over-all strength, and that strength cannot be artificially eliminated. Even total disarmament would leave a nation with a "war potential" that could be mobilized after a declaration of war. International quarrels would not be discontinued by the abolition of armaments. Second, no disarmament treaty could eradicate man's knowledge of nuclear physics and his ability to reconstruct an atomic or hydrogen bomb, if need be. In any event, even an elimination of nuclear weapons would leave countries possessing such vast resources and skills as the United States and the Soviet Union with more than enough mobilizable power to conduct a long and very destructive war.

The belief that disarmament is the solution to war in the state system is based on the assumption that the arms race causes wars: In order to protect itself, a nation increases its military strength; another nation, seeing this, builds up its military power to guard against a possible attack; the ensuing arms race develops its own momentum and creates a war psychology; at a favorable moment, therefore, when one country feels that it is stronger than the other—or believes that the other side is beginning to pull ahead—it will attack. The interaction among the contestants is thus seen to produce an arms spiral that, when it reaches a critical point, automatically precipitates hostilities in a sort of "spontaneous combustion." But because in the state system arms accompany competition, the critical question is why wars sometimes occur and sometimes not. The answer requires a look at the political reasons.

To attribute wars to arms is to confuse cause and effect. An arms race does not obey a logic of its own. It cannot be seen as an autonomous process divorced from the political context in which it occurs. Capabilities cannot be artificially separated from intentions. Military power serves the political ends of the state.[12] An arms race reflects political tensions between nations; it does not cause these tensions. Armaments are needed by states to protect what they consider to be their interests. Nations do not fight because they possess arms. Rather, they possess arms because they believe it might someday be necessary to fight. Indeed, it can be shown that, when nations involved in political quarrels fail to arm themselves, they invite aggression. While it is true that when power confronts power there may be danger, it is certain that when power meets weakness there will be far greater danger. It is all too easy to point to conflicts and attribute them to arms races. It is much more difficult to point to wars that were prevented because nations guarded themselves.

Since arms are a *symptom* of interstate political conflict, it is an illusion to expect nations to disarm as long as conflict persists. *The prerequisite for disarmament would be political agreement on the issues separating the nations involved in the arms race.*[13] How can nations be expected to agree to the elimination or reduction of the instruments with which they seek to protect themselves or gain their ends? If nations cannot settle their political differences, they cannot end the arms race. If these differences could have been resolved, the arms race would never have begun. In the absence of reliable substitutes for the armed power with which states can defend and seek their objectives, states need arms. This, in turn, is bound to color their disarmament proposals. If a nation is already stronger than its opponent, it will want to preserve and even enhance this superiority, and its disarmament plans will contain this built-in bias. If a nation is weaker, it will want to catch up with and, if possible, surpass its opponent, and its disarmament proposals will reflect these objectives. The former state's attempt to freeze the *status quo* will be a source of anger and frustration to a revisionist state; the latter's effort to erode the *status quo* by changing the power relationship will be a source of annoyance and worry to the state that profits from the *status quo. Disarmament negotiations in these circumstances become merely another form of the arms race itself, the aim of each nation being an increase in its relative power position.*

It could not be otherwise. In the state system, each nation must defend itself in case of attack. The possibility of war being inherent in the

[12] On the nature of the arms races, see Samuel P. Huntington, "Arms Races: Prerequisites and Results," in Carl J. Friedrich and Seymour E. Harris, eds., *Public Policy: A Yearbook of the Graduate School of Public Administration, Harvard University* 7 (Cambridge, Mass.: Harvard University Press, 1956): 41–86; Hedley Bull, *The Control of the Arms Race*, 2d ed. (New York: Praeger Publishers, 1965), pp. 6–12; Colin S. Gray, "The Arms Race Phenomenon," *World Politics*, October, 1971, pp. 39 ff; and *idem*, "The Urge to Compete: Rationales for Arms Racing," *World Politics*, January, 1974, pp. 207 ff.

[13] Merze Tate, *The United States and Armaments* (Cambridge, Mass.: Harvard University Press, 1948), makes this point very well in analyzing the only reasonably successful disarmament agreement, the Washington Naval Conference of 1921–22.

conflict of national wills, each state must pay attention to its armed strength. As Salvador de Madariaga has remarked: "All disarmament conferences are bound to degenerate into armament conferences. In all of them discussion is based on the assumption of war, and they all reveal the inevitable conflict between the ardent endeavors of the delegations present, each of which has for its main aim to secure the highest possible increase of its relative armaments in a general reduction of absolute forces, if such a reduction there must be."[14] A parable of a disarmament conference held by animals illustrates this point. The animals, according to the story, having decided to disarm, convene in order to discuss the matter. The eagle, looking at the bull, suggests that all horns be razed. The bull, looking at the tiger, says that all claws should be cut short. The tiger, looking at the elephant, is of the opinion that tusks should be either pulled out or shortened. The elephant, looking at the eagle, thinks that all wings should be clipped. Whereupon the bear, with a circular glance at all his brethren, says in tones of sweet reason: "Comrades, why all these halfway measures? Let us abolish everything—everything but a fraternal, all-embracing hug." Not only do countries need arms but, because of their importance, they usually cannot agree on the ratio of power that ought to exist between them.

Since the lack of mutual trust is the principal impediment to agreement on disarmament, the United States since 1945 has proposed inspection as a *substitute* for this distrust. States are not going to rely on good faith for the implementation of whatever accords may be reached. In the nuclear era, the United States has argued, this is especially true. Any disarmament involving strategic nuclear arms is in itself an incentive to cheat; to gain an advantage over the adversary might result in a significant political "payoff." But the Soviet Union until 1974 consistently rejected American calls for inspection and denounced them as attempts at espionage. (It is doubtful, however, that Washington would have been any more willing to tolerate Soviet personnel inspecting American industrial plants and military installations than Moscow was willing to tolerate American inspectors doing the same thing in Russia.) While the consequence was to compel both sides to rely primarily on remote means of inspection in the arms control area, which became increasingly feasible with newer technology, the conflict over inspection demonstrated the underlying distrust and suspicion that inspection was supposed to overcome. Mutual confidence, in short, is the necessary prerequisite for inspection to work; it is precisely the absence of this confidence that—given the conflicts of interests among states—makes statesmen feel it imperative to possess arms. And this is exactly where the problem lies: Arms in an essentially anarchical state system serve

14 Salvador de Madariaga, *Disarmament* (New York: Coward-McCann, 1929), pp. 62–63. For an account of the disarmament negotiations as part of the postwar arms race, see John W. Spanier and Joseph L. Nogee, *The Politics of Disarmament* (New York: Praeger Publishers, 1962).

useful functions, and without reliable alternatives to achieve the same purposes potential adversaries are unlikely to surrender or accept any significant restrictions of their arms. It is perhaps symbolical that the very first disarmament conference in 1899 was called by the Czar, who, financially strapped, feared a decline of Russian power as Germany armed its forces with new artillery. Needless to say, Germany was unwilling to forgo the strengthening of its armies.

Why then, besides the fundamental reason of seeking a power advantage, do states pursue disarmament? A second reason is propaganda. Disarmament is like motherhood, the flag, and apple pie. Who can be against such things? Does not everyone desire them? Disarmament conjures up an image of peace and harmony among states, a willingness to coexist amicably and resolve disputes with reason, to act with restraint and radiate goodwill and to show concern for all men, not just one's own nation. Disarmament is good, moral, clean, and virtuous; to be against disarmament is to be for war, conflict, and national egotism, against humanity. And which nation wants to be labeled a warmonger? Thus disarmament is an issue in which diplomacy concerns itself to a very large extent with what we earlier called one of diplomacy's side-effects: propaganda. Since the effects of war in our age would be catastrophic there was widespread support throughout the world for at least some form of disarmament; on the other hand, because each of the superpowers tended to see the adversary's disarmament proposals as attempts by the latter to enhance his security while weakening his own power position—in contrast to one's own increasing awareness of all parties' common interests in arms control—neither was really willing to accept the other's proposals. But because of the popularity of disarmament as an issue, they were unwilling to reject them without suffering a severe propaganda defeat. Disarmament plans therefore frequently tended to contain a "joker" that the opponent could not possibly accept.[15] The joker served a dual function: to compel a rejection of the entire plan and thus place the onus for the resulting diplomatic deadlock on the other side, and to protect the vital interests of the proposing side.

A third reason for disarmament negotiations is economic. Earlier we talked of the choice governments, especially governments of great powers, must make between guns and butter. The arms bill for the superpowers is enormous, continuous, and, with increasing technical complexity—at least in Western economies—going up constantly. Since World War II, the United States and the Soviet Union have produced nearly $20 trillion in GNP, approximately $15 trillion in the United States and the rest in Russia. Of this amount, more than $2 trillion has been spent on arms, about $1.3 trillion by the United States, and an estimated $1 trillion by Russia.[16] In 1968, during the Vietnam War, the U.S. defense budget was 42.5 per cent of the total federal budget; in 1974 it was 27.9

[15] *Ibid.*
[16] Department of State news release, August, 1972.

per cent, which was less than 6 per cent of the U.S. GNP. The fact that this percentage was the lowest since before the Korean War suggests that for about two decades the U.S. defense budget ran higher, nearer 10 per cent. The defense budget is, not surprisingly, a source of contention in America. As Senator McGovern, the Democratic aspirant for the Presidency in 1968, said during the defense budget debate in 1972:

> Our people are alert to threats abroad. But they are equally concerned with the deterioration of our society from within.
>
> They see decaying cities, wasted air and water, rampant crime, crumbling housing and failing transportation. . . . And they are tired of seeing their needs starved to underwrite corrupt governments overseas, to pay more than our share of alliances with the rich nations of Europe and to buy shiny new airplanes that don't fly, guns that don't fire and missiles that only increase the terror.
>
> I suggest that the most serious national security questions today involve such questions as the health of our people, the quality of our schools, the safety of our streets, the condition of our environment, the vitality of our economic system and most of all the confidence of our society that this nation cares about its own.[17]

But it is not just the superpowers and their allies who spend large sums on arms. The developing countries, too, are buying arms, including the most advanced conventional arms, on a large scale, for both their protection and their prestige.[18] The poor countries, therefore, are ironically getting poorer—in part, at least—because they are buying more weapons. In 1974 India, for example, exploded a nuclear device and, despite its claim that it had no intention of building a nuclear force, thereby starkly raised the issue of an underdeveloped country's national priorities. As the world's newest nuclear power, India was a country with a population of 580 million and growing at a rate of 13 million a year. Approximately 30 per cent were illiterate. Its industrial production was stagnant. Three-fourths of its university graduates could not find employment, and unemployed intellectuals are a sure source of trouble. The *New York Times*, in an editorial, was very blunt. It remarked that India had placed "considerations of national power and prestige above the needs of its people," that the Indian explosion was "another monument to human folly" in general, and the appropriate reaction should be "one of despair that such great talent and resources have been squandered on the vanity of power, while 600 million Indians slip deeper into poverty. The sixth member of the nuclear club may be passing the begging bowl before the year is out because Indian science and technology so far have failed to solve the country's fundamental problems of food and population."[19] Perhaps these words smack a little too much of the moral out-

17 *New York Times*, August 2, 1972.
18 See, for example, "Poor Nations Spend Fortune on Arms Purchases," *ibid.*, pp. 1, 14, for the situation as these nations entered the 1970's.
19 *Ibid.*, May 20, 1974.

rage of a nation that already had the bomb; yet they do address the basic dilemma: The cause of disarmament is very often advanced not only in order to increase the amount of domestic "butter" but also with the idea that the rich countries could give the money they would normally spend for their weapons to the poorer nations for their economic development.

In the final analysis, however persuasive the economic reason for disarmament, the consideration of security is greater (and for the superpowers the economic reason may be satisfied to some degree by arms control, especially if SALT I and II are followed by reductions of forces). Symptomatic of disarmament's failure to solve the problems of interstate conflict is the fact that disarmament negotiations do not even occur until nations are locked in political struggle, and by then it is too late. Settlement of differences, political agreement, and the existence of some degree of mutual confidence and trust are the ingredients necessary for a successful disarmament agreement among states that expect that they may go to war with one another. In their absence, disarmament negotiations are bound to fail since the conflicting nations will feel that, in the absence of reliable substitutes, they need arms for their defense and realization of their goals.

Yet fervent advocates of disarmament tend to minimize the political obstacles to disarmament, reflecting the attitude that there *is* a solution to the arms race. The overriding issue is preventing the death of the earth. Because the problem of the arms race is stated in these apocalyptic either-or terms, it becomes a matter in which there can be no choice: Because it is a problem that *must* be resolved, it becomes a problem that must be *resolvable*. To admit that it might in fact not be possible to disarm would be so negative as to discourage further efforts to seek agreements; instead, it would encourage a complacency that could only end in disaster. Consequently, in this view, obstacles blocking the way to disarmament are not recognized as insurmountable; they are merely difficulties to be overcome. If the problem of nuclear fission was solvable, why could not human ingenuity—applied to the abolition of weapons rather than to the production of ever more destructive ones—solve the problem of disarmament? Why should man not apply his reason for once to constructive rather than destructive purposes?

Because disarmament is so desirable, its advocates conclude that it is technically and politically possible.[20] Disarmament may not be the usual way to resolve conflicts, and politicians may reject the idea outright as "impractical and impossible," but the uniqueness of our times demands bold solutions. However impossible disarmament may have been in the past, there is no alternative to it today. The search for disarmament is therefore not an idealistic but a highly realistic policy; the admonition to "love thy neighbor" becomes: "Love thy neighbor *if* you love your-

[20] Robert Gilpin, *American Scientists and Nuclear Weapons Policy* (Princeton, N.J.: Princeton University Press, 1962).

self."[21] No great power can afford *not* to love its neighbor if it values its own life. The world must not destroy itself simply because the leaders of these powers still think in outdated terms of "national interests" rather than in realistic terms of the "common interests of mankind" in preserving peace. What the world needs is not more old-fashioned "power politics," which in the past always led to war, but imaginative and radical solutions. Nuclear bombs make it mandatory for statesmen to change habits and ways of thinking inherited from a prenuclear age. If the world is not to be engulfed in nuclear flames, political leaders must be objectively concerned with the needs of humanity, regardless of their own subjective prejudices and national ideologies, which pale into insignificance beside the overwhelming central issue of survival.

Implicit in this line of thinking is a clear-cut division between those who have a vested interest in the preservation of the nation-state—after all, what jobs would there be for soldiers, diplomats and "merchants of death" if the nation-state and arms were abolished?—and the vast mass of "humanity." The former obviously oppose disarmament and cannot successfully participate in negotiations, for their patterns of thought reflect the state system. But the future of the world demands that statesmen think as though the state system has *already* been transcended.

---

[21] Herz, *International Politics*, p. 333.

10 Peace Through the Transformation of the State System

World Government and the Abolition of Conflict

If disarmament is defeated by the existence of the state system, would not the *abolition* of that system safeguard the future existence of mankind? The argument for disarmament thus often spills over into an argument for world government. Governments preserve peace and maintain law and order on the domestic scene. If a government could be created that would supersede the governments of sovereign nations, could it not, like national governments in their spheres, ensure global peace once and for all? It is often argued, by analogy, that under the American Articles of Confederation, the states retained their sovereignty and continued their quarrels. But under the Constitution, the states were reduced in status to nonsovereign members of a new federal system in which the national government applied the national law directly to individuals and had the responsibility and the authority to ensure domestic tranquility. Could one not then argue, as advocates for world government do, that the American Constitutional Convention was the Great Rehearsal[1] for a global convention that would transfer the sovereignty of all nations to a world government whose purpose would be to ensure global peace through the establishment of the "rule of law"? Such partisans seem to believe that wherever a "legal order" is established—that is, where government applies the law directly to its citizens—government becomes a peace-keeping institution. What leads them to this conclusion? One analyst has suggested that the attractiveness of certain words, and the meanings often attributed to them, explain the magnetism of world government for many people:

[1] Emery Reves, *The Anatomy of Peace* (New York: Harper & Row, 1945), pp. 253–70. See also Carl Van Doren, *The Great Rehearsal* (New York: Viking Press, 1948), for American Constitutional nation-building as an example for the world.

270

A clue may perhaps be found in the intimate association between the idea of world government and the fashionable theme of world rule of law. *Law* is a key word in the vocabulary of world government. One reacts against anarchy—disorder, insecurity, violence, injustice visited by the strong upon the weak. In contrast, one postulates law—the symbol of the happy opposites to those distasteful and dangerous evils. Law suggests properly constituted authority and effectively implemented control; it symbolizes the supreme will of the community, the will to maintain justice and public order. This abstract concept is all too readily transformed, by worshipful contemplation, from one of the devices by which societies seek to order internal relationships, into a symbolic key to the good society. As this transformation takes place, law becomes a magic word for those who advocate world government and those who share with them the ideological bond of dedication to the rule of law—not necessarily in the sense that they expect it to produce magical effects upon the world, but at least in the sense that it works its magic upon them. Most significantly, it leads them to forget about politics, to play down the role of the political process in the management of human affairs, and to imagine that somehow law, in all its purity, can displace the soiled devices of politics. Inexorably, the emphasis upon law which is characteristic of advocates of world government carries with it a tendency to focus upon the relationship of individuals to government; thinking in legal terms, one visualizes the individual apprehended by the police and brought before the judge.[2]

So apart from the seductive quality of certain words and the images they produce in people's minds, the key argument of world government proponents is that peace in society relies primarily upon the creation of a government that, with its superiority of power, will be able to enforce the law upon individuals. This, however, exaggerates the coercion needed to maintain law and order; it also shows that world government advocates misunderstand the function of government. Admittedly, a government's power does play a role in preserving peace. To repeat an earlier phrase, a peaceful society is—at least to a degree—a policeful state. At the same time, however, as we also saw in our analysis,[3] this power is not the principal factor for peace, particularly in democratic societies. There have been simply too many civil wars, *coups d'état*, and revolutions to place as much trust as world federalists do in the establishment of government as a solution for the disorder inherent in the international system. Rather, peace results from the political negotiations and compromises required by the constantly changing internal distribution of power among conflicting interests within a common political culture. It is not the policeman or judge who plays the principal role in preserving peace; it is the politician.

The American example of nation-building—from confederation to federation—as a Great Rehearsal is good evidence that the mere creation

---

[2] Inis L. Claude, Jr., *Power and International Relations* (New York: Random House, 1964), pp. 260–61.

[3] See Chapter 3.

of government as a solvent of conflict is misleading. The reason is apparent from the Preamble of the Constitution, which declared that the purpose was to establish a "more perfect union." In other words, there was already a union, a union formed during the long colonial period and validated by the War of Independence; and it only needed to be made "more perfect." By 1787 Americans already shared one language, a common cultural tradition, and a democratic heritage. "The thirteen colonies formed a moral and political community under the British Crown, they tested it and became fully aware of it in their common struggle against Britain and they retained that community after they had won their independence. . . . The community of the American people antedated the American state, as a world community must antedate a world state."[4] The final test of this Union came during the Civil War, which had to be fought before the Union could become a durable political community. It is, then, precisely this absence of an equivalent sense of global sense of community or political culture comparable to that existing in most contemporary Western states that makes it impossible to establish a world government.

More ironically, in an essentially anarchical or Hobbesian state system, one that exists in a state of potential war, the only world government, if it could be established, would be a world dictatorship. When a sense of community is absent, the only government capable of restraining the various nations would have to concentrate immense power, thus creating what Hobbes called a Leviathan. This is not what world federalists want, however; they desire a democratic world state. But a constitutional or limited government based upon the consent of the governed, assumes— as shown by the U.S. experience—a pre-existing community. Thus world government advocates are caught in an insoluble dilemma: to emphasize the urgency of transforming the existing state system they describe the latter in Hobbesian terms, as we did in establishing our first-level model; but then they describe the result they want in democratic terms and reject the logical consequence of their own earlier analysis. Thus world government may be not only nearly impossible to create, but even not desirable—at least for democrats.

Lately, however, new and appealing arguments have been heard, if not on behalf of a world government, at least on behalf of a variety of global institutions. Man may not yet possess the broad community on which to build the central federal government to govern mankind, but, it is asserted, he does share common concerns. His social and economic problems are immense and cut across frontiers, so that it may be said that man increasingly lives in a "world without borders"; and, while a world government clearly does not yet exist to cope with these problems, there is an obvious need for the establishment of a series of global institutions

---

[4] Hans J. Morgenthau, *Politics Among Nations*, 4th ed. (New York: Knopf, 1967), pp. 498, 499. See also Crane Brinton, *From Many One* (Cambridge, Mass.: Harvard University Press, 1948).

to cope with the specific issues that arise in the different economic and social areas.[5]

First, almost all nations are engaged in trying to enhance their prosperity or wealth. And this is especially true of the developed Western nations, which were intensely preoccupied during the 1960's with ever greater "consumerism," raising their standards of living with more and more cars, color television, air conditioners, and new varieties of food in ever fancier individually wrapped plastic packaging. Second, the result was a corresponding reduction of such finite resources as fresh water, mineral reserves, energy, arable land, living space, and recreation centers. One indication that man's voracious appetite, especially that of the species Americanus, is pressing against the earth's fixed reserves of fossil fuels was the so-called energy crisis of 1973, with its clear demonstration of both the interdependence of all countries and the inability of any single nation to handle problems broader than national. The crisis endangered the whole basis of modern industry, threatening high unemployment, major inflation, and the end of economic growth and a whole way of life, with its dependence on everything from the large automobile to the electric knife and shaver. For non–oil producing underdeveloped countries, with their already oversized populations, increasing at ever faster rates, and their difficulty in growing enough food, the far higher costs of fuel and increasingly scarce fertilizer endangered their development and possibly threatened starvation for many of their peoples. Third, even for those countries with industry and high standards of living, the by-products of "better living through industry"—pollution of air, lakes, and rivers, the killing of birds and fish, and accompanying diseases for man such as emphysema—have become a major source of consternation and concern. Fourth, when the mass demand throughout the world for social justice, equal rights, and individual dignity is added to these problems, the global impact of the problems of hunger, poverty, unemployment, environment, and an increasing gap between rich and poor countries is fairly obvious. But the institutions to deal with these essentially global problems are still primarily national and reliance for their resolution placed upon international cooperation.[6] Thus, it is claimed by the proponents of a "world without borders" or, in Brzezinski's terms, of "planetary humanism,"[7] a gap exists between technology and its social and economic effect on the one hand and international institutions to cope with these problems on the other—with the single exception of the

[5] Lester R. Brown, *World Without Borders* (New York: Vintage Books, 1973). See also Charlotte Waterlow, *Superpowers and Victim* (Englewood Cliffs, N.J.: Prentice-Hall, 1974); Miriam Camps, *The Management of Interdependence* (New York: Council on Foreign Relations, 1974); and Seyom Brown, *New Forces in World Politics* (Washington, D.C.: Brookings Institution, 1974).

[6] See President Ford's speech to the U.N. urging a global strategy on energy and food. *New York Times*, September 19, 1974.

[7] Zbigniew K. Brzezinski, "U.S. Foreign Policy: The Search for Focus," *Foreign Affairs*, July, 1973, p. 712.

multinational corporations, which are not, however, held responsible by any public international bodies. Thus the well-being of mankind is at stake, dependent as never before on tackling problems on a worldwide scale in an allegedly highly interdependent world,[8] while the basic question remains: Can a new world order with the appropriate institutions be created by the nations of the world before it is too late? A former U.N. Secretary-General has said:

> I do not wish to seem overdramatic but I can only conclude from the information that is available to me as Secretary General that the members of the United Nations have perhaps ten years left in which to subordinate their ancient quarrels and launch a global partnership to curb the arms race, to improve the human environment, to defuse the population explosion and to supply the required momentum to development efforts.
>
> If such a global partnership is not forged within the next decade, then I very much fear that the problems I have mentioned will have reached such staggering proportions that they will be beyond our capacity to control.[9]

In the final analysis, the advocates of total disarmament and the proponents of world government and other global institutions as solutions to the problems of coexistence and minimum human needs in the state system have much in common. Both assume that the alternative to either "common sense" solution is disaster. The abolition of all weapons, the transformation of the state system and the weakening of sovereignty may involve risks, but disaster from nuclear warfare or overpopulation or environmental damage or the drying up of resources is unthinkable. And no "sane" man hesitates between such risks and the certainty of catastrophe. It's a simple "either-or" problem, and the solution is just as simple. All men need do is realize the peril to their existence, the stark alternatives, and the urgency of implementing the remedy. Unfortunately, the fact that a goal seems necessary and desirable does not render it attainable. Neither "solution" is, in fact, the quick and easy remedy that advocates for each claim it to be.

Supranational Community-Building Through Functionalism

If the establishment of a world government by means of federation on the basis of the American nation-building model, or creating global institutions to deal with mankind's common and pressing problems, is

---

[8] The crucial question of interdependence is examined by Edward L. Morse in "The Transformation of Foreign Policies: Modernization, Interdependence, and Externalization," *World Politics*, April, 1970, pp. 371 ff., and in his case study *Foreign Policy and Interdependence in Gaullist France* (Princeton, N.J.: Princeton University Press, 1973); and Richard Rosecrance and Arthur Stein, "Interdependence: Myth or Reality?" *World Politics*, October 1973, pp. 1 ff.

[9] The foreboding words of U.N. Secretary-General U Thant were reported by James Reston, *New York Times*, October 22, 1970.

hardly likely to occur in the near future, is there any other way of over-coming nationalism and building such a government with a supportive global community that presumably would allow such a government to be democratic rather than dictatorial? A number of political scientists decided to study this issue empirically. How had political units in the past integrated into larger political organizations whose authority then supreseded that of its original? And how were these historical cases relevant to the contemporary problem of integrating nation-states into a larger supranational political community? Note the three words we have just used: "integrating," "supranational," and "community." Karl Deutsch, who together with several associates analyzed various cases of the integration of political units in the *preindustrial* era, defined integration as "the attainment, within a territory, of a 'sense of community' and of institutions and practices strong enough and widespread enough to assure, for a 'long' time, dependable expectations of 'peaceful change' among its population."[10] Closely related is the term "supranational," which refers to the formation of a community and institutions *supra*, or above, those of the integrating states; the community would have the authority to make political decisions on behalf of the states, obligating their obedience (as the U.S. federal government has an authority superior to that of the individual states). "Supranational," then, is not to be confused with the word "international" and used interchangeably. An international organization is a piece of machinery, as we have already seen in the U.N., to help states among themselves; decisions that emerge are produced by negotiation and compromise among the states, not imposed upon them from above. Finally, according to Amitai Etzioni, a "political community," is

> . . . a community that possesses three kinds of integration: (a) it has an effective control over the use of the means of violence (though it may "delegate" some of this control to member-units); (b) it has a center of decision-making that is able to affect significantly the allocation of resources and rewards throughout the community; and (c) it is the dominant focus of political identification for the large majority of politically aware citizens.[11]

Among states the threat to use violence remains a key element in the resolution of differences; but the chief characteristic of a supranational organization is that intimidation and war are no longer used by its member states as a method of bargaining over important issues. The anarchical model of the state system, which focuses on negotiations through threat and counter-threat, or force and counterforce, is no longer applicable. Deutsch has therefore called such an enlarged supranational organ-

[10] Karl Deutsch *et al.*, *Political Community and the North Atlantic Area* (Princeton, N.J.: Princeton University Press, 1957), p. 5.
[11] Amitai Etzioni, *Political Unification* (New York: Holt, Rinehart & Winston, 1965), p. 4.

ization a "security-community."[12] Historically, he distinguishes among two kinds: a *pluralistic* security-community, composed of a number of states that retain their national autonomy while forming certain specific and subordinate agencies to enable cooperation on particular matters (as America and Canada or Norway, Denmark, and Sweden), and an *amalgamated* security-community in which the states surrender autonomy to a new set of political institutions, as Italy or Germany at the time of unification. Of the two, Deutsch found that pluralistic security-communities were easier to realize and were more durable; amalgamated security-communities were harder to form and more likely to fail.

The movement toward a united Europe since World War II, the principal and largest historical experiment by industrialized states in supra-nation-building, falls in the latter classification, although in reality it is closer to the former. But what we are interested in first, and what Deutsch and his colleagues were interested in, are the *conditions* which are essential for a successful amalgamated security-community. Not surprisingly, a number of these conditions which had been present in the preindustrial amalgamations were also present in the more contemporary experiment that began in 1950 with the formation of the European Coal and Steel Community (ECSC) and produced, eight years later, the European Economic Community (EEC) or Common Market. And it is on this important—if not revolutionary—experiment that we shall concentrate.

One condition was a compatibility of values and expectations among the amalgamating states. This was certainly true of the Inner Six; all were pluralistic societies (although Germany and Italy had recently been fascist states), and each had representative political institutions. In the larger countries, West Germany, France, and Italy, as well as in smaller Belgium, Christian Democrats who shared a European outlook of and similar views on social welfare and other issues were in control of the key government positions. A second condition was that the political elites of the integrating countries felt that their way of life was distinctive. The Iron Curtain was more than a political division; it also separated the "West" from the "East," thereby forming two different geographical and cultural entities. Christian Democrats were particularly disposed to think of the East-West conflict in terms of the historic struggle between Christendom and the "barbarian" invaders from the East (such as the Mongols and Turks). Russia, often in the past regarded as non-European, now fitted this latter role, and, for the Christian Democrats, the defense of "civilization" once again required Western countries to subordinate their own differences, this time to unite in the struggle against Communist Russia.

A third condition of particular significance in amalgamation has been the expectation of economic benefit. For the Inner Six this was to be realized in two ways: the formation of a single common market by the

[12] Deutsch *et al.*, *Political Community*.

elimination of all trade barriers, import quotas and other restrictions among themselves; and the establishment of a common tariff wall to protect this market. Industry would then have an enormous potential market, and efficient energetic enterprises presumably would expand and modernize their plants to take advantage of this enlarged market. By the same token, inefficient plants unable to compete—and unwilling to make the effort—would be closed. But business in general would profit, thus European integration would be in the interest of business. Labor would acquire a similar stake in this New Europe as production rose and the level of employment and real wages followed suit. To be sure, workers in the less efficient industries would lose their jobs, and they might have to be moved to other areas in search of new employment. But in general the Common Market would produce more jobs. The consumer would also benefit from the expanding economy. As he saw national economic barriers tumble and industry increasingly convert to the principles of mass production—large-scale production at reasonable cost and with wages sufficiently high to enable the consumer to buy in volume—he, too, would recognize the pocketbook advantages of the Common Market.

These, then, are some of the principal conditions for the existence of a supranational community. Others are superior economic growth and a marked increase in the political and administrative capabilities of the participating units, unbroken links of social communication, a broadening of the political elite, mobility of persons, and a multiplicity of ranges of communication and transaction.[13]

But how about the *process* of integration? How does it occur? Functionals think they know. David Mitrany, the father of this school of thinking, assumed that the vertical divisions between states, which produce conflict and war, could be overcome by *horizontally* tying the various functional areas of the economies of different countries together in order to resolve their common social, economic, and humanitarian needs.[14] These needs, he felt, could be regarded as essentially nonpolitical and noncontroversial since they were concerned with such values as welfare and social justice, not national security and prestige. As each area of need was tackled, a transfer of each state's authority to supranational institutions would occur; as the satisfaction of more needs is undertaken, more and more authority is transferred to the international institutions. Sovereignty is thus whittled away until at some point nations would find themselves brought very close by this ever expanding web of activity, greater stake in peace, and transfer of national authority to the new supranational organs. In Frederick Schuman's apt phrase, integration of the various functional areas would bring "peace by pieces."[15] Mitrany

---

[13] *Ibid.*, pp. 46–58.

[14] David Mitrany, A *Working Peace System* (London: National Peace Council, 1946).

[15] Quoted by Inis L. Claude, Jr., *Swords into Plowshares* (New York: Random House, 1964), p. 376.

called it a "working peace system," distinct from a peace safeguarded by a balance of power; clearly, as with the "world without borders" approach, his emphasis is on social and economic tasks that cut across national boundaries, establishing supranational institutions to which governments relinquish their authority to deal with these functions. In Mitrany's own words, "the problem of our time is not how to keep nations peacefully apart but how to bring them actively together."[16]

Ernst Haas was the first to study this process of integration in great detail after the Europeans had started their movement toward forming a greater Europe. Like Mitrany and Jean Monnet, the French master planner of the New Europe, Haas found the driving force behind integration to be economic self-interest. There had to be "something in it for everyone." Haas also emphasized, as did the French government in launching ECSC, the importance of approaching the question of integration step by step. Rather than attempting immediate integration of the entire economy of all member nations—which would have been politically impossible to implement—they suggested selection of the coal and steel sector. In 1950, French Foreign Minister Robert Schuman proposed that the Six pool their coal and steel industries in the European Coal and Steel Community. The choice of coal and steel, the backbone of industry, was deliberate, for it would interweave German and French heavy industry to such an extent that it would become impossible to separate them. Germany would thus never again be able to use its coal and steel industries for nationalistic and militaristic purposes. The political and military power of the Ruhr would no longer be accessible for purely German purposes. War between Germany and France would become not only unthinkable but impossible under these circumstances. Because the coal and steel sector forms the basis of the entire industrial structure, the isolation created by the establishment of ECSC was artificial. It was for this very reason, Haas suggested, that it would have an economic "spillover" effect. ECSC would exert pressure on the unintegrated sectors of the economy; and as the benefits of the pooling of heavy industry became clearly observable, these sectors would follow suit. The Coal and Steel Community, in brief, was seen as the first stage of an attempt to create a wider market in one particular area of the economy. It was expected that this approach would be gradually extended to other functional areas of the economy, such as agriculture, transportation, and electricity, with the eventual creation of a federal European state with a huge market and a highly developed mass-production system.

This economic spillover occurred in 1958, when the Six established the Common Market. Their aim was the formation, over a twelve- to fifteen-year period, of an economic union. During this time, all tariffs, quotas, and other restrictions hampering trade among themselves would be completely eliminated; in turn, they would establish a common tariff on imports from outside the EEC. Furthermore, they would gradually

[16] Mitrany, *Working Peace System*, p. 7.

abolish restrictions on the movement of labor, capital, and services within the community and set up a number of funds to help realize the Common Market. Finally, the Six established a third community, Euratom, for the generation of industrial energy. Together, ECSC, EEC, and Euratom constituted the European Political Community.

Fundamentally, the theory of functional integration rested on the theory of free trade. Each nation would specialize in those commodities it could produce best, and the resulting trade would maximize consumer choice and national prosperity for all the concerned nations. It was in the results of this free trade, however, that the significant ingredients of integration were to be found. One was the economic spillover from one sector of the economy to another. The other and more important effect, which Haas stressed as being of central importance, was the *political* spillover. If there was to be a Common Market, and if it was to be more than just a customs union, there had to be a uniform set of rules to govern the economic and social policies of the member countries.[17] For example, if one nation should adopt a deflationary policy, its industries would be able to undersell those of its five partners and capture their markets. Clearly, this kind of development had to be guarded against. Or if a nation, while abolishing its tariffs for a specific industry, then subsidized that industry's production or imposed an internal tax on competitive foreign goods, it would gain an obvious advantage for its own industry. Such discrimination by a government therefore had to be forbidden. Uniform rules could not be established, however, simply by preventing deviant behavior; they required affirmative action. Because prices reflect production costs, which in turn partly reflect national regulation of wages, hours, working conditions, and social welfare programs, the industries of a nation with lower standards would possess a great advantage over competitors in the neighboring states. A single set of standards in such areas as minimum wages, maximum hours, and welfare programs was thus considered a necessity. In addition, since workers would be able to move from one country to another in their search for employment and better jobs, there had to be a single social security program for all six nations. If labor was to be mobile, its welfare programs had to be community-wide. In turn, the increasing need to harmonize the social and economic policies of the Six would demand a single institutional center for policy formulation in Continental Europe. Common policies would require common institutions with supranational authority.

In real terms, such supranational authority, Haas said, "starts to come into play when a state agrees . . . to carry out decisions to which it is

[17] Two of the better early analyses of the harmonization of national policies were Michael Shanks and John Lambert, *The Common Market Today—and Tomorrow* (New York: Praeger Publishers, 1962), pp. 56–105, and U. W. Kitzinger, *The Politics and Economics of European Integration* (New York: Praeger Publishers, 1963), pp. 21–59. See also Emile Benoit, *Europe at Sixes and Sevens: The Common Market, the Free Trade Association, and the United States* (New York: Columbia University Press, 1961).

itself opposed. Most obviously, such a situation arises when it has agreed to be outvoted if necessary by other states—either by a simple or by some weighted or qualified majority."[18] Common institutions with supranational authority extending beyond trade and tariff matters play a central role in furthering the larger political community. Because of this stress on institutions, Haas's theory of functionalism, as distinct from Mitrany's, has been renamed neo-functionalism. It states:

> If economic integration merely implied the removal of barriers to trade and fails to be accompanied by new centrally made fiscal, labor, welfare, and investment measures, the relation to political integration is not established. If, however, the integration of a specific section (e.g., coal and steel), or of economics generally (e.g., the "General Common Market") goes hand in hand with the gradual extension of the scope of central decision-making to take in economic pursuits not initially "federated," the relation to the growth of political community is clear.[19]

The development of a political community is most readily demonstrated by interest group activity. In a developed economy federated into a supranational system, those whose interests are affected by the decision-making institutions, adversely or otherwise, will organize to lobby at the supranational level in order to influence particular decisions. Hence, an economic institution affects the political level, expanding the scope of the full community. One is reminded of the United States, where various interests lobby at the state and the federal level. In an open, pluralistic society, interest groups and political parties (as aggregates of interest groups) will normally tend to act at whatever level of government important political policies are decided, and this has indeed been the aim of the EEC. It was this interaction between the decision-making institution and the lobbying of the multitude of interest groups, then, that was of vital importance to the political integration of the Six.[20] But in the long run the self-interest of the various groups will not suffice. A truly federal Europe must have popular support as well, and the political spillover is also intended to achieve this:

> As the process of integration proceeds, it is assumed that values will undergo change, that interests will be redefined in terms of a regional rather than a purely national orientation and that the erstwhile set of separate national group values will gradually be superseded by a new and geographically larger set of beliefs. . . .
> As the beliefs and aspirations of groups undergo change due to the necessity of working in a transnational institutional framework, mergers in values and doctrine are expected to come about, uniting groups across former frontiers. The overlapping of these group aspirations is finally thought to result in an accepted body of "national" doctrine, in effect

[18] Kitzinger, *European Integration*, pp. 60–61.
[19] Ernst B. Haas, *The Uniting of Europe* (Stanford, Calif.: Stanford University Press, 1958), pp. 12–13.
[20] *Ibid.*, p. xiii.

heralding the advent of a new nationalism. Implied in this development, of course, is a proportional diminution of loyalty to and expectations from the former separate national governments. Shifts in the focus of loyalty need not necessarily imply the immediate repudiation of the national state or government. Multiple loyalties have been empirically demonstrated to exist.[21]

Based upon "the logic of integration," the EEC was designed to develop into a United States of Europe through three stages: the first stage was a *customs union*; the second, an *economic union*; and the final stage will be the *political union*.

The fundamental assumptions underlying this logic were threefold: first, that economic and social problems could be separated from political and security issues (this distinction is also sometimes made, as we know, in terms of "low" policy and "high" policy); second, that the ever widening vested interests and habits of cooperation formed in the low policy area could be transferred to the high policy area; and three, that there will be a massive shift of loyalty from national allegiance to the new supranational community as citizens—producers, laborers, farmers, and consumers—realize the economic benefits from the new and larger community.

The ups and downs of the European movement reflect on the validity of these assumptions. It has been suggested, for example, that the very economic success of the Six may, ironically, be one of the greatest obstacles to the political spillover. As the individual national wealth of the participants rose, the urgency of further integration declined. Thus, contrary to the functional analysis—which emphasized that the fulfillment of some needs would result in the growth of support for the integration of other sectors of the economy and the further growth of the political institutions—economic gains through the realization of the customs union may lead to the protection of the *status quo* and a reduction in support for further integration.[22] Indeed, the final irony may well be that the citizens and interest groups who gain economically from the European movement attribute these benefits largely to their governments, thereby once more enhancing the confidence in the nation-state so many had seemingly lost as a result of defeat in World War II and the post-war economic collapse.

Thus national loyalties remain; only in the long run may generational changes result in greater attraction to a New Europe for those born after World War II, whose values are by and large said to be post-bourgeois.[23]

[21] *Ibid.*, pp. 13–14.

[22] Explained as the concept of "equilibrium"; see Leon N. Lindberg and Stuart A. Scheingold, *Europe's Would-Be Polity* (Englewood Cliffs, N.J.: Prentice-Hall, 1970). See also Joseph S. Nye, Jr., *Peace in Parts* (Boston: Little, Brown, 1972).

[23] Ron Inglehart, "An End to European Integration?" *American Political Science Review*, March, 1967, pp. 91–105, and *idem*, "The Silent Revolution in Europe: Intergenerational Change in Post-Industrial Societies," *American Political Science Review*, December, 1971, pp. 991–1017.

(Bourgeois values were largely concerned with material and physical security, whereas post-bourgeois are concerned more with belonging and intellectual and esthetic satisfaction, and adherents of the latter tend to be more cosmopolitan than parochial—nationalist—in their identity.)

Even more important, high policies and low policies proved harder to separate in reality than in theory, because theory did not take into account nonpolitical or technical issues. Nor should this have occasioned surprise. Inis Claude has asked:

> Is it in fact possible to segregate a group of problems and subject them to treatment in an international workshop where the nations shed their conflicts at the door and busy themselves only with the cooperative tools of mutual interests? Does not this assumption fly in the face of the evidence that a trend toward the politicization of all issues is operative in the twentieth century?[24]

Even where distinctions were recognized between low or welfare or prosperity policies and high or security policies, however, states remained jealous guardians of their sovereignty, national identity, and military strength; the more an economic policy seemed to infringe on security issues, the greater the difficulties in forming a united policy and the less likely was it that the cooperative habits learned in the low-policy area would be transferred to high policy. France and the other five countries might pool their coal and steel producing facilities (and even here France had the high-policy goal, however, of trying to ensure itself against German rearmament and aggressive policies), but it was quite another story when it came to pooling their foreign or defense policies for a common European policy.

The functionalist belief in "the victory of economics over politics" had, therefore, incorrectly minimized the significance of political decisions and the will of individual leaders and nations, such as the Christian Democratic Premiers and Chancellors of Italy, France, and West Germany who initiated the European integration movement, or de Gaulle who slowed it down. Indeed, a study of Britain's entry into the Common Market demonstrates with great force that this decision was not—and could not be—the result of the interplay among the various subnational interest groups; the decision was clearly a high-policy decision, based upon broader political criteria than merely economic interests, however important these were too.[25]

A third critique, which Britain's entry into the Common Market, as well as the original Inner Six's impetus toward European integration, illustrates, is that Haas's functionalism has also ignored the state system and the differing roles the various participating nations perceive for

[24] Claude, *Swords into Plowshares*, p. 385.

[25] Robert J. Lieber, "Interest Groups and Political Integration," *American Political Science Review*, March, 1972, pp. 53–67, and, in more detail, *idem, British Politics and European Unity* (Berkeley: University of California Press, 1970).

themselves. Thus, after World War II, in an external environment dominated by the two superpowers, Europe saw that it would be helpless unless it integrated and became stronger once again; and for France, as we saw, it was a means of gaining equality with the "Anglo-Saxons" and later, during the de Gaulle era, to become a leader of Europe against an American-dominated Atlantic Community. And, of course, it was the United States that spurred the European movement in order to add Europe's power to the Western scales in the balance with the Soviet Union. Similarly, as the threat from the East has diminished, there has been a loss of the momentum the original integration movement possessed. As the defeated, conquered, and discouraged Continental states recovered and the unique circumstances in which integration was launched has passed, the larger vision seems to have dimmed somewhat. Will a withdrawal of large numbers of American troops, a renewed sense of insecurity, and growing Russian military might to the East help reinvigorate this vision?

The need for a common policy was dramatically illustrated during the early 1970's. On the one hand, there were indications of new life in the European union movement. First, the Six became the Nine, as Britain, Ireland, and Denmark entered in 1973 (Norway refused). Second, the enlarged Community met and defined its long-term goal of union by 1980. As Theo Sommer has suggested, the Europe that may emerge will not be the original Europe I with its supranational institutions; nor does it seem likely that it will be de Gaulle's Europe II, whose essence was nationalistic. Europe III will in all probability focus on the cooperation of governments leading to negotiated collective policies. The building blocks of Europe will remain the states, but the Community will speak more and more with one voice, although in different tongues, to the outside world.[26] Third, the Community gave some evidence of its ability to move toward united foreign policy positions, as in its response with "a single voice" on economic issues to the Kissinger call for a new Atlantic Charter in 1973.

On the other hand, other events called into question the degree of cohesion of the EEC and even its future viability. France undermined an agreement on economic and financial union; Britain and West Germany quarreled bitterly about the contribution each nation was to make to a fund to help the poorer regions of Europe develop to the level of the more advanced (in this case, British regions to be financed largely by the Germans, the British insisted); and when the Arab oil boycott was imposed against the Netherlands for its pro-Israeli stand in the 1973 war, the other eight members abandoned the Netherlands like a hot potato instead of sharing their oil with their fellow member. In addition, Paris, London, and Bonn each struck out on their own to make their separate deals with the Arabs for oil as each placed its national interest

[26] Theo Sommer, "The Community Is Working," *Foreign Affairs*, July, 1973, pp. 748–49.

before the Community's common interests; and finally, the new British Labour Government announced it opposed Britain's membership on the terms previously negotiated by the preceding Conservative Government. The European Economic Commission, in a surprisingly frank declaration on the State of the Common Market, in February 1974, therefore declared at some length:

> Europe is being put to the test. It is faced with a new situation which is pitilessly highlighting its weakness and its dependence, but which is also revealing how badly it is in need of unity.
>
> It is facing this situation in a state of crisis: A crisis of confidence, a crisis of will and a crisis of lucidity. . . .
>
> Now that it is put to the test, Europe must show the world its common resolve. Over the last few weeks, setbacks and failures have, on the contrary, disturbed us and have raised doubts as to the will of the governments to make progress and as to the ability of our institutions to fulfill their tasks.
>
> For instance, the European regional development fund, that very symbol of solidarity, has still not been set up, despite the commitment, entered into at Paris and Copenhagen, to set it up before the end of 1973.
>
> For instance, the community has not yet managed to define its position in relation to the rest of the world on certain of the major issues which it is discussing.
>
> At a time when international relations are undergoing a far-reaching transformation, with vital consequences for us all, is there a single European country which can exercise real influence and carry weight comparable to that of a united Europe?[27]

These and other questions concerning the additional cost of oil, the resulting balance of payment deficits all member states would confront, and the measures that would be taken to remedy these deficits without harming economic growth, employment, and social justice, the Commission suggested, required a single economic strategy. Would Europe show a will to unite, or would it flounder? That was the question.

But there is another way of looking at this question. Europe is engaged in an experiment of "supra-nation" building whose complexity is even greater than that of the United States in a simpler day. Considering the far shorter period the Europeans have had, it is perhaps extraordinary not that the emerging European Community has so far been unable to overcome national resistance more quickly but that the disappearance of national interests should have been expected so quickly. The danger will come if, as in their recent behavior, the member governments no longer seem to believe that community action can fulfill their purposes better than individual national action. For the Commission, as the executive of the EEC, does not yet possess the authority to deal with the important issues confronting the European states, and the various

---

[27] "State of the Community," *European Community*, April, 1974, pp. 12–14.

governments have in their recent actions hardly demonstrated the will to do so in common as "Europeans."

Given both the shortcomings of neo-functionalism as a theory and its ambiguous results in practice, the question arises whether the European experiment could be applied in other areas so that regional integration could be the basis for a world government. According to Haas, who differs somewhat with Deutsch, the factors favoring integration are an urban-industrial level of development, a pluralistic society in which the masses express their aspirations and grievances through interest groups and political parties, political elites competing with one another for control of the government, and relations between elites and masses that are governed by constitutional and democratic rules. Clearly, the European experience with functionalism is therefore not applicable to the underdeveloped countries, with their low degree of industrialization, tenuous national integration, and absence of pluralism and democracy. Thus the prospects for the East African Community or the Central American Common Market would appear to be bleak. Yet the reason for their continued existence would seem to be precisely their low level of economic development, which, in turn, exerts pressure for modernization through economic integration. And high politics again played a large role in the decision of the less developed countries to integrate. "The evidence from the East African and Central American cases clearly suggests that, for less developed countries, economic integration is better conceptualized in terms of high politics than its welfare equivalent in Western Europe," Roger Hansen notes. "[I]t is clear that in the present international system . . . industrialization might be considered as a prerequisite to any meaningful high-political role performance. . . . Western European nations could afford to treat economic integration as a matter of welfare politics without foreclosing their high-politics option because each started from a significantly industrialized base. The case is quite other in the less developed regions of the world."[28] Thus the functional model, analyzed in the context of the European experience, would seem to be limited in its applicability in practice, as well as in explanatory capacity for non-Western areas. And yet, Robert Lieber has observed:

> Even with such extensive criticism of the functionalist theory of integration, we are still left with what one of its sharpest critics has termed an empirical theory of considerable analytic power and predictive ambition. . . . It effectively calls our attention to the way in which integration can grow as an unintended product of incremental decisions; it identifies the spillover process that does operate within the realm of welfare politics; it indicates how integration can thrive despite divergent interests and orientations; and it correctly predicts group behavior across national boundaries. Functionalism offers a useful means for making sense of the

[28] Roger D. Hansen, "Regional Integration: Reflections on a Decade of Theoretical Efforts," *World Politics*, January, 1969, pp. 260–61.

complex and sprawling integrative enterprise. It provides organizing concepts and helps us to formulate questions, explanations and even predictions. We are thus considerably better off than if we approached this enterprise with only a critical stance and no theory at all.[29]

But as a process of achieving a world state and community its utility remains a question mark.

The Multinational Corporation, the New Globalism, and the Transnational Actor

In contrast to international and supranational organizations, transnational actors may be defined as organizations that carry on "significant centrally directed operations in the territory of two or more nation-states." For example, a gigantic business enterprise such as General Motors, American-controlled and -directed, carries on its activities in many different countries. Such a corporation's interests and perspectives are broader than merely national, as it pursues its purposes *across* international boundaries in many different markets. While, to be sure, business organizations, banks, churches (notably the Catholic Church), and revolutionary groups are not new to the international scene, the years since World War II have seen a vast proliferation and growth in size of transnational actors, as well the extension of their operations to a virtually global scale. Lester Brown, in comparing the size of the multinational corporation (MNC) with the size of nation-states, ranks them according to gross annual sales and GNP respectively. He found the first 22 entries are the 22 largest nations, ranging from the United States to Argentina. Number 23 is General Motors, followed by Switzerland and Pakistan; Standard Oil of New Jersey and Ford Motors rank 27 and 29. Of the top 50, 41 are nations and 9 are MNCs; of the second 50, 18 are nations and 32 are MNCs. In the top 100, countries barely outnumber corporations, 59 to 41.[30] Another indicator of size reveals that Standard Oil of New Jersey has three times more employees overseas than the State Department and a tanker fleet larger than that of Russia.

What has made it possible to talk of a "transnational organizational revolution in world politics"?[31] It is especially modern means of fast transportation and communication, plus the technical and organizational capabilities to operate across long distances. Particularly in the

---

[29] Robert J. Lieber, *Theory and World Politics* (Cambridge, Mass.: Winthrop Publishers, 1972), pp. 49–50.

[30] L. Brown, *World Without Borders*, 213–15, 216.

[31] Samuel P. Huntington, "Transnational Organization in World Politics" *World Politics*, April, 1973, pp. 333 ff. See also Luiz Simmons and Abdul Said, eds., *The New Sovereigns* (Englewood Cliffs, N.J.: Spectrum Books, 1974), and Charles P. Kindleberger, ed., *The International Corporation* (Cambridge, Mass.: MIT Press, 1970).

business area, because of the emergence of strong consumer economies in many countries plus the contemporary significance of high-technology industries like electronics and pharmaceuticals this revolution has become very visible. As noted earlier, extensive American capital investment and business growth have taken place in Europe, a growth so large (from $3.8 billion in overseas investments in 1950 to $32.2 billion in 1970) that one can speak of *two* American economies, one in the United States and the other in Europe; and the latter runs second to the former in the non-Communist world as the largest economy. American corporations, used to operating in the many U.S. states with their different regulations, have adapted better than their European competitors to operating within the Common Market; European firms, which have historically confined themselves to protected national markets, have consequently lagged behind American corporations.[32] The transnational business organization, operating in multiple markets—which is why the term "multinational business" is usually used—mobilizes and shifts its resources from one country to another as needed; in response to its aim of seeking maximum profits, the firm regards the various national markets as just parts of a single larger one in which capital, technology, and other resources are shifted across boundaries according to the needs of the entire market. American firms, thinking in regional terms, have thus become more "European" than the European ones; the largest corporations in Europe are American.[33]

The capacity to operate in several markets has given rise to a great deal of speculation about the impact of such transnational or multinational actors on the state system. Our entire analysis up to this point has focused on the nation-state as the chief actor in an anarchical international environment. Given the size, wealth, and future growth of the MNC, observers ask whether such organizations are independent actors on the world scene who not only may be mankind's best hope for abolishing poverty but also may provide the principal impetus for creating the world community the state actors seem unable to. George Ball, a former Under Secretary of State, has asserted that the MNC, which he calls "Cosmocorp," has outgrown the state; national boundaries are too confining for its activities.[34] Unlike traditional imperialist theory, which argued that the state opened up new lands for business to exploit, the new business corporation seeks not territorial and political control but access to different markets. In this multinational context, the Cosmocorps's managers are viewed as the new globalists," the "advance men" of "economic one-worldism" who view the globe as a single market. Dependent upon foreign states for permission to produce and sell within

[32] Robert L. Pfaltzgraff, *The Atlantic Community* (New York: Van Nostrand Reinhold, 1969), pp. 108–10.

[33] *Ibid.*, p. 80.

[34] George W. Ball, "Cosmocorp: The Importance of Being Stateless," *Atlantic Community Quarterly*, Summer, 1968, p. 168.

their frontiers, these managers regard the nation-state and assertive militarist foreign policies as contrary to their own interests. Their primary loyalty is, in a real sense, to the corporation rather than to the nation; the corporation's interests take precedence over the national interest. In brief, MNCs need peace; national rivalries are economically too costly from their perspective. MNCs, the devil of imperialist theory, become the angels of the new order, for they act as a major restraint on foreign adventures as peace and profit become interdependent.[35] Thus the MNCs threaten to replace the nation-state as the most visible and potent actor on the world scene.

The contrary view holds that these rumors of the imminent death of the state are premature for two reasons. The first is that politics still precedes economics—that is, the transnational revolution is to a large extent a reflection of America's great power and influence throughout most regions of the world. In its conflicts with Russia and China, the United States has used alliances in every region to effect the containment of these two Communist countries. American military and political organizations, as well as private economic ones, came in the wake of commitments to Western Europe, the Middle East, South Asia, and East Asia, as well as Latin America, America's historic sphere of influence. Robert Gilpin has argued that "political values and security interests are the crucial determinants of international economic relations. . . . Throughout history each successive hegemonic power has organized economic space in terms of its own interests and purposes."[36] While it is true that transnational actors are the product of modern technology, it was American power that created the conditions for their expansion. Most MNCs are American-controlled. The implication is that a reduction of America's role in the world will witness a decline of their activities, although not those of the increasing numbers of European and Japanese firms.

The second reason why the state may well survive the challenge of the new transnational business actor is that, while some conflict between the two is unavoidable, they need each other. Their conflict is complementary.

> It is conflict not between likes but between unlikes, each of which has its own primary set of functions to perform. It is, consequently, conflict which, like labor-management conflict, involves the structuring of relations and the distribution of benefits to entities which need each other even as they conflict with each other. The balance of influence may shift back and forth from one to the other, but neither can displace the other.[37]

Indeed, the transnational actor strengthens rather than weakens the state since the former needs the latter's permission for access to its ter-

[35] Barnet, *The Roots of War* (Baltimore: Penguin Books, 1973), pp. 229–38.

[36] Robert Gilpin, "The Politics of Transnational Economic Relations" in Robert O. Keohane and Joseph S. Nye, Jr., eds., *Transnational Relations and World Politics* (Cambridge, Mass.: Harvard University Press, 1972).

[37] Huntington, "Transnational Organization," p. 366.

ritory. The multinational corporation may well be a leading reason for the increasing role of the state in economic affairs and the extension of state power in the economic realm. In Europe, for example, governments intervene in the economic sphere in order to create domestic competitors to counterbalance the size and influence of U.S. corporations; governments remain sensitive to retaining national control over their economies and are concerned that their goals not be upset by corporate decisions made on a multinational basis. As John Fayerweather has noted, "at critical points every nation-state finds that its objectives of national military security, domestic economic stability, protection of particular national groups, and even national pride become more important than potential economic increments from full participation in global economic optimization."[38]

How can these two contradictory views be evaluated? On the one hand, it is correct that on occasions the corporations follow policies that are contrary to those of the home nation. For example, American companies invested millions of dollars in Europe establishing and expanding their activities there, while simultaneously the U.S. government wanted to reduce the dollar outflow in order to cut the balance of payments deficit. A more dramatic instance came to light during the 1973 war between Israel and Egypt and Syria when the Arabian American Oil Company, the world's largest petroleum producer, refused to supply oil to U.S. military forces in the Mediterranean and other areas of the world on instruction from Saudi Arabia, its only source of crude oil. Aramco, composed of four of the largest American oil companies, claimed it really had no choice but to follow Saudi instructions. As a result, the Defense Department had difficulty in obtaining oil for military forces at a time when the course of the Israeli-Arab hostilities posed the danger of a U.S.-Soviet confrontation (which did in fact come). Was Aramco's compliance with Saudi Arabia's embargo against the United States for its support of Israel a flagrant instance of a lack of corporate patriotism or merely evidence of the sound business practice of loyalty to the company first?

On the other hand, Aramco's behavior illustrates that the presence of a transnational actor on a state's territory reinforces that state, which controls the access to its national markets. A country that does not want American investments can keep them out, like Japan for much of the post–World War II period, or regulate foreign-owned subsidiaries, as do France and Britain. In any case, American-owned corporations abroad are subject to the laws and commands of the host country.[39] When Argentina in 1974 wanted to sell thousands of vehicles made by Ford, General Motors, and Chrysler subsidiaries in that country to

---

[38] John Fayerweather, "The Internationalization of Business," *Annals of the American Academy of Political and Social Science*, September, 1972, pp. 6–7.

[39] Raymond Vernon, *Sovereignty at Bay* (New York: Basic Books, 1971), pp. 241–47.

Cuba, it was not the companies that blocked the deal; they wished to respond to Argentina's policy. It was the U.S. government that opposed the deal until Argentina threatened to nationalize the companies. Aramco responds obediently to the wishes of Saudi Arabia, even if this results in helping the Arabs in their economic warfare against the United States. Clearly, this MNC, like other such MNCs, is hardly a docile instrument of "U.S. imperialism," serving national policy by preying upon other nations' resources and undermining the capacity of their governments to do what they wish for the welfare of their peoples.[40] Rather, although the MNC may have its headquarters in the United States and have captured a sizable part of the American market, it has in a genuine sense become "denationalized," belonging not to any one nation but to the many nations in which it operates and responds to markets.

The corporations essentially are not interested in politics; they prefer just to be left alone to do their business. This means that an MNC will work with a democratic government in a democratic society and—despite the howls of its critics—with despotic and even racist governments in other countries (just as the Catholic Church has historically come to terms with virtually every conceivable type of government in order to have access to their territory to save the souls of their citizens).[41] In the short run, the MNCs reinforce the *status quo* in the societies in which they operate; in the long run, however, they may help to undermine the *status quo* by being examples of a new technology, ideas, social and cultural values, and ways of life that challenge the less developed countries' more traditional culture, just as Western colonialism initially provided the stimulus for change. Robert Gilpin's conclusion is this:

> There is little evidence to substantiate the argument that the multinational corporation as an independent actor has had a significant impact on international politics.
>
> While the evidence is indisputable that the multinational corporation is profoundly important in the realm of international economic relations, its political significance is largely confined to its impact on domestic politics where it is an irritant to nationalistic sentiments. . . .
>
> Where these business enterprises have influenced international political relations, they have done so, like any other interest group, by influencing the policies of their home governments. . . .
>
> Contrary to the argument that the multinational corporation will somehow supplant the nation-state . . . it is closer to the truth to argue that the role of the nation-state in economic as well as in political life is increasing and that the multinational corporation is actually a stimulant to the further extension of state power in the economic realm.[42]

[40] For the imperialist and exploitative character of MNCs, see Ronald Müller, "Poverty Is the Product," *Foreign Policy*, Winter, 1973–74, p. 71 ff. and his book with Richard J. Barnet, *Global Reach* (New York: Simon & Schuster, 1974).

[41] Ivan Vallier, "The Roman Catholic Church: A Transnational Actor," in Keohane and Nye, eds., *Transnational Relations*, pp. 135–40.

[42] Gilpin, "Politics of Transnational Economic Relations," pp. 68–69.

The "state centric" model of international politics is thus likely to remain our principal explanation of what occurs in the international environment. Yet in the long run will not these new economic transnational actors become the "new sovereigns"? MNCs, which by their presence help preserve the *status quo* in any of the countries they are doing business in—or help slowly to undermine the *status quo*—are very clearly transnational *political* actors. Among other things, they may also expunge the distinction between the high politics of national security and prestige and the low politics of prosperity as MNCs become increasingly active in this latter area and governments, in response, extend their control over their economies because of their sensitivity to economic issues and the desire to preserve national control over them. The state, still supreme, therefore may not be replaced by the MNC; rather, the state over the long run may more and more find the MNC a worthy competitor.

Furthermore, while the MNC is at present probably the most significant new nonstate actor to appear in the state system, other actors—particularly self-styled revolutionary groups, whose acts include terror, assassination, and the threat and use of violence—have already taken on a degree of prominence that may be enhanced in the future if such groups feel that the predominant state system cannot satisfy grievances and claims that they assert to be legitimate.[43] The proliferation of such noneconomic transnational actors may make it increasingly difficult in the future to focus on the state system as a model in our attempts to understand international politics. Indeed, since we defined international politics in terms of the interactions among states, we might, as Keohane and Nye do, substitute the words "world politics," since this will compromise more than the sum of interstate relations; it will also include inter–transnational actor and state–transnational actor relationships.

Such groups as the various Palestinian organizations, with their hijacking of planes, assassinations of individuals, and murders of groups like the Israeli Olympic team members in Munich in 1972 or the children at Maalot in 1974; or the Irish Republican Army, with its bombs and letter-bombs in London; and others have already shown that they cannot be ignored as actors. And this is so for at least two reasons. One reason has to do with the nature of a state system composed of actors whose basic concern is their security and who keep one another in check and restrain the actual use of violence among themselves primarily by threatening one another with their military power. Many of these more militant groups, whether they are called freedom fighters or terrorists, clearly do not place primary emphasis on their survival; although their claim of being willing "to die for their cause" has not always at the moment of truth been borne out, their fervor on behalf of their conceptions of jus-

---

[43] Louis R. Beres, "Managing Power in a Changing World System," unpublished paper, and J. Bowyer Bell, "Contemporary Revolutionary Organizations" in Keohane and Nye, eds., *Transnational Relations*, pp. 153–68.

tice, their dedication to a cause, and their occasional willingness to sacrifice their own lives mean that their scale of values is different from that of state actors. In turn, this means that what in our age has become known as deterrence—in this case, punishment by conventional force if deterrence should fail—cannot work well. Who are the members of such groups? Where are they? How can they be seized and punished? The difficulty is compounded if such groups live within the borders of states (e.g., Lebanon, which has to tolerate them; Syria, which is sympathetic to them; or Jordan, which has squashed them with some success) other than their targets, and the retaliation has to cross official state frontiers.

The second reason they cannot be ignored is, as we have stressed up to this point, that states become socialized by the system and learn "the rules of the game" by which nations play. The absolute significance of this was seen in the manner the two nuclear superpowers have managed their adversary partnership. The leaders of the two nuclear giants and their respective top-level bureaucracies have through trial-and-error *learned*—and there is no better word for it—enough about one another's behavior that they almost trust one another, if not each other's intentions, at least to the extent of expecting "responsible behavior" in moments of confrontation. Just as both fear the dispersion of nuclear arms because they consider that some of the nuclear newcomers may be "irresponsible"—juvenile delinquents, if you will, among the maturer, more experienced, responsible nuclear adults—and will by their behavior introduce all sorts of misperceptions, misunderstandings, and miscalculations, so it must be recognized that some nonstate actors will immensely complicate the calculations of statesmen and make it far more likely that violence will occur, in which states sympathetic to the nonstate actor's cause may become involved.

The appearance, growth, and possibly increasing significance of all nonstate actors, economic or not, violent or not, may thus have a profound impact on a state system, already extremely difficult to manage, that lives with the constant possibility that the instrument of its preservation, war, may paradoxically be the instrument of its destruction. Can such a system cope with the possibility that some day desperate revolutionary groups may even acquire and use such conventional arms as rockets that zero in on airplane engines (the British Army turned out in force to patrol London's main civilian airport when it was rumored that some Arab guerrillas had obtained such Russian-made portable missiles from a sympathetic Arab state and intended to shoot down a few jetliners) or even obtain nuclear devices in order to get their way as in *Thunderball*, the James Bond novel? Certainly, it cannot be denied that when a transnational organization resorts to economic boycotts and airline hijackings to impose its demands, it is behaving politically.

In the meantime, the new actor who has become important and has transformed the bipolycentric system into a tripolycentric one is China. In a world that was not ready for disarmament or world government, one in which states had not yet been subordinated in significance to global economic corporations, it is the new state system dominated by America, Russia, and Communist China that statesmen have to deal with; neither they nor the outside analyst quite know what its rules of behavior will be or whether it will be a stable or an unstable system.

11 Tripolarity and the Limits of First-Level Analysis

Bipolarity, Multipolarity, and Stability Reconsidered

It is often said that the state system that emerged officially with President Nixon's visit to Peking is tripolar. In our earlier terms we would call it tripolycentric, but, whichever term we use, the focus is on the Big Three relationship. Our analysis will examine this triangle and attempt to show how a model can be used to suggest what some of the rules of behavior are likely to be and whether such a system will be stable or not.[1] In the process, we will also assess the principal thesis of our entire first-level analysis: that the structure of the system determines the behavior of states.

But first we must look back at our analysis of bipolar and multipolar models. Two problems confront the analyst of tripolar international politics. One is that he does not know whether tripolarity is essentially bipolarity plus one, or a multipolar system because it contains more than two poles and is, therefore, by definition no longer bipolar. Which system is tripolarity more likely to resemble? (We shall later focus on the three principal poles in the contemporary system and not all the other centers of decisions; hence we shall not use the term tripolycentrism.) The second problem is that, even if this issue is decided, which is the more stable system? Before our lengthy analysis of the nuclear balance, we saw that international politics theorists had generally held that bipolar systems were unstable—more prone to erupt into violence because of the bipolar confrontations and crises, the temptation to launch preemptive strikes, the belief in domino theories, and the incentive to

[1] This chapter is based on Joseph L. Nogee, "Polarity: An Ambiguous Concept," paper delivered at the 1973 Convention of the American Political Science Association and in *Orbis*, Winter 1974, and "International Politics in a Tripolar World," paper delivered at the 1972 Convention of the Southern Political Science Association.

undermine the adversary's camp while holding one's own together. Conversely, multipolarity's more complex and flexible system was more likely to avoid crises and the possible eruption of war precisely because of its allegedly greater maneuverability; moderation, self-restraint, and stability were therefore built into systems with five or more poles (most theorists agreed that five seemed to be the minimum number of poles required for a multipolar system; if that is so, tripolarity systems are obviously not multipolar).

But the impact of nuclear weapons since 1945, as analyzed in earlier chapters, has led a number of theorists to question these conclusions about which system is more stable. They have specifically focused on the issue of attention. Deutsch and Singer, as we saw earlier, argued that it is precisely the fact that in a bipolar system the two powers concentrate on each other all the time that accounts for the mutual reinforcement of hostile perceptions and feelings. Whatever validity this generalization may have had in prenuclear systems, the reverse seems nearer the truth in nuclear bipolarity. It is, according to Kenneth Waltz, precisely because there are no distractions that the two states can guard against one another's attempts to cross the frontier lines between their respective spheres and avoid war. Aware of their capacity to incinerate one another, they have spent immense intellectual and economic resources on analyzing and effecting deterrence, crisis management, and limited war. "Rather a large crisis now than a small war later is the axiom that should precede the statement, often made, that to fight small wars in the present may be the means of avoiding large wars later."[2] Whereas in the prenuclear age a state might have been tempted to overestimate its own power and underestimate that of its opponent, nuclear arms have compelled American and Soviet policy-makers not to commit such errors, and this has had a restraining effect. Or, to put it another way, nuclear bipolarity has produced the stability previously attributed to non-nuclear multipolar systems because the contestants could devote full time to preserving the balance between them *and* devote equal care to acting with the self-restraint and caution required by modern arms.

Conversely, nuclear multipolarity may now be characterized by instability. If the management of a nuclear world requires complete attention, then the less attention one state pays to another potentially hostile one, the greater the danger there is of a catastrophe. The greater the uncertainty as power and alignments change, and the larger the number of different national policy-making elites involved, the higher the possibility of accident, miscalculation, and escalation of conflicts. Nuclear multipolarity has lost the advantages of bipolar simplicity, the certainty of alignments and of where "frontiers" are, and the increasing ability of the two sets of leaders to learn how to handle their various confrontations. Ciro Zoppo has summed up:

[2] Kenneth N. Waltz, "The Stability of a Bipolar World," *Daedalus*, Summer, 1964, p. 884.

Asymmetries in capabilities, military doctrines, and national goals might well become intolerable in a multipolar international system characterized by fluidity of political orientation or alignment and by latent breakthroughs in military technology. Initial experience with military nuclear development suggests that fledgling and adversary powers may not reach deterrent sufficiency at an even pace or with strategic symmetry. The complexity of deterrent calculations would be severely magnified for all powers in the system. Shifting deterrent relationships could confuse the signaling of intentions between the superpowers at tactical and strategic levels.[3]

More specifically, one can calculate the matter of nuclear diffusion quantitatively, on the basis of the capacity of various nations to manufacture nuclear weapons. Besides the present six members of the "nuclear club," countries such as West Germany, Italy, Japan, and Switzerland are all industrialized, have this capacity (even underdeveloped India achieved it), and have not yet ratified the nonproliferation treaty; other possibilities are Brazil, Argentina, Iran, Israel, Egypt, Pakistan, South Korea, and some other nations.[4] In addition, there are a number of countries that have research reactors to train scientific personnel; among them are Yugoslavia, Poland, Rumania, Taiwan, Turkey, and the Philippines. Such a quantitative estimate is, however, open to question. For one thing, a few bombs or missiles constitute neither an effective deterrent nor a credible retaliatory force and, in Soviet opinion at least, do not affect the crucial American-Soviet strategic balance.[5] In addition, the extremely high cost of the crucial factor, the delivery system, is not usually counted as part of the cost estimate in calculating the price of obtaining a minimal nuclear strike force. The United States could afford to go through the five stages from subsonic bombers to supersonic bombers to stationary missiles (liquid and solid fuels) to mobile missiles and, finally, from missiles with a single warhead to multiple warheads. But Britain could not. Whether other nations will in the future abandon their desire for nuclear arsenals and delivery systems because of the immense cost remains to be seen. This cost could be reduced, of course, by basing national deterrents on missiles from the start; and the cost could be even further reduced if the rate of technological change in delivery systems should ever slow down or be stabilized by agreement among the major powers.

But in the final analysis much will depend on political factors and what effects the nuclear nonproliferation treaty, which was not signed by

[3] Ciro E. Zoppo, "Nuclear Technology, Multipolarity and International Stability," *World Politics*, July, 1966, p. 601.

[4] See *The Nth Country Problem and Arms Control* (Washington, D.C.: National Planning Association, 1960). The latest USACDA agency estimate is contained in the *New York Times*, July 4, 1974.

[5] Roman Kolkowicz *et al.*, *The Soviet Union and Arms Control: A Superpower Dilemma* (Baltimore: The Johns Hopkins Press, 1970), pp. 70–115.

France and China, will have.[6] Will the treaty mean, for instance, that nations aspiring to great-power status will not be tempted to enter the nuclear arms race? How many states will still believe, despite the treaty, that nuclear weapons are the sole deterrent against another nuclear-armed power, particularly if they feel that they will not be protected by one of the nuclear superpowers in a crisis? How many nations, great or small, will believe that nuclear arms will enhance their bargaining power and, therefore, their influence on the regional or global levels sufficiently to be worth the cost of violating the nonproliferation treaty? More specifically, in the context of national security, will not the Chinese nuclear presence eventually compel Japan and perhaps Indonesia to produce their own bombs for security? If Israel should develop a bomb, will not Egypt follow suit? And in terms of prestige, can West Germany and Italy really afford not to build their own, just as India felt it could not forswear a weapon already owned by China?

The big question, of course, is what is likely to be the impact if at least a dozen nations—and perhaps twice that many—should like India go nuclear despite the nonproliferation treaty's attempt to limit the diffusion to the original three members plus France and China. Will it destabilize or stabilize the situation? In terms of statistical probabilities, of course, nuclear proliferation will tend to be a destabilizing factor. The more nations possessing the bomb, the greater the possibility that an accident, miscalculation, or even deliberate attack by an irresponsible national leader will touch off a local war in which the nuclear giants may become involved. In the words of President Kennedy:

> I ask you to stop and think for a moment what it would mean to have nuclear weapons in many hands—in the hands of countries large and small, stable and unstable, responsible and irresponsible, scattered throughout the world. There would be no rest for anyone then, no stability, no real security, and no chance of effective disarmament. There would only be increased chances of accidental war, and an increased necessity for the great powers to involve themselves in otherwise local conflicts.[7]

There is also the additional danger of a catalytic war in which a third power, say, China or Cuba, launches a few missiles against one of the two nuclear giants. The latter, believing the attack came from its chief opponent, strikes a retaliatory blow. As a result, the United States and Russia devastate each other while the third party emerges unharmed and in a stronger position.

[6] See Leonard Beaton and John Maddox, *The Spread of Nuclear Weapons* (New York: Praeger Publishers, 1962); Leonard Beaton, *Must the Bomb Spread?* (Baltimore: Penguin Books, 1966); Raymond Aron, "Spread of Nuclear Weapons," *The Atlantic Monthly*, January, 1965, pp. 44–50; George Liska, *Nations in Alliance* (Baltimore: Johns Hopkins Press, 1962), pp. 269–84; George H. Quester, *The Politics of Nuclear Proliferation* (Baltimore: Johns Hopkins Press, 1973); and *idem*, "Can Proliferation Now Be Stopped?" *Foreign Affairs*, October, 1974, p. 77 ff.

[7] Quoted in *New York Times*, July 27, 1963.

It may, of course, be objected that these dangers are more speculative than real. It has been suggested, for instance, that a "two-tier" system— the two superpowers on the top tier, the others below—will be stable.[8] Such a system is, in a sense, already in existence in the contemporary world of the six nuclear powers. Why should this two-tier system become less stable when one, two, or half a dozen or more secondary nuclear states are added to this number? Is it likely that the latter would dare attack either of the giants, each of which has virtually invulnerable missile systems vis-à-vis secondary nuclear powers? An attack would be tempting fate, because either could wipe out the aggressor even after absorbing the first strike. With their invulnerable retaliatory systems, both superpowers could delay a retaliatory attack; each would have time in which to ascertain whether its opponent had in fact launched the attack, and, if not, who had. Attacking a superpower, in brief, would not be worth the risk of discovery.

Furthermore, is there any reason why the two superpowers need to become involved if two small nuclear powers, say Israel and Egypt, engage in a nuclear conflict? Would not both have every reason to dissociate themselves from the belligerents? Past behavior would seem to indicate that neither the United States nor Russia will permit any other country to involve it in a conflict that risks its survival. If Moscow would not let Peking involve it in its quarrel with the United States over Formosa because that might have precipitated a superpower nuclear confrontation, it is highly unlikely that it would allow non-Communist client states—in whose survival its stake is presumably less than in a formally fraternal state—to do so. In addition, it is certain that the impact of nuclear diffusion will not be symmetrical. If Switzerland or Sweden acquired nuclear arms, it would be within the context of a genuinely neutral foreign policy. Neither state is likely to increase the instability of the state system, for neither is an active aggressive participant on the international stage. But even in the case of non-neutrals, the pattern of deterrence between the two nuclear giants might be reproduced between the smaller nuclear states if the rate of nuclear diffusion were approximately the same among potential adversaries. When the leaders of secondary states realize the awesome destructive power of the atom, they, too, may learn to think of nuclear arms only in terms of deterrence.[9] The pax atomica might in this case provide eternal secular peace, and a multipolar system might then be called stable after all. But this conclusion remains debatable.[10]

---

[8] Liska, Nations in Alliance, pp. 272–77.

[9] Albert Wohlstetter, "Nuclear Sharing: NATO and the N + 1 Country," Foreign Affairs, April, 1961, pp. 357–58.

[10] Balanced analyses will be found in William B. Bader, The United States and the Spread of Nuclear Weapons (New York: Pegasus, 1968), and Alastair Buchan, ed., A World of Nuclear Powers (Englewood Cliffs, N.J.: Prentice-Hall, 1966).

Tripolarity and the Rules of the System

A model of tripolarity is probably closer to bipolarity than multipolarity in a *nuclear* system in that a triangular structure is more apt to preserve peace. In such a relationship, each pole will have at least two incentives for self-restraint and moderation in its behavior. The first is that total nuclear war between any two poles would weaken the participants so catastrophically that the third pole would attain a dominant systemic position. The "victorious power," if there were to be one, would confront the third power, still untouched by the nuclear havoc, and even if that power were to possess an inferior strategic nuclear capability—as China is likely to have for some time—it would dictate the terms of peace. Second, not only will each pole be opposed to such an outcome, but each will also wish to prevent the emergence of a dominant coalition composed of the other two poles. (One need but recall America's almost paranoid fear of confronting a joint Sino-Soviet bloc, Peking's hysteria at the thought of a joint American-Soviet attempt to isolate the new China, and intense Soviet suspicions and apprehensions over Sino-American *rapprochement*.) Such a coalition could result only if any of the three exhibited unduly aggressive behavior. Self-restraint is, in short, a wise policy for each pole.[11] As a broad generalization, it can probably be hypothesized that, *whereas in a bipolar system the great fear of each power is becoming militarily inferior lest the opponent achieve military superiority and a dominance that may not be reversible, in a tripolar system the fear of each pole is diplomatic isolation.*

Thus, in a tripolar structure system-maintenance places maximum incentive on abstention from the kinds of confrontation and lower-level military engagement that might escalate and erupt into a nuclear conflagration, including nonintervention in each other's spheres of influence, and relative moderation in each pole's demands and behavior. Each pole is also likely to concentrate its attention and energies on its relations with its two rivals, for to become too involved outside the triangular structure and neglect its relationships with the other two poles may be disadvantageous.

The heart of the rules of behavior has been stated by Michel Tatu:

1. The existence of "adversary number one" leads to "objective collusion" with number two.

[11] Some of the best writing on tripolarity has been done by Ronald Yalem, who believes it is likely to prove unstable. See his "Tripolarity and the International System," *Orbis*, Winter, 1972, pp. 1051 ff., and "Tripolarity and World Politics," *The Yearbook of World Affairs 1974* (London: London Institute of World Affairs, 1974), pp. 23 ff.

2. Each of the three players aims to reduce collusion between the others to a minimum.
3. At the same time, it is in the interest of each to bluff or blackmail his chief adversary by threatening collusion with the other.
4. The surest way for any of the three to provoke the other two into collusion is to display undue aggressiveness.[12]

Notice Tatu's use of the word "collusion." Although the term denotes an underhanded intention, this is not necessarily the case. Two powers may well seek a *rapprochement* on some particular issue such as arms control for reasons having little or nothing to do with power number three. Nevertheless, the latter is likely to be suspicious of the motives of the other powers and therefore perceives "collusion," whether in fact it exists or not. What Tatu really means is that, although B and C move closer together against A, whom both fear may otherwise gain hegemony, each in order to keep his potential partner "honest" will on certain occasions move—or seem about to move—toward A; and A, to prevent a possible alliance of B and C against himself, will in turn seek to exploit differences and conflicts of interests between them, offer a few "carrots" as rewards, and, swinging his stick, ominously suggest that if B and C move closer each will jeopardize good relations with himself. As the *Economist* has illustrated:

Of course, there can still be specific agreements between any two of the three: between Russia and America about Berlin, for instance, or about the size of their missile armouries; between China and America about the future of Taiwan; perhaps even between Russia and China about their border. But from now on the main aim of the policymakers in Washington and Peking and Moscow will be to make sure that none of them is left with the short end of the stick. The diplomacy of the next ten years will be a search for a local accommodation here, and a temporary collaboration there, in which each of these three powers will be trying to become one of a twosome and to avoid finding itself a permanent onesome.[13]

A nuclear tripolar system, then, promises to be stable, perhaps more stable than a two-pole system, for it need not be quite so sensitive to slight increments of power by any pole as the emphasis shifts from continuous crises toward maneuver, from rigid confrontation to flexibility. Whereas in a bipolar system each state felt that it must match the other, in a tripolar system some gain in power can be permitted because, if the increase should become too threatening to the other two poles, they are likely to combine their power. If one of the poles has been aligned with

[12] Michel Tatu, *International Negotiation: The Great Power Triangle, Selected Comment,* Subcommittee on National Security and International Operations of the Committee on Government Operations, U.S. Senate, 92d Congress, 1st session (Washington, D.C.: Government Printing Office, 1971), p. 11.
[13] *Economist,* September 11, 1971. For elaboration, see William E. Griffith, *Peking, Moscow, and Beyond* (Washington, D.C.: Center for Strategic and International Studies, 1973).

the pole seemingly bent on expanding its power, it will shift toward the third pole; or else the third pole, because it can throw its power in the scales of the weaker one, may be in a position to act as a moderator in the dispute. *Rational calculations of power and self-interest, not ideology, will be the basis of each pole's foreign policy.* (As with bipolar and multipolar systems, one can of course demonstrate that tripolarity will be unstable, largely on the basis of the temptation of two poles to divide the third and revert to bipolarity, plus the fact that the addition of one more pole to the two existing ones will multiply the relationships—and therefore the number of conflicts—in the system threefold as each pole will have a relationship with each of the other two poles: China ⟶ U.S./U.S.S.R., U.S.S.R. ⟶ U.S./China, U.S. ⟶ U.S.S.R./ China. Thus there are more possibilities of conflict.)[14]

The Definition of a Pole

It is all very well for a model to suggest certain rules of behavior and tell us whether a particular system will be stable or not. But in the "real world," does it make much sense to talk of a tripolarity that includes China as a "pole?" China, after all, is not in the same power league as Russia and America. Rather, it is primarily an agrarian country with a low level of technological-industrial development, has a conventional military strength that cannot match that of the other two superpowers, and possesses a strategic nuclear capability that is very modest by American and Russian standards. How, by common-sense judgments about the power standings of nations, can China even be considered a "half-pole" making, instead of tripolarity, a two-and-a-half pole system? If China is considered a pole, why are not France and England poles as well, since they too have small nuclear forces? The attempt to answer these questions shows how theorists of international politics differ among themselves on such a fundamental issue as the definition of a pole, as they do on questions of stability.

Perhaps the most common criterion by which power is measured is military power and more specifically, since 1945, nuclear power. If strategic nuclear striking strength were really the key—and it seems to be the foremost badge of superpower status—we probably should have characterized the post–World War II system as unipolar since the Soviet Union did not test an atomic device until 1949 and did not have an ability to strike the United States until the late 1950's; it was not until the early 1970's that Russia attained what is now called "parity." Indeed, only now can we designate the system as bipolar, given the superiority

[14] Yalem, "Tripolarity and International System"; *idem*, "Tripolarity and World Politics"; and Morton Kaplan, "Variants on Six Models of the International System," in James N. Rosenau, ed., *International Politics and Foreign Policy*, rev. ed. (New York: Free Press, 1966), pp. 294–95.

of the United States and U.S.S.R. over all other nuclear states. Until it attained that parity, the Soviet Union kept the balance for most of this period with a minimal deterrent capability against the United States plus a massive aerial and ground striking capability against Western Europe; thus Moscow held London and Paris hostage for American restraint. Had Washington been willing to risk sacrificing Western Europe, Moscow would have been unable to deter the superpower across the Atlantic.

Today it is China that occupies a vastly inferior strategic power position. The United States and the Soviet Union possess a first-strike capability against China; China has none. The two superpowers also possess a second-strike capacity; China's is very limited. Against Russia China has greater strength, because China has deployed a limited number of MRBMs and IRBMs, which can reach large sections of Asian Russia and even European Russia. (Moscow does, of course, have the right to build up to 100 ABMs. If effective and deployed, such ABMs can possibly limit the damage a Chinese strike could inflict against the parts of Russia around Moscow.) Against the United States, China can use its missiles only against American forces in Asia, as well as allies and friends; a sufficient Chinese ICBM capability, able to inflict unacceptable losses in the United States proper, is years off. But for China it may not be necessary to match the two superpowers right away. Russia too, after all, lagged behind the United States, and Peking, like Moscow earlier, can deter the United States by threatening Japan, Australia, New Zealand, Thailand, and other states (possibly including India, which China could perhaps threaten and hold hostage to help to deter Russia, which has signed a treaty of friendship with India). Furthermore, even a small number of ICBMs, which can destroy 5 million to 10 million Americans, is probably enough to help deter the United States in most situations that are likely to arise. China is likely to benefit, after all, from the special circumstance of its position in the triangle. With its far smaller, yet growing, nuclear strike force, it could weaken either Russia or America enough—or at least policy-makers in Moscow and Washington would fear that possibility—so that it might leave one of them much weakened and impair its capacity to inflict unacceptable damage upon the other.[15] Thus China's deterrent ability probably has a greater capacity to dissuade both superpowers than the numbers of its ICBMs would suggest. China may someday achieve strategic parity, but a far smaller force, one it can afford financially, may serve it well for some time to come. A relationship of mutual deterrence among the Big Three will in the meantime emerge.[16]

[15] Harry G. Gelber, "The Impact of Chinese ICBMs in Strategic Deterrence," *Orbis*, Summer, 1969, pp. 413–414, and *Nuclear Weapons and Chinese Policy*, Adelphi Paper No. 99, International Institute for Strategic Studies, London, 1973.

[16] Hedley Bull, "The New Balance of Power in Asia and the Pacific," *Foreign Affairs*, July, 1971, p. 673.

Yet, to the degree that nuclear forces are thought of in terms of negative power—the capacity to deny rather than to gain—it may again be suggested that military power in general and strategic power in particular are a necessary but not a sufficient criterion for determining which state is a pole. Frequently economic wealth is advanced as a broader gauge of a state's power. Wealth obviously bears a relationship to military power, since the richest states presumably can afford to buy the most military power. Indeed, wealth can buy power of all kinds, and this remains important for distinguishing the superpowers from the secondary powers. Britain cannot afford to build a sizable nuclear force or to keep up with the ever changing state of the art in delivery systems and warheads. It had a choice to make between trying to keep up with the leading members of the nuclear club and developing a sufficient conventional capacity to defend Britain's many other interests; its failure to make this choice, its decision to have some of each, meant that in 1956, for instance, it did not have a nuclear force to deter Soviet threats of rocket attacks against London (Washington had to tell Moscow not to try that one) nor the conventional capabilities to occupy the Suez Canal and present the world with a *fait accompli*. The United States and the U.S.S.R. can mobilize both kinds of forces in sizable quantities, plus large amounts of other power, such as economic-technical assistance, if they wish to use these means as diplomatic tools. Thus a state's gross national product—the total value of its production and services—has frequently been used as a relatively accurate and measurable means of comparing the power of different states.

GROSS NATIONAL PRODUCT
(at current market prices and exchange rates, $ billions)

Year	U.S.A.	U.S.S.R.	Japan	West Germany	France	Britain
1952	350	113	16	32	29	44
1955	399	136	23	43	35	54
1958	455	178	32	56	50	65
1961	520	213	51	81	65	77
1965	685	269	88	115	99	100
1968	865	339	142	135	127	103
1969	931	364	166	151	142	110
1970	976	403	198	189	149	121
1971	1,050	422	221	217	164	135
1972	1,152	439	317	259	202	141

SOURCE: International Institute for Strategic Studies, *The Military Balance 1973–1974*, p. 79, for selected years, corrected for 1971–72.

The table just above shows the following: (1) the clear-cut distinction between the superpowers and secondary powers over a two-decade period; (2) the ranking of the principal and secondary actors listed, which stand pretty much as most observers would rate them without knowing their GNP figures; (3) the leveling-off of the Soviet effort to catch up with the United States economically, indeed, the widening of the GNP gap between them; and (4) the fact that, of the secondary powers, only Japan is catching up with the superpowers economically, having reached a position right behind the Soviet Union and threatening to overtake it within a decade or two, although that prediction predated the post-1973 energy crisis.

Japan's GNP is far higher than China's, which is not listed in the above table. Specifically, in terms of GNP, Japan at the beginning of the 1970's was approximately three times stronger than China, seventeen times more powerful than Indonesia, and 50 per cent more so than the entire rest of the region, composed of fourteen other nations, including China. (China's GNP, however, is greater than that of all the thirteen other countries put together, excluding Japan.)[17] Yet this Japanese-Chinese comparison demonstrates at the same time the limits to which GNP figures can be reliably utilized to measure power—indeed, how misleading they can be. China possesses nuclear weapons and, being a totalitarian state, controls the allocation of resources in order to concentrate on whatever objectives it chooses, such as a nuclear capability at the cost of larger domestic investments. Japan is economically far superior and is likely to enhance its economic lead over China. However, Japan has no nuclear forces and only a small conventional self-defense force; whatever influence it has is based solely on economic strength. Indeed, Japan is probably the first major power—by all the indices of population, industry, education, technical skills, and so forth—in history to attempt to project influence on the basis of its capacity to produce the goods many countries crave rather than as a military power with a self-defined political role.[18] Japan is not so much a nation as a large trading company—or, as some wag has called it, Sony Incorporated. Japan may, therefore, be an *economic* superpower, but politically and militarily it is only a potentially great power, still searching—and not too hard at that—for a role after years of American tutelage. More broadly, GNP reveals little about a nation's unity, the stability of its government, popular morale, military doctrine, and quality of diplomacy, which are relevant in analyzing a nation's power and foreign policy. Yet, as with military power, despite limitations economic productivity remains a rough indicator of power and a convenient shorthand means for comparisons.

There is another reason why adding up the various components of

[17] Donald C. Hellmann, *Japan and East Asia* (New York: Praeger Publishers, 1972), pp. 32–33.

[18] *Ibid.* See also Robert E. Osgood, *The Weary and The Wary* (Baltimore: Johns Hopkins Press, 1972), and Adelphi Papers 95 and 97: Kunio Muraoka, *Japanese Security and the United States,* and Maratako Kosaka, *Options for Japan's Foreign Policy* (London: International Institute for Strategic Studies, 1973).

power will not suffice. The United States, for example, from 1919 to 1939 was undoubtedly the world's greatest power—had it been willing to mobilize its power and use it; but it was not, preferring to return to an earlier isolationist position made temporarily possible again by Germany's defeat and the absence of threat to France and Britain until the late 1930's. The United States, refusing to be a political and military player, therefore ranked behind the various European powers, including Russia and Japan in that period. The question, in short, is one of motivation. That is what differentiates China, on the one hand, from Japan and the Europe of the Common Market, on the other; China has the determination to play a primary role in Asia, as well as in other geographical and ideological (Communist) subsystems. Neither Japan nor Europe yet possesses the assured sense of identity of China or has yet been able to define for itself the political roles it wishes to play; they are both still dependent upon the United States for their defense, although they possess the industrial strength, technological and scientific skills, and manpower to develop great power—that is, an ability largely to defend themselves. Thus being an economic superpower is insufficient *unless* this economic potential is married to political will, for it is this will that converts potential into actual power. In the absence of such a determination to play a political role, a potential pole like Europe, with a population larger than Russia's or America's, remains a stake over which the real superpowers contest rather than an influential actor in itself.[19]

The most significant factor in this element in what Spiegel has called "motivational power" is the nature of the regime, as is apparent in the change of regimes from Czarist Russia to Soviet Russia, from Weimar (democratic) Germany to Nazi Germany or from Nationalist China to Communist China.[20] Such transformations are, in general, more significant in their impact upon national goals than are changes in the leadership of the same regime. This motivation in foreign policy may be roughly measured by such indicators as the percentage of the GNP spent in such areas as defense and foreign aid, the percentage of the population serving in the armed forces, the number of diplomats and other foreign policy and defense officials sent to other countries, the number and level of official visitors sent abroad, return visits by foreigners, and official radio broadcasts beamed to foreign countries. David Wilkinson has specifically distinguished between two broad classes of states, one characterized by the presence of a conscious, policy-controlling will, the other by its absence. He hypothesizes that "the more one finds of this kind of hostile, dynamic leadership, the more its nature and peculiarities explain policy, while the less one finds of such 'will,' the more one will be able to explain policy by referring to traditions, history, and stable bureaucratic habit. Conversely, abrupt shifts of policy should

[19] George F. Kennan, "Europe's Problems, Europe's Choices," *Foreign Policy* (Spring 1974), pp. 13–14.
[20] Spiegel, pp. 71–78.

more often than not coincide with the presence or appearance of a leadership of this kind."[21] In any event, this will to play an active and major role in the international system means that a pole becomes deeply involved in both the competitive and the cooperative relations that characterize the power struggles in the state system. "A pole like the magnetic metaphor from which the term comes must repel and attract. . . . Nations between whom there are no vital conflicts of interests cannot be considered polar antimonies."[22] Thus, as Nogee goes on to suggest, a pole is not only to be defined (1) in terms of its inherent components of power but also (2) in terms of an external relationship of rivalry and cooperation.

Only the United States, the Soviet Union, and China pursue such policies of rivalry and cooperation with one another. Japan and Western Europe are allies of the United States; neither is actively competing with Russia and China, against whom they remain protected by the United States. Some, like Brzezinski, separate this triangle into two, one of which concerns itself with such political-military issues as security and arms control, the other of which is composed of the leading industrial countries—America, Western Europe, and Japan—and is obviously concerned with economic issues. The first triangle's emphasis is on conflict, the second's on cooperation.[23] Yet the economic-financial relations among the industrialized countries, one, are hardly without conflict and, two, spill over into NATO and U.S.-Japanese relations. It may be useful, then, to distinguish between different kinds of issues, but how analytically helpful this distinction may be is debatable, given the difficulty of really separating them. In any event, once again we see some of the difficulty in defining the pole and then defining who the principal actors in the system are. Some—including President Nixon—have talked of a five-pole world; others arrive at the number by looking at different geographical areas, as Alastair Buchan did when he asserted that in Europe there are three poles (the United States, the U.S.S.R., and the Europe of the Common Market) and in Asia there are four (the United States, the U.S.S.R., China, and Japan).[24] Clearly, political scientists cannot even agree on such a fundamental concept as a pole. If, as Nogee has claimed, a pole remains an ambiguous concept, we shall not be very wrong if we claim that at present three poles remain dominant while the Europe of the Nine and Japan continue to search—not too eagerly—for a role in the international system.

[21] David Wilkinson, *Comparative Foreign Relations* (Belmont, Calif.: Dickenson, 1969), p. 27.

[22] Nogee, "International Politics in Tripolar World," p. 13.

[23] Zbigniew Brzezinski, "The Balance of Power Delusion," *Foreign Policy*, Summer, 1972, pp. 57–58.

[24] Alastair Buchan, *Power and Equilibrium in the 1970's* (New York: Praeger Publishers, 1973), pp. 91–105.

Stability: Counting Poles?

If we can agree that China is a pole, we must still return to the basic question about tripolarity: Will it be stable, as was suggested earlier? Our entire discussion throughout first-level analysis has emphasized a relationship between the number of poles and the stability or instability of the system. We saw that some analysts suggest that bipolarity is unstable and multipolarity stable; other analysts conclude just the opposite. Maybe the principal reason for this disagreement is, as Joseph Nogee has suggested, that any system can be stable or unstable depending on the presence of other factors besides two, three, or more poles.[25]

Earlier, admittedly, we concluded that tripolarity would also probably be a stable system. Let us briefly analyze such a system and see whether this is correct or not. Although no actual global tripolar system has recently existed, a tripolar subsystem has—the Europe of the 1930's. It was regionally tripolar in terms of power. On one side were Britain and France, both *status quo* powers; Britain was clearly the leader, France the follower, unwilling to act unilaterally without British support. On the second side was the Soviet Union, a revisionist state, which had in 1928 launched the first of its programs to industrialize and militarily strengthen itself. And on the third side of the triangle was Germany, joined after March, 1938, by Italy as its junior partner. The relationship was also tripolar ideologically: liberal democracy, communism, and fascism. Instead of each pole's need to prevent a coalition of the other two by behaving in a restrained manner and thereby preserving the peace, the system produced great uncertainty, anxiety and instability—and, eventually, war.[26]

When Russia joined the League of Nations and signed treaties with France and its ally, Czechoslovakia, in an antifascist coalition, Germany felt isolated and encircled. Instead of moderating German behavior, the drawing together of Paris and Moscow provided Hitler with the reason, or at least the justification, for marching into the Rhineland in 1936, which bolstered his image in the West as a staunch anti-Communist. When Germany and the Western allies seemed to resolve their difference, as at Munich, and gave the impression of joining together to save European civilization from Bolshevism, the Soviet Union felt isolated and began its quest for an alliance with Hitler. The resultant Nazi-Soviet Pact against plutocratic and bourgeois democracy was the pre-

[25] Nogee, *Polarity*, pp. 18–20.

[26] Among other books, see John Wheeler-Bennett, *Munich* (London: Macmillan, 1948); Keith Eubank, *The Origins of World War II* (New York: Crowell, 1969); A. J. P. Taylor, *The Origins of the Second World War* (New York: Premier Books, 1963); and A. L. Rowse, *Appeasement* (New York: Norton, 1963).

lude to war. The pact divided Poland between the two revisionist powers, gave Russia extra time to prepare itself for war, and permitted Hitler to think about one war at a time, first against Britain and France, and then against Russia.

Why did European tripolarity fail to prevent the outbreak of World War II and not create a system of peace with built-in self-restraints? One principal reason was the inability of the two *status quo* powers to decide who was their chief adversary, Germany or Russia. An essential ingredient for preserving peace in any multipolar system is the isolation of the principal source of possible disturbance. But the Franco-Soviet treaty, whose purpose was supposed to be the containment of Germany, had little chance of being implemented, given, among other reasons, French anti-Communist sentiments stemming largely from domestic sources and the suspicions of the Soviet Union's Western neighbors that the Russians would stay and impose their regime upon them once the Red Army marched across their lands to come to grips with the German Army. Even before Munich, London had frowned upon the Franco-Soviet treaty. After Munich, British apprehensions about Soviet purposes led London to move so slowly and at such a relatively low diplomatic level in its negotiations with Moscow about a possible alliance against Germany that Hitler had plenty of time to sign Stalin up first; and Stalin must by then have preferred Hitler to Chamberlain, whose intentions toward Russia and willingness to stand up to Germany were questionable. The British leader and his associates seemed unable to make up their minds whether Russia should be used against Hitler to save Europe from Facism or Nazi Germany be used as a bulwark to protect Europe from the Red virus. Hitler's pose as an anti-Bolshevik was not shattered until the Nazi-Soviet Pact.

A second reason for the instability of the European system during the 1930's was the presence of a risk-taker.[27] Hitler has often been portrayed as irrational, a man determined to attain his goals whatever the risks and costs. Actually, the image is contrary to fact: The German leader always carefully calculated power relationships. He was keenly aware of Germany's weaknesses, and this dictated his chief tactic of dividing his opponents. Before the war, he successfully used the claims of national self-determination, fear of Bolshevism, and the bilateral treaty to separate and paralyze his opponents; after the war erupted, his technique was the *Blitzkrieg*, quickly destroying his enemies one at a time before they could cooperate and mobilize their potential power, which, Hitler knew (and the general staff kept reminding him in case he ever forgot), was greater than that of Germany. Yet if the Führer was not the reckless leader of his public reputation, he did have strong nerves and was quite willing to test his opponents' will. Hitler had a sharp eye for the psychological weaknesses of his adversaries and was particularly adept at ex-

[27] William J. Newman, *The Balance of Power in the Interwar Years 1919–1939* (New York: Random House, 1968), pp. 155–62.

ploiting British and French fears of war. By 1939, after a series of political tests over German rearmament, the Rhineland reoccupation, the Austrian *Anschluss,* and the Sudetenland, his estimation of his Western adversaries' will and resolution was so low that the belated British commitment to the defense of Poland lacked credibility. As a risk-taker, had he not taken greater gambles in prior years? And had he not always been successful as his enemies retreated from every challenge?

Third, the two Western powers committed a double mistake: they underestimated their own strength and greatly overestimated Nazi Germany's; more significantly, they misunderstood its leader's intentions. Would Hitler be satisfied once his claims of self-determination had been met, or were his purposes less limited? Chamberlain's policy of appeasement assumed that Hitler accepted the European system and that he merely aimed at certain readjustments of the distribution of power so that specific German needs would be met. Further, if the system satisfied what the English leader believed to be Germany's legitimate interests, Hitler, in his turn, would presumably reciprocate by recognizing the Western countries' legitimate interests, thus limiting his own demands and, in general, playing by the rules.[28] This policy was doomed to failure since the Führer rejected the bourgeois world with its compromises and bargaining, and used its principles and techniques only to undermine it. Above all, Nazi Germany's aims went beyond the rather limited goals prescribed by national self-determination. The British Prime Minister misread his adversary's goals, partly because Hitler shrewdly presented Germany's demands as limited and justified by the Allies' violation of their own principles at Versailles in 1919. Chamberlain, like many others in Britain, saw Hitler as the rather crude spokesman for legitimate German grievances stemming from the allegedly harsh, unfair, and punitive Versailles *diktat.* In short, Hitler was not really an aggressor; Germany had been mistreated by the West, and it was up to the West to make amends if the Third Reich was to become a reliable and stable member of a new Concert of Europe composed of London, Paris, Berlin, and Rome.

Fourth, Britain and France as the *status quo* powers also disagreed on what the *status quo* meant. Britain, until 1939, would commit itself only to the defense of France's frontier with Germany (a meaningless commitment since it would have no choice but to go to war if Germany invaded France) but not to France's allies in Eastern Europe. Because after 1925 France refused to take any actions not endorsed by London, this French attempt to contain Germany was unworkable. It might have been unfeasible anyway, for France's Maginot Line psychology and military planning were at odds with this alliance system, but Britain ensured its failure because it approved of changes in the East European territorial *status quo*; indeed, it regarded these as essential if peace were

28 Arnold Wolfers, *Britain and France Between Two Wars* (New York: Norton, 1966), pp. 270–303, and Newman, *Balance of Power,* pp. 164–65.

to be preserved. More seriously, although Russia was presumably a stronger ally against Germany than its smaller Western neighbors, the implementation of the Franco-Soviet alliance depended upon British approval. Finally, British opposition to Italy's attempt to conquer Ethiopia was instrumental in driving Mussolini into Hitler's arms. Earlier the Italian dictator had opposed the Nazi attempt to seize Austria; in 1938 he did not. Mussolini's switch, however, might have occurred anyway, given his ideological rapport with Hitler and Italy's revisionist ambitions. And Italy was a power in name only.

Finally, the third pole—Soviet Russia—also blundered in its calculations. Spurred on by Munich, which Stalin viewed as the West's attempt to open Hitler's road to the east, he signed his own Munich in the form of the Nazi-Soviet Pact, which attempted to redirect Hitler westward. Long before the war, Stalin had talked of staying out of a future war among the capitalist states, letting them exhaust one another and then dictating the peace. Stalin, like Churchill and the German generals, confidently assumed that the French army could stand up to the *Wehrmacht*. Whether Stalin had aligned Russia with France during the middle 1930's in order to pursue a genuine containment policy together with France remains unknown; if this had been the reason, it was clearly no longer valid by 1939. The Russian leader, as already suggested, reciprocated Britain's distrust of him, and it seems that, even had Chamberlain "sincerely" sought an alliance, acted with dispatch, and flown to Moscow as he did three times to Hitler, Stalin would simply have strung him along in order to speed Hitler's signature on the alliance he really wanted.

To sum up: This brief analysis would reinforce our proposition that an abstract deductive model will be of only limited utility in helping foreign policy observers analyze the patterns of behavior by the principal actors in an actual tripolar system. World War II was not an "inevitable" result of the tripolar European systems. Churchill called it the "unnecessary war." Indeed, most critics feel that the war was avoidable and that German power could have been contained had its adversaries, especially Britain, acted differently. Thus peace or war, stability or instability, seems to be less a matter of the number of poles *per se* than poles *plus* such other factors as the national objectives of the principal actors, the domestic sources of foreign policy behavior, and the policy-makers' perceptions of the nature of the external system and the threats posed to their countries. If, for example, a traditional conservative such as Streseman had been Germany's Chancellor in the 1930's, Chamberlain's policy in all likelihood would have worked; but the Prime Minister's misperception of Hitler as a nationalist who did not wish to destroy the European system, only to improve Germany's position in it, spelled the doom of the appeasement policy. Thus had Germany's policy been only what it appeared to be, or had British policy more correctly analyzed Hitler's real ambitions and demonstrated more firmness, war might have been avoidable. Of course, such an alternative policy would have had to presume that British public opinion would have supported a containment of Nazi Germany. After the fantastic loss of life in 1914–18 and the intense desire to avoid another such bloodletting, plus the post-Depression domestic problems of class hostilities and continued high unemployment, a tough foreign policy was unlikely. It needed a Munich and its failure to restrain Hitler's intentions to underline that the issue was Britain's security, not Germany's legitimate grievances.

More specifically, from a policy point of view, the 1933–39 period showed that in a tripolar system containing two principal revisionist powers, one of which was energetically expansionist (Germany) and the other rhetorically committed to long-range transformation of the system (Russia), the *status quo* power's strategy must include the following: the identification and isolation of the chief threat to the balance; agreement on the nature of the principal adversary's threat, the location of their own vital interests, and avoidance of major involvement in areas of secondary interest against secondary adversaries or their potential allies; and the demonstration of sufficient power and determination to deter the risk-taker and attract the cooperation of the other revisionist pole. But whatever they should have done, an analysis of European tripolarity in the 1930's supports Nogee's contention that, while first-level analysis can suggest that the number of poles will limit the alternative policies states can pursue and thus influence their strategies in the system, this is not the same as saying that the distribution of power or the structure of the system determines state behavior. For, in different words, it asserts that first-level analysis must be supplemented by second- and third-level analyses.

PART THREE

National Systems
and
Decision-Making

12 National and Elite Styles in Foreign Policy: American and Soviet Perceptions and Behavior

The American National Style

The game of international politics has, up to now, been analyzed in terms of the interactions among the states that together compose the state system. To do so, we have had to assume that the member states are alike in interest, motivation, and internal structures. Hence, in focusing on the pattern of action and reaction among these actors, we began where domestic policy left off. In using the systemic level of analysis, we therefore have had no reason to look inward—except in those instances when states did not do what they should have done. While this assumption about the identical nature of states is conceptually useful for our first level of analysis, it does not suffice—as noted in our analysis of tripolarity—if we wish to analyze and more fully understand the actual behavior of states. For each state has a "picture in its head" of the world and its role. Each wears "colored glasses," because it possesses a repertory of acts and responses derived from its domestic and foreign experiences. Thus each perceives "reality" selectively because of its particular "Weltanschauung" (world view) or "cognitive map"; in practice, each has a corresponding "operational code" or "national style."[1]

This method of analyzing foreign policy is based on the assumption that the manner in which policy-making elites see the world and define their aims is decided within the framework of a nation's political culture. American policy, like Russian policy, derives from a set of attitudes

[1] An exhaustive analysis of the American "style" may be found in Stanley Hoffmann, *Gulliver's Troubles, or The Setting of America's Foreign Policy* (New York: McGraw-Hill, 1968), Part II, pp. 87–213. See also Hans J. Morgenthau, *In Defense of the National Interest* (New York: Alfred A. Knopf, 1951); Robert E. Osgood, *Ideals and Self-Interest in America's Foreign Relations* (Chicago: University of Chicago Press, 1953); George F. Kennan, *American Diplomacy 1900–1950* (Chicago: University of Chicago Press, 1951); and John Spanier, *American Foreign Policy Since World War II*, 6th ed. (New York: Praeger, 1973).

toward politics and political conflict in general and international politics in particular, conceptions of how and to what extent historical development can be molded, and ideas of the methods to advance national objectives. But whereas the Kremlin's perceptions and behavior stemmed from the revolutionary framework held by its dictatorial leaders, Washington's have been influenced more by nationally shared values and beliefs and the historical experience of American democracy. The concept of style, in brief, can assist an analyst in clarifying how a nation and its policy-makers are likely to view a specific situation, the alternative courses of action that will be seen, and the option selected. It can therefore be very helpful in analyzing a particular situation, although it is not a substitute for examining institutional and other pressures that shape the final decision.[2]

Perhaps fundamental in America's experience was its lengthy isolation from the quarrels of the great European powers. For almost a century, it was able to devote itself to domestic tasks: strengthening the bonds of national unity, westward expansion, absorbing the millions of immigrants attracted by the opportunities of the country, and industrializing and urbanizing an entire continent. This freedom to concentrate on internal affairs cannot be explained entirely as the result of the Atlantic Ocean and weaker neighbors to the north and south. As a democratic nation, America's internal orientation must also be explained by the preferences of the electorate. As was hypothesized earlier, citizens in a democracy are primarily concerned with their individual and family well-being. All Western democracies, responding to public demands, have consequently become welfare states.[3] Demands for spending time in the armed forces or for paying higher taxes to finance international obligations are bound in this context to be viewed as burdens. And foreign policy will, on the whole, be considered a distraction from the primary domestic tasks. The American's intense concern with private and material welfare and his almost compulsive striving for economic success—the measure of his self-esteem—have been noted since Tocqueville. If, in an egalitarian society, a man is judged primarily by his material achievements, because these indicate his ability and therefore bring him social respect, he will concentrate on "getting ahead." Money becomes the symbol of status and prestige; it is a sign of success, just as a failure to earn enough money is considered a token of personal failure.

Given such a profound inward orientation, the United States turned

[2] Alexander L. George, "The 'Operational Code': A Neglected Approach to the Study of Political Leaders and Decision-Making," *International Studies Quarterly*, June, 1969, pp. 190 ff.

[3] The hypothesis offered by Klauss Knorr and others about democratic behavior, discussed in Chapter 2, is generally supported by Gabriel A. Almond, who, in *The American People and Foreign Policy* (New York: Praeger Publishers, 1960), strongly emphasizes the "extraordinary pull of domestic and private affairs even in periods of international crises." See particularly Almond's Chapter 3, his summation of the American value orientation, pp. 48–50.

its attention to the outside world only when it felt provoked. The external threat had first to constitute so clear a danger that it could no longer be ignored. This point cannot be overemphasized: The United States rarely initiated policy; the stimuli responsible for the formation of foreign policy usually came from beyond America's frontiers. The result historically was that U.S. foreign policy was essentially both reactive and discontinuous, an impatient response to external pressure when there was a "clear and present danger," and a return to more important domestic affairs as soon as the danger had passed. Long-range involvement commitments and foreign policy planning therefore tended to be difficult.

The American attitude was further characterized by a high degree of moralism and missionary zeal stemming from the nation's long consideration of itself as a unique and morally superior society. The United States was the world's first democracy committed to the improvement of the life of the common man. It was a post-European society, and Americans were the "chosen people." The New World stood for opportunity, democracy, and peace; the Old World for poverty, exploitation, and war. Lincoln phrased it briefly and aptly when he said that America was "the last best hope on earth." Woodrow Wilson in World War I and Franklin Roosevelt in World War II expressed much the same feeling. Just as in 1862 the United States could not remain half free, half slave, so, in 1917 and again in 1941, the world could not continue half free, half slave. Each war was considered as an apocalyptic struggle between the forces of darkness and the forces of light.[4] Moralism in foreign policy thus reflected the awareness and pride of a society that believed it had carved out a better domestic order, free of oppression and injustice. This was truly a society in which the *vox populi* was the *vox dei*.

Isolationism from European "power politics"—not isolationism from Latin America or Asia—was therefore basically a means of safeguarding American morality and purity. Self-quarantine was the best way to prevent the nation from being soiled and tainted by Europe's undemocratic domestic institutions and foreign policy behavior. The American experiment had to be safeguarded against corruption by power politics, and withdrawing from the state system and providing the world with an example it could adopt was therefore the only correct course. On the other hand, once it became impossible to remain aloof in this century, the country went to the other extreme by launching crusades. As a self-proclaimed superior country—morally and politically—the United States could remain uncontaminated only by eliminating those who might in-

[4] Paul Seabury, in *The Rise and Decline of Cold War* (New York: Basic Books, 1967), pp. 39–45, has some fitting quotes, especially a poem by Archibald MacLeish, celebrating the *pax americana* as a preamble to the *pax humana* during World War II. The moralism of a postwar Secretary of State, John Foster Dulles, is discussed well by William L. Miller, "The 'Moral Force' Behind Dulles' Diplomacy," *Reporter*, August 9, 1956.

fect it. Thus, once the nation had been provoked, it tended to act as a missionary power and sought to make the world safe for American democracy by democratizing or Americanizing it into peaceful facsimiles of itself. American crusading, like isolationism, sprang from the same source.

A third characteristic follows from those liberal democratic values upon which the nation was founded and the resultant high degree of moralism: a depreciation of power politics with its connotations of conflict, destruction, and death.[5] Strife is considered abnormal and only transitory; harmony is the normal condition among states. The use of power within the national political system is made legitimate only by democratic purposes; its employment in the state system as well can be justified only by a moral cause. Specifically, in the state system this means that power cannot be employed, at least without arousing guilt feelings, unless the nation confronts a morally unambiguous case of aggression. And when that happens, it must completely eradicate the immoral enemy that threatens the nation and its democratic principles. The presumption is that democracies are peaceful states because the people who elect their rulers and suffer the hardships of war are peace-loving, hence the eruption of hostilities is attributable to authoritarian and totalitarian states whose rulers, unrestrained by democratic public opinion, wield power for their own personal aggrandizement. Their removal therefore becomes a condition for peace and the end of power politics itself. Thus, while the exercise of power by American democracy might be sinful, salvation could be gained by the very nobility of its purpose. Paradoxically, war, the ultimate instrument of power politics, becomes justified because it is presumably the means for its own abolition. In Woodrow Wilson's famous phrase, America fights wars to end all wars. Peace is normal; war is abnormal, cruel, and senseless, and it would not have erupted but for the aggressor, who, as a criminal, must be punished for his deviant behavior. American power is "righteous power." Ironically, therefore, its only morally justifiable and emotionally satisfying wars, fought with a reasonable degree of public unity and support, are total wars. For all their fantastic destructiveness and loss of life, they raise few moral qualms.

The fact that, twice in this century, the United States has successfully dealt its enemies total defeat has strengthened yet another attitude: that the United States is omnipotent and, once engaged in a conflict, could "lick anyone in the system."[6] Indeed, even in the country's earlier history, America's actions had met with quick success whenever it had been drawn into the international arena. At one time or another, it had

[5] Robert E. Osgood, *Limited War* (Chicago: The University of Chicago Press, 1957), pp. 28–45, focuses on this point in explaining the difficulties the nation has in conducting limited wars.

[6] Denis W. Brogan, "The Illusion of Omnipotence," *Harper's*, December, 1952, pp. 21–28.

beaten the British, the Mexicans, the Spaniards, the Germans, and the Japanese. Moreover, America had never been invaded, defeated, or occupied (as most other nations had been); it had, to be sure, committed mistakes, but with its great power it had always been able to rectify them. To a nation in which one popular slogan expressed confidence in doing "the difficult today, the impossible tomorrow," failure would be a new experience. America's history had been a witness to victories only; its unbroken string of successes seemed evidence of national omnipotence. This attitude of American invincibility tended, of course, to be reinforced by its many domestic successes. Thus, historically, America was a unique country for, with the single exception of the Civil War, it never learned the meaning of tragedy. Few other states have managed to avoid defeat and conquest. This has meant that policy-makers have usually not been deterred from most actions by thoughts of failure; but had failure in fact happened, they could have expected a major political reaction. For if the country were indeed all-powerful, public opinion would understand such a failure or defeat only in terms of governmental incompetence or treason. The nation could not have admitted that the situation it had become involved in might not be resolvable by the proper application of force.

A closely related attitude has been America's pragmatism. Again, it has been part of the nation's experience that when problems arose, they were solved by whatever means were at hand. Americans have always been pretty much a "how to do it" people and, indeed, prided themselves on their problem-solving abilities. Europeans might have invented radar or the jet engine, but it was Americans who then refined and developed these inventions, produced them on a large scale, and marketed them better than the countries of origin. All problems were solvable; it was only a matter of "know-how." The question was not *whether* but *how*—and how quickly at that. This approach to foreign policy might appropriately be called the engineering approach to external problems. This reinforces what Robert Tucker has characterized as a general Western attitude:

A pragmatic or instrumental approach to world problems typifies the Western policy-maker. Not theoretical conceptions enabling him to relate policy to the general trends of events, but know-how in the face of concrete problem-situations is what he typically emphasizes. He wants to "solve" the immediate, given concrete problem that is causing "trouble," and be done with it. Accordingly, diplomatic experience—always of great importance, of course—is exalted as the supreme qualification for leadership in foreign policy. For experience is the royal road to know-how. It teaches the statesman how to negotiate with the Russians, how to coordinate policy with the allies, how to respond to emergencies, and so on.

In facing foreign-policy problems it is not the Western habit to attempt first of all to form a valid general picture of the world-setting events in which the problems have arisen. The tendency is rather to isolate the given problem-situation from the larger movement of history and ask: what can and should we do about it?[7]

More specifically, this means that the United States tackles each problem as it arises. In the abstract, this makes sense. After all, until a situation has occurred and the "facts" are in, how can one react? The trouble is, by the time sufficient facts are in the situation may well be so far developed that it is too late to do much about it or, if one does, the difficulties just abound. America's quest for certainty, in other words, is carried too far. Policy-making should, in essence, mean tackling problems early enough so that one's influence can still be usefully brought to bear; but usually this can be done only when there is still insufficient information. By the time the situation is clear, a crisis is already at hand, and it is too late for any effective action short of applying military power; it may even be too late for that. Pragmatism, in brief, reinforces the reactive and discontinuous nature of the American conduct of foreign policy, along with the emphasis on the immediate and short-run to the detriment of longer-run policy considerations.

These are but a few U.S. attitudes toward international politics; they by no means exhaust the list. The question is, in what ways have they affected U.S. behavior? During World War II, they led the United States to divide nations between those who were "peace-loving" (the United States, the U.S.S.R., and Great Britain) and "aggressors" (Germany, Italy, and Japan). The former had to completely destroy the latter by seeking the latter's unconditional surrender. Therefore, the two Western democracies crusaded for a total victory. Once that objective had been achieved, the aggressors were to be entirely disarmed and the peace preserved by the cooperation of the peace-loving nations within the new United Nations. Power politics would be ended; alliances, spheres of influence, and balances of power, said President Roosevelt shortly before his death, were to be replaced by international organization, which represented an alternative and better means for preserving peace. The evil nations having been defeated, no new aggressors were expected. Russia, an ally, was certainly not expected to become an adversary. Good nations/bad nations, power/international organization, war/peace were the mutually exclusive and simple dichotomies.

Thus, although Soviet behavior had already changed by the time hostilities ceased, a period of eighteen months was to elapse before American policy toward Russia was reassessed. Perhaps such a re-evaluation could not have been undertaken any earlier. The American public's attitude toward the Soviet Union was still generally friendly and hopeful about peaceful postwar cooperation. Furthermore, its desire for peace was too strong. The United States wished to be left alone to occupy itself once more with domestic affairs and the fulfillment of American so-

[7] Robert C. Tucker, *The Soviet Political Mind* (New York: Praeger Publishers, 1963), pp. 181–82.

cial values. The end of the war presumably signaled the end of power politics and the restoration of normal peacetime harmony among nations. The emphasis was, therefore, on rapid demobilization. "We want our daddies," cried America's children, and the cry was heard in Congress and the White House. Only when Britain pulled out of the eastern Mediterranean and there was no longer any countervailing power on the European Continent, and only after continued Soviet denunciations and vilifications of the United States and Britain did Washington again commit itself. For this commitment to be made, a large external stimulus was needed.

U.S. identification of Russia as an enemy was the result of Russian actions. U.S. attitudes affected U.S. behavior patterns only *after* the nation had become so engaged. Once that had occurred, however, American moralism was transformed into militant anti-Communism. This was hardly surprising, particularly during the period of extensive and intensive bipolarity. For the antithesis between American democratic values and Soviet Communist values was striking; it was a clear case of good against bad, and it fitted the traditional dichotomy of New World democracy versus Old World autocracy. The impact on the resulting containment policy was readily visible. American policy, for instance, put off any political settlement with Russia until after Communism had "mellowed"—that is, changed its character. Until then, negotiations were thought to be useless not only because of the expansionist aims of the Soviet leadership but also because such diplomatic dealings with the devil in the Kremlin would be immoral. The recognition of Communist China in this atmosphere of anti-Communism became impossible, and China's intervention in Korea only confirmed America's appraisal of Communist regimes as evil, even though America had itself precipitated this intervention by its march up to China's frontier with North Korea.

Similarly, if Communism *per se* was the enemy, then America had to oppose it everywhere—at least where counterbalancing American power could presumably be effectively applied—regardless of whether the system was intensively bipolar or relaxed, or whether the area to be defended was of primary or secondary interest to U.S. security. Almost equally indiscriminately, the United States supported any anti-Communist regime, regardless of whether it was democratic—a Franco, a Chiang Kai-shek, a Diem or Thieu, to name but a few among many. And viewing Communism as truly wicked, the United States viewed all Communist states as uniformly evil. Hence, the recognition of differences among Communist states—and the exploitation of these divisions—was delayed. The impact of nationalism as a divisive factor within the Communist world was played down in the face of the belief that all Communist states were equally immoral. Above all, the issue of foreign policy tended to be posed in terms of a universal struggle between democracy and totalitarianism, freedom and slavery. Thus, at the beginning of the cold war, President Truman stated the issue in Greece as follows: "Totalitarian regimes imposed on free people, by direct or indirect aggression, undermine the foundations of international peace and hence the security of the United States"[8]—although Greece, for all its political and strategic significance, could hardly be classified as a democracy. Presidents after Truman followed his precedent, as American commitments became virtually global.

Because this anti-Communist justification for American foreign policy was in its declaratory statements unqualified by time, place, or circumstance, anti-Communism came back to haunt the policy-makers, especially Democratic ones, as they found that, regardless of preference, they were committed to "tough" policies with little regard for maneuver because, in a two-party system, the "in" party was fearful of being charged with improperly protecting American interests and "coddling Communism." In the wake of Nationalist China's collapse, the Truman Administration thus found itself attacked as "soft on Communism." Indeed, the unquestioned assumption that the United States was omnipotent suggested that the basis for America's failure in China was treason within its own government. For if the nation was omnipotent, it could not be its lack of strength that accounted for its "defeat." It could not be that there was a limit to the nation's ability to influence events far away from its shores. Such setbacks must have been the result of American policies: China fell because the "pro-Communist" administrations of Franklin Roosevelt and Harry Truman had either deliberately or unwittingly "sold China down the river." This charge, which came primarily from the strong conservative wing of the Republican Party (including Joseph R. McCarthy and Richard M. Nixon), was simplicity itself: America's China policy had ended in Communist control of the mainland; Administration leaders and the State Department were responsible for this policy; therefore, the government must harbor Communists and Communist sympathizers who "tailored" American policy to advance the global aims of the Soviet Union.[9] Disloyal American statesmen were responsible for the "loss" of China; it was to them, not to China, that the collapse of Nationalist China was due. Low Nationalist morale, administrative and military ineptitude, and repressive policies that had alienated mass support had nothing to do with it; nor did superior Communist organization, direction, morale, and ability to identify with popular aspirations. Omnipotence, confronted by failure, tended to produce conspiratorial interpretations.[10]

[8] Quoted by Joseph M. Jones, *The Fifteen Weeks* (New York: Viking, 1955), p. 272.

[9] Tang Tsou, *America's Failure in China* (Chicago: University of Chicago Press, 1963), pp. 538–41. For a case study of the accusation of a leading State Department figure by Senator McCarthy, see McGeorge Bundy, *The Pattern of Responsibility* (Boston: Houghton Mifflin, 1952), pp. 201–20.

[10] The repetitious pattern of charges of conspiracy in American political life is elaborated in Richard Hofstadter, *The Paranoid Style in American Politics* (New York: Vintage Books, 1967).

The subsequent conduct of the Korean War provides a good example of the influence of anti-Communism upon foreign policy. The Truman Administration's decision to advance into North Korea was undoubtedly influenced by the fact that a midterm Congressional election was coming up; a victory in Korea could deflect accusations of "softness" on Communism and permit the Democrats to present themselves as vigorous anti-Communist crusaders and defenders of America. The subsequent Chinese intervention, which produced a stalemate at the 38th Parallel—the line on which the war had started—certainly led to a renewal of these charges. One consequence was that Truman could not sign an armistice that accepted the prewar partition of Korea, for this would allegedly represent a peace without victory and would mean risking a Democratic defeat in the coming 1952 Presidential election. Truman was trapped. He could not extend the war without risking greater escalation, casualties, and costs; nor could he end the war. The continuing and frustrating battlefield stalemate was a major factor in the Republican victory in 1952. Only President Eisenhower, who as a war hero could hardly be accused of being an appeaser, could sign a peace accepting the division of Korea.

Similarly, when in 1960 it became popular "to stand up to Castro," Presidential candidate Kennedy dramatized his anti-Communism with vigorous attacks on Castro and suggestions that the Cuban "freedom fighters" be allowed to invade Cuba. When he came into office, he found that the Eisenhower Administration had been planning what he had advocated. Despite his own later uneasy feelings about the CIA-planned and -sponsored invasion, he felt he could not call it off. If the operation was canceled and the news were leaked by its proponents in the government, as well as by the Cuban exiles who had been trained for this invasion and would, in the event of cancelation, be returning to the United States from their overseas training camp, he would stand exposed as being less anti-Communist than his predecessor, as a President who lacked nerve.[11] So, with some changes, he permitted the operation to proceed despite misgivings that turned out to be correct. It was a humiliating personal and national experience for the Administration and, ironically, left Kennedy vulnerable to the accusation that he was unwilling to stand up to the Communists because he would not use American forces to eliminate Castro. Thus, as the situation in Vietnam proceeded to disintegrate later in 1961, it is not surprising that the President would introduce American military "advisers," particularly when the Bay of Pigs had been quickly followed by inaction at the time of the erection of the Berlin Wall and, in Laos, by the agreement to form a coalition government, which the Communist Pathet Lao soon violated by quitting the government in order to attack it.

An additional result of the fear of Communism was the pathological

[11] Theodore C. Sorensen, *Kennedy* (New York: Harper & Row, 1965), pp. 330–32.

domestic proportions it reached. "Reds" were seen not only in government but in the universities, labor unions, churches—everywhere. Communism was portrayed as an all-powerful demonic force seeking to subvert and destroy the American way of life; it had to be rooted out. In this climate of opinion, particularly in the early and middle 1950's, Congress and the state legislatures supported official investigations of private citizens, schools, and government agencies. They demanded "loyalty oaths" from government employees and passed laws directed against subversion and any activities that appeared to be unpatriotic or "un-American." Some states passed "speaker-ban laws," attempting to dictate the policies of state universities concerning visiting lecturers. These were but some of the indications of the extent to which the fear of Communism led to "McCarthyism," or widespread witch-hunting, and anti-Communist zeal took precedence over common sense, academic freedom, "due process," and the spirit of the United States Constitution.[12]

In view of these happenings, it is not surprising that critics of America's most agonizing war, the Vietnam war, see the American intervention in terms of this continued anti-Communism, even though the bipolarity of the cold war days has passed.[13] U.S. policy-makers had lived through the sternest days of the American-Soviet conflict, and they still thought in terms of the "old myths"; given their anti-Communism, they could not see the war as a national struggle for unity. Given the Democrats' memories of the consequences of seeming to be "soft on Communism," a Democratic Administration would particularly wish to avoid the charge of having "lost" Vietnam. Then, too, it was seduced by illusions of omnipotence. After all, where had American power ever failed? Such optimism was expressed most strongly by the civilian policy-makers. When a leading civilian government official was told that eliminating the guerrillas in Vietnam might take as long as it had in Malaya, he curtly responded: "We are *not* the British."[14] Indeed, the assumption was that Hanoi was fearful lest the United States use its power and that, should America indicate its willingness to use it, Hanoi would desist from directing and helping the Vietcong, leaving the latter for Saigon and Washington to mop up. In brief, a major war to prevent the loss of South Vietnam and, in the Administration's opinion, the consequent loss of Southeast Asia, might be averted if North Vietnam could be con-

[12] Richard H. Rovere, *Senator Joe McCarthy* (New York: Harcourt, Brace, 1959). The atmosphere of this period in American history is well reconstructed in Eric F. Goldman, *The Crucial Decade* (New York: Knopf, 1956), pp. 113–44, and Fred J. Cook, *The Nightmare Decade: The Life and Times of Senator McCarthy* (New York: Random House, 1971).

[13] For criticisms of American "globalism," see J. William Fulbright, *The Arrogance of Power* (New York: Vintage, 1967); Edmund Stillman and William Pfaff, *Power and Impotence* (New York: Vintage, 1967); and Ronald Steel, *Pax Americana* (New York: Viking, 1967).

[14] Bill Moyers, President Johnson's special assistant from 1963 to 1966, reports this comment in an interview with *Atlantic* magazine, reprinted in Robert Manning and Michael Janeway, eds., *Who We Are* (Boston: Little, Brown, 1969), p. 262.

vinced of U.S. determination; in the event of noncompliance, Hanoi would be subjected to ever increasing coercion and force. Thus a slow squeeze on Hanoi began in 1964 while the Administration started contingency planning for American air strikes to begin in early 1965.[15]

In Vietnam, U.S. pragmatism combined with a belief that the proper techniques could solve all problems, and the result was the resort to force. Most policy-makers characteristically regarded the subsequent war as essentially a "military" war in which superior fire power and helicopter mobility would enable America to destroy enemy forces. The political aspects of the war, above all the basic land reforms needed to capture the support of the peasantry, were by and large ignored, and therefore no South Vietnamese Government could win popular support. Indeed, the unpopular successive regimes in Saigon seemed almost irrelevant. The fact that counterguerrilla war can be conducted successfully only if political conditions are ripe was ignored. On the contrary, the erosion of governmental authority in Saigon in early 1965 removed the last obstacles to the large buildup of U.S. ground forces and offensive operations. America intended to conduct the war as if it were a conventional, although limited, war. The resulting large-scale search-and-destroy operations rarely found large enemy forces to "chew up"; the enemy, usually informed where U.S. forces would land by the prelanding fighter or artillery bombardments of an area, frequently vanished, leaving behind only frustrated American commanders. Indiscriminate use of air power and artillery fire, which destroyed many Southern hamlets, did little to help create the peasant support needed to win a counterrevolutionary war. It was also apparent from the beginning that the war in South Vietnam could not be won. Instead of examining the political reasons indigenous to South Vietnam, the policy-makers told themselves that the reason it could not be won was primarily military: the infiltration of North Vietnamese troops and weapons. The bombing of the North was expected to remedy this by pounding it into submission. The bombing did not, however, decrease the volume of men and supplies flowing southward, nor did it destroy the people's morale or pressure Hanoi into ending the war. Quite the contrary. Techniques employed in a political vacuum were bound to fail.

As hostilities in Vietnam therefore dragged on and as U.S. casualties and impatience grew,[16] American politics witnessed the reappearance of

[15] For details, see the inside account as revealed in *The Pentagon Papers*. Also see the careful reconstruction of the beginning of the 1965 bombing campaign in Alexander L. George *et al.*, *The Limits of Coercive Diplomacy* (Boston: Little, Brown, 1971), pp. 144–200.

[16] Larry Elowitz and John W. Spanier, "Korea and Vietnam: Limited War and the American Political System," *Orbis*, Summer 1974, pp. 510–34, and John E. Mueller, *War, Presidents and Public Opinion* (New York: Wiley, 1973), who comes to the startling conclusion that the war had no *independent* impact on President Johnson's declining popularity, although the rate of this decline was the same as for Truman in the Korean War. See also Milton J. Rosenberg *et al.*, *Vietnam and the Silent Majority* (New York: Harper & Row, 1970).

a characteristic dichotomy: those who advocated further escalation in the hope of attaining a clear-cut military victory and those who proposed a withdrawal because victory seemed elusive. Indeed, this typical either/or response was frequently advocated by the same persons. Thus, President Johnson found himself increasingly subject to opposing policy pressures. One was to escalate the war; to appease this pressure, which came mainly, as during the Korean War, from conservative and hawkish elements in the Congress, he did in fact escalate. This tended to be momentarily popular, but eventually it rebounded when it failed to achieve victory. On the other hand, he was pressed to withdraw, but this risked leaving his Administration open to the charge of "appeasement." If he chose the middle course of neither expansion nor retreat, domestic opinion would further bifurcate, leaving the center weaker than ever. Whatever he did, the President was trapped. And he could count on little aid from his own party, which was deeply divided.

Not only did the all-or-nothing attitude erode President Johnson's support, leading him to withdraw from seeking a second term of office and producing a Republican victory in the 1968 Presidential election (just as Truman had not run for another term after succeeding Roosevelt, and Eisenhower had defeated Stevenson); it also led to widespread disillusionment with foreign policy and the use of power, especially the use of force. Power politics, it has been suggested, has historically been considered wicked, something engaged in only by the states of the Old World. American power had to be righteous power. Vietnam, where the action could be watched nightly on television in "living color," seemed only to prove again that, in the exercise of power, the nation had been carried away and had forsaken its moral tradition. Driven by an anti-Communism that exaggerated the cohesiveness and threat of the "Sino-Soviet bloc," tempted to intervene in many places and make widespread commitments in the name of anti-Communism, and aligning itself with many a disreputable reactionary regime in the name of freedom, the United States appeared to have violated its own democratic and liberal professions. Thus, the use of power in Vietnam reawakened guilt feelings. Power was a corrupting factor. It was better to concentrate on domestic affairs and return to a historic and venerable duty, that is, complete the unfinished tasks of American society, create a truly democratic nation in which the gap between profession and performance would be minimal, and, as in the early days of the Republic, serve as an example for all mankind.

If power is evil and its exercise tantamount to abuse, providing an example of a just and democratic society to the world was the moral thing to do. In the words of Senator Fulbright, Chairman of the Senate Foreign Relations Committee until 1974, power had made the United States "arrogant," and he counseled that the United States should therefore focus its attention and resources "to serve as an example of democracy to the world" and "overcome the dangers of the arrogance of power." More specifically, "the nation performs its essential function not in its capacity as a *power* but in its capacity as a *society*."[17] Ronald Steel, in criticizing the *pax americana*, has said the same thing more eloquently:

> It is now time for us to turn away from global fantasies and begin our perfection of the human race within our own frontiers. There is a great deal to do at home within a society which a century after the liberation of the slaves still has not been able to grant the Negro full equality, a society which has been plagued with violence in the streets and guilt in the heart, which has achieved unprecedented material riches and yet is sick from a debilitating alienation, where the ideals of American democracy are mocked by the reality of racial prejudice, where individual decency is in constant conflict with social irresponsibility, where prosperity has assured neither justice nor tolerance, where private affluence dramatizes the shame of public squalor, where wealth has brought psychoanalysis, and where power has bred anxiety and fear. This is a society whose extraordinary achievements are now being overshadowed by the urgency of its unfulfilled promises and by dangerous strains in its social fabric.
>
> America's worth to the world will be measured not by the solutions she seeks to impose on others, but by the degree to which she achieves her own ideals at home. That is a fitting measure, and an arduous test, of America's greatness.[18]

Thus the optimistic faith that America, with its great power and missionary zeal, could improve the world was replaced by a mood of disillusionment as, in the wake of Vietnam, it appeared that the wicked world beyond its borders could not be quickly or totally reformed and that the attempt would corrupt the nation. The characteristic cycle, then, seems to begin with a commitment and an attempt to reform the world, which is eventually replaced by a mood of cynicism about whether the world is worthy of being saved by this country, a fear the nation will lose its soul in the effort, and a renewed determination to concentrate on America and improve national life so that the presumed superiority and greater morality of the American way of life will once more radiate to the world and be worthy of imitation. Setting an example for the rest of the world, instead of adulterating its own purity with power politics, is then said to be America's task. The American approach to foreign policy thus seems to remain one of dichotomies: either peace or war, abstention or total commitment, no force or maximum force, and, last but not least, passionate crusading or disillusioned withdrawal.

The moralistic gladiator of today converts into the repentant sinner tomorrow and then swings back again the day after. But as gladiator or repentant sinner, as a defender of orthodoxy or a critic of official policy, the moralism of his political thinking remains constant; so does his expectation that his country can regenerate mankind—by force or by example. Only the American passion for victory remains constant. The

---

[17] Fulbright, *Arrogance of Power*, pp. 256–58.
[18] Steel, *Pax Americana*, pp. 353–54.

right and left both share it. Both march for victory and peace, one by seeking to Americanize the world—thereby redeeming a wicked planet from corruption, the other by withdrawing America as much as possible from the universe (with the exception of aid to the underdeveloped countries, where erasing poverty is viewed as a humanitarian and moral task) in order to avoid being tainted by it. Each assumes that it is in the power of the United States to defeat the enemy or to bring about harmony among nations all by itself. One asks *Why Not Victory?*, the other suggests *The Peace Race*. Both are committed to the proposition that what America wills, it can attain; it needs only the will to achieve its aim. This testimony to American omnipotence, impatience, and moralism would suggest that old, deep-lying attitudes and values—and *especially* basic emotions—continue to exercise a profound impact upon American foreign policy.

Soviet Elite Style

Since foreign policy decisions are not made by nations but by a few decision-makers, some analysts have suggested that perhaps the styles or operational codes of the elite, the small group that makes policy, may be analytically more valuable. The United States has frequently been called a one-class society, not that there were not other classes, but that the basic values of American society were essentially middle-class. De Tocqueville said that America was born middle-class. Thus, for this country, one can argue that the policy elite and the masses do share a fundamental set of beliefs, values, and attitudes. But in other countries, where class structures are more rigid or the elite, even if not a class, is clearly divided from the people in general, elite beliefs and values may provide a significant clue to the decisions a state has—or will—make. This is particularly true for the Soviet elite, with its ideological outlook or *Weltanschauung*.

Almost all debates on Soviet policy revolve around the fundamental issue of the Soviet leaders' self-proclaimed adherence to the official ideology of Marxism-Leninism. Are these leaders really motivated by Communist ideology, or do they merely use it to justify and expand their power? Are they bent on fomenting a world revolution, or are they trying only to increase the strength of Russia as a nation? Are the men in the Kremlin revolutionaries or nationalists? It was suggested earlier in the context of the distribution-of-power analysis that ideologies are, by and large, justifications for what states feel they must do to preserve and enhance their security interests in the state system. In that context, ideologies are instruments to rationalize what would have been done even in the absence of a particular ideology. Ideology is not a motivating force. Thus the Soviet leaders think in terms of the same "national interest" that motivates the behavior of other nation-states. Ideology, it is said, has not led Moscow to adopt any policy that Russian "national interest" did not demand. It has been merely a means for promoting that interest. The manipulation of this ideology to justify any and every change of foreign and domestic policy only "proves" that it is too flexible to be a guide to action.

The opposing contention holds:

> To dismiss ideology as an irrelevant criterion to an understanding of the political conduct of Soviet leaders . . . would be to assume that it is possible to build up a large organization ostensibly dedicated to certain explicit objectives, in which individuals are promoted on the basis both of their professional ability and their demonstrable ideological dedication, but in which an inner sanctum operates, makes decisions with a complete disregard of the ideological principles of the movement, indeed remains immune to the constant pressures for ideological justification, and cynically disregards the official creed.[19]

Ideology in this context is what we earlier called an analytical framework that "organizes reality" for its devotees. It is through the ideological lenses that the latter selectively perceive the world, define and understand it, and decide how to act in it.

Ideology for the Soviet leaders may well be defined as "a comprehensive, consistent, closed system of knowledge, to which its adherents turn to get answers to all questions, solutions to all their problems."[20] Marxism-Leninism as a *Weltanschauung* provides for its believers an all-encompassing picture, a complete explanation of man, society, and history. As a total conceptual framework, it embraces not only economics and politics, but philosophy, science, the arts, and even spiritual matters. No sphere of life is exempt. In addition, it provides a complete critique of existing society and projects the desired future state of existence. Marxism-Leninism is deeply rooted in the belief that almost all social evils are the products of the private ownership of property and the profit motive; simultaneously, it incorporates an apocalyptic image of the future in which its values and domestic structure will come to be universal. The ideology is thus concerned with extensive social change; as Marx said, his purpose was not merely to philosophize about the world but to change it. The ideology is also official, and its interpretation is the task of the Party leaders, who regard their reading of the ideology as embodying the only true view of society and history; as "true believers," such ideologues have been quite dogmatic. Finally, it follows that this kind of ideology is mutually exclusive with any other ideology; by its very nature it is intolerant of contrary beliefs—even, if not especially, when different interpretations of The Truth have been offered by co-believers. These, as we already know, are dismissed as heretics who have deserted "the faith."

[19] Zbigniew K. Brzezinski, *The Soviet Bloc* (Cambridge, Mass.: Harvard University Press, 1967), pp. 388 ff.

[20] Herbert J. Spiro, *Government by Constitution* (New York: Random House, 1959), p. 180.

This stress on ideology as the key factor in the determination of foreign policies of a great power such as the Soviet Union obviously does *not* mean that, in a specific situation, Soviet leaders go to the library and find a statement of what to do clearly spelled out in Marx's *Das Kapital*. It means only that as its first function the ideology provides them with a way of perceiving and interpreting "reality"—with *their* model of the world. Second, it is a total critique of contemporary society, which is condemned as utterly evil and beyond redemption. Third, it defines the long-range, historically appointed purpose the revolutionary movement seeks to achieve. And finally, it legitimates the authority of the leaders of the movement and sanctions the actions they take in seeking their objectives. The assumption, in brief, is that ideology is a motivating force and not merely a rationalization.

After they seized power in 1917, therefore, the new Soviet leaders felt that they represented a *novus ordo seculurum*. It was the prevailing capitalist order that was responsible for the mass of men living in poverty, ill health, and ignorance domestically, and it was capitalism that was the main reason mankind was cursed by war. Thus man could be freed from economic exploitation, political subjugation, and frequent interstate violence only by the destruction of capitalism. The Soviet leaders also believed in History, according to which the laws of economics, which had been discovered by Karl Marx, doomed capitalism; the proletarian revolution, which would usher in a better and more peaceful Communist world, was inevitable. Yet, in fact, Russia's new revolutionary leaders were pessimists at heart. They tended to see their country as a sanctuary, while the rest of mankind was cursed by capitalism. But they were not really convinced that the course of History was ordained or, rather, that History knew the direction in which it was supposed to go. After all, the proletarian revolution was supposed to have occurred in a highly industrialized society in which the working class constituted a majority. But that had not happened because labor, seduced by higher wages and a rising standard of living, had betrayed the proletarian cause. Hence, professional revolutionaries—who, as middle-class professionals and intellectuals, had remained dedicated to the vision of a world without oppression, injustice, and war—had seized power in the name of the proletariat in Russia, an economically backward peasant society, in order to establish a base from which the global regeneration of mankind could start. The "true believers" would have to give History a helping hand by engineering revolutions and imposing the faith that would make man free and ensure his secular salvation. Soviet Communism was thus from the beginning pervaded by a profound self-doubt that, if left alone, History might not in fact give birth to proletarian revolutions. The extension of Communism had therefore to be consciously and constantly pursued. Domestic justice and international peace could be realized only if the old order were swept away throughout the entire state system. All men had to be liberated from social tyranny and the scourge of war.

This meant that Soviet Russia had become a revolutionary power. It denied the legitimacy of what it regarded as the prevailing capitalistic order and the right of non-Communist states—which, by definition, were said to be capitalist—to exist. The basic assumption of the balance of power, however, is precisely each state's right to exist, regardless of its domestic structure. *By claiming universal applicability for its values and ways of organizing domestic society, it made the domestic structures of all other states the central issue of the state system.* The revolutionary state had to extend the revolution to all other states and convert them to the faith "that makes men free"; this was its historic *duty*. Only the worldwide victory of the "new order" could lead to the establishment of a universal society in which man for the first time in history would be truly free from oppression, need, and war.

We already know that no state in a pluralistic system can feel absolutely secure; yet, while obviously greatly concerned with its security, it does not normally feel so insecure that it becomes completely preoccupied with its survival and seeks universal domination, thereby eliminating the threats from all other states. It seeks security within a balance of power system that guarantees its right to exist, as well as the survival of other states. Conflicts are therefore limited and pragmatic; no state seeks another's total destruction. Each recognizes the right of the other states to exist. But different domestic structures tend to introduce conflicting values and goals into the system, and the political relations among states begin to be conducted according to conflicting interpretations of *the legitimacy of the system and the existence of its component members*, the acceptable limits of ambition, and the proper methods of carrying on these relations. This, in turn, means that the conflict tends to become total. If one state feels compelled to destroy the domestic structures of other states and transform them according to its own ideological values, that state must seek a monopoly of power. It cannot be interested in preserving a balance and the prevailing state system. It seeks to overthrow the balance as a prerequisite to remaking that system in its own image.

In a brilliant and eloquent passage, George Kennan has described how this revolutionary approach to foreign policy made a "mockery of the entire Western theory of international relationships, as it evolved in the period from the seventeenth to the nineteenth centuries":

> The national state of modern Europe, bitterly as it might feud with its neighbors over the questions of *relative* advantage, was distinguished from the older forms of state power by its abandonment of universalistic and messianic pretensions, by its general readiness to recognize the equality of existence of other sovereign authorities, to accept their legitimacy and independence, and to concede the principle of live and let live as a basic rule in the determination of international relationships. . . .
>
> It was this theory that the Bolsheviki challenged on their assumption of power in Russia. They challenged it by the universality of their own

ideological pretensions—by the claim, that is, to an unlimited universal validity of their own ideas as to how society ought to be socially and politically organized. They challenged it by their insistence that the laws governing the operation of human society demanded the violent overthrow everywhere of governments which did not accept the ideological tenets of Russian Communism, and the replacement of these governments by one that did. . . .

The significance of this situation has been somewhat obscured by those Western historians and commentators who have been unable to perceive any difference in principle between the attitude of the Soviet Union toward the Western countries and that of the Western countries toward the Soviet Union. After all, they have said, were not the Western governments equally hostile to Russia? Did they not attempt to overthrow the Soviet regime by their intervention in 1918–1919? Could the challenge to existing concepts of international relations properly be laid only at the Soviet door? Was not the Western rejection of socialism as a conceivable governmental system just as important in the breakdown of the established theory of international life as the Soviet rejection of capitalism?

It is my belief that the answer to these questions is "No." Any unclarity on this point can lead to a grievous misunderstanding of some of the basic elements of Soviet-Western relations. There were, in those initial years of Soviet power, some very significant differences between anti-Sovietism in the West and the hostility which the Soviet leaders entertained for the Western powers. This hostility from the Communist side is preconceived, ideological, deductive. In the minds of the Soviet leaders, it long predated the Communist seizure of power in Russia. Anti-Sovietism in the West, on the other hand, was largely a confused, astonished, and indignant reaction to the first acts of the Soviet regime. Many people in the Western governments came to hate the Soviet leaders for what they *did*. The Communists, on the other hand, hated the Western governments for what they *were*, regardless of what they did. They entertained this feeling long before there was even any socialistic state for the capitalists to do anything to. Their hatred did not vary according to the complexion or policies or actions of the individual non-Communist governments. It never has. . . .

Surely, this approach cannot be equated with that of the pragmatic West, where for forty years the argument over the attitude to be taken toward Soviet power has revolved around the questions of interpretation of the behavior of the Soviet regime. There have undoubtedly been individuals here and there in the Western countries whose hatred of what they understood to be socialism has been so great that they have felt it should be rooted out with fire and sword, on straight ideological grounds, wherever it raised its head. But such people, surely, have been few; and I do not think that their views have ever been dominant in any of the major Western governments. . . . Had the Soviet leaders contented themselves from the outset with saying that they felt that they knew what was good for Russia, and refrained from taking positions on what was good for other countries, Western hostility to the Soviet Union would never have been what it has been. The issue has never been, and is not today, the right of the Russian people to have a socialistic ordering of society if they so wish; the issue is how a government which happens to be socialistic is going to behave in relation to its world environment.[21]

Marxism-Leninism, then, first of all gave the new rulers of *Soviet* Russia a comprehensive analytical framework; in its terms, the Soviet leadership has perceived the world, defined the principal operational social and economic forces, discriminated between friend and foe, established Moscow's *long-range* goals, and provided a continuing commitment to them. This was the crucial difference: Unlike the Czars, Soviet policy-makers perceived national security in the context of their long-range offensive aims. In the days before Tito and Mao, Moscow conceived of Soviet security in universal terms; no lasting national security could be achieved until all states were Communist. The new Soviet Russia was the base for a world revolution and the nucleus of a future proletarian world order.

Second, and following logically, the ideology clearly defined the enemy as the capitalist states. The revolutionary state, by definition, is committed to the elimination of the old order. The struggle to achieve this must be prosecuted with vigor and persistence; to relax from this historical struggle is tantamount to a betrayal of the revolutionary mission. Victory over capitalism is the *raison d'être* of the movement. This does not mean that "peaceful coexistence" until the moment of victory is impossible. There is no special emphasis in Communist doctrine on the use of force, as in Nazi doctrine.

> The Kremlin is under no ideological compulsion to accomplish its purposes in a hurry. Like the Church, it is dealing in ideological concepts which are of long term validity, and it can afford to be patient. It has no right to risk the existing achievements of the revolution for the sake of vain baubles of the future.[22]

Soviet doctrine does not, therefore, reject temporary relaxation of the struggle if time is needed to recoup one's strength or build greater strength; nor does it frown upon accords with adversaries. These are viewed as tactical changes required by the "ebb and flow" of prevailing circumstances; but the ultimate objectives remain. The question is not whether these objectives are to be abandoned, only how they can best be realized. The struggle must go on, for the long-range aims are given and unchangeable; only the methods to be employed are flexible. Cooperation and negotiations do not mean the end of conflict; rather, they are ways of conducting it.

Third, as just suggested, this total conflict between the Soviets and the non-Communist world was perceived as irreconcilable and unending—until the moment of victory. The basic "fact" of history was the exist-

---

[21] George F. Kennan, *Russia and the West Under Lenin and Stalin* (Boston: Little, Brown, 1961), pp. 179–83. Emphasis in original. Used by permission of the publisher.

[22] Kennan, *American Diplomacy 1900–1950*, p. 118.

ence of a condition of continuing and irreconcilable conflict between classes or, more specifically, between states controlled by antagonistic classes. Politics was not a means of reconciliation.[23] It was an unending series of "campaigns" whose aim was to defeat the capitalist enemy. The only question was *kto—kovo?* ("Who, whom?" meaning "who will destroy whom?").[24] Marxism-Leninism, to reemphasize, conferred upon the commissars aims the Czars had never possessed and infused Soviet policy with a compulsion to exploit all opportunities to expand whenever these presented themselves and whenever such attempts to assist history did not endanger the base of the revolution. "The main thing," Kennan has said, "is that there should always be pressure, increasing constant pressure, toward the desired goal."[25] At the same time, no risks were to be taken which might endanger the home of the revolution.

The impact of this ideological image of the external world and the nature of politics greatly enhanced the degree of suspicion and fear among states that already existed as a result of the system's anarchical nature. It was this additional measure of skepticism and apprehension that, for example, made it as impossible to achieve after World War II the *modus vivendi* arrived at after 1815. Perhaps the most significant characteristic of the Soviet leaders' thinking was the distinction they made between objective and subjective factors. The former were those fundamental economic and *objectively existing forces* that determined the social structures and political behavior of any state. Thus any Soviet leadership was bound to see the international environment as *extremely* hostile and instill in it a deep distrust of any Western state, however benevolent its expressed intentions; indeed, since it assumed that the Western states were out to destroy it—as it was bent on destroying them—its attitude toward what it saw as a capitalist-dominated system bordered on paranoia. Consequently, it was immaterial during World War II whether Stalin subjectively or personally liked Roosevelt. For Stalin *knew* that the deeper objective forces of the economic substructure, upon which the social and political superstructure rested, would really determine Roosevelt's actions: The American President was merely a puppet—even if a likable puppet—of Wall Street; governmental decisions simply reflected the "laws" of capitalism.

Thus, in 1941–45, Moscow saw the United States as but a temporary ally; once Germany was defeated, America, as the strongest Western capitalist power, would be Russia's principal enemy in the continuing

[23] " 'Compromise,' which is the daily product of our political system, is an evil word in the Soviet vocabulary, the word 'reasonable' has no real equivalent in Russian, and, more fundamentally, Soviet leadership feels that its moral right to rule rests on the 'correctness' of its analyses." Philip E. Mosely, *The Kremlin and World Politics* (New York: Vintage Books, 1960), p. 296.

[24] Nathan Leites, *A Study of Bolshevism* (New York: Free Press, 1953), pp. 27–63, and Robert Strausz-Hupé et al., *Protracted Conflict* (New York: Harper & Row, 1959), pp. 21–22.

[25] Kennan, *American Diplomacy 1900–1950*, p. 118.

struggle with capitalism. The United States, thinking in the terms of its historic approach to international politics, saw World War II as a temporary dislocation of the normal, peaceful condition among nations. After the conclusion of hostilities, American policy-makers expected to live in harmony and friendship with the Soviet Union. The chief American objective in Europe in 1941–45 was the strictly military goal of Germany's unconditional surrender in the quickest possible time. The aim was total victory and the elimination of Hitler. A postwar balance of power against Russia played no role in the formulation of American wartime planning and strategy. Soviet policy, however, foreseeing postwar conflict, remained highly suspicious of the West, and, in the wake of the retreating German armies, Russia quickly consolidated its hold on Eastern Europe in a successful attempt to extend its power.

Stalin, after all, was not suspicious of just American capitalists.[26] He was suspicious of his colleagues as well—so much so that when they were invited to dinner, as Khrushchev later revealed, they were never sure they would be returning home. And he was suspicious of the Red Army soldiers who had seen Eastern Europe and Germany—as destroyed as these were—because he feared they might be infected with the bourgeois virus; so he ordered them to be "re-ideologized." Many Russian prisoners of war were shipped to Siberia for this task, never to be seen again. Stalin was even fearful of his writers, artists, and musicians. It would have been a miracle if, in these circumstances, Stalin had not been suspicious of the Western states, no matter how benevolent their intentions.

Ironically, given Stalin's expectations, the war years had created a great reservoir of good will toward the Soviet Union both in America and in Western Europe. Russia had borne the brunt of the German armies, and the heroism of the Red Army and the Russian people was acclaimed everywhere. Stalin, the dictator who had collaborated with Hitler in 1939–41, became "Uncle Joe," as American leaders talked of a new era of good relations with Russia. In America and Britain, hopes for the postwar period were high; in France, where the Communists had played a leading role in the resistance movement, Russia was also much admired. By and large, the Soviet Union was described in glowing terms —virtually as a democracy—just as it was later pictured in almost satanic terms. Concerned as Russia was about its security in Eastern Europe, given this atmosphere, it should have been easily reassured. Had the Soviet Union left Poland, Hungary, Rumania, and Bulgaria internally autonomous while securing control of their foreign policies, as it did in postwar Czechoslovakia, it could have avoided arousing and alienating America and Britain. The Western states accepted the Soviet contention that Eastern Europe was Russia's security belt. But they felt that coalition governments that included Communists could be friendly to the Russians *and* to the West. Eduard Beneš in Czechoslovakia seemed

[26] Adam B. Ulam, *Expansion and Coexistence* (New York: Praeger Publishers, 1968), pp. 398–402.

a symbol of this model for Eastern Europe—until the Russians overthrew his coalition government.

Thus the Soviets emptied the reservoir of good will quickly. Why? No doubt one reason lay in the fact that the ideology, exclusive and intolerant, was incompatible with, and hostile toward, an open society and multiple competing groups. But this only accounts for the Soviets' wholesale conversion of the East European states into satellites. What about the *timing* of the Soviet moves? This cannot be explained only by the presence of the Red Army throughout most of the area; above all, it was the result of the ideologically induced expectation that the immediate postwar period would be one of social and political upheaval and, therefore, would be an opportune time for the extension of Soviet power. It was anticipated that the United States would suffer another depression once war production ceased and, as a result, it would withdraw once more into its traditional isolationist posture. During the war, Roosevelt had in fact told Stalin that American troops would be withdrawn from Europe within two years of Germany's surrender. At the same time, Russia knew that the instability of Europe once Germany was defeated would not last forever, and American capitalism would eventually recover. Thus the opportunity brought on by the fluidity of the immediate postwar situation had to be seized.[27]

It may be true that much of Russia's expansionist policy in the wake of the retreating German armies can actually be explained in systemic terms. But it can hardly be doubted that the Soviet leaders' perception of the capitalist states as permanently hostile made it impossible for them to believe in the professions of good will and friendly intentions by President Roosevelt. And their perception of the Soviet Union's role in the world made it impossible for them to abstain from exploiting the weaknesses they found to Russia's south and west in an effort to extend socialism from one country to a larger area. Thus, the relative security the Soviet leaders could have gained for Russia by acting more cautiously was squandered by their own ideological thinking and ideologically induced behavior. First they aroused British and then American opposition; high international tension was in good part, then, due to ideology rather than mere power distribution.

Communist ideology has also influenced the behavior of non-Communist states, as during the interwar period. The French effort—aided by France's allies in Eastern Europe—to contain Germany illustrates this point. In addition to its alliance with the members of the Little Entente, France signed a treaty with Russia; it, in turn, signed one with Czechoslovakia. But the French were never to implement the alliance. In 1938, France's Little Entente partners suspected that if they ever let the Red Army pass through their territories to come to the aid of the Czechoslovak Government, it would never leave. As for the French, they were

[27] *Ibid.*, p. 410, and Paul E. Zinner, "The Ideological Bases of Soviet Foreign Policy," *World Politics*, July, 1952, pp. 497–98.

highly suspicious of Communist Russia, in part because of the sizable French Communist Party and the French bourgeoisie's fear of social revolution, and in part because of the government's fear that if it aided Czechoslovakia Moscow would stand by until France and Germany had weakened each other sufficiently to leave Russia in the predominant position on the Continent. Yet France and Czarist Russia had been allies before World War I. It was only after that conflict and the ensuing Bolshevik Revolution that French-Soviet relations became so loaded with mutual suspicions because of the Communist nature of Russia's leadership that no meaningful alliance was possible.

In Great Britain as well, interwar actions were influenced by strong suspicions of Russian motives. When, after Munich, Chamberlain's British government responded to pressures from Churchill and other anti-Munich Conservatives and sought an alliance with Russia, it was so suspicious of Soviet revolutionary aims that it moved at a snail's pace; probably to its relief, Hitler signed up Stalin first. During World War II, these suspicions were reduced because Roosevelt and Churchill tended to see Russia as primarily a Czarist state. Various factors influenced this assessment: the apparent identity of Soviet aims with traditional Russian foreign policy objectives (for example, its concern for the security of Eastern Europe and its search for a warm-water port); the Soviet stress on the "Great Fatherland War," which highlighted Russian nationalism and tended to obscure Soviet Communism; the dissolution of the Comintern; the replacement of the "Internationale" with a Russian national anthem; the relaxation of restrictions upon the church; and the West's own hope that the wartime cooperation would mitigate, if not remove, Soviet suspicions of the West—particularly if the West proved its sincerity by recognizing Russia's historic security interests. Even the anti-Communist Churchill of the prewar period had talked of a postwar peace guarded by the "Four Policemen"—the United States, Britain, Russia, and China: "I wished to meet the Russian grievance, because the government of the world must be entrusted to satisfied nations, who wished nothing more for themselves than what they had. If the world government were in the hands of hungry nations, there would always be danger."[28] If they were jointly to preserve the peace, all four states would have to be satisfied. Churchill's assumption was that, while Stalin might be hungry, his appetite was limited and an appropriate meal could therefore be served to satiate him. Uncle Joe was merely an heir to Nicholas II. This assumption was, to be sure, more hope than reality. But it was a genuine hope. Perhaps wartime cooperation would erode Soviet suspicions and fear about Western intentions; in any event, the attempt to win Russia's friendship had to be made if a major postwar conflict was to be avoided.

Not until the Allied invasion of France, in June, 1944, would Church-

[28] Winston S. Churchill, *Second World War*, Vol. V: *Closing the Ring* (Boston: Houghton Mifflin, 1948), pp. 363, 382.

ill's apprehensions about Communist policy become reawakened by Russia's behavior in Eastern Europe. But it was the postwar Labour Government that would take the initiative in mobilizing opposition to Soviet moves in Europe (although revisionists tend to forget this). Even then, Washington was still hopeful. Indeed, throughout the war years and immediately thereafter, Washington thought of itself as a mediator between Moscow and London. Assuming that Russia and Britain would police the Continent, Washington preferred to act as the impartial referee between two friends whose ambitions clashed in Eastern Europe and the Eastern Mediterranean. Not until the Truman Doctrine did the wartime assumption about Russia as a state with legitimate and moderate aims become replaced by an assumption that its aims were of a greater scope and the recognition that America would have to take the initiative in organizing the West to contain Russian power.

If Communist ideology intensified the suspicions already stemming from the nature of the state system, such suspicions were not limited to Soviet attitudes toward the Western powers (and their reciprocal attitude toward Moscow). For the Soviet Union was also suspicious of other Communist states, as was revealed when, right after the war, Stalin expelled Tito—a loyal Stalinist until then—from the Soviet bloc. It was revealed even more dramatically in Communist Russia's whole relationship with Communist China, where it simply proved impossible for these two giants of the Communist world to maintain a long-term mutually beneficial alliance. Conflicts among Communist nations were supposed to be nonexistent, for antagonism between states was ostensibly the result of the competing interests of their dominant classes. Because Communist states were professedly classless societies, no strife between them should have occurred. But the problem was that the Soviet Union was no longer the only powerful Communist state and that its monopoly over defining the "truth"—that is, its total control of decision-making —was being challenged. In part, Moscow had only itself to blame for this undermining of its authority. One of the functions of Communist ideology is to legitimize those who hold authority. Communist ideology was therefore intended to legitimize the Soviet leaders both as the rulers of the Soviet Union and—when the Soviet Union was the only socialist state—as the directors of the international Communist movement. Just as there can be only one Pope, there can be only one source of ideological pronouncements in a secular movement like Communism. Moscow was this infallible source. But Peking challenged Moscow's papal authority and monopoly of political wisdom. In the resulting inter-Party conflict, each contender claimed to possess the correct interpretation of history and to be the true interpreter of the Party theology. Thus, within years of Stalin's death, each denounced the other for heresy. Claiming to be the fundamentalists, the Chinese saw themselves as remaining true to Marxism-Leninism, which they felt Moscow had betrayed. Moscow, the Communist Rome, and Khrushchev, the new Communist Pope (and later Brezhnev), were thus challenged by Mao Tse-tung's Eastern Orthodox Church. How could China possibly follow a nation whose Communism was "phony," whose revisionist domestic policies were "rapidly swelling the forces of capitalism" inside Russia,[29] and whose foreign policy was aligning itself with the United States against China at this time?[30]

Compromise on common policies between *Communist* Russia and *Communist* China was to be an insuperable obstacle. In matters of doctrine, where the purity of the theology is at stake, would not a policy of give and take contaminate that purity? How can mutual adjustments be made between two members of a movement in which differences of emphasis become issues of loyalty to the faith? How could Moscow's primacy, the Kremlin's infallibility, and its doctrinal purity be made compatible with Peking's desire for co-primacy, Maoist infallibility, and Chinese ideological fundamentalism? The Western allies, themselves pluralistic societies, can cope with pluralism and diversity. But the Communist states cannot, because domestically their parties impose a uniform pattern in accordance with their ideological interpretation. Each is a totalitarian society precisely because the Party claims that it is the bearer of the revealed "truth," which must be imposed upon the society because "the truth will make men free." Conversely, all heresy must be ruthlessly eliminated. How then can two such states, each convinced that its interpretation of the truth is the only correct one, coexist? Non-revolutionary great powers at least share a degree of toleration. If they are allies, like France and America, they can resolve differences as mere conflicts of interests without the additional burden of an unresolvable superimposed conflict between "good" and "evil." Nor, where differences of interest continue to exist, do they affect the totality of their relationship and necessarily lead to a virtually complete rupture. However, the self-righteous—for the righteous in arguments always tend to become self-righteous—exhibit no such tolerance. When ideology is so intimately linked with power, as it is in Communist policy and decision-making, then there can be only one "correct" answer. Divergent policies cannot be compromised, and these differences will affect the entire range of their relations. The flavor of the resulting bitterness between Moscow and Peking in their papal quarrel over who is orthodox and who is heretical can only be savored through their own incredible verbal exchanges:

> After Stalin's death [say the Chinese] Khrushchev, a capitalist-roader in power hiding in the Soviet Communist party . . . usurped party and government power in the Soviet Union. This was a counter-revolutionary *coup d'état* which turned the dictatorship of the proletariat into the dic-

29 *New York Times*, July 14, 1964.
30 *Ibid.*, February 6, 1966.

tatorship of the bourgeoisie and which overthrew socialism and restored capitalism. [The Soviet Union is] a dictatorship of the German fascist type, a dictatorship of the Hitler type.[31]

Matters have gone so far [replied the Soviets] that Hitler's raving about the need to "save" the people from the "Slav threat" has been taken out of the mothballs. The people in Peking emulate the ring-leaders of the Nazi Reich in attempting to portray the Soviet Union as a "colossus with feet of clay. . . ."

By their actions the Peking leaders leave no doubt that they strive to use the heroic freedom struggle of the peoples in their global intrigues that stem from the Great Han dreams of becoming the new emperors of "The Great China" that would rule at least Asia, if not the whole world.[32]

In these circumstances, it is clear that the essence of any give and take is blocked by the insistence on doctrinal purity. One "correct" answer demands a single center of political authority and ideological orthodoxy. *Any relationship between Communist states must therefore be hierarchical in nature; it cannot be one of equality.* Either Moscow or Peking must be the source of Communist theological interpretation *and* the source of policy in most, if not all, issue areas.

A Comparison of American and Soviet Styles

On the eve of the cold war, it should be clear by now, the styles of the two superpowers contrasted sharply. With regard to their respective perceptions of the nature of politics—especially their images of conflict—the American emphasis on an international harmony of interests stands in stark contrast to the state system's emphasis on the inevitability of conflict and differences of interests among states. The former view regards conflict as an abnormal condition, the latter perceives harmony as an illusion. The United States, long isolated from Europe and therefore not socialized into the state system, did not accept the reality and permanence of conflicts among its members. Differences between states were not considered natural, and certainly not deep and long-range; rather, they were attributed to wicked leaders (who could be eliminated), authoritarian political systems (which could be reformed), or misunderstandings (which could be straightened out if the adversaries approached each other with sincerity and empathy). Once these obstacles had been removed, peace, harmony, and good will would reign supreme. The Soviet emphasis, on the other hand, is on the inevitable nature of conflict with capitalist states. Conflict is not the result of wicked capitalist political leaders; they might be very decent and likable men, but the point is not their personality but the systems they represent. Nor is conflict the result of a misapprehension; there is nothing accidental

---

[31] *New York Times*, May 3, 1970.
[32] *Ibid.*

about it. Real peace and harmony will come only after capitalism, the real cause of rivalry between states, has been eliminated and replaced by world Communism; until then, it is only natural, indeed imperative, to exploit existing competition and conflict to advance Soviet Russia's cause.

Above all, America has always considered itself a morally and politically superior society due to its democratic culture. This has meant that its attitude toward the use of power internationally has been dominated by the belief that the struggle for power did not exist or could be avoided by isolating oneself from it or could be eliminated by crusading against those countries indulging in power politics. Moralism in foreign policy proscribed the use of power in peacetime lest one became tainted; it could be employed only in confrontations with unambiguous aggression, transformed then into an obligation to fight on behalf of righteous causes. In short, power, internationally just as domestically, can be legitimated only by democratic purposes; otherwise, its exercise would be evil and would necessarily arouse guilt feelings.

The Soviet belief in unceasing and irreconcilable conflict means an acceptance of power as an instrument of policy, a means dedicated to the pursuit of the end of Communism. But this power is used with care and restraint:

> [The Kremlin] has no compunction about retreating in the face of superior force. And being under the compulsion of no timetable, it does not get panicky under the necessity for such retreat. Its political action is a fluid stream which moves constantly, wherever it is permitted to move, toward a given goal. . . . But if it finds unassailable barriers in its path, it accepts these philosophically and accommodates itself to them. The main thing is that there should always be pressure, increasing constant pressure, toward the desired goal. There is no trace of any feeling in Soviet psychology that that goal must be reached at any given time.[33]

The Soviet use of power is not, therefore, subject to cyclical swings from isolationism to crusading and back again, as used to be the American pattern. Power is the raw material of international politics, to be applied discriminatingly and cautiously toward the achievement of specific and less-than-total objectives in each challenge and/or response. Its use arouses no sense of guilt; the issue is whether it is successfully employed to advance Soviet goals. It is used to probe for soft spots in the adversary's positions; if countered, it is called off, however humiliating. "Adventurism" and "romanticism" which might provoke the enemy too greatly and endanger the base of the world revolution are to be abjured.

But perhaps the most telling symptom of American's national style in conducting foreign policy is that, after every major war, the reasons for the country's participation in struggle and bloodshed have been reinterpreted. These revisionist histories have certain common themes: The conflicts in which the nation had become entangled did not in fact

---

[33] Kennan, *American Diplomacy*, p. 118.

threaten its security interests; it became involved because the politicians saw a menace where none existed, and this illusion had been promoted by propagandists who aroused and manipulated public opinion, by soldiers with bureaucratic motives, and, above all else, by bankers and industrialists—the "merchants of death" of the 1930's, the "military industrial complex" of the 1960's—whose economic interests benefited from the struggle. America's engagements in the two world wars of this century (as in the cold war later) were mistakes; they were really unnecessary or immoral, if not both. The evil enemy yesterday identified as the aggressor and *provocateur* thus apparently did not represent a threat to American security at all; to the contrary, the threat turns out to have been from within, not from without. In brief, but for certain *domestic forces*, the United States could have continued to isolate itself from international politics.

Revisionism, symbolically enough, is perhaps then the deepest symptom of the aversion to "power politics." Revisionism, the distinguished American diplomatic historian Dexter Perkins has written, always seeks to convince the public that "every war in which this country has been engaged was really quite unnecessary or immoral or both; and that it behooves us in the future to pursue policies very different from those pursued in the past."[34] What is most striking about the revisionists' claims that the cold war was avoidable (a conclusion derived from their sole emphasis on second-level analysis) is that they really believe that, but for America's purported anti-Communism and lack of sensitivity to Russian interests, the superpower conflict would not have erupted—as if, in the state system (according to our first-level analysis) conflict was not inherent *regardless* of the internal nature of the powers that, after World War II, had to arrange a new power distribution to provide a modicum of safety and stability in an anarchical international system.[35] The revi-

[34] Dexter Perkins, "American Wars and Critical History," *Yale Review*, Summer, 1951, pp. 682–95.

[35] For some of the revisionist history placing the responsibility for the beginning of the cold war upon the United States, see among others D. F. Fleming, *The Cold War and Its Origins*, 2 vols. (Garden City, N.Y.: Doubleday, 1961); Gar Alperovitz, *Atomic Diplomacy: Hiroshima and Potsdam* (New York: Vintage Books, 1967); William A. Williams, *The Tragedy of American Diplomacy* (Cleveland: World, 1959); Gabriel Kolko, *The Politics of War: The World and United States Foreign Policy, 1943–1945* (New York: Random House, 1968); and Thomas G. Paterson, *Soviet American Confrontation* (Baltimore: Johns Hopkins Press, 1973).

Evaluations of the Fleming-Alperovitz thesis, which directly blames American anti-Communism (the Williams-Kolko school finds the fault in the imperialistic nature of American capitalism) may be found in Arthur Schlesinger, Jr., "The Origins of the Cold War," *Foreign Affairs*, October, 1967, pp. 22–52; J. L. Richardson, "Cold War Revisionism: A Critique," *World Politics*, July, 1972, pp. 579 ff.; and John Spanier, "The Choices We Did Not Have: In Defense of Containment," in Charles Gati, ed., *Caging the Bear* (New York: Bobbs-Merrill, 1974), pp. 128 ff. The Gati book is an evaluation of Kennan and Containment, twenty-five years after his "X" article. Finally, particularly for an assessment focusing on the economic interpretations of U.S. policy, see Robert W. Tucker, *The Radical Left and American Foreign Policy* sionists have instead written the new Versailles "guilt" literature. Just as, in the 1930's, British and French revisionist historians suggested that, but for the harsh Versailles Peace Treaty imposed upon Germany in 1919, Germany would not be threatening the peace of the world, so contemporary revisionists have suggested that the cold war was totally America's fault. In short, but for Versailles there would have been no Hitler; and because of the injustice of Versailles, Britain and France should have felt guilty and without any *moral* right to deny Nazi Germany its "legitimate claims." Similarly, but for U.S. anti-Communism, Stalin's fears and suspicions would not have been aroused and there would have been no need for the Soviet-American clash of interests; Stalin had only Russia's limited and legitimate interests in mind.

A change in *American* behavior is thus the remedy. If America abandons its anti-Communism, there will be no need for cold wars, interventions, or large military budgets. Instead, it can build the truly just society at home, a wiser and more moral policy.

> The reluctance, or the inability, to face the humiliating facts of international life is as noticeable in America as it was in the Britain of 30 years ago—at least among the young and the intellectuals. When they could no longer see their country as the noble, disinterested guardian on the ramparts of freedom, when the competitive pursuit of security could no longer be glamorized as a fight for the highest values, many sought refuge in the old illusion that one only has to recognize the beam in one's own eye to remove the splinter from that of one's opponent and thus live happily together forever after.[36]

Such an attitude, which seeks to deny the reality of international struggle and suggests it can be avoided, is not to be found among the characteristics of Soviet style.

A Critique of National and Elite Styles

Finally, there remains the basic question: Is there really such a thing as national style? How can one be sure that when a decision is made it is the result of a national style? For one thing, can we distinguish between the style of a single nation and that of several nations whose governments and political systems are similar? Robert Tucker, in emphasizing pragmatism, talked of this characteristic of policy-making as Western, not just American; the British have long been proud of what they refer to as their pragmatism in foreign affairs. George Kennan has always focused

---

(Baltimore: Johns Hopkins Press, 1971). For an analysis that suggests either poor scholarship or deliberate distortion of the documents, see Robert J. Maddox, *The New Left and the Origins of the Cold War* (Princeton, N.J.: Princeton University Press, 1973).

[36] J. H. Huizinga, "America's Lost Innocence," *New York Times Magazine*, January 26, 1969, p. 82.

on the international behavior of democracies, not merely America's crusading style. Fred Iklé, in comparing Western and Soviet negotiating techniques, notes certain features as distinctively Western: letting the opponent determine the issues to be negotiated; being shy about making counter-demands; fear of offering unacceptable proposals; and denying oneself available threats. Why? Because the Western negotiating style, heavily influenced by compromise and conciliation at home, believes in meeting conflicting demands halfway, in splitting the difference; not to do so is considered improper, and to make counter-demands or invoke threats is immoral. Good will and a sincere commitment to settle are believed to be the right way of doing things—although, for example, not exploiting a threat may leave one's own interests unsatisfied, not stating a seemingly unacceptable demand will make it so to the opponent, fortify his commitments because the expectation will be not to yield, and narrow the parameters of the Western diplomatic position (or, as we saw in Berlin after 1958, the refusal to state counter-demands left only Soviet demands on the books, which in turn meant that any compromise would have undermined the West's own position. Luckily, it was part of the Russian style to "ask for a whole loaf where they could get a half a loaf —and end up with nothing").[37]

Interestingly enough, as in Iklé's analysis of Western and Soviet diplomacy, Western states' national styles tend to be lumped together while the Soviet style is treated as distinctive. When dealing with regimes whose outlooks are all characterized by a Marxist-Leninist perspective, we no longer in fact talk of how the Communists do this or that; rather, we talk of Soviet Communists, Chinese Communists, Yugoslav Communists, and Rumanian Communists to stress how national attitudes infuse the perceptions of any set of Communist leaders. Yet, can we really deny that certain American or British ways of perceiving and handling foreign policy problems are not uniquely national, or that certain forms of behavior are not common to most, if not all, Communist elites?

A second problem is more obvious: Are we not really talking of the style of the policy-makers rather than the nation? Policy is decided by a relatively few people on behalf of the nation; the people do not make policy. At best, they have the opportunity to change their leaders every few years if, in retrospect, they did not like the government's policies; public opinion may also affect policy in between elections. But by and large the public—in a democracy at least—reacts to decisions after they are made and sets the outer limits within which the responsible officials make their decisions. Would it not, therefore, be analytically more useful to focus on these officials, as we did when we defined the Soviet style largely in terms of the ideological preferences and outlook of the Kremlin leaders, rather than a broad national style? Do the few who make pol-

[37] Fred Iklé, *How Nations Negotiate* (New York: Harper & Row, 1964), pp. 238–53.

icy share national preferences and attitudes and ways of behaving? The difficulty of distinguishing an elite style from a national style is evidenced particularly in the Soviet case where it ought to be easier to separate the Communist and national elements.

Is Russian expansion due to Soviet or Russian influences? Is Communism merely a tool of a long-standing, pre-Bolshevik expansionist tradition? Edward Crankshaw, a close British observer of Russian affairs, argues that "Russia has been an expanding power since the foundation of the Muscovite state in the fourteenth century"[38] because of strategic, economic, and missionary factors. Like Halle earlier, Crankshaw suggests that Russia has been expansionist for essentially defensive reasons because it is not protected as England and the United States are by oceans, or Italy and Spain by mountain barriers. "The Russians voyaged across the (Russian) plain, much as Tudor seamen explored the oceans. It is hard to know where to stop. If the Muscovites themselves had not expanded outwards from their centre and deep into the plain, their neighbors would have done so in their place."[39] Russian leaders, with no natural barriers for protection, have thus become obsessed with security and expanded along lines of least resistance to keep "the enemy at the gates" as far away as possible.[40] Economic reasons, especially the search for maritime outlets, plus Moscow's vision of itself as the Third Rome (the real heir to Christian leadership and exponent of the true Christian faith after the fall of Constantinople), reinforced this expansionist tradition and even gave it a strong missionary or messianic touch. Experience in the state system, geographical position, strategic and economic reasons, in short, are all concrete, specific, and material. By contrast, ideology tends to be verbal, broad, and subject to many different and usually conflicting interpretations; indeed the practical relevance of ideology for making foreign policy decisions is indeed questionable. Is ideology not invoked more as a rationalization for decisions than a cause for them? What, then, is Soviet in Soviet Russian foreign policy? What is Russian? What in U.S. policy is American and what is unique to the policy-making elite; indeed—if we wish to be even more empirical and careful in our analysis—what is unique to liberal policy-makers like Truman or Kennedy as distinct from more conservative ones like Eisenhower or Nixon?

Third, does not the concept of national style assume that characteristics carry over from one generation to another? Yet common sense tells us that, even if there is such a thing as national style, some of its characteristics will change over time. Vietnam, it has been suggested, was the product of a crusading style; but, some critics have suggested, this costly tragedy may at least have the beneficial result of sobering this country

[38] Edward Crankshaw, *Cracks in the Kremlin Wall* (New York: Viking Press, 1951), p. 58.
[39] *Ibid.*, p. 59.
[40] *Ibid.*, p. 60.

up, of changing its style so that in the future American policy-makers will take a longer and harder look at what are their vital interests, will not define an adversary by ideology alone but by who he is and how strong he is and which of the American interests, if any, he threatens, and to what degree. In short, the U.S. missionary style will, it is hoped, be tempered, and the United States, having finally been socialized by the state system, will behave more like other nations (which, of course, then raises the question again of what will be American about how the United States conducts itself internationally?). Does the Nixon and Kissinger emphasis on the balance of power in fact mean that national style has already been largely abandoned?

Elite style is also subject to change as perceptions change. Soviet commentators and ideologues have shown increasing awareness that the American Government, rather than being simply an instrument of Wall Street, has a high degree of autonomy on foreign policy issues.[41] The bourgeoisie might share common interests and attitudes, but it is internally divided about which foreign policies to pursue. Thus the idea of a united, cohesive group of monopoly-capitalists possessing a single external policy view, enacted on their behalf by their "executive committee," has been replaced by an analysis that focuses on Washington as at least semi-independent of Wall Street. And Washington itself is now divided into different sets of policy-makers with varying interests and viewpoints on the conduct of foreign policy. Instead of an organized "power elite," there is a pluralistic decision-making system. The Soviets see U.S. policy-makers basically divided into two groups, which reflect the division within the bourgeoisie itself: There are the "realists" and the "madmen" or "maniacs."[42] The former wish to avoid a war, are cautious, seek a reduction of international tension, and view American power and influence as limited; the latter prefer military solutions to international problems, are militantly anti-Communist, and seek a *pax americana*. But nonbourgeois groups, such as trade unions and churches, have also been recognized as seeking to influence policy.

By and large, then, American foreign policy as conducted by the realists is seen as aimed not at destroying the Soviet Union and risking nuclear warfare but at preserving the state system and peaceful coexistence with Russia. In terms of our own previous analysis of the changed nature of American-Russian relations, Moscow views the contemporary pattern as a limited adversary relationship of conflict *and* cooperation. Although the Soviets are still committed to the vision of a Communist world, they perceive this as more and more in the distance. In the early

[41] William Zimmerman, *Soviet Perspectives on International Relations, 1956–67* (Princeton, N.J.: Princeton University Press, 1969), pp. 214–18. Also for Kennan's own reassessment of Soviet foreign policy, see "Mr. X Revisited: An Interview with George Kennan" and "Mr. X Reassessed: The Meaning of Containment," in Charles Gati, ed., *Caging the Bear* (New York: Bobbs-Merrill, 1973), pp. 27, 40.

[42] Zimmerman, *Soviet Perspectives*, pp. 221–25.

1960's, Khrushchev still believed there would be significant advances toward that goal during the next two decades; within a few years, his successors were stressing the several centuries it had taken capitalism to supplant feudalism. In short, the leaders of the Soviet Communist Party —like the leaders of the British Labour Party after the war—have become increasingly "socialized" by the state system. Indeed, "it is to structural changes in the Soviet Union's position in the international system that one must look, first of all, for an explanation of the evolution of Soviet perspectives on the international system.[43] As one of the two superpowers, the Soviet Union has increasingly acted as other great powers have always done—that is, it has shown a keener concern about its place in the existing system than about the conversion of this system into a new order. Since it has become a "have" power, an equal to the United States, Moscow's interest in comanaging the state system in whose survival it has acquired a vested interest has risen. And this reason was reinforced by nuclear weapons, which made it necessary to think of "peaceful coexistence" in more than tactical terms.[44] Revolutionary ambitions had to be adjusted to the realities of the existing system.

Fourth, these results from the confrontation of style and reality raise the question of how the outside observer can distinguish between a nation's style in its external behavior and just the plain responses to the distribution of power in the state system and the compulsion a state feels to respond to certain existing pressures. We noted earlier that, when Britain, France, and Germany collapsed after World War II, the United States emerged as the only counterbalancing power to the Soviet Union in Eurasia. The emerging bipolarity was the cause of the containment policy. To be sure, the ability of American policy-makers to mobilize popular support for this policy in terms of the traditional Old World/New World, authoritarian/democratic dichotomy was very helpful in these circumstances; but can it be claimed that but for America's style, a style that included the arousal of the sleeping giant whenever wicked nondemocratic regimes appeared to threaten him, that the United States would not have reacted as it did in the context of external bipolar pressures?

And this question surely raises the fifth and final question about national style as an analytical tool: Is that style, to the extent it exists, defined by what the policy-makers say, by what they do, or by what particular patterns of behavior they and their predecessors have exhibited before, whether such patterns may be attributed to specific national

---

[43] *Ibid.*, p. 282.

[44] The risk-taking in Soviet foreign policy from 1955 to 1966 is analyzed by Michael P. Gehlen, *The Politics of Soviet Coexistence: Soviet Methods and Motives* (Bloomington, Ind.: Indiana University Press, 1967), pp. 116–27, and Hannes Adomeit, in Adelphi Paper 101, *Soviet Risk-Taking and Crisis Behaviour: From Confrontation to Coexistence* (London: International Institute for Strategic Studies, 1973).

values and historical experiences or to elite ideological beliefs and perceptions? Does the United States really act according to a style or does it merely verbalize in a certain way in order to disguise a policy pretty much dictated by "power politics" and first-level considerations? Is Russia's "adversary partnership" relationship with the United States consistent with its ideological outlook, or is ideology merely invoked to justify a policy dictated by the necessity of coexistence in a nuclear state system? Peking certainly has left no doubt that it feels Moscow has betrayed the faith by its relationship with Washington. But, then, has not Peking done the same thing because of typical balance of power calculations?

The Clash of Systemic Socialization and Style

For all of the analytical problems inherent in the concept of style, its impact on foreign policy is hard to deny altogether. Indeed, one way of interpreting a state's foreign policy behavior is to see it as the product of the interactions and tensions between systematically and stylistically influenced behavior. As suggested, for both the Soviet Union and the United States, the effect of the system has been a moderating or restraining one; the system has tended to socialize both states, regardless of their internal natures. If that is true, the Soviet Union finds itself today in a paradoxical position. As a *Communist* state, it was increasingly confronted by situations that, from the point of view of a *national* state, were counterproductive.[45] It was clear that the expansion of Communism to states Moscow did not control was not necessarily a blessing. To have an ally like China was to need no enemies. It was Peking, not Washington or London or Bonn, that actually claimed Russian territory. It was Mao who challenged the Kremlin's leadership of the Communist movement and called for the overthrow of its rulers. And it was the Chinese who wanted Moscow to be more militant and risk its survival for the sake of the cause. Indeed, Communist expansion in Asia was of questionable value to Russia if it did benefit China. Hence, Soviet help for Hanoi was in large measure motivated by the desire to establish Soviet influence and counteract Peking. Closer relations with India, including Moscow's nonaggression pact with India in 1971, was a part of the Soviet Union's attempt to build up countervailing power to China. Even the events within the Communist states of Eastern Europe became crises when they threatened the bonds of the Warsaw Pact and,

[45] This point is incisively made by Adam B. Ulam, "Communist Doctrine and Soviet Diplomacy: Some Observations," *International Negotiation* (testimony before the Jackson Subcommittee on National Security and International Operations of the Committee on Government Operations, United States Senate) (Washington, D.C.: Government Printing Office, 1970), pp. 4–6.

possibly, the domestic evolution of the Soviet political system beyond a point the Kremlin felt it was safe to tolerate.

It was the non-Communist states, especially during the 1950's and 1960's, that, by contrast, proved to be some of Russia's most reliable means for expanding its influence and eroding that of the West. To that end, some of the Arab states, for example, were, until 1973, more useful to Moscow than the fraternal states. Had Russia tried to subvert one or more of the Arab states, it would probably have alienated the more important states, thereby reducing Soviet influence. Indeed, it was the seizure of power in the Sudan by the Communist Party shortly after Sadat succeeded Nasser that led to the first breach with Moscow. On the whole, it was safer and politically more profitable to exploit Arab hostility toward Israel and the United States. Yet it was also a Soviet apprehension that if it supplied Egypt with offensive arms demanded, an Arab-Israeli war would result, precipitating a Soviet-American confrontation; Soviet leaders therefore decided not to send such weapons. In turn, this compelled Sadat to turn to Washington to resolve his problems. Thus, state-system reasons also set limits to the expansion of Soviet influence in this instance.

This is not to say that Moscow has yet entirely surrendered the idea of the irreconcilable hostility of capitalism, even though it was increasingly negotiating both explicitly and tacitly with Washington to help preserve the peace and to do something about the dangerous and costly armaments race. As Adam Ulam has said:

> Political and psychological exigencies compel the Soviet regime to persist in [its] official and unrealistic view of the world: Communist China, while temporarily hostile, cannot in the long run have interests antagonistic to the USSR, whereas the United States, while not an immediate threat to Russia, must be considered a constant danger because of the nature of her system. [The reason is] the psychological inability of the Soviet leaders to admit to their people, perhaps even to themselves, the true dimensions and dangers of the Chinese problem. To do so would be to reveal how obsolete are the premises of Communism in today's world, to acknowledge unmistakably that the main danger to the security of the USSR comes not from the capitalists but from the growing power of a fellow Communist state. This acknowledgment, in turn, *would challenge the domestic rationale of the Communist regime, the whole structure of the Soviet power, the position of the ruling elite*–all this would be put in jeopardy.[46]

Nevertheless, Soviet Russia in the 1970's is increasingly behaving like a traditional great power. This does not mean, of course, that American-Soviet rivalry will soon come to an end and be replaced by a harmonious relationship. For, as the state system level of analysis has suggested, the great powers, given their sense of insecurity and their concern with

[46] *Ibid.*, pp. 3–4. Emphasis added.

power, will remain the primary actors on the international stage. Russia, even as a nonrevolutionary state, will continue to be one of the world's two greatest powers, with ambitions and interests of its own—which in many areas and on many issues are bound to clash with those of the other superpower. Indeed, Soviet power has been growing. Today, Russia has more land-based strategic missiles than the United States; it is rapidly building up its nuclear submarine fleet and constructing a sizable surface fleet (including helicopter and aircraft carriers, as well as landing barges), which has been moved into the Mediterranean, the Red Sea, and the Indian Ocean—from which long-range naval patrols can be extended beyond Singapore—and has shown "the flag" in the Caribbean as well as the Gulf of Mexico.

Three questions are raised by this vast increase of Soviet power. First, will the Soviet Union with its new-found strategic strength, and the enhanced sense of self-confidence this is likely to confer upon its rulers, make greater demands and seek to use its power to realize more political dividends—as Khrushchev sought to do by exploiting a yet nonexistent growing nuclear missile might in the late 1950's and early 1960's? Second, will such assertiveness and risk-taking—as well as the ability to limit American options in local crises—be enhanced by the ability to extend conventional power across the oceans to almost any area of the world? Communist Russia, like Czarist Russia, has basically been a land power whose possibilities of expansion were largely limited to areas bordering on its frontiers. Even as one of the two superpowers to emerge out of World War II, Russia failed to assert its claim to administer one of Italy's ex-colonies in North Africa; and even as a nuclear superpower, it failed in the early 1960's to hold its advance position in Cuba or to consolidate its influence in the Congo or Ghana. Russia remained landlocked. But "naval power has historically been more flexible and more easily available to pursue particular objectives than land-based strength. We talk as though 'gunboat diplomacy' was . . . outdated. . . . But that depends on the purposes and determination of those who have the gunboats."[47] Thus, Soviet Russia may well show two elements of continuity with Czarist Russia: expansion on land into territorially contiguous regions (in contrast to Western European maritime expansion) and avoidance of collisions with a superior power.

The third question is whether such a siege mentality is not useful to a regime seeking to preserve its domestic structure in the face of challenges from artists and intellectuals, the questioning attitude of many youths, and the increasing sense of nationalism among important Soviet minorities. By equating even the tolerance of dissent, as in Czechoslovakia, with a threat to the survival of the Communist regime, foreign adversaries provide the regime with the justification it needs to reimpose stricter censorship and persecute nonconformists. Russia's growing

[47] Max Beloff, "Russia's Foreign Policy: Cycle of Mistrust," *Interplay*, February, 1971, pp. 10–20.

strength at a time of an increasing American mood to retract commitments may make this an attractive policy. Will the increase of Soviet military strength and the decreasing attraction of both the ideology and the Soviet political system at home and abroad then tempt the Soviet leadership to follow the advice of Shakespeare's Henry V—"to busy giddy minds with foreign quarrels"?[48] How Russia, now a power with a stake in the system and no longer a fervent revolutionary state, will use its growing power thus remains a key question.

The state system has also raised a key question for U.S. foreign policy. As noted earlier, American foreign policy has in the past been characterized by its crusading style. The United States, it was argued, as essentially an inward-oriented society that concentrates on domestic affairs and welfare issues, considers foreign policy burdensome and distracting. Therefore, in order to mobilize public support for external ventures, the struggle for power and security endemic in the state system had to be disguised as a struggle for the realization of the highest values. Because, from the beginning of its existence, the United States has felt itself to be a post-European society—a New World standing as a shining example of democracy, freedom, and social justice for the Old World—anti-Communism was an obvious means for mobilizing Congressional and public support for postwar policy. *America could thus practice "power politics" while disguising it as "ideological politics."*[49] Power politics needed ideological justification in a nation that had always felt power was evil and corrupting. Just as, domestically, power was legitimated by the democratic purposes for which it was used, so externally its employment had to be justified in terms of making the world safe for democracy. In short, after 1945 anti-Communism did not define American foreign policy objectives; rather, American democracy needed it to conduct a traditional foreign policy.

If anti-Communism served as an instrument of internal mobilization, its "feedback" upon the foreign policy it was intended to serve was, as we know, frequently harmful because of the competitive nature of American party politics. The obvious conclusion therefore might well be that the decline of anti-Communism would be beneficial for American foreign policy. Vietnam deeply disillusioned the nation about anti-Communism; the war having been justified in its name, the reaction is

---

[48] In the final analysis, here as in subsequent chapters, the questions we ask and the interpretations we present of the behavior of political systems depend on how the individual scholar looks at these systems. For a representation and analysis of how leading American scholars of the Soviet Union have interpreted Soviet behavior —from "The Great Beast" to "The Neurotic Bear," with a middle position of "The Mellowing Tiger"—see William Welch, *American Images of Soviet Foreign Policy* (New Haven, Conn.: Yale University Press, 1970), together with Jan F. Triska, "Soviet Foreign Policy Studies and Foreign Policy Models," *World Politics*, July, 1971, pp. 704 ff.

[49] Huizinga, "America's Lost Innocence," perceptively analyzes the problems confronting the United States once it can no longer disguise "power politics."

that the price has been too high. Before Vietnam, the nation could be mobilized to stop Communist aggression; since Vietnam, the concern has been not to become engaged in further adventures overseas. Even more fundamentally, anti-Communism has been weakened by the increasing political pluralism of the former Sino-Soviet bloc.

In a bipolar world, power politics was easy to moralize precisely because the bipolarity was one of power and values. Globalism, which made sense as long as any Communist expansion meant an addition to Soviet strength, could thus be explained in terms very understandable to Americans—democracy versus dictatorship. However, it was one thing to "fight Communism" as long as there was only one Communism to fight, and another to fight it once Communism was a many-splintered thing. Which Communism did the country "fight"? Were all Communist states, *because* they were Communist, its enemies? Or did America now have to distinguish among them and see which were hostile, friendly, or neutral and, therefore, which might or might not pose a threat to American interests? More specifically, the question was: What changes in the distribution of power could America, in these new circumstances, safely allow, and where, if anywhere, and against whom, did it still have to draw "frontiers"? Answers to these questions were more difficult than during the simple days of bipolarity, because each situation would confront policy-makers with alternative policies, thereby arousing great debates, possibly intense controversy, and social division within the United States. In such debates, anti-Communism was no longer particularly useful as a means of eliciting popular support and uniting the nation.

The key question for the future conduct of American foreign policy, therefore, is whether—in the absence of anti-Communism—the United States will "dirty" its hands by playing power politics, straight and unadorned; or will it, after having become disillusioned by Vietnam and disenchanted with a world in which the forces of good no longer face the forces of evil in a simple confrontation, continuously sway between moral crusadism and moralistic isolation?[50] Will not the real test of America's capacity to play a leading role in preserving the global balance, therefore, come in our era, after Vietnam? When power politics was synonymous with ideological politics, it was easy to be a leader and organize various coalitions whose basic task was to push back when pushed. But can a nation that has historically condemned power politics adapt its outlook and style, once it is no longer possible to justify foreign policy in terms of ideological crusades, and "play the game by no other name"? Will the "balance of power" logic of the Nixon-Kissinger team arouse the kind of support and passion that a foreign policy justified by moral principles used to? Can an Administration on the basis of power arguments, on the one hand, maintain overseas commitments and large military budgets

---

[50] See Donald R. Lesh, *A Nation Observed* (New York: Potomac Associates, 1974), for a series of Gallup polls on American attitudes toward foreign affairs, especially the increase of isolationalist attitudes.

and, on the other hand, simultaneously seek improved relations with Russia and China? In an atmosphere of *détente,* will these policies not seem contradictory? And, of course, even if the United States could conduct its foreign policy in terms of power calculations, would that—for a democracy—be desirable? Alastair Buchan, an Englishman, has argued that "it would be a sorry world and one that risked alienating not only the lesser powers but our own younger generation as well if they were asked to believe that a balance of power is the highest political achievement of which the new great powers are capable."[51]

[51] Alastair Buchan, *Power and Equilibrium in the 1970's* (New York: Praeger Publishers, 1973), p. 111.

13 Imperialism: The Marxist and Devil Versions

American Imperialism

Since the idea of national and elite styles, although it seems quite persuasive, leaves some rather basic questions unanswered, some analysts have suggested falling back on a more time-honored analytical framework for an explanation and prediction of a nation's foreign policy: the Marxist-Leninist theory of imperialism. Especially in the wake of the Vietnam war, which seemed unexplainable to many observers in terms of the balance of power and vital American security interests, imperialism appears to be a more convincing explanation of U.S. policy. Imperialism, unlike our other explanatory concepts, may not be helpful in interpreting all states' foreign policies, but it may provide insights into the motivational basis of a capitalist state's foreign policy. For, if power politics seemed unpersuasive in accounting for American intervention in Vietnam, perhaps the "real reason" for the intervention lay in the nature of the U.S. economy. The fundamental significance of the economy, the basis of production, employment, and prosperity, could hardly be doubted; its needs might therefore be a better "clue" for understanding U.S. foreign policy in general and Vietnam particularly. There was nothing vague about imperialism, as there was about national style; it pointed straight to the nature of the economy and what Marxists call "the mode of production" as *the* cause of American policy. In the words of Gabriel Kolko, a historian:

> The way Americans define the causes of the Indochina debacle will determine whether they shall be intellectually prepared to anticipate future crises. Conventional wisdom still attributes America's role in Vietnam to accidents or bureaucratic myopia, thereby slighting the real meaning of the consistency of American interventions in the Third World in suppressing radical forces and preserving semicolonial societies.
> Vietnam was an "accident" along a much older, intrinsically dangerous

354

route only insofar as Washington's goals there far exceeded its power to attain them, and it eventually became profoundly dysfunctional to the U.S.'s global priorities and needs. But to divorce Vietnam and numerous interventions from the specific goals of American capitalism in the world, assuming that the needs and values of capitalism are irrelevant to the range of policy options decision-makers consider, is sanctioned ideology but poor history and debilitating to our capacity to anticipate our future.

War, from preparations through aftermath, is the central element in defining the essential quality of capitalist societies as well as their relative power throughout this century, and it has also become the main catalyst to revolutionary movements and changes in vast areas.[1]

The Marxist Background:
The Class Struggle and the Gravediggers

Marxism arose as part of a general protest movement, which ranged from revolutionary anarchism to Utopian Socialism, from the Luddites to the Christian Socialists, against nineteenth-century industrial capitalism. While industrialization was eventually to lead to rapidly rising standards of living for the masses, the principal concern in its early stages was sustained economic growth. The reason for this is inherent in the process of industrialization itself, for industrialization basically seeks to accumulate capital (or, as economists term it, capital goods)—that is, factories, machinery, and other durable equipment. This, of course, oversimplifies the nature of industrialization. If it is basically a process of economic growth, it is also vastly more than that; without an accompanying cultural, political, and social revolution uprooting the old rural and static society, no industrial revolution can occur. In short, the industrialization of a society is more than a "technical" problem. Nevertheless, the essence of industrialization remains the increase of a society's industrial capital, for it is this capital that, when combined with human labor, permits a society to increase its productivity. The machine allows the worker to raise his industrial output, producing in a day what he might otherwise have produced in a week. His higher productivity can then more adequately meet consumer demands for whatever goods are required. The result is better living conditions.

Ironically, capital can be accumulated only if consumption is postponed. In order to build a factory, expand an already existing factory, or buy more machinery, a businessman must invest money. But where does he obtain this money? The answer to this crucial question is that the sum he invests comes primarily out of his profit. Although he could simply save this money, his desire for more profit leads him to reinvest it. And to acquire the maximum degree of profit, he pays his workers as little as possible and makes them work as long as possible. Otherwise, his

[1] Gabriel Kolko, "A War From Time to Time," *New York Times*, March 6, 1973. Emphasis added.

profit margin would be lower, and he would not be able to invest as much money—which, in turn, would slow down the rate of industrialization. The industrial working class thus pays a large share of the price of industrialization. The farmer, too, pays a price, for if industrial wages are to be kept low, the cost of staples in the laborer's diet must also be kept to a minimum. This process of industrialization is essentially the same, no matter what the nature of the economic system. Even a Communist society accumulates capital in this manner; there, however, it is the state rather than the private entrepreneur that accumulates the capital and squeezes it out of the general population.

The terrible effects of industrialization on the workers in the nineteenth century have been vividly described in many works, including Marx's *Kapital*. Edmund Wilson, in his depiction of the arrival of Friedrich Engels in Manchester, described it thus:

He saw the working people living like rats in the wretched little dens of their dwellings, whole families, sometimes more than one family, swarming in a single room, well and diseased, adults and children, close relations sleeping together, sometimes even without beds to sleep on when all the furniture had been sold for firewood, sometimes in damp, underground cellars which had to be bailed out when the weather was wet, sometimes living in the same room with pigs; ill nourished on flour mixed with gypsum and cocoa mixed with dirt, and their wailing children with laudanum; spending their lives, without a sewage system, among the piles of their excrement and garbage; spreading epidemics of typhus and cholera which even made inroads into the well-to-do sections.

The increasing demand for women and children at the factories was throwing the fathers of families permanently out of work, arresting the physical development of the girls, letting the women in for illegitimate motherhood and yet compelling them to come to work when they were pregnant or before they had recovered from having their babies, and ultimately turning a good many of them into prostitutes; while the children, fed into the factories at the age of five or six, receiving little care from mothers who were themselves at the factory all day and no education at all from a community which wanted them only to perform mechanical operations, would drop exhausted when they were led out of their prisons, too tired to wash or eat, let alone study or play, sometimes too tired to get home at all. In the iron and coal mines, also, women and children as well as men spent the better part of their lives crawling underground in narrow tunnels, and, emerging, found themselves caught in the meshes of the company cottage and the company store and of the two-week postponement of wages. They were being killed off at the rate of fourteen hundred a year through the breaking of rotten ropes, the caving-in of workings due to overexcavated seams and the explosions due to bad ventilation and to the negligence of tired children; if they escaped catastrophic accidents, the lung diseases eventually got them. The agricultural population, for its part, deprived by the industrial development of their old status of handicraftsmen and yeomen who either owned their own land and homes or were taken care of with more or less certainty by a landlord on whose estate they were tenants, had been transformed into wandering day laborers, for whom nobody took responsibility and who were punished by jail or transportation if they ventured in times of need to steal and eat the landlord's game.

It seemed to Engels that the medieval serf, who had at least been attached to the land and had a definite position in society, had had an advantage over the factory worker. At that period when legislation for the protection of labor had hardly seriously gotten under way, the old peasantry and hand-workers of England, and even old petty middle class, were being shoveled into the mines and the mills like so much raw material for the prices their finished products would bring, with no attempt even to dispose of the waste. In years of depression the surplus people, so useful in years of good business, were turned out upon the town to become peddlers, crossing-sweepers, scavengers or simply beggars—sometimes whole families were seen begging in the streets—and, almost as frequently, whores and thieves.[2]

Marxism was one legacy of this Industrial Revolution. Specifically, it was one of many moral protest movements against the cruelties and miseries suffered by the workers. Such exploitation of man by man had to be ended, for it violated the whole Western humanitarian tradition from its Judaeo-Christian beginnings to the French Revolution. The equality of man was meaningless in a society so deeply divided into the privileged few and the underprivileged many. The dignity and freedom of the individual could possess little reality for the majority of men paid only subsistence wages, if they found any employment at all. Capitalism had enslaved man in economic bondage.

A system based on production for the "profit of the few" had to be changed to production for the "use of the many." To be sure, capitalism had brought mankind great benefits. And no one praised its success more than its greatest critic: "The bourgeoisie, during its rule of scarce one hundred years," Marx wrote in the *Communist Manifesto*, "has created more massive and more colossal productive forces than have all preceding generations together. Subjection of nature's forces to man, machinery, application of chemistry to industry, and agriculture, steam-navigation, railways, electric telegraphs, clearing of whole continents for cultivation, canalisation of rivers, whole populations conjured out of the ground—what earlier century had even a presentiment that such productive forces slumbered in the lap of social labour?"[3] But though the bourgeoisie had created the industrial machinery, the bourgeoisie was itself the greatest obstacle to mass production for the benefit of society. For Marx, capitalism's assumption that industry could abolish poverty

[2] Edmund Wilson, *To the Finland Station* (Garden City, N.Y.: Anchor Books, 1953), pp. 134–36. Used by permission of the author. For revealing documents of the period, see E. Royston Pike, *"Hard Times": Human Documents of the Industrial Revolution* (New York: Praeger Publishers, 1966), and Albert Fried and Richard M. Elman, eds., *Charles Booth's London* (New York: Pantheon, 1968).

[3] Arthur P. Mendel, *The Essential Works of Marxism* (New York: Bantam Books, 1961), pp. 17–18.

once and for all by providing man with his basic necessities was errone-
ous, for an economic system based upon the profit motive could result
only in an inequitable distribution of the income. It was the desire for
profit that was the cause of the workers' poverty and degradation, and
profit was the outcome of private control over the means of production.
Capitalism therefore had to be replaced by a more just system—socialism
—if the "acquisitive society" were to be transformed into a society that
concerned itself with social justice for the underprivileged. In a socialist
society, the working class would own the means of production and hence
would receive a fair share of the national income.

But Marxian socialism was more than a moral protest movement; it
was also "scientific." Indeed, Marxism could be defined as that school of
socialism which seeks to prove that the coming of socialism is inevitable.[4]
In that respect, Marxism was a national outgrowth of the general Western belief in the inevitability of progress and the equally widespread
equation of progress with improvement. This optimistic faith was itself
an offspring of the eighteenth-century Age of Reason. A reaction to medieval society and philosophy, the Age of Reason—the Enlightenment
—stood in direct contradiction to the religion-dominated and tradition-
bound ethos of feudal Europe. The Enlightenment substituted reason
for God, and the material world became man's chief concern; the creation of a better life for himself, his chief goal. The perfect society was to
be created here and now. Man's condition, the result not of sin but of
ignorance, would be altered through reason, not Grace. The master of
his own fate, man could create the kind of world he wanted because God
had given him the reason with which he could build a paradise on earth;
secular rather than spiritual activities were to be the chief focus of man's
strivings. The Enlightenment posited a rational universe, which could
be mastered through knowledge. Knowledge would reveal comprehensi-
ble laws. Once these laws were discovered, all problems of human existence could be solved. This is why the Age of Enlightenment stressed
"materialism," defined in this context simply as "realism," as the rational inquiry into man's secular universe in order to discover the laws of
that universe, composed of matter.

Marx inherited this mental "set" and it was as a realist that Marx
claimed the capitalist system was historically doomed. Capitalism asserted that the individual responded to economic self-interest in the
same way an individual atom responded to gravity. Given this self-interest as man's basic motivation, the "economic laws" that would maximize society's economic benefits were the laws of supply and demand
operating through the free market. The capitalist argument was simple.
The individual wishes to augment his wealth; his desire for profit therefore leads him to produce whatever product consumers demand. Naturally, he will try to charge as much as possible. But because others, in

4 Alfred G. Meyer, *Communism*, rev. ed. (New York: Random House, 1967),
p. 12.

their search for profit, may produce the same item, his price must be competitive. If he charges more than they do for the same item, no one will buy his product. And what price can he get? Each producer, hoping for increased sales, will try to undersell his competitors. But no producer can sell at less than cost and still stay in business. And if his costs are higher than his competitors', he must go out of business or find a more efficient method of production. The market's free competition thus has four results: It supplies the products the consumers demand, it sells these goods at a minimal cost to the consumers, it provides profit for the producers, and it ensures that only efficient operations remain in business. The "economic laws" channel each individual's self-interest in socially beneficial directions, and the competitive mechanism of the market provides for the "greatest good of the greatest number." The free market thus theoretically guarantees a harmony of interest between producers and consumers.

Marx accepted this description of the capitalist market and focused his criticism on what he considered the market's central feature: namely, that it transformed all relationships between individuals into exchange or monetary relations. In a market society, it seemed to him, this was the only meaningful bond between individuals. The consumer, to obtain the goods he wants, offers a cash incentive; the producer, to sell his goods, responds to the consumer's demand. Men are thus linked to each other as buyers and sellers through money; but they are also linked as employers and employees, and again the relationship is a monetary one. For, in fact, the employer *buys* labor power, which the worker sells in order to obtain money with which to buy the goods necessary to sustain himself. For Marx, this was the distinguishing feature of capitalism: the fact that not only goods but *men* were sold on the market. Indeed, human labor was sold like any other product. The bourgeoisie, as Marx bitterly said, "has left no other bond between man and man than naked self-interest, than callous 'cash payment.' . . . It has resolved personal worth into exchange value, and in place of the numberless indefeasible chartered freedoms, has set up that single, unconscionable freedom—Free Trade."[5]

In the end, the exploitation of the workers is the result of this sale of men as commodities. Like laissez-faire economists, Marx maintained that the value of a product was equivalent to the amount of labor expended in its production. How then, he asked, did one derive profit? If the exchange value of a product equaled its labor cost, then profit could be gained only by raising the price above the market value or by paying the worker less. And this latter option, he maintained, was precisely the case. The worker received only a subsistence wage—enough to keep him alive and able to work and reproduce; to the employer, his labor was worth no more than the amount it took to keep him alive. The difference

[5] Quoted in *ibid.*, p. 15.

between what he should have been paid in terms of the cash *value* of his labor in the product and what he was actually paid represented the profit, or "surplus value."

The significance of Marx's theory of value lies in its sociological implications. His analysis of the free market emphasizes not just the production and exchange of commodities, but the *social organization* for production. Capitalists and proletariat need each other; both classes are compelled to cooperate. Each contributes a specific function: one the capital goods, or what Marx called the "means of production," the other the labor power. But if the two classes are functionally interdependent, they are also mutually antagonistic. The capitalists exploit the proletariat because the market transforms all human relationships—whether buyer-seller or employer-employee—into exchange, or monetary, relations. The capitalists, to maximize their profit, will squeeze as much surplus value out of labor as possible; and although they constitute only a minority of the population, they can continue their exploitation of the majority because they own and control the means of production and, thus, the power of the state.

Political philosophers from Aristotle onward had analyzed the interaction between private power and the control of the state. It has long been understood that groups organize to protect their interests and extend their reach to the political arena. In some ways, Marx was reasserting this interpretation when he stated that the bourgeoisie controlled not only economic but also political power. But for Marx it was more than an attempt to manipulate the apparatus of the state by private interests: The state was, in Marx's words, nothing but the "executive committee of the bourgeoisie," the superstructure built on, reflecting and reinforcing the economic arrangement (capitalism) in the substructure. Hence, the state would perpetuate capitalist exploitation of the proletariat. The result could be no less than a class struggle between the exploiter and the exploited. Nor was this class struggle, according to Marx, unique to capitalism. In every economic system, the "forces of production" produced corresponding "relations of production," or social structure. In the Greek and Roman slave system, which succeeded the stage of "primitive communism" (primitive society, in which all production and appropriation had been communal), there were the slaveowners and the slaves; in medieval feudalism, the landowners and the serfs; and in industrial capitalism, the capitalists and the proletarians. In each, the superstructure—the state and the law, the moral and religious code, even art and family life—reflected and reinforced the economic base. Every economic system was divided between the "haves" and the "have-nots," and all were consequently racked by the class struggle.[6] Because the political system was controlled, a political solution to the class struggle was foreclosed; political reforms were meaningless, for in the end the haves

[6] *Ibid.*, pp. 13–14.

would never willingly relinquish control. Would the worker ever achieve abundance and freedom from his "economic slavery"? Not by ameliorating reforms. Still, argued Marx, the "laws of economics" assured his liberation.

Such stress on economic determinism was hardly surprising, as it was the era of industrialization, an era preoccupied with capital accumulation. To the businessman, wealth, profit, and success were synonymous. To the worker, who scratched out a bare existence by laboring fifteen hours or more a day, economics was even more vital—a matter of survival. In an age in which the masses were still desperately poor but were beginning to see that such poverty could be ended, the economic causes of conflict seemed obvious.

The bourgeoisie and the proletariat, then, were not fated to face each other eternally. "Judgment day" for the capitalist class would come, Marx said; for the proletarian revolution was *historically inevitable*. The economic forces that had earlier caused the death of the slave and feudal systems were destined to do the same for capitalism. From the theory of surplus value, which for Marx was the axle around which the capitalist wheel revolved, Marx derived three economic laws, which explained the behavior of the system—and doomed it. The first was the law of "capitalist accumulation." Each capitalist, seeking to maximize profit, expands his output in order to sell more than his competitors. To do this, each must hire more workers, but as the labor supply is bought up, labor costs will rise and, in turn, cut into profits. Each employer must therefore install labor-saving machinery to reduce costs and preserve profit margins. Thus he accumulates capital. But he is simultaneously working against himself. His source of surplus value is the very worker whom he must now replace. The increasing proportion of machinery to labor therefore produces the very thing the introduction of machinery was supposed to prevent: a decline in profits. The second law—the "concentration of capital"—follows logically. The competitive process that results from the struggle for profits drives the weaker capitalists into bankruptcy, thereby concentrating capital in fewer and fewer hands. Eventually, this process ends in the establishment of monopolies. Together, these two laws produce the third, the law of "increasing misery." On the one hand, as the capitalists are driven out of business and the workers are displaced by machinery, there is large-scale unemployment, and, simultaneously, an increase in the size of the proletariat caused by the entry into it of these capitalists who have lost out. On the other hand, the capitalist, compelled to compensate for his falling profits, must intensify his exploitation of the workers by further decreasing their subsistence wages. Because the unemployed—Marx called them the "industrial reserve army"—have no other means of existence, they have little choice but to accept work at any price. The wage level is then driven down for all workers. Surplus value again increases, but only for a time. The competitive process begins again, further decreasing profit, concentrating capital, and increasing the proletariat's size and misery. And by a series of recurring crises, each more severe than the preceding one, capitalism arrives at the final stage of its development—the proletarian revolution.

Capitalism, Marx held, would thus be its own gravedigger—for through industrialization it fathers the very class that will overthrow it when it reaches economic maturity. The laws of the free market, ironically, will result in the overthrow of its advocates. The forces of production will then no longer be privately owned. The exploitation of man by man will be ended forever, for society will no longer be divided into "haves" and "have-nots." Industry, publicly owned by the "dictatorship of the proletariat," will be used for the proletariat's benefit. The dictatorship, however, was to be only temporary. Once its principal purpose—the liquidation of the bourgeoisie—was accomplished, and private property, the source of class formation and the class struggle, eliminated, the state was to "wither away" and a new period of history would begin. Man would then be able to live in harmony, and the classless society would finally fulfill the ideals of fraternity, liberty, equality—and affluence—for the vast majority.

The Failure of Marxism

The fundamental error committed by Marx was that he confused capitalism with democracy. Because the state was the "executive committee" of the bourgeoisie, he said, capitalism could not reform itself; the parliamentary institutions of capitalist states were merely the façade for the "dictatorship of the bourgeoisie." According to Marx, the bourgeois minority would continue to use the power of the state—the police and the army—to preserve its dominance over, and exploitation of, the proletariat, and to quell any worker disturbances or riots. This state of affairs would end only on the day the proletariat rose up to overthrow its exploiters; because reform within the system was impossible, revolution was the only means of changing that system. This conclusion was perhaps natural at the time Marx wrote, for the bourgeoisie was politically very powerful and the reform movement very weak. Certainly, ruling groups or classes have not in the past willingly surrendered their power. The French Revolution, exemplifying a bourgeois revolution against the traditional order, seemed to be good evidence to support this contention.

Marx was mistaken though, for democracy and capitalism, while closely related, are not identical. His mistake stemmed from his failure to distinguish between democratic ends and means. Certainly, in his own mind, he was committed to democratic ends: the inalienable rights of the individual and social justice for all men. Indeed, his basic charge against capitalism was that it frustrated the realization of the aims proclaimed by the French Revolution, that it was unjust, indeed inhuman;

nourished by the greed of the few, it led to the exploitation of the many. Democracy could flourish only in the postcapitalist stage of socialism, after private property had been abolished. Marx's attack on capitalism was basically, therefore, a moral attack, "an anguished protest against the materialist spirit of capitalism, against the profit motive, against the mechanization and dehumanization of all classes of people in the service of industrial production."[7] Because political power was controlled exclusively by the ruling bourgeoisie, Marx did not hold out any promise of popular relief and amelioration. Consequently, he resorted to an economic interpretation of history to prove the "inevitability" of socialism: The "laws of economics" had already determined the doom of capitalism. In taking this view, Marx not only underestimated the importance of politics, but failed to grasp the essential relationship between democratic ends and the democratic process. For an essential corollary of the commitment to the rights of the individual—to individual liberty and equality—is that individuals sharing common values and interests have the right to organize to advance their goals. A society in which men can thus express their interests—whether organized as interest groups or as social classes—is pluralistic. Democracy can therefore be seen largely as a method or process: It provides for the adjustment and accommodation of the constantly conflicting interests inherent in any multi-interest political system.

What is, above all, obvious about "democracy as a method of self-government" is that it rejects the claim that man is a prisoner of fate, that his life is determined by forces or "laws" beyond his control. Rather, democracy assumes that man is a reasonable free agent who can to a large degree—although perhaps not to the degree supposed by the Enlightenment—determine the kind of society in which he lives. If purportedly historical or economic laws produce results he does not like, he can change the results. If, for instance, the laissez-faire market results in monopolies, unemployment, and low wages, man can remedy this by altering the manner in which the market operates. He is not the victim of the laws of the market. Once he determines the purposes an economy should serve in terms of his value preferences, he can then seek their realization through the political process.

This was exactly what happened in the late nineteenth century as the free market became progressively less free, while capital concentrated, just as Marx had foreseen. Competition resulted in industrial and commercial monopolies that dominated the market and controlled the levers of government. There was bound to be a political reaction. Any group holding a monopoly of power will use that power for its own purposes; unrestrained by any countervailing power, which is the basis of democratic freedom, it will abuse that power. Not only will other interests be neglected, but the dominant group will be in a position to exploit the

[7] Robert V. Daniels, *The Nature of Communism* (New York: Random House, 1962), pp. 12–13.

interests of other groups—for example, workers' wages and farmers' food prices (which can both be kept low), and consumers' needs (for which prices can be kept high). All these groups, having no means of effective protest, will seek to organize politically to gain satisfaction. In Marx's age, big business was the dominant force in politics, and he thus believed that the bourgeoisie controlled the state and reform would be impossible. But he failed to recognize the "political law" that power begets counterbalancing power. As other interests—farmers, laborers, and so forth— began to organize to avoid being controlled by business, democratic governments, reacting to the votes and needs of their citizens, began increasingly to interfere with the laws of the market—*not* in order to destroy capitalism, but to make it *responsive* to the needs of all groups. Democracy, in short, began to "socialize" capitalism—that is, to make it socially responsible.

Thus democracy avoided the violent revolution Marx had forecast for it. Monopoly capitalism might well have precipitated such a revolution had it been left unreformed. Too many social groups did feel exploited. If a democratic reform movement had not responded to their grievances and needs, there would have been no alternative left to them but to seek satisfaction outside the system by nondemocratic and violent means. Capitalism, if it was to survive, had no choice but to accept democratic reforms. By accepting them, indeed, it consolidated its position, for its response to popular needs won it popular allegiance. Thus, by meeting the aspirations of the workers, it "derevolutionized" them. As labor's economic situation improved, it began to have a vested interest in the *preservation* of capitalism. Industry obviously also played a vital role in this process, not only by its acceptance of political reforms but by contributing to the rise in real wages that followed the early phase of industrialization. Industrialists ultimately realized that more profit could be earned if goods were mass-produced and reasonably priced so that workers with sufficiently high incomes could buy them. Thus, democracy and industry were gradually able to satisfy labor's demands. As a result, the labor parties in Central and Western Europe abandoned the concept of the proletarian revolution. Revolution was replaced by democratic gradualism and peaceful change via the ballot box. And revolutionary Marxism became evolutionary socialism.

The word "socialism" has had unsavory overtones in the United States, where it was long equated with "anticapitalism" and "un-Americanism." Nevertheless, even America, as a democratic nation, has to a large extent "socialized" its economy so that the market produces socially acceptable results. Actually, the same types of reform of the market structure that have been introduced in Europe under the socialist label have been instituted in the United States with no set ideological basis. One merely has to substitute the term "social progress" for socialism.

The Populist and Progressive movements, the New Nationalism, the New Freedom, the New Deal, the Fair Deal, the New Frontier, and the

Great Society have all advanced their programs in the name of social progress. Whether American "socialism" is known as the welfare state, welfare capitalism, or even "people's capitalism"—as President Eisenhower once suggested—is largely irrelevant. What is significant is that most Americans have come to accept in practice many of the ideas that Europeans consider socialist. For example, some students attending a state university may condemn "socialism" without stopping to think that they are receiving their education in a tax-supported, "socialistic" institution. Yet many of them would not have access to higher education—generally believed to be a prerequisite for economic opportunity and social advancement—were they unable to attend a school whose tuition charges are considerably lower than those of the private universities. State universities, which are indeed socialist in nature, are a logical outgrowth of the democratic dedication to equal opportunity for all individuals.

Democratic socialism and welfare capitalism have in general resorted to three types of measures to make the market more socially responsible. First, they have redistributed income through such measures as minimum-wage laws, legalization of collective bargaining, social security, farm price supports, and, above all, the income tax. Second, primarily through indirect planning—monetary controls, tax adjustments, and deficit financing—they have sought to control business cycles, particularly the downswings with their high levels of unemployment. Third, they have established some supervisory control over the major sectors of industry by antitrust legislation, regulatory commissions, and—in the case of self-styled socialist governments (postwar Britain)—nationalization. But even the nationalization effected by Britain was hardly revolutionary. Far from expropriating all private property, the government nationalized only a small segment of industry; while this included such a strategically important area as steel, it was generally composed of economically decaying industries—such as coal, the nationalization of which had been recommended not by the Labour but by the Conservative Party. Nationalization, in brief, has served basically as a utilitarian measure. It has done so little to change management-labor relations that European trade unions have become disenchanted with it. The German Democratic Socialists have dropped the idea from their party platform, and the right wing of the British Labour Party wants to drop it, too. European socialist parties have become essentially programatic and peaceful progressive parties committed to the welfare state for all classes. The proletarian revolution and the proletarian state have been forgotten.

Leninism, Imperialism, and Stalinist Rule

It was inevitable that Marxists would question the failure of the proletarian revolution to occur. Democratic reform was the one answer they would not accept. Something that was evil could not be made less evil by "reform." Perhaps its outward appearance could be altered, but it would remain basically unchanged. If capitalism was still evil and if it remained an exploitative order, why had it not collapsed as Marx had predicted? The usual explanation for the failure of the revolution was that the workers' rising living standards gave them a vested interest in the capitalist system. That was the principal reason why democratic socialists had given up their plans to overthrow capitalism. In Lenin's view, however, a movement that abandoned the revolution and sought to acquire a larger share of the capitalist pie was no longer Marxist. Lenin recognized that the higher wages of the workers had undermined their proletarian consciousness and made them reform-minded in terms of improving their material standards; they had developed what he called a "trade-union consciousness." The crucial question posed by this development was: What had made it possible for the capitalists to raise paychecks rather than, as predicted, being forced to decrease them further?

The ability of capitalism to reform itself having already been excluded, the answer had to be found in external circumstances. Colonialism, or imperialism, provided the key.[8] The "internal contradiction" of capitalism—the class struggle between the bourgeoisie and the proletariat—had been resolved by capitalism's indulgence in imperialism. It was imperialism that had changed the first and third laws of capitalism. The second law remained correct: Capital *was* concentrated in fewer and fewer hands. The era of imperialism was, indeed, the era of monopoly capitalism. But the law of capital accumulation, which forecast the declining rate of profits, had been reversed. Imperialism was the source of huge profits—so huge, in fact, that Lenin called them "superprofits." Colonies provided inexpensive raw materials and cheap labor. They also augmented the market in which goods produced in the metropolitan country could be sold and provided greater investment opportunities for surplus capital.

It was now clear why the European workers' living standards had risen, despite the law of increasing misery. For the protelariat had shared in the society's enormous increase of wealth. In the age of imperialism, capitalism could afford to make economic concessions to its laboring class in order to gain its support. It could even permit political concessions. Once the workers' allegiance to the capitalist system had been won, they could even be allowed to vote, as voting was meaningless when the choice was between two parties representing the capitalist class; their only choice was which group of capitalists should exploit them, not whether by means of a free vote exploitation could be abolished. The working class became increasingly "embourgeoised," losing its revolutionary drive and spirit and taking on a vested interest in the preservation of capitalism. This commitment to capitalism was reinforced

[8] V. I. Lenin, *Imperialism, the Highest Stage of Capitalism*, rev. ed. (New York: International Publishers, 1939).

by the proletariat's new and intense nationalistic feelings. Hostile to the capitalist class in the preimperialist phase, the proletariat acquired this nationalism as it came to identify its interests with capitalist imperialism.

Lenin's explanation for the failure of the proletarian revolution implied pessimism about the future. While imperialism continued, the capitalists would reap sufficient superprofits with which to "buy" the support of the working class. Only if these profits were eliminated would the capitalists have to resume their preimperialist domestic exploitation. Then the class struggle would resume and, finally, result in the proletarian revolution. This was exactly what Lenin predicted, for, through imperialism, the "inner contradiction" of capitalism had been projected on a global scale. Just as the capitalist class had exploited the proletarian class for profit, the capitalist countries now exploited the proletarian (colonial) countries for "surplus value." Imperialism had, by its conquest of most non-Western areas, transformed the fight against capitalism into a global conflict. The domestic class struggle was now an international class struggle. Indeed, because the uprising of the workers in developed capitalist nations had come to depend upon the elimination of colonial holdings, the prerequisite for the proletarian revolution in capitalist countries now became the anti-imperialist revolution of the precapitalist colonial countries. "National liberation" became Communism's most immediate task.

Lenin thus turned Marx upside down. The proletarian revolution would now begin in nonproletarian societies. The workers' revolution would arise in lands whose economies were basically agrarian, where peasants (not workers) constituted the vast majority of the population. Marx had said that the proletarian revolution would occur spontaneously when the capitalist economy became mature. Lenin now observed that when the economy had become mature, the capitalists avoided the revolution by the policy of imperialism. The consciousness of the proletariat was in these circumstances transformed from revolutionary to reformist. Conversely, the proletarian mood—the awareness of people that, being poor and miserable, they are exploited—became most highly developed in the colonial countries. Thus, where Marx had stated that economic maturity *and* political consciousness were parallel developments that would precipitate the proletarian revolution, Lenin now asserted that they were *inversely* related in the age of imperialism. The contrast was stark: Marx had stressed *economic* maturity as the prerequisite for the revolution. Lenin now emphasized *political* consciousness. Stalin later said, in his lectures on Leninism:

> Where will the revolution begin? Where, in what country, can the front of capital be pierced first?
>
> Where industry is more developed, where the proletariat constitutes the majority, where there is more culture, where there is more democracy—that was the reply usually given formerly.
>
> No, objects the Leninist theory of revolution; *not necessarily where*

industry is more developed, and so forth. The front of capital will be pierced where the chain of imperialism is weakest, for the proletarian revolution is the result of the breaking of the chain of the world imperialist at its weakest link; and it may turn out that the country which has started the revolution, which has made a breach in the front of capital, is less developed in a capitalist sense than other, more developed, countries, which have, however, remained within the framework of capitalism.[9]

Global Imperialism and Vietnam

The Marxist analysis of American capitalism and imperialism usually begins with the "men of power"—the men who make the decisions. The large corporations supply the foreign policy decision-makers, who, once in office, maintain their connections with their industrial firms and their allied law and banking firms. These men form a small, cohesive group whose career experiences and expectations for the future color their perceptions. Business, therefore, serves as the fount of the personnel and assumptions underlying foreign, as well as domestic, policies. As servants of corporate capitalism, seeking profits both at home and abroad, they hold to a policy of "free world imperialism." To quote Gabriel Kolko's words once more:

> . . . foreign policy decision-makers are in reality a highly mobile sector of the American corporate structure, a group of men who frequently assume and define high level policy tasks in government, rather than routinely administer it, and then return to business. Their firms and connections are large enough to afford them the time to straighten out or formulate government policy while maintaining their vital ties with giant corporate law, banking, or industry. The conclusion is that a small number of men fill the large majority of key foreign policy posts. Their many diverse posts make this group a kind of committee government entrusted to handle numerous and varied national security and international functions at the policy level. Even if not initially connected with the corporate sector, career government officials relate in some tangible manner with the private worlds predominantly of big law, big finance, and big business.[10]

Being the world's most powerful capitalist country, America has become the great capitalist exploiter of the underdeveloped areas of the world. Accordingly, U.S. neocolonial control of their resources is absolutely essential for the continued health of the U.S. economy.[11] With

[9] Joseph Stalin, *The Foundations of Leninism,* quoted in Mendel, *Essential Works of Marxism,* pp. 228–29. Emphasis in original.

[10] Gabriel Kolko, *The Roots of American Foreign Policy* (Boston: Beacon Press, 1969), pp. 3–26; Richard J. Barnet, *The Economy of Death* (New York: Atheneum, 1969), pp. 87–97; and G. W. Domhoff, *The Higher Circles: The Governing Class in America* (New York: Vintage Books, 1971), pp. 111–55.

[11] Kolko, *Roots of American Foreign Policy,* pp. 48–87, and Carl Oglesby and Richard Shaull, *Containment and Change* (New York: Macmillan, 1967), pp. 72–111.

only 6 per cent of the world's population, America produces nearly 50 per cent of the world's goods. To manufacture only the items for which it possesses the raw materials would reduce the capitalists' profits, cause large-scale unemployment, and reopen the class struggles, which would climax in proletarian revolution in America. The "new" nations therefore function essentially as they did before they were granted formal political independence (hence the term "neocolonial"). They are still enchained as suppliers of raw material for the most advanced industrialized capitalist nation. To sum up: A capitalist state, such as the United States in the contemporary world, *must* expand abroad if its rulers wish to stave off domestic revolution.

But this does not mean, the proponents of the imperialist theory assert, that American expansion began with the end of World War II. It began with the founding of the Republic.[12] "The internationalist stance was taken once and for all. True, we went eagerly westward into the continent, slaughtering and cheating Indians as no Henrik Verwoerd [a former Prime Minister of South Africa] or even Ian Smith [Prime Minister of Rhodesia] ever slaughtered and cheated the blacks of Africa." Thus, even while expanding westward, American imperialism looked outward. The Monroe Doctrine laid the basis for American economic and political control over the whole Western Hemisphere. A few decades later, the United States extended its economic control across the Pacific to China with the Open Door Policy. America's business—then as now—was Business. The flag followed trade and investments. The whole world became the Western frontier, and it has remained so ever since. In this context, it was American capitalism that precipitated the conflict with Russia. Stalin is absolved of all responsibility, because "before him [in 1945] towered a demanding United States, history's most violent nation . . . in the prime of its superpower."[13] More specifically, the United States precipitated the cold war by seeking to push Russia out of Eastern Europe, its security zone, and even strove to weaken and undermine the Soviet Union itself before, in its strengthened postwar position, it could become the nucleus of a new postcapitalist world order. In the resulting cold war with Russia—and later China —anti-Communism was invoked to justify American imperialism and to condemn the striving for political and economic independence by the underdeveloped nations, upon whose continued exploitation the prosperity of the United States depends. As a result, the United States has become the citadel of the *ancien régime,* the supporter of reactionary dictatorships and military cliques throughout this Third World to prevent the rise of nationalist and revolutionary regimes that would claim national control over their resources and foreign investments on behalf of their people, who under imperialism continue to suffer poverty and misery. Interpreted in this global manner, the war in Vietnam was un-

[12] E.g., see Oglesby and Shaull, *Containment and Change*, p. 48.
[13] *Ibid.*, p. 49.

avoidable, despite its costs and despite the fact that South Vietnam was of so little economic value to the United States. The stake was nothing less than American control of the economies of the underdeveloped countries. Should Vietnam demonstrate that a genuinely nationalist, revolutionary movement could throw off the imperialist shackles, it would set an example for all the other colonial countries. Therefore, Washington had to intervene to crush the Vietcong. If South Vietnam fell, a *global* domino reaction would follow.[14]

The logical conclusion of such analysis holds a Vietcong victory and an American defeat to be the preconditions for the eventual emergence of a world in which despotism, hunger, and war will be abolished. And the end of American imperial control will also permit the emergence of a truly just and peaceful America, for, once the capitalists have lost their huge profits, the resulting mass dissatisfaction will produce the revolutionary conditions that will finally liberate the American people. Imperialism, the last stage of capitalism, brought into play to avoid the revolution, disintegrates as its chains collapse in the areas that are economically most underdeveloped but politically most conscious of their exploitation and, therefore, most revolutionary.

A Critique of the Leninist Interpretation

How valid is this Marxist-Leninist imperialist theory as a general means of explaining and predicting a nation's foreign policy, specifically U.S. foreign policy? Perhaps a fundamental criticism would be that conflict and war occurred among independent political units—empires, city-states, or dynasties—long before industrial capitalism. How then can one attribute wars in general to economic causes and especially to the profit motive? Once it is admitted that perhaps not all wars are due to capitalism, the thesis is itself gravely weakened and can no longer stand as a broad explanatory generalization; even where it can be shown that a specific war may have been profitable, can one even say that this consequence of a war was the motivation for its occurrence? And even if one could say that for certain wars, does this justify raising these instances to a universal historical law, economically predetermined? In any event, most Western colonial expansion occurred in the period from the sixteenth to the eighteenth century, the period before industrial capitalism. Indeed, even most of the strife and hostilities that occurred in the nineteenth century or during the period of industrial capitalism to which Lenin attributed colonialism and war—the three Prussian wars against Denmark, Austria, and France; the Russo-Turkish and Russo-Japanese wars, and World War I—can hardly be attributed to capitalist rivalries. In fact, Russia and Italy, active imperialist states, were not even capitalist. And countries such as Switzerland and the Scan-

14 Kolko, *Roots of American Foreign Policy*, pp. 85–87.

dinavian countries managed to find markets and raw materials without acquiring any colonies.[15] Soviet behavior in the post–World War II period throws even more doubt on the relationship between industrial capitalism and war.

Second, and contrary to Lenin, other students of Western imperialism have claimed that

> . . . international friction over private investments has been a good deal more frequent and dangerous where private investments have been pressed into service as instruments, tools, of a larger political purpose which the investments themselves did not originate. Investments used in the quest for national glory, and the like, have been more productive of international friction in the past than investments actuated solely by private profit motives.[16]

Specifically, colonial acquisition often served the state's political rather than economic purposes. In a state system in which states felt insecure and had to concern themselves constantly with their power relative to the power of potential adversaries, colonies represented more than profit. They enhanced a nation's prestige. For Germany, nationally unified only in 1870, far later than the other great powers, colonies were a means of gaining a "place in the sun." Not only were some of those in the South Pacific not profitable, but it had to spend money to maintain them.[17] This was money considered well spent because colonies to the great powers were like atomic bombs since 1945, a sign of rank and power. Only Austria-Hungary before 1914 had no colonies; it was a sign of its weakness and decline, which were to lead it to precipitate World War I in a last desperate effort to stay alive. On the other hand, for France, defeated by Germany in 1870, colonial expansion in Africa became a way of regaining a lost status and disguising a national humiliation. For France, facing a Germany with a far larger population, the manpower

[15] Benjamin J. Cohen, *The Question of Imperialism* (New York: Basic Books, 1973), p. 67.

[16] Eugene Staley, *War and the Private Investor* (Garden City, N.Y.: Doubleday, 1935), pp. xv–xvi.

[17] One interesting feature of the expansionist phase of American foreign policy at the turn of the century was the strong belief of the progressive spokesmen who were its advocates in Social Darwinism and the "white-man's-burden" philosophy. They had a large measure of contempt for the materialistic emphasis of American life, and were concerned lest the vigor and spirit of America be sapped by a slothful and easy life. Their devotion was primarily to the martial virtues, heroism and glory, not material values. In contrast, American industry opposed any Cuban adventure at the turn of the century. Not until the United States acquired the Philippines were American businessmen suddenly overcome by the vision of millions upon millions of potential Chinese customers, just as the missionaries were overwhelmed by the vision of saving so many heathens. The former dream was quickly recognized as an illusion, and the attention and resources of American industry were refocused on the intensive exploitation of the domestic American market. See Richard Hofstadter, *Social Darwinism in American Thought*, rev. ed. (Boston: Beacon Press, 1955) and Julius W. Pratt, *Expansionists of 1898* (Baltimore: Johns Hopkins Press, 1936).

of the colonies meant more soldiers to balance its big neighbor's army. While Tunisia might therefore "pay off" economically, the colonies in equatorial Africa generally did not; the French Government had other purposes in mind in acquiring them.

Thus, while economics should not be discounted as a motive for Western nineteenth-century imperialism, it should not be exaggerated either, for, very clearly, the state system and power considerations were then—as before—fundamental in explaining state expansion. Benjamin Cohen, in a detailed analysis of imperialist theory and Western colonialism, finds the taproot of imperialism in the anarchical organization of the international system. "Nations yield to the temptations to domination because they are driven to maximize their individual power position" by their sense of uncertainty and insecurity.[18] Imperialism, which Cohen defines as "any relationship of effective domination or control, political or economic, direct or indirect, of one nation over another," is the offspring of competing national sovereignties.[19] The "logic of dominion" is a rational operational strategy for a nation to adopt in these circumstances.

But even if capitalism cannot generally be held responsible for interstate conflicts and wars, and even if power and prestige were important factors in the colonialism of the late nineteenth century, does this mean that *American capitalism after World War II* cannot be held to blame for the outbreak of the cold war and, what is even more important in the radical critique of U.S. foreign policy, the alleged subjugation of the Third World? On the cold war, we can be brief since we have already examined the causes of American-Soviet rivalry and found them in the state system and the emerging bipolarity after Germany's defeat. Not only had the United States, as yet unsocialized by the state system, during the war sought to overcome the Kremlin's suspicions of the West in order to lay the foundations for postwar cooperation and peace; but as the war drew to a conclusion the principal concern of American policymakers was not to eliminate the self-proclaimed bastion of world revolution and enemy of Western capitalism, nor to push Russia out of Eastern Europe and convert that area into a market for American corporations (even had that desire existed, poverty-stricken Eastern Europe would not have been a very profitable market for American goods), but to forestall a complete return to the historic position of isolationism. The public mood was all too evident in the hasty military demobilization, the riots of some overseas units that felt that their demobilization was not rapid enough, and the cries of America's children heard both in Congress and the White House: "We want our daddies." (One group of servicemen sent the President, whose hometown was Independence, Missouri, a telegram with the memorable line: "Give us our independence or you'll go back to yours.") For the United States to have pursued

18 Cohen, *Question of Imperialism*, p. 245.
19 *Ibid.*, p. 16.

the assertive foreign policy complete with atomic threats that the revisionists have claimed it did, would have required a dictatorial disregard for the widespread demands of public opinion, which very definitely set the outer limits on what the Administration could have done.

It was not until a year and a half after World War II ended that the Truman Doctrine was enunciated. Only after further attempts to reconcile differences with Moscow, after continued Soviet pressure, denunciations, and vilifications, was containment launched. Hostile Soviet behavior was the reason for the gradual shift of American policy and public opinion from amity to enmity; American policy was not the product of a virulent and pre-existing anti-Communist ideology, and therefore not comparable to Soviet policy, which, in addition to its historical roots, reflected an anticapitalist animus that predated both the Bolshevik Revolution of 1917 and subsequent Western anti-Soviet behavior. Even before the Bolshevik leaders seized power, they had already judged capitalist states as hostile simply because they *were* capitalist.

But what of the charge of American domination of the Third World, which is the cause of their continued poverty and misery, as well as military interventions as in the Dominican Republic and Vietnam and more subtle economic-political interventions in countless other countries, such as Greece and Brazil, where U.S. imperialism supports what Kolko picturesquely calls the "local *compradors* [sharks] and oligarchies"?[20] Is the U.S. economy so dependent on the underdeveloped countries' natural resources that it can neither control them nor afford to give them independence lest they withhold their resources and thereby lower the rate of economic growth, employment, and prosperity with the likely result of large-scale unemployment, an end to the economic "trickle-down" from the corporations' "superprofits," and therefore massive social and political unrest as a prelude to the proletarian revolution?

Clearly, the United States, with more than half of the world's productive capacity, does need extensive natural resources to stoke its industrial machinery. Kolko has argued it is not even the total volume of resources that the United States imports that is the cause for U.S. imperialism in the Third World. The American economy is "so intricate that the removal of even a small part, as in a watch, can stop the mechanism."[21] Each ton of steel, he cites as an example, requires the addition of about 13 pounds of manganese. "The same analogy is true of the entire relationship between the industrial and so-called developing nations: The nations of the Third World may be poor, but in the last analysis the industrial world needs their resources more than these nations need the West."[22] Quite apart from the questionable latter half of this assertion—questionable because for the Third World the West, and espe-

[20] Kolko, *Roots of American Foreign Policy*, p. 86.
[21] *Ibid.*, p. 50.
[22] *Ibid.*

cially the United States, remains a principal source of the technology and "know-how" they need for diversifying their economies and creating self-sustaining growth—the American dependence on the underdeveloped countries as a general proposition simply does not wash. In the case Kolko cites of manganese, for example, he himself suggests its availability from Brazil, India, Gabon, and South Africa, as well as more than half the world's known reserves in Russia and China.

There is simply no evidence, one, that Communist countries are in the least reluctant to sell their resources to the capitalist West; two, that nationalist regimes in the Third World will not sell their resources to the West—although, as the Arabs have shown, these countries do want higher prices or what they consider a fairer return for the resources that keep Western industry running; three, the sources of these raw materials are numerous and in many cases in politically safe areas. It is, in any case, unlikely that all these sources will cut off their supplies to the West or the United States at the same time. As Robert Tucker has caustically noted, "Radical intellectuals may harbor such romantic notions but governments, revolutionary governments included, do not" because they need the capital.[23] Finally, the United States already possesses many of the raw materials it needs. One need but look at current attempts to find new sources of energy, more fully exploit domestic U.S. oil deposits, and clean up an old source, coal, of which the United States has a vast supply. As President Nixon's phrase "Operation Independence" suggests about the energy problem, "not only does the evidence fail to bear out the argument of dependency but it points in the opposite direction to an economy that is remarkably self-sufficient, so much so that a policy of autarchy represents a very real possibility."[24]

What is true for America's alleged dependence on Third World natural resources is equally true for America's similarly alleged need of the underdeveloped countries for market and investment opportunities. American exports find their principal markets in the rich Western states, not the poor countries that cannot afford to buy much. The United States, Britain, France, West Germany, and Japan have not since 1945 suffered from a lack of consumer purchasing power! In 1968, American exports represented 4 per cent of the GNP; 67 per cent of these went to Western Europe, Canada, and Japan, while exports to the underdeveloped states decreased between 1955 and 1968.[25] Most goods stayed at home. American investments also went primarily to Western industrial countries, even though Washington attempted to control the outflow of dollars to minimize the impact on the balance of trade. Direct investments abroad as a percentage of the total investment was 6 per cent; when compared with domestic corporate profits, the return on for-

[23] Robert W. Tucker, *The Radical Left and American Foreign Policy* (Baltimore: Johns Hopkins Press, 1971), p. 126.
[24] *Ibid.*, p. 120.
[25] *Ibid.*, pp. 134–36.

eign investment was 9.3 per cent.[26] Most investments also stayed at home to stoke the growth of the economy.

The real blow to the theory of imperialism surely comes in the Middle East: Here very clearly the oil companies who, according to the theory, should have determined U.S. policy in the area, have had virtually no influence at all. American policy has been consistently favorable to Israel; the oil companies obviously have favored the Arabs. Even after that policy became more even-handed after 1973, the Nixon Administration was heavily influenced by the desire to avoid yet another Arab-Israeli War, which might lead to Soviet-American involvement and possible nuclear war. In 1973 the two superpowers almost did clash as the Soviets apparently threatened to send in their troops unilaterally as the Israelis were about to defeat the Egyptians again. If the Israeli-Arab differences could not be resolved, if their conflicts of interests continued to smolder, and if the Arabs would go to war again and in another military clash be humiliated once more, the world might witness a Soviet-American confrontation on the brink of nuclear war, as Moscow would protect its clients and Washington would oppose a military intervention.

And finally, even on its own terms, the imperialist interpretation of postwar American policy is dubious. But for Hanoi and the Vietcong, its advocates are in fact arguing, the exploitative character of American neocolonial control would continue, preventing the industrialization of backward nations. Even in Latin America, the area usually cited as the one in which America presumably most effectively extends its imperialist tentacles, Communist Cuba and the increasing number of emerging national-socialist—and often military—regimes would suggest the tenuousness of the self-perpetuating character of "American imperialism." Indeed, if, as the critics themselves say, the issue in Vietnam was nationalism, it was questionable whether the outcome of that conflict would have either bolstered the cause of revolutionary Marxism or reduced the size of America's global empire any more than have other nationalist governments that established their independence prior to Vietnam's "war of national liberation."[27] In any event, ultimate refutation of the thesis of capitalism as the cause of the war in Vietnam came from that citadel of capitalism, the stock market: Wall Street quotations rose each time it appeared that the war might be nearing an end. Peace, not war, was profitable. And once the Nixon Administration had moved toward *détente* with Russia, it was the business community that became one of its strongest advocates and supporters—just as it had looked forward to close American-Russian relations after 1945. There was money in it. It was not the capitalists who had precipitated the cold war; nor did they oppose *détente*.

[26] *Ibid.*, pp. 126–31.

[27] George Lichtheim, *Imperialism* (New York: Praeger Publishers, 1971), pp. 145–50.

In brief, an analyst who wishes to use the capitalist-imperialist model cannot simply posit an economic motivation because it seems persuasive to him and because whatever situation he then wishes to explain seems plausible in the light of such an economic analysis. While it is true that economic factors have on occasion contributed to interstate conflict and war, so have other factors. The real question, then, is whether war can be explained primarily or exclusively in economic terms. In order to do that, the analyst must show that economic motives were actually converted into aggressive and expansionist policies, including the outbreak of hostilities. As Vernon Van Dyke has argued, "Those who approach the question of the causes of imperialism and war through a study of the formulation and execution of foreign policies in concrete situations rarely emerge with an answer that is exclusively economic. Almost always noneconomic factors are found to be heavily involved, and very often they appear to play a decisive role."[28]

For example, can a policy conclusion about "American imperialism" be drawn merely from the identity of certain actors? To ask merely a few key questions: Were the men whom Kolko listed the *cause* of the government's policy or were they merely the *effect*—that is, were they attracted to government service when the nation perceivd itself to be endangered? And if it can be shown that they flocked to the government in 1940 when the enemy was on the right, not on the left, can their motivations really be said to derive from an anti-Communist ideology; or did it stem from a concern with national security, whether the threat came from the right or left? And, in any event, when men go from their Big Business, Big Law, or Big Finance offices to the State or Defense Department, do not their perceptions of their roles change and, therefore, their outlook and policy preferences? Is it not more likely that as a man's role (the behavior that is expected from him in a specific position, be it as a father, professor, or Secretary of State) changes, predictions of his behavior solely on the basis of past roles or class identification are likely to be off the mark. The expectations of society, of his political superiors and peers, as well as his own perception of that role will be among factors affecting his behavior. A Secretary of State coming from a corporation law firm will define his role by his view of what it entails and the view of his new "reference group." Secretary of State Acheson's perceptions of the international system and the Soviet Union's aims after World War II were not influenced by his previous legal experience on behalf of big business. He certainly did not consider himself to be the spokesman for corporate capitalism and the architect of free world imperialism. Not the demands of the economic system but his image of the state system impressed him and governed his actions.[29]

[28] Vernon Van Dyke, *International Politics*, 2d ed. (New York: Appleton-Century-Crofts, 1966), p. 110.

[29] Dean Acheson, *Present at the Creation* (New York: W. W. Norton, 1969), and

The Military-Industrial Complex

The explanation of American foreign policy in terms of the machinations of a military-industrial complex, like the imperialist one, is also based on the identity of the principal participants: Again, little is said about the policy process itself; once the main participants have been listed and the alleged policy outputs noted, a cause-and-effect relationship is assumed. The military-industrial complex thesis is simplicity itself: It holds that certain forces have profited economically and politically from the cold war and therefore favor continued high international tensions and large-scale armament programs.[30] These forces, as the term suggests, include, first of all, the professional military, whose role, status, and share of the budget all depend on "peace not breaking out," and second, the managers of the industrial corporations that serve the military and gain handsomely by it. The relationship is one of mutual need. Some of the industries are extremely dependent on the services: Lockheed Aircraft, General Dynamics, McDonnell-Douglas, and Boeing would not survive without military orders. They employ large numbers of retired officers to help solicit contracts and find out what kinds of weapons the military wants. Others, like General Motors, International Business Machines, or Standard Oil of New Jersey, add to their annual profits although they are not strictly dependent for their economic well-being on the production of arms. The military, in turn, needs the corporations, especially those that are virtually public corporations, for they have the managerial talent, technological ability, and production lines the military needs. They are its arsenals.

Other groups, however, also possess a vested interest in the continuation of the cold war. They include those whom Barnet has labeled as "national security managers," composed not only of the military but also, more influentially, the "militarized civilians" or "homicidal bureaucrats."[31] These men come from the world of corporations, high finance, and corporate law, are its servants, and keep America in "permanent war," both because America's economic goals are necessarily expansionist

Ronald J. Stupak, *The Shaping of Foreign Policy: The Role of Secretary of State as Seen by Dean Acheson* (New York: Odyssey Press, 1969).

[30] Sidney Lens, *The Military-Industrial Complex* (Philadelphia: Pilgrim Press, 1970); Barnet, *Economy of Death*; Ralph Lapp, *The Weapons Culture* (Baltimore: Penguin Books, 1968); William Proxmire, *Report from Wasteland* (New York: Praeger Publishers, 1970); Seymour Melman, *Pentagon Capitalism* (New York: McGraw-Hill Book Co., 1970, and *The Permanent War Economy* (New York: Simon & Schuster, 1974); and Adam Yarmolinsky, *The Military Establishment* (New York: Harper & Row, 1971). The most balanced treatment is Yarmolinsky's.

[31] Richard J. Barnet, *The Roots of War* (Baltimore: Penguin Books, 1973), pp. 13–22.

and because these civilians perceive the world and operate in much the same way as the professional military. "The principal militarists in America wear three-button suits."[32] Examples cited include Secretary of State Acheson, who before Korea counseled a build-up of military strength and later was the first to recommend fighting in that country; included too is Secretary of State Dulles, who built up America's extensive alliances outside of Europe. Having embraced the military's "realism," these men and their subordinates have gained a sense of accomplishment, public stature, and deference, as well as contacts for their later professional lives; they therefore do not favor a relaxation of the international tensions or a resolution of conflicting interests which are their *raison d'être*. This is true of the fourth segment outside of the government as well: the labor unions, whose members find employment and paychecks in the defense industries; the universities, whose physical and biological scientists are engaged in government "research and development" and whose social scientists are contracted for policy-oriented studies; and the various states whose economic growth is spurred by military installations and defense plants. Indeed, few segments seem exempt: Local real estate dealers, contractors, and retail merchants all profit by the population expansion that defense installations bring to their communities.

Defense is thus good business. Vested interests pervade American life and this is reflected by their representatives in Congress, the fifth element composing the MIC. Mobilizing support for arms production and a tough international stand is easy. Until recently, anti-Communism was the means for enlisting the evangelistic spirit and enthusiasm of the American people; their crusading behavior served the national security managers well. Few Congressmen asked questions about the defense budget or argued for lower force levels, different strategies, and fewer weapons. To do so was to risk being accused in the next election of neglecting the nation's defenses against Communism; to risk one's constituents' welfare; to risk the disapproval of colleagues, many of whom had bases and defense industries in their constituencies and were officers in the reserves and some of whom controlled one's political future in Congress; and to risk the ultimate accusation, that of being unpatriotic —"un-American."[33] Defense spending, in any event, has benefited the entire economy. It has constituted a huge subsidy underwriting the stability and growth of the economy. Without it, the nation could expect sizable unemployment and a decline of profits. America, in short, cannot afford peace. Too many powerful participants in the policy process have a stake in the system as it now operates; hence, the world's first

[32] Barnet, *Economy of Death*, p. 79.

[33] The correctness of these assumptions by advocates of the "military-industrial complex" argument, and more broadly, Congressional voting behavior in relationship to defense issues, is analyzed in Bruce M. Russett, *What Price Vigilance?* (New Haven, Conn.: Yale University Press, 1970).

democracy, dedicated to man's life, is now committed to an "Economy of Death." Private enterprise has been replaced by "Pentagon Capitalism" and a "Weapons Culture"; and the efficiency of the private sector has been replaced by a highly inefficient "military socialism." Weapons are produced years after their target dates—if produced at all—and all too frequently they turn out to have poor reliability and be excessively expensive. The "overruns" on cost estimates often run into the billions.

The military-industrial complex (MIC) interpretation of American foreign policy—like the earlier imperialist interpretation—makes a very satisfactory explanation for its advocates. It provides them with a key that allegedly unlocks the mysteries and problems of the world, for it constitutes a complete analysis of all domestic and foreign events. Economics to Western man seems such an obviously fundamental force. To an American especially, the striving for monetary success and material abundance (even for those who deliberately reject its pursuit) is ever present. Explanations of American domestic politics have often relied heavily upon assumptions about economic competition among business, labor, agriculture, and the military. Americans are the "people of plenty," and America's politics is largely a question of the division of this bounty. Thus, an analysis of American foreign policy in terms of the quest for profits by big corporations suggests a tangible and demonstrable underlying motivation.

As with the imperialist theory, the MIC thesis omits all, or at least very much, analysis of the state system; the thesis rests in a vacuum. Hence, this interpretation takes on much of the conspiratorial tone of the virtually identical "merchants of death" interpretation of why the United States went to war in 1917.[34] The financiers, the munitions manufacturers, and the Eastern Establishment, with its anti-German and pro-Britain sentiments, were to blame for U.S. entry into that war. In other words, but for those groups, the United States could have stayed neutral and spared "the people" a war. German hegemony in Europe and the threat it constituted to American security were ignored. The

---

[34] A characteristic view of the role of the military was of "the alliance of the military with powerful economic groups to secure appropriations on the one hand for a constantly increasing military and naval establishment, and on the other hand, the constant threat of the use of that swollen military establishment in behalf of the economic interests at home and abroad of the industrialists supporting it. It meant the subjugation of the people of the various countries to the uniform, the self-interested identification of patriotism with commercialism, and the removal of the military from the control of civil law."

Interestingly enough, this statement, which could have been spoken by a liberal Senator or a representative of Students for a Democratic Society, is from Senator Nye's investigations, held during the 1930's, which attributed our involvement in World War I to the military-industrial complex of its time. "Munitions Industry," *Report on Existing Legislation*, Senate Report No. 994, Part 5, 74th Congress, 2d Session (Washington, D.C.: GPO, 1936), pp. 8–9. Quoted in Hans Morgenthau and Kenneth Thompson, eds., *Principles and Problems of International Politics* (New York: Knopf, 1950), pp. 62–63.

contemporary version of this thesis also defines those forces with a vested interest in the cold war, and it too suggests that if political control were exerted over them, the American people could once more live in peace, cut the defense budget, reduce military influence in government, and rearrange the priorities between foreign and domestic policies. Both explanations assert that, if America but wills abstinence, it can abstain.

How this variant of the illusion of omnipotence could provide for a disengagement from continuous armaments races and conflicts abroad is hard to understand, however, if there are in fact so many millions of both influential and working Americans who benefit from their continuation. Indeed, there is a contradiction at the heart of the MIC. On the one hand, it is suggested that American foreign policy is too interventionist, too committed, too expensive, and distorts national priorities. What gives the MIC argument much of its emotional appeal is that America's allegedly overextended and dangerous policy is contrary to the interests of the vast majority of Americans who would benefit by the cutback of external commitments and concentration on domestic affairs to make America a better place for all to live in; the MIC is, in fact, presented as a conspiracy blocking the majority's "real interests." On the other hand, almost every group in the United States would seem to have a cash interest in international tension, including the flower-growers who supply the flowers for battle monuments; if this is true, the nation would have an interest in continued cold war policies, and it is therefore hard to understand how this policy can be changed. Yet it has been changed: the percent of the gross national product spent on defense is today lower than at any time since before the Korean War in 1950, defense-related employment is half of the 10 percent it was during the 1950's, a number of large aerospace firms have been in serious financial trouble (Lockheed being rescued from bankruptcy by the government), and defense profits down compared to non-defense earnings.[35] And whether defense spending was a needed crutch for the economy is at least debatable; if the skilled personnel and technology devoted to weaponry had been devoted instead to the growth of the non-military sector of the economy (assuming no external threat), would not the economy have grown more rapidly?

A better perspective on the military-industrial complex can be gained if it is viewed in the context of the state system. In a bipolar system in which both powers, regardless of their domestic structures or values, were highly sensitive to the slightest shift in the balance of power lest it result in the opponent's hegemony, the emphasis was on demarcating spheres of influence and on defusing confrontations and managing crises. Not surprisingly in these circumstances, policy-makers were con-

[35] Philip Odeen, "In Defense of the Defense Budget," *Foreign Policy*, Fall, 1974, pp. 94–95.

cerned with their nation's military strength. Nor should it be surprising that civilians, especially Secretaries of State, would advocate a military build-up or the fighting of a limited war like Korea. They were, after all, presumed to be the Presidents' chief foreign policy advisers, and the nation's objectives and the means to achieve them were bound to be of concern to them. Ideally, policy balances means and ends. The "militarized civilians" may thus advocate the development of a new weapon or military doctrine, or the use of higher force levels, just as they may advocate the opposite if, as in matters of arms control or lower perceived external threats, they feel such a course to be necessary or desirable.

Besides being affected by the extensive and intensive bipolarity of the period from 1945 through the Cuban missile crisis, policy-makers were also affected by the continuously and rapidly changing technology. The fear of a technological breakthrough by the opponent was bound to worry those whose main concern was deterrence of an enemy believed to be expansionistic. As technology invents ever newer delivery systems, a series of arms races is at least understandable. For deterrence to remain effective, the offense had to stay ahead of the defense; the deterrer could never leave his adversary in doubt that the second-strike forces could get through and eradicate him. In short, the military influence in the policy process reflected the international situation the United States confronted; and given the responsibility of policy-makers in a bipolar nuclear system and the nature of modern technology, they were going to play it conservatively. With the nation's security at stake, great risks were unlikely.

In addition to the state system and technology, the MIC thesis conveniently ignores both the actual policies pursued and the actual policy process. During the early years of the cold war, the principal instrument of national policy was economic aid. Not until the Korean War erupted and the fear of other possible Communist military attacks, particularly by the Red Army in Europe, heightened the Truman Administration's estimation of the external threat to American security did American and NATO rearmament begin in earnest. After Korea, the fiscally and politically conservative Eisenhower Administration again cut back military spending drastically (as a percentage of an annually growing gross national product). Its desire to balance budgets at lower spending levels and its conviction that the United States could spend itself into bankruptcy (documented by quotes attributed to but never uttered by Lenin to the effect that America could be defeated in this manner without a shot ever being fired) led it to concentrate its spending on the Air Force, with its capacity for "massive retaliation." On the whole, during the Truman and Eisenhower years, military appropriations and strategy were decided by the "remainder method"—that is, the sum left after the national income had been calculated, the cost of domestic programs provided for, and nonmilitary foreign policy expenditures decided.[36] Only since Kennedy have administrations decided the defense budgets in an opposite fashion: by first deciding national strategy, and from this deducing the missions of the various services, the weapons they needed, and the over-all cost.

Throughout, civilian policy-makers always remembered the maxim that if you listened to a doctor you were never healthy, or a minister, never without sin, or a military man, never secure. Consequently, while the services were consulted, they rarely stopped grumbling about all the weapons they did *not* receive. The result was that, given a limited budget, they had to compete among themselves for money and weapons. The Defense Department's constituents—the industrial corporations and the political supporters of the services and corporations in Congress —were, it is true, also involved in the policy process, although not necessarily in the way usually asserted. For example, while it is normally believed that congressmen whose constituencies include industries producing military hardware will vote for high military budgets, the voting records of such Congressmen do not support this thesis; many, indeed, vote for lower defense budgets. The principal correlation is between voting for arms and those representatives whose districts or states include military bases.[37] In any event, to the degree that corporations supported weapons production and Congressmen voted for the military, their role was basically limited to supporting a particular service in its conflicts with the other services for contracts *after* the basic issue of funds and strategy had been decided by the President, whose control over the military was, in fact, strengthened by this intense interservice and intercorporate rivalry. He ruled because they were so deeply divided. There was no military-industrial complex, dictating higher budgets, more weapons, and more hawkish foreign policies, but *a number of* military-industrial complexes that were usually in competition with one another.

For the Presidents, then, the principal factors affecting decisions remained their perceptions of the deterrent balance and technology. Even when Soviet military strength rose, it took some *action* by Russia or its friends to bring about an American build-up. It took a Korean attack or a threat over Berlin to raise the executive and legislative branches' perception of an external threat and to make it politically feasible to suggest that, in view of the enhanced danger to national security, new domestic programs or greater funding of the old ones could be postponed or new taxes with which to buy more weapons would receive popular support. Before Korea, Truman refused to enhance the nation's military capability; but Eisenhower, even after Sputnik, did little, despite grave warnings about a potential missile gap and SAC's new

---

[36] Samuel P. Huntington, *The Common Defense* (New York: Columbia University Press, 1961), and Walter Millis, *Arms and the State* (New York: Twentieth Century Fund, 1958), Part Two.

[37] Russett, *What Price Vigilance?*

vulnerability. It was the liberally oriented Kennedy Administration that launched a large missile production program and limited war preparations in order to give itself policy options after Khrushchev's tough behavior at the Vienna summit meeting and the renewed Soviet challenge in Berlin. The Nixon Administration was virtually alone among postwar administrations in deciding upon major arms production and deployment in the absence of an obvious and visible security threat— and this is one reason for the vigorous criticisms it received. In response, it could only assert the possibility of grave future danger; but in the absence of aggressive Soviet behavior, it could not prove its case. It was therefore unable to rally widespread political support and still the critics of its plans for deployment of ABMs and MIRVs, both weapons whose utility was in any event hard to demonstrate, as the test of their effectiveness lay in their nonuse.

One key point also follows from the bureaucratic decision-making model (which will be presented in the next chapter): The military does not generally live up to its popular bloodthirsty and warlike image. Hitler once remarked of the German military that before he became the Führer he thought he would have to put a leash on his soldiers and hold them back; instead he had constantly to push them forward. An army or navy is a bureaucracy. It is obviously interested in the expansion of its capabilities and influence in decision-making, but like any bureaucracy it has a tendency to play its safe. War, as the Prussian general Clausewitz has said, is a gamble; it is risky and can spell defeat for a country and a loss of influence, if not collapse, of the military bureaucracy. It is, in a real sense, easier to play soldier in peacetime. For example, the U.S. Army perceived its prime role in the post-1945 period to be the defense of Europe. Feeling that it never received sufficient resources, the army was always aware that commitments would outrun its strength; generally, therefore, it was not particularly enthusiastic about adding new commitments. It preferred to concentrate on what it believed to be its primary obligations.

For another example, the army (and, for that matter, the other services) did not advocate intervention in Korea; it was the civilian leadership that felt it necessary to intervene. After China's entry into that war, when pressure to retaliate against China became intense—from MacArthur in the field and from the Republican Party—it was the military as a whole that took a leading role in opposing this move. Russia was the primary enemy; the United States should not, therefore, invest excessive resources against a secondary enemy and weaken itself in such a struggle. The air force, for instance, opposed using its big bombers for attacks against China since if too many were shot down it would weaken the air force's deterrent capacity against the Soviet Union. In short, the services have hardly been war dogs straining at the leash, seeking to promote futher commitments and interventions.

Korea was not the only example. The military was not the prime force proposing the Bay of Pigs operation; the blockade of Cuba a year later; or the Dominican intervention; nor, despite the military headquarters established in Saigon with Kennedy's commitment of military advisers, was the military in Washington too enthusiastic about a Vietnam intervention. After what had been to it a disillusioning experience in Korea —a limited war in which the military felt it had been improperly restrained politically—a clique called the "Never-Again Club" was formed. When asked from time to time about its judgments about a possible intervention, as in Laos in 1961, the services asked for a virtually free hand so that presumably they would not be "shackled" again, unable to win. The civilian response was hardly surprising: No. Thus the military relieved itself of any responsibility in case of disaster from nonintervention and tried to place full blame for that eventuality on its civilian superiors. On the other hand, once the latter had decided to intervene *with* limits, the military went in and, hardly unexpectedly given what it had to do, sought to increase its strength and a relaxation of restraints to enhance the pressure on the enemy.

On the whole, therefore, it is probably correct to say that the MIC thesis is primarily a "devil theory," a polemical tool rather than an analytical one. The writings of the MIC theorists tend to run to a pattern: They decry both the nature and methods of American foreign policy, what the United States has done to the world, how it has done it, and the price it has paid in terms of delaying the fight against poverty and injustice at home. They hold the military, business, and their "servants" in Congress responsible for starting the cold war and/or continuing hard-line policies and escalating the arms race; in brief, the MIC is invoked to discredit the policies and institutions responsible for these policies. Someone must be to blame for the mess; clearly international tension and domestic injustice are not in the majority's interests. Logically, therefore, it follows that this minority of privileged men act as a conspiracy. Note also that the logic of this argument is backward: The substance of the policies is condemned first; the MIC analyst then reasons from that back to those allegedly to blame. The whole argument rests on the rather questionable ground of guilt by association: If someone has an interest in arms, bureaucratically or economically, this must be the cause of arms races and increased international tensions. Arms do acquire vested domestic interests, but this does not necessarily mean that arms races are initiated by those interests, or that they will stoke such a race and prevent its slowing down or cessation. The 1972 ABM treaty, for example, was further reduced by the 1974 protocol agreed to at the Brzehnev-Nixon summit meeting that year; a lot of jobs and some vested interests, including some in the Soviet military, lost out in these agreements, which were made by two determined political leaders who could not be blocked. In the final analysis, if studied empirically, the policy-process is quite different: pluralistic, competitive, open, and *legitimate*— exactly what the imperialist and MIC explanations deny.

14   Decision-Making and Perceptions

The decision-making approach to understanding the foreign policy of a country makes the basic assumption that one needs to look at the specific men and departments officially responsible for making external policy.[1] For when we talk of a state's doing this or that, we are really talking about those men and the policy decisions they make and how they implement them. The state, in short, equals the official policy-makers whose decisions and actions are the policies of the state. The decisions they make are the "outputs" of the domestic political system. By focusing on the decision-makers, this approach emphasizes how they *see* the world. What is important, after all, is not what the international system is really or objectively like, but how the policy-makers subjectively perceive it. For it is on these perceptions that they act or, for that matter, do not act; reality, in this perspective, does not exist by itself, independent of the policy-maker's definition of the external situation.

As we saw much earlier, the balance of power analysis could prescribe what Chamberlain should have done to counter Hitler in the 1930's, but not what he did. By failing to look at the Prime Minister and his advisers, within the Cabinet and outside of it, and to analyze their perceptions of Hitler, Nazi Germany's goals, and the Versailles Peace treaty, first-level analysis could not by itself tell us as outside observers why the British did what they did and did not do, why they bungled and brought on the very war they had hoped to avoid. Such an analysis was thus not very helpful. Similarly, even if another concept could properly explain some particular event, as the concept of national style can account for the American intervention in the Vietnam war, such an explanation may be

[1] See Roger Hilsman, *To Move a Nation* (Garden City, N.Y.: Doubleday, 1967); Graham Allison, *The Essence of Decision* (Boston: Little, Brown, 1971); Morton H. Halperin, *Bureaucratic Politics and Foreign Policy* (Washington, D.C.: Brookings Institution, 1974); and Morton H. Halperin and Arnold Kanter, eds., *Readings in American Foreign Policy* (Boston: Little, Brown, 1973).

rejected as too broad and vague. How can one say national style is responsible for the war in the absence of looking more closely at the men who made that decision, which departments they served in (e.g. the Defense Department), the pressures within the organization to intervene or not to intervene, and legislative and public pressures. Since national style presumably affects all policy-makers alike, does this mean that the Vietnam intervention was inevitable? If not, then despite the alleged impact of American style, do we not have to examine the men, sometimes described as "the best and the brightest" men America had to offer, who made the decisions to intervene?

One model of decision-making—the rational actor model—has been central to first-level analysis, which represents each state as a unified actor who makes his choices in foreign policies in four clearly separate steps: one, he selects the objectives he wishes to achieve and values he expects to maximize; two, he considers the alternative means of achieving these aims; three, he calculates the likely consequences of each of the courses of action he might adopt; and four, he selects the one that has the best prospect of attaining the desired aims. Thus, as Henry Kissinger wrote in 1957, if U.S. policy sought security and peace, it could not rationally rely on a strategy of massive retaliation against the U.S.S.R. when confronted with limited challenges. To respond in this manner would only ensure U.S. suicide; not to respond at all would be tantamount to surrender. Both courses of policy were, therefore, irrational. The only rational and feasible option in these circumstances was a "limited war" response.[2] This rational model, as ought to be clear, underlies not only much of the analyses of international politics and specific foreign policies, but other spheres of decision-making as well. Not only in the "games nations play," with their informal rules, but clearly in other games as well, whether they too have informal rules, such as in courtship or politics (Watergate, for instance, clearly violated generally understood norms of conduct), or more formal rules, as in football or chess, each player must make a set of decisions if he is to "win" in a competitive situation. He usually has several options; he must at each point in the game decide which play is the best one in terms of his goals.

The other model is that of governmental politics. It focuses on the executive branch of government and especially the bureaucracies whose official responsibility is to formulate and execute the nation's foreign policy. The emphasis is on the pluralistic nature of decision-making since the executive branch is in fact a "many-splintered" thing; so is the legislature, at least in free countries; and outside in society are the many interest groups, mass media, and various publics who together constitute public opinion. The bureaucracy is thus placed in its broader governmental and societal setting. Making policy in these circumstances comes, on the one hand, through conflicts among many actors with different perceptions, perspectives, and interests and, on the other hand, through reconciling these differences. These two elements of the policy struggle will determine who gets what and when. Such a political way of making policy generally applies to program policies, which express continuing goals and involve a continuing set of actors, including the Congress, because program policies usually need funding.

Graham Allison has aptly illustrated the difference between rational and bureaucratic policy-making.[3] When in the late 1950's the Soviet Union tested its first ICBM, Washington became very concerned about a missile gap favoring Moscow. American policy-makers, using the rational model, thought that Russia would exploit this technological breakthrough, mass produce ICBMs, and use them to pressure the United States to concede territorial changes in Central Europe, specifically in the symbolically significant western half of Berlin. If the same American policy-makers had used the pluralistic policy-making model, they would have been more cautious in drawing this conclusion. The Red Army controlled the missiles, and it was unlikely suddenly to abandon its traditional definition of its role in favor of strategic deterrence with ICBMs. Such a shift of role within the army would certainly have been accompanied by an observable policy struggle as those officers whose functions would have been downgraded would have fiercely resisted. Similarly, the development of a large ICBM force would have required a vast transfer of funds from other services and their requirements, thereby creating noisy quarrels. The different models, then, offered quite different assessments of what the Soviets would do and implied quite different prescriptions for American defense and foreign policies. The incoming Kennedy Administration, acting upon the rational model, initiated larger missile deployment than it might otherwise have done; the Russians' reaction, after the Cuban missile crisis, was the extensive build-up that has resulted in their achievement of strategic parity.

Crisis Decision-Making

For the two types of decisions we discussed earlier, the rational actor model is probably the most relevant in explaining and understanding crises decisions. Crises, as already suggested, are characterized by a number of features: a perceived threat to vital interests, usually surprise, and a sense of urgency to make decisions.[4] Overhanging the situation, in which one state has confronted another with a demand for a change in the *status quo*, is the possible use of violence, possibly a nuclear war. One

[3] Graham T. Allison, "Conceptual Models and the Cuban Missile Crisis," *American Political Science Review*, September, 1969, p. 716.

[4] Oran Young, *The Politics of Force* (Princeton, N.J.: Princeton University Press, 1968), pp. 6–15, and Charles F. Hermann, ed., *International Crises* (New York: Free Press, 1972).

characteristic of the decision-making process is, therefore, that the decisions will be made at the very top of the governmental hierarchy by the President and his closest advisers. Some will be his statutory advisors, such as the secretaries of his chief foreign policy agencies, others will be men both in and out of government whose judgment the President particularly trusts. Thus, during the potentially very explosive Cuban Missile Crisis of 1962, the Executive Committee, which managed the crisis, listed as its members the President and Vice-President, the Secretaries of State and Defense; their seconds-in-command; the Director of the CIA; the Chairman of the Joint Chiefs of Staff; the President's Special Assistant for National Security Affairs; and certain other individuals such as the Secretary of the Treasury; the Attorney General (the President's brother); his Special Counsel, perhaps the President's closest friend after his brother; an Ambassador just returned from Moscow; and President Truman's former Secretary of State.[5] During the 1972 spring offensive of North Vietnamese troops, when the defeat of the South Vietnamese Army seemed imminent, the decision-making process was more narrowly confined. Partly as a result of the concentration of foreign policy decision-making in the White House under Henry Kissinger, partly as a result of the President's style as a "loner," and partly as a result of the Nixon tactic of confronting a Senate increasingly critical of the continuation of the Vietnam war with *faits accomplis* (which could not be done if leaks occurred prior to action), the decision-making seems to have been confined largely to the two men, although formally the members of the National Security Council were consulted.[6]

A second characteristic of crisis decisions is the central role of the President; it is he who, more than anyone else, interprets events and evaluates the stakes in the crisis. Kennedy's and Nixon's "readings" of the nature of the situations they confronted, the consequences these situations might have upon U.S. security and their own political futures and ability to lead the nation were responsible for their actions. (The latter two can hardly be separated, for the external challenges, as Presidents see them, do not really leave them with a choice of accepting a personal loss of prestige without accepting a loss of national prestige. For a President of the United States personal and national cost calculations tend to become identical.) Kennedy saw the installation of Soviet missiles in Cuba as a personal challenge with damaging national effects. In response to earlier Congressional and public clamor about possible Soviet offensive missiles in Cuba—as distinct from ground-to-air or -ship defensive missiles—Kennedy had publicly declared that the United States

---

[5] For the Cuban missile crisis, see Elie Abel, *The Missile Crisis* (New York: Bantam Books, 1966); Alexander L. George *et al.*, eds., *The Limits of Coercive Diplomacy* (Boston: Little, Brown, 1971); and Robert F. Kennedy, *Thirteen Days* (New York: Norton, 1969).

[6] Tad Szulc, "Behind the Vietnam Cease-Fire Agreements," *Foreign Policy*, Summer, 1974, pp. 39–40.

would not tolerate offensive missiles on the island 90 miles off the Florida coast. Intended primarily as a declaration to cool American domestic criticism which had come largely from Republicans, Kennedy's statement had also led Moscow to respond that it had no intention of placing missiles in Cuba; Russia had more than enough missiles at home. Thus the President had initially de-emphasized the possibility that the Russians would install such weapons in Cuba and Moscow had then signaled it understood Kennedy's declaration; in private, it had further reassured him that it had no intentions of installing missiles anywhere outside of the U.S.S.R. Kennedy was thus publicly pledged to act if the Russians lied—as it turned out—unless he wished to be publicly humiliated. If he did not act in these circumstances the Soviet leader would not believe other pledges and commitments the President had made or was obligated to fulfill by virtue of their existence when he had acceded to the Presidency. At least, this is how the President perceived the situation.

The consequences were adjudged very dangerous by Kennedy, who already feared that Khrushchev interpreted previous acts by Kennedy—the abortive Bay of Pigs invasion of Cuba and the inaction of U.S. troops when the Berlin Wall went up—as acts signaling a lack of will, an absence of sufficient resolution and determination on the part of the United States to defend its vital interests. Khrushchev talked openly of America's failure of nerve. The United States, in his view, talked loud but carried a small stick. In this context, it was not so much the effect of the Soviet missiles upon the military equation between the two powers, although that was important; it was the political consequences of the *appearance* of a change in the balance of power that were deemed critical by Kennedy. The Soviet Union was supposed to be on the short end of the missile gap. But American inaction would, Kennedy feared, be widely recognized as a persuasive answer to the U.S. claims of missile superiority, would lead allied governments to fear that in the new situation in which America would be highly vulnerable to nuclear devastation they could no longer count on the United States to defend them, and above all it might tempt the Soviets to exploit this situation and seek to disintegrate America's alliances—especially NATO, since Khrushchev had already restated his determination to eject the Western allies from West Berlin. If Khrushchev got away with Cuba, why should he take seriously Kennedy's pledge to defend West Berlin? And if he did not, would not Soviet and American troops soon be clashing in an area where they would be hard to separate?

The real irony of the Cuban missile crisis is that Kennedy was also determined that during his years in office he would try to seek a more stable and restrained basis of coexistence with the Soviet Union. This long-range goal, which hardly had the massive support it has today, could not be realized if Khrushchev would not take Kennedy seriously and felt he could push him around; then serious negotiations, recognizing each other's legitimate interests, would be impossible. Thus a major change in the cold war atmosphere was at stake in addition to America's reputation for power and willingness to keep commitments already given; domestically, of course, another "defeat" in Cuba, a discrediting of Kennedy's foreign policy, was bound to effect Kennedy's personal standing with his party, the Congress, and the public and to lead to, among other things, strong right-wing Republican pressures to be more forceful in the future and endangering the New Frontier's liberal domestic reforms.

Nixon in Vietnam also saw the central issue as America's reputation for power or prestige.[7] When he came into office, there was little question that American opinion was weary of the high cost, especially in casualties, of the Vietnam war. The cost seemed totally disproportionate to the continuation of a war that promised no successful end in the near future. For Nixon, the crux of the problem was not whether the United States got out of Vietnam but, as he repeatedly stressed, how it got out. If America's chief adversaries, Russia and China, were to be deterred and contained, if fruitful negotiations were to occur on arms control with Moscow and opening up relations with Peking, and if a more stable and peaceful "structure of peace" were to be worked out with those two capitals, then America's perceived reputation in the two major Communist countries was the crucial factor. If the United States were humiliated in Vietnam, it would be viewed as a "pitiful, helpless giant" that could be pressured, with which one need not negotiate seriously on a basis of the mutual recognition and acceptance of legitimate security interests, and that offered few attractions as a potential partner to either Russia or China against the other.

Nixon's strategy was, therefore, to "Vietnamize" the war. This meant that the South Vietnamese Army would increasingly take over the fighting, but it would receive large-scale U.S. air support to preserve a non-Communist government in South Vietnam. If public opinion would support a low-cost strategy in casualties for the United States, if the pressure for America to get out completely could be greatly reduced at home, then Hanoi would presumably gain an incentive to negotiate a compromise settlement of the war. Confronted by the continued participation in the war of U.S. air power and—it was hoped—an increasingly better trained South Vietnamese Army equipped by the United States, with its hopes for an all-out victory in the South dimming as the costs of the war continued to drain its strength, Hanoi would prefer to end the hostilities rather than continue fighting, and settle for political competition to gain a share of the power in Saigon.

It was this strategy that faced disaster in the spring of 1972, just after Nixon's dramatic visit to Peking and just before his extremely important visit to Moscow to negotiate limitations on defensive and offensive missiles and other key topics. Nixon, like Kennedy, rejected the possibility

[7] Besides the earlier Szulc article, the Nixon decision has been reconstructed from the *New York Times* of the period and Henry Branden, *The Retreat of American Power* (Garden City, N.Y.: Doubleday, 1973).

of inaction, even though the Moscow summit meeting with its potential for dramatically changing the nature of the U.S.-Soviet adversary-partnership for the better might be jeopardized if he took strong action against the Soviet Union's fraternal socialist state. But the President felt that Moscow, having supplied Hanoi with much of its modern paraphernalia of war, such as ground-to-air missiles and tanks for its current conventional offensive, should have restrained Hanoi just before the summit. As Nixon perceived the situation, whether or not Moscow was aware of the timing of Hanoi's offensive, the fact was that the offensive seriously endangered Nixon's Vietnamization policy and this would humiliate him on the eve of vital negotiations; and the President did not intend to enter these negotiations under the cloud of defeat and failure. The failure of Vietnamization also would, of course, discredit the President's prestige and leadership at home. Thus Nixon, who had already ordered the bombing of North Vietnam, now ordered the additional step of mining its harbors to stop incoming Russian and Chinese supplies. Johnson had always refused to take this step; the risk of a confrontation with Moscow was too high. Did the latter not have the right to supply its friend? Would Washington have permitted Russia to blockade its supplies to South Vietnam? In any event, Nixon took the risk of a confrontation. Negotiations with Hanoi had not gotten anywhere; Vietnamization did not seem much more successful. The President, therefore, re-Americanized the war and by risking a direct confrontation with the U.S.S.R. hoped to compel it to pressure Hanoi to settle the war—if the U.S.S.R. wanted better relations with the United States. The Russians did not call off the Moscow summit meeting.

Nixon apparently did not consider other courses of action; he rejected inaction if that was the price for the Moscow summit. Kennedy did consider alternative responses to the Soviet missiles, everything from diplomatic pressures and a secret approach to Castro to surgical air strikes on the missiles, invasion, and blockade. However, feeling strongly that he had to act in order to impress Khrushchev, Kennedy chose the blockade as the option most likely to attain the removal of the Soviet missiles. While the blockade could not by itself achieve this objective, it was a sign of American determination, permitted the United States the option of increasing the pressure on Moscow later if Moscow did not remove its missiles, provided a relatively safe middle course between inaction and invasion or an air strike, which might provoke the Russians, and placed on Khrushchev the responsibility of deciding whether to escalate or de-escalate. It is significant to note that thanks to a U-2 "spy plane," the Administration had a whole week to debate the meaning and significance of the Russian move, what its military and political effects were likely to be on U.S. security interests, what the different courses of actions open to the United States were, and which was most likely to achieve the removal of the Soviet missiles without precipitating nuclear war. Many crises simply do not afford such time for preparation and the careful consideration of the many alternative actions possible. Even during the missile crisis, the initial reaction of most of the President's advisers was to bomb the missile sites. Slowing down the momentum of events, therefore, becomes crucial if impulsive actions are to be avoided.

Nixon apparently made his decision to bomb and mine in Vietnam during the week before he announced it—that is, after Kissinger had flown to Moscow to talk to Russia's leaders and after he had, upon the latter's urgings, met privately with Hanoi's top negotiator in Paris—to no avail. At a subsequent Nixon meeting with his principal Cabinet officers, only the Vice-President and Secretary of the Treasury Connally were strongly in favor of attacking North Vietnam; the Secretaries of State and Defense and the Director of the CIA were opposed or unenthusiastic. Kissinger was apparently of two minds on the issue. Nixon thus had less time than Kennedy had in Cuba, more like Truman after the North Korean invasion of South Korea, or Kennedy when the Berlin Wall went up, or Johnson when the internal Dominican situation erupted and the Embassy began reporting the likelihood that "Castro Communists" might gain control—in short, more like the typical crisis.

As one might imagine, a third characteristic of crises is the subordination of bureaucratic interests to the need to make a decision to safeguard the "national interest." The crisis is accompanied by a sense of urgency to make a decision, as well as the perception by the policy-makers that the nation's security is at stake and the possibility of war looms threateningly. Moreover, decision-making has risen to the top level of the government, and the men in these positions, while reflecting their departmental viewpoints, do not necessarily feel themselves limited to representing these perspectives. Organizational affiliation is not *per se* a good predictor of their stands; such senior participants on occasions such as crises behave in a manner more like "players" than "organizational participants." Robert S. McNamara did not reflect the Joint Chiefs' readiness to bomb and invade during the Cuban missile crisis (just as later in Vietnam he was increasingly to disagree with their views and recommendations); he became the leading advocate of the blockade. Other players in that crisis did not even represent foreign policy bureaucracies —the two closest men to the President, the Attorney General and the President's Special Counsel, along with the Secretary of the Treasury and the ex-Secretary of State, for example, represented themselves and only themselves. Thus the bureaucratic axiom that "you stand where you sit" is not necessarily correct, at least during crises.

Finally, crisis decision-making is characterized by Congressional noninvolvement. Congressional leaders are usually called in and informed of the President's decision just before he announces it publicly. This is done as a matter of courtesy. But their advice is not requested. Presidents consider themselves more representative than any Senator or House member and as representative as Congress as a whole. Interestingly enough, Kennedy, after informing a Congressional delegation of his decision to blockade Cuba, did ask for its opinions. When the response was to question the blockade's utility and advocate an air strike instead, Kennedy reacted angrily. After the Congressmen left, he consoled himself by saying that had they had more time to think it over, they, like he, would also have decided on the blockade. If Presidents assure themselves like this, why indeed consult members of the legislative branch? In any event, in crises what choice do they have but to support the only President the country has at the moment?

Decision-Making as a Pluralistic Power Struggle

The governmental model of decision-making is composed of multiple actors. These are, first of all, the three branches of the federal government. In foreign policy matters, the principal participants are the executive and the legislative branches. Within these institutions, there are a multitude of departments, organizations, staffs, committees, and individuals. Within the executive branch, for example, there are the senior foreign policy departments (State, Defense, CIA), the junior departments (AID, U.S. Information Agency, and Arms Control and Disarmament Agency), departments whose jurisdictions are basically domestic but that on specific issues deal occasionally with foreign policy issues that fall within their expertise (Treasury, Commerce, Agriculture), and finally, the President, his Assistant on National Security Affairs, plus his staff. Similarly, Congress is "splintered" into the Senate and the House, and each is further divided into different party groupings and committees.[8] The table on page 394 shows some of the committees in the U.S. Congress that deal with foreign policy issues.

In foreign policy, however, the relationship of Congress to the President differs significantly from the relationships that exist in domestic policy. In the latter, Congress tends to delay and obstruct Presidential policies; in foreign policy, Congress was, until Vietnam, usually *supportive*. Throughout most of the postwar period, Congress has followed the President's lead in foreign policy, and its role has been essentially reactive and peripheral. The executive initiated and devised foreign policies, which Congress rarely rejected; primarily, its role was to legitimate policies devised by the executive, either in the original or in some amended form.[9] The record of American foreign policy since 1945 shows clearly that all major Presidential initiatives, from the Truman Doctrine

[8] For elaboration, see John Spanier and Eric M. Uslaner, *How American Foreign Policy Is Made* (New York: Praeger Publishers, 1974).

[9] Former Secretary of State Dean Acheson offers some amusing and somewhat sarcastic comments on the way Senator Vandenberg, during the crucial days after 1945, helped to legitimate Presidential policy. *Present at the Creation* (New York: Norton, 1969), p. 223.

and Marshall Plan to the Alliance for Progress and the Nuclear Anti-Proliferation Treaty, have been accepted and supported by Congress.[10]

COMMITTEES OF CONGRESS DEALING WITH FOREIGN POLICY ISSUES

Committee	Subjects
Foreign Relations (Senate)	General conduct of foreign policy; declarations of war; treaties
Foreign Affairs (House)	
Armed Services (Senate and House)	Military affairs; defense budget
Interstate and Foreign Commerce (Senate and House)	Transportation, shipping, telecommunications
Appropriations (Senate and House)	All programs requiring funding; defense budget; budget for running bureaucracies
Government Operations (Senate and House)	Investigations of executive branch by legislative branch, including foreign policy questions
Banking, Housing, and Urban Affairs (Senate)	International monetary policy; authorizations for Export-Import Bank
Banking and Currency (House)	
Aeronautical and Space Sciences (Senate)	Space program
Science and Astronautics (House)	
Judiciary (Senate and House)	Immigration and naturalization
Ways and Means (House)	Reciprocal trade agreements; tariffs
Finance (Senate)	
Public Works (Senate and House)	Matters affecting public land and water (e.g., development with Canada of Saint Lawrence Seaway)
Rules (House)	Setting of legislative agenda for all bills in the House

This pluralism is supplemented by organized groups representing many areas of economic, ethnic, racial, and religious interest. In foreign policy, however, "it is questionable, in fact, whether we are really entitled to talk about group influence on 'foreign policy'; with very rare exceptions, the influence of nongovernmental groups is on particular, discrete, rather highly specialized matters, which, even if they may be deemed to be within the foreign policy field, are very far from consti-

[10] James A. Robinson, *Congress and Foreign Policy-Making*, rev. ed. (Homewood, Ill.: Dorsey Press, 1967). For the early postwar period, see Daniel S. Cheever and H. Field Haviland, Jr., *American Foreign Policy and the Separation of Powers* (Cambridge, Mass.: Harvard University Press, 1952), pp. 106 ff.

tuting or defining that field."[11] The reasons for the more limited role of pressure groups in external matters is easy to understand. Such groups have knowledge and experience in great abundance on internal affairs, but on foreign policy issues they rarely show comparable information and skill. These are, however, possessed by the foreign policy experts, and this provides a powerful counter to lay involvement. In addition, whereas interest groups are regularly consulted by their respective executive departments as domestic legislation is drawn up (they are, after all, the departments' clientele), in foreign policy the departments involved tend to be their own constituencies and spokesmen. Institutional interests within the government therefore predominate over associational interests outside it. The responsible agencies have their own experts and are in contact with other experts, be they at the RAND Corporation or at Harvard University. Thus, while there is a fairly stable structure of societal interest groups concerned with domestic policies, the comparable structure in the area of foreign policy is weak and, at times, ephemeral.

Conflict in this area, then, is essentially institutional; and, because the President is both the nation's chief diplomat and the Commander-in-Chief of its armed forces, this conflict occurs primarily within the executive branch, between executive departments responsible for foreign policy formulation and implementation.[12] We should probably talk of these various actors as actors in different organizational settings—the Department of State versus Defense, executive versus Congress or, even more specifically, the European desk in State versus the Asian desk, the air force versus the army, the Senate Foreign Relations Committee versus the Armed Services Committee—because each one approaches a specific problem from its distinct perspective. Each of the bureaucracies, institutions, and other interested groups develops intense organizational identifications, and all are determined not only to survive but to expand their influence in the policy process; furthermore, each, viewing a problem from its special perspective, is likely to develop strong convictions about the content of policy. This is particularly true when "national interests" are involved and a department feels it has a vital contribution to make. Institutional struggles between the executive and legislative branches, as well as conflicts within each branch and within executive departments, are consequently the norm.

This policy process is often condemned as "parochial," the assumption being that more comprehensive solutions—and, hence, more correct solutions—to all policy problems could be found were it not for the selfishly motivated and narrowly conceived points of view held by the

[11] Bernard C. Cohen, "The Influence of Non-Governmental Groups in Foreign Policy-Making," in Andrew Scott and Raymond Dawson, eds., *Readings in the Making of American Foreign Policy* (New York: Macmillan, 1965), pp. 96–116.

[12] See Samuel P. Huntington, *The Common Defense* (New York: Columbia University Press, 1961), pp. 123 ff., for defense policy formulation.

various participants in the foreign policy process. Such a view ignores the fact that, in any pluralistic institution, different institutional and policy convictions compete; thus there are competing policy recommendations offered as solutions to whatever problems are being considered, and these recommendations will represent a fairly broad spectrum of choice. Just as in a democracy different groups and individuals have the right to articulate their values and interests, so the various parts of the executive establishment articulate their own policy views and seek to protect their own interests. The issue is not whose policy position and recommendations are correct; *there clearly is not a single correct policy. The issue is how to reconcile conflicting interpretations of what the correct policy ought to be.* This reconciliation of the policy preferences of the various "players" is complicated by the many players outside the executive branch.

The result of this institutional pluralism is that the policy process is one of reconciling conflict, of attempting to build a "consensus" or majority "coalition" among opposing views in order that decisions can be made and supported. Negotiating thus occurs throughout the executive branch as officials and agencies in one department seek support in another, or attempt to enlist the aid of the President or his advisers in achieving their goals. It is a process of widening the base of support within the executive and then seeking further support in the two houses of Congress, gaining allies through continual modifications of the proposed policy as concessions are made to potential allies in order to meet their specific aspirations and objections and put together a majority coalition. Indeed, because decision-making is fundamentally a matter of negotiations within a pluralistic governmental structure, the policy process is indeed a matter of multiple decisions and approvals over a period of time. The official policy "output" that emerges represents the victory of one coalition formed across institutional lines over an opposing coalition; membership in these coalitions tends to shift from issue to issue.

Roger Hilsman has compared this policy process to the behavior of states in the international system.[13] Politics, Hilsman has said, is characterized by these features: one, the existence of multiple groups or organizations; two, an accompanying set of different and conflicting perspectives, values, and interests; and three, different amounts of power. Thus policy is not only a matter of which points of view seem the most pertinent and "correct"; it is also a matter of power. The resulting policy struggle—as international politics—might be summed up as a struggle among the different actors in terms of their conflicting power and purposes; the intragovernmental negotiations involved in this struggle are every bit as difficult and tedious as intergovernmental bargaining.

The characteristics of the conflict and the coalition-building process affect the policy output. One of the most important results of this con-

---

[13] Hilsman, *To Move a Nation,* pp. 552–55.

tinuous bargaining within the "policy machine" is that policy moves forward one step at a time and tends to focus on momentary concerns and short-range aims.[14] This is usually called incrementalism. Another word is "satisficing." Policy-makers, this words suggests, do not, each time they have to make a decision, sit down and go through the rational procedure of decision-making. They do not try to isolate which values and interests they wish to enhance, examine all the means that might achieve these goals, calculate the consequences of each, and then select the one most likely to be successful. Policy-makers have neither the time nor the resources to go through this process. Instead, they pick the policy that is likely to be the most satisfactory; and they judge this by whether a policy has been successful in the past. If a policy has been satisfactory up to that point, why not another step forward on the same path? The presumption is that what worked in the past will work now, as well as in the future. In addition, once a majority coalition has been forged after hard struggle and probably much "bloodletting," a "winning" coalition will normally prefer modification of existing policy to another major fight. The assumption is, of course, that there will be policy outputs. This is not necessarily true. The negotiating process among different groups with conflicting perspectives and vested interests can produce a stalemate and paralysis of policy.

As a result, policy tends to sway between incrementalism and crisis, either because incrementalism could not adequately cope with a developing situation or because stalemate produces no policy at all. It might be said with reasonable correctness that during "normal" periods low external pressure on the policy machine favors the continuation of existing policies; during crises, a high degree of pressure tends to produce innovative reaction. This may be because a stalemated policy machine needs an *external "trigger"* to undermine a coalition supporting the *status quo*. A crisis may shake coalitions loose, awaken a sufficiently great sense of danger to dampen, even if only for a short time, the pluralistic struggle and create a feeling of urgency—and therefore of common purpose—among the various participants in policy-making. Additionally, as already suggested, crisis policy is decided in an inner circle composed of the President and a few top officials and trusted advisers; at a time of perceived danger, these officials function relatively free of departmental viewpoints and interests, which are likely to be subordinated to the perceived need for rapid decision-making. The usual process of consensus or coalition-building is, in brief, short-circuited.[15] There are, then, two policy processes: the pluralistic advocacy system and the crisis management system, the latter composed of the top officials (Assistant Secretaries and up), the former, of a broader mix of interests.

[14] Charles E. Lindblom, "The Science of Muddling Through," *Public Administration Review*, Winter, 1959, pp. 79–88.
[15] Theodore J. Lowi, *The End of Liberalism* (New York: Norton, 1969), pp. 160–61.

Thus, it took a Pearl Harbor to harness the strength of the United States and direct it toward warding off the German and Japanese threats to the nation's security. Symbolically, after December 7, 1941, Franklin Roosevelt, who had called himself "Dr. New Deal"—the physician called in to cure a sick economy—became "Dr. Win-the-War." Similarly, after World War II, it was the overwhelming Russian threat that allowed Truman to mobilize the country for containment; before the threat became so obvious that it could no longer be ignored, Truman had been unable to take the necessary countermeasures. And again, it took a Castro, with his attempts to stir anti-American revolutions in Latin American countries, to produce an Alliance for Progress in order to help relieve some of the problems producing revolutionary situations in the Southern Hemisphere.

A further characteristic of the policy process, and implicit in our analysis so far, is its time-consuming nature. Incrementalism suggests a policy machine in low gear, moving along a well-defined road rather slowly in response to specific short-run stimuli. A proposed policy is normally discussed first within the executive. It then passes through official channels, where it receives "clearances" and modifications as it gathers a broader base of support on its way "up" the executive hierarchy to the President. The constant conferences and negotiations among departments clearly slow the pace. The process takes even longer when policy needs Congressional and public approval. In domestic policy particularly, potential opponents can occupy many "veto points" to block legislation within Congress; such veto points are the House Rules Committee, other House and Senate committees, which hold hearings on particular legislation, and the floor debates and votes in both chambers. The advantage normally lies with those who oppose a specific piece of legislation, because it is difficult to jump all the hurdles along its route to passage. In foreign policy, there are no clearly definable "veto points," as in domestic affairs, but the path of executive policy-making is no speedier. Given this slow negotiating policy process, the formidable obstacles and great effort needed to pass major policy, old policies and the old assumptions upon which they are based tend to survive longer than they should. For example, policy based on the assumption that the Communist world was cohesive continued even after the Russian-Chinese conflict had surfaced in the late 1950's, and preoccupation with strategic deterrence persisted long after the need for a limited war capacity had been painfully demonstrated by Korea. Domestically, it can be argued that urban decay, racial discrimination, environmental pollution, and overpopulation are all problems that went neglected for such long periods that crises were bound to occur. Indeed, it may well be that many of the nation's external and internal problems cannot be solved by a time-consuming process that does not produce policy until conflicts between clashing interests have been resolved and compromises struck. In the end, time—the ingredient that large-scale governmental policy processes consume in abundance—may run out, and the government, confronted by ever more problems and incapable of meeting them with sufficient effectiveness and timeliness, may find itself "overloaded," perhaps breaking down under the strain.

The competition among the various groups involved in the policy process that tries to "sell" their products is also likely to place a premium on attractive and appealing packaging and advertising. This means that, rather than present complex and sophisticated reasons for advancing a particular policy position, advocates will try to make their policy more acceptable by oversimplifying the issues at stake, tying their product up with a pretty moral ribbon, and overselling it by asserting that it will definitely solve the buyer's problems, which the sellers may also exaggerate in their sales pitch in order to enhance the consumer's feeling that he absolutely needs the policy product being offered him.[16] In foreign policy, the presentation of issues in terms of Communism versus anti-Communism, of good against evil, hardly helped the understanding of the real issues involved and made it difficult to adjust policies to a changing international environment and a changing Communist world. The threat of Russia, simply as a great power, was real enough; a Communist Russia, moreover, somewhat intensified this threat. Nevertheless, the menace of "international Communism" was exaggerated, in part because it was a most effective device, used to persuade various governmental agencies to accept certain recommended policies as well as to mobilize majority support, in Congress and the country, for governmental policies once these had been decided.

More specifically, as Halperin and Kanter have suggested, the biases inherent in the decision-making system help determine which decisions are made. If anti-Communism was the bias—the belief that Communism was expansionistic and aggressive, that it had to be contained rather than appeased, that military force was to be used to effect containment wherever and whenever necessary—those who tried to "sell" their policy preferences in terms of these "shared images" had a good chance of putting together a majority coalition. On the other hand, those whose preferences questioned these assumptions lost out. Other writers have said the same thing more crudely: They have suggested that those who were the toughest anti-Communists, posing as the most vigorous "operators" who would get things done, won the bureaucratic and the wider governmental struggle. Bureaucratic *machismo* is the easiest way to sell policy.

All advocates of specific policy preferences especially seek to sell their products to their potentially best customer—the President. His approval and support is obviously decisive. Hence, the competition is intense. All important policies are likely to come up for the President's attention and decision. The President, as the sole nationally elected official, holds the only position in which all the many considerations bearing on policy can

[16] *Ibid.*

be balanced off against one another. There is no other point at which conflicting views and interests so converge; in his office, nonmilitary and military programs, foreign policy and domestic claims conflict, are weighed, and are compromised. Yet the very fact that the President is central in the policy process and the demands upon his time are therefore overwhelming means that he cannot give many policies the time they deserve—indeed, he may have little time for them until a crisis erupts. A distant problem will usually be ignored or receive scant attention until it reaches a crisis level; then the problem will be managed.

One further characteristic of American foreign policy decision-making is its public nature. In a democracy, this is inevitable. While policy may be made primarily by the executive, the confines of this policy are established by public opinion. No British Government before 1939 could have pursued a deterrent policy toward Hitler, and no American Government before the fall of France could have intervened in Europe to preserve the balance of power. In general, however, public opinion tends to be permissive and supportive as far as the Presidential conduct of foreign policy is concerned.[17] Aware of its lack of knowledge, information, and competence in an area remote from their everyday involvement—in the more familiar area of domestic policies, public opinion is much more structured and knowledgeable—the public looks to the President for leadership. Only when setbacks arise or painful experiences that pinch the voters' toes occur will public opinion react, broadly clarify the limits of its tolerance, and perhaps punish the party in power. But even if most of the time public opinion does not act as a restraining factor, policy-makers are always aware of its existence, however amorphous it may be. Because mass opinion does not tend to take shape until *after* some foreign event has occurred, it can hardly act as a guide for those who must make policy; nonetheless, the latter will take into account what they think "the traffic will bear," because they know that if a decision is significant enough there is likely to be some crystallization of opinion and, possibly, retribution at the polls.

On the other hand, policy-makers not surprisingly exploit foreign policy issues for domestic political purposes. Peace is a particularly profitable issue. Thus, to win a Presidential election, an Eisenhower promises "to go to Korea," implying that he can end the war; and running on a peace platform four years later, he has to torpedo America's two closest allies in Suez. Johnson halts the bombing of North Vietnam just before election day in an attempt to help Hubert Humphrey beat Richard Nixon. (Given the closeness of the election results, it has been suggested that,

[17] Francis E. Rourke, "The Domestic Scene," in Robert E. Osgood, ed., *America and the World: From the Truman Doctrine to Vietnam* (Baltimore: Johns Hopkins Press, 1970), pp. 147–88; William R. Caspary, "The 'Mood Theory': A Study of Public Opinion and Foreign Policy," *American Political Science Review*, June, 1970, pp. 536–47; and James N. Rosenau, "Foreign Policy as an Issue Area," in Conference on Public Opinion and Foreign Policy, *Domestic Sources of Foreign Policy* (New York: Free Press, 1965).

had the bombing stopped earlier, Humphrey, whose campaign was on the upswing toward the end, might have won.) And almost every President (and several Presidential candidates) since Truman has sought to meet the Soviet leaders at a summit conference—and, since Nixon, the Chinese Communist leaders also—for such conferences, with their aura of peace, their promises of a better future based on improved personal relations between American and Soviet (or Chinese) leaders, and their appearance of promoting a more secure world for all mankind, offer considerable domestic capital.

The ABM and Vietnam

These are by no means all of the characteristics of the foreign policy process in the federal government, but they are the most evident. If we consider the Johnson Administration's decisions on the ABM and Vietnam, they are clearly visible.[18] Opposed to the ABM were Secretary of Defense McNamara and Secretary of State Rusk, plus the ACDA; all felt that the decision to deploy an ABM would mean a spiraling and costly arms race that would also destroy all chances for a stabilization of American-Soviet deterrent balance. McNamara believed that an American decision to deploy the ABM would virtually preclude any possibility of initiating arms limitations talks with the Soviets. He was also skeptical of the technical feasibility of the proposed ABM. The Secretary, however, was in a minority position within his own department on the question of feasibility. The Pentagon's Office of Defense Research and Engineering, concerned with modern weapons development, and its Office of Systems Analysis both supported deployment. Within Defense, only the Office of International Security Affairs joined McNamara in opposition to the ABM.

The principal bureaucratic supporters of the ABM were the armed services. In contrast to most defense issues, the ABM debate found the three services united in their support for a weapons system. While the army, navy, and air force each "saw a different face of ABM and reached different conclusions,"[19] the very fact of this interservice agreement is worth noting. Previously, McNamara had used divisions among the services to prevail on issues of defense spending. However, the united front compelled the Secretary to go above the services and appeal directly to the President. Thus different departments and, indeed, different bureaus within the various departments all saw different "faces" of the same ABM problem and had different stakes in the issue.

Others too had interests and stakes in ABM. Supporting the services

[18] This section relies heavily on the account by Morton H. Halperin, "The Decision to Deploy the ABM: Bureaucratic and Domestic Politics in the Johnson Administration," *World Politics*, October, 1972, pp. 62 ff.

[19] *Ibid.*, pp. 67–69.

were several senior members of the Senate Armed Services Committee, including the chairman, Richard Russell, and such other influential members as John Stennis and Henry Jackson. These Senators were supporters of Johnson's Vietnam policy and had been friends of the President when he had been the Democratic Majority Leader in the Senate during the Eisenhower Administration. Indeed, Johnson had served with them on Armed Services and trusted their judgment. He was particularly close to Russell.

In arguing their case, proponents and adversaries often stressed different factors. Supporters stressed the fact that the Soviets had already developed such a system, that it threatened America's deterrent capacity, and that the ABM would save American lives. They argued that an ABM would provide the Americans with an extra bargaining chip in any negotiations on a mutual defensive weapons limitations. Opponents, on the other hand, were less concerned about the Soviet deployment of ABMs than with the potential for a new arms race. Another factor that concerned the opponents more than the supporters was the price tag. Estimates of the cost of an ABM system ranged from $30 billion to $40 billion.

In these circumstances of opposing pressures, no decision was possible at a level below the President; only he could decide. But a President's stakes are greater than anyone else's, and his perspective is different from that of any other player. For one thing, he needs to maintain unity in his administration. The President therefore wanted to avoid, if at all possible, a direct break with McNamara. The two men were already at odds over Vietnam, but the President still valued his Secretary of Defense too highly to reject his advice out of hand. Since McNamara viewed the ABM choice as a direct confrontation between himself and the Joint Chiefs of Staff, a decision to deploy the system would be taken as a direct rejection by the Secretary. In addition, a President also needs Congressional support for his foreign and domestic policies. Thus a negative decision on the ABM would alienate key Senators, who were also long-time friends and former colleagues whose opinions and convictions Johnson respected. But a President is also more than the chief officer of an administration and chief legislator drawing up most of the legislation to be submitted to Congress. He is also head of his party, and, therefore, concerned with his own re-election and his party's future fortunes at the polls. The Republicans were already talking of an ABM gap, threatening to do to the Democrats what Kennedy and Johnson had done to Nixon in 1960 with the "missile gap" issue—using the symbolically potentially powerful charge of neglecting the nation's defenses. Johnson, who had not yet decided not to run again for the Presidency, had to be worried about the possible impact of such an accusation.

But these considerations still do not comprise all the considerations and pressures a President must take into account. A President knows that in the final analysis it is he who is responsible for the country's security and protection; others can advise him, but only he can make the required decisions, and it will be he who will be judged not only by the people he governs but by history.[20] And this is his ultimate stake. He will go down in history in line with Washington, Jefferson, Lincoln, the two Roosevelts, Truman, and others; no one who occupies the White House (or its equivalent in other countries) can possibly ignore his future historical reputation. Thus Johnson, whose involvement in Vietnam was at the time already arousing popular and Congressional criticisms and clouding his historical status, was keenly interested in a major arms limitation agreement with the Soviet Union to help his standing politically at the time and historically in the future; he needed a major breakthrough in the area of international reconciliation.

In this situation, given the "falls" he saw in the ABM issue and the stakes he had it, yet confronted by conflicting pressures, the President would ideally have preferred to make no decision at all and allow the proponents and opponents of ABM to reach some kind of compromise among themselves. The problem of gaining the President's support for one of the contending coalitions is thus not limited to getting to the President to enlist him but, confronted with cross-pressures, includes getting him to make any decision at all. His tendency is to procrastinate or to make only a "minimal decision." Warner Schilling's delectably apt phrase, used in connection with another important Presidential decision, is "How to Decide Without Actually Choosing."

> The President did make choices, but a comparison of the choices that he made with those that he did not make reveals clearly the minimal character of his decision. It bears all the aspects of a conscious search for that course of action which would close off the least number of future alternatives, one which would avoid the most choice.[21]
> . . . One of the major necessities of the American political process [is] the need to avert conflict by avoiding choice. The distribution of power and responsibility among government elites is normally so dispersed that a rather widespread agreement among them is necessary if any given policy is to be adopted and later implemented. Among the quasi-sovereign bodies that make up the Executive the opportunities to compel this agreement are limited.[22]

Harry Truman put this need for gaining support if a policy was to be decided and later carried out in fewer and more picturesque words: "They talk about the power of the president, how I can push a button and get things done. Why, I spent most of my time kissing somebody's ass."[23]

The critical question thus became: what would be the nature of this compromise? At least a part of the answer became clear in a meeting

[20] Halperin, *Bureaucratic Politics and Foreign Policy*, pp. 81–82.
[21] Warner R. Schilling, "The H-Bomb: How To Decide Without Actually Choosing," in Halperin and Kanter, eds., *Readings in American Foreign Policy*, p. 253.
[22] *Ibid.*, p. 255.
[23] Quoted in *Time*, January 25, 1968.

Johnson and McNamara had with Soviet Premier Kosygin at Glassboro, New Jersey, in June, 1967. Johnson pressed the Soviets for a date for the opening of arms limitations talks. This would allow him to postpone the decision on the ABM. But Johnson did not receive an answer. Kosygin, in a meeting with Johnson and McNamara, described the Soviet ABM as a defensive weapon and, therefore, unobjectionable. The ABM, as a weapon that would save lives, was in the Russian Premier's judgment a good weapon that would not destabilize the arms balance, and was thus not a proper subject for SALT. McNamara's principal objection to the ABM had now been refuted by the Soviets. Consequently, Johnson no longer saw the ABM as a possible stumbling-block in beginning arms limitations talks.

So Johnson made his minimal decision: a small anti-Chinese ABM system. McNamara announced the decision in a contradictory speech: On one hand, the Secretary of Defense announced that the most effective way a Soviet ABM could be overcome was by saturating the defense with offensive missiles—suggesting that this was what the Soviets could do to the United States as well—but on the other hand, in case the Chinese were as irrational as their militant revolutionary rhetoric at that time seemed to indicate, a small ABM system might help deter such a strike. In one sense, McNamara had won a major victory against the Joint Chiefs of Staff and ABM supporters in Congress who favored the nationwide anti-Soviet (and more expensive) ABM system. The very fact that McNamara made the speech indicated that he had by no means suffered a major defeat on this issue. He could view the President's decision as leaving open the possibility that the system would never be deployed at all if the Russians would later agree to a mutual defensive weapons limitation. The Administration had *not* come out in support of deployment, but only for increased funding for the procurement of certain ABM parts that would require a long lead time. On the other hand, the very fact that the Administration had publicly changed its position represented a victory for ABM supporters in Congress and the Joint Chiefs. Proponents of the more extensive system viewed the Administration's change in position as a hopeful sign and expected that they could accomplish their goal later. There were as yet no "winners" or "losers." Compromises had prevented that; the fight was to continue into the Nixon Administration, which decided that, in the absence of any agreement on the Soviet SS-9, it wanted a minimal protection for its Minutemen missiles and a bargaining chip for the forthcoming SALT talks.

If the ABM decision is a good illustration of how a decision emerges from the interactions of multiple actors with conflicting perspectives and different stakes in the ABM issue, the Vietnam war is an excellent example of the incremental nature of policy-making. A commitment of sorts to Vietnam had begun during the period when the French were engaged in retaining their colonial control after World War II. After an initial period of nonsupport fór this colonial effort, the United States began to supply economic and military assistance to the French in return for French support of American policy in Europe, an area of vital interest to the United States. This aid was stepped up after the outbreak of the Korean War and China's later military intervention. It was during this period, just after Communist China's birth and alliance with Russia and the war in Asia, that the bipolar image of the world—bipolar in terms of power and ideology—held by American policy-makers seemed to possess considerable validity (it was certainly shared by Moscow and Peking). Since the expansion of any Communist country's power was thus viewed in Washington as an expansion of Communist Russia's power, and a gain of power and security for Russia was equated with a loss of power and security for the United States, it is not surprising that the collapse of Vietnam was viewed in terms of a domino image. If Vietnam fell the rest of the dominoes in Southeast Asia were expected to fall. The other countries of the area either would turn toward a pro-Communist neutralism or would themselves become taken over as a result of Communist revolutionary war or Communist pressures from outside.

The Second Indochina War, which began in the late 1950's, was thus to be a problem for the Kennedy Administration. But Kennedy, during his years in office, never really had time for Vietnam. He was swamped by other foreign policy crises, as well as by an increasingly tense racial situation domestically. Cuba, Berlin, Laos, Vienna (where he had a tense confrontation with Khrushchev), and the Alliance for Progress preoccupied him. Vietnam was not then a crisis, although it was a deteriorating situation. Because of Kennedy's essentially bipolar view of the international conflict, his perception of "wars of national liberation" as instigated by Moscow, and his desire to avoid further foreign policy setbacks and accusations of being soft on Communism, he committed military advisers to help shore up Saigon and avoided making a clear-cut decision about what to do in Vietnam. After Kennedy's assassination, Johnson too sought to procrastinate, hoping for the best even while planning escalation. His time was primarily devoted to restoring calm and unity in the wake of national tragedy, to passing the largest volume of progressive domestic legislation in this century, and to the forthcoming election campaign.[24] The President's experience, expertise, and interest were domestic. Johnson's attempt to win time and convince Hanoi of the futility of persisting in the struggle may have been understandable, but in the meantime, South Vietnam neared total collapse. By early 1965, procrastination was no longer feasible. The choice had become one of either withdrawing from the war or expanding and escalating it. Johnson at this point decided to follow what he and his advisers saw as a continuing American commitment to Saigon begun under Truman,

[24] Tom Wicker, *JFK and LBJ: The Influence of Personality Upon Politics* (Baltimore: Penguin Books, 1969), pp. 151–82.

continued under Eisenhower, escalated by his predecessor with the sending of 16,500 American military personnel, and expanded by himself with his decision to order air strikes against the North after the alleged attack on two U.S. destroyers in the Gulf of Tonkin in August, 1964.[25]

In brief, Johnson inherited a situation in which only *ad hoc* decisions had been made in response to immediate problems. Only piecemeal economic and military commitments had been made; each constituted the minimally necessary step to prevent a Communist victory.[26] At no point were the fundamental questions and long-range implications of an increasing Vietnam involvement analyzed: Was South Vietnam vital to American security? Would its fall represent the consolidation of one country under a nationalist leader or constitute a "falling domino" in the Communization of all of Southeast Asia? Did the political situation in South Vietnam warrant or preclude American intervention? Were political conditions both in the United States and in South Vietnam conducive to effective military action? How large a commitment would the United States be required to make, and what costs should be expected? What role should Saigon and its forces play? If these questions were even asked by President Kennedy and other responsible foreign policy officials as they sent military advisers into South Vietnam—thus creating a powerful military bureaucracy in Saigon that had a vested interest in succeeding and fed deliberately over-optimistic reports to Washington in order to acquire more arms, men, and money—the answers did not provide guidelines for the policies that were ultimately followed. The assumption was that South Vietnam was vital, a test of the credibility of America's commitments and power. Policy was built upon that assumption. The approach was incremental and, as the overall situation deteriorated badly, Johnson, like Kennedy, continued to react to the symptoms of the problem and applied short-range solutions: first, covert operations, then increasingly frequent "retaliatory" air strikes against North Vietnam, followed by around-the-clock bombing, and, finally, when none of these measures worked to compel Hanoi to "cease and desist" in the South, the use of U.S. ground forces in South Vietnam.

Yet counterrevolutionary warfare is political first and military second; its success depends upon the development of a relationship of trust and support between the government and its citizens. The failure of Diem, followed by the American agreement to depose him and its tacit acceptance of his murder, convincingly demonstrated that the political situa-

---

[25] See *New York Times*, June 13, 14, 1971, and Joseph C. Goulden, *Truth is the First Casualty: The Gulf of Tonkin Affair—Illusion and Reality* (Chicago: Rand McNally, 1969).

[26] Chester L. Cooper, *The Lost Crusade* (New York: Dodd, Mead, 1970); Hilsman, *To Move a Nation*, p. 413 ff.; and, especially, David Halberstam, *The Best and the Brightest* (New York: Random House, 1972), a good although not unbiased over-all account of the incremental nature of the U.S. commitment. See also Daniel Ellsberg, *Papers on the War* (New York: Simon & Schuster, 1972), for the impact of domestic anti-Communism on this incrementalism.

tion in South Vietnam was not conducive to a successful termination. Indeed, intervention was frequently advocated also for boosting the South Vietnamese Government's morale! But how American intervention would supply that government with the will and determination to fight was never discussed; should morale in Saigon not have been a prerequisite for U.S. help? In any event, a sizable contingent of American advisers was already involved, and American prestige had been committed. The war had already become Americanized.

At this point, the tendency of the policy process to oversell—aided by President Johnson's obvious political interest in ending the war as quickly as possible, certainly by 1968—gave military considerations the upper hand. Thus, despite much evidence to the contrary, the war was generally considered to be a modified and limited form of conventional warfare. For example, in 1962, General Wheeler, then Army Chief of Staff and later Chairman of the Joint Chiefs, said, "Despite the fact that the conflict is conducted as a guerrilla warfare, it is nonetheless a military action. . . . It is fashionable in some quarters to say that the problems of Southeast Asia are primarily political and economic rather than military. I do not agree. The essence of the problem in Vietnam is military."[27] American commanders in Vietnam agreed. Vietnam would not be much different from Korea. It was just a matter of Americanizing the war a little more than it already was. The Joint Chiefs of Staff assured Johnson that a couple of years and 200,000 troops should do it. (The sloppy evaluation by the JCS and its advice to Johnson contrasted strongly with the approach of Army Chief of Staff Matthew B. Ridgway, who in 1954 had sent teams to Vietnam to calculate what it would take if the United States should intervene. His report to President Eisenhower, a former general himself, was a principal reason the United States stayed out of the war at that time.)[28]

In any case, Secretary of State Rusk largely concurred with the conclusion that Vietnam would be essentially a conventional war and that since it would therefore be a military affair he should stay out of it. Walt W. Rostow, the Presidential assistant for national security affairs, was particularly concerned with the problem of supplies infiltrated from external areas or "sanctuaries" and therefore suggested that only attacks on the "ultimate source of aggression" would bring such a war to an end. The Central Intelligence Agency (whose predictions about what would happen if America intervened were remarkably accurate), the State Department's Bureau of Intelligence and Research, Assistant Secretary for Far Eastern Affairs Averell Harriman, and some of the bright young Turks he had brought with him into that bureau, as well as certain military officers in the Pentagon working in the area of counterrevolutionary strategy and tactics, contested this interpretation. But their efforts were

27 Hilsman, *To Move a Nation*, p. 426.
28 Melvin Gurtov, *The First Vietnam Crisis* (New York: Columbia University Press, 1967).

in vain and gradually most of them, especially in State, lost their jobs or were replaced, or simply lost much of their influence, as did the CIA.[29] In these circumstances, it is not surprising that the air force managed to oversell what bombing North Vietnam would accomplish. One cannot, in a sense, blame the military. Officers generally believe—and should believe—in the efficacy of their service. It is their civilian superiors who should know better.

The public nature of decision-making has been especially evident in the case of the Vietnam war, certainly more so than in the Johnson ABM decision. But, apart from Johnson's general knowledge that a long war would not be popular, public opinion was not much of a guide at the beginning of Johnson's escalation. What was important throughout 1964 and the first months of 1965 was how the President perceived public, as well as Congressional, opinion: His conclusion was that neither the general public nor its representatives wanted the United States "to lose South Vietnam to Communism." Such an evaluation was not without support. He received overwhelming approval for his action during the Gulf of Tonkin episode and, by and large, he continued to receive majority approval during the initial period of open intervention. Nonetheless, Johnson never went to the public or to Congress to explain either the seriousness of the situation as he perceived it in South Vietnam or the necessity, as he saw it, of large-scale U.S. intervention—and very probably a long war. The increasing intervention was thus not accompanied by much public debate, although neither was there much public criticism. But the longer the war lasted, the greater the dissatisfaction with American policy became, and the more extensive and intensive were the criticism and dissent expressed both in Washington and in the country as a whole. Administration officials frequently explained their policy; officials who disagreed sometimes resigned, more often leaked their viewpoints or expressed them to newspaper correspondents. Members of Congress articulated their views more and more. Well-known Democratic and Republican liberals voiced their increasing opposition. Senator Fulbright held Senate Foreign Relations Committee hearings giving critics, frequently ex-government officials and concerned and knowledgeable scholars, a forum.[30] The senator also offered his own wide-ranging critique of American foreign policy in two books.[31] Two other Senators went directly to the public: Eugene McCarthy, who decided to oppose President Johnson in the primaries; and, after McCarthy's surprisingly strong showing in New Hampshire, Robert Kennedy, President Johnson's principal rival in the party and by then already a powerful critic of the war, who also entered the primaries to contest

[29] Halberstam, *The Best and the Brightest*, pp. 361–78.

[30] *The Vietnam Hearings* (New York: Vintage Books, 1966).

[31] J. William Fulbright, *Old Myths and New Realities* (New York: Vintage Books, 1964), and *idem, The Arrogance of Power* (New York: Vintage Books, 1967).

Johnson's renomination. The Republican leadership, on the other hand, increasingly attacked the Administration for its military restraint and advocated the full unleashing of American air power; in these attacks, they were joined by a number of powerful conservative Democrats, especially in the Senate.

Criticism and dissent were, of course, not limited to Washington. Support and, more often, opposition spread to many college campuses and cities. Demonstrations, teach-ins, marches, vigils, and, on occasion, riots accompanied this widening opposition. The Administration, of course, counterattacked.[32] General Westmoreland and Ambassador Lodge, for example, were called home and appeared before Congress and the public—on such shows as "Meet the Press"—where they presented optimistic forecasts and belittled Vietcong achievements; and the President gave speeches defending his policies and denouncing his critics as "nervous nellies." After the Vietcong's Tet offensive had revealed the fallaciousness of official optimism regarding a victorious conclusion to the war, the criticisms grew even more widespread and pointed. The press was by then very hostile, and Congressional opposition to mobilizing larger reserves and an even more costly war was clear. The immediate issue around which much of the debate revolved was the bombing of North Vietnam. Initiated to bring Hanoi to the negotiating table, its cessation became the precondition Hanoi set for any talks about ending hostilities. On March 31, 1968, the President announced the bombing halt that, most significantly, signaled an end to the previously open-ended commitment to Vietnam, implicitly acknowledged repudiation of a military victory as the objective, and began the shift of ultimate responsibility for the conduct of the war to Saigon. He also announced he would not run for a second term. This example leaves little doubt that the longer an issue persists the more will Congressional and public opinion become involved (in contrast to a crisis, which is by and large handled by the President and a few of his most trusted advisers and is over quickly).

In summing up, a number of points need to be made about decision-making models. First, as the Johnson decision giving the go-ahead on an anti-Chinese ABM system illustrates only too well, not all decisions are easily explainable in terms of the rational actor model. Johnson's decision might not have been made but for domestic political pressures, since the President really was primarily interested in starting the SALT talks and avoiding another expensive and possibly destablizing arms race in defensive and offensive weapons. But the individual "foreign policy" decision that emerges from this bureaucratic system, set in its turn in the broader governmental system,

---

[32] The battle within the executive over Vietnam, and especially over halting the bombing of North Vietnam, is told in some detail in Townsend Hoopes, *The Limits of Intervention* (New York: McKay, 1969).

. . . is not necessarily "policy" in the rational sense of embodying the decisions made and actions ordered by a controlling intelligence focusing primarily on our foreign policy problems. Instead it is the "outcome" of the political process, the government actions resulting from all the arguments, the building of coalitions and countercoalitions, and the decisions by high officials and compromises among them. Often it may be a "policy" that no participant fully favors [for the system is] more responsive to the internal dynamics of our decision-making process than to the external problems.[33]

Second, the model by emphasizing "games bureaucrats play" tends to slight the role of the President in the making of noncrisis decisions; he is merely one of many players.[34] To be sure, he may be a "first among equals," but the emphasis is on the limits of his ability to impose *his* decisions, the constraints placed upon *him* by the other players. Johnson did not want an ABM but was pushed into taking his first minimal step; in Vietnam, all the bureaucratic forces impelled him to greater intervention. Sometimes, as is almost implicit in the bureaucratic analysis, the President seems to become the tail that wags the bureaucratic dog.

Some of President Nixon's foreign policy decisions showed that this is not necessarily true for noncrisis decisions. Nixon made himself preeminent in decision-making. Like some of his predecessors who had also wanted to be their own Secretaries of State, he seized for himself certain specific policy areas (e.g., SALT) or policies (e.g., negotiating the end of the Vietnam war and *rapprochement* with China). "The ability of bureaucracies to independently establish policies is a function of Presidential attention. Presidential attention is a function of Presidential values. The Chief Executive involves himself in those areas which he determines to be important."[35] Thus, in contrast to the bureaucratic model's emphasis, it is more correct to say that to a large degree bureaucratic influence is a function of Presidential—and, it ought to be added, Congressional and public—inattention. In terms of crisis and noncrisis policies this means that the bureaucracy plays its largest role in routine day-to-day affairs, its smallest during crises.

But, in addition, President Nixon concentrated foreign policy decision-making authority in the White House by making his Special Assistant on National Security Affairs a kind of supersecretary of foreign affairs, giving him a fairly sizable staff, and clearly ignoring the bureaucracy or subordinating it to the White House; the staff presented the bureaucracy with questions on any area or policy it wanted policy papers on, gathered them together, evaluated the alternative policies recommended,

[33] J. M. Destler, *Presidents, Bureaucrats and Foreign Policy* (Princeton, N.J.: Princeton University Press, 1972), pp. 64, 74.

[34] See Stephen D. Krasner "Are Bureaucracies Important?" *Foreign Policy*, Summer, 1972, pp. 159–79, for an incisive critique of the bureaucratic model.

[35] *Ibid.*, p. 168.

and, once the best policy had been picked, sent it back to the bureaucracy and tried to ensure its implementation.[36] The Nixon experiment was an attempt to institutionalize rational policy-making. As he had said, "I refuse to be confronted with a bureacratic consensus that leaves me no options but acceptance or rejection and that gives me no way of knowing what alternatives exist."[37] Foreign policy decisions that were primarily the outcome of bureaucratic infighting and compromise rather than rational responses to the perceived external challenges and problems confronting the nation were to be avoided. Bureaucratic interests, while not totally eliminated, were thus greatly limited and subjected to Presidential perspectives and interests—at least, until Watergate.

Third, it needs to be repeated that this analytical approach is comparative. While we used the American Government as an example, pluralistic decision-making is equally valid for analytical purposes using the Soviet or British Government for illustration. In Russia, too, there are multiple bureaucratic interests behind the totalitarian facade: Party, army, police, and industrial and agricultural interests, all of which have their spokesmen to represent their needs and grievances. Thus conflict among "interest groups" occurs in the Soviet Government, but, in contrast to the American Government, these bureaucracies are unable to mobilize legislative and popular support for their policy preferences, perhaps even against the Party. Outside the government, groups such as the trade unions do not have an autonomous existence but exist within a system in which the Party controls appointments, promotions, and demotions. But within these constraints of Soviet Government policy is also made through coalition-building.[38]

In the British Government, despite the Prime Minister's control over his Parliamentary followers because of the disciplined nature of British parties, he must first resolve differences within the Cabinet among members who represent different institutional and associational interests. Then he woos the backbenchers because he cannot lead his party where it does not want to go. Thus a Prime Minister tends to avoid innovations in policy unless he has gained support from his Cabinet colleagues and the rank and file. "Seldom will a prime minister try to force a decision widely and genuinely unpopular in his party. The prime minister must preserve the unity of the party, for it is not possible for him to perpetuate his rule by constructing a series of majorities whose composition varies from issue to issue [as in the United States]. He is, therefore, constrained to crawl along cautiously, to let situations develop until the necessity of

[36] Destler, *Presidents, Bureaucrats, Foreign Policy*, pp. 119–53.

[37] *Ibid.*, p. 119. Also see Alexander L. George, "The Case for Multiple Advocacy in Making Foreign Policy," *American Political Science Review*, September, 1972, pp. 751 ff.

[38] Zbigniew K. Brzezinski and Samuel P. Huntington, *Political Power: USA/USSR* (New York: Viking Press, 1964), pp. 196–97.

decision blunts inclinations to quarrel about just what the decision should be."[39] Thus incrementalism seems to be as much a feature of British as American government. Continuity of policy, slow adjustment to changing circumstances, policy deadlocks, and evasion of issues until they become crises are features held in common. Innovations in policies are few and far between.

Finally, it needs to be added that this model holds several policy implications for international negotiations. For one thing, it suggests how difficult they are likely to be, quite apart from the substantive complexity of the problems being negotiated. For misunderstandings, failures of communication, disappointed expectations, and the failure of negotiations between two countries may easily result, because each set of national foreign policy-makers is so deeply engaged in its own bureaucratic and governmental "games" that it is not paying sufficiently close attention to the other side. Thus, even between countries as close as Britain and the United States, negotiations can break down because Londoners are negotiating with other Londoners in trying to make policy, and Washingtonians with other Washingtonians, "Their self-absorption is a day-and-night affair; it never flags. They calculate accordingly and act to suit. So do their counterparts inside the other government. . . . Comprehension of the other's actual behavior is a function of their own concerns."[40] Therefore, the outcome of interallied negotiations is the product of the interactions of intragovernmental negotiations. For example, in the Skybolt affair (discussed earlier in connection with de Gaulle's veto of Britain's entry into the Common Market), "our men [did not] consistently conceive themselves and Londoners as players in two intricate and subtly different bargaining arenas, interacting on each other by and through the side-effects of their internal games."[41] Between adversaries, the problems are likely to be even greater, especially where one side may know less about the other's government than about his ally's; nondemocratic governments tend to hide their intragovernmental differences better than democratic ones. Yet, because our model would suggest that such differences exist even in dictatorships, the Nixon Administration agreed to a whole series of projects with the Soviet Union in order to give parts of its bureaucracy vested interests in cooperation with the United States. Thus, should the political leadership decide at any future time once more to confront the United States, multiple segments of the bureaucracy would be counted on to restrain it. The key question, of course, is who would control whom?[42]

[39] Kenneth N. Waltz, *Foreign Policy and Democratic Politics* (Boston: Little, Brown, 1967), pp. 59–62.

[40] Richard E. Neustadt, *Alliance Politics* (New York: Columbia University Press, 1970), p. 66.

[41] *Ibid.*, p. 138. Also see Michael J. Brenner, "Strategic Interdependence and the Politics of Inertia," *World Politics*, July, 1971, pp. 635 ff.

[42] See Chapter 16 for further analysis of this issue.

15 The Less Developed Countries: The Primacy of Domestic Concerns

Deprivation, Desperation, and Degradation

The right of national self-determination, born in the West but denied by the Western powers in their overseas territories, became a key issue in the postwar world. Throughout Asia and Africa former colonies sought national independence, and most of them gained it. The common denominator of this global nationalist revolution was a fundamental assertion to be "free from" the control of the former colonial power. From the beginning, colonialism had held the seeds of its own destruction. The humiliation and resentment of foreign domination stirred a "reactive nationalism" that asserted itself in terms of the values with which the Westerner justified his rule—national self-determination, dignity, and equality. The nation would be master of its own destiny; no one would ever dominate it again or treat it condescendingly as "second-class."

Accompanying this drive for national independence was the determination to achieve a higher standard of living and abolish the abject poverty and misery of past centuries. For in the economically underdeveloped countries, man continued to live basically on subsistence agriculture because he did not possess the modern tools—the factories, the machinery, the dams, and so forth—with which to increase his productivity. Even more important, he lacked the cultural values, the social structure, and the political order necessary for industrialization. However, underdeveloped nations do not necessarily lack natural resources. In that sense they can be separated into those underdeveloped countries that are very wealthy like the Arab oil states and those that either own less desirable raw materials or possess very little of nature's wealth in their soil; indeed, many of the latter are themselves, like the industrialized countries, victims of the higher oil prices. But the hallmark of an underdeveloped society, in contrast to a developed one, lies in its inability to attain *con-*

413

tinued economic growth. The dividing line between developed and underdeveloped (or developing, in recognition to the slow progress being made) societies is usually pegged at an average annual income per person of $500. For the 70 per cent of the world's population living in the new nations, the per capita income figure is far lower—less than $250 a year or 65 cents a day.

In contrast, the annual average per capita incomes in Western Europe, Japan, and the United States by the end of 1973 were astronomical, in excess of $3,000, or $8.21 a day. Moreover, these incomes are constantly on the rise, while those of the underdeveloped nations are at a virtual standstill. The industrial West had the capital for further growth; the new nations suffer from a lack of capital. But the dividing line between developed and underdeveloped countries is not limited to economics; it is reflected in the differences between low and high infant mortality, long and short life expectancy, availability of such items as cars and housing (and even further, the availability of bath or showers and water supply in the house), calorie intake per person (malnutrition stunts physical and mental growth and creates a generally listless condition), and uses of energy (in 1970, the underdeveloped nations, with a population double that of the industrial countries, used only one-seventh of the total energy produced).

For the affluent white middle-class American, who has forgotten what it is like to be poor—and who spends a minimum of $100 per year on recreation, as well as about $500 on tobacco and food—it is impossible to conceive of the life led by a typical family in a developing nation. Robert Heilbroner has graphically conveyed what such an existence would mean to a suburban family living on a $9,000–$10,000 income.

We begin by invading the house of our imaginary American family to strip it of its furniture. Everything goes: beds, chairs, tables, television set, lamps. We leave the family with a few old blankets, a kitchen table, a wooden chair. Along with the bureaus go the clothes. Each member of the family may keep in his "wardrobe" his oldest suit or dress, a shirt or blouse. We will permit a pair of shoes to the head of the family, but none for the wife or the children.

We move into the kitchen. The appliances have already been taken out, as we turn to the cupboards and larder. The box of matches may stay, a small bag of flour, some sugar and salt. A few moldy potatoes, already in the garbage can, must be hastily rescued, for they will provide much of tonight's meal. We will leave a handful of onions, and a dish of dried beans. All the rest we take away: the meat, the fresh vegetables, the canned goods, the crackers, the candy.

Now we have stripped the house: the bathroom has been dismantled, the running water shut off, the electric wires taken out. Next we take away the house. The family can move to the toolshed. It is crowded, but much better than the situation in Hong Kong, where (a United Nations report tells us) "it is not uncommon for a family of four or more to live in a bedspace, that is, on a bunk bed and the space it occupies—sometimes in two or three tiers—their only privacy provided by curtains."

But we have only begun. All the other houses in the neighborhood have also been removed; our suburb has become a shantytown. Still, our family is fortunate to have a shelter; 250,000 people in Calcutta have none at all and simply live in the streets. Our family is now about on a par with the city of Cali, Colombia, where, an official of the World Bank writes, "on one hillside alone, the slum population is estimated at 40,000 —without water, sanitation, or electric lights. And not all the poor of Cali are as fortunate as that. Others have built their shacks near the city on land which lies beneath the flood mark. To these people, the immediate environment is the open sewer of the city, a sewer which flows through their huts when the river rises."

And still we have not reduced our American family to the level at which life is lived in the greatest part of the globe. Communication must go next. No more newspapers, magazines, books—not that they are missed, since we must take away our family's literacy as well. Instead, in our shantytown we will allow one radio. In India the national average of radio ownership is one per 250 people, but since the majority of radios is owned by city dwellers, our allowance is fairly generous.

Now government services must go. No more postman, no more fireman. There is a school, but it is three miles away and consists of two classrooms. They are not too overcrowded since only half the children in the neighborhood go to school. There are, of course, no hospitals or doctors nearby. The nearest clinic is ten miles away and is tended by a midwife. It can be reached by bicycle, provided that the family has a bicycle, which is unlikely. Or one can go by bus—not always inside, but there is usually room on top.

Finally, money. We will allow our family a cash hoard of five dollars. This will prevent our breadwinner from experiencing the tragedy of an Iranian peasant who went blind because he could not raise the $3.94 which he mistakenly thought he needed to secure admission to a hospital where he could have been cured.

Meanwhile the head of our family must earn his keep. As a peasant cultivator with three acres to tend, he may raise the equivalent of $100 to $300 worth of crops a year. If he is a tenant farmer, which is more than likely, a third or so of his crop will go to his landlord, and probably another 10 per cent to the local money lender. But there will be enough to eat. Or almost enough. The human body requires an input of at least 2,000 calories to replenish the energy consumed by its living cells. If our displaced American fares no better than an Indian peasant, he will average a replenishment of no more than 1,700–1,900 calories. His body, like any insufficiently fueled machine, will run down. That is one reason why life expectancy at birth in India today averages less than forty years.

But the children may help. If they are fortunate, they may find work and thus earn some cash to supplement the family's income. For example, they may be employed as are children in Hyderabad, Pakistan, sealing the ends of bangles over a small kerosene flame, a simple task which can be done at home. To be sure the pay is small: eight annas—about ten cents—for sealing bangles. That is, eight annas per gross of bangles. And if they cannot find work?Well, they can scavenge, as do the children of Iran who in times of hunger search for the undigested oats in the droppings of horses.[1]

It is not surprising that, as Pakistan's Finance Minister has said, for the children who survive the age of five in the underdeveloped countries, life is matter of "deprivation, desperation, and degradation. It is an intense, but mercifully a short struggle, as their life expectancy is no more than thirty years."

The Westernization of the Intelligentsia

While the developing countries generally tend to blame Western capitalism for these conditions, the role played by the West in forging their nationhood cannot be ignored. For one, it was the "territorialization" by the colonial powers that defined the present frontiers of these nations. The Western powers drew arbitrary lines on a map, often straight through tribal or ethnic boundaries, and then imposed a single administrative and legal structure upon the territory. All who lived within this structure were treated as if they belonged to a single nation. A graphic example of the impact of such actions on the new nations is seen in the case of Indonesia. When Indonesia received its freedom, it did not receive as part of its territory Dutch New Guinea, or West Irian. The Dutch claimed that the people of New Guinea were ethnically, racially, and culturally distinct from Indonesians. Nevertheless, Indonesia persisted until, in 1963, it acquired West New Guinea. The territory had been part of the old Dutch East Indies empire, and Indonesia defined its territorial limits in terms of the former imperial frontiers. Similarly, India, in its quarrel with China over precisely where the Sino-Indian boundary lies in the Himalayas, defined its claim in the context of the line drawn by the British colonizers.

Another by-product of colonialism was the construction of harbors, roads, railroads, airports, telephone and telegraph lines, and factories, and the development of natural resources. These provided what economists call the infrastructure, or capital overhead—the prerequisite for any major industrialization.[2] To be sure, the Europeans did not undertake these projects for the benefit of the natives. The roads and railroads carried the resources or crops from the interior to the harbors; they were also used for troop movements to quell uprisings and riots. Nevertheless,

[1] Robert L. Heilbroner, *The Great Ascent* (New York: Harper Torchbooks, 1963), pp. 23–26. Used by permission of the publisher and A. D. Peters & Co.

[2] The disruption of the traditional colonized society by Western economic behavior is analyzed in Max F. Millikan and Donald L. M. Blackmer, eds., *The Emerging Nations* (Boston: Little, Brown, 1961), pp. 3–17, and Immanuel Wallerstein, *Africa: The Politics of Independence* (New York: Vintage Books, 1961), pp. 29–43.

their impact upon the traditional native economy and society was disruptive. In the cities, the traditional patterns of life and expectations of the vast majority of the peasants who had migrated from the land were altered. The European-built centers of government, business, and communications offered the peasants who came there to work a new way of life and new values. Urban life provided the "demonstration effect."[3] The Europeans lived better and longer. Why, the natives wondered, could they not live as well and as long? They could hardly avoid awareness of the technical and scientific knowledge, tools, and skills that had given the Europeans their higher material standards, as well as their power. Why, the natives asked themselves, could they not learn these secrets of science? One thing was especially noteworthy: Europeans believed that one could improve life here on earth rather than accept poverty as one's fate.

The urge to transform backward societies into modern societies and economies thus began with the European introduction of urbanization, industry, a wage labor force, and an exchange economy. But the most significant contribution of Western colonialism was the education of the social groups that were determined to lead their shackled nations into freedom and modernize their backward countries. A relatively small and youthful group, this nationalist intelligentsia produced the leadership of revolutionary movements in the underdeveloped countries. The members of this intelligentsia were doctors, journalists, civil servants, lawyers, and so forth; what they have had in common has been their "Westernization." Educated in Europe or America, or in Western schools in their own countries, they learned the Westerner's ways—his language, dress, and conduct. Even more significant, in the course of their professional training they learned to think in characteristically Western rational and secular terms. This "scientific" and "material" pattern of thought holds revolutionary implications. As it did for their eighteenth-century European *confrères*, for the rising intelligentsia of the underdeveloped states it provided an escape from the traditions, customs, and privileges that held their societies in the tight grip of economic, social, and political backwardness. Materialism, with its simple but powerful message that man is the master of his own destiny, became for them an exhilarating philosophy of intellectual liberation from religious superstition; it substituted rationalism for obsolete traditions and institutions. It was the absence of just such a material attitude that was responsible for their nations' economic underdevelopment.

Education, then, was the chief means by which Western political and social thought was diffused to non-Western areas. As one political analyst has observed: "The future will look back upon the overseas imperialism of recent centuries, less in terms of its sins of oppression, exploitation, and discrimination, than as the instrument by which the spiritual,

[3] Barbara Ward, *The Rich Nations and the Poor Nations* (New York: Norton, 1962), p. 54.

scientific, and material revolution which began in Western Europe with the Renaissance was spread to the rest of the world."[4]

It is because of this Westernization, then, that the members of the intelligentsia became leaders in the nationalist and modernizing movements of their countries. For it confronted them with a personal emotional and psychological dilemma that "politicized" them and turned them to revolutionary politics (which may be difficult for an American to understand, accustomed as he is to consider professional middle-class men solid, reliable, and satisfied burghers—at least until the last few years, when some of his sons became revolutionary). But, unlike his Western counterpart, the non-Western intellectual was not a product of his society's organic social development. As the "returned student," he was literally a stranger in his own country, an outcast who had broken with the ways of his society. A Westernized foreigner to his own people, he remained a native—with all that the word denotes—to the colonial power. He was, so to speak, born into one world, living in another, and belonging to neither. He was an isolated and lonely figure with no sense of belonging, his life suspended between the foreign colonial rulers and his own custom-bound people.[5] That the intellectual, facing such an acute psychological crisis, should become revolution-oriented is not surprising. For only in revolutionary politics could he find a new home. Disoriented because he had been deprived of his old values, he found in the "nation" a new sense of belonging. He therefore became a member of the "party of national independence" in order to overthrow the Western colonizer and then to close the vast gap between his own backward nation and a "twentieth-century nation" by "Westernizing" it.

In addition, the non-Western intellectual, because he was cut off from his own society, was denied the recognition, social status, and respect a person of his attainments would expect from his community. To most of his countrymen, he was a stranger whose whole pattern of think-

[4] Rupert Emerson, *From Empire to Nation* (Cambridge, Mass.: Harvard University Press, 1960), p. 6.

[5] "The term 'intelligentsia' [is thus] used to denote specifically those intellectuals who are experiencing internal conflict between allegiance to traditional cultures and the influence of the modern West. Within these terms of reference it is not the amount of knowledge or education that determines membership in the intelligentsia. . . . No man, no matter how learned, is classified as a member of the intelligentsia if he has retained his identity with his national background. As long as he remains integrated in his society and accepts the values of that society as his own, he is likely to remain essentially a conservative without that revolutionary spark which . . . would class him as a member of the intelligentsia. If, on the other hand, he is an intellectual who has felt the impact of Western civilization and has been drawn into the vortex of conflicting ideas, he enters the ranks of the intelligentsia. . . . Within the intelligentsia, however, rebelliousness is a common characteristic. Beset with doubts about traditional cultural values, its members have felt a driving need to search for something new." Klaus Mehnert, "The Social and Political Role of the Intelligentsia in the New Countries," in Kurt London, ed., *New Nations in a Divided World* (New York: Praeger Publishers, 1964), pp. 121–22.

ing and life was foreign. Instead of acquiring status in the traditional manner—by age, family, rank, or land ownership—he depended on his own achievements. If he were a Westerner, he would gain social recognition and advancement in terms of authority and financial rewards. But he was living in an economically backward nation where there were few outlets for his professional skills. What kind of a career could a journalist expect in a country of illiterates, or a doctor in a superstitious culture that preferred witch doctors? He thus became an unemployed, frustrated intellectual. His education raised his aspirations too high for a society in which his opportunities for a productive life and satisfaction of his ambitions were thwarted. "There is no more explosive political material than the doctor who knows what modern medicine can do but does not have the facilities to put his knowledge to work; or the teacher who must teach, if at all, without textbooks; or the engineer without access to capital equipment; or the businessman without a place of business; or the politician without a following that understands what he is talking about."[6] In the modern, urban-industrial nation that he and his fellow intellectuals would create, he would live a useful life. His skills could be fully utilized and properly rewarded in terms of position, power, and pay.

The intellectual's yearning for security and a sense of belonging, as well as for status and a productive life, also instilled in him a populist or "socialist" concern for the people's welfare. His cultural isolation from the mass of his own countrymen, the very countrymen for whom he sought national independence, fed his need for communion with them and his sense of service to them.[7] Only by dedicating himself to their welfare could he regain his identification with them and find an outlet for the genuine sense of compassion that their misery stirred within him. "The people" became his standard; all that he did or wanted to do he justified with reference to "the people."[8] The intelligentsia thus advanced itself as the group that would lead the people out of the wilderness of servitude, backwardness, and destitution into the paradise of national independence and the twentieth-century welfare state. Whereas in the West intellectuals have generally been spokesmen for a particular class or interest, allowing the professional politician, the aristocrat, the businessman, or the trade union leader to represent them, in the non-Western area the intelligentsia is the ruling class.[9]

But as intensely aware as the first generation of leaders were of the

[6] Eugene R. Black, *The Diplomacy of Economic Development* (New York: Atheneum, 1963), p. 12.

[7] For example, see Jawaharlal Nehru, *Toward Freedom* (New York: John Day, 1941), pp. 352–53.

[8] Mehnert, "Role of Intelligentsia," p. 130.

[9] Harry J. Benda, "Non-Western Intelligentsias and Political Elites," in John H. Kautsky, ed., *Political Change in Underdeveloped Countries* (New York: John Wiley, 1962), p. 237.

underdeveloped condition of their countries, and as determined as they have been to initiate development, they have faced almost insuperable obstacles to the necessary economic "take-off" and self-sustaining economic growth. A lack of national cohesion, a far too rapidly growing population, a dearth of capital, and a traditional social structure and values all have impeded the modernization of their societies, with the result that grave foreign policy implications have ensued.

The Absence of National Unity

The Westernized intellectuals may have become rulers of new nations, but few of their subjects share their nationalism. Concepts of a nation, of national loyalty, of a national government that makes decisions for the benefit of the entire community, of national laws and regulations that take precedence over local government and tradition are all new and strange to most of the peoples of the underdeveloped areas. The first requirement of the leaders of the new nations has been to construct the very nation in whose name they revolted against colonial domination. They must be "nation-builders" in order to give reality to the nation they have long felt inside themselves. But their masses have never lived in a "nation." Their lives have been rooted in smaller communities and their first loyalty is to the tribe, to the region, or to religious, racial, or linguistic groups.[10] Loyalties are parochial and attitudes are particularistic. These stand as formidable barriers to the formation of a sense of national consciousness and a devotion to national symbols and, in fact, may reach such an intensity, either alone or in combination, as to cause civil war. Men from other regions will be regarded not as fellow nationals with whom one shares loyalty to nation, language, historical memories (beyond the memory of colonial rule), and hopes for the future, but as "strangers," "foreigners," "outsiders." Disunity rather than unity is the spirit of the new nations. The communities created by the colonial powers may have become "national" in the sense that the people living within these areas desired to rid themselves of foreign rulers. But their common resentment and aspiration to be free did not develop into a shared allegiance to the nations whose frontiers had been artificially drawn in previous centuries by Europeans.

The crucial problem of integrating the diverse masses into the new nation, of forming a national consensus, is therefore not an easy one. Race is one element impeding this "integrative revolution." For example, many of the countries of Southeast Asia, such as Thailand, Malaya, and Singapore, contain numerous and sizable minority groups, and chief

[10] See particularly Emerson, *From Empire to Nation*, pp. 89–187, 295–359; Clifford Geertz, "The Integrative Revolution," in Clifford Geertz, ed., *Old Societies and New States* (New York: Free Press, 1963), pp. 105–57; and Walter Connor, "Nation-Building or Nation-Destroying?" *World Politics*, April, 1972, pp. 319 ff.

among these are the overseas Chinese.[11] Almost everywhere in Southeast Asia, the Chinese are the middlemen. They are the distributors of consumer goods, the bankers, the investors, the shopkeepers. And while they dominate Southeast Asia's economic life, the Chinese, by retaining their language and customs, have tended to isolate themselves; they remain foreigners in the nations where they live. Centuries of Chinese invasion and conquest of the area have left a residue of suspicion that is only added to by this cultural isolation. The result is fear, jealousy, discrimination, and accusations of "alien exploitation." The renewed pride of the Chinese in the new China—not because it is Communist but because it is a China that can no longer be humiliated by other nations—exacerbates an already tense situation. Consequently, the Chinese may look to Peking for protection against native restrictions, discrimination, and reprisals. (Many, of course, have ambiguous feelings, because the New China is militantly antibourgeois.) Whether the overseas Chinese can be assimilated and integrated into the national lives of the nations of Southeast Asia is an open question.

There are also religious animosities. When these turn into religious wars and lead to the massive dislocation of millions of people and the slaughter of hundreds of thousands, they seem incomprehensible—at least to a Western world that has long forgotten the Thirty Years' War. This was what happened when South Asia, upon gaining its independence, was partitioned into Hindu India and Moslem Pakistan because the Moslem minority wanted its own nation. The division was accompanied by a great bloodbath. Over half a million people died, or were murdered.[12] Religious divisions do not, of course, have to be disastrous. But internal dissension that hampers "nation-building" does occur in a nation such as Lebanon, which is evenly divided between Moslems and Christians, or Burma, with its religious differences between the Karens and the Moslem Arakanese. And in Nigeria, the religious differences between the Moslem Yorubas and the Christian Ibos did nothing to diminish the intensity of a conflict that was also based on tribal, regional, and economic divisions.

Regional differences tend to be a further divisive factor, and this is particularly true if they are accompanied by uneven distribution of re-

[11] The Malaysian Government is in fact considering amending its constitution to outlaw any talk about Malay-Chinese racial divisions. *New York Times*, March 2, 1971. See also Richard Hughes, "I Am Chinese! I Live in the Southern Ocean," *New York Times Magazine*, August 4, 1963, p. 61, and A. Doak Barnett, *Communist China and Asia, Challenge to American Policy* (New York: Harper & Row, 1960), pp. 172–210. For a fictional treatment of racial divisions, see Anthony Burgess, *The Long Day Wanes* (New York: Ballantine Books, 1965). For the Chinese Communist views of this problem, encouraging the overseas Chinese to adopt local nationality and use local languages, see Stephen Fitzgerald, *China and the Overseas Chinese* (Cambridge, England: Cambridge University Press), 1972.

[12] Michael Brecher, *Nehru: A Political Biography* (New York: Oxford University Press, 1959), pp. 362–63.

sources and wealth. A case in point is Indonesia, which is a nation of islands, the main ones being Java (on which the capital, Jakarta, is located), Sumatra, Celebes, most of Borneo, and about half of New Guinea. Sumatra is the source of Indonesia's oil and rubber wealth, and the Sumatrans have little use for the Javanese, whom they feel they are subsidizing. The inhabitants of Celebes, on the other hand, are suspicious of both the Javanese and the Sumatrans. Finally, the people of West Irian have little, if anything, in common with the people of the other islands. As can be seen in Indonesia or in the conflict between what used to be West and East Pakistan (now Bangladesh), as well as in some of the new African countries, such as Zaïre and Nigeria, "Regionalism is understandable because ethnic loyalties can usually find expression in geographical terms. Inevitably, some regions will be richer than others, and if the ethnic claim to power combines with relative wealth, the case for secession is strong"[13]—as, in fact, happened in Pakistan, the Congo, and Nigeria.

As if the three factors of disunity named thus far were not sufficient, there is yet a fourth—tribalism. Particularly in Africa, the tribe is still the psychological, economic, and political reality to many, for it is the social organization closest and most familiar to them. The colonial powers—particularly the British, who ruled their colonies "indirectly" (through the traditional chiefs), helped to preserve this tribalism. The African tribes generally are not, as might be thought, small groups of a few hundred or thousand members. The larger tribes, if they lived in the United States, would be considered ethnic or national minority groups.[14] The problem is less the large numbers of tribes than the large size of some tribes. As a result, the cohesion of the new nation may be weakened by the desire of tribal chieftains to invoke the same claim of national self-determination that the intelligentsia previously invoked on behalf of the nation. Additionally, because the Europeans often split up tribal groups when they drew up their artificial boundary lines in the conference rooms of Berlin, London, and Paris, the new nations' frontiers tend to be unstable. Tribes freely cross frontiers in search of water and grazing lands; one part of a tribe may try to break away from its "nation" to join the rest of the tribe in the neighboring nation. The result may be a frontier war, as neither nation can allow secession, which would weaken if not disintegrate its statehood.

The new nations' lack of political and cultural cohesiveness is symbolized best by the language problem. For language is one of the most important factors in forming and preserving a sense of nationalism, and uniformity of language not only helps men to communicate with one

---

[13] Wallerstein, *Africa*, p. 88.

[14] See James S. Coleman, "The Character and Viability of African Political Systems," in Walter Goldschmidt, ed., *The United States and Africa* (New York: Praeger Publishers, 1963), pp. 49–50.

another but also promotes common attitudes and values. In turn, a feeling of group consciousness and common interests is stimulated; men learn to think in terms of "we," as opposed to the "they" who speak a different language and have different ideas.

The language problem is perhaps best illustrated by the case of India. India has at least twelve major languages, each of which is spoken by more than a million people.[15] In addition, there are twenty-four tribal languages or dialects, each spoken by more than 100,000 people, and sixty-three non-Indian languages, of which English is the most widely spoken. An Indian commission investigating this linguistic problem found that regional cultures based on language communities were more intelligible to the average Indian than Indian nationalism. If India is the most extreme case, it is nonetheless not unique. The lack of a common language is a problem in almost all the new nations, and the prospects for national cohesion in these circumstances are certainly not promising. The question for these new nations is less whether they will develop economically than whether they will survive as national entities. For when people obey racial, religious, or tribal authority instead of legitimate national authority, which group controls the central government can be perceived by the various groups as a matter of life and death, precipitating secession and civil war.

Overpopulation and the Malthusian Problem

The second problem the modernizing intelligentsia confronts is that of overpopulation. Not all underdeveloped nations, to be sure, have this problem, but for the many that do it places in question whether they can make any economic progress at all. Obviously, if there are always more mouths to feed, all or most of the increment in national income is likely to be eaten up. World population has already passed the 3 billion mark and is increasing at an annual rate of just over 2 per cent. On the average 207,000 children are born each day, and almost 1.5 million per week. But Europe averages an increase of only 0.8 per cent (this excludes Russia, with a 1.1 per cent), and the American rate is 1.3 per cent. It is in the underdeveloped areas that the rate is highest: 2.9 per cent for Latin America (7 million people per year), 2.3 per cent for Asia, and 2.5 per cent for Africa. India's birth rate is enough to fill a city the size of New York every year; its total population is more than 400 million. China's annual new population would permit it to add another Canada every year; its population, already estimated at 700 million, is expected to reach the billion mark by the year 2000, if not earlier. In 1900, there was one European for every two Asians; in 2000, the ratio will probably

[15] See Selig S. Harrison, "The Challenge to Indian Nationalism," *Foreign Affairs*, July, 1956, p. 624.

be one to four. It is also estimated that by 2000 there will be two Latin Americans for each North American—and this is based on a 300 million population for the United States.

This, then, is the "population explosion." It was in 1830 that world population reached 1 billion. By 1930, it had doubled; by 1970, the total was 3.5 billion people, and nearly half of the world's population were under twenty. By the year 2000, the population is expected to rise to 7 billion people. After that, an additional billion will be added every five years or less if the present rate of population increase continues.[16]

The underdeveloped countries have thus come face to face with the realities of the Malthusian problem: the constant hunger and grinding poverty that result when the population grows faster than do the means of subsistence. More than 150 years ago, the Reverend Thomas Malthus, who was also an economist, predicted this fate for the Western world—unless population growth was limited either by "positive checks," such as wars or epidemics, which result in a high death rate, or by "preventive checks," such as sterilization or contraception, which result in a low birth rate. The great economic progress in the West—despite the huge population increase since 1800—seemed to refute Malthus: Agricultural production provided a plentiful supply of food, and industrial production raised the standard of living to new heights. Hence, for years, Malthus's dire prediction was ignored by all save the most diehard pessimists.

Unfortunately, the conditions that confront the underdeveloped nations are quite dissimilar from those experienced by the West. One of the chief differences is that the Western countries had far smaller populations when they began industrializing, and their subsequent population increase did not outdistance their economic gains. Ironically, the pattern existing in the non-Western countries was to a significant degree brought about by the colonial powers. In the precolonial period, the Malthusian "positive checks" had, in their own cruel way, maintained some sort of balance between population and resources. The typical age-old pattern was simple: Once a tribe had eaten up most of the available food in the area it inhabited and had overfarmed the land so that soil erosion had begun, it would invade the preserve of neighboring tribes. In ensuing battles, members of both tribes would be killed off, thus decreasing the number left to be fed. Periodic famine and pestilence also helped to maintain a balance between births and deaths. This seemingly eternal cycle of peace and population growth succeeded by violence and population decline was broken by entry of the colonial powers. Preserving peace

---

[16] Text of President's Message to Congress on World Planning of Population Growth, *New York Times*, July 19, 1969. Some smaller countries have however shown a substantial decline in birthrates, as shown by Michael S. Teitelbaum, "Population and Development," *Foreign Affairs*, July, 1974, p. 746, which analyzes the range of possible solutions to these twin problems.

in the areas they ruled and introducing modern medicine, these powers upset the balance: More of the newborn survived, and people lived longer; populations began to increase at much greater rates.

The West also introduced contraceptive devices, but knowledge and use of birth-control methods spread very slowly, in part because of religious opposition and in part because of tradition. Nonetheless, some governments, such as the Indian Government, have instituted public education campaigns in family planning, financed research to discover a cheap and effective means of contraception that the untutored can use, and encouraged sterilization. In 1963 India's goal was to reduce the birth rate by more than one-third within a decade, from 42 per thousand population to 25; by 1973 the figure reached was only 38 per thousand, and the target date was extended until 1980. India's financial problems, even before the fantastic rise in oil prices it had to pay after 1973, however, were so immense that despite an annual increase of 13 million people it cut its birth-rate programs as part of a stringent economy campaign—even though any fruits of development will be endangered by this fast-growing population.

Despite this example, however, at the 1974 international conference on world population problems, the underdeveloped countries were hardly willing to recognize that their growth, which is doubling their population every 20 years, was a problem. They shifted the focus of attention from birth control, emphasis of which they felt was an infringement of their sovereignty, to economic and social development. Arguing that the fuller exploitation of the world's resources could comfortably support ten times the present global population of 4 billion, they placed responsibility principally upon the industrialized nations to waste fewer resources to support their already very high standard of living and accelerate the development of the less developed countries. Despite the dissimilarity of the situation, they emphasized that as in the West, a declining birth rate would come as modernization occurred. The central question, therefore, remains: Can these countries develop, given the fact that the pace of economic growth must surpass their fast-rising populations?

It may well be that the unceasing productivity of children may produce wide-spread starvation. Malthus may yet be proven correct. Unable to grow enough food themselves, this rapid population increase may not only strangle the underdeveloped countries' modernization but pose some political and moral questions for all Western nations: Will they tighten their own belts in order to avert extensive starvation throughout the Third World? Will Americans, for example, cut back the fertilizer they use in their gardens, cemeteries and golf courses to send it abroad to help these countries grow more food? Will they pay the higher food prices in a world where demand seems to be exceeding supply or insist to their elected representatives to feed America first and at reasonable prices? Thus, for the underdeveloped nations, the following maxim will be painfully true: "Industrial revolutions may be defeated by Malthusian counterrevolutions."[17] Fertility, once the key to survival, seems to have become mankind's curse. Who said "love makes the world go around"?

The Lag in Capital Formation

Alongside problems caused by the gap between national leaders and tradition-bound masses and by overpopulation are the overwhelming problems of backward, if not stagnant, economies. It is upon such a base that the new nations must build an industrial economy that will banish poverty, bring material abundance, end their economic dependence on the former colonial powers, and give them international standing. Industrialization, to put it another way, is a symbol of modernity. It is also a means of escaping a past in which these countries were largely "raw-materials appendages" to the industrial powers. Vitally concerned with the economic "take-off" and the transition of a modern society, the underdeveloped nations must somehow obtain the requisite capital for capital accumulation.

The underdeveloped nations are basically exporters of primary products or raw materials. Most of them, moreover, possess only a single major product for export. Theoretically, they should be able to earn sufficient capital from their exports to carry out large-scale industrialization. For, as Western nations continue to consume more, their demand for raw materials should rise correspondingly. In practice, however, things have not usually worked out that way. It is their dependence on the export of raw materials that has limited the earning capacities of the underdeveloped countries. For their exports rise or fall with every fluctuation of the Western business cycle. As the Mexicans used to say, "A sneeze in the American economy could lead to pneumonia in Mexico." Moreover, advanced Western technology in many instances has made it both possible and profitable to develop synthetics or other substitutes. Industries are thereby released from the dependence on many natural raw materials; in turn, as demand decreases, prices drop. In addition, even where there are no substitute materials, as competition among underdeveloped countries exporting the same raw material increases, prices are driven down further.

The dilemma of underdeveloped countries is agonizing. They desperately need capital. They rely on their raw material exports to earn this capital. But the harder they work to enlarge their volume of exports to enhance their earnings, the more prices fall. At the same time, because they do not produce enough food for their rapidly growing popu-

[17] Alexander Gerschenkron, *Economic Backwardness in Historical Perspective* (New York: Praeger Publishers, 1965), p. 28.

lations, they must import the food they need. They must also import the machinery required to start their industrialization—Western machinery, whose prices are, on top of everything else, always rising. Exports of raw materials then, do not seem a likely route of escape from poverty for the underdeveloped countries. American farmers faced a similar bind at a time when farm prices were low: They overproduced in order to enhance their earnings, thus glutting the market, forcing prices even lower, and reducing the farmers' living standard far below that of the city dweller. The domestic laws of the laissez-faire market, having produced politically unacceptable results, were therefore amended to guarantee farmers higher prices and a decent standard of living through parity prices; internationally, this has not been done.

Not, that is, until the Arab boycott of the West during the Yom Kippur War in 1973 when the Arab and non-Arab producers raised their oil prices drastically. To what extent their ability to get together and jointly raise their prices will serve as an example to the other raw material producing countries remains unknown. On the one hand, the industrial countries remain dependent on iron, lead, tungsten, aluminum, chromium, manganese, nickel, tin, zinc, mercury, platinum, and other items (the United States spent $5 billion on metal imports in 1970; by 1985 this figure is estimated to reach $18 billion; and by 2000, $44 billion). If the key raw materials producers can, like the Arab oil producers, organize producers' associations and dramatically increase their prices, they would have a far greater capacity to finance their own economic growth and modernization. They would be receiving on the international market the equivalent of the farm subsidy.

On the other hand, if the impact of such a rise in prices will stoke the already high Western inflation and lead to a recession and major reduction in the demand for natural resources, their prices are likely to slump as the producers compete again for the industrial markets. Thus it remains unclear whether the non–oil producing underdeveloped countries can form cartels and quadruple prices in those raw material areas where there are more than just a few producers (who are easy to organize) and substitutes are unavailable. Moreover, it is these countries that are themselves hardest hit by the oil price hike. Not only do their own energy bills rise substantially at a time when they are not yet exporting at premium prices—probably leading to a reduction of needed oil and other imports with all the consequences this will have on their economies and societies—but they will also have to pay far higher prices for fertilizer (made from oil), which is in itself already in short supply, or face possible large-scale starvation in a world whose production is not keeping pace with the demands of a rapidly rising population; in turn, this is forcing up food prices all over the world, prices most new nations cannot afford, and what is bought is paid for in foreign currencies they have not earned enough of. Thus, even if they raise raw material prices to exploit the West's needs, as well as to pay for their own higher energy bills, "resource diplomacy" may still not be the likely route of escape from poverty for the underdeveloped countries as their rates of economic growth, already lagging, decline even further.

Nor can many underdeveloped countries rely on private foreign investments. Private Western—and especially American—capital for foreign investment is drawn to investments that will yield relatively good profits in a reasonable period of time. Such expectations cannot on the whole be realized in underdeveloped economies, for industrialization is a long-range process. Moreover, the basic prerequisite for economic growth is capital overhead: schools, roads, railroads, ports, hospitals, housing, and power.[18] Education, housing, and public health services do not yield rapid economic returns, but they are essentials whose contribution would, in the long run, pay off. Public funds are thus necessary in the early stages of economic development, for only when this infrastructure is in place will private capital be attracted by the possibilities of more rapid economic growth in the future. Money is attracted to money, not to poverty.

In addition, many leaders of new nations are not particularly enthusiastic about attracting private capital, at least in the first stages of national development. To them, colonialism and capitalism are in a sense synonymous, and consequently they tend to be hostile toward private enterprise, suspecting that it might forge new economic chains for their enslavement. "Real" political freedom is equated with economic independence. The new nations are constantly on guard against the possible establishment of foreign control by what they call "neocolonialism." Economic nationalism, as in Chile, Bolivia, and Peru, is thus a popular policy. Additionally, capitalism is, in the minds of many, linked to "dog-eat-dog" competition, high profits for a privileged few, and exploitation and subsistence existence for the many. Viewing capitalism largely in terms of its nineteenth-century behavior during the early years of industrialization, many leaders of the new nations believe in "socialism"; they are especially concerned that heavy industry—steel, rubber, chemicals, and so forth—the backbone of an advanced economy, should be publicly rather than privately controlled. Thus, even where private capital might be attracted to underdeveloped nations, investors fear their firms may be expropriated and nationalized, or subjected to discriminatory taxes or to currency controls that prevent the withdrawal of profits; and, of course, the contingency of violent nationalist agitation is ever present. Only recently have some nations, like Egypt, reassessed the desirability of attracting foreign private investments.

Another source of capital formation is through internal savings. In the West, capital was mobilized primarily by private businessmen, although governments played an important role in support of the business

[18] See Millikan and Blackmer, eds., *Emerging Nations*, pp. 46–53; and Walt W. Rostow, *The Stages of Economic Growth* (London and New York: Cambridge University Press, 1960), p. 21–26.

community by such means as capital outlay (the roads and canals mentioned earlier), protective tariffs, allowance of a high degree of industrial concentration, and pursuit of vigorous antilabor policies. All this assured high profits and thereby stimulated the process of capital accumulation, which required a vast inequality of income to succeed. Those with high incomes, because they could not consume all their earnings, saved and invested a considerable amount. In the mid-twentieth century, however, the idea of having a small minority of businessmen earn large profits at the expense of their countrymen finds little favor. More important, even if the twin prejudices against private capital and minority privilege did not exist, from whom could one squeeze the savings? The overwhelming majority of the populations of the underdeveloped countries live on the land and are engaged in subsistence farming. It would be difficult to depress their primitive standards of existence further, at least without resorting to totalitarian techniques. By contrast, the West possessed a wealthy class even before industrialization began.

To be sure, many of the underdeveloped countries (especially those in Latin America) do have a wealthy class—the large landowners who cooperated with the colonial power not only because it was profitable to do so but also because it guaranteed the stability of the traditional society and their own position at the top of the social hierarchy. While this class usually possesses great wealth, members tend to spend it largely in ostentatious living and in foreign travel and foreign investments; they are generally quite content with their way of life and are not much concerned with the welfare of the peasants. Nor are they interested in industry, as it would destroy the existing society and with it their own social position and their economic and social privileges.

More generally, however, traditional society lacks the secular orientation that produces the idea of material progress, individual achievement and reward, and vertical social mobility. Yet these are prerequisites for any sustained effort at saving and capital formation. A very apt demonstration of the largely extrasecular nature of life in a traditional society is the fact that in many underdeveloped countries necessary functions involving trade and money had to be left to "outsiders," or "foreigners." Thus, in Southeast Asian countries, most of the commerce has been in the hands of the Chinese minorities; and in sub-Saharan Africa, business has largely been left to the Indians.

The same traditionalism of society and culture also handicaps agricultural modernization. Although the overwhelming majority of the populations of the underdeveloped nations live on the land, the peasants in most countries cannot produce enough food. The great emphasis on industrialization has too often led to a neglect of agriculture. To the leaders of these countries, agriculture means poverty; it also is a constant reminder of their past colonial subjugation, of their former status as a supplier of raw materials. Yet agriculture remains vital, and food production must be raised dramatically to feed the growing population, both rural and urban-industrial, and to earn foreign exchange with which to buy required goods and services—or, at least, to decrease the amount of foreign currency spent on food imports. Economic growth, in short, requires *both* industrial and agrarian development. Instead of being separate and distinct processes, they are intertwined. An industrial revolution cannot occur without the provision of extra food, and to raise food production above the subsistence level requires the application of machinery and science to farming.

This is a far from simple task in traditional societies, where peasants have for centuries tilled the soil by the same methods. Unlike the Western farmer—who produces cash crops for a market and is therefore alert to technical innovations that might increase his production, enabling him to buy the other goods he needs, including food items he does not grow himself—the peasant is a subsistence farmer, producing in the main for his family only, exchanging with his village neighbors any surplus he may have for things he needs. Usually, the peasant is the last person to be touched by the currents of modernization. Poorly educated and physically isolated from the growing urban centers, he lacks contact with the latest trends in politics, with the new intellectual and technical currents that sweep the cities. The peasant is subject mainly to conservative influences: to religion, which tells him that he must bear his lot patiently and prepare himself for the hereafter; and to the landowner, who is the local political leader and the man to whom the peasant traditionally pays deference as well as portions of his crop. Not surprisingly, it is usually the city-dweller who is the activist and organizer of revolutionary movements; the peasant tends to be politically passive.

This does not mean that the peasant lacks grievances, which can be manipulated by revolutionary leaders in the attempt to break the power of the landowners and to undermine the existing society. For the peasant has an intense "land hunger." He wants to own the land he tills. But most of the land that peasants hold by tenure is owned by a few wealthy landlords. In Latin America as a whole, 90 per cent of all land was owned by 10 per cent of the landowners,[19] years after Castro had already taken over power in Havana. Moreover, land tenure systems are frequently subject to such abuses as excessive payments in crops (generally from 10 to over 50 per cent, and in some cases even 90 per cent) or in work to be done on the landlord's estate. On the other hand, peasants who own their own land are handicapped by the small size of their holdings as well as by their crude methods of work. Hence, even if he owns his land, the backward and impoverished peasant, compelled to borrow money in order to survive, can do so only by paying a money-lender—usually the local landowner—extremely high interest rates (rang-

---

[19] Tad Szulc, *The Winds of Revolution* (New York: Praeger Publishers, 1965), pp. 54–55.

ing from 20 to 40 per cent, or even higher). The peasants are thereby condemned to live in a state of continual indebtedness.

Thus the technical backwardness of the peasant, his small holdings of land, and the concentration of landownership all stand as formidable obstacles to agricultural development. Consequently, the overthrow of the old landowning class is not just a matter of social justice. It is a functional political and economic prerequisite for modernization if a nation is to bring to power men whose aim it is to industrialize; to destroy the traditional social structure, founded upon a grossly uneven distribution of wealth; and to channel savings into industrialization and permit agrarian reform.

Fundamentally, this means that the peasant must be granted his own land. But the redistribution of land is only the beginning. In most areas, the density of the population is likely to result in too many small farms —or what has been called "postage-stamp cultivation." Even if the peasant is taught more modern farming methods, receives proper credit facilities, gains a market for which to produce, and produces more of the high yield and protein richer wheat varieties which characterize the "Green Revolution," his crop production may still be insufficient, given the increasing population and small farms which are simply too unproductive; mechanical equipment is both too costly and too inefficient for use on small farms. There are no easy solutions, then, even after the political and social barriers are overcome. Collectivization of the land has not been too successful where tried, largely because of bitter peasant opposition; after almost half a century, agriculture remains the weakest area in the Soviet economy. Perhaps the Japanese type of farmer-operated cooperatives for credit, processing, and marketing is a feasible way of permitting the farmer to maintain his own plot of land, even if relatively small, while extending to him the advantages of a larger unit.

In any case, whatever the size of the farm, if the peasant is to till his soil and produce a surplus that can be siphoned off to feed the city population, it is absolutely essential that a good part of the population be moved off the land. It is the population growth that has crowded the land with small, inefficient subsistence farms. With fewer peasants on the land, it would be possible to concentrate land in larger farming units and thereby raise the over-all output. At the same time, such a shift of population could provide the necessary labor force for a growing industrial sector. In these two ways, agriculture can produce capital. For the peasant, whether he stays on the land or moves to the city, is a creature of habit. His whole way of living and his traditional values will change only gradually. Yet change they must if the needs of commercial agriculture and of the pattern of urban-industrial life are to be met. Basically, then, what is needed in the underdeveloped nation is a transformation in modes of thought, beliefs, and perceptions—in short, a cultural revolution.

The Cultural and Political Transformation

It should be obvious by now that the term "economic development" presents a one-dimensional picture of the process involved when a traditional rural society undergoes the transition to an advanced modernized nation. For "economic development" implies that the only requirement is industry, that industrialization follows automatically from capital formation, and that mobilizing this capital is therefore the crucial problem. But that is a vast oversimplification—if, indeed, not a distortion—of the complex realities of modernizing a traditional society. Industrialization is more than simply building steel mills and constructing dams. It is, *above all else,* a change in people's values, aspirations, and expectations. The necessary changes are not just economic; they are political, social, and cultural as well. Economic development is, in brief, multidimensional; it aims at the complete transformation of society.

Because the modernization that underdeveloped countries are currently undergoing is in some respects comparable to earlier Western development, it would perhaps be instructive to review briefly some of the principal changes involved in the transition from medieval feudalism to the more "modern," centralized monarchical states. It has been pointed out previously that the traditional societies do not regard economic activity as a prime concern of life. Surprising as it may be, even in Western history money-making was not always the chief pursuit. In the Middle Ages, religion was man's principal concern. His earthly existence was merely a short prelude to eternal life, for which he prepared himself by adherence to the moral code of the Church. Every aspect of his behavior was subjected to the spiritual authority of the Church, and, in the economic sphere, the Church condemned the charging of interest rates—a basic necessity on a monetary economy—as usury. The desire for profit was equated with greed, and economic competition simply was not part of the accepted way of life.[20]

This attitude toward interest and profits was, of course, inimical to business. Economic competition, profits, savings, investments, and the whole concept of economic growth were alien ideas in the Middle Ages. The merchant and craft guilds, which existed in the towns that had grown up by the eleventh century, functioned to prevent competition and regulate the economic life of the town. Membership in a guild was a prerequisite to the establishment of oneself in "business" as a craftsman, and it was no easy task to become a member. The guilds regulated the age at which apprenticeship began, the cost and duration of training, and the number of apprentices each guild master could have at any specific time. Thus no master could acquire more helpers than his com-

[20] See R. H. Tawney, *Religion and the Rise of Capitalism* (Baltimore: Penguin Books, 1947), p. 35.

petitors and thereby threaten their survival. Moreover, the guilds regulated prices—which, according to the Church, had to be "just." A merchant was expected to be satisfied with a price that covered no more than the cost of materials plus labor.[21] Economically, socially, and politically, the aim of medieval life—apart from its overriding religious purpose—was stability, security, and subsistence for everyone. Nowhere was this more evident than in the countryside, where the vast majority lived. There the manor was the center of organized life and loyalties. Feudalism, which lasted from approximately 850 to 1200, arose after the collapse of Rome and later, Charlemagne's empire. The dissolution of these larger political units of economic and social organization resulted in widespread chaos, disorder, and violence. The resulting search for security led to the establishment of the manorial system whose function was not only to produce food for its inhabitants but also to provide them with a government and protection. The lord of the manor, whose title and position derived from his ownership of the land, filled many functions. He was governor, judge, and military defender; in the absence of a central government, no one else could undertake these tasks. But the lord of the manor was not an entrepreneur. The manor did not produce for a national market; agricultural methods and practices were dictated by custom, and only enough food for local subsistence was grown.

The serfs owned no land; nor could they buy it. Land was inherited, and it was the basis of the entire social order. The lords, precisely because they owned the land, were the social, political, and military elite. There was no chance for the landless serf or his children to acquire land and rise socially. The lord-and-serf relationship involved mutual responsibilities and obligations. In return for the stability and security provided by the lord, the serfs performed the manorial labor. Bound to the land, they owed their master certain traditional services, such as working in his fields and paying him taxes (these were paid in kind with a part of the crop grown by the serf on the lord's land). There was no exchange economy; the medieval economy was essentially a "natural" one.

Thus, in order to modernize, Europe had to shift its emphasis from the spiritual afterlife to the temporal, replace the landowning nobility with a class concerned with capital accumulation, achieve a more fluid social structure that permitted upward mobility on the basis of achievement, and, finally, create a larger framework of political, social, and economic organization. None of these changes came quickly. The first thorough break with the medieval attitude came with Calvinism. The heart of Calvinist doctrine, predestination, stated that God had already selected those who would gain salvation. All others were condemned to damnation and could do nothing to redeem themselves. The Calvinists naturally believed that they were among the few slated for salvation in the hereafter. In the meantime, they would dedicate their life on earth

[21] *Ibid.*, pp. 37, 38, 43.

to the glorification of God, demonstrating their spiritual devotion to Him—not just by prayer, but by action. Calvinism, in contrast to Catholicism, did not reject secular activities as unimportant; rather, it assigned priority to them. The vigor with which a person pursued his "calling" was a token of his dedication to God and his own spiritual worth.

As wealthy as a man might become, though, he could never forget that he was "ever in the great Taskmaster's eyes." He was exhorted not to spend his money frivolously but to save it and use it to produce more and even greater "good works." Industriousness, profits, savings, and investments were thus legitimized by religion. Thrift, character, and hard work represented the Calvinist's earthly trinity. A man's energy had to be focused on pursuing the work to which God had called him. He was to shun luxury, leisure, entertainment, and sexual enjoyment. In order not to succumb to temptation and become morally corrupted, he had to exercise stringent discipline over his weaknesses and emotions.

It is hardly surprising that the "Protestant ethic" and capitalism became so closely identified, for Calvinism dictated a "new scale of moral values and a new ideal of social conduct." It was but a short way from Calvin to Adam Smith, whose theory of capitalism was based upon a recognition of the acquisitive passion the Church had earlier condemned. Smith accepted the desire for gain as a fact of life, calling it "enlightened self-interest." Laissez-faire capitalism was merely to harness this acquisitive instinct to the public welfare:

> Calvin did for the bourgeoisie of the sixteenth century what Marx did for the proletariat of the nineteenth. . . . He set their virtues at their best in sharp antithesis with the vices of the established order at its worst, taught them to feel that they were a chosen people, made them conscious of their great destiny in the Providential plan and resolute to realize it. The new law was graven on tablets of flesh; it not merely rehearsed a lesson, but fashioned a soul. Compared with the quarrelsome, self-indulgent nobility of most European countries, or with the extravagant and half-bankrupt monarchies, the middle classes, in which Calvinism took root most deeply, were a race of iron.[22]

This rise of capitalism and the bourgeoisie was, furthermore, accompanied by the centralization of political power in the state. The bourgeoisie settled in the new towns on or near rivers and roads, and were thus well located for the conduct of trade. They considered themselves free men, not subject to the control of the local lord. The consequent town-country, feudal nobility—commercial middle-class conflict forged an alliance between the king and the bourgeoisie. Because of the decentralization of power in medieval Europe, the king had been the supreme lord largely in name only. To consolidate power in his hands, he had to break the power of the nobility, upon whom he was dependent for his

[22] *Ibid.*, p. 39.

wealth and army. The bourgeoisie proved to be an alternative source of wealth. It was willing to furnish money and give the king its allegiance, for its aims coincided with his. First, it sought town charters specifying the citizens' freedom and their rights. Second, it wanted a larger area in which to trade. A powerful monarchy and the establishment of a sovereign state were thus in its interests. By the early sixteenth century, England, France, and Spain were already ruled by strong kings. The greater size, the single code of law, security of travel, a common set of weights and measures, and a common currency were all to the pecuniary advantage of the bourgeoisie.

The bourgeoisie particularly benefited from the king's desire to enhance the power and prestige of the new state. As the index of power was wealth—with which the monarch could pay the bureaucracy administering the state, maintain a strong army, or build a sizable fleet—mercantilism aimed at the development of a more self-sufficient economy. State policy was to maximize exports and minimize imports. Governments subsidized everything from porcelain manufacturing to armaments production; and this ever growing economy in turn provided the economic foundation for the increasing political and social cohesion of the state. Governments also sponsored the great voyages of exploration and granted charters to trading companies to exploit the wealth of the New World and the Orient. The result was a shift in trade from the Mediterranean to the Atlantic. Gold, silver, jewelry, spices, tobacco, ivory—and, of course, slaves—were transported to Europe from the new lands, most of which were colonized. This "commercial revolution" transformed Europe into the economic center of the globe, the cockpit of world power. But the result would not have been achievable without the prior change of values and social structure plus the establishment of a central government.

The Domestic Sources of Foreign Policy

The foreign policies of the new nations, like their domestic policies, reflect their preoccupation with nation-building. Indeed, it has been said that for a "new state, foreign policy is domestic policy pursued by other means; it is domestic policy carried beyond the boundaries of the state."[23] And what are the specific conditions that so largely influence the conduct of foreign policy? The first is the intensely felt nationalism of the new leaders. Their memories of colonialism and the long—and sometimes bloody—colonial struggle were not erased on the day they achieved independence. For the first generation of leaders, the past *is* the present, and their vivid memories make them jealous guardians of their nations' newly won independence.

[23] Robert C. Good, "Changing Patterns of African International Relations," *American Political Science Review*, September, 1964, p. 638.

More significantly, the nationalism of the new states—and this is particularly true of those who become the nation's first set of leaders—is not merely the product of past subjugation. More important than the memories of colonialism is the problem of achieving postindependence national cohesion. The new nation has shared only the experience of colonial rule, and it was the single purpose of gaining national freedom that enabled the various groups constituting the colonized "nation" to cooperate. Once the colonial power is ejected, these groups have little sense of belonging to a distinct cultural entity with certain shared expectations about its future. Once the opponent who united them is gone, there is little else to hold them together as a political, economic, and administrative entity; the centrifugal forces then begin to exert their pulls.[24] Ironically, the resulting disintegration is given impetus by the very principle of national self-determination in whose name the anticolonial revolution was carried out.

A second factor affecting foreign policy concerns economic development. For all new nations, the response to the revolution of rising expectations is of crucial importance. The degree to which these expectations are satisfied will be proof of the effectiveness of the new national government. Economic development produces a better life for the citizen; the significance of this is its *political* payoff. To the people of a new nation not yet solidly knitted together, the nationalist intelligentsia has to prove that what it is seeking to establish will be beneficial to them. Otherwise, why should they transfer their loyalty to it? Economic development can in this way help strengthen the fragile bonds of national unity. It can also contribute to this goal in other ways. An industrial economy, because of the specialization and division of labor, ties different sectors of a country together; men of different ethnic backgrounds and religious beliefs work together because of the imperative of economic interdependence. As these men interact economically, travel to other sections of the country, and communicate with people in

---

[24] It may be useful to recall in this connection that, although the United States had been united by the struggle against the colonial ruler, it returned to its pre-independence "tribalized" existence after the Revolutionary War was concluded. A man's loyalty was to his state. The first Union was a Confederation in which each state remained sovereign. The central government possessed neither an executive nor an independent judiciary; the Congress represented the states, and each state cast one vote. Important decisions required nine votes, and even then the resulting laws depended for their execution upon the will of the state governments. Congress had no authority to tax, to regulate commerce, or to negotiate effectively with foreign countries. The various states conducted independent relations with foreign powers, issued their own currencies, and constructed tariff walls at the expense of their neighbors. It soon became clear that the Articles of Confederation needed to be replaced by a national constitution and the "firm league of friendship" transformed into a "more perfect union" if the United States was to survive. Yet the strength of state loyalties over national loyalty remained very much in evidence even after this decision was made. Madison, a Founding Father, could be rebuked in the House of Representatives for using the word "national," a term so suspect that it had *deliberately* been omitted from the Federal Constitution.

different areas, they become more aware that they are all part of one nation and that unity is essential if their common hopes for the future are to be realized. An advancing economy also creates a new pattern of interests. The old farming interests are supplemented by a host of new economic and professional interests. In this context, individuals define their roles less in terms of prior ethnic or religious allegiances than in terms of their "interests." This rise of new social classes (the urban middle and working classes) is of key significance, for such groups or classes are nationwide rather than regional. Men thus become nationally self-conscious.

A third factor concerns the enormous extent of social ferment that accompanies modernization as tradition and customs collapse, a ferment that can lead to a continuing cycle of revolution. Because the old ways of doing things no longer suffice, new ways must be adopted. The result for most people is bewilderment and intense frustration. They find it difficult to adjust the behavior and attitudes of a lifetime to the changing environment. The peasant's sense of security (which stems from knowing his place in society) and his sense of belonging (which results from being part of an old way of life) collapse—particularly in the case of the peasant who is forced off the land and herded into the city and the new factory, where he must learn the values and habits of industrial civilization. He resents the factory with its discipline and monotony, long hours and low pay, and he hates the vast slums where he lives in filth, poverty, and disease, with tens of thousands of other uprooted peasants. He feels degraded. As a peasant, poor as he was, he at least felt he had a status and a role in society; as a peasant-worker, torn loose from his traditional moorings and submerged in the anonymity of the labor force, he feels the denial of his individuality.[25] He has become an isolated atom in a mass society.

[25] Marx, who confused capitalism as a mature economic system with the early phase of capital accumulation under any economic and political system, caught the essence of these peasant-laborers' protest. The bourgeoisie, he said, "has pitilessly torn asunder the motley feudal ties that bound man to his 'natural superiors,' and has left remaining no other nexus between man and man than naked self-interest, than callous 'cash payment.' . . . It has resolved personal worth into exchange value." Marx might more appropriately have used the words "Industrial Revolution" for "bourgeoisie." Indeed, he did say: "Owing to the extensive use of machinery and to division of labor, work of the proletarians has lost all individual character, and, consequently, all charm for the workman. He becomes an appendage of the machine. . . . Modern industry has converted the little workshop of the patriarchal master into the great factory of the industrial capitalist. Masses of laborers, crowded into the factory, are organized like soldiers. . . . Not only are they slaves of the bourgeois class, and of the bourgeois state; they are daily and hourly enslaved by the machine, by the supervisor, and, above all, by the individual bourgeois manufacturer himself. The more openly this despotism proclaims gain to be its end and aim, the more petty, the more hateful, and the more embittering it is." Quoted in Arthur P. Mendel, ed., The Essential Works of Marxism (New York: Bantam Books, 1961), pp. 15, 19–20; see also Adam B. Ulam, The New Face of Soviet Totalitarianism (Cambridge, Mass.: Harvard University Press, 1963), pp. 19–20.

The peasant who stays on the land is subject to similar frustration, hostility, and impatience. His transformation is from a subsistence peasant producing for his family to a commercial farmer producing for a market. He now must learn to operate new farm machinery and try new methods. If herded into collectivized farms, he will also feel deprived of "his" piece of land and his personality. Furthermore, he is resentful if, with the exception of the crop he needs to feed his family, the state takes away his increased yield to feed people in the cities and to earn foreign exchange. Thus his consumption, like that of the factory laborer, does not materially improve.

In the past, both groups were constantly told by leaders of independence movements that, once the colonial rulers were ousted, life would improve. But this better life cannot come for a long time, because capital formation requires postponement of consumption. The greater the gap between expectation and satisfaction becomes, the greater his frustration. Only a gradual closing of this gap, affecting him in terms of some improvement in his own life, plus the finding of some roots and personal security, can relieve this dissatisfaction. Thus, a society in transition is teeming with discontent, bewilderment, and insecurity.

A fourth factor compounds the problems of the new nations—namely, that the Westernized nationalist leader has often in the past been a stranger in his own land because his acquired Western values alienated him from his own culture. Thus, the assertion of nationalism not only enabled the masses to identify themselves with him and by extension with the nation, but also allowed him to identify himself with his people. The leader, as a Westernized man, knows that he has more in common with his former rulers than with the people in whose name he speaks. Before independence, he achieved identification through his leadership of the nationalist movement. After independence has been gained for "his" people, he cannot relax this nationalist stance. His need to identify with the people is stronger than ever.

How does the nationalist intelligentsia try to cope with these problems? One way is to "nationalize" the people—to inculcate in them a sense of national consciousness and loyalty, recognition of the national government as *their* government, of its laws as the laws of the nation reflecting their will and requiring *their* adherence. The majority must acknowledge that they are citizens of one nation and that the national government has the legitimate authority to make decisions on behalf of the entire population. Such a popular consciousness cannot be developed overnight. An entire people must, in a sense, go to school—to learn their nation's language and history (much of it mythical, devised for the purpose of fostering a sense of national identification) and to be brought into the mainstream of national life. Only then will the national symbols stimulate deeply felt emotion; only then will a truly national community emerge.

In the meantime, if the nation is to hold together the leader must act as a substitute "hero," the single person who more than anyone else symbolizes in his person the new nation.[26] He led the preindependence nationalist movement—he was the man who for years agitated for freedom, propagated its mythology, and went to jail for it. He and the nation are in a very real sense identical. As "the founder of the nation," he can indeed say *"la Nation, c'est moi."* For without his symbolic presence, the unity of the new nation would erode. Loyalty can usually be felt more keenly for an individual who incorporates an idea—such as the "nation"—than for the idea itself. One is flesh and blood, the other an abstraction. The hero in a new nation is a transitional figure in a transitional society. He serves the indispensable function of encouraging a shift from the traditional, parochial loyalty to the tribe or region to the broader loyalty of the still abstract nation-state. The hero possesses charisma—"a quality of extraordinary spiritual power attributed to a person . . . capable of eliciting popular support in the direction of human affairs."[27] He is, in fact, a *substitute* for the real nation and for the national institutions that have not yet been built, and he also confers legitimacy upon the new nation and its government.

This hero is usually supported by a single party as a principal instrument of national integration.[28] Unlike Western political parties, whose primary function is to represent the various interests within the nation, the rationale of the single party in a developing country is twofold: first, it is an effective way to socialize the traditionally "tribalized" people on a national basis. With the masses in the towns and countryside organized in provincial and local cells, the party, by drawing them into contact with national political life, tries to instill in them a sense of identification as citizens of a distinct national community. Just as the charismatic hero replaces the traditional chieftain, the nation is supposed to replace the tribe. For the party claims that it represents the nation. And opposition to the hero and the party is generally considered tantamount to treason. The second rationale of one-party rule is its presumed efficiency in mobilizing the economic and human resources of the nation for the purpose of modernization. As one African leader has said:

> Once the first free government is formed, its supreme task lies ahead—the building up of the country's economy, so as to raise the standards of the people, to eradicate disease, to banish ignorance and superstition. This, no less than the struggle against colonialism, calls for the maximum united effort by the whole country if it is to succeed. *There can be no room for difference or division.* In Western democracies, it is an accepted

[26] Wallerstein, *Africa,* p. 98.

[27] *Ibid.,* p. 99.

[28] Three-fourths of Africa's 345 million people, for example, lived under one-party rule in 1970—that is, twenty-nine out of forty states. *New York Times,* June 14, 1970.

practice in times of emergency for opposition parties to sink their differences and join together in forming a national government. *This is our time of emergency*, and until our war against poverty, ignorance, and disease has been won, we should not let our unity be destroyed by a desire to follow somebody else's "book of rules."[29]

By American standards, such a one-party system is of course undemocratic. In the United States, the opposition is a loyal opposition whose allegiance is to the same nation and values as the governing party. But in a new African nation, the opposition's allegiance is often regional and tribal, and it thus represents the centrifugal forces in the society. In these circumstances, a change in the form government toward greater democracy could result in the disintegration of the state. The choice is *not* democracy or dictatorship, but nationhood or disintegration.[30]

The leaders of new states confront problems that are so vast that rather than concentrate on their domestic needs they may prefer to play a dramatic role on the international stage. This may, in fact, help them "nationalize" their people. Since the only force that united the people was hatred of the former colonial power—and this "reactive nationalism" tends to lose its force as a socially cohesive factor soon after independence—the only way of arousing the people and keeping them united is to continue the struggle against European colonialism or "imperialism" in general. The more tenuous the bonds uniting the members of the society, the more ardent will be the campaign against the "vestiges of imperialism." By asserting that the nation is once more threatened by the Dutch or the French or the British—if not by all the Western states acting jointly as "NATO imperialists"—the leaders again seek to arouse their people and unite them against a common external danger. Thus, anticolonialism does not end with the achievement of national freedom. The struggle for independence must be continued until a measure of national unity has occurred.

The nationalist role of the leaders is also intended to divert popular attention from the domestic scene. At home, only painfully slow progress can be realized; the task is bound to be a long and arduous one, and the masses will tend to become increasingly restless and dissatisfied. The gap between their rising expectations and satisfaction seems unbridgeable as increasing numbers of people become politically conscious and make demands for the satisfaction of their needs, even during the initial capital-accumulation phase. In addition, the increased movement from the country to the impersonal and unfamiliar cities disrupts the traditional loyalties and ties of the people; unable to find substitutes, they live isolated in a mass society. Thus the pressure on the national leaders that results from the continuing need to improve living conditions and build the new nation is unrelenting. Unable to satisfy popular demands,

[29] Julius Nyerere, quoted in Paul E. Sigmund, Jr., *The Ideologies of the Developing Nations* (New York: Praeger Publishers, 1963), p. 199. Emphasis in original.
[30] Wallerstein, *Africa*, p. 96.

the leaders and their governments suffer a decline of prestige and support. In order to preserve or recapture the people's support, stay in power, and stabilize the government, the leaders' temptation to assert themselves in foreign policy becomes irresistible. In circumstances of economic stagnation, cultural alienation, and governmental insecurity, external adventure proves to be a useful tool. "If Castro were to act on the advice of theorists of economic development," Henry Kissinger has said, "the best he could hope for would be that after some decades he would lead a small progressive country—perhaps a Switzerland of the Caribbean. Compared to the prospects of leading a revolution throughout Latin America, this goal would appear trivial, boring, perhaps even unreal to him."[31]

For the leader, a nationalist foreign policy is, in addition, a psychological imperative. Without nationalism, he lacks personal roots, security, and communication with "his" people. The result of all these factors is that the political leaders will be tempted to preserve their power by externalizing domestic dissatisfaction; foreign scapegoats will be needed to relieve internal stresses and strains. It is easier for leaders to play a prominent and highly visible international role before their countrymen than to undertake the hard and difficult work of modernizing their nations. The people can take pride in their leaders'—and hence, their nation's—new status and identity in an international society that, under colonialism, had denied them importance and dignity as a nation and a people.

The Characteristics of the New Nations' Foreign Policy

Basic to a new nation's anticolonial nationalism is its nonalignment (once referred to in the United States as nonentanglement, or isolationism). The new nation seeks to discover and enhance its personality and, in so doing, refuses to ally itself with the former colonial ruler and, in fact, abstains from permanent diplomatic or military identification with any great power. Indeed, it gains self-recognition by asserting itself—at the very minimum on a verbal plane—against the great powers. Having gained independence, it must preserve its separate identity.

In fact, nonalignment is not as easy to define as it may seem. The Yugoslavs consider themselves nonaligned; so do the Egyptians, Indians, Ethiopians, Malaysians, and Tunisians. Yet, the dispositions of these countries range from sentiments that might be described as pro-Soviet to those that might be called pro-American. In a way, the problem of classifying the varieties of nonalignment is one of time. A regime may be looking eastward one moment and be normalizing its relationship with the West next. Indonesia may burn the United States Information Agency office one day and destroy and kill members of the Communist

[31] Henry A. Kissinger, *American Foreign Policy* (New York: Norton, 1969), p. 40.

Party a day later. Egypt may one day seem a Soviet pawn—indeed, in 1971 it formalized its association with a treaty of friendship and cooperation—but a year later it throws out the Soviet advisers and within two more years its President has re-established diplomatic relations with the United States and called the American-Jewish Secretary of State his "good friend" and "miracle worker." Aid supplied by one side often comes only after the other has refused to give it. Nonalignment is even more a matter of issue areas.[32] One such area is the military. Egypt and India thus received vast amounts of military equipment from Russia, but Singapore is willing to make its naval base available to the West in case of hostilities, and Tanzania relies upon the former mother country's (Britain's) military to restore domestic order. Yet all consider themselves nonaligned. Some countries seek and gain such military aid from both sides. The same is true for such other areas as economic assistance and trade, as well as diplomatic and ideological issues. Thus country A may be leaning westward because it places a high priority on democratic values, receives most of its military hardware from the West, gets about equal amounts of economic aid from both sides, and gravitates more toward Western than Soviet diplomatic positions (although, in fact, a country like India, democratic tradition notwithstanding, often seems to gravitate the other way). Country B, by contrast, is politically sympathetic to the East, from which it receives military hardware, obtains much of its economic aid and trade from the West, and leans notably eastward on diplomatic issues (although again, a one-party state like Egypt, with its "Arab Socialism," can switch from its pro-Soviet stance and shift its nonalignment more toward the United States, as well as dismantle much of its brand of socialism in order to release private initiative and attract foreign investments while retaining some public ownership over certain sectors of the economy). Even when a nonaligned country, however, seems to lean more toward Russia or America, one must be careful: "Pro-Soviet" may reflect a general attitude and preference on the part of the nationalist leaders, but it may also indicate positions which these countries would have taken even in the absence of a cold war—such as anticolonialism or anti-apartheid—and with which the Soviets seek to identify themselves. The same goes for a country that seems pro-American: Anwar Sadat is an Egyptian nationalist first, and if he leans toward the United States it is because in his view Washington can help him achieve his goal of recovering Egyptian lands lost in 1967 better than Moscow because Washington, not Moscow, has influence in Israel.

Nation-building through the rejection of the European colonial powers, as discussed previously, was formalized by America's Monroe Doctrine. More than a century later, Colonel Nasser of Egypt was to be particularly successful in awakening Egyptian—indeed, Arab—national-

[32] Cecil V. Crabb, *The Elephants and the Grass* (New York: Praeger Publishers, 1965), pp. 20–38.

ism through a foreign policy that hinged on the rejection of the colonial nations. His seizure of the Suez Canal in 1956 in response to what he felt was America's neocolonial treatment of Egypt was characteristic. In the face of Egyptian actions of which it disapproved—an arms agreement with the Soviet Union signed in late 1955, a stepped-up campaign to overthrow the pro-Western governments of Iraq and Jordan, the recognition of Communist China, and an intensification of the virulence of its verbal onslaught against the West in general—the United States had withdrawn funds pledged for the Aswan Dam.

Already acclaimed as the new Saladin of the Arab world for his Soviet arms deal—"this one bold stroke [with which] he declared his independence of the West and proclaimed his leadership of the Arabs"[33]—Nasser now nationalized the Suez Canal and announced that Egypt would build the dam with the money earned by the canal. It would be the symbol of an Egypt freed from colonial humiliation and servility:

> Citizens, we shall never allow the imperialists or the oppressors to have a hold over us. We shall never allow history to repeat itself. We have marched forward to build Egypt strongly and surely. We march forward to political and economic independence, we march forward towards a strong national economy for the masses of the people. We march forward to work. If we look back, we do so only to demolish the relics of the past, to demolish the relics of oppression, servility, exploitation and domination. We look back at the past to put an end to its effects. No, O citizens, as the rights revert to their owners, now that our rights in the Suez Canal have reverted to us after 100 years, we are building the real foundations of sovereignty and the real edifice of grandeur and dignity.[34]

During his life, it was said of Nasser that "his power and influence rest on his ability to symbolize Arab nationalism as an idea and as a practical force. As he walks on the world stage, millions of Arabs see him playing the role they would like to play and doing the things they would like to do. . . . When he challenges the great powers and takes daring risks in the name of Arab 'rights and dignity,' and gets away with it, the Arab masses feel an emotional lift and a satisfaction that no Arab leader has given them within memory."[35] The accuracy of this depiction was verified in the vivid scenes of anguish at the time of his death.

If nonalignment in the East-West conflict is the basic principle of a new nation's foreign policy in its search for self-recognition, opposition to great-power bases or involvement in its territory is a second aspect of its quest for national identity. And such opposition can range from shrill verbal attacks to regional aggression or expansion. In the American case,

[33] John C. Campbell, *Defense of the Middle East*, rev. ed. (New York: Praeger Publishers, 1961), p. 73.

[34] Quoted in Royal Institute of International Affairs, *Documents on International Affairs, 1956* (London: Oxford University Press, 1959), pp. 111–12.

[35] Charles D. Cremeans, *The Arabs and the World* (New York: Praeger Publishers, 1963), p. 25.

the leaders of the young republic could well recall that, during the seventeenth and eighteenth centuries, four European wars had involved the colonies,[36] and they were determined to avoid future repetition. No more wars were to be fought in the New World by the European powers. The Monroe Doctrine made it unmistakably clear that the hemisphere was no longer an arena for European colonization or intervention. At the same time, the early years of the Republic were spent eliminating the last vestiges of British, French, and Spanish power in territories considered to belong to the United States. The opposition by today's new states to great-power presence in their areas is equally vehement. The establishment under U.S. sponsorship of the Middle Eastern Treaty Organization (the Baghdad Pact) in the 1950's provides a revealing example. Nasser saw the alliance as an attempt by the Western powers to preserve their former colonial domination of the Middle East. Britain, he said, having lost its controlling influence in Egypt, had merely shifted its base of control to Iraq. Thus the Baghdad Pact provided Nasser with a visible, proximate target to boost his own and Egypt's role throughout the Arab world: his denunciation extended to all Arab regimes not sufficiently militant. More conservative Arab states, governments with formal ties to the West or, as Israel, those simply declared to be "beachheads for American imperialism"—all became his targets. As Nasser wrote:

> The pages of history are full of heroes who created for themselves roles of glorious valor which they played at decisive moments. Likewise the pages of history are also full of heroic and glorious roles which never found heroes to perform them. For some reason it seems to me that within the Arab circle there is a role, wandering aimlessly in search for a hero. And I do not know why it seems to me that this role, exhausted by its wanderings, has at last settled down, tired and weary, near the border of our country and is beckoning to us to move, to take up its lines, to put on its costume, since no one else is qualified to play the part.[37]

Nasser, seeking his own identification with the Egyptian people and Arab masses in general, was only too willing to play that heroic role, and circumstances—the Western regional presence and, especially, Egypt's discouraging domestic situation—provided him with the opportunity to fulfill his conception of the Arab's manifest destiny.

A third feature of the new nation's nationalistic, sometimes xenophobic foreign policy is its propensity to lecture the colonial powers about their international manners—that is, to moralize. This may in part be considered a realistic policy: to compensate for their lack of strength

[36] King William's War, 1689–97 (War of the League of Augsburg); Queen Anne's War, 1702–13 (War of the Spanish Succession); King George's War, 1744–48 (War of the Austrian Succession); and the Seven Years' War, 1756–63 (French and Indian War).

[37] Gamal Abdel Nasser, *Egypt's Liberation* (Washington: Public Affairs Press, 1955), pp. 87–88.

with a pose of "spiritual superiority." Morality may be a weak state's only weapon, particularly in its relationship with nations in which public opinion is accessible to external influence and must be considered by the policy-makers. If the state system "could be made to function on moral principles, the inequality of strength between states would become inconsequential."[38] But the new nations are not wholly opportunistic in their use of morality. Younger generations generally tend to criticize and reject the ways of their elders. It is a kind of arrogance: weak and inexperienced as they may be, they can at least feel morally superior. Self-righteousness is a luxurious and delicious feeling. This was certainly true of the youthful United States, which saw itself as the beacon of liberty, an example to the world.

And just as the new nations call themselves socialists, meaning that their societies are committed to the welfare of all their citizens, so the new United States proclaimed what, *for its time*, was a "left-wing" ideology—that all men are equal, that they possessed certain inalienable rights, and that government should be by consent of the governed. And, like most of today's new nations, the United States did not limit its rejection of the colonial order to political structure and values; the economic system was repudiated as well. Thus, just as "capitalism" is rejected today because it is held responsible for colonial "exploitation," so the United States reacted against the British mercantilist system, which had assigned to the colonies the status of suppliers of raw materials. Finally, just as the new nations have given nonalignment a moral content, so America's repudiation of the Old World's power politics was couched in moral terms. Isolationism or nonentanglement was a policy by which America would quarantine itself not only from Europe's social structure but also from its "old fashioned" international habits. The two were thought to be organically linked. Power politics—considered equivalent to war—was the "sport" of European princes unrestrained by democratic public opinion. Only democratic nations, whose leaders were responsible to the people, could be peaceful. As Thomas Jefferson exclaimed, diplomacy was "the pest of the peace of the world . . . the workshop in which nearly all the wars of Europe are manufactured."[39]

Naturally, the Europeans returned these compliments, calling the United States arrogant, naive, and hypocritical: arrogant because, as in the Monroe Doctrine, it addressed the powers of Europe as an equal; naive because, as a young republic, it had yet to learn the facts of life; and hypocritical because, as a self-proclaimed beacon of the virtues of the democratic ways of life, the "land of liberty" was the last to outlaw slave traffic, denied its Negroes their "inalienable" human rights, practiced lynching, ruthlessly removed its Indians from fertile lands to make

[38] Werner Levi, "Ideology, Interests, and Foreign Policy," *International Studies Quarterly*, March, 1970, p. 11.

[39] Quoted in Felix Gilbert, *To the Farewell Address* (Princeton, N.J.: Princeton University Press, 1961), p. 72.

room for white settlers, and was not averse to using a little "power politics" in order to win further territory in the Southwest and West. In much the same way, India under Nehru set itself up as spiritually superior, as the shining example of the virtue of practicing nonviolence in international affairs, and offered the United States frequent lectures on power politics and the immoral use of force. As the United States had attributed Europe's wars to petty jealousies and rivalries, so too did India see the causes of the cold war. Meanwhile, at home (where another form of segregation, the caste system, has been part of India's traditional culture for centuries and, though legally abolished, still has great social force), the new nation had some second thoughts about trying its own hand at power politics, even resorting to the use of force in Kashmir, Goa, and, more recently under Madame Gandhi, in Bangladesh, where India's successful military intervention ensured the breakup of Pakistan, India's chief rival for supremacy on the subcontinent. The Indian atomic explosion in 1974 near the Pakistani border was symbolic of India's claim to dominance and Pakistan's subordinate status.

A fourth characteristic of new nations' foreign policy is an attempt to expand its regional influence, even by the use of violence. While this characteristic hardly applies to most of the new nations, in several instances it has been strikingly displayed. Thus former President Sukarno of Indonesia, trying to unify several major islands and hundreds of little islands of the Indonesia he inherited from the Dutch, did everything but declare formal war on Malaysia, already an independent nation, as an appendage of British colonialism! Similarly, another former ruler, Nkrumah of Ghana, pursued a Pan-African policy to combat neocolonialism, which allegedly is keeping Africa divided and subservient to the Western states who formerly controlled them directly and are now seeking to do so indirectly. And Nasser during his rule of Egypt launched a militant Pan-Arab policy seeking to overthrow pro-Western regimes and replace them with governments loyal to him. The existence of Israel, defined by him as an output of Western imperialism, became a handy external scapegoat. If Israel had not existed, Nasser, in his attempts to nationalize the political consciousness of his people and divert their attention from the internal grievances resulting from economic mismanagement, would have had to invent it.

Thus, the domestic instability accompanying modernization spills over into the international arena. When a new nation with tenuous bonds of unity fragments, or when, to avoid such a domestic schism and to defuse the domestic dissatisfactions accompanying the nation's manifold growing pains, the nationalist intelligentsia—insecure in its power—tries to use foreign policy adventures to establish national cohesion and preserve its own popularity and power, it is likely to attract the Soviet Union and the United States. These difficulties attract the two superpowers because of the possibility that they may bring to power a group inimical to the interests of one of them, with the additional possibility that a regional expansion to the benefit of the other may occur. If one of the two nations is unwilling to tolerate what, in terms of the global balance of power, it may consider a local or regional setback, it will intervene; or, if it fears that its own nonintervention will invite its opponent to intervene, the result may be a preventive intervention. In both cases, it risks counterintervention.

From the systemic point of view, the behavior of the new states may seem "irresponsible." But the crucial point is precisely that their leaders feel little sense of responsibility for the stability of the system. Their principal preoccupation is domestic and, as one student of the impact of nationalism upon Europe in the last century has remarked, not until nationalists become "at least partially content with an existing state of internal affairs [will] they be willing to act as responsible members of an international community."[40] But a "society in the agonies of domestic transformations is not likely to regard international determinants as decisive. . . . External policies are merely instrumental to internal purposes and rarely are internal programs fashioned in response to the international environment."[41] Only when "emergent" nationalists become "mature" nationalists can international influences be expected to work. The European system had sufficient difficulties integrating Italy and Germany before World War I; it never did assimilate the several new states that arose in the interwar period out of the ashes of the Austro-Hungarian Empire. Yet the post–World War II era has witnessed the rise of almost three score of new nations.

Underdeveloped Countries and Economic Aid

Under such circumstances, one obvious question is whether economic aid speeds the modernization process and shortens the time it takes for the new states to reach the mature nationalist phase. Though all the facts are not yet in, we do have a considerable amount of information with which to venture an answer. Foreign aid has, after all, been with us for a good many years. In a sense, the very distribution of power in the postwar state system enhanced the ability of the new nations to attract needed funds. During the days of bipolarity, the superpowers were unwilling to risk total war, and each, therefore, hoped to defeat its opponent in the developing areas. Foreign aid as an instrument of policy in this contest was, in the nuclear age, considered a substitute for arms: "In our times, economic activities are not an alternative [to war]; they are a substitute. They are no longer a preferable alternative to clearly feasible war and to equally despicable but apparently dispensable power politics. They are instead a substitute for practically self-defeating major war,

[40] Richard Rosecrance, *Action and Reaction in World Politics* (Boston: Little, Brown, 1963), p. 209.
[41] *Ibid.*, p. 299.

and they are more than ever an instrument of the again respectable politics of power."[42] In short, foreign aid became for a while an instrument of economic warfare.

The Soviet aid program began in 1954–55 and, until approximately 1964,[43] was concentrated in just a few countries. Aid was given to states that were either politically vital (such as India) or strategically located (such as Afghanistan). In particular, aid was given those states that, possessing both these qualities, were also "troublemakers"—such as the United Arab Republic, Iraq, Algeria, and Cuba. Moreover, the Soviets did not necessarily ask for the economic justification of a project as a condition for aid. Thus they furnished aid to build such projects as the Aswan Dam for the United Arab Republic and a steel mill for India, in each case responding to a request by the host country for such support rather than initiating the proposed program. They were not especially concerned with how a particular project fitted into a country's over-all plan for development. If a project served Soviet purposes, it received support. One such purpose was public notice, and hence the Soviets spent their money on highly visible projects—not only the high dam at Aswan but also paving Kabul's main street and supplying the Afghans with buses, or building sports stadiums in Rangoon and Jakarta. They were also quite willing to send the new states modern weapons, which provided the recipients with the symbols of a modern nation and the illusion of national strength or, as in the Arab case, made them close allies in a joint effort to dislodge Western influence from the Middle East.

The Soviet aid program relied heavily on credits, while the United States relied largely on grants. It was often argued that the former had a distinct psychological advantage over the latter. Unlike grants, which supposedly had a tendency to make the recipient feel he was accepting charity, credits, it was claimed, enabled the borrower to retain his dignity; because he was paying for the loan, he would feel that he was engaged in a normal business transaction of mutual benefit to both parties. Moreover, the Soviet loans were extended at an interest rate of 2–2.5 per cent, while American loans generally carried at least a 4–5 per cent charge. The lower Soviet rate allowed the Russians to accuse the West of exploiting the developing countries in typical capitalist fashion and to stress the advantage to a developing country of Soviet aid. On top of this, the Soviets seemed more willing to accept repayment of their loans in local currency or in the form of the recipient country's exports, which often helped to relieve a surplus of cotton, rice, fish, or sugar and to preserve the country's slim dollar or sterling reserves. Yet, while the So-

[42] George Liska, *The New Statecraft* (Chicago: University of Chicago Press, 1960), p. 3.
[43] See Joseph S. Berliner, *Soviet Economic Aid* (New York: Praeger Publishers, 1958), pp. 179–80, and Hans Heymann, Jr., "Soviet Foreign Aid as a Problem for U.S. Policy," *World Politics*, July, 1960, pp. 525–40.

viet loan policy may have appeared to have many advantages to the developing nation, it was in fact geared to specific Soviet purposes, which actually had little to do with the recipient's well-being. The Soviets used loans not to preserve the recipient's sense of self-respect but to keep down costs; a loan program is always less expensive than an outright grant. Moreover, because loans must be repaid, the number of applications is limited. Equally important, loans establish bilateral trading relationships with the recipients; thus the Soviet Union obtained commodities it needed.

The Soviet Union's aid program was not as successful as one might have thought. The results speak for themselves. Soviet aid to a particular country has often been initiated at a point when relations between the recipient and the West were poor. Aid to Iraq was begun after that nation's pro-Western government had been overthrown by a new nationalist government, which, having denounced Western "imperialism" and withdrawn from METO, was very much "open" to new sources of support. When Guinea opted to leave the newly formed French Commonwealth and France accordingly withdrew all its aid, Soviet rubles began to pour into the country. As Egypt grew increasingly anti-Western in the mid-1950's, opposed METO, and sought to overthrow pro-Western governments throughout the Arab world, the Soviet bloc offered Egypt a huge supply of modern weapons. When the United States then retracted its offer to build the Aswan Dam, in part because of Egypt's new close ties with the Soviet Union, the Soviets took over financing of the project.

Yet Iraq did not go Communist, and the new government eventually arrested the Iraqi Communist leaders. Sékou Touré of Guinea sent the Russian Ambassador home for allegedly plotting to overthrow his government and then began to re-establish his relations with France. And Nasser, and his successor as well, arrested Egyptian Communists and even denounced Russia on several occasions. In no developing nation has Soviet aid resulted in the acceptance by local leaders of Soviet dictation on domestic or foreign policy—except in Cuba, where the Communists were already in power *before* the Soviet aid program began. But even Castro, while receiving about $1 million a day, has castigated Moscow for refusing to support revolutionary action in Latin America.[44]

Why did the Soviet Union have such limited success with its aid program in exploiting the new states' anti-Western emotions? One reason is Soviet performance. The Soviets have at times failed to deliver the quantity of goods promised, engaged in questionable practices (such as reselling Egyptian cotton at lower than world market prices and thereby both competing with and underselling Egypt's own cotton)[45] and delivered poor-quality crude oil, wormy wheat, and unsatisfactory machinery. Some of these failures might, indeed, have been expected. The

[44] For a well-balanced analysis of the early years of Soviet aid, see Barbara Ward, "The Other Foreign Aid Program," *New York Times Magazine*, June 17, 1962.

[45] Berliner, *Soviet Economic Aid*, pp. 171–77.

Soviets generally perform best in the area of heavy industry, where they have considerable experience, rather than in light industry or the production of consumer items. Soviet experience in agriculture, already an Achilles' heel in the Soviet economy, had little applicability to the tropical farming of most of the underdeveloped areas. Yet these defects of the Soviet aid program should not be overstressed. Not only has the American program suffered like failures, but the Soviet program also has had certain advantages over its American counterpart.[46] The Soviets, not needing Congressional approval of annual foreign aid appropriations, have been able to commit themselves for years in advance, thus allowing the recipient nation to plan a long-range economic program. They have also had the flexibility to exploit favorable new situations as these have arisen; no legislature allocates aid money for specific projects. The Soviet Government can also mobilize its best engineers and technicians if it so desires, for there are no private Russian corporations whose higher wages attract top talent away from government-sponsored aid projects. Finally, no citizen or official, ethnic group, or farm lobby in the Soviet Union embarrassed the government by denouncing the aided country or by attempting to block an aided nation's efforts to pay its debts through the sale of farm goods of which the Soviet Union already possesses a surplus or of manufactured items in competition with its own products.

But Soviet aid since 1954–55 has not achieved more politically principally because its long-range political aims did not coincide with the aspirations of the developing countries. Short-range Soviet goals may well have been compatible with their aims of national independence and nonalignment in foreign policy. Indeed, one of the attractions of Soviet aid was that it strengthened the newly independent nation by lessening its otherwise exclusive dependence on the former mother country or on the United States. But Soviet—and certainly Chinese Communist—longrange aims diverged sharply from the objectives of the new states. These nations have keen memories of their long colonial subjugation; they were not about to substitute Soviet or Chinese colonialism for the Western variety. Their nationalism was directed against *any* foreign control. This posed a real dilemma for the Soviets. Wherever the Soviets have not interfered in its domestic politics, they have enjoyed good relations with the recipient nation—as, for instance, with India. But where the Soviets have sought to pressure a government to support Communist positions or have even gone so far as to attempt to overthrow the government, the result has been the jailing of local Communists, the expulsion of the Soviet Ambassador, or the surveillance of Communist technicians supervising the aid programs.

For the United States, the aid program's principal purpose—after it was switched from Europe to the non-Western nations and, again, until about the middle 1960's—stemmed from the cold war aim of halting

[46] Heymann, "Soviet Foreign Aid," pp. 538–39.

Communism. Indeed, the term "economic aid" is actually something of a misnomer,[47] as the giant portion of American aid since the Korean War has been *military aid* to support the armies of allied nations around the Sino-Soviet periphery: Nationalist China, South Korea, South Vietnam, Pakistan, and Turkey. Admittedly, such military assistance is a form of economic aid; for, if its army is being supported, the recipient nation spends less of its own money on its military forces and can instead invest more heavily in its economic development. (This, of course, presumes it would invest in a military force even without aid—a fair presumption, given the internal factors, noted earlier, that lead to domestic instability.)

Another form of aid might—for want of a better term—be called "bribery" aid. Much of the aid extended to Latin American republics before the Alliance for Progress could be included in this category. Dollars, as well as military equipment, sent to these countries under the guise of economic development or hemispheric collective self-defense, were actually intended to "buy" the support of the ruling classes and the military, neither of which was particularly interested in modernization. The United States was preoccupied in Europe, Asia, and the Middle East—that is, anywhere but Latin America, whose grave social, political, and economic problems were ignored until Castro suddenly and dramatically drew attention to the vulnerability of the United States in its own backyard. Up to that point, the United States had been interested primarily in preserving hemispheric stability and securing votes in the United Nations. Latin American armies, hardly threatened by the Russian or Chinese military and useless as fighting machines anyway, could nevertheless be strengthened to deal with unrest at home.

But the most significant form of aid, in view of the almost global scope of the "revolution of rising expectations," has been that given for *capital development*.[48] American policy-makers, fearful that the Soviets could exploit the transitional period between the traditional society and the beginning of a self-sustaining economy, were naturally anxious to promote economic growth. They feared that some of the more important new nations, should they fail to transform themselves into unified, urban, industrialized societies, might adopt Communism in order to organize themselves for modernization more effectively. Implicit in the American promotion of economic growth was the assumption that poverty would benefit the Communist cause. The revolution of rising expectations could not be allowed to turn into a revolution of rising frustrations.

Conversely, it was frequently assumed—as with Russia—that eco-

[47] For the classification of aid generally followed here, see the excellent article by Hans J. Morgenthau, "A Political Theory of Foreign Aid," *American Political Science Review*, June, 1962, pp. 301–9.

[48] For an excellent study of U.S. aid programs, see Joan M. Nelson, *Aid, Influence and Foreign Policy* (New York: Macmillan, 1968).

nomic development would nurture a more open society and democratic institutions,[49] and that this, in turn, would ensure peaceful international behavior. While these assumptions are questionable, it is true, as already suggested, that democracy cannot develop amid conditions of poverty. As Aristotle pointed out, "Poverty is the parent of revolution and crime"; "when there is no middle class, and the poor greatly exceed in number, troubles arise, and the state soon comes to an end." Aristotle believed political stability depended upon the absence of extremes of wealth and poverty: "Thus it is manifest that the best political community is formed by citizens of the middle class, and that those states are likely to be well-administered, in which the middle class is large, and stronger if possible than both the other classes, or at any rate than either singly; for the addition of the middle class turns the scale, and prevents either of the extremes from being dominant."[50] In other words, widespread moderate affluence is a prerequisite for democratic government. When the majority of men live in dire need—and are aware that a better life is possible but see no signs of any improvement—democratic government will not establish roots. A higher national income, and a more equitable distribution of that income, are more likely in a developed economy, and such economies do tend to promote democracy. The society that can afford to "deal everyone in" can afford to be democratic.[51] Economic growth does not, of course, automatically produce a democratic society—Germany and Japan in the 1930's and the Soviet Union today being obvious examples. In each of these cases, an economically developed nation has been controlled by an authoritarian or totalitarian regime bent on regional or global expansion. The values of freedom and democracy are not the necessary result of economic development. But if economic development is not *a sufficient* condition to ensure the maturation of a democratic society, it nevertheless remains *a necessary* condition.[52]

This promotion of favorable domestic developments in the new nations was, of course, closely related to the hope that a conflict between the older and newer states was avoidable. Amercan policy-makers generally assumed that a world divided between rich and poor nations was incompatible with U.S. interests. It was the nineteenth-century Western society of the wealthy few and the destitute masses that Marx wrote

[49] This was an implicit assumption, never made explicit in the doctrine of foreign aid. The reasons for this are analyzed in Robert A. Packenham, "Developmental Doctrines in Foreign Aid," *World Politics*, January, 1966, pp. 194–225, and *idem*, *Liberal America and the Third World* (Princeton, N.J.: Princeton University Press, 1973).

[50] William Ebenstein, ed., *Great Political Thinkers*, 3d ed. (New York: Holt, Rinehart & Winston, 1960), p. 105.

[51] David M. Potter, *People of Plenty* (Chicago: University of Chicago Press, 1954), pp. 118–19.

[52] See Black, *Diplomacy of Economic Development*, pp. 19, 23. For a general analysis of the conditions necessary for democracy to flourish, see Seymour M. Lipset, *Political Man* (Garden City, N.Y.: Doubleday, 1959), pp. 45–67.

about in the *Communist Manifesto*. He merely projected this actual social division into the future when he prophesied the demise of capitalism. Most of the Western nations, however, managed to avoid the "inevitable" proletarian revolution by redistributing their national incomes, stabilizing their economies, and regulating their large industrial corporations. Democracy, by reforming capitalism, derevolutionized labor and gained its allegiance to a form of welfare capitalism, or social democracy, in which labor shared in the general improvement of living standards. The same kind of maldistribution of income now plagues the underdeveloped world. The question is whether what Marx called "the specter of Communism" has been defeated domestically only to reappear now and defeat the bourgeois West internationally.[53]

Since the middle 1960's, however, there have been significant changes in both American and Soviet aid policies. This is due to a number of reasons. Both of the superpowers have become increasingly aware that "instant development" is an unrealistic expectation. Modernization is a very long and very complex progress, not to be achieved in a "Decade of Development" (as the 1960's were designated by the United Nations), or by the transfer of factories and machinery to a cultural environment unable to cope with modern industry and its accompanying social, political, and psychological needs. The long haul, the efforts already made, and the disappointing results have both tired and disenchanted the two principal competitors. Both have also realized that aid does not necessarily buy allies or votes. The Soviet Union, specifically, became increasingly disillusioned with the more radical leaders it once sought as partners against the West. Many of them had, by 1965, been deposed; but additionally, in each instance the new regime stated that one of the principal reasons for the *coup d'état* had been economic stagnation and domestic chaos. Furthermore, the receivers of Soviet aid often did not pay back their loans. The United States, on the other hand, grew more sophisticated; while coming around to accepting nonalignment even before the fall of radicals such as Ben Bella in Algeria, Nkrumah in Ghana, and Sukarno in Indonesia, it has been less than enchanted with those who have often bitten the hand that fed them. Finally, bipolarity has passed. In an era of increasing superpower negotiations (rather than confrontations) and of growing acceptance of their respective spheres of influence, the competition for the Third World has seemed less urgent, particularly as other external commitments and demands on resources as well as domestic needs came to be more pressing.

American aid has, as a result, been on the decline. Since 1966, Presidential requests for economic and military aid have been cut by about $1 billion a year. Relative to the nation's increasing ability to pay as the

<hr>

[53] This thesis has been re-examined in a general re-evaluation of the U.S. foreign aid program by Samuel P. Huntington in "Foreign Aid for What and for Whom?" *Foreign Policy*, Winter, 1970, pp. 161–89, and *idem*, "Does Foreign Policy Have a Future?" *Foreign Policy*, Spring, 1971, pp. 114–34.

gross national product rose, the aid "burden" declined. In the late 1940's, Marshall Plan aid took 2.75 per cent of the GNP. By the beginning of the 1970's, nonmilitary aid reached a low of 0.29 per cent of the GNP, the lowest of all major donor countries. The comparison of American aid with that of other countries was already striking in 1968. Between 1956 and 1961, development aid had been increasing rapidly; it increased more slowly up until 1967, and then, in 1968, began to decline.

OFFICIAL DEVELOPMENT AID AS A PERCENTAGE OF THE
GNP OF MAJOR COUNTRIES (1968)

France	0.72	United States	0.38
Australia	0.57	Canada	0.28
Netherlands	0.54	Sweden	0.28
Britain	0.42	Japan	0.25
West Germany	0.42	Italy	0.23
Belgium	0.42		

SOURCE: Organization for Economic Cooperation and Development and the Development Assistance Committee. From Lester B. Pearson, *Partners in Development: Report of the Commission on International Development* (New York: Praeger Publishers, 1969), p. 148.

During his years in office, President Johnson proposed a major change in development programs: In effect, it constituted a further reduction in the size of U.S. aid. What he suggested was a shift from support for industrialization to support for the areas of health, education, and food production—in short, a shift to a "bare bones" *technical assistance program*. By the time President Nixon took office, this emphasis on technical assistance at the expense of long-term capital aid was reinforced; so was the emphasis on private investment. Only the humanitarian rhetoric of foreign aid remained to uplift. The President, to be sure, made such generally approved recommendations as separating military from economic aid and increasingly channeling more—and eventually most—loans for development through international institutions such as the World Bank, the various regional banks, and UNCTAD. This would, it was hoped, leave the United States less vulnerable to charges of using its aid to advance American political and strategic aims, and perhaps it would also satisfy those senators who argued that bilateral aid had involved their country too deeply in the affairs of too many countries, especially Asian countries. But little was said about committing larger funds—say, the .7 per cent of the GNP recommended in 1969 by an international commission headed by Canada's ex-Prime Minister and former Foreign Minister, Lester Pearson. Greater emphasis was clearly to be placed on technical assistance and even more on a larger role for American private enterprise. A main criterion for future aid was to be

economic rather than political: Could the recipient mobilize his resources and adopt policies that would make sound use of the proffered
funds?

The Soviet Union has followed suit. Indeed, ideologically, the shift in
attitude to foreign aid since 1964 has been a startling confirmation of our
earlier analysis of Soviet "revisionism."[54] In the early 1960's, the Soviet
counsel to the new states was drawn straight from Marxism-Leninism:
Expand the public sector of the economy in order to gain control over
the economy; expropriate and nationalize private foreign and domestic
firms to keep profits for reinvestment that would otherwise go into private hands at home or abroad; and orient economic relations toward
Russia and its friends to break the alleged Western imperialist economic
chains of subjugation that have kept nations underdeveloped. All this
has changed. Soviet aid policy now also emphasizes the economic criteria
more heavily than the political. Conversely, it has de-emphasized, in a
very un-Marxist fashion, the scope of state control and nationalization
of industry, has suggested that private capital—including *Western* capital—has an important role to play in the modernization of the new nations, and has pointed out that more balance is needed between industrial and agrarian development. The amount of Soviet aid has also
fallen off.

Thus, while for both superpowers economic effectiveness has become
more important, it has come to be especially so for the Soviets, because
the United States has always been concerned with economic rationalism.
This is not to say that political considerations are not now significant—
as, for instance, in Soviet aid to the Arab countries. But what it does
mean is that both nations wish the recipients of their aid to place greater
emphasis on putting their economic houses in order. Presumably each
expects political benefit from this; probably neither will be pleased if
needed reforms in the program, however, are accompanied by a change
from a friendly to a hostile disposition on the part of the recipient country. Clearly, both now use economic aid, as great powers before them
did, to keep or gain influence rather than to bring about radical changes
in the new nations' domestic structures. One might say of the American
program, as has been said of the Russian one, that the efforts to make aid
economically more telling is "not in order to lessen the influence of 'socialist' economies [or of mixed economies, as in the United States] but
to improve its chances and popularity."[55] Nevertheless, the amounts of
economic aid with which this will be sought will be smaller than at any
time since World War II. Indeed, foreign aid does not even cover the
extra costs of oil the underdeveloped nations have had to pay since the
Arabs raised the price in 1973.

[54] Elizabeth Kridl Valkenier, "New Trends in Soviet Economic Relations with the
Third World," *World Politics*, April, 1970, pp. 415–32, and *idem*, "New Soviet
Views on Economic Aid," *Survey*, Summer, 1970, pp. 17–29.

[55] Valkenier, "New Soviet Views," p. 29.

Military Rule, Political Legitimacy, and Second-Generation Leadership

The prospects for modernization in many underdeveloped countries are thus not very bright. The central problem of the political system's legitimacy remains especially crucial. Not surprisingly, without it new states continue to be unstable and are racked by civil wars, *coups d'état*, revolutions, and assassinations. Nor is it surprising that the trend in the non-Western areas in these circumstances is toward military control and government. A number of conditions favor this increasing military intervention in politics.[56] First is the low level of legitimacy in the new states. Whereas in a modern society with a tradition of civilian institutions, the military would find it difficult to justify seizing power and demanding public obedience (or proving it possessed legitimate authority), in a new country in which political obligation still follows largely along subnational ethnic, religious, and racial lines, the military can seize power. Instead of being regarded as a usurpation, such a seizure can claim legitimacy if the embryonic political institutions and the politicians seem to have failed. Civilian leadership, overwhelmed by the massive problems confronting it, has often proved itself inept and indecisive. In addition, the one-party systems may not have possessed the necessary organizational cohesiveness and discipline to mobilize their populations for the hard tasks of modernization. More frequently, in the absence of any opposition, they grow lax, self-indulgent, and corrupt. Political instability, deteriorating or stagnant economic conditions, plus perhaps national humiliation, tend to undermine popular faith in the politicians, political institutions, and "politics," and the people turn toward the army, the symbol of the nationhood it is sworn to defend. The army, opposed to the lack of discipline and widespread dishonesty in government, and usually somewhat contemptuous of politicians (certainly incompetent ones), often interprets public opinion in this way, for it tends to perceive itself as the public's protector and guardian. In a sense, the army, having no real function as a major defense force and wanting something to do, starts to behave as a political party. And, having the means to seize power, it becomes an effective party.

A second condition favoring domestic military intervention is the low

[56] General analyses of the role of the military in new nations are Morris Janowitz, *The Military in the Political Development of New Nations* (Chicago: University of Chicago Press, 1964); S. E. Finer, *The Man on Horseback* (New York: Praeger Publishers, 1962); John J. Johnson, ed., *The Role of the Military in Underdeveloped Countries* (Princeton, N.J.: Princeton University Press, 1962); Samuel P. Huntington, *Political Order in Changing Societies* (New Haven, Conn.: Yale University Press, 1968), pp. 192–263; and Edward Feit, "Pen, Sword and People: Military Regimes in the Formation of Political Institutions," *World Politics*, January, 1973, p. 251 ff.

level of economic development. Again, a Western army, regardless of its organizational and technical sophistication, could not run a society as complex as Britain or the United States—probably not "even" New York City. When, after 1945, the army ran the occupation of Germany, for example, it did so only with the help of the top men in American business and professional life. Even then, its responsibility was limited to repair and reconstruction work. But in a far less developed society the military may be technically more competent than the civilians. Armies are, by and large, microcosms of modern industrial societies. They are technically and rationally oriented to their occupational activities. They cannot function without engineers, mechanics, communications specialists, and so forth; even the operation of jeeps, tanks, guns, and other military equipment by the ordinary soldier demands elementary "industrial" skills. Military units have, in fact, on occasion been used for such tasks as the construction of roads, bridges, and harbors—recalling the role of the U.S. Corps of Engineers in the development of the American West.

Third, armies in new nations may be in the best position to organize the nation for its "take-off" and to surmount the turbulent transition from the traditional agrarian to modern society. An army is founded on centralized command, hierarchy, and discipline, the very characteristics Communist Parties, whether loyal to Moscow or Peking, claim would allow them, and only them, to modernize an underdeveloped nation successfully and rapidly.[57] The army may, in fact, be the only organization that can compete with the Communists in their capacity to break the power of the land-owning classes, carry out land reforms, organize the nation's human and natural resources for development, and control the unhappy masses from whom capital savings must be collected. In addition, the real power in many of the new states' armies lies with the younger, highly nationalistic officers, who are dedicated personally and institutionally to the modernization of their nations. In the past, their senior officers came from the landed upper class, which had a vested interest in preserving the traditional society; this is true, for example, for a number of armies in Latin America. But today it is not the generals but the captains who play the key role in control of the army. As sons of small landowners and low-grade civil servants, they consider themselves the true "sons of the land" and despise the traditional ruling class where it still governs. They are aware of the comparative weakness of their army, a weakness reflecting not merely the absence of modern weapons but the pre-industrial nature of their society. They also know from experience that whereas, in a traditional society, a man's status was decided at birth, in the Westernized or modern army, personal advance-

[57] It has also been argued, however, that the army's role is less likely to be influenced by characteristics of its internal organization as by the political and social conditions of the society in which it exists. In some societies, it will play a "progressive" role, in others a conservative one. Huntington, *Political Order in Changing Societies,* pp. 221–22.

ment is possible. For this reason, they, as young and ambitious individuals whose prospects of social advancement and economic reward are cut off as long as the civilian society is highly stratified, often entered the army, where their status in many cases was determined not by birth and family but by ability and hard work. The fact that there was a relationship between effort and reward in the military served to point up the injustice of the surrounding civilian society and the need for reform. Thus, the younger military leaders tend to share the nationalistic and modernizing desires of the Westernized secular intelligentsia; indeed, they are usually referred to as the "military intelligentsia" or the "intelligentsia in uniform."[58]

Even if some military governments, with their frequently civilian expert advisers, should be more successful than civilian governments in organizing their societies for economic take-off—and the evidence is that up to now they have had the same lack of success as civilian-controlled governments[59]—the problem of *democratic* political development still remains. Even if the controlling party or army should voluntarily relinquish power —which, again, may not necessarily happen—its stewardship will have tended to strengthen the authoritarian tradition the new nation inherited from the colonial period, a tradition reinforced by the nation's modernization. The one-party (or military government's) "tutelary democracy" may thus remain tutelary, and democracy may become nothing more than a façade hiding the reality of an authoritarian civilian or military regime.

The issue of democracy is not, however, a *real* issue, for the new states lack the prerequisites for the conduct of a democratic government: a relatively high standard of living, mass literacy, a sizable and stable middle class, a sense of social equality, and a tradition of tolerance and individual self-reliance. The real issue for the new states is not a democratic restraint of power and an emphasis upon various freedoms but the harnessing of sufficient power to hold the nation together and set it on the way into the twentieth century—which requires hard work, austerity, and self-control—while seeking to legitimate the new nation and the national government's authority. A Western political analyst has put it as follows:

> The peoples of the West advanced toward democracy by very slow and gradual stages which included long periods of rule by absolute monarchs and despots, benevolent or otherwise. The achievement of ordered societies, reasonably in agreement on those basic elements of social cohesion necessary for the functioning of democracy and well started on the path

[58] The degree to which the military leaders' perception of their role is influenced by the values they learned in Western military academies is suggestively analyzed in Robert M. Price, "A Theoretical Approach to Military Rule in the New States," *World Politics*, April, 1971, pp. 399–430.

[59] Eric A. Nordlinger, "Soldiers in Mufti," *American Political Science Review*, December 1970, p. 1131 ff.

of economic development, was in good part the product of the firm authoritarian rule which bridged the transition from the Middle Ages to the contemporary world.

For a backward people precariously moving out from under colonialism into independence with all the problems of economic development still ahead of them, it is highly doubtful that the sovereign remedy is a full-scale installment of democracy as the latter has evolved in advanced and prosperous Western societies. Democracy implies far-reaching freedoms, and an opposition; but the prime requirement is not for more freedoms but for discipline and hard work, not for opposition but for a national consolidation of all forces and talents. This is all the more true in countries such as Nigeria or Malaya where the opposition is likely to be made up of parties formed on tribal, racial, or religious lines, deepening inner divisions at a time when the essential need is strong and unified management. The achievement of coherent national unity can properly be set as the first goal since it is an indispensable condition for internal order and security and for representative government as well.[60]

The related problem for foreign policy is whether the military men and civilian leaders, where they are still in power (and not as mere front men for the army), will have the will and the stamina to turn inward and deal painstakingly with their nations' domestic problems. Many of the more radical, aggressive first-generation leaders have been deposed, usually by the army and usually, as suggested, for their internal economic failures and corruption. This has been a hopeful sign. Perhaps more new states will, like Indonesia, turn away from regionally aggressive policies to concentrate on domestic "problem-solving."[61] But perhaps they cannot, given the almost insuperable nature of the domestic problems, or will not. Thus foreign policy may remain the continuation of domestic politics by other means—or, in one author's pithy summation, they will remain "weak but not meek."[62]

[60] Rupert Emerson, *From Empire to Nation*, pp. 289–90.

[61] For a gloomy view of the future of Southeast Asia—and by implication other developing areas—see Gunnar Myrdal, *Asian Drama*, 3 vols. (New York: Twentieth Century Fund, 1968).

[62] Peter Calvocoressi, *World Order and the New States* (New York: Praeger Publishers, 1962), p. 34.

16 Modernization, Elite Perceptions, and the Prospects for Peace

Homogeneity and Modernization

Just as state system analysis suggests its own remedies for alleviating or eliminating the consequences of the competitive quest for power and security, so the second and third levels of analysis also commend solutions for the dangerous results of interstate conflict stemming from the varying domestic structures and perceptions by policy-makers.

Many political systems have perceived in themselves solutions to the problems of international politics. Thus, after the French Revolution in 1789, presuming that power politics was the offspring of selfish princes and that "the people" who had to fight and die were peaceful, democrats asserted that harmony among states and peace would follow once the Revolution had overthrown the small group of rulers who profited by a state system composed of authoritarian states. After the Bolshevik Revolution, the Communist leadership felt that, once the minority of capitalists in the Western states had been overthrown and the people could no longer be exploited and sent off to war for their rulers' benefit, there would no longer be any reason for hostilities among states. Leon Trotsky, the new Foreign Commissar, said that he took the job so that he would have more time for his Party activities; all he had to do, he felt, was to publish the secret treaties signed by the Czarist regime and call for the poor and the downtrodden to rise up and revolt.[1] Then he could close the Foreign Office—permanently! "Rulers bad, people good" seemed to be a common diagnosis of the ills of the world; and "all power to the people," or at least to their representatives—whether self-proclaimed or elected—appears to have been the prescribed remedy.

Even more fundamentally, the similarity of domestic structures has been presumed to produce a moderate, stable, peaceful state system.

[1] Edward Hallett Carr, *The Bolshevik Revolution, 1917–1923* (London: Macmillan, 1953), p. 16.

Stability would be the result not only of the balance of power but also of the homogeneity of the domestic structures of its leading members. For where the individual political systems were similar, the aims of the states, their assessments of what constitutes a tolerable, if not always reasonable, demand, their ideas of the legitimate methods of resolving differences, and their evalutions of historical trends were likely to be similar as well.

Modernization, it is sometimes suggested implicitly (if not explicitly), will be the contemporary remedy for the heterogeneity of social structures and political and economic systems. In this respect, economic development has taken the place of nineteenth-century laissez-faire economics; then, as so often today, economics was identified with social harmony and the welfare of all men, while politics was equated with conflict, war, and death: Just as the "good society" would be the product of free competition, so the peaceful international society would be created by free trade; an international laissez-faire policy would benefit all states just as a national laissez-faire policy benefited each individual within these states. Consequently, people all over the world had a vested interest in peace if they were to carry on their economic relations. Trade and war were incompatible. Trade, moreover, depended upon mutual prosperity—the poor do not buy much from one another. War impoverishes and destroys, creating ill will among nations, while commerce benefits all the participating states; the more trade, the greater the number of individual interests involved. Commerce was, consequently, nationally and individually profitable and created a vested interest in international peace. War, by contrast, was economically unprofitable and therefore obsolete. Free trade and peace, in short, were one and the same cause.

A modern replica of this identification of economics with peace may be found in the former Presidential adviser W. W. Rostow's interpretation of "the stages of economic growth." Rostow suggests that all states, like individuals from birth, pass through certain stages as they mature. These are: the traditional society, whose economy is agrarian and static; the pre–take-off phase, in which economic growth starts; take-off, in which economic development becomes a continuing matter; maturity, in which the economy diversifies; high mass consumption; and last, a post–mass consumption society, in which economic concerns and quantitative concerns give way to a much greater focus on the quality of individual and social life.

Rostow suggests that, in the first two stages, states are not yet sufficiently strong to resort to war. But during the transition from a traditional, socially fragmented society to a modern urban-industrialized society, the political leaders tend to invoke nationalism. And this nationalism tends to give rise to regional aggression.

> Historically, it has proved extremely tempting for a part of the new nationalism to be diverted on to external objectives, notably if these objectives looked to be accessible at little real cost or risk. These early aggres-

sive exercises were generally limited in objective, aimed at territories close to the new nation's own borders—within its region—rather than directly at the balance of Eurasian power: thus, the American effort to steal Canada during the French wars; Bismarck's neat military operations against Denmark, Austria, and France from 1864 to 1871; the Japanese acquisition of primacy in Korea in 1895; and the Russian drive through Manchuria to Vladivostok, leading to the test of strength with resurgent Japan in 1904–5.[2]

The modern version of this "bloody shirt" politics is a product of the need to enhance national cohesion for the purpose of modernization and was found in the first-generation leaders of independence movements—the Ben Bellas, Nassers, Sukarnos, Nkrumahs, and, to perhaps a lesser extent, the Nehrus. Rostow cautions us to be reasonably cheerful about this stage of development, for in the past these external adventures gave way as the task of modernizing the economy and society absorbed more time and energy. In short, Rostow provides us with a certain historical perspective on our age. The behavior of some of the new nations is merely part of a passing phase.

Of course, even when passed, peace is not guaranteed. During the take-off stage, the state's resources would still be relatively limited, and its expansion would therefore tend to be regional. But once a state is industrially developed and powerful, it can, if it so chooses, pursue far greater expansion. Germany, Japan, and Russia chose such a course. Nonetheless this stage coincides with the high mass-consumption phase that is supposed to make the principal states alike and the world less war-prone. Hence, domestic preoccupations and affluence will become the society's chief concerns, not foreign policy and war. Values, too, will change. During this stage, man is no longer regarded as an object for exploitation or aggression; the emphasis is on his dignity and welfare.

In this context, according to Rostow, Russia in the early 1960's was a nation seeking to convert its maturity into world primacy by postponing or damping the advent of the age of high mass consumption: "But in essence Communism is likely to wither in the age of high mass consumption."[3] Not just Russia, according to this logic, but China too someday will become a peaceful member of the state system; not just militant Communist states, but new, economically underdeveloped, socially fragmented, and politically unstable states will join the ranks of well-behaved, international system-maintaining states as their emergent nationalism is transformed into a mature, cooperative nationalism.

[2] For the effects of economic growth on society, see W. W. Rostow, *The Stages of Economic Growth* (New York: Cambridge University Press, 1960), p. 113 and idem, *Politics and the Stages of Growth* (Cambridge, England: Cambridge University Press, 1971). For a comparative study of Russia and America and an evaluation of the possibilities of "convergence" between these two highly industrialized societies, see Zbigniew K. Brzezinski and Samuel P. Huntington, *Political Power: USA/ USSR* (New York: Viking Press, 1964).

[3] Rostow, *Stages of Economic Growth*, p. 133.

Stalinism as a Technique of Modernization

The possible erosion of totalitarianism in Russia needs to be understood in the context of the birth and growth of the Soviet system itself. As we saw earlier, Lenin's theory of imperialism explained why the proletarian revolution had not occurred in a mature, industrial country but in an underdeveloped, nonindustrial country that did not have a politically conscious proletarian majority. This shift of the first phase of the proletarian revolution from economically advanced capitalist countries to economically underdeveloped, precapitalist, agrarian societies had a profound impact upon Communism. The working class could no longer be trusted, because its consciousness had become corrupted by "bourgeois reformism." It was unreliable and could not be expected to fulfill its historically appointed task. Since the proletariat had in effect betrayed the revolution, the responsibility of carrying it out would have to be assigned to the "vanguard of the proletariat," a small party of professional revolutionaries.[4] Completely different from a democratic party, whose basic function is to aggregate the nation's various interest groups, this was a party of "true believers," of men like Lenin who had remained loyal to the cause. It was they who were now to be the "defenders of the faith," the sole guardians of the proletariat's consciousness. Dedicated and incorruptible, they became the self-appointed instrument of History in the implementation of the revolution and the destruction of the world bourgeoisie. Communism, self-proclaimed as a majority movement, thus transformed itself into a minority struggle. A revolution that was to have been spontaneous and inevitable as capitalism matured economically became a revolution engineered by a highly conscious vanguard in an economically backward country whose industrial working class constituted a small minority.

Political consciousness and will had obviously prevailed over economic determinism. Equally clear, the reason they had prevailed was that Communism was racked with intense and constant self-doubt as to whether the revolution would in fact occur. History had to be helped along because it was not following its natural course. The revolution would not be the result of material conditions; rather, it would be the product of a few men's faith and work. A small group of the elect—in the Calvinist sense—would make sure the revolution occurred. Just as the Calvinists knew the "will of God," so the Leninist revolutionaries knew the "objective laws of history." Each set of leaders knew "the truth," and be-

[4] V. I. Lenin, *What Is To Be Done? Burning Questions of Our Movement* (New York: International Publishers, 1929). On the development of the Party before 1917, see Bertram Wolfe, *Three Who Made a Revolution: A Biographical History* (New York: Dial Press, 1948); and on the Party's development until just after Stalin's death, see the definitive volume by Leonard Schapiro, *The Communist Party of the Soviet Union* (New York: Random House, 1959).

cause this truth would save man from sin and damnation, each had the right—even the duty—to impose its rule in order to rescue man. Conversely, each movement distrusted the very mankind to whose service it claimed dedication. Man, weak and corruptible, had to be protected from Satan or capitalism. If necessary, he had to be coerced to "save" himself.[5]

Given this elitist, antidemocratic attitude, it was "inevitable" (in the best Marxist sense) that the vanguard of the proletariat should, as a party of the select, function without any inner democracy. As a minority party, it could never win full power by legitimate means; such power had to be seized by revolution. But such a campaign to seize the reins of government could be successful only if this professional revolutionary vanguard was organized as a general staff. Centralized leadership, hierarchical organization, strict discipline, and obedience all the way down the chain of command were absolutely necessary. Moreover, everything had to be subordinated to the objective of winning power. Disagreements or factionalism within this military-like elite were intolerable. The generals could not plan and implement a campaign if the colonels and majors—and even other generals—were constantly dissenting. The generals, especially the chief of staff, had to decide policy and be given unquestioning obedience. The "Party line" was absolute for all members. To gain outside support—a general staff without an army is impotent—the Communist Party had to learn to exploit all resentments of different groups or classes and direct these against the government; all aspirations blocked by the government were to be manipulated in order to bring it down. Alliances could be made with any group or class if they brought the final goal nearer. Such alliances must also be broken when they no longer served their purpose. The main point was flexibility of tactics, since the end—power—justified the means. As the capture of power would destroy the heretical old society and supposedly usher in the new and better society—a truly moral society in which all men would for the first time in history be really free and equal—all means could be used to achieve this goal. If the means were immoral, the morality of the end provided the justification.

By capturing power in an unindustrialized society, the Party stamped upon the nation the character it had acquired in its struggle to win that power. These features were to be reinforced once the Party took power as it sought to impose "from above" its proletarian class-consciousness upon the unrevolutionary working class and tradition-bound peasantry. The resulting political system, which grew into full bloom under Stalin, came to be seen by many Western observers and analysts as unique, and was termed totalitarian.[6] It was held to differ greatly both from democra-

---

[5] This comparison of Calvinism and Communism is elaborated in Alfred G. Meyer, *Marxism* (Cambridge, Mass.: Harvard University Press, 1954), pp. 6–9.

[6] The post-Stalin period, dealt with later in this chapter, demonstrated that the system was not immune to change, or so "totalitarian" that it could prevent the

cies and from traditional dictatorships or autocracies of the past.[7] A constitutional democratic system, it was suggested, places three kinds of restraints on political power: formal (as defined by a constitution, bill of rights, and the existing body of law); informal (stemming from the pluralistic nature of the society); and cultural (resulting from the behavior patterns of the society). Traditional dictatorships or autocratic governments remove the formal restraints, and therefore, like totalitarian systems, they have arbitrary rule and a lack of political and civil rights—although even in this respect autocratices, while frequently oppressive, are still not as arbitrary as totalitarian governments. Autocracies do not select a whole part of their population according to class or racial criteria and then systematically liquidate it.[8] Generally, they do not eliminate all freedoms[9] or execute most of the opposition leaders.[10] In any case, autocracies rarely attempt to eliminate the informal restraints. Indeed, they tend to be based on a coalition of existing groups or classes—for example, an alliance of landed nobility, army, and church—which are themselves carriers of the cultural restraints. Only if a group resists is it likely to be subjected to pressure and some of its leaders arrested. But autocracies do not generally possess a government party that can reach down into society and organize, control, and manipulate all facets of the lives of the

---

rise of other groups, which the political leaders then had to accommodate. Nevertheless, for the Stalin period, in which the society was to relearn its new values and undergo industrialization, the term totalitarian remains appropriate.

[7] Totalitarianism is analyzed as a unique system by Carl J. Friedrich, ed., *Totalitarianism* (Cambridge, Mass.: Harvard University Press, 1954); Carl J. Friedrich and Zbigniew K. Brzezinski, *Totalitarian Dictatorship and Autocracy*, 2d ed. (New York: Praeger Publishers, 1966); and William Ebenstein. *Totalitarianism* (New York: Holt, Rinehart & Winston, 1962).

[8] Thus, the Soviets shipped off to Siberia at least 5 million kulaks (relatively prosperous peasants) as part of a policy aiming at the "liquidation of the kulaks as a class." About 1 million perished, and many of the remainder died during the next years because of the hardships resulting from forced labor. Hugh Seton-Watson, *From Lenin to Khrushchev* (New York: Praeger Publishers, 1960), pp. 156–59.

[9] "In tsarist Russia there was no freedom of the press in the Western sense. But antigovernment books and papers did circulate. Russian was the first language into which Marx's *Das Kapital* was translated from the German and, in 1912, *Pravda*, the organ of Lenin's Boshevik group, was openly published in tsarist Russia. . . . If the government allowed such revolutionary materials to be circulated, it goes without saying that liberal and democratic doctrines in books and periodicals were widely circulated without much official hindrance." Ebenstein, *Totalitarianism*, p. 25.

[10] "Lenin's own experience as a political exile in Siberia (1897–1900) illustrates the difference. He was not imprisoned behind barbed wire, and he did no forced labor. He could move about freely within a prescribed area, he played chess regularly with police officials, he practiced law for the benefit of poor peasants. He even finished his book *Development of Capitalism in Russia* while in exile. Furthermore, he maintained excellent health during his stay in Siberia, married there, and was able to think and plot for the future. His main complaint, like that of other political exiles, was not cruelty or hard labor, but boredom. . . . Stalin also was banished to Siberia. Again the relative mildness of tsarist political repression is illustrated by the fact that Stalin managed to escape on three occasions, a feat unthinkable today." *Ibid.*, p. 24.

people. They are primarily interested in controlling their citizens' political activities, although they often tend to define "political" quite broadly. The pluralistic nature of the society is by and large left alone. The basic aim is to preserve the domestic political *status quo*. Family life, professional and business activities, and religious affiliations are usually considered private affairs—if they do not spill over into the political arena.

In vivid contrast, the very first act of a totalitarian regime after it assumes control and suspends all constitutional limitations on governmental power is to destroy this social pluralism. All political parties and professional associations are declared illegal. The aim is to eliminate all organizations standing between the party and the individual. The society is then rebuilt with new organizations created and controlled by the revolutionary party. No group is left outside the scope of party control. Old social norms are destroyed to enable the party to mold the society in accordance with its own ideological norms. Unlike the old-fashioned autocracy, with its interest in maintaining the domestic *status quo*, totalitarianism is future-oriented because it is committed to carrying out a social revolution in terms of its ideological norms.

From this determination to transform society follows the attempt, in practice not always successful, to assert complete control over every aspect of the individual's life. A militant and exclusive faith is bound by its very nature to seek to politicize all phases of life. A movement that seeks to convert man to the true faith cannot exempt any facet of his life from its supervision. A monopoly of truth, wisdom, and virtue must produce a monopoly of political control over all economic, social, cultural, scientific, and spiritual matters. The distinction between a man's private and public lives is eliminated. Ideally, it is not enough, as in an autocracy, that the citizen does not break the law, engage in opposition political activities, or read forbidden books and newspapers. He cannot merely obey the party's orders while not believing in its mission. No church, extrasecular or not, with an exclusive faith likes to allow the right to disbelieve. And the Communist Party, as a revolutionary party, is comparable to a "church in the very obvious sense that it is the institutionalization of belief. It is the organization which bears and propagates the faith. In power, it assumes the exclusive right to teach belief. Within the Party one belief—the official version of Marxism-Leninism— has a doctrinal monopoly: one church, one faith."[11] Under traditional authoritarian governments, such an exclusive and demanding faith was unknown. But in a totalitarian system, even the Boy Scouts become the

[11] Robert V. Daniels, *The Nature of Communism* (New York: Random House, 1962), p. 331. Thus Trotsky defended his oppositionist position with a declaration of loyalty: "My party—right or wrong. . . . I know one cannot be right against the party . . . for history has not created other ways for the realization of what is right." Quoted in Schapiro, *Communist Party of Soviet Union*, p. 284. See also the brilliant fictional account of how one Old Bolshevik leader is finally led to confess in Arthur Koestler, *Darkness at Noon* (New York: New American Library, 1948).

Young Pioneers and, later, the Komsomol. They may still go camping and parading, but their principal function is the ideological indoctrination and training of the boys from whom future leaders will be selected. Similarly, art and literature must reflect the revolutionary spirit of "socialist realism"; abstract art or dissonant music are denounced as "bourgeois decadence."

In addition to this task of remolding society in accordance with a set of ideological tenets or "revealed truths", the new rulers in an economically backward society, as Russia was in 1917, are committed to a second function: the organization and concentration of the society's resources for industrialization. It must industrialize not only so that the nation can become stronger and wealthier, but also so that the Party can legitimate its power. The Party must create the proletariat in whose name it made the revolution. It therefore organizes the same capital accumulation for which it so harshly criticized capitalist systems. And capital accumulation, even when it is called "socialist construction," is by its very nature a cruel process. The Communist leaders can no more avoid squeezing the masses, including the proletariat, for savings than could their capitalist predecessors. In fact, their means of capital accumulation are harsher. Capitalism in the West was tempered by the growth of democracy. The political process provided channels through which the workers' social protests could be heard; with the acquisition of the vote, they could gain redress of their major grievances.

But in an underdeveloped country industrializing under Communist Party control, there is no independent political channel through which the masses can seek amelioration. The Party is committed to industrialization—and rapid industrialization at that; it intends to drive the population toward that end as rapidly as possible. Incentives, controls, terror, propaganda—all are employed to speed industrialization or at least to maintain its speed. At the same time, the subsistence, or near-subsistence, wages of the worker and peasants assure high "surplus values." The government's monopoly of political power, mass communications, and instruments of force, which make this quick industrialization possible, also allow it to control popular dissatisfaction. By an ironic quirk of history, Stalinist Russia thus ends up fashioning itself in Marx's image of capitalism and becomes transformed into state capitalism. And it is the Party leaders, rather than the capitalists, who become the new ruling class.[12] This very political development also disproves Marx in his fundamental criticism that private ownership of the means of production and private profit are the basic causes of the workers' miseries during the era of bourgeois industrialization. Actually, the exploitation of the masses is the product not of capitalism, but of the early phase of industrialization. But paradoxically, Soviet Communism had thereby become a technique for the purpose of modernization—like capitalism!

[12] Milovan Djilas, *The New Class* (New York: Praeger Publishers, 1957), pp. 37–69.

The Post-Stalinist Transformation and Ideological Erosion

If totalitarianism had been effective in spurring Soviet industrialization, it was also becoming clear that by the time of Stalin's death in 1953 industrialization and the nature of Soviet society were becoming increasingly incompatible. Communism, as a technique of political organization—that is, of bringing all the resources of the community together and focusing them on one task, industrialization—had transformed Russia into the second most powerful country in the world. But the cost was enormous—not only in terms of human lives, but also in terms of the vitality of the economy and its ability to function effectively and efficiently. Stalin's rule had become highly personal and extremely arbitrary. The pillars of Stalin's totalitarianism had been the Party, the technical-managerial personnel spawned by industrialization and the need to administer its results, the secret police, and the army. Stalin, however, had ruled primarily through the secret police and a widespread use of terror. Even the Party had become subordinated to the police, the principal instrument with which Stalin had, in the 1930's, eliminated all opposition to himself within the Party. It had been the secret police that Stalin had used to carry out his collectivization of the peasantry and his vast program of industrialization during the 1930's; so, too, had they been used to effect the extensive purges in 1936–38 of the top personnel in the Party, the economic apparatus, the army, and even the secret police organization itself.

But by the time of Stalin's death this police-directed system was in serious trouble. In order to achieve rapid industrialization, the workers had been compelled to work hard at low wages. While there were actual forced-labor camps into which millions of Russians were thrown, mostly for political reasons, the Soviet Union was really one massive forced-labor camp where workers had no right to protest, where they were subjected to excessive labor discipline and speedups, and where they lived in austerity and fear. The peasants who had not been removed from the land to the factory were just as harshly treated; in fact, Stalin tried to squeeze even more out of them than he did out of the workers. But his pervasive police supervision, the arbitrary power of arrest, and the fear of "being sent to Siberia," if not executed, had by the early 1950's brought the Soviet Union to a point of diminishing economic returns.

Fear is a potent incentive. Beyond a certain point, though, it tends to paralyze a system. Fear may have made Stalin feel secure, as no one could dare to oppose him, but it could not stimulate the initiative, creativity, and imagination needed to direct large-scale industrial and scientific efforts. How could industry be expected to increase its productivity when there was such fear and the standard of living was so low that even threats of increased terror and of exile to Siberia ceased to be effective?

How could science—particularly nuclear physics—flourish in an atmosphere that discouraged critical inquiry and innovation? Popular dissatisfaction, ideological disillusionment, and a pervasive fear of assuming responsibility were thus the principal results of the use of terror. No industrialized society could function effectively in this manner. Thus, ironically, the Soviet system was itself the victim of the "inherent contradictions" that Soviet political leaders, quoting Marx, were so fond of seeing within the capitalist economy. Moreover, it was a typically Marxian contradiction, one between the industrial-economic substructure and the political-social superstructure. In short, Stalinism, as a method of modernization, seemed to have become outmoded by the industrialization it had fostered. "Stalinist methods—police terror, the slave labor camps, the periodic decimation of the ruling elite through arrests and executions, and the clumsy centralized bureaucratic regulation of all areas—proved uneconomical and politically ineffectual in promoting the growth of Soviet society."[13]

A mature industrial society cannot be ruled by terror. Rather, a developed society like the Soviet Union makes demands of its own, and the Party as the ruling elite must meet them. The first imperative for the Party is that, in order to encourage productivity, it must grant workers higher pay and an opportunity to improve their living conditions. In a nation that has concentrated its energies on industrialization through decades of enforced self-denial and constant toil, it is natural that there would be an intense popular desire for better working conditions, shorter hours, more pay, better housing, and more consumer products. And this material demand of the masses also has a nonmaterial corollary that expresses itself in a desire for a life that is less arbitrary, with fewer restrictions, some opportunity for changing jobs, more freedom to travel, and toleration of a certain degree of nonconformity. In short, in order to enlist people's willingness to work and to encourage the initiative and creativity needed for the operation of a complex economy, the political system must offer some material incentives as well as a degree of personal security and freedom.

The second imperative for the Party is to enlist the support of the growing "middle class" produced by industrialization. This class, composed by and large of the scientists, engineers, executives of light and heavy industry and of the agricultural sector, and technicians of all varieties, is indispensable for the operational efficiency of the economy. As experts in various fields of competence, its members are the the managers. If one were to compare the sociopolitical structure of the Soviet Union with an American corporation, it might be said that it shares the divorce of ownership and management characteristic of American industry: The Party represents the board of directors; it owns the corporation because it holds most of the shares—in fact, all the shares. The man-

[13] Wolfgang Leonhard, "Internal Developments: A Balance Sheet," *Problems of Communism*, March–April, 1963, p. 7.

agers are the salaried employees responsible for the daily operations of the corporation. Their reward is a high salary, social standing, and authority to achieve their economic targets, be it a certain quantity of goods or profit ratios. Their tenure is judged in terms of their successful meeting of these targets. In the Soviet Union, these functional experts also wish to improve their living conditions, acquire more leisure time, and gain some degree of autonomy and a guarantee against a return of the police state.

Finally, the third imperative for the Party is that it must educate its subjects. Illiterates cannot man machines—or become scientists or industrial executives. Industry increasingly demands trained manpower rather than unskilled labor. Education is thus a fundamental prerequisite of an urbanized and modernized society.

The question was whether the three imperatives would gradually erode the foundations of the Soviet totalitarian state. Eventually, of course, this question will apply to the Chinese state as well. Would an increasingly affluent population not threaten the future of the Party itself? If one of the major reasons for the Party's claim to power was that it could quickly industrialize the nation and provide its citizens with a better life, what justification would it have for staying in power once that industrialization had been accomplished? What need would there be for the Party to espouse Communist ideology and to talk of world revolution in a mass-consumption society? An industrialized and urbanized society in which the populace has a reasonably high standard of living is not as much concerned with ideology as it is with its own well-being and with the protection of political rights against the arbitrary acts of the government—at least if the Western experience of affluence *and* democracy can serve as any sort of a guide. This increasing concern with "welfare" to enlist popular support and participation in society thus suggests both a shift in the allocation of resources, with greater stress on consumer goods, and a spreading lack of ideological concern—indeed, ideological boredom—in the mass of the population. And once the appetite for more consumer goods and a better standard of living has been partially met, the appetite for the satisfaction of even greater needs will have been whetted.

The rise of the various functional elites or interest groups[14] tends to reinforce the emphasis on consumer goods and greater restraint on arbitrary rule. For the "Red executives" demand a high standard of living and some security of job tenure. As men with skills whose services the Party needs and rewards, they become members of the privileged "new class." Hence, they gain a vested interest in the system; one key conse-

14 On the role of interest groups see H. Gordon Skilling, "Interest Groups and Communist Politics," *World Politics*, April, 1966, pp. 435–51; Philip D. Stewart, "Soviet Interest Groups and the Policy Process," *World Politics*, October, 1969, pp. 29–50; and H. Gordon Skilling and Franklyn Griffiths, eds., *Interest Groups in Soviet Politics* (Princeton, N.J.: Princeton University Press, 1973).

quence of this is that, fearful of jeopardizing their hard-earned position and prosperity and wishing to pass these on to their children, the elites will seek to restrain adventurous foreign policies that might jeopardize the security, if not survival, of the Soviet Union—and with it their status and roles within the Soviet system.

Furthermore, these elites become increasingly "de-ideologized." For the process of industrialization that created them also requires that they become more technically and professionally oriented. The Soviet military provides a good example. Nowhere had the stultifying impact of Stalinist terror been more noticeable than on military thinking and doctrine, which, after World War II, stressed that the "permanently operating factors"—the stability of the rear, the morale of the army, the quantity and quality of divisions, the weaponry of the army, the organizational ability of the army commanders—would decide the outcome of a future war. This formulation was, of course, truistic and largely meaningless, since a nation with superior morale, armed forces, and economy would obviously be the victor. Yet it took no account at all of the impact of nuclear technology. If the permanently operating factors were decisive, then the possibility of a surprise atomic attack was obviously merely a transitory and nondecisive factor. To write off the effects of a surprise attack in an age of nuclear weapons and rapid delivery vehicles was to enshrine Soviet *pre*nuclear experience as a permanent guide to action in the nuclear age. At best, according to Stalin, a surprise attack could gain only temporary success. Had not the experience of the German surprise attack on the Soviet Union in 1941 "proved" its futility? Stalin's interpretation, in fact, claimed the Soviet World War II strategy would be the winning strategy in future full-scale wars.

Hence, while the Soviets developed nuclear arms, this did not mean they fully understood the revolutionary impact of the new technology. There was little discussion in Soviet military journals of the radically changed strategic posture. Yet the experience of World War II was hardly relevant to the new challenge posed by the United States. As a result, Soviet military doctrine simply failed to develop an *inter*continental strategy that included in its formulation a realization of the innovative nature of nuclear weapons. Instead, the Soviets merely criticized the American evaluation of the decisive importance of surprise attack and nuclear bombs. Not until after Stalin's death did they re-evaluate their own strategic doctrine. And only then did Soviet military strategists admit that World War II did not provide a model for future wars and that a surprise nuclear attack could be decisive. For the first time, Soviet officers talked of "the laws of war as armed conflict," and armed conflict was then to be discussed *per se*, independent of the Party's teachings on the causes of wars. The same laws of war applied to all participants in combat. The hydrogen bomb obviously had the same impact on a Communist target as on a capitalist one. In short, once the Stalinist mold was broken, Soviet military doctrine could adjust itself to "reality" without being "blinded" by ideology. Since then, Soviet strategic debates—between traditionalists and radicals,[15] or conservatives and pragmatists[16]—have reflected the same kind of doctrinal and service interests that exist in the United States. All this represented a significant breakthrough. The laws of war, like the laws of chemistry or engineering or industrial management, were recognized as being the same for all industrial societies. It followed from this that if the experts were to apply their expertise in a professionally competent manner, ideological and political control had to be minimized.

The functional specialization of the various Soviet elites also changes the role of the political leadership. This is a consequence of the division of labor inherent in a sophisticated and advanced economy that creates numerous elites, each with its own professional and organizational interests. These, in turn, will be reflected in the emergence of various factions within the Communist Party, because most of the leading members of these "interest groups" are enrolled in it. The pluralistic nature of industrial society thus emerges *within* the power structure of the totalitarian Party. Before industrialization began, the Party had been the only organized group and its word was law. But the economy's growth created new groups, each possessing its own interests. In such circumstances, the Party loses its monopoly of authority and is compelled to share it. Indeed, increasingly it must judge among the groups' conflicting interests and competing claims—whether for larger military forces or more investments in heavy or light industry or agriculture—and play a mediating role. In short, behind the outer totalitarian form this pluralism creates the substance of a Western-type checks-and-balances system that itself restrains the power of the Party leadership to do whatever it wants.

If greater affluence, technical expertise, and professional competence undermine ideology and the one-party state, education administers the final blow. Once a man is encouraged to "think for himself" as an engineer or scientist, will this not become a habit in ideological and political matters, too? As early as 1957, Allen Dulles, then Director of the U.S. Central Intelligence Agency, noted:

> Knowledge is not an inert substance. It has a way of seeping across lines and into adjacent compartments of learning. The Soviet leaders . . . cannot illuminate their scientific lecture halls and laboratories without also letting the light of truth into their history and economics classrooms. Students cannot be conditioned to turning off their analytical processes when the instructor changes a topic. [Consequently] men and women who have their critical faculties sharpened are beginning to question why

[15] Raymond L. Garthoff, *Soviet Strategy in the Nuclear Age*, rev. ed. (New York: Praeger Publishers, 1962); Herbert S. Dinerstein, *War and the Soviet Union* (New York: Praeger Publishers, 1962); and Thomas W. Wolfe, *Soviet Strategy at the Crossroads* (Cambridge, Mass.: Harvard University Press, 1964).

[16] Roman Kolkowicz *et al.*, *The Soviet Union and Arms Control* (Baltimore: Johns Hopkins Press, 1970), pp. 38–39.

the Russian people cannot be freed from rigid Communist Party and police-state discipline, given a greater economic share of the fruit of their labors, and allowed to participate—at least by an effective expression of consent—in their own governing.[17]

The implications for foreign policy of this theory of economic development are of particular interest. For the conclusion is that Soviet foreign policy will once more become *Russian* foreign policy. The erosion of the missionary ideology, the increasing demand for more butter rather than guns, the rise of a privileged, and essentially conservative, managerial class, the restraints placed by the new checks-and-balances system upon the Party leaders, who are no longer of the generation that made the revolution and, therefore, have less zeal and sense of commitment to world revolution than their predecessors, all contribute to the derevolutionization of the Soviet Union. Revolutionary proclamations thus become a matter of routine articulation of an increasingly irrelevant liturgy; rhetoric aside, the Soviet Union is increasingly being transformed into a typical nation-state, concerned more with the protection of Russian *national* interests than with the advancement of Communist interests. Soviet foreign policy, like that of other states, reflects the domestic structure and political pressures; and with the "end of ideology," its revolutionary refusal to recognize the right of states to enjoy different social and political persuasions also ends. The changing external behavior of the Soviet Union in the post-Stalin period, particularly since 1962, is therefore interpreted as more than merely a tactical shift; rather, it is alleged to reflect the changing nature of the Soviet system and the corresponding changes in its foreign policy goals.

The Relationship of Economic to Political Development

It would seem that the significant relationship, the one that will allegedly most affect the issue of war or peace, will be the tie between economic and political development. Will the larger Communist states, as they modernize, become increasingly pluralistic and less arbitrary domestically, more moderate in their external behavior? Will the new states be able to unify themselves, achieve a self-sustaining growth, and attain a degree of social and political stability? Finally, as industrial states pass beyond the stage of affluence, what kinds of values will replace the Calvinistic doctrines of a developing society, and how will this affect the conduct of foreign policy? In brief, what are the relationships between economic growth, political development, social equilibrium, and a peaceful foreign policy?

[17] Allen W. Dulles, "The Communists Also Have Their Problems," speech delivered on September 19, 1957, quoted in Samuel Hendel, ed., *The Soviet Crucible* (New York: Van Nostrand, 1959), pp. 505–8.

The problem is that we do not really know the answers to these questions. The few attempts at building theories of modernization have been based largely upon Western experience, and, because the United States and England have been posited as the model of a modern system, they have reflected a kind of egocentric stance. These two nations have been *the* most highly developed societies—politically, economically, and socially. They have served as examples other nations could—and obviously would—imitate if they wanted to become modern, affluent societies. (These theories were, by the way, generally written before the awareness and popularity of the environmental-cost-of-industrialization thesis.)

Some of these concepts of modernization also reflect a non-Marxist version of economic determinism. Whereas Marxism predicted that, when socialism replaced capitalism, peace would follow, this later approach suggests that this will occur only when societies become modern. Economic and technological factors make their own demands, and the industrial way of life molds society accordingly; it presumably overcomes differences of political structures, historical experiences, and cultural values, and produces similar political systems. Even such authors as A. F. K. Organski, who have stressed the political stages of development, have accepted this primacy of economics.[18] While stressing the differing roles governments play at various stages—such as unification, industrialization, or welfare—politics is nonetheless seen as a function of certain stages of economic growth. But whether all industrialized and urbanized societies are indeed so similar that they can be embraced by the concept of "modern society" is a doubtful assumption. America and Russia, for example, are unlikely to "converge" as virtually identical societies.

Perhaps most disturbing in the concept of development is the notion, often left unspoken, that at the end of the process of development stands a democratic society. In a way, this expectation may not even seem unreasonable. Western states were not always democratic, and we certainly know from history that only among "people of plenty"—where the "plenty" is reasonably equitably distributed among most classes or sections of society—can democracy flourish. By comparison, the lack of a middle class and the existence of a social imbalance between the privileged few and the deprived majority provide ideal breeding grounds for political instability and revolution. Yet we also know from the examples of Germany and Japan that modernization does not by itself produce political democracy; rather, it can strengthen a basically semifeudal authoritarian system. The United States still refers to "grass roots" democracy—that is, to American democracy's agrarian origins; modernization may have strengthened this democratic system, but it did not produce it. Thus the assumption that modernization will result in a decline of totalitarianism remains to be proved.

The Communist Party in Russia has, for example, retained control

[18] A. F. K. Organski, *The Stages of Political Development* (New York: Knopf, 1965).

over the economic managers, secret police, and military. This continued supremacy is historically perhaps not surprising, if one contrasts the evolution of the Russian and Soviet systems with that of the West. There, industrialization occurred in societies that were already pluralistic. Even in the age of royal absolutism, more than one center of power existed in the state: the nobility, the Church, and the burghers. The monarch's dependence on support from one or more of these groups led him to grant concessions ranging from the Magna Charta for the nobility to charters for towns. He was therefore anything but absolute. In reality his authority, although great, was limited. The evolution of constitutional monarchies and democracies was, in a sense, inevitable. It was in this context that Western industrialization and the growth of the middle class occurred. Russia, by contrast, never had a pluralistic tradition. Throughout its history it had been a unicentered state, with the Czars functioning as the secular rulers of the state and as the heads of the Orthodox Church. The Russian nobility, while administering the civilian and military levers of power through which the Czars maintained their dominion, never attained the degree of independence from the Crown that the nobility in most Western states was able to grasp. It would have been inconceivable for the Russian aristocracy to rebel against the Crown and compel a Czar to sign a Russian Magna Charta. Nor did the small Russian bourgeoisie, which developed with Russia's industrialization during the late nineteenth century, ever establish its independence from the autocracy. The Communists not only inherited this tradition of state control and direction, they have up to now further strengthened it during their drive to modernize the Soviet Union. Indeed, the commissars, as several Czars before them, have on occasion imported Western technology without its effecting—in the sense of liberalizing or creating a more pluralistic society—the domestic political nature of these regimes in any major way.

The Soviet political system has thus hardly eroded. Nevertheless, neither is it the same system it was under Stalin. Whether one calls it post-totalitarian or the "new face" of Soviet totalitarianism,[19] an evolution has clearly occurred. Totalitarianism—implying a totality of power and the impossibility of the rise of distinct elites or interest groups that would influence the decision-making process—can no longer be regarded as monolithic. All the elites accept (at least, they do not challenge) the legitimacy of the Party's policy-making authority.

> . . . within the party there is a hidden struggle for power, a subterranean rivalry over policy and the public interest, sometimes bursting into the open in purge and counterpurge. In the absence of an effective representative body, and also of independent and competing parties, the single party must fill many roles performed in other systems by various institutions

[19] Adam B. Ulam, *The New Face of Soviet Totalitarianism* (New York: Praeger Publishers, 1965), and *idem, The Unfinished Revolution*, (New York: Random House, 1960).

and, above all, must serve as a broker of competing group interests. In the post-Stalin era, with the circle of decision-making widening and public discussion less restricted, the party chiefs must more and more give attention to forming a consensus among competing policy groups, specialist elites, differing viewpoints within the party, professional and other associations, and broader amorphous social groupings.[20]

Soviet totalitarianism has thus not shown itself immune to change. What seems to have emerged is a state that is more stable, somewhat more bored with ideology, and somewhat less arbitrary; prominent dissidents are sent into exile abroad, where they lose their sting, or placed in psychiatric institutions since disagreement is tantamount to wrong thinking, clearly a psychiatric disorder! Essentially Russia has emerged as a hierarchical, highly centralized, bureaucratic society in which many of the assumptions of Marxism-Leninism, while widely and implicitly accepted (as many Westerners unthinkingly accept the values of Christianity), seem on the whole increasingly irrelevant to daily individual life and the manifold problems of running a complex and urbanized and industrialized society.[21] In the long run, then, the post-Stalin development of the Soviet Union is changing the Soviet political system, but its long-run evolution remains hard to predict.

It is this issue, therefore, as we saw much earlier, that was part of the debate on the Nixon-Kissinger policy of *détente:* Should the U.S. lower tensions with the U.S.S.R. and ignore Soviet domestic repression? The proponents of *détente* argue that in the long run this will help enhance the Soviet standard of living, relax the totalitarian system somewhat more, and weaken further any Soviet expansionist motives. Or must *détente,* as its critics maintain, be accompanied by internal Soviet liberalization? For, they argue, the U.S. must be true to its own democratic values, and a regime that refuses its citizens the right to emigrate or dissent and blocks free exchanges of people and ideas with the West is a regime which remains hostile to the West. This means it would have no scruples about reverting to confrontation after a period of *détente* during which it relaxed the West's guard and took advantage of its technology, credit and trade to reinvigorate its industry for renewed tests of strength. Thus the relationship of the regime, internal changes, and external behavior remains a fundamental point of debate about the nature of the *détente* with the U.S.S.R.

In what remains among the more thoughtful and sophisticated analyses of the dynamics of modernization, C. E. Black has talked of *seven* patterns of modernization.[22] Black's criteria for classification are political

---

[20] Skilling, "Interest Groups," pp. 448–49.

[21] Alfred G. Meyer, *The Soviet Political System* (New York: Random House, 1965). For judicious analyses of contemporary Russia, see Frederick C. Barghoorn, *The USSR* (Boston: Little, Brown, 1966), pp. 362–87, and John S. Reshetar, Jr., *The Soviet Polity* (New York: Dodd, Mead, 1971).

[22] C. E. Black, *The Dynamics of Transformation* (New York: Harper & Row, 1966), pp. 90–128.

and social, rather than economic, and cover five points. They are: first, whether the transfer of political power from traditional to modernizing leaders in a society occurred earlier or later relative to other societies (in the former, for example, problems would be confronted more pragmatically, while, in the latter, modernization becomes intertwined with the acceptance or rejection of foreign models); second, whether the modernist challenge to the traditional elite was internal or external; third, whether a society enjoyed a continuity of territory and population or had experienced a regrouping of land and peoples; fourth, whether a society beginning modernization was self-governing or had experienced colonial rule; and fifth, whether such a society had sufficiently developed its institutions to adapt them to a modern society. Accordingly, Black's first pattern of modernization is limited to Britain and France; the second pattern comprises their white "offshoots," the United States, Canada, Australia, and New Zealand; third are the European states that modernized after the French Revolution; fourth are the Latin American states colonized by the European states least inclined to modernize; fifth are Russia, China, Japan, and other non-Western societies, indirectly influenced in their modernization by the Western example; and the last two patterns comprise the countries in the former colonized areas. All in all, the relationship of economic growth to political evolution and to external behavior would seem to be far more complex than was once thought by some social scientists.

Leadership, Misperception, and Mental Health

Leaders, as we saw in our analyses of style and decision-making, are the key personalities and play the principal roles in policy formulation and implementation. What is particularly important is the images the nation's chief decision-maker and his key advisers hold of the external world and of their country's aims and role in the international system. No issue has done more than Vietnam to spotlight critically this issue of how the principal decision-makers of a country view the world beyond their own national boundaries. Johnson and Nixon were said to be "cold warriors." Unable to overcome their anti-Communism, they perceived the world—especially the Communist world—through distorted lenses and therefore pursued policies unsuited to the contemporary world. "The deficiencies of American foreign policy, epitomized by Vietnam but evident in events in many other parts of the world, result from faulty modes of thought rather than from defects of personality or errors of execution." Washington is still living on the "intellectual capital" accumulated in 1947 even though "these policies have become obsolete, and the United States has been unable to devise new policies capable of dealing successfully with the issues of a different age."[23] Correct perceptions of

[23] Hans J. Morgenthau, A New Foreign Policy for the United States (New York: Praeger Publishers, 1969), pp. vii, 3.

the fragmentation of the Communist nations and of the nature of the war in South Vietnam would presumably have resulted in a more accurate assessment of American interests in Vietnam, and that in turn would have precluded the massive intervention of 1965. In broader terms, what is frequently implicit in this approach is the assumption that international conflicts and tensions are the product of *misperception*. It is this emphasis on mistaken perceptions of policy-makers that constitutes the essence of much of the writing by scholars on perception and images of the world. Much of this writing betrays a strong normative bias, for it tends to suggest that conflicts among states have no "real" causes and would be resolvable if the policy-makers were but willing to correct their misperceptions.

Ralph K. White is typical of this misperception school. "Misperceptions might explain how normally sane human beings can unwittingly, without intending the consequences, involve themselves step by step in actions that lead to war."[24] War is thus a mistake when it erupts. Misperception or distorted "cognitive maps," therefore, provides the only sensible explanation of why states continue to resort to warfare when the world "desperately wants to avoid it" and "only a madman could start a war." White, indeed, entitles his opening chapter "Misperceptions as a Cause of Two World Wars," suggesting that the two most significant twentieth-century wars were mistakes and the world would have been better off had they not occurred. (E. H. Carr in 1939 wrote that this view, while characteristically Anglo-Saxon, will be news to Czechs and Poles who owed their national existence to World War I, to the French who regained Alsace-Lorraine in 1918, or the Germans who had been successful in 1866 and 1870 and only regretted they had lost World War I.[25]) These misperceptions of reality, White stresses, are the result of six forms of distortion:

(1) A diabolical enemy-image
(2) A virile self-image
(3) A moral self-image
(4) Selective inattention
(5) Absence of empathy
(6) Military overconfidence[26]

Let us look at two prominent American statesmen as examples. In a biography of Dean Acheson, one of the two distinguished Secretaries of State who served President Truman, Gaddis Smith has argued that the assumptions underlying Acheson's thoughts and policy advice were "an

---

[24] Ralph K. White, *Nobody Wanted War* (Garden City, N.Y.: Doubleday, 1968), p. 3.

[25] Edward Hallett Carr, *The Twenty Years' Crisis 1919–1939* (New York: Macmillan, 1961), pp. 51–52.

[26] White, *Nobody Wanted War*, p. 6.

extraordinarily articulate expression of thoughts which guided American foreign policy for a third of a century after outbreak of the Second World War. An appraisal of Acheson must therefore be an appraisal of the nation's behavior in world affairs for an entire generation."[27] Thus, in Smith's interpretation, Acheson's general image of the world and what ought to be America's role in it was shared by other Secretaries of State, including his successor John Foster Dulles, as well as such later Presidents as Johnson and Nixon with their blunders in Vietnam. All these cold warriors, it is argued, were heavily influenced by their generation's experiences and perceptions. The postwar American leaders were the offspring of the 1930's; Hitler and Munich, as well as the Nazi-Soviet Pact, were etched into their minds. More specifically, one lesson this generation felt it had learned from the interwar period was that America's isolationist stance had helped bring on World War II, as surely as American participation in Western Europe's defense after World War I (a kind of post-1918 NATO directed against Germany) would have helped deter Hitler. Isolationism was therefore no longer a feasible policy; expansionistic totalitarian movements, Nazi or Soviet, had to be contained. A second lesson was that appeasement only whetted a dictator's appetite; it was better to stand firm against his demands and "present arms"; Soviet policy was expansionist and aggressive and had to be resisted, by force if necessary. Thus, "driven by the ghost of Hitler,"[28] by the memories of the failure of trying to understand the enemy's viewpoint, of making concessions from a position of weakness, of failing to match the adversary's military strength, this generation had learned that "peace cannot be preserved by good intentions and a small army." Acheson therefore approached U.S.-Soviet relations as a deadly contest in which a gain in power for the former was good, a gain for the latter bad. Negotiations with the devil were to be avoided. Soviet totalitarianism had to be contained, its expansionist attempts dammed up, until some day it would mellow. Inflexible U.S. policies, distrust of all Russian and other Communist states' aims and interests, and an inability to recognize the diversity of the Communist world were purportedly the result; so was the unnecessary continuation of the cold war, it is suggested.[29]

Whereas analysts like Fulbright and Smith emphasize misperceptions due to learning the wrong lessons of history, others like Ole Holsti and Townsend Hoopes attribute them to other factors. In focusing on Acheson's successor, they emphasize Secretary of State Dulles's rigid personality plus his equally inflexible anti-Communist viewpoint. Their view was well expressed by a British Ambassador to Washington during the Dulles period:

[27] Gaddis Smith, *Dean Acheson* (New York: Cooper Square Publishers, 1972), p. 414.

[28] *Ibid.*, p. 423.

[29] Gaddis Smith, "The Shadow of John Foster Dulles" *Foreign Affairs*, January, 1974, pp. 403–8.

Three or four centuries ago . . . it was not rare to encounter men of the type of Dulles. Like them, in vigorous and systematic reflection, he had come to unshakeable convictions of a religious and theological order. Like them, he saw the world as an arena in which the forces of good and evil were continuously at war. Like them, he believed that this was the contest which supremely mattered.[30]

Characteristic of this mentality, Hoopes has entitled his biography of the Secretary *The Devil and John Foster Dulles*.[31] Communism was the devil. More analytically, Holsti argues that Dulles drew a distinction between the Russian state and the governing Communist Party, between Russian national interests and Marxist-Leninist ideology with its universal revolutionary goals, the Russian people and the Soviet leaders. The consequence of these distinctions, Holsti claims, was that in Dulles's mind America's quarrel was with the Soviet leadership whose aims reached beyond Russia's legitimate and limited interests; the United States had no conflict with the Russian people, who, if they had been represented by a democratic rather than a totalitarian government, would be following only Russia's limited national interest instead of global expansionist purposes. These were the cause of the cold war. American policy had to prevent this expansion of "atheistic Communism" and be constantly wary of Communist attempts to relax the West's guard.

Given Dulles's black/white image of the world—and this is of central importance to the misperception approach—all incoming information would be filtered through his particular perceptual lenses; all information that fitted into his preconceived image was selected while information that did not fit was filtered out. The image thus remained intact. Psychologic is the term sometimes used to describe this tendency to see what we want to see and reject contrary evidence; psychologists call it a "reduction of cognitive dissonance." The consequence, Holsti argues, is that various Soviet pronouncements and moves, including a major reduction in the size of the Red Army during Dulles's tenure as Secretary of State were rejected as possible concessions and attempts to relax tensions because they only served to reinforce Dulles's pre-existing picture of Soviet Russia as an aggressive and expansionist state. A more flexible personality might have been more receptive to new and conflicting information and, it is implied, to a lessening or end of the Soviet-American conflict.

Sometimes, instead of attributing misperceptions to individual leaders' images or personalities, analysts attribute them to nations as a whole. Nations, says John Stoessinger, "live in darkness." Great gaps appear be-

[30] Quoted by Ole R. Holsti, "Cognitive Dynamics and Images of the Enemy: Dulles and Russia," in Holsti *et al.*, *Enemies in Politics* (Chicago: Rand McNally, 1967), p. 37.

[31] Townsend Hoopes, *The Devil and John Foster Dulles* (Boston: Atlantic/Little, Brown, 1973).

tween image and reality as men and nations respond not to realities but to fictions—what Fulbright called "myths"—which they themselves created. "[G]reat nations struggle not only with each other, but also with their perceptions of each other."[32] These misperceptions are not easily changed. As in pluralistic decision-making with its incremental policy momentum, change comes largely after a disaster like Vietnam; only at such moments are old perceptions and policies re-examined. In the absence of disaster, however, China's or America's or Russia's self-images and images of one another and other states remain intact. Clearly, nations are in need of "light" and enlightenment.

One popular version of this theme is that of the "mirror-image,"[33] which goes something like this: Two adversaries find it impossible to resolve, for example, an arms race because they bring to the negotiating table the distrust, suspicion, and fears they have acquired as opponents. As antagonists, each has come to believe that it represents wisdom, virtue, and morality, and that the other side is not only the embodiment of evil but seeks its destruction. The United States views the Soviet Union as a Communist dictatorship that exploits its masses at home and is bent on a global crusade for Communism. The Soviet Union is equally convinced that the United States is a dictatorship of the bourgeoisie that has enslaved its proletarian majority at home and seeks to export capitalism abroad by force. Americans, of course, know how false this image of the United States is. At the same time, the Soviets would contend that they do not exploit their masses, that the austerity of the period of intensive industrialization is being replaced by increasing attention to the welfare of Soviet citizens, and that in international politics they seek only to be left alone to complete their industrial revolution; their large armies and powerful rockets are needed only because of the threat of an American attack (paralleling the U.S. claim that its military forces are needed only to deter a Soviet attack). It is on the basis of these distorted images, then, that both act belligerently, thereby bringing the world to the precipice of utter destruction—and for no "sane" reason. As Erich Fromm has said, each side views the other "pathologically"—in terms of paranoia, projection, fanaticism, and Orwellian "doublethink."[34] Fromm, like others, thinks of war and peace in terms of individual psychology and analyzes war as a deviation comparable to personal psychotic behavior. In such terms, objectively there is no reason for conflict, and it would not exist but for man's distorted perceptions, unhealthy attitudes, and outmoded ways of thinking.[35]

[32] John Stoessinger, *Nations in Darkness* (New York: Random House, 1971), p. 5, and *idem*, *Why Nations Go to War* (New York: St. Martin's Press, 1974).

[33] Ralph K. White, "Images in the Context of International Conflict," in Herbert C. Kelman *et al.*, eds., *International Behavior: A Social-Psychological Analysis* (New York: Holt, Rinehart & Winston, 1965), pp. 238–75.

[34] Erich Fromm, *May Man Prevail?* (New York: Doubleday, 1961).

[35] For the use of an analysis of alleged distorted U.S. perceptions of the Soviet

Sometimes, it would seem that peace is but a matter of mental health. Some political analysts, in fact, have tried to psychoanalyze leading personalities (such as President Wilson, or the first postwar Secretary of Defense, James Forrestal, who committed suicide, and President Nixon) and, in the process, have found personality traits that adversely affected—or could so have affected—their conduct in office. We are all aware that among policy-makers, as among the rest of us, there are normal amounts of hostilities, repressed urges, and anxieties that could be channeled into policy. Not surprisingly, therefore, one psychologist, after noting that many of the Nazi leaders could be professionally diagnosed as mentally ill, has suggested that a person entrusted with leadership, domestic or international, should first receive a psychological test; such testing to sort out the normal from the maladjusted would be devised and administered by a group of psychiatrists and clinical psychologists to minimize the possibility of error.[36] If a President and other leaders have personal physicians on their staff to take care of their physical health, why not psychiatrists as well to watch over their mental health? One clinical professor at Stanford University Medical School has attributed the eruption of World War I to the "birth-maimed, mother-hating, vain, insecure, strutting, ridiculous adult adolescent," William I, who ruled Germany, and Czar Nicholas II, "weak of will . . . dominated by his wife, Alexandria, who was the slave of the dissolute monk, Rasputin." And World War II was the result of the Versailles peace, which was made by Wilson, who "was not mentally sound," and British Prime Minister Lloyd-George, "a manic-depressive"; and the actions during the 1930's of dictators like Stalin, "a sociopath, a moral imbecile," and Hitler, a "paranoid." Insanity obviously holds the scepter![37] Another well-known M.D. suggests that if Abraham Lincoln had been helped to deal with his "inner conflicts," the Civil War could perhaps have been avoided; and if Nixon had had a psychiatrist on his staff, "Watergate might not have had a chance to develop."[38] Rulers ought obviously to be "psychologically disarmed" if we are all to remain safe and sane. It has been seriously suggested in this connection that new drugs capable of controlling emotions and aggressive behavior might, indeed, prove to be a helpful supplementary technique to curb leaders' hostile impulses.

The problem with this solution is threefold. First, in many cases the psychiatrists would differ among themselves; who, then, would psychoanalyze the psychiatrists, not only to ensure that *they* were of "sound"

Union as an attack upon the foundations of "realist" thinking, see Anatol Rapoport, *The Big Two: Soviet-American Perceptions of Foreign Policy* (New York: Pegasus, 1971).

[36] Otto Klineberg, *The Human Dimension in International Relations* (New York: Holt, Rinehart & Winston, 1964), pp. 65–66.

[37] Russell V. Lee, "When Insanity Holds the Scepter," *New York Times*, April 12, 1974.

[38] Thomas P. Szasz, "The Dominion of Psychiatry," *New York Times*, November 20, 1973.

mind and "reasonable" judgment but also to determine *which* opinions were "correct"? How can the citizens of a nation be assured that the psychiatrists' judgments about their leader's psychological fitness and character are valid and reliable, and not an expression of their personal political preferences under the guise of expert opinion, as the nuclear scientists often expressed their individual political views when they were requested to give objective, technical advice on arms control issues? Even if the psychiatrists could keep their political biases out of their professional opinions, however, the additional question that must be asked about a leader is not just whether he suffers a current mental or character deficiency but whether he is likely to develop one in the future. What degree of risk of a future mental breakdown or character flaw should be regarded as acceptable before he can be certified fit for office?[39]

Second, it is one thing to psychoanalyze a historical figure at a distance—a hazardous undertaking in itself—and quite another to conclude that a man's mental state affected his formulation of objectives and his choice of means in an injurious manner. Stalin may have been paranoid, as Khrushchev claimed, but in his behavior he was hardly rash or prone to disastrous miscalculation (and when he did miscalculate, he did it much as *any* policy-maker might have done). Indeed, even though as outside observers we might be tempted to label Stalin's foreign policy, with its fantastic suspicion of other states, as paranoid, ordinary intelligence cautions us: Was such policy due to a personality problem, or to the ideological framework through which Stalin perceived the United States as an enemy, or to the totalitarian system in which he held absolute power and yet continuously feared those who might overthrow him, or to the natural suspicion of a ruler aware of the nature of the state system and Russian history? Stalin, in brief, may have had a distorted image of America, but this does not mean that his misperception was the offspring of a sick personality.

Third, the idea of mentally sanitizing leaders, perhaps by coming up with a character profile—like James Barber's fourfold character typology —in order to eliminate those who do not fit the "safer" typologies from even being nominated for office smacks of Plato's exclusion from government of all those who are incorrectly trained. But do psychiatry and behavorial engineering really have better answers to the historic problem of power than, for example, the one given by many of the more prestigious political theorists throughout the ages and practioners like the American Founding Fathers, who relied upon balances of power among competing interests, parties, and institutions? Contending groups participating in the policy process tend to reduce, if not eliminate, views that reflect compelling personal needs. Even if one important policy-maker held opin-

---

[39] Alexander L. George, "Assessing Presidential Character," *World Politics*, January, 1974, p. 237, a review essay on James D. Barber, *The Presidential Character: Predicting Performance in the White House* (Englewood Cliffs, N.J.: Prentice-Hall, 1972).

ions based upon extremely distorted perceptions, it is unlikely that these views would survive the continuous confrontation with more "realistic" policy prescriptions. "Insofar as a decision is made within a group context in which the individual's decision or attitude is visible to others, the opportunity for a decision or attitude to perform personality-oriented functions will be limited."[40] While there is no guarantee that what Janis has called "groupthink"[41]—a unified policy position that emerges after insufficient consideration of alternative policy options—will not occur, it need not happen and can be guarded against, as Presidents like Roosevelt, Kennedy (especially during the Cuban missile crisis, although not the abortive Bay of Pigs invasion the year before), and Nixon have repeatedly demonstrated.

Some of these comments would apply especially to crisis decision-making. As we saw in the Cuban missile crisis case, the Kennedy Administration had a number of options: to do nothing, a protest at the United Nations, blockade, air strike, and invasion. While the blockade was finally settled upon, the air strike was recommended in the early stages by a number of the President's advisers, who, upon more consideration, changed their minds. All the alternative courses of action were carefully sifted. Indeed, to promote the frankest possible discussion, the President absented himself from many of the discussions; his presence and opinions when he was present tended to stifle opposing or critical views. The collective decision-making tended to filter out distortions of perception and irrational judgments. Admittedly, the decision-making went on within a larger framework in which the Soviet action and its meanings were defined. Some critics of Kennedy undoubtedly feel this framework was itself distorted and judge an action that could have blown up mankind because of a few missiles as bordering on the irrational.[42] Thus, even were these critics to agree that Kennedy handled the situation with skill, they would still hold that their judgments on American policy and their outlook on world politics differed from his and presumably were more accurate. But whose perception is in fact more accurate?

Clearly, in the Cuban crisis, time was an important variable. Had the crisis decision been made in a great hurry, it might well have been the wrong decision. For example, an air strike might have killed Russians, humiliating Khrushchev and compelling him to react to avenge Russian honor. But even had the decision been made more quickly than it actually was, and even had it been a disastrously wrong decision, one still

[40] Sidney Verba, "Assumptions of Rationality and Non-Rationality in Models of the International System," World Politics, October, 1961, p. 103.

[41] Irving L. Janis, Victims of Groupthink (Boston: Houghton Mifflin, 1972). See George, "The Case for Multiple Advocacy in Making Foreign Policy," and I. M. Destler, Presidents, Bureaucrats and Foreign Policy (Princeton, N.J.: Princeton University Press, 1972), for analyses of how "groupthink" can be avoided.

[42] Richard J. Barnet, The Economy of Death (New York: Atheneum, 1969), pp. 84–85.

could not say that hostility and other psychological needs of some policy-makers had been channeled into the policy product. In any event, rarely do states act as quickly as individuals. "There is thus little counterpart among states to the verbal or physical slap in the face which is sometimes experienced by persons and which usually provokes various types of quick and violent behavior."[43]

But if we eliminate psychiatrists and their paraphernalia, we are still left presumably with the leader's misperceptions, whatever their origins. One difficulty with analyses like those of Dulles is, however, that they reconstruct only from public statements how individual policy-makers saw reality in general and certain situations in particular. Another, more severe problem is that of knowing whether a policy-maker's image of an adversary can be attributed to a rigid personality, religious attitudes, false historical analogy, or the thinking he absorbed from experience in the state system. As was suggested much earlier, in a system characterized by a high degree of mistrust, even a defensive act may well be interpreted by the opponent as hostile. The result, of course, will be the growth of mutually held hostile images that on the whole tend to resist contradictory evidence (because states are doing more than one thing at a time, no evidence in any case is likely to be wholly contradictory); indeed, friendly gestures may be dismissed as attempts to hoodwink one into relaxing one's guard, or else as signs of weakness. The greatest difficulty, however, stems from the possibility that *the analyst is merely substituting his own judgment for that of the policy-maker. In other words, as a critic of official policy, he tends to attribute this policy to the distorted views of decision-makers (whereas his own are assumed correct) and therefore concludes that the remedy is to correct their false images of their adversaries.* If, in short, those who formulate policy were more "flexible," continuously "testing reality" and adjusting their perceptions to reality (generally, the reality of the critics), there would presumably be no reason for conflict.[44] It cannot be denied, of course, that decision-makers, like most individuals, tend to see the world through colored glasses and by and large select the fact that will fit and confirm their preconceptions. But it is also true that "if we consider only the evidence available to a decision-maker at the time of decision, the view later proved incorrect may be supported by as much evidence as the correct one—or even by more."[45]

Nevertheless, it remains popular to explain conflict as if it were the offspring of falsely held images by one of the parties to a conflict and

[43] Bernard Brodie, *Escalation and the Nuclear Option* (Princeton, N.J.: Princeton University Press, 1966), p. 139.

[44] For example, see Ross Stagner, *Psychological Aspects of International Conflict* (Belmont, Calif.: Brooks/Cole Publishing Co., 1967), pp. 1–16, and Klineberg, *Human Dimension.*

[45] Robert Jervis, "Hypotheses on Misperception," *World Politics*, April, 1968, p. 460.

perhaps by both. Not that such images are not present, as our earlier analyses of America's national style and Soviet perceptions and elite style have shown. But in opposition to the assertion that such images cause or greatly magnify conflict, it might more correctly be asserted that the opposite is true: *Conflict among states demonstrates not so much that the adversaries misunderstand one another as that they understand each other too well.* While Chamberlain misperceived the nature of Hitler's aims, Britain appeased him; but once the Prime Minister's misperceptions had been corrected by events—contrary to White—Britain declared war on Germany. It was Roosevelt's incorrect image of Stalin's Russia that resulted in a policy that concentrated on Germany's defeat and undertook no measures in anticipation of the postwar balance of power. As Soviet Russian power expanded in the wake of Germany's defeat and led to pressures on Iran and Turkey after 1945, it was Truman's correct perception of what had to be done in a two-power world that produced the containment policy. Indeed, as suggested earlier in the book, if the two superpowers had shared the same political and economic systems, their rivalry would still have erupted; fearful of each other, each was concerned with enhancing his power and security through the establishment of a new balance of power now that Germany and Japan had been defeated. America's role in Europe after Hitler's defeat was no different from Britain's role after Napoleon's defeat; on both occasions, Russia—once Czarist, once Communist—threatened to achieve hegemony despite its toll of casualties and suffering in the preceding war.

Yet within a year of the Truman Doctrine, the United States was proffering help to Tito's Yugoslavia after his break with Stalin, the first of several attempts to "build bridges" to Eastern Europe, which began in earnest in 1956 at the time of the Polish and Hungarian upheavals. Similarly, after Nationalist China's collapse in 1949, the allegedly indiscriminately anti-Communist Acheson recognized the potential of differences between the two Communist giants and planned, once Chiang on Formosa had been eliminated by Mao, to recognize the new Chinese regime. Even during the Korean War, Acheson had felt that the crossing of the 38th Parallel was safe *because* Peking was already too absorbed with the Russian threat to the North to pay much attention to events in Korea.

As the situation changed again, the United States and the U.S.S.R. began to cooperate with one another on arms control; they shifted from a total adversary relationship to a limited adversary relationship. Perhaps one of the best examples that perceptions change with external circumstances has been President Nixon's pursuit of *détente* with Russia and *rapprochement* with China. During the 1950's, Nixon had been a militant anti-Communist; no so-called psychohistorical analysis has yet satisfactorily explained how a man so allegedly loaded with misperceptions, character defects, and inner anguish could have conducted such a flexible, nonideological, pragmatic balance of power policy.[46] In addition, Peking's revolutionary anticapitalist posture and rhetoric did not stand in the way of improvement of relations with the United States when its fraternal Russian ally appeared as a potential attacker; nor did it inhibit it from supporting (capitalist) European integration and a strong (capitalist) NATO to balance Russian power in the West. Marx and Mao had become subordinated to the balance of power. As Hans Morgenthau has commented more generally, "the assumption that the issues of international conflict, born as they are of misunderstandings, are but imaginary and that actually no issue worth fighting about stands between nation and nation" is wrong.

> Nothing could be farther from the truth. All the great wars which decided the course of history and changed the political face of the earth were fought for real stakes, not for imaginary ones. The issue in these great convulsions was invariably: who shall rule and who shall be ruled? Who shall be free, and who, slave?[47]

And a Final Word on Concepts

We began this work by setting up an analytical framework. It is perhaps appropriate, then, to end by commenting on that framework. First, it should be apparent that all three levels of analysis are necessary if international politics is not to be analyzed in an oversimplified fashion. The state-system model may greatly help us understand the outbreak of the cold war, but by itself it cannot tell us the reasons for the scope and intensity of conflict. On the other hand, to attribute the eruption of the American-Soviet conflict solely to the Kremlin's anticapitalism or solely to Washington's anti-Communism is to ignore the power and security dilemma confronting all powers in the state system. It is, in short, to neglect the environment in which states live. The result is not only a too restricted understanding of state behavior, it is also a misreading of history that could, if extended, result in a misreading of the future. Hence, to suggest, as do American revisionist writers, that but for an alleged American anti-Communist animus that predated Soviet postwar behavior there would have been no cold war is to ignore the ongoing realities of the state system. In the absence of a first-level perspective, the cold war is bound to be misunderstood. For it is then viewed solely as an offspring of American anti-Communism or Soviet anticapitalism, or Truman being tough rather than conciliatory, or Stalin's paranoia, rather than the continuation of the age-old game of "power politics," which the members of the state system are compelled to play by the very nature of the system. Yet, if the reasons for this conflict are perceived in-

[46] Bruce Mazlish, *In Search of Nixon* (New York: Basic Books, 1972).

[47] Hans J. Morgenthau, *Politics Among Nations*, 4th ed. (New York: Knopf, 1967), p. 504.

correctly, the lessons drawn from it—lessons that will influence future policy since policy-makers tend to base policy on past experience—will also be incorrect.

Second, while usually we need all three levels of analyses, this does not mean that all three levels are equally important. Depending upon the situation to be analyzed, different levels may be most significant. In part, this is a matter of the investigator's judgment about which level is likely to be the most fruitful for his analysis. Thus, even though one analyst might give the greatest weight to the structure of the state system and the least to personality, such a weighting cannot be applied across the board, regardless of the circumstances to be examined. For example, however much one can explain and understand post–World War II American foreign policy by the changing distributions of power in the external environment in which the United States had to live with other states, such an analysis is incomplete. For American decision-makers, having successfully used anti-Communism to mobilize public and Congressional support once Soviet postwar aims became clear, found themselves trapped by a competitive two-party system; the mere possibility that the out-party might accuse the in-party of being "soft on Communism" drove it (especially the Democrats) to pursue more militant policies and allowed it less flexibility in policy decisions. The combined impact of elections and accusations—that is, domestic politics—thus contributed greatly to pre-emptive actions such as the Dominican intervention or the 1965 intervention in Vietnam. These were undertaken in large part to forestall opposition-party assaults on the Administration's foreign policy conduct.

Third, different levels of analysis may yield conflicting interpretations. First-level analysis, based upon the structure or hierarchy of power in the system, equates those who are most powerful with those who are most active. A small country under normal conditions is not going to be a principal troublemaker, no matter what its ideology or aims; it is the big and powerful countries whose conflicts will disturb the system. And strength derives from industry and modern technology. But our second-level developmental scheme held out the expectation that modernized nations equaled more peaceful societies. A world of urbanized industrial states would be one of consumer satisfaction and citizens' inward orientation and, therefore, one in which "war no longer paid." Thus, will a multipolar world—very likely a nuclear multipolar world—be more dangerous or more peaceful?

Or, to cite another instance, according to the second-level capitalist interpretation, the American intervention in Vietnam is viewed as the logical product of the American profit-seeking economic system. In terms of third-level analysis, the war is the result of the policy-makers' distorted perceptions of the state system. Thus according to the former interpretation, the outbreak of war or the avoidance of war is a question of the system; changing leaders makes no difference since they are the products and instruments of that system. Whether a Johnson or a Mc-Govern is President is not important as a reason for the U.S. military involvement in Vietnam; the system determined that. It is an illusion that "one simply replaces individuals in office with other men . . . rather than solving problems with an altogether new system"[48] that will behave in a quite different manner—in the instance above, for example, a socialist system, which would not be prone to military interventions and an expansive, aggressive foreign policy because it would not be committed to the search for economic profit abroad. According to the perception thesis, however, who is President is important, indeed the key factor. The "system," whatever it may be, is not an automaton moving along some predetermined path; countries with the same type of system do not all act alike. Who its leaders are is significant; a Johnson will intervene in Vietnam, a McGovern will not. Systems are not beyond human control and will; leaders' choices of policy direct the system.

Fourth, while the various levels of analysis and the concepts at each level are intended to help the analyst understand state behavior better —regardless of whether the observer approves of that behavior or not—a particular level and certain concepts can be used to cast blame. Thus, we observed earlier the fascination with economic explanations as the root causes of conflict and war, particularly the capitalist-imperialist interpretation. More often than not, such explanations are invoked polemically, as simple explanations cutting through the complexity of reality allegedly revealing the "true" motivations behind policy; usually dividing the world between the privileged and the poor, the haves and have-nots, the exploiter and the exploited, and the evil few and the good, decent, oppressed majority, these explanations become morality tales allowing their user to castigate, denounce, and accuse—and usually, to offer equally simple solutions. What is important in this matter is the awareness that the levels can be used in this unanalytical and polemical manner, and to guard against it.

Fifth, concepts change. Bipolarity in the prenuclear period has traditionally been equated with instability and multipolarity with stability. Nuclear weapons, however, have led to a reassessment of these correlations. Nuclear bipolarity may be more stable than nuclear multipolarity. In short, however valid and persuasive any concept may seem at a given moment, it ought to be re-examined regularly, because in a world of rapidly changing conditions a concept true today may be wrong tomorrow. Some of the developmental or modernization concepts with their series of steps of economic growth and political stages, based upon Western historical experience and Western society—and more specifically, American society—as the model that non-Western nations would reach when

[48] Gabriel Kolko, *The Roots of American Foreign Policy*, p. 134.

they some day become modern, are already being reassessed as scholars learn more about the variety of Western experiences, as well as those of the new non-Western states.

Finally, an analysis of international politics can be no better than the concepts employed, irrespective of the levels of analysis. But many of the concepts needed for a study of contemporary international politics are still young—for instance, those concerning modernization, regional integration, and deterrence. To understand the fast changing world in which we live, the social scientist has been compelled to grope for such new concepts. Even our language is sometimes new, reflecting the inadequacy of older terminology in dealing with some of the unique problems of our time. To take only one example, our military vocabulary now includes terms virtually unknown before World War II: nuclear exchange and stalemate; mutual deterrence; credibility; "soft" and "hard" weapons; passive and active defenses; pre-emptive, first, and second strikes; assured destruction; countervalue, counterforce, and damage-limiting strategy; spasm, accidental, and limited wars; escalation; Nth-country problem; nuclear proliferation; arms control; tacit agreement; nuclear blackmail; crisis management; nuclear threshold; and overkill. This intellectual ferment is likely to continue and to help us broaden and deepen our insight into our environment as our conceptual tools become more refined and sophisticated.

In the meantime, this generation, like earlier generations, will be called upon or condemned to live with an ambiguous reality, and it will have to forswear both cynicism and illusion in trying to define it. To do this is to live dangerously. It must simultaneously avoid a seductive but futile escape into nostalgia for the past and an imperious rage at a world that will not conform to its vision. Instead it, like its predecessors, must learn to live in a world where the constant is neither war nor peace, where the millennium remains a distant dream, and where the threat of a nuclear Armageddon is an ever present fear. The beginning of wisdom is to understand, even if only a little bit more, the most difficult of all worlds— the *real* one. It is to that end that this book is dedicated.

A Selective Bibliography

Introduction to International Politics

Aron, Raymond. *Peace and War.** Garden City, N.Y.: Doubleday & Co., 1966; London: Weidenfeld and Nicolson, 1966. Paperback ed., Praeger.

Carr, Edward H. *The Twenty Years' Crisis 1919–1939.** New York and Basingstoke: The Macmillan Co., 1961. Paperback ed., Harper Torchbooks.

Deutsch, Karl. *The Analysis of International Relations.** Englewood Cliffs, N.J.: Prentice-Hall, 1968.

Dougherty, James E., and Robert L. Pfaltzgraff, Jr., *Contending Theories of International Relations.** Philadelphia: J. B. Lippincott Co., 1971.

Farrell, R. Barry, ed. *Approaches to Comparative and International Politics.** Evanston, Ill.: Northwestern University Press, 1966.

Herz, John H. *International Politics in the Atomic Age.** New York: Columbia University Press, 1962.

Hoffmann, Stanley. *Contemporary Theory in International Relations.* Englewood Cliffs, N.J.: Prentice-Hall, 1960.

Kaplan, Morton A. *System and Process in International Politics.** New York: John Wiley & Sons, 1964.

———, ed. *New Approaches to International Relations.* New York: St. Martin's Press, 1968.

Knorr, Klaus, and James N. Rosenau, eds. *Contending Approaches to International Politics.* Princeton, N.J.: Princeton University Press, 1969.

Knorr, Klaus, and Sidney Verba, eds. *International System: Theoretical Essays.** Princeton, N.J.: Princeton University Press, 1961. (This is the book form of the October, 1961, issue of *World Politics.*)

McClelland, Charles A. *Theory and the International System.** New York: The Macmillan Co., 1966.

Morgenthau, Hans J. *Politics Among Nations.* 4th ed. New York: Alfred A. Knopf, 1967.

---

* Indicates paperback.

491

NEUMANN, SIGMUND. *Permanent Revolution.** 2d ed. New York: Praeger Publishers, 1965.

ROSECRANCE, RICHARD. *Action and Reaction in World Politics.* Boston: Little, Brown & Co., 1963.

ROSENAU, JAMES N., ed. *Domestic Sources of Foreign Policy.* New York: The Free Press, 1967.

————, ed. *International Politics and Foreign Policy.* 2d ed. New York: The Free Press, 1969.

————, ed. *Linkage Politics.* New York: The Free Press, 1969.

SINGER, J. DAVID, ed. *Quantitative International Politics.* New York: The Free Press, 1968.

WALTZ, KENNETH N. *Man, the State, and War.** New York: Columbia University Press, 1959.

WOLFERS, ARNOLD. *Discord and Collaboration: Essays on International Politics.** Baltimore: The Johns Hopkins Press, 1965.

ZAWODNY, J. K. *Guide to the Study of International Relations.** San Francisco: Chandler Publishing Co., 1966.

DETERRENCE, ARMS CONTROL, AND CRISES

ABEL, ELIE. *The Missile Crisis.** Philadelphia: J. B. Lippincott, 1966. Paperback ed., Bantam.

ABSHIRE, DAVID M., and RICHARD V. ALLEN, eds. *National Security.* New York: Praeger Publishers, 1963.

Atomic Energy Commission. *The Effects of Nuclear Weapons.* Rev. ed. Washington, D.C.: Government Printing Office, 1962.

BADER, WILLIAM B. *The U.S. and the Spread of Nuclear Weapons.** New York: Pegasus, 1968.

BEATON, LEONARD. *Must the Bomb Spread?* Baltimore: Penguin Books, 1966.

BLOOMFIELD, LINCOLN P. *Khrushchev and the Arms Race.* Cambridge, Mass.: The MIT Press, 1966.

BRENNAN, DONALD G., ed. *Arms Control, Disarmament, and National Security.* New York: George Braziller, 1961.

BRODIE, BERNARD. *Strategy in the Missile Age.** Princeton, N.J.: Princeton University Press, 1959.

BUCHAN, ALASTAIR, ed. *A World of Nuclear Powers?** Englewood Cliffs, N.J.: Prentice-Hall, 1966.

BULL, HEDLEY. *The Control of the Arms Race.** 2d ed. New York: Praeger Publishers, 1965.

EDWARDS, DAVID V. *Arms Control in International Politics.** New York: Holt, Rinehart & Winston, 1969.

ETZIONI, AMITAI. *The Hard Way to Peace.** New York: Collier Books, 1962.

————. *Winning Without War.** Garden City, N.Y.: Doubleday & Co., 1964.

FRYKLUND, RICHARD. *100 Million Lives.* New York: The Macmillan Co., 1962.

GEORGE, ALEXANDER L., et al. *The Limits of Coercive Diplomacy.** Boston: Little, Brown & Co., 1971.

GREEN, PHILIP. *The Deadly Logic.** Columbus: Ohio State University Press, 1966. Paperback ed., Schocken.

HADLEY, ARTHUR T. *The Nation's Safety and Arms Control.* New York: The Viking Press, 1961.

HUNTINGTON, SAMUEL P. "Arms Races: Prerequisites and Results," in CARL J. FRIEDRICH and SEYMOUR E. HARRIS, eds., *Public Policy.* Cambridge, Mass.: Graduate School of Public Administration, Harvard University, 1958.

KAHN, HERMAN. *On Thermonuclear War.* Princeton, N.J.: Princeton University Press, 1960.

———. *Thinking About the Unthinkable.** New York: Horizon Press, 1962. Paperback ed., Avon.

KAUFMAN, WILLIAM W. *The McNamara Strategy.* New York: Harper & Row, 1964.

KENNEDY, ROBERT F. *Thirteen Days.** New York: W. W. Norton & Co., 1969. Paperback ed., Signet.

KISSINGER, HENRY A. *The Necessity for Choice.** New York: Harper & Row, 1961.

———, ed. *Problems of National Strategy.** New York: Praeger Publishers, 1965.

KNORR, KLAUS. *On the Uses of Military Power in the Nuclear Age.* Princeton, N.J.: Princeton University Press, 1966.

KNORR, KLAUS, and THORNTON READ, eds. *Limited Strategic War.* Chicago: University of Chicago Press, 1957.

LAPP, RALPH E. *Kill and Overkill.* New York: Basic Books, 1962.

LEFEVER, ERNEST W., ed. *Arms and Arms Control.** New York: Praeger Publishers, 1962.

LEVINE, ROBERT A. *The Arms Debate.* Cambridge, Mass.: Harvard University Press, 1962.

MANDER, JOHN. *Berlin.** Baltimore: Penguin Books, 1962.

MILLIS, WALTER, *et al. World Without War.** New York: Washington Square Press, 1961.

OSGOOD, CHARLES E. *An Alternative to War or Surrender.** Urbana: University of Illinois Press, 1962.

OSGOOD, ROBERT E., and ROBERT W. TUCKER. *Force, Order, and Justice.** Baltimore: The Johns Hopkins Press, 1967.

ROSECRANCE, RICHARD N., ed. *The Dispersion of Nuclear Weapons.* New York: Columbia University Press, 1964.

SCHELLING, THOMAS C. *Strategy of Conflict.** Cambridge, Mass.: Harvard University Press, 1960. Paperback ed., Oxford (London).

SCHELLING, THOMAS C., and MORTON H. HALPERIN, *Strategy and Arms Control.** New York: Twentieth Century Fund, 1961.

SNYDER, GLENN H. *Deterrence and Defense.* Princeton, N.J.: Princeton University Press, 1961.

SPANIER, JOHN W., and JOSEPH L. NOGEE. *The Politics of Disarmament.** New York: Praeger Publishers, 1962.

SPEIER, HANS. *Divided Berlin.* New York: Praeger Publishers, 1961.

YOUNG, ORAN. *The Politics of Force.* Princeton, N.J.: Princeton University Press, 1968.

LIMITED WAR—CONVENTIONAL AND REVOLUTIONARY

GALULA, DAVID. *Counterinsurgency Warfare.* New York: Praeger Publishers, 1964.

GIAP, VO NGUYEN. *Banner of People's War: The Party's Military Line.* New York: Praeger Publishers, 1970.

————. *People's War, People's Army.** New York: Praeger Publishers, 1962. Paperback ed., Bantam.

GREENE, T. N., ed. *The Guerrilla—and How to Fight Him.** New York: Praeger Publishers, 1962.

HALPERIN, MORTON H. *Limited War in the Nuclear Age.** New York: John Wiley & Sons, 1963.

HEILBRUNN, OTTO. *Partisan Warfare.* New York: Praeger Publishers, 1962.

HIGGINS, TRUMBULL. *Korea and the Fall of MacArthur.* London and New York: Oxford University Press, 1960.

HUNTINGTON, SAMUEL P., ed. *Changing Patterns of Military Politics.* New York: The Free Press, 1962.

KAUFMANN, WILLIAM W. *Military Policy and National Security.* Princeton, N.J.: Princeton University Press, 1956.

KISSINGER, HENRY A. *Nuclear Weapons and Foreign Policy.** New York: Harper & Row, 1957. Abridged paperback ed., Norton.

Mao Tse-tung on Guerrilla Warfare. Translated and with an Introduction by SAMUEL B. GRIFFITH. New York: Praeger Publishers, 1961.

MEYER, KARL E., and TAD SZULC. *The Cuban Invasion.* New York: Praeger Publishers, 1962.

OSANKA, FRANKLIN M., ed. *Modern Guerrilla Warfare.* New York: The Free Press, 1962.

OSGOOD, ROBERT E. *Limited War.* Chicago: University of Chicago Press, 1957.

PARET, PETER. *French Revolutionary Warfare from Indochina to Algeria.* New York: Praeger Publishers, 1961.

PARET, PETER, and JOHN W. SHY. *Guerrilla in the 1960's.** Rev. ed. New York: Praeger Publishers, 1962.

PYE, LUCIAN W. *Guerrilla Communism in Malaya.* Princeton, N.J.: Princeton University Press, 1956.

SPANIER, JOHN W. *The Truman-MacArthur Controversy and the Korean War.** Cambridge, Mass.: Harvard University Press, 1959. Rev. paperback ed., Norton.

TAYLOR, MAXWELL D. *The Uncertain Trumpet.* New York: Harper & Row, 1960.

THAYER, CHARLES W. *Guerrilla.** New York: Harper & Row, 1963.

TRINQUIER, ROBERT. *Modern Warfare.* New York: Praeger Publishers, 1964.

TURNER, GORDON B., and RICHARD D. CHALLENGER, eds. *National Security in the Nuclear Age.** New York: Praeger Publishers, 1964.

WHITING, ALLEN S. *China Crosses the Yalu.* New York: The Macmillan Co., 1960.

WOLF, ERIC. *Peasant Wars of the Twentieth Century.** New York: Harper & Row, 1969.

THE VIETNAM WAR

COOPER, CHESTER L. *The Lost Crusade*. New York: Dodd, Mead & Co., 1970.

DRAPER, THEODORE. *Abuse of Power*.* New York: The Viking Press, 1967.

FALL, BERNARD B. *Street Without Joy*. 3d rev. ed. Harrisburg, Pa.: The Stackpole Co., 1963.

————. *The Two Viet-Nams*. 2d rev. ed. New York: Praeger Publishers, 1967.

————. *Viet-Nam Witness, 1953–66*. New York: Praeger Publishers, 1966.

GURTOV, MELVIN. *The First Vietnam Crisis*.* New York: Columbia University Press, 1967.

HOOPES, TOWNSEND. *The Limits of Intervention*.* New York: David McKay Co., 1969.

OBERDORFER, DON. *Tet*. Garden City, N.Y.: Doubleday & Co., 1971.

The Pentagon Papers.* Chicago: Quadrangle, 1971. Paperback ed., Bantam.

PFEFFER, RICHARD M., ed. *No More Vietnams?** New York: Harper & Row, 1968.

PIKE, DOUGLAS. *Viet Cong*.* Cambridge, Mass.: The MIT Press, 1966.

SCHLESINGER, ARTHUR M., JR. *Bitter Heritage*.* Boston: Houghton Mifflin & Co., 1967. Paperback ed., Fawcett Crest.

SCHOENBRUN, DAVID. *Vietnam*.* New York: Atheneum, 1968.

SCHURMANN, FRANZ, et al. *The Politics of Escalation in Vietnam*.* Boston: Beacon Press, 1966. Paperback ed., Fawcett Premier.

SHAPLEN, ROBERT. *The Lost Revolution*.* New York: Harper & Row, 1966.

TANHAM, GEORGE K. *Communist Revolutionary Warfare*. Rev. ed. New York: Praeger Publishers, 1967.

THOMPSON, SIR ROBERT. *No Exit from Vietnam*. New York: David McKay Co., 1969.

ALLIANCES

BEER, FRANCIS A., ed. *Alliances*.* New York: Holt, Rinehart & Winston, 1970.

FRIEDMAN, JULIAN R., et al. *Alliances in International Politics*.* Boston: Allyn & Bacon, 1968.

LISKA, GEORGE. *Nations in Alliance*. Baltimore: The Johns Hopkins Press, 1962.

RIKER, WILLIAM H. *The Theory of Political Coalitions*.* New Haven, Conn.: Yale University Press, 1962.

NATO

ARON, RAYMOND. *The Great Debate*.* Garden City, N.Y.: Doubleday & Co., 1965.

BEER, FRANCIS A. *Integration and Disintegration in NATO*. Columbus: Ohio State University Press, 1969.

BELOFF, NORA. *The General Says No*.* Baltimore: Penguin Books, 1964.

BUCHAN, ALASTAIR. *NATO in the 1960's*. Rev. ed. New York: Praeger Publishers, 1963.

CALLEO, DAVID. *The Atlantic Fantasy.** Baltimore: The Johns Hopkins Press, 1970.

COTTRELL, ALVIN J., and JAMES DOUGHERTY. *The Politics of the Atlantic Alliance.** New York: Praeger Publishers, 1964.

DEUTSCH, KARL, et al. *France, Germany and the Western Alliance.** New York: Charles Scribner's Sons, 1967.

GROSSER, ALFRED. *French Foreign Policy Under de Gaulle.** Boston: Little, Brown & Co., 1967.

HANREIDER, WOLFRAM. *The Stable Crisis.** New York: Harper & Row, 1970.

————. *West German Foreign Policy.* Stanford, Calif.: Stanford University Press, 1967.

HOFFMANN, STANLEY. *Gulliver's Troubles or The Setting of American Foreign Policy.** New York: McGraw-Hill Book Co., 1968.

KAISER, KARL. *German Foreign Policy in Transition.** London and New York: Oxford University Press, 1968.

KISSINGER, HENRY A. *The Troubled Partnership.** New York: McGraw-Hill Book Co., 1965. Paperback ed., Doubleday Anchor.

KLEIMAN, ROBERT. *Atlantic Crisis.** New York: W. W. Norton & Co., 1964.

KNORR, KLAUS, ed. *NATO and American Security.* Princeton, N.J.: Princeton University Press, 1959.

KRAFT, JOSEPH. *The Grand Design.* New York: Harper & Row, 1962.

NEUSTADT, RICHARD E. *Alliance Politics.* New York: Columbia University Press, 1970.

NORTHEDGE, F. S. *British Foreign Policy.* New York: Praeger Publishers, 1962.

OSGOOD, ROBERT E. *NATO: The Entangling Alliance.* Chicago: University of Chicago Press, 1962.

PFALTZGRAFF, ROBERT L., JR. *The Atlantic Community.** New York: Van Nostrand Reinhold Co., 1969.

RICHARDSON, JAMES L. *Germany and the Atlantic Alliance.* Cambridge, Mass.: Harvard University Press, 1966.

STEEL, RONALD. *The End of the Alliance.* New York: The Viking Press, 1962.

WHITE, THEODORE H. *Fire in the Ashes.* New York: William Sloane Associates, 1953.

WILCOX, FRANCES O., and H. FIELD HAVILAND, JR., eds. *The Atlantic Community.* New York: Praeger Publishers, 1963.

FUNCTIONALISM AND COMMUNITY-BUILDING

DEUTSCH, KARL, et al. *Political Community and the North Atlantic Area.* Princeton, N.J.: Princeton University Press, 1957.

ETZIONI, AMITAI. *Political Unification.** New York: Holt Rinehart & Winston, 1965.

HAAS, ERNST B. *The Uniting of Europe.* Stanford, Calif.: Stanford University Press, 1958.

KITZINGER, U. W. *The Politics and Economics of European Integration.** New York: Praeger Publishers, 1963.

LICHTHEIM, GEORGE. *The New Europe.** 2d ed. New York: Praeger Publishers, 1964.

LIEBER, ROBERT J. *British Politics and European Unity.* Berkeley: University of California Press, 1970.

LINDBERG, LEON N., and STUART A. SCHEINGOLD. *Europe's Would-Be Polity.** Englewood Cliffs, N.J.: Prentice-Hall, 1970.

SHANKS, MICHAEL, and JOHN LAMBERT. *The Common Market Today—And Tomorrow.** New York: Praeger Publishers, 1963.

INTERNATIONAL ORGANIZATION

BAILEY, SIDNEY D. *The United Nations.** New York: Praeger Publishers, 1963.

BLOOMFIELD, LINCOLN P. *The United Nations and U.S. Foreign Policy.** Boston: Little, Brown & Co., 1960.

BLOOMFIELD, LINCOLN P., et al. *International Military Forces.* Boston: Little, Brown & Co., 1964.

BOYD, ANDREW. *United Nations.** Baltimore: Penguin Books, 1963.

BURNS, ARTHUR LEE, and NINA HEATHCOTE. *Peace-keeping by U.N. Forces.* New York: Praeger Publishers, 1963.

CALVOCORESSI, PETER. *World Order and New States.* New York: Praeger Publishers, 1962.

CLAUDE, INIS L., JR. *The Changing United Nations.** New York: Random House, 1967.

———. *Power and International Relations.* New York: Random House, 1964.

———. *Swords into Plowshares.* Rev. ed. New York: Random House, 1964.

DALLIN, ALEXANDER. *The Soviet Union at the United Nations.* New York: Praeger Publishers, 1962.

FRYE, WILLIAM R. *A United Nations Peace Force.* Dobbs Ferry, N.Y.: Oceana Publications, 1957.

HAAS, ERNST B. *Beyond the Nation-State.** Stanford, Calif.: Stanford University Press, 1964.

HAMMARSKJÖLD, DAG. *Servant of Peace.* Edited by WILDER FOOTE. New York: Harper & Row, 1963.

KAY, DAVID A., ed. *The United Nations Political System.** New York: John Wiley & Sons, 1967.

LASH, JOSEPH P. *Dag Hammarskjöld.* Garden City, N.Y.: Doubleday & Co., 1961.

MILLER, LINDA B. *World Order and Local Disorder.* Princeton, N.J.: Princeton University Press, 1967.

MILLER, RICHARD. *Dag Hammarskjöld and Crisis Diplomacy.* Dobbs Ferry, N.Y.: Oceana Publications, 1961.

NICHOLAS, HERBERT G. *The United Nations as a Political Institution.** 2d ed. London and New York: Oxford University Press, 1962.

NYE, JOSEPH S., JR. *Peace in Parts.* Boston: Little, Brown & Co., 1971.

STOESSINGER, JOHN G. *The United Nations and the Superpowers.** New York: Random House, 1966.

WILCOX, FRANCIS O., and H. FIELD HAVILAND, JR., eds. *The U.S. and the U.N.* For the Johns Hopkins University, School of Advanced Studies, Washington, D.C. Baltimore: The Johns Hopkins Press, 1961.

Transnational Actors

Keohane, Robert O., and Joseph S. Nye, Jr., eds. *Transnational Relations and World Politics.* Cambridge, Mass.: Harvard University Press, 1972.

Kindleberger, Charles P., ed. *The International Corporation.* Cambridge, Mass.: MIT Press, 1970.

Muller, Ronald, and Richard J. Barnet. *The Earth Managers.* New York: Simon & Schuster, 1974.

Vernon, Raymond. *Sovereignty at Bay.* New York: Basic Books, 1971.

Comparative Foreign Policy

Brzezinski, Zbigniew K., and Samuel P. Huntington. *Political Power: USA/USSR.** New York: The Viking Press, 1964.

Macridis, Roy C., ed. *Foreign Policy in World Politics.** 3d ed. Englewood Cliffs, N.J.: Prentice-Hall, 1967.

————. *Modern European Governments.** Englewood Cliffs, N.J.: Prentice-Hall, 1968.

Northedge, F. S., ed. *The Foreign Policies of the Powers.** New York: Praeger Publishers, 1969.

Waltz, Kenneth N. *Foreign Policy and Democratic Politics.** Boston: Little, Brown & Co., 1967.

Wilkinson, David O. *Comparative Foreign Relations.** Belmont, Calif.: Dickenson Publishing Co., 1969.

Communism

Bober, M. M. *Karl Marx's Interpretation of History.** New York: W. W. Norton & Co., 1965.

Daniels, Robert V. *The Nature of Communism.** New York: Random House, 1962.

Hunt, R. N. Carew. *The Theory and Practice of Communism.** Rev. ed. Baltimore: Penguin Books, 1963.

Lichtheim, George. *Marxism: An Historical and Critical Study.** 2d ed. New York: Praeger Publishers, 1965.

Marcuse, Herbert. *Soviet Marxism.** New York: Columbia University Press, 1958. Paperback ed., Random House Vintage.

Mendel, Arthur P., ed. *The Essential Works of Marxism.** New York: Bantam Books, 1961.

Meyer, Alfred G. *Leninism.** Cambridge, Mass.: Harvard University Press, 1957. Paperback ed., Praeger.

————. *Marxism.* Cambridge, Mass.: Harvard University Press, 1954. Paperback ed., University of Michigan Press.

Popper, Karl R. *The Open Society and Its Enemies.** Vol. II: *High Tide of Prophecy.* Princeton, N.J.: Princeton University Press, 1950. Paperback ed., Harper Torchbooks.

Wilson, Edmund. *To the Finland Station.** New York: Harcourt, Brace & Co., 1940. Paperback ed., Garden City, N.Y.: Doubleday Anchor Books, 1953.

THE COMMUNIST WORLD

BARNETT, A. DOAK. *Communist China and Asia: Challenge to American Policy.** New York: Harper & Row, 1960.

———, ed. *Communist Strategies in Asia.** New York: Praeger Publishers, 1963.

BOYD, R. G. *Communist China's Foreign Policy.** New York: Praeger Publishers, 1962.

BROMKE, ADAM, ed. *The Communist States at the Crossroads.* New York: Praeger Publishers, 1965.

BRZEZINSKI, ZBIGNIEW K. *The Soviet Bloc.** Rev. ed. Cambridge, Mass.: Harvard University Press, 1967.

CRANKSHAW, EDWARD. *The New Cold War.** Baltimore: Penguin Books, 1963.

DUTT, VIDYA P. *China and the World.** New York: Praeger Publishers, 1966.

FLOYD, DAVID. *Mao Against Khrushchev.** New York: Praeger Publishers, 1964.

HALPERIN, MORTON. *China and the Bomb.** New York: Praeger Publishers, 1965.

HINTON, HAROLD C. *Communist China in World Politics.* Boston: Houghton Mifflin Co., 1966.

HSIEH, ALICE LANGLEY. *Communist China's Strategy in the Nuclear Era.** Englewood Cliffs, N.J.: Prentice-Hall, 1962.

HUCK, ARTHUR. *The Security of China.** New York: Columbia University Press, 1970.

HUDSON, G. F., *et al.*, eds. *The Sino-Soviet Dispute.** New York: Praeger Publishers, 1961.

IONESCU, GHITA. *The Break-Up of the Soviet Empire in Eastern Europe.** Baltimore: Penguin Books, 1965.

LALL, ARTHUR. *How Communist China Negotiates.** New York: Columbia University Press, 1968.

LOWENTHAL, RICHARD. *World Communism.** London and New York: Oxford University Press, 1966.

MEHNERT, KLAUS. *Peking and Moscow.** New York: G. P. Putnam's Sons, 1963.

NORTH, ROBERT C. *The Foreign Relations of China.** Belmont, Calif.: Dickenson Publishing Co., 1969.

PENTONY, DEVERE E., ed. *China, the Emerging Red Giant.** San Francisco: Chandler Publishing Co., 1962.

———, ed. *Red World in Tumult.** San Francisco: Chandler Publishing Co., 1962.

SALISBURY, HARRISON E. *War Between Russia and China.** New York: W. W. Norton & Co., 1969. Paperback ed., Bantam.

SCHWARTZ, HARRY. *Prague's 200 Days.* New York: Praeger Publishers, 1969.

SKILLING, H. GORDON. *The Governments of Communist Eastern Europe.** New York: Thomas Y. Crowell Co., 1966.

WINDSOR, PHILIP, and ADAM ROBERTS. *Czechoslovakia 1968.** New York: Columbia University Press, 1969.

WINT, GUY. *Communist China's Crusade*.* New York: Praeger Publishers, 1970.

ZAGORIA, DONALD S. *The Sino-Soviet Conflict, 1956–1961*. Princeton, N.J.: Princeton University Press, 1962.

THE SOVIET POLITICAL SYSTEM

ARMSTRONG, JOHN A. *Ideology, Politics, and Government in the Soviet Union*.* 3d ed. New York: Praeger Publishers, 1973.

BARGHOORN, FREDERICK. *Politics in the USSR*.* Boston: Little, Brown & Co., 1966.

BRUMBERG, ABRAHAM, ed. *Russia Under Khrushchev*.* New York: Praeger Publishers, 1962.

CRANKSHAW, EDWARD. *Khrushchev's Russia*.* Rev. ed. Baltimore: Penguin Books, 1962.

DEUTSCHER, ISAAC. *Stalin*.* London and New York: Oxford University Press, 1949.

DJILAS, MILOVAN. *The New Class*.* New York: Praeger Publishers, 1957.

EBENSTEIN, WILLIAM. *Totalitarianism*.* New York: Holt, Rinehart & Winston, 1962.

FAINSOD, MERLE. *How Russia Is Ruled*. Rev. ed. Cambridge, Mass.: Harvard University Press, 1963.

FRIEDRICH, CARL J., and ZBIGNIEW K. BRZEZINSKI. *Totalitarian Dictatorship and Autocracy*.* 2d ed., rev. New York: Praeger Publishers, 1966.

LEONHARD, WOLFGANG. *The Kremlin Since Stalin*.* Translated by ELIZABETH WISKEMANN and MARTIN JACKSON. New York: Praeger Publishers, 1962.

MEYER, ALFRED G. *The Soviet Political System*. New York: Random House, 1965.

MOORE, BARRINGTON, JR. *Soviet Politics: The Dilemma of Power*.* Cambridge, Mass.: Harvard University Press, 1950. Paperback ed., Harper.

RESHETAR, JOHN S., JR. *The Soviet Polity*.* New York: Dodd, Mead & Co., 1971.

SCHAPIRO, LEONARD. *The Communist Party of the Soviet Union*.* New York: Random House, 1960.

SETON-WATSON, HUGH. *From Lenin to Khrushchev*.* New York: Praeger Publishers, 1960.

SHUB, ANATOLE. *The New Russian Tragedy*.* New York: W. W. Norton & Co., 1969.

TUCKER, ROBERT C. *The Soviet Political Mind*.* New York: Praeger Publishers, 1963.

ULAM, ADAM B. *The New Face of Soviet Totalitarianism*.* Cambridge, Mass.: Harvard University Press, 1963. Paperback ed., Praeger.

———. *The Unfinished Revolution*.* New York: Random House, 1960.

SOVIET FOREIGN AND MILITARY POLICY

ASPATURIUN, VERNON V., ed. *Process and Power in Soviet Foreign Policy*. Boston: Little, Brown & Co., 1971.

BRZEZINSKI, ZBIGNIEW K. *Ideology and Power in Soviet Politics*.* Rev. ed. New York: Praeger Publishers, 1967.

DALLIN, DAVID J. *Soviet Foreign Policy After Stalin*. Philadelphia: J. B. Lippincott Co., 1961.

DINERSTEIN, HERBERT S. *War and Soviet Union.** Rev. ed. New York: Praeger Publishers, 1962.

GARTHOFF, RAYMOND L. *Soviet Military Policy*. New York: Praeger Publishers, 1966.

―――. *Soviet Strategy in the Nuclear Age.** Rev. ed. New York: Praeger Publishers, 1962.

GEHLEN, MICHAEL P. *The Politics of Coexistence*. Bloomington: Indiana University Press, 1967.

HORELICK, ARNOLD L. and MYRON RUSH. *Strategic Power and Soviet Foreign Policy*. Chicago: University of Chicago Press, 1966.

KENNAN, GEORGE F. *Russia and the West Under Lenin and Stalin.** Boston: Little, Brown & Co., 1961. Paperback ed., NAL.

KOLKOWICZ, ROMAN, *et al. The Soviet Union and Arms Control.** Baltimore: The Johns Hopkins Press, 1970.

LEDERER, IVO J., ed. *Russian Foreign Policy.** New Haven, Conn.: Yale University Press, 1962.

LEITES, NATHAN. *The Operational Code of the Politburo*. New York: McGraw-Hill Book Co., 1951.

―――. *A Study of Bolshevism*. New York: The Free Press, 1953.

MACKINTOSH, J. M. *Strategy and Tactics of Soviet Foreign Policy*. London and New York: Oxford University Press, 1962.

MOSELY, PHILIP E. *The Kremlin and World Politics.** New York: Random House, 1960.

PENTONY, DEVERE E., ed. *Soviet Behavior in World Affairs.** San Francisco: Chandler Publishing Co., 1962.

SHULMAN, MARSHALL D. *Beyond the Cold War.** New Haven, Conn.: Yale University Press, 1965.

―――. *Stalin's Foreign Policy Reappraised.** Cambridge, Mass.: Harvard University Press, 1963. Paperback ed., Atheneum.

SOKOLOVSKY, V. D., ed. *Military Strategy: Soviet Doctrine and Concept.** New York: Praeger Publishers, 1963.

STRAUSZ-HUPÉ, ROBERT, *et al. Protracted Conflict.** New York: Harper & Row, 1959.

TRISKA, JAN F., and DAVID D. FINLEY. *Soviet Foreign Policy*. New York: The Macmillan Co., 1968.

ULAM, ADAM B. *Expansion and Coexistence.** 2d ed. New York: Praeger Publishers, 1974.

VON LAUE, THEODORE. *Why Lenin, Why Stalin?** Philadelphia: J. B. Lippincott Co., 1964.

Washington Center of Foreign Policy Research. *Two Communist Manifestoes.** Washington, D.C., 1961.

WOLFE, THOMAS W. *Soviet Power and Europe, 1945–1970.** Baltimore: The Johns Hopkins Press, 1970.

―――. *Soviet Strategy at the Crossroads*. Cambridge, Mass.: Harvard University Press, 1964.

ZIMMERMAN, WILLIAM. *Soviet Perspectives on International Relations, 1956–1967*. Princeton, N.J.: Princeton University Press, 1969.

AMERICAN FOREIGN POLICY

ADLER, SELIG. *The Isolationist Impulse.** New York: Abrams, 1957. Paperback ed., Collier Books.
———. *The Uncertain Giant.** New York: Macmillan, 1966. Paperback ed., Collier Books.
ALMOND, GABRIEL. *The American People and Foreign Policy.** New York: Praeger Publishers, 1960.
ALPEROVITZ, GAR. *Atomic Diplomacy: Hiroshima and Potsdam.** New York: Random House, 1967.
BROWN, SEYOM. *The Faces of Power.** New York: Columbia University Press, 1968.
DIVINE, ROBERT A. *The Reluctant Belligerent.** New York: John Wiley & Sons, 1965.
FEIS, HERBERT. *Churchill-Roosevelt-Stalin.* Princeton, N.J.: Princeton University Press, 1957.
GATI, CHARLES, ed. *Caging the Bear.* New York: Bobbs-Merrill Co., 1973.
GILBERT, FELIX. *To the Farewell Address.** Princeton, N.J.: Princeton University Press, 1961.
HALLE, LOUIS J. *The Cold War as History.* New York: Harper & Row, 1967.
HILSMAN, ROGER. *To Move a Nation.** Garden City, N.Y.: Doubleday & Co., 1967. Paperback ed., Dell.
HOWE, IRVING, ed. *A Dissenter's Guide to Foreign Policy.** New York: Praeger Publishers, 1968. Paperback ed., Doubleday Anchor.
JONES, JOSEPH M. *The Fifteen Weeks.** New York: The Viking Press, 1955. Paperback ed., Harcourt.
KENNAN, GEORGE F. *American Diplomacy 1900–1950.** Chicago: University of Chicago Press, 1951. Paperback ed., Mentor.
———. *Memoirs.** Boston: Atlantic-Little, Brown & Co., 1967.
KOLKO, GABRIEL. *The Roots of American Foreign Policy.** Boston: Beacon Press, 1967.
LIPPMANN, WALTER. *U.S. Foreign Policy.* Boston: Little, Brown & Co., 1943.
LISKA, GEORGE. *Imperial America.** Baltimore: The Johns Hopkins Press, 1967.
MORGENTHAU, HANS J. *In Defense of the National Interest.* New York: Alfred A. Knopf, 1951.
———. *A New Foreign Policy for the United States.** New York: Praeger Publishers, 1969.
MUELLER, JOHN E. *War, Presidents, and Public Opinion.* New York: John Wiley & Sons, 1973.
OGLESBY, CARL, and RICHARD SHAULL. *Containment and Change.** New York: The Macmillan Co., 1969.
OSGOOD, ROBERT E. *Ideals and Self-Interest in America's Foreign Relations.** Chicago: University of Chicago Press, 1953.
SEABURY, PAUL. *The Rise and Decline of the Cold War.* New York: Basic Books, 1967.
SMITH, GADDIS. *American Diplomacy During the Second World War.** New York: John Wiley & Sons, 1966.

SNELL, JOHN L. *Illusion and Necessity.** Boston: Houghton Mifflin Co., 1963.

SPANIER, JOHN. *American Foreign Policy Since World War II.** 6th ed. New York: Praeger Publishers, 1973.

STEEL, RONALD. *Pax Americana.** New York: The Viking Press, 1967.

TSOU, TANG. *America's Failure in China.** Chicago: University of Chicago Press, 1963.

TUCKER, ROBERT W. *Nation or Empire?** Baltimore: The Johns Hopkins Press, 1968.

————. *The Radical Left and American Foreign Policy.** Baltimore: The Johns Hopkins Press, 1971.

MEMOIRS AND BIOGRAPHIES OF AMERICAN STATESMEN
AND ADMINISTRATIONS

ACHESON, DEAN. *Present at the Creation.** New York: W. W. Norton & Co., 1969. Paperback ed., Signet.

BEAL, JOHN R. *John Foster Dulles.* New York: Harper & Brothers, 1956.

BYRNES, JAMES F. *Speaking Frankly.* New York: Harper & Brothers, 1947.

EISENHOWER, DWIGHT D. *White House Years: Mandate for Change.** Garden City, N.Y.: Doubleday & Co., 1963. Paperback ed., NAL.

————. *White House Years: Waging Peace.* Garden City, N.Y.: Doubleday & Co., 1965.

FERRELL, ROBERT H. *George C. Marshall.* New York: Cooper Square Publishers, 1966.

GERSON, LOUIS L. *John Foster Dulles.* New York: Cooper Square Publishers, 1967.

HOOPES, TOWNSEND. *The Devil and John Foster Dulles.* Boston: Atlantic/ Little, Brown and Co., 1973.

SCHLESINGER, ARTHUR M., JR. *A Thousand Days.** Boston: Houghton Mifflin, 1965. Paperback ed., Fawcett Crest.

SORENSEN, THEODORE C. *Kennedy.** New York: Harper & Row, 1965. Paperback ed., Bantam.

TRUMAN, HARRY S. *Memoirs.** 2 vols. Garden City, N.Y.: Doubleday & Co., 1958. Paperback ed., Signet.

FOREIGN POLICY DECISION-MAKING
(INCLUDING MILITARY-INDUSTRIAL COMPLEX)

ALLISON, GRAHAM T. *Essence of Decision.* Boston: Little, Brown & Co., 1971.

BARNET, RICHARD J. *The Economy of Death.** New York: Atheneum Publishers, 1969.

————. *The Roots of War.** Baltimore: Penguin Books, 1973.

CHEEVER, DANIEL S., and H. FIELD HAVILAND, JR. *American Foreign Policy and the Separation of Powers.* Cambridge, Mass.: Harvard University Press, 1952.

COOK, FRED J. *The Warfare State.** New York: Collier Books, 1964.

CRABB, CECIL V., JR. *Bipartisan Foreign Policy.* Evanston, Ill.: Row, Peterson & Co., 1957.

DAHL, ROBERT. *Congress and Foreign Policy.** New York: Harcourt, Brace & Co., 1950. Paperback ed., Norton.

GILPIN, ROBERT. *American Scientists and Nuclear Weapons Policy.** Princeton, N.J.: Princeton University Press, 1962.

GRABER, DORIS. *Public Opinion, the President, and Foreign Policy.** New York: Holt, Rinehart & Winston, 1968.

HALPERIN, MORTON. *Bureaucratic Politics and Foreign Policy.* Washington, D.C.: Brookings Institution, 1974.

HALPERIN, MORTON, and ARNOLD KANTER, eds. *Readings in American Foreign Policy.* Boston: Little, Brown & Co., 1973.

HILSMAN, ROGER. *The Politics of Policy Making in Defense and Foreign Affairs.** New York: Harper & Row, 1971.

HUNTINGTON, SAMUEL P. *The Common Defense.** New York: Columbia University Press, 1961.

JANIS, IRVING L. *Victims of Groupthink.* Boston: Houghton Mifflin, 1972.

LAPP, RALPH. *The Weapons Culture.** New York: W. W. Norton & Co., 1968. Paperback ed., Penguin.

LENS, SIDNEY. *The Military-Industrial Complex.** Philadelphia: Pilgrim Press, 1970.

LENTNER, HOWARD H. *Foreign Policy Analysis.* Columbus, Ohio: Charles E. Merrill Publishing Co., 1974.

PROXMIRE, WILLIAM. *Report from Wasteland.* New York: Praeger Publishers, 1970.

RADWAY, LAURENCE I. *Foreign Policy and National Defense.** Glenview, Ill.: Scott, Foresman & Co., 1969.

ROBINSON, JAMES A. *Congress and Foreign Policy.** Rev. ed. Homewood, Ill.: The Dorsey Press, 1967.

ROSEN, STEVEN, ed. *Testing the Theory of the Military-Industrial Complex.* Lexington, Mass.: Lexington Books, 1973.

RUSSETT, BRUCE M. *What Price Vigilance?** New Haven, Conn.: Yale University Press, 1970.

YARMOLINSKY, ADAM. *The Military Establishment.* New York: Harper & Row, 1971.

UNDERDEVELOPED COUNTRIES AND MODERNIZATION

ALMOND, GABRIEL A., and JAMES S. COLEMAN, *The Politics of the Developing Areas.* Princeton, N.J.: Princeton University Press, 1960.

BERLINER, JOSEPH S. *Soviet Economic Aid.* New York: Praeger Publishers, 1958.

BLACK, C. E. *The Dynamics of Modernization.** New York: Harper & Row, 1966.

BLACK, EUGENE R. *The Diplomacy of Economic Development.** New York: Atheneum, 1963.

BURKE, FRED G. *Africa's Quest for Order.** Englewood Cliffs, N.J.: Prentice-Hall, 1963.

CAMPBELL, JOHN C. *Defense of the Middle East.** Rev. ed. New York: Praeger Publishers, 1961.

CHAMBERS, WILLIAM N. *Political Parties in a New Nation.** London and New York: Oxford University Press, 1963.

CRABB, CECIL V. JR. *The Elephants and the Grass.* New York: Praeger Publishers, 1965.

CREMEANS, CHARLES D. *The Arabs and the World.** New York: Praeger Publishers, 1963.

DEUTSCH, KARL W., and WILLIAM J. FOLTZ, eds. *Nation-Building.* New York: Atherton Press, 1963.

DRAPER, THEODORE. *Israel and World Politics.** New York: The Viking Press, 1968.

EMERSON, RUPERT. *From Empire to Nation.** Cambridge, Mass.: Harvard University Press, 1960. Paperback ed., Beacon.

FICKETT, LEWIS P., ed. *Problems of the Developing Nations.** New York: Thomas Y. Crowell, 1966.

FINER, S. E. *The Man on Horseback.* New York: Praeger Publishers, 1962.

GEERTZ, CLIFFORD, ed. *Old Societies and New States.* New York: The Free Press, 1963.

GERSCHENKRON, ALEXANDER. *Economic Backwardness in Historical Perspective.* Cambridge, Mass.: Harvard University Press, 1962. Paperback ed., Praeger.

GOLDSCHMIDT, WALTER, ed. *The United States and Africa.** Rev. ed. New York: Praeger Publishers, 1963.

GORDON, BERNARD K. *The Dimensions of Conflict in Southeast Asia.** Englewood Cliffs, N.J.: Prentice-Hall, 1966.

HEILBRONER, ROBERT L. *The Great Ascent.** New York: Harper & Row, 1963.

———. *The Making of Economic Society.** Englewood Cliffs, N.J.: Prentice-Hall, 1962.

HODGKIN, THOMAS. *African Political Parties.** Harmondsworth, England: Penguin Books, 1961.

HUNTINGTON, SAMUEL P. *Political Order in Changing Societies.* New Haven, Conn.: Yale University Press, 1968.

JANOWITZ, MORRIS. *The Military in the Political Development of New Nations.** Chicago: University of Chicago Press, 1964.

JOHNSON, JOHN J., ed. *The Role of the Military in Underdeveloped Countries.* Princeton, N.J.: Princeton University Press, 1962.

KAUTSKY, JOHN H., ed. *Political Change in Underdeveloped Countries.** New York: John Wiley & Sons, 1962.

LEGUM, COLIN. *Pan-Africanism.** Rev. ed. New York: Praeger Publishers, 1965.

LEVI, WERNER. *The Challenge of World Politics in Southeast Asia.** Englewood Cliffs, N.J.: Prentice-Hall, 1968.

LIEUWEN, EDWIN. *Arms and Politics in Latin America.** Rev. ed. New York: Praeger Publishers, 1961.

LIPSET, SEYMOUR M. *The First New Nation.* New York: Basic Books, 1963.

LISKA, GEORGE. *The New Statecraft: Foreign Aid in American Foreign Policy.* Chicago: University of Chicago Press, 1960.

LONDON, KURT, ed. *New Nations in a Divided World.** New York: Praeger Publishers, 1964.

MCCORD, WILLIAM. *The Springtime of Freedom.** London and New York: Oxford University Press, 1965.

MCKAY, VERNON, ed. *African Diplomacy.** New York: Praeger Publishers, 1966.

MARTIN, LAURENCE W., ed. *Neutralism and Nonalignment*. New York: Praeger Publishers, 1962.

MILLIKAN, MAX F., and DONALD L. M. BLACKMER, eds. *The Emerging Nations*.* Boston: Little, Brown & Co., 1961.

ORGANSKI, A. F. K. *The Stages of Political Development*. New York: Alfred A. Knopf, 1965.

PYE, LUCIAN W. *Politics, Personality, and Nation-Building*.* New Haven, Conn.: Yale University Press, 1966.

ROSTOW, W. W. *Stages of Economic Growth*.* London and New York: Cambridge University Press, 1960.

RUSTOW, DANKWART A. *A World of Nations*.* Washington, D.C.: The Brookings Institution, 1967.

SCHMITT, KARL M., and DAVID D. BURKS. *Evolution or Chaos*.* New York: Praeger Publishers, 1963.

SHILS, EDWARD A. *Political Development in the New States*.* 's-Gravenhage, The Netherlands: Marten & Co., 1962.

SIGMUND, PAUL E., ed. *The Ideologies of the Developing Nations*.* 2d rev. ed. New York: Praeger Publishers, 1972.

STALEY, EUGENE. *The Future of Underdeveloped Countries*.* Rev. ed. New York: Praeger Publishers, 1961.

SZULC, TAD. *The Winds of Revolution*.* Rev. ed. New York: Praeger Publishers, 1965.

VON DER MEHDEN, FRED R. *Politics of the Developing Nations*.* Englewood Cliffs, N.J.: Prentice-Hall, 1964.

WALLERSTEIN, IMMANUEL. *Africa: The Politics of Independence*.* New York: Random House, 1961.

WARD, BARBARA. *Five Ideas That Change the World*.* New York: W. W. Norton & Co., 1959.

———. *The Rich Nations and the Poor Nations*.* New York: W. W. Norton & Co., 1962.

ZARTMAN, I. WILLIAM. *International Relations in the New Africa*.* Englewood Cliffs, N.J.: Prentice-Hall, 1966.

PERCEPTION AND PSYCHOLOGY

FRANK, JEROME D. *Sanity and Survival*.* New York: Random House, 1968.

HOLSTI, OLE R., et al. *Enemies in Politics*.* Chicago: Rand McNally Co., 1967.

KELMAN, HERBERT C., ed. *International Behavior*. New York: Holt, Rinehart & Winston, 1965.

KLINEBERG, OTTO. *The Human Dimension in International Relations*.* New York: Holt, Rinehart & Winston, 1964.

RIVERA, JOSEPH H. DE. *The Psychological Dimension of Foreign Policy*. Columbus, Ohio: Charles E. Merrill Publishing Co., 1968.

STAGNER, ROSS. *Psychological Aspects of International Conflict*.* Belmont, Calif.: Brooks/Cole Publishing Co., 1967.

STOESSINGER, JOHN G. *Nations in Darkness*.* New York: Random House, 1971.

———. *Why Nations Go to War*. New York: St. Martin's Press, 1974.

WHITE, RALPH K. *Nobody Wanted War*.* Garden City, N.Y.: Doubleday & Co., 1968.

Index